D1478407

A Respectable Ditch

JAMES T. ANGUS

A History of the Trent-Severn Waterway
1833–1920

McGill-Queen's University Press   Kingston and Montreal

© McGill-Queen's University Press 1988
ISBN 0-7735-0597-0

Legal deposit 1st quarter 1988
Bibliothèque nationale du Québec

Printed in Canada

This book has been published with the help of a grant from the Social Science
Federation of Canada, using funds provided by the Social Sciences and
Humanities Research Council of Canada.

All maps were prepared by Iain Hastie.

Graphic Design: Peter Dorn, RCA, FGDC

Page i: Stepping lock gates in Gamebridge Lock, 1906. (Trent-Severn Waterway
Office [TSWO], Peterborough)

Canadian Cataloguing in Publication Data

Angus, James T. (James Thomas), 1928-
    A respectable ditch : history of the Trent-Severn Waterway, 1833-1920
    Includes index.
    Bibliography: p.
    ISBN 0-7735-0597-0
    1. Trent-Severn Waterway (Ont.) – History.
    2. Canals – Ontario – History.   I. Title.
    HE401.T74A64 1988   971.3'15   C87-090222-9

For Scotty

Contents

Nichol Hugh Baird.
(Courtesy Mrs A. Foley,
Toronto)

Hamilton Hartley Killaly.
(Public Archives Canada [PAC]#/s963A)

Kivas Tully. (PAC/S17140)

Preface

In some respects the history of the Trent-Severn Waterway resembles the history of Canada. One parallels the other. The same political and economic tensions that have constantly beset the country can be identified in the canal's story: defence against American invasion, free trade versus tariff protection, private enterprise or government intervention, the problem of moving vast quantities of grain from the central plains to deep-water ports, freight rates, energy production and who should control it, and the obsessive preoccupation with federal and provincial responsibilities. What follows is a record of how these national questions affected the development of a waterway that the country could ill afford and only a handful of people wanted. Consequently, this is not a story about transportation or engineering. It is a book about politics – the politics of dreamers.

The passage of the first small boat through the waterway in July 1920 marked the realization of a dream older than the nation itself and, like the dream that gave birth to Canada, rooted in realism. The dream was to connect Lake Ontario to Georgian Bay with a navigable watercourse that would be shorter and more protected than the longer route through the Great Lakes. Much of the work was already done. Nature had carved a natural channel between the pre-Cambrian bedrock and the intersecting strata of limestone, as it funnelled the melt-water from the Wisconsin Glacier into the Atlantic Ocean. When the ice had gone, a necklace of small lakes remained, strung along a cascading river under the jaw of the Canadian Shield. The Indians discovered the necklace and for centuries employed it as a canoe route. The French learned about it from the Indians and used it for exploration. The British understood its strategic importance; they surveyed it. But it was the early settlers who saw the economic significance of the natural waterway and sought ways to develop it. This book is about their efforts, and the efforts of their children and grandchildren.

The book is an attempt to give a fitting scope to a rather long subject, to treat it as a whole. I was less concerned with how the canal was built than why. I have tried to discover the underlying causes for what happened during those 150 years by assessing the impact of national and international forces on the motives and actions of the canal's builders.

So my primary interest has been with the participants themselves, who included some of Canada's greatest leaders. Every governor-general of British North America, from Sir Guy Carleton, who ordered the first survey, to Lord Sydenham, who cancelled the first construction in 1841, was intimately involved with early decisions about the waterway. Every prime minister of Canada, from Sir Francis Hincks, who tried to sell the decaying locks and dams in 1850, through Sir John A. Macdonald, who revived the scheme in 1883, and Sir Wilfrid Laurier, who toyed with it, to Sir Robert Borden, who finally completed it, was trapped in the political webs spun by this most persistent public project. But the most important participants were the countless little-known Canadians who, for one reason or another, promoted the scheme and doggedly pushed it to a conclusion. This is their story.

As I researched and wrote, I became as obsessed with sorting out the details of their story as they were with promoting and developing the waterway. I have tried to describe their successes and failures as they struggled against forces that were bigger than themselves, pursuing a vision that most other Canadians could never see. I have tried to present the problems they faced as they saw them, to analyse their goals as they set them, and to explain their actions against a background of larger economic and political issues. I have told everything as it happened. The reader will discover that some of what the participants did was worthy, even inspiring; some things were sordid and deplorable too. But it was only the means that were sometimes reprehensible; the end was always noble. Consequently some of the better-known participants may emerge as quite different from previous portrayals.

Most of what follows is new. Nearly all the material has been drawn from unpublished sources. I searched through hundreds of government records, letters, and newspaper stories. I examined private papers. I read all the Commons debates on the Trent Canal from 1874 on, the year debates were first published. I studied all the public accounts from 1832 to 1923. The dollar figures quoted are the figures reported to Parliament by successive auditors-general. Sterling has been converted to decimal currency using the exchange rate of five dollars to the pound. Documentation of the facts will be found in the Notes. Only the interpretation of the facts may be questioned; I take full responsibility for that.

Richard B. Rogers.
(PAC/C10309)

Commissioners, Quebec
Bridge inquiry, 1907 – 8.
Left to right: J. Galbraith,
Henry Holgate, J.G.G. Kerry.
(Courtesy Col. A.J. Kerry,
Woodstock, England)

Acknowledgments

This book has been published with the help of a grant from the Social Science Federation of Canada, using funds provided by the Social Sciences and Humanities Research Council of Canada. I am most grateful to the Social Science Federation for this support. I must also express my gratitude to Lakehead University for providing financial assistance in the preparation of the manuscript.

Many others assisted in the production of this book. I gratefully acknowledge the invaluable assistance provided by the staffs of the Public Archives of Canada, the Archives of Ontario, the Toronto and Peterborough public libraries, and the Trent-Severn Waterway Office in Peterborough. A special word of thanks is due to Virginia Taylor and Vivian Nyssonen, librarians of Lakehead University, for their help in locating numerous government documents.

My thanks, too, to Col. A.J. Kerry for providing information about his father, J.G.G. Kerry, to Mrs A. Foley for the picture of her late husband's illustrious ancestor, Nichol Hugh Baird, and to Mrs Herbert Geale of Peterborough for making available valuable background material on her father, R.B. Rogers. To the many friends and acquaintances who know and love the Trent-Severn Waterway and who encouraged me to complete the work, I owe a debt of gratitude.

Joan McGilvray, co-ordinating editor at McGill-Queen's, who guided the manuscript (and me) through the intricacies of publication, and John Parry, my copy-editor, whose dedication to accuracy astonishes, deserve my special gratitude.

Finally to Pat Barclay for editorial assistance and to Eleanora Bailey and Sheila Wilson, who typed several versions of the manuscript, I express my thanks.

Running logs through dam at Buckhorn. (Public Archives Canada (PAC#/ ACC 11747-4)

PART ONE

The Colonial Years: 1833–41

The Inland Waters:
Proposed Transportation Routes 1835

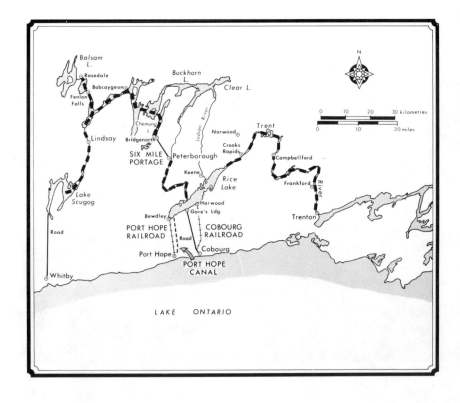

CHAPTER ONE

James Bethune's Waterway

On the afternoon of 1 June 1833, somewhere in the frontier town of Peterborough, Upper Canada, probably at the back of Bethune's store on the corner of Charlotte and Water streets, six men sat down at a table. Spread out in front of them was a map of the Newcastle District. Beside the map were two sealed envelopes. In the envelopes were tenders for constructing a wooden lock at the shallow rapids where Sturgeon Lake drained into Pigeon Lake, called "Bobcajionunk" by the Indians but corrupted to "Bobcaygeon" by white men.

When the men opened the envelopes and chose one of the tenders, a train of events would be set in motion that would extend over four generations and involve hundreds of public meetings, dozens of petitions, countless editorials and newspaper letters, the formation of several canal associations, and a march of thousands of delegates on Ottawa. This same train of events would prompt hundreds of speeches in Parliament, force the passage of numerous statutes and orders-in-council, call for several commissions and investigations, launch dozens of surveys, and produce engineering innovations and construction masterpieces, but also some blunders, scandals, and damaged reputations. The discontinuous series of events originating with the construction of a lock at Bobcaygeon would comprise the longest-lasting public enterprise ever undertaken in Canada, which in the end would create a canal extending from Lake Ontario to Georgian Bay and costing $24 million but which, when finished in 1920, would be used in its entirety by few except some wealthy American yachtsmen and a few adventurous Canadian canoemen. The Bobcaygeon lock, started in 1833, was the first phase in construction of what later became known as the Trent Canal.

The men gathered in Peterborough that June afternoon were commissioners named in a special act of the legislature of Upper Canada, with authority to borrow $10,000 to be spent on the improvement of "the Navigation of the River Otonibee [sic] ... and also the adjacent waters leading to Mud Lake and Scugog Lake."[1] Authority was given to the commissioners for "receiving plans, tenders, estimates, and of contracting for and superintending the work and labour."[2] They had, in fact, been given carte blanche to improve the navigation of the district as they saw fit, because the improvements would be "manifestly advantageous to the surrounding Settlement, and ... greatly extend the benefits of Commerce."[3] (Sterling was used in Upper Canada until 1858 when decimal currency came into general use. For the sake of consistency dollar equivalents will be quoted throughout the book.) Unstated in the legislation was the fact that the improved navigation would also be manifestly advantageous to the seven commissioners, all of whom had vested interests in the improvements that they were empowered to make. Some owned large tracts of land on the waterway, bought cheaply for speculative purposes; some owned businesses that were dependent upon improved navigation. All but one of the commissioners were loyal supporters of the government, but, regrettably, none of them knew anything about hydraulic engineering or about lock construction. None of this bothered the commissioners or the majority of legislators. Appointment of commissioners to supervise public projects, regardless of conflicts of interest, was the way things were done in 1833, when the distinction between public needs and private wants was never very clearly perceived.

The form of colonial government established in Upper Canada by the Constitutional Act of 1791 permitted such blatant misuse of political power as was being exercised by the commissioners that afternoon. Fearful of the democratic principles that led to revolution and the loss of the Thirteen Colonies, the British government deliberately tried to control democracy in what was left of British North America after 1783. But, inevitably, the calculated weakening of the popular element in the colony only strengthened the control of a colonial aristocracy and thus contributed more to the abuse of power (and eventually to rebellion) than to the intended maintenance of constitutional authority and social order.

Not only had the government no cabinet ministers responsible to Parliament, but there were also few skilled administrators and technical staffs to manage the day-to-day business of government, which by 1833 had increased substantially. There was, for example, no department of public works to plan, design, supervise, co-ordinate, and finance the many public projects required in a pioneer state where transportation facilities in the form of roads, bridges, harbours, canals, and, later, railroads were badly needed.

The normal process by which a needed local facility came into existence was for a group of settlers to petition the lieutenant-governor, asking for government support for the project. Petitions were sent to the legislative assembly, which in turn referred them to a select committee with power to summon witnesses, hear evidence, and call for papers. If a request had merit, the select committee recommended that legislation be prepared and the amount of financing to be authorized, through loans, grants, or the sale of debentures. For major public works projects, the enabling legislation provided for the establishment of a board of commissioners with full authority to plan, manage, and finance the work. If the legislative council (upper house) and the lieutenant-governor approved, the legislation became law and the work was carried out under the supervision of commissioners, serving as a local public works mini-department with powers that, although somewhat limited by the legislation, were generally quite broad. Commissioners, usually named in the act, were selected from among the leading citizens of a community more for their political allegiance than technical expertise. Frequently they included those who initiated the project. Such was the process that brought the six commissioners to the meeting in Peterborough that June afternoon.

One commissioner, from Peterborough, was Col. Alexander McDonell, a militia officer and immigration and crown land agent and a nephew of Alexander McDonell, Roman Catholic bishop of Kingston and member of the legislative council since 1831. Settlers spoke well of Commissioner McDonell, a hero of the War of 1812 and, although Roman Catholic, a loyal supporter of the Church of England–dominated government. Pioneer settler John Langton said McDonell was "generally liked."[4] The Hon. Peter Robinson, commissioner of crown lands, whom McDonell assisted in locating Irish immigrants in the Peterborough area in 1825, called him an "intelligent and respectable young man."[5] Now, as immigration and crown land agent, under Robinson, McDonell assisted new settlers in finding their chosen lots in the bush, settled boundary disputes, and mediated grievances between settlers and the government at York. In 1834 McDonell would seek a seat in the legislative assembly as a Conservative candidate in the new riding of Peterborough. When he promised the electors gathered at Sully (now Harwood) on Rice Lake that if he were elected "their welfare and interest should ever command his warmest advocacy and regard,"[6] they not only cheered him but also voted for him. So in addition to being immigration and crown land agent, McDonell became a commissioner of public projects, a member of the legislative assembly, and later a justice of the peace. Thus did power concentrate in the hands of a few in the 1830s.

Since no restrictions in land speculation were placed on government officials, McDonell had used his positions to acquire some prime pieces of property for both himself and his relatives. Some lots, like the 1,200 acres on Sturgeon Lake purchased for his uncle, Bishop McDonell, had been bought fairly at public auction but very cheap, because no one, it seems, wanted to bid against such a popular man. An improved waterway would increase the value of McDonell's property.

Another commissioner was John Huston of Cavan, a justice of the peace, militia officer, and surveyor. Having surveyed townships in the area in the early 1820s, he knew the District of Newcastle better than anyone. In 1833, as a public land surveyor, he reported through McDonell to Peter Robinson who, since 1827, had been commissioner of crown lands and surveyor general of Upper Canada. Huston, too, owned large tracts of land. The increased settlement that the waterway was expected to produce would provide plenty of work for his transit and level, to say nothing of the inflation in the value of his land.

Commissioner John Hall was a moderate Reformer and resident of Peterborough. He had just acquired water power rights at Buckhorn Falls, where he was about to build a dam and mill. Regular steamship service on Chemung and Buckhorn lakes would be immensely advantageous to him.

Commissioner Col. Robert Brown, a gentlemen farmer, owned a large tract of land near Peterborough. A loyal supporter of the ruling Family Compact, Brown was for some years commanding officer of a battalion of militia known as the Fourth Northumberland Fusiliers.

Commissioner Thomas Need had just purchased several hundred acres of land at Bobcaygeon. The proposed canal and lock would run through his property. A dam would create a head for the mill he was planning to build.

William Whitla, who, with his brother George, owned property at the rapids just below Peterborough to which they gave their name, was also listed as one of the commissioners in the legislation. Since his name did not appear on any advertisement or reports by the commission, it is doubtful if he actually served, and he may not have attended the June meeting.

Finally, there was Commissioner James Gray Bethune, "great man" of the district and architect of the scheme. Bethune came from United Empire Loyalist stock, his father, the Reverend John Bethune, having fled after the American Revolution from South Carolina to Montreal, where he established the first Presbyterian congregation in Canada in the 1820s. John Bethune's third son, James Gray, settled in Cobourg, where his entrepreneurial skills contributed much to the early development of the Newcastle District. A man of considerable personal charm and inde-fatigable drive, he "stood high in the confidence of both the government and the people,"[7] at least for a time. While others talked about one developmental scheme or another, Bethune acted. His first commercial venture was a store and post office in Cobourg. Later he branched out into real estate, banking, and transportation. By 1830 he was operating schooners on Lake Ontario and providing stage coach service to Rice Lake. He was an agent for the Canada Company but also ran his own real estate business, acquiring large tracts of land for himself as be bought and sold property for others. He managed the Cobourg branch of the Bank of Upper Canada and for a time acquired the trust of everyone in the district; monied immigrants placed their funds in his hands for safekeeping, and he acted as a sort of savings bank for the poorer classes. Bethune energetically promoted public works too. He was largely responsible for securing government legislation in 1833 authorizing the expenditure of $20,000 to construct a bridge across the mouth of the Trent River to replace the less than efficient ferry service there. On behalf of a group of businessmen, Bethune promoted and received a charter for a railroad from Cobourg to Rice Lake which, had it been built, would have been the first in Upper Canada. Bethune was a director of the Cobourg Harbour Company, a private outfit for which he acquired government grants. Although he would later change his opinion of Bethune, John Langton's first impression of him was that he was one who had "done more for the Newcastle district than any other living man."[8]

Bethune's most lasting contribution to the district was the construction of what turned out to be the first lock on the waterway that later became known as the Trent Canal. Some have wondered why, if the government had intended to build a canal connecting Lake Ontario and Georgian Bay, the first lock was built at Bobcaygeon, roughly in the centre of the waterway, where at the time of its construction only three people lived. Actually, the lock at Bobcaygeon constructed in 1833 had nothing to do with the later, much-talked-about Trent waterway. The first lock was conceived in the fertile mind of the canny Bethune as part of a plan for providing transportation into the hinterland; it was not connected in any way with canalization of the Trent River. In fact, the Bobcaygeon lock was planned at a time when Bethune neither wanted the Trent River navigation improved nor believed that it would ever happen.

Peter Robinson's settlement of Irish immigrants in the Peterborough area in 1825, augmented by a steady influx of settlers in the years following, created a compelling need for transportation facilities. In 1833 natural waterways provided the most practical and cheapest means of transportation; therefore it was natural that the chain of inland lakes beginning with Rice Lake and extending westwards through the Newcastle District would be seen as a logical conduit for moving goods and people in and out of the interior. Improvements with dams to raise water levels, locks to bypass rapids, and dredging to deepen shallow spots would make this natural waterway even more serviceable. But the problem in 1832 was how to get access from Lake Ontario to Rice Lake and its chain of connecting lakes. The Trent River was the natural outlet of the system, and many believed that a canalized Trent provided the only logical means of entry. But James Bethune did not accept this view.

Between 1815 and 1827 several surveys, ordered by the imperial government to locate a defence route through the interior of Upper Canada, coincided with the advance of settlement up the Trent. These surveys, especially the Catty survey of 1819, which proved that no satisfactory alternative to the Trent existed, aroused high expectations among settlers that the Trent River-Lake Simcoe route would be chosen. Active but not very serious agitation for the Trent's development began as early as 1820. In that year, John Bannister, who had received a grant of 800 acres at the present site of the Hiawatha Indian village on Rice Lake (later acquired by Bethune for taxes), suggested in a letter to the lieutenant-governor that a government lottery was "the only probable method to collect so large a sum, as the contemplated work will require."[9] Bannister's proposal, which does not seem far-fetched in this day of government-sponsored lotteries, received no consideration. In 1827, Thomas A. Stewart and other settlers petitioned for improvements of the inland waters. Their petition produced no immediate results, but it did keep expectations for a water communication alive.

Access to the inland waters by way of the Trent River had many drawbacks. To render navigable this twisting 67-mile-long river with its many falls, rapids, and shallows would be both technically difficult and expensive. The province, already burdened with heavy debts, could not afford to finance such a costly undertaking. And the enthusiasm that some expected the imperial government to have for undertaking the work had been dampened by the experience with Col. By's recently completed Rideau Canal; it had originally been estimated to cost $2,370,000 but had cost the British treasury over $4 million. Although well built, the canal proved to be of dubious military worth and, because of its location, of no commercial value at all.

Even if the money could be found and the construction difficulties overcome, there was still a question of the benefit to be derived from an improved Trent River. A boat ascending the 67-mile stretch of river would upon entering Rice Lake have travelled only about 12 miles from the Lake Ontario ports of Cobourg or Port Hope – a fact pointed out somewhat caustically by Hamilton Killaly, commissioner of public works, when he cancelled the first canalization scheme in 1841.

While these problems were being contemplated by residents in the district and policy-makers at Toronto, the enterprising Bethune, who saw that money could be made immediately in the transportation business, ignored the Trent, considering it an unlikely prospect; he concentrated on developing another route into Rice Lake, of which there were at least five possibilities. There were two roads: a road from Port Hope to Bewdley on the southwest end of Rice Lake, hacked out of the bush in 1819 and later extended around the lake to Peterborough, and the road from

Cobourg to Sully over which Robinson had hauled the Irish immigrants in 1825 and that had been improved by the Canada Company in 1827 at a cost of $3,000. Three other proposals were being discussed as alternatives to the Trent. A group of businessmen in Port Hope petitioned in 1832 for a permit to build a railroad from Port Hope to Bewdley. Another group of Port Hope residents was proposing that a canal be dug through the Oak Ridges moraine from Rice Lake to Port Hope by way of Smith's Creek. Finally, as mentioned earlier, a group in Cobourg headed by the energetic Bethune petitioned for a charter to construct a railroad from Cobourg to Rice Lake. Any one of the latter three proposals would have been superior to the Trent River scheme from the standpoint of cost and facility of engineering. Any one of them would have been adequate to handle the inland trade, which in the 1830s was not very heavy. But as will be demonstrated later, because of local rivalries and competition none of them was built at a time when it would have been most useful for settlement purposes. In any event, Bethune, always an opportunist, decided not to wait for a resolution of the competition over the selection of routes. He took advantage of the existing facilities and in 1832 planned his own transportation network into the back country.

Bethune's plan was patterned on the centuries-old portage principle, incorporating both land and water transport. His plan called for transporting passengers and freight from Cobourg to Rice Lake by stage (later by rail); at Sully the goods would be transferred to a steamer which would carry them to Peterborough, already developing as the principal distribution centre for the surrounding communities. From Peterborough, freight and passengers destined for points west would be transported by stage and wagon to Bridgenorth to connect with a regularly scheduled steamer on Chemung Lake. Locks and short canals would be built at Bobcaygeon and Purdy's Mill (Lindsay) to extend the route as traffic required. Thus all settlements bordering the Back Lakes would have direct access to the front. This plan was practical and made good sense for the times. Designed to satisfy the immediate commercial and agricultural needs of the district, it was not intended to be part of the grandiose scheme for linking Lake Ontario to Georgian Bay that others in the district were prophesying. In 1832 Bethune put the first phase of his plan into operation.

In January he laid the keel of the steamboat *Pemedash* at Sully on Rice Lake; in the spring the tiny, tub-like, wood-burning side-wheeler was launched, and that summer daily service to Whitla's Rapids, a point on the Otonabee River just below Peterborough, commenced. By the following summer Bethune had the Cobourg-Peterborough section of his system fairly well organized. Warehouses had been built at Cobourg and at the landing in Peterborough where goods and luggage were stored free of charge. To permit the flat-bottomed *Pemedash* to proceed, with some manual assistance, all the way to Whitla's Rapids, even in periods of low water, rocks were removed "from sundry parts"[10] of the Otonabee River at a cost of about $750. Bethune then placed a notice in the *Cobourg Star* announcing daily steamer service between Peterborough and Sully. The notice informed travellers that the *Pemedash*, with Capt. Cleghorn in command, left Peterborough every morning at 8 a.m. (except Sunday) and returned from Sully in the early evening. A connecting stage left the Steamboat Hotel in Cobourg, also at 8 a.m., to convey passengers to Sully, and five to ten heavy wagons departed from the Cobourg harbour warehouse every morning at half past six "for the conveyance of merchandise and luggage directed toward Peterborough and other parts of the interior."[11] During the shipping season of 1833 the *Pemedash* (renamed the *Otonabee* later that summer) made 136 round trips between Peterborough and Sully. She transported, in total, 172 barrels of pork and potash and 374 tons of general merchandise. The number of passengers carried is not known.

In the summer of 1833 Bethune was ready to initiate the second phase of his transportation chain. In June a sister steamer to the *Pemedash*, the *Sturgeon*, was launched at Bridgenorth, intended to "ply between Bridgenorth and the Bobcaygeon Falls through Chemong, Buckhorn and Pigeon Lakes, calling at several intermediate places."[12] During periods of high water she would attempt to ascend the Pigeon River as far as Cotnam's Landing (now Omemee) in Emily township. When the lock at Bobcaygeon was completed, her route would be extended to Cameron Falls and up the Scugog River to Purdy's Mill. The *Sturgeon* made her maiden voyage to Bobcaygeon on 5 September. Between that date and 20 November, when navigation closed for the season, she made 61 round trips. In all, that first season she carried 60 barrels of pork and 55 tons of general freight, much of it delivered to the construction crew already at work on the Bobcaygeon lock.

Bethune intended to develop the waterway as a private profit-making venture, but before he constructed any costly locks or carried out other expensive improvements he sought a measure of protection for his investment. He wanted, in fact, monopoly use of the waterway. To this end he petitioned the lieutenant-governor in the fall of 1832. He would be willing, he said, to spend a considerable sum in the improvement of the waterway, provided he could be indemnified by being authorized for a number of years to collect tolls on the various boats and vessels that would navigate the waters. When others learned about Bethune's request, they opposed it. Thomas Ward of Port Hope, who happened to own a good deal of land at Bridgenorth, collected signatures for a petition asking the lieutenant-governor to deny Bethune's request and to have the improvements carried out as a public enterprise instead. Ward and his friends asked that a sum of money to be expended on the waterways be granted by the legislature and placed in the hands of a commission. Both petitions were handed over to a select committee chaired by George S. Boulton of Cobourg. Boulton was hardly a disinterested arbiter.

Boulton and his relatives, although men of personal honour, typified the reason why the government of the day was odiously referred to as the "Family Compact." A family of lawyers and politicians, the Boultons wielded considerable political influence in Upper Canada. D'Arcy Boulton, the father, was an English barrister who emigrated to Upper Canada in 1797. By a special act of the legislature in 1803, he was created a barrister in Upper Canada; in 1805 he was appointed solicitor-general, in 1814 attorney-general, and in 1818 a judge of assize. D'Arcy's second son, John Henry, who practised law at York, acquired in succession his father's former portfolios: solicitor-general in 1818 and attorney-general in 1829. John Henry was also a member of the legislative assembly, elected in 1830 to represent Niagara. The third son, George S., practised law in Cobourg. He, too, was a member of the legislative assembly, representing Durham County from 1831 to 1841.

Short in stature but long in vision, George S. Boulton had good reason to want the waterway improved. A survey of the Crown Land Patent Records for Upper Canada reveals that Boulton owned thousands of acres of land scattered throughout the district but principally along the route of the proposed waterway. Much of his land had been acquired as surveying grants, but a good deal of it had been bought cheaply at public auction after 1826, when the government of Upper Canada decided to end all free land grants and to begin land sales. This policy was designed to increase provincial revenues but coincidentally served to the benefit of the Family Compact landowners as well. As long as free land was available, they had difficulty selling off their large land holdings, but because of the changed policy, Family Company stalwarts like Boulton, Burnham, and Rubidge reported their property in the district to have doubled in value. An improved waterway would increase land values even more. When the political pressure for a through waterway began to build in 1834, Catharine Parr Traill estimated that her husband's property in Douro had increased in value "in a three-fold degree."[13] Thomas Need reckoned that the start of the Bobcaygeon lock quadrupled the value of his land.

Need's property at Bobcaygeon was originally owned by Boulton who, in 1825, had acquired as a surveying grant several hundred acres of prime land at the Bobcaygeon Rapids in the very spot through which a future canal would run. At the time that Boulton's select committee was deliberating over the Bethune and Ward petitions, Boulton was negotiating with Need for the purchase of this land. A lock at Bobcaygeon would facilitate the sale. Thus Need could write in *Six Years in the Bush*, when referring to the Bobcaygeon lock, "Such an undertaking I had in some degree anticipated when I selected my land."[14]

Boulton offered a compromise to Bethune, which was reflected in the select committee's report and later incorporated into the legislation that Boulton drafted. Bethune would not be given a monopoly over the vital waterway, which would remain under public control, but would get the improvements necessary for operating his steamer service. The committee recommended to the legislature "that [$10,000] be granted, and placed in the hands of commissioners, to be expended for the completion of the proposed improvement."[15] Bethune and Need were both named commissioners. The purpose for which the money could be spent was left sufficiently vague to allow the commissioners to make any improvements they, i.e. Bethune, wished. The money was to be raised through the sale of debentures and given to the commissioners in the form of a loan. Principal and interest on the loan were to be redeemed through tolls, dues, and rates which the commissioners were empowered to collect on boats and freight moving through the waterway. Everyone was pleased with the legislation, which was passed on 13 February 1833. Bethune would get the improvements his transportation business required, paid for by public funds. Ward was happy to have the waterway remain under government control. Need was happy because he got the property at Bobcaygeon that "had every prospect of rapid progress."[16] And Boulton got $3,750 from Need for land that had not cost him anything.

Although seven commissioners had been appointed by the legislature to supervise the improvements, it was, in fact, exclusively Bethune's project – a fact that a select committee reporting to the legislature in 1836 pointed out, noting that "James G. Bethune being the only active commissioner was permitted to draw and pay over the money as he thought proper and take upon himself the principal direction of the work."[17] The necessary authority to proceed with the work having been granted, Bethune, as always, acted quickly. In March, he placed advertisements in the leading newspapers of the province, inviting tenders on the following works: building a lock at Bobcaygeon, constructing a lock at Purdy's Mill, dredging the Otonabee River, and clearing a navigable channel up Cavan Creek as far as Taggest's Mill. Persons tendering on the two locks were required to post bonds and to demonstrate, with appropriate references, that they could do the work. The deadline for receiving tenders was 1 June.

On 1 June, Bethune called a meeting of the commissioners to examine the tenders. The response to the advertisement was disappointing. Only two tenders were received, both for the Bobcaygeon lock. As the tender of Pierce, Dumble and Hoar, carpenters in Cobourg, was the lowest, the commissioners agreed to consider it.

On 3 June, Bethune arranged financing for the improvements through the Bank of Upper Canada, which bought four government debentures, in amounts of $2,000 each, at 6 per cent interest. The act had authorized security on the debentures, both principal and interest, to be given only in the form of tolls to be collected from the proposed improvements, but the bank was not satisfied with this. Consequently, it demanded collateral security by a mortgage on Bethune's real estate in Peterborough. Bethune signed over his property, and the money was given to him personally, not to the commissioners. This bizarre arrangement would cause considerable controversy a little later, when both the lock and Bethune's business interests failed.

On 10 June, Bethune took the other commissioners to Bobcaygeon to examine the site of the proposed lock, which had just been surveyed by Cobourg land surveyor Frederick P. Rubidge, who also drafted the specifications for the lock and canal.

Another meeting of the commissioners was called in Peterborough on 1 July, at which, according to Thomas Need, "several plans and estimates were proposed and taken into consideration and one or two important improvements ordered to be carried into effect."[18] The improvements were the lock at Bobcaygeon, a contract for which was awarded to Pierce, Dumble and Hoar, and dredging in the Otonabee River. No tenders having been received for the badly needed improvements in the Otonabee River, it was decided to appoint John Heard, a friend of Bethune's, "to engage hands, provide the necessary craft and implements and superintend the work."[19] In late August, Heard and his crew began dredging. Shoals below Whitla's Rapids were cleared, permitting the *Pemedash* to steam unimpeded to Peterborough. This work cost about $1,915.

On 25 July, Pierce, Dumble and Hoar signed a contract for $8,000 for building the Bobcaygeon lock. The contractors arrived at Bobcaygeon on 2 August, and work on the Trent canal's first lock began immediately.

CHAPTER TWO

The Bobcaygeon Lock

The first Bobcaygeon lock was a disaster. Although the principle of a hydraulic lift lock is simple, construction of the one at Bobcaygeon proved more difficult and more costly than either Bethune or the inexperienced contractors realized. The lock itself was well enough built, but because of engineering errors and serious miscalculations in water levels, the contractors could not get water into it and for four years the lock remained totally useless.

A hydraulic lift lock (the prototype was invented by Leonardo da Vinci in the fifteenth century) is designed in such a way as to create a step between two water levels, allowing vessels to be raised or lowered from one level to the other. Falls or rapids caused by the natural drop between two bodies of water are bypassed with a canal, dug in opposite directions from each body of water. The lock is built into the canal at the point where the two levels meet, creating a step equal to the difference between the surface elevations of the two connected waters. The juncture between the levels can be established at any point suitable for the insertion of the lock, but digging the canal requires accurate engineering based on precise measurements and a knowledge of the high- and low-water levels in the reaches above and below the falls. To ensure a constant water level in the canal for navigation purposes, a control dam is built across the natural waterfall.

A lock is a box-like structure with gates at each end and valves or sluices that allow the box to be filled or drained of water when the gates are shut. When the upper valves are open and the lower valves are closed, the lock fills to the level of the upper reach. The valves are then closed and the gates leading into the upper reach opened, permitting entry of a boat into the lock. The boat having entered, the upper gates are then closed and the lower valves opened, allowing the water in the lock to drain to the level of the lower reach. When the lock has been drained, the lower gates can be opened, permitting the boat to proceed on its way. The difference between the upper and lower levels determines the lock's "lift."

Lock gates have to be very strong to withstand the great pressure, and they need to be as watertight as possible to allow the lock to fill and drain properly. To produce watertightness, the closed gates fit on a mitre sill, situated on the floor of the lock. The depth of the water over the mitre sill has to be sufficient to accommodate the draft of the boat. Today locks are built of poured concrete and steel gates. In earlier times, locks were made of wood or blocks of limestone masonry with gates constructed of oak timber.

Frederick P. Rubidge, who designed the Bobcaygeon lock, apparently knew little more about lock construction than the general principles outlined above. His lock specifications, drafted for the guidance of the contractors, were very sketchy. They called merely for a lock 120 feet long between the gates and 28 feet in width. The lift was estimated to be 10 feet "more or less," which was considerably off. The side walls of the lock were to be made of 15-inch by 12-inch oak and pine timbers; the gates were to be 17 feet wide and 15 inches thick, built of oak timbers and covered with two-and-a-half-inch pine planks. There were to be four valves, two at each end, 2 feet, 9 inches square. The upper valves were to open into the bottom of the lock "from the outside in a safe and substantial manner," and the lower valves were to be located in the lower gates. The lock was to be placed at the lower end of a canal to be cut through the rock "from the headwater of the Bobcaygeon River."[1] The canal was to be 50 feet wide at the surface and 36 feet wide at the bottom and capable of holding four feet of water. Its length and hence its precise location were unspecified.

At first everything went well enough. Most of the first summer was spent in cutting the canal and preparing timber and planking for the lock. The materials were available on the spot or from nearby Purdy's Mills, but tools, equipment, and supplies had to be brought 21 miles from Peterborough in wagons and barges, until the *Sturgeon* was placed in service in September. Many of the labourers were recruited from the nearby settlements in Ops and Emily townships. The work was highly labour-intensive, and although wages were low, the primitive nature of construction required many man-hours of work, creating a labour bill much higher than the contractors had anticipated.

The canal had to be cut through limestone rock. When the surface cover had been removed, shallow holes were drilled in the rock with crude bits and sledge hammers; the holes were filled with black powder, which when ignited blasted the rock apart. The loose rock was then carted out of the cut in barrows and hand carts. It was back-breaking, sometimes dangerous work. It was also time-consuming. Costs mounted. Flies, especially swarms of "blue devils," that filled the warm August air were a constant source of irritation to the workers. Later, heavy rains impeded the work. A very wet season "prevented the waters from subsiding to their normal level," causing the constructors "much extra expense and loss of time."[2] The weather finally forced suspension of work on 14 November, and the contractors were given an extension of time on the contract.

Despite difficulty with the weather, work had progressed remarkably well. In just over three months half the contract had been completed, and the work had a salutary effect on the district. In reporting progress to the lieutenant-governor on 16 November, the commissioners were able "to observe with pleasure the beneficial influence the commencement of these works has exerted in promoting settlement." They pointed out with pride that "a number of very respectable settlers had gone in," and there was a "great demand for locations." Seeing their property values increase daily, the commissioners predicted that when the works were completed, providing the advantages of steam navigation, the district would "acquire a degree of prosperity and importance to which it could not otherwise have attained."[3] Indeed Bethune, the transportation baron, must have appeared to many in the district as a miracle worker.

But alas! In the spring, just about the time the contractors were returning to work at Bobcaygeon, James Bethune became a "defaulter and insolvent."[4] All his assets, including the funds for the Bobcaygeon works, were frozen.

Always a better promoter and doer than bookkeeper and accountant, Bethune kept his financial records in a deplorable state of disorder: bank, business, personal, and public works accounts were so thoroughly confused that even he had difficulty sorting them out when his creditors moved to foreclose on him. It was his banking interests that brought about his downfall. Uncertainty in us banking circles in 1834, reluctance of Canadian banks to extend credit, stringent government regulations governing the issue of paper currency, and the fact that the Bank of Upper Canada did not pay interest on deposits, encouraging immigrants to keep their gold locked away in strong boxes, caused a great shortage of cash in Upper Canada in the early 1830s. With little money in circulation, a depression set in and business ground to a halt.

Settlers who had placed their sovereigns in Bethune's bank for safe keeping tried to recover them, but regrettably many of the sovereigns were not there. On audit, the bank was found to be $15,000 short. Some of the shortage could probably be accounted for by faulty bookkeeping, but some of it undoubtedly resulted from funds being funnelled off, temporarily, into one of Bethune's business ventures. Bethune claimed that the bank had been robbed, but many thought that he had stolen the money himself. No criminal charges were laid, but Bethune lost his bank managership and with it the confidence of the government and his creditors. His debts were large, estimated by some to be as high as $80,000.

Alarmed, his debtors, large and small, wanted immediate repayment, but Bethune could not raise the cash. While many, including the government, owed him money, he was not able to collect from them, partly because cash was scarce, partly because his accounts were in such confusion that he was not exactly sure what was owed him, and partly because his enemies had no desire to rescue him from impending bankruptcy. His health gave way under the strain, preventing him from sorting out his financial affairs, and unfortunately, as he confessed to Peter Robinson, "there was no person that could attempt to make up the accounts but [him]self."[5] Meanwhile, he was "pestered from morning until night for small sums,"[6] his name was vilified, his character was denigrated (Langton now called him a "most reckless and unprincipled speculator"),[7] and, to make matters worse, he was not able "to dispose of any property, real or personal."[8] His property was valued at upwards of $300,000.

Hoping to regain the confidence of the government, the key to his salvation, Bethune declared as a Conservative candidate in Northumberland in the autumn election of 1834. He spoke to electors gathered at Sully about the immediate interests of the district "for up to two hours with a fluency and eloquence" that under the circumstances of his predicament "astounded even his warmest friends ."[9] The election was close, but despite Bethune's eloquence, the Reformer, Dr John Gilchrist, outpolled him.

Then, as he had predicted in August, his "time of appointing"[10] arrived. Civil suits followed bankruptcy. Still unable to pay his debts, the "Great Man" suffered the ignominy of being carted off to prison at Amherst in the spring of 1836. In time he was able to straighten out his accounts, collect his debts, sell his property, pay his creditors, and extricate himself from prison. He moved to Rochester, New York, where in 1841 at the age of 48 he died, a sickly and dispirited man. But legal disputes growing out of the chaos he created in financing the Bobcaygeon lock would linger long after his death.

Bethune's bankruptcy created a serious, immediate problem for the contractors at Bobcaygeon. Because the account for the works was in Bethune's name and not the commissioners', it was frozen along with all his other accounts. Since no more money could be advanced, the contractors had either to pay the workers out of their own pockets or to suspend the work. To make matters worse, it had become clear that the contract was underbid. Although they faced the risk of losing considerable money, and perhaps not even being paid for the work already done, Pierce, Dumble and Hoar decided to complete the lock anyway.

As early as January, the sharp-eyed John Langton had detected weaknesses in the design of the works. In a letter to his father, he predicted that "though the canal is progressing, the whole plan in my opinion is so radically bad that until it is altered entirely the steamer will never get up into Sturgeon Lake."[11] The commissioners and the contractors apparently did not share Langton's pessimism. On 11 June, Hall and some of the other commissioners visited the works and, according to Need, "were much pleased with what they [had] seen."[12] Not until 4 November, when water was let into the canal to test the lock, was Langton's assessment proved correct.

"Misfortune on misfortune," Need wrote in his diary, "the canal gives in several places and leaks so bad that the water will not rise."[13] The limestone bed of the canal was full of fissures and crevices; as the water ran down the canal, it simply disappeared into the deep cracks, none of it reaching the lock which sat like an empty wooden bucket at the bottom of a dry well. For three days, Need and the workers tried to remedy the situation "by damming up part of the canal in order to avoid the most considerable leaks,"[14] but without success. "My efforts are unavailing ... the canal sinks down in another place at the bottom and the water escapes,"[15] a frustrated Need wrote for posterity. He finally stopped trying to staunch the leaks.

Even if the canal had not leaked, the lock would still have been practically useless. By a miscalculation in the levels, the lock had been set too high, the top of the lower sill being placed on the same level as the low-water level at Pigeon Lake; therefore, for several weeks of the year, boats would not have been able to leave or enter the lock. But even if the lock had been properly levelled, there was yet another problem: the dam built across the rapids to divert the flow from Sturgeon Lake into the canal had not been made high enough "to retain a sufficient head of water over the shallows above."[16] Thus boats would not have been able to enter the canal from the Sturgeon Lake end at low water.

When making a survey of the waterway the following summer, Baird found the works at Bobcaygeon "entirely useless." Tactfully, he attributed the errors to "some unaccountable oversight."[17] John Langton's judgment was more blunt. He called the work "an apology for a lock, which the stupidity (if in some cases it be not worse) of the Commissioners has imposed."[18]

The mistakes made in the Bobcaygeon works were the result of faulty engineering done by a land surveyor inexperienced in lock construction, but responsibility for them lay with the commissioners, none of whom seemed willing to accept it. As no specific length for the canal or precise location for the lock had been determined, no testing of the bedrock had been carried out, and the lift was estimated to be about 10 feet when in reality it was only 5 feet 5 inches, clearly the "surveying and plotting"[19] reported to have been done by Rubidge in May 1833 were only superficial. The specifications given to Pierce, Dumble and Hoar were not sufficiently detailed for reasonable tendering, let alone accurate construction. Nor was there adequate supervision. Bethune did not visit the site once after construction had started. John Hall and Alexander McDonell saw the works only once or twice. John Huston was at Bobcaygeon a couple of times, but primarily to survey Need's property and to subdivide it into lots. Need, being on the spot, was the only commissioner to take an active interest in the works. He visited the construction site almost every day, but training for the ministry had ill prepared him for supervising such a complex engineering project.

Peter Robinson was concerned about the apparent lack of canal levels from the beginning. In late September 1833, after construction was well under way, he wrote to Bethune about them. In responding to Robinson on 28 September, Bethune agreed that "the work could not proceed"[20] without the levels, and he assured Robinson that he had written to Alexander McDonell and Deputy Provisional Surveyor John Smith to take the levels immediately. By then it was early October, and because of an unusually wet autumn, the levels in the lakes had reached unprecedented highs. A knowledge of high-water levels is very important in canal and lock designing, but a knowledge of low-water levels is even more crucial, especially in a waterway that has no form of water control but natural ones. Although one can easily determine a high-water level on an unfamiliar lake from water stains on the rocks and shoreline vegetation, it is virtually impossible to determine low-water levels by sight. In the absence of any historical data for Pigeon and Sturgeon lakes, low-water levels could be only estimated, and these were incorrectly estimated from the base of abnormal highs. This simple error in calculation probably accounted for the incorrect placement of the lower sill and the wrong elevation of the Sturgeon Lake dam. It was the fault of the surveyors and ultimately that of the commissioners, but not of the contractors.

On 23 November, long after the contractors had departed, Need wrote to Bethune, Boulton, and John Hall to ask what was to be done about the faulty lock, but he got no response. Bethune was in seclusion, recovering from an emotional collapse occasioned by his financial difficulties and recent rejection at the polls. Apparently none of the other commissioners wanted to assume responsibility either, as the contractors complained that they "were unable to procure the attendance of any of the commissioners to examine or accept" the work [21] The contractors did not think that they should be held responsible for the errors; further, they were $3,830 in debt. At their own expense, they employed a civil engineer who examined the work and confirmed that it was "finished and executed as well or better than the contract and specifications bound them"; the engineer judged also that "the work was taken at too low a rate."[22] Armed with this evidence, the contractors petitioned the lieutenant-governor for redress.

The legislature accepted the recommendation of a select committee that examined the grievance and awarded the contractors the $3,830 in compensation they had requested.

And so the lock at Bobcaygeon, which had started a-building with the offer of such great promise for the future, turned out a bitter disappointment. A total of $13,830 had been wasted. Thereafter, Thomas Need would concentrate on building his mills and developing his property into the village of Rockeby. [23] John Langton and other residents of Sturgeon Lake would continue to curse the commissioners every time they bulled their heavy scows through Bobcaygeon Rapids – more difficult now because of a useless dam and an even more useless lock. Until his release, James Gray Bethune would languish in Amherst prison, where he complained that because "bed, sofa and office furniture occupied so much," he had "but nine feet square left for exercise."[24] The slow-moving *Sturgeon*, which had been humiliated by losing a race with Langton's rowboat in May 1834, was last sighted at Bobcaygeon Rapids on 9 November, unable to enter the lock that had been specially built for her. Then she vanished from history.

Later many others would champion the cause of the waterway. Four years after the failure of the first lock, a second, improved lock would be placed in operation at Bobcaygeon. The second lock would be the true first lock of the Trent canal.

CHAPTER THREE

The Question of Routes

Bethune's precipitate move to develop a private transportation network through the Back Lakes triggered intense public reaction in the district. His initial success aroused a spate of anger, jealousy, and competition which, in turn, produced an avalanche of petitions and a series of "moves" instigated by groups that desired a transportation route, especially from Lake Ontario to Rice Lake, that would be advantageous to themselves.

First, there were the farmers, mill owners, and lumberers who lived along the Trent River; they saw the Trent as the only logical access to Rice Lake. They wanted the waterway principally because the farmers would benefit from the cash-paying jobs the development work would create, the lumberers would benefit from the improved facility for moving timber to the Quebec market, and all the river communities would prosper in a myriad of ways by the commerce that the waterway would bring. But development of the Trent River would be costly and would have to be undertaken as a public enterprise. This was the main objection to it and the principal reason why the imperial government abandoned the scheme and why earlier petitions by settlers to have the river canalized had been ignored.

A second group comprised the businessmen in Cobourg, most of whom were directors and stockholders in the Cobourg Harbour Company. These men planned to open up the district with a railroad from Cobourg to Rice Lake. Produce from the interior and iron from a mine at Marmora would be transported by steamer to Sully and thence to markets on Lake Ontario and Montreal, by way of Cobourg harbour. This would be a private venture with profits going to the shareholders of the railroad and harbour companies. James Bethune was the leader of this group.

A third group, in Port Hope, planned to charter a private canal company. Its canal, connecting Port Hope with Rice Lake, would funnel produce and profits through Port Hope.

Finally, there were the residents of Peterborough and the developing settlements to the northwest. Although generally favouring the historic proposal for the development of the Trent River, this group really did not care which outlet to Lake Ontario was chosen. Its principal objective was to get a system of locks and canals constructed through the Back Lakes – preferably all the way to Lake Simcoe – so that they could move their produce out to markets.

The giant strides made by Bethune in securing legislation for his own transportation business goaded all the groups into action, all at the same time and each against the others. The Port Hope and Trent River groups, while not supporting each other, were united in their opposition to Bethune and his gang of railway promoters in Cobourg. The railway promoters, in turn, sought to block any canal from Rice Lake to Lake Ontario that would compete with the railway for the limited trade in the district. "There is so much favouring of interest about this [question of route] that one has to be constrained,"[1] Nichol Hugh Baird reported to the lieutenant-governor in November 1833. This was probably the understatement of the year. Though public petitions had been ignored in the past, many wondered how 'an unprincipled speculator' like Bethune could build steamboats, receive government grants for a lock, and even have the audacity to request monopoly privileges on a waterway that belonged to the people. The answer lay where the answer to all puzzling questions about the Trent canal would lie – in the perplexing riddle of politics.

Before reorganization of the political boundaries in Upper Canada at Union in 1841, the Newcastle District was comprised of the adjacent counties of Durham and Northumberland. The developing townships at the north of the district, in what later became Peterborough and Victoria counties, were attached to Northumberland and Durham for administrative purposes. The proposed Trent waterway, which from the beginning had strong political ramifications, snaked through the back of the district, cutting across the two ridings of Durham and Northumberland. Most of the Trent River, the Otonabee River, and the Back Lakes, to a point almost as far west as Bobcaygeon, lay in Northumberland; the section from Bobcaygeon to the Talbot River, including Lake Scugog and the Scugog River, was in Durham. Before the general election of 1834, only one member represented Northumberland, but two men, George S. Boulton of Cobourg and John Brown of Port Hope, represented Durham.

Brown was a promoter and director of the Port Hope Canal Company; he naturally favoured the Port Hope route over either the Trent River canal or the Cobourg railway. Boulton was a director of the Cobourg Harbour Company and soon to be a director of the Cobourg and Rice Lake Railroad Company. He was opposed to both the Trent River and Port Hope routes; the Trent because of the cost involved and the Port Hope Canal because of its potential competition with his vested interests in Cobourg.

Neither Brown nor Boulton was antagonistic to Bethune's plan to build locks in the Back Lakes, as long as he did not obtain a monopoly over the waterway. His locks and canal would facilitate the transport of produce to and from the interior and Rice Lake. From that point on, the expectation of the two men differed. It was Brown's hope that the freight would pass out to Lake Ontario through the proposed Port Hope Canal. Boulton, however, anticipated the freight would move over the proposed Cobourg railway. Consequently, when Boulton's committee recommended Bethune's scheme in the legislature, Brown voted for the bill. The people who lived along the Trent, however, were not satisfied.

Boulton, being the leading political figure in the district, came under intense public criticism for pushing Bethune's scheme in the legislature and ignoring the interests of those who lived along the Trent. So he decided that the time had come to awaken, with a splash of cold, financial reality, those who dreamed of a canalized Trent River. Thus, on 7 November 1832, when he knew that Bethune's petition for financial support was coming before the legislature, Boulton announced in the House that he was going to "move for an address to His Excellency ... requesting him to take the necessary measures for the survey, by a competent engineer, of the River Trent, from its mouth to Rice Lake, in order to ascertain the practicability and expense of a Canal."[2] After a heated debate on 3 February 1833, the legislature agreed to defray the expenses of the survey, and finally, on 13 February, the same day the act authorizing Bethune's scheme was passed, the lieutenant-governor informed the House that he would "order Surveys and Estimates ... be made by persons properly qualified to perform the service."[3] On 19 March Lt.-Col. Rowan, private secretary to the lieutenant-governor, wrote to Nichol Hugh Baird, then living in Montreal, to ask him if he would make the survey. Baird agreed, but no date was set. Time passed. Meanwhile, tenders were called and work began on the Bobcaygeon lock.

Residents in the Peterborough area grew impatient. Hoping to capitalize on the momentum generated by Bethune's lock building, they organized a promotional meeting at the King's Arms Hotel in Peterborough, on 27 August. The meeting, which was attended by many of the leading citizens of the area, including John Hall and John Huston, unanimously resolved that: "the time has now arrived when improvement of the navigation of the River Trent has become an object of vital importance to this district and that measures should be taken to press upon the Legislature the necessity of procuring a correct survey and estimate ... and of directing its immediate attention to the object of such vast importance to the interests of the Province, both political and commercial."[4]

The immediate result of the meeting, which was the first of hundreds that would be held through the years, was to hasten Baird's survey. Baird arrived at the mouth of the Trent River on 7 September and began examining the falls and rapids and estimating the cost of overcoming them.

While only 37 years of age, Nichol Hugh Baird had a good deal of civil engineering experience, particularly on canals. Born in Glasgow, Scotland, on 26 August 1796, he was the oldest son of Hugh Baird, superintendent of the Forth and Clyde Canal. Nichol Hugh began the study of engineering in 1816, apprenticing under his father, from whom he acquired the types of skills that gave Scots an international reputation for engineering excellence. Indeed, Tsar Nicholas I, who inherited, along with the Russian crown in 1825, a tradition dating back to Peter the Great of borrowing from the West both its technical skills and stylistic inspiration, employed young Baird for a time, to undertake some reconstruction projects in St Petersburg. Later, in 1828, Baird emigrated to Canada to become clerk of works on the Rideau Canal construction. In 1831 he married Mary Telfer White, daughter of Andrew White, a prosperous Montreal contractor who had built sections of the Rideau Canal. When Rowan's letter arrived, the Rideau Canal had been completed and Baird was supervising construction of the bridge of Trenton. Devising ways of taming the tortuous Trent River offered just the challenge Baird was looking for. He hired Frederick P. Rubidge of Cobourg to assist with the survey.

The principle that Baird proposed using for overcoming the several obstacles on this "grand and available stream"[5] was that of damming the rapids and overcoming the rises with locks and, where necessary, short canals. He estimated that the work would require 43 locks and 17 dams. The cost he placed at $1,167,236 for wooden dams and masonry locks 134 feet long and 34 feet wide, with 5 feet of water over the sills. He reckoned that it would take four years to complete the work. He submitted his report on 28 November and with it offered advice that his commission had not called for. He did, in fact, what every succeeding engineer connected with the Trent canal, except one, would do: he promoted it, pointing out "a few of the advantages likely to accrue from the fulfilment of such a measure."[6] These included "relieving the country immediately contiguous and the region beyond from the land-locked predicament in which they now are ... increase in the value of the many thousands of acres on and contiguous to its banks ... facility for the transport of lumber ... incalculable advantage this Province would derive from the Marmora iron works being set in operation ... an incalculable benefit to the settlements around the Rice Lake, Ottonabee [sic] River, and the Lakes beyond."[7] Finally, projecting into the future, he pointed out "that the navigation carried into Rice Lake is comparatively speaking communication carried into Lake Huron."[8] He volunteered the opinion that the cost of construction could be recovered from tolls, estimated from timber alone to be $30,000 annually, and from property taxes, to which every land-owner between the Trent's mouth and Lake Simcoe "would cheerfully sub-mit."[9] It seems that Baird wanted very badly to secure the job of superin-tending the proposed works.

When word reached Port Hope that Baird was at work on the Trent River, the residents of Port Hope became active. The Port Hope people were convinced that a cost comparison of the two routes would favour Port Hope, which they argued would not only provide the same com-mercial benefits to the interior as the Trent, but also had the advantage of being much shorter (only 14 miles). On 4 October Capt. Richard Bullock, farmer and justice of the peace, forwarded a petition on behalf of the town to the lieutenant-governor, asking him "to direct that the civil engineer employed on the Trent survey do also survey the proposed [Port Hope] canal."[10] Lt.-Gov. Sir John Colborne asked Baird to conduct the survey, but he declined, giving as an excuse that he would "be occupied for some time on the Trent Survey."[11] Actually, Baird was becoming interested in the Cobourg railway. Later he would survey the route for the railway and subscribe for stock. He recommended a young engineer named Robert Maigny for the Port Hope survey.

Next, the railway promoters in Cobourg, in the process of petitioning the legislature for a charter, launched a campaign, probably instigated by the wily Bethune, to scupper both the Port Hope and Trent River canals. The *Cobourg Star* printed a lead editorial on 30 October, denounc-ing the Trent and supporting the Cobourg and Rice Lake Railroad. It pointed out that the obstacles in the Trent were found (by Baird) to be immense, and "the amount of capital required to form locks and canals ... is calculated at [$1.5 million] – a sum [exaggerated] of such magnitude that it is unlikely that the government will be induced to undertake this improvement.[11] "Fortunately," the editorial continued, "the construction of a railroad, against which there are no material obstacles could effectively accomplish communication between the front and the back country with no heavy tax on the country's resources."[12]

Port Hope wasted no time in counteracting the initiatives of the *Cobourg Star* on behalf of the railroad. A general meeting was conven-ed at the Mansion House Hotel in Port Hope on Tuesday, 26 November, at which a series of canal resolutions was adopted. The resolutions pleaded for government support for the Port Hope Canal, arguing that it "would not mitigate [sic] against the proposed grand scheme of opening the Trent," pointing out "that reports so ingeniously circulated to the disadvantage of this place and the Trent are absurd and malicious," and reasoning "that no railroad whatsoever from Rice Lake to any part of Lake Ontario [could] equal any advantage of a direct water communication."[13] Copies of the resolutions were sent to all the leaders in government.

Because there was no immediate positive sign that the government would build them a canal, the Port Hope promoters thereafter decided to charter their own canal company and build a canal themselves, possibly with some government assistance.

Meanwhile, residents on the Trent engaged in political activity of their own to make sure that the Trent River route was not forgotten. Encouraged by Baird's favourable report, William Robertson, a lumberer who resided near the mouth of the Trent, collected 230 signatures for a petition "praying that the River Trent may be made Navigable."[14] Robertson's petition was tabled in the legislature on 7 January 1834 by the member from Hastings.

Finally, on 30 January 1834, the lieutenant-governor transmitted to the House of Assembly Baird's long awaited report of his survey of the Trent River, the results of which were by then common knowledge. In tabling the report, His Excellency directed "the attention of the House to the advantages that [would] be derived by opening the navigation for steam vessels from Rice Lake to Healey's Falls."[15] In singling out just one portion of Baird's report, the lieutenant-governor was undoubtedly influenced by George S. Boulton and the promoters of the Cobourg and Rice Lake Railroad, because opening navigation from Rice Lake to Healey Falls would serve the interests of the railroad and very few others.

Baird had proposed dividing the Trent River into five sections for construction purposes. The fifth and cheapest section, estimated by Baird to cost about $35,000, extended from the top of Healey Falls to Rice Lake. To render this section navigable, Baird had proposed building a dam at the head of the falls to drown out the shallows in the river above and one dam and a lock at Crooks' Rapids (now Hastings). The distance from Healey Falls to the Marmora iron works at Blairton was only about nine miles.

Iron deposits had been discovered at Blairton in 1816. Early attempts to develop the property had been unsuccessful, because of the difficulty of transporting the heavy ore by wagon to a smelter at Belleville. In 1831, a group of men from Montreal, encouraged by prospective markets for iron for military and naval needs as well as commercial uses such as railroads, incorporated the Marmora Foundry Company with a view to reopening the Blairton mine. Opening the Healey Falls – Rice Lake section of the Trent River would solve the company's transportation problems, as pig iron produced in its foundry could be hauled easily to Healey Falls, loaded into barges, towed across Rice Lake to Sully, and transported thence to Lake Ontario markets on the Cobourg and Rice Lake Railroad.

Baird's report and Robertson's petition were referred to a select committee chaired by George S. Boulton. Four days later, on 3 February 1834, Boulton reported back to the legislature. As might be expected, he recommended that the Healey Falls – Rice Lake section be undertaken at once and that the sale of debentures for $39,060 be authorized for the purpose. Robertson's petition was ignored, although development of the lower Trent was not ruled out at some future date "deemed advisable by the Legislature."[16] The recommendation was manifestly prejudicial to the Cobourg Railroad and perhaps to some future Port Hope Canal, but it did not recommend itself to the people on the lower Trent or to the residents of Peterborough and the Back Lakes. The report was not acted upon.

On 6 March, two acts – one incorporating the Port Hope and Rice Lake Canal Company, the other incorporating the Cobourg Rail Road Company – passed the legislature. Also on that day, Maigny submitted his survey and estimate for the Port Hope Canal.

Maigny's plan called for 35 wooden locks, 70 feet long and 14 feet wide, averaging a 10-foot lift with 5 feet of water over the sills. The total cost he estimated at $507,130 – less than half the cost of Baird's proposed Trent River improvements.

At that point, the controversy surrounding the various proposals became quiescent for a time, because Sir John Colborne decided that before doing anything, he would visit the district to see the waterway for himself. In the mean time, Bethune launched the *Sturgeon* on Chemung Lake and work on the Bobcaygeon lock proceeded towards its calamitous conclusion.

Sir John Colborne had arrived at York in November 1828, to take over the lieutenant-governorship of Upper Canada from Sir Peregrine Maitland. A brilliant soldier who had distinguished himself in the Napoleonic War, Sir John resembled his former commander, the Duke of Wellington, in both appearance and disposition. This soldier-statesman with a Wellingtonian temperament was ideally suited for the task of governing the colony, then seething with political unrest. Sir John was soon regarded as "being a plain straight forward sort of person" who, when he had taken a fancy to a particular township, "produced the happiest results."[17] The residents of the District of Newcastle, many of whom were Tories, looked favourably on Colborne, whom they believed championed their causes and whose visit they thought would produce the happiest results for them.

Colborne started his six-day tour of the district from Port Hope, on 11 September 1834. His trip took him by stage through Cavan township to Peterborough; then, accompanied by Thomas A. Stewart and Alexander McDonell, he travelled through Chemung and Buckhorn lakes to the site of John Hall's developing mills at Buckhorn Falls; next he went to Bobcaygeon, where he inspected the work of the lock and where he dined and slept at Need's house. The next day he travelled by canoe to Fenelon Falls to visit Jameson, Wallis, and Langton. On the following day he proceeded through Cameron and Balsam lakes and walked about a dozen miles through the bush to see the Talbot River – the natural link between the Back Lakes and Lake Simcoe. His return journey took him back through Peterborough to Rice Lake, on the *Pemedash* to Bewdley, and overland back to York. Colborne was delighted with what he had seen, being impressed with both the number and the calibre of the "aristocratic" settlers whom he had met. According to John Langton, he promised "to send ... up plenty of settlers next year."[18]

This promise was interpreted by the "aristocratic" settlers as support for the waterway, which they saw as essential to their plan for creating a system of tenant farming in the northern wilderness.

The outcome of the general election held at Sully on 6 and 9 October had a profound effect on the ever-shifting sand of canal politics. The Reformer, Dr John Gilchrist of Keene, was elected to replace Archibald McDonald in the south riding of Northumberland; the new riding established in the back townships returned Alexander McDonell of Peterborough. Boulton and Brown retained their seats in Durham. The residents of Peterborough and the other interior communities now had, in McDonell, a direct voice in the legislature, and McDonell had support in the legislative council through his uncle, the Roman Catholic bishop of Kingston, owner of 1,200 acres of land on Sturgeon Lake, which required only adequate water communication to increase its value to its full potential. Thomas A. Stewart had been appointed to the legislative council in 1833, thus adding another powerful voice to those who lobbied for extension of the waterway into the Back Lakes.

Colborne's visit put the political football into scrimmage once more. Hoping that Colborne was sufficiently convinced of the merits of a developed Trent system, John Hall, whose Buckhorn mills were isolated at the moment but lay on the route of the proposed waterway, called a meeting in Peterborough on 1 November to push the scheme once more. A petition was drafted calling for "connecting the waters of Lake Huron with those of Lake Ontario by canal or otherwise"[19] and suggesting that if provincial funds were not adequate that Parliament apply to the imperial government for support. (The 'or otherwise' foreshadowed a recommendation for an alternative system that Baird would soon make). Hall collected 730 signatures on his petition, which was tabled in the legislature by McDonell on 23 January 1835 as one of his first legislative actions. The petition was referred to a select committee consisting of Gilchrist, Samson, and McDonell himself. This committee recommended to the House, and the House agreed, "that a competent engineer be employed to examine the most eligible route for a canal between Lake Simcoe and Rice Lake."[20] So once again Rowan wrote to Baird, asking him to conduct a survey, and once again Baird rented a canoe and set off through the Back Lakes, on 18 June, to find the most eligible route for the canal. Many thought that the much-talked-about waterway would at long last become a reality. But not for a while yet.

The truth of the matter is that the government, or at least many influential men in it, while recognizing the need to yield in some way to the intense public pressure coming from the region, did not want the Trent drainage system developed. For one thing, the cost would be enormous. But the main opposition came from the directors and shareholders of the Welland Canal Company, many of whom were members of the Family Compact. Ever since its opening in 1829, the Welland Canal had experienced financial difficulty. Revenue from tolls was insufficient to pay for routine maintenance, let alone provide profits, and capital for expansion was hard to find. The company needed the assistance of government to keep it afloat. (On 6 March 1834, the same day the Port Hope and Rice Lake Canal Company and the Cobourg Rail Road Company were incorporated, the legislature passed an act authorizing purchase, by the government, of $250,000 worth of Welland Canal Company stock.) William Hamilton Merritt, founder of the company, had been for years advocating development of the St Lawrence River canals, which he saw as the best means of recapturing the trade lost to New York with the completion of the Erie Canal in 1825 and, incidentally, of improving the fortunes of the Welland Canal. He was not enamoured of the prospect of squandering a large sum of money on the Trent waterway, which he regarded as purely local improvement.

The other directors of the Welland Canal Company agreed with Merritt. They were willing to spend a few thousand pounds for cheap wooden locks to facilitate the movement of produce through the Back Lakes of the Newcastle District. They were willing even to tolerate a privately constructed canal between Rice Lake and Port Hope, on the small scale recommended by Maigny, so long as the canal served local transportation needs. But there was no possibility of their agreeing to the government building another provincial canal connecting Lake Huron and Lake Ontario that would divert future traffic from the upper Great Lakes away from the anaemic Welland. Opposition by promoters of the Welland Canal would frustrate the efforts of those who promoted the Trent canal for the next 70 years.

The Port Hope and Rice Lake Canal Company had been counting on government grants for the success of its endeavours, and when these were withheld the company was doomed. Thus, for the time being, Port Hope ceased to pose a threat to the Trent, but 60 years later the Port Hope Canal would rise, like the phoenix from its ashes, to challenge the Trent route a second time.

In 1835, the Cobourg Rail Road Company seemed to have better grounds for optimism about its chances of competing successfully with the Trent River development for access into Rice Lake. On 3 July, the promoters of the railroad gathered in the Steamboat Hotel in Cobourg "to take into consideration the best means of availing themselves of the act of incorporation."[21] A temporary board of directors was elected, a stock book was opened, and $23,250 of the authorized $200,000 of capital stock was subscribed for by the "gentlemen present."[22] The first task of the temporary board was to hire Baird, who had just completed the Lake Simcoe survey, to lay out the route of the proposed railroad. Baird, accompanied by Frederick P. Rubidge, commenced taking levels for the railroad on 26 August, "starting from the Harbour Company's warehouse on the east pier."[23] *The Cobourg Star* confidently predicted that "in two years ... stock in the Cobourg and Rice Lake Railroad is likely to prove anything but a losing concern."[24]

It must have been with considerable chagrin that Baird sat down in his study in Montreal in early September to review his field notes and sketches of the Lake Simcoe survey and to prepare his estimate. His report, which was to be submitted before the opening of the next session of Parliament, would reveal that a canal from Rice Lake to Lake Simcoe would require 32 locks and 13 dams and would cost, at a minimum, $1,310,340. Added to the Trent River estimate, this would mean constructing 75 locks and 30 dams, at a total cost of $2,477,575. And there was still the line from Lake Simcoe to Lake Huron to be surveyed, before the full cost of the through waterway could be known. Baird knew contemporary canal politics as well as anyone, and he knew that his proposal with its rich estimate would sit uncomfortably with the abstemious legislature. But he did want to see the waterway developed; therefore, before submitting his official report with a litany of reasons why the Trent waterway should be constructed, he decided to submit an interim report with a more palatable proposal.

Baird's interim proposal called for a line of communication using a combination of water transportation and railroads, anticipating the "piggy-back" method of transport effected between railroads and trucks in the twentieth century. He proposed specially designed steamers that would "admit of a train of cars being transported ... with their holdings"[25] to ply the intermediate waters. This was the same portage principle followed by Bethune, substituting railroads for stage coaches. Baird estimated that this "combined principle" would reduce construction costs by about $1.5 million and would allow the communication to be completed in three years. His proposal, like Bethune's plan, made good sense and might have been adopted, if the government had had any serious intention of developing the route, or if the local promoters had not continued to press for the more unrealistic all-water system, ending up with no system at all. The saving in cost notwithstanding, Baird's combined principle probably reflected a personal interest, too. If canalization of the Trent River proved too costly, as seemed likely, the Cobourg railroad could easily serve as the rail link at the eastern extremity of a possible combined system. Perhaps this explains why Baird purchased stock in the Cobourg Rail Road Company even though he was publicly and vigorously promoting development of the Trent River. In any case, as his commission required, he submitted a detailed report for an all-water communication in December. Naturally, publication of his report set off another round of political activity.

Now the commercial interests of Kingston entered the controversy. Baird's recommendation that the Trent-Simcoe waterway to Lake Huron be developed as a logical continuation of the Rideau Canal appealed to the commercial instincts of the businessmen in Kingston, and had from the earliest days. In 1794, Governor Simcoe reported that "the Merchants of Kingston [were] turning their eyes to this route as forming ... a very practicable Communication between Lake Huron and Montreal."[26] Now, 40 years later, there was Kingston, sitting at the entrance to the recently completed Rideau Canal, but little traffic passed through its harbour; most of the Lake Ontario trade moved out through Oswego, just across the lake from Kingston, down the Erie Canal to the Hudson River and on to New York. Baird's report revived the Kingston merchants' interest in the Trent. They envisioned Kingston as the hinge in Baird's proposed transportation arc that would garner trade on Lake Huron and the upper lakes, funnel it through the Trent system to Lake Ontario, carry it up the Rideau to the Ottawa River, and move it downstream to Montreal.

In mid-December 1835, a public meeting was called by the principal businessmen in Kingston to support the alleged thrust of Baird's report, although none could have read it at the time. The group resolved that a petition be prepared "praying theLegislature to adopt such measures for opening the navigable communication between the Bay of Quinte and Lake Huron as may be found most advantageous to the country."[27]

Early in the following January, the Kingston *Chronicle*, with Baird's report now in hand, published a two-part editorial calling for development of the Trent River and lambasting the promoters of the Cobourg railroad and the Port Hope Canal for their "jealousy of the undertaking" and for being the "main cause of its delay if not of its defeat."[28]

Meanwhile, the residents of Peterborough, fearing that their interests might lose out in the acrimonious dispute over the selection of the exit route, held another meeting. They demanded that a communication be opened up "from Harvey and Verulam to Peterborough" and further (not caring whether the Trent, Cobourg, or Port Hope was the ultimate choice) called for navigation to be improved "from Peterborough to any point on Rice Lake."[29]

Next, Thomas A. Stewart collected 650 names for his second petition to the legislature in less than a decade. Addressed to his fellow legislators, Stewart's petition prayed "that this House will not fail to grant a sufficient sum for commencement of the contemplated improvements between Lake Simcoe and the Bay of Quinte."[30] Alexander McDonell tabled the petition on 29 January.

With the hope of resolving the competing demands within some kind of rational provincial perspective, the legislature established a standing committee "upon the subject of canals and internal improvements."[31] on 23 January. Dr John Gilchrist, MLA for Northumberland, was elected chairman of the committee of which William Hamilton Merritt was also a member. Very early in its deliberations, the committee examined the question of improvements in the District of Newcastle.

Curiously, many Tories and Reformers in Parliament were united in their opposition to the development of the Trent, the Tories to protect the Welland Canal, the Reformers to protect the proposed railroad from a government-sponsored competitor. But the Cobourg Rail Road Company dearly wanted the lock at Hastings for the iron trade, and there were the communications needs of the citizens of Peterborough and the Back Lakes, vigorously advanced by Alexander McDonell and Thomas Stewart, to be considered – transportation facilities that incidentally would create another source of freight and revenue for the railroad.

Thus on 3 March 1836, Gilchrist presented a recommendation from the standing committee that accommodated the interests of the residents of Peterborough and the Back Lakes, the Cobourg Rail Road Company, and himself. Using Baird's estimates, the committee recommended that $80,000 be appropriated by the legislature, this "trifling sum"[32] to pay for a lock and dam at Hastings, a lock and dam at Whitla's Rapids (now Scott's Mills lock), a renovated lock and dam at Bobcaygeon, and a lock and dam at Purdy's Mills. These improvements would open up almost 170 miles of navigation – from Healey Falls to Peterborough and from Hall's Mills at Buckhorn to Lake Scugog; the 6 miles between Peterborough and Chemung Lake would "probably be connected ... by railroad."[33] Thus "the agricultural products as well as iron from the Marmora works would find a cheap and speedy transit overland by a railroad from Cobourg or canal from Port Hope,"[34] the committee assured the legislature. The recommendation was really an update of the report submitted by George S. Boulton in 1834, but expanded to include improvements from Peterborough through the Back Lakes to win the support of McDonell and Stewart. Gilchrist had a personal reason for wanting a lock built at Hastings. A dam there would raise the level of Rice Lake, backing the water up the shallow Indian River and making it navigable as far as his mill and distillery at Keene. Gilchrist's report, like Boulton's earlier one, made no recommendations regarding the lower Trent River except to suggest that opening the upper section would lessen the expense of construction on the lower sections, "when it may be considered expedient to commence the same."[35] The legislature adopted the report and asked Gilchrist to prepare the legislation. The bill was presented to the House and passed on 24 March, but not without a little difficulty. The bill named eight commissioners, many of whom where shareholders in the Cobourg Rail Road Company, including Gilchrist himself, but only three of them were Reformers. An attempt was made to amend the legislation by adding the name of Wilson S. Conger, a Cobourg merchant, a Reformer and director of the Rail Road Company, to the list. The amendment failed by a single vote, but the bill passed with a large majority. For reasons that will be explained later Sir Francis Bond Head, Colborne's successor, refused royal assent to the bill.

The Trent River lobby did not give up pursuing development of the lower Trent. In the general election held in July, Dr Gilchrist was rewarded for his machinations by being voted out of office. He was replaced by a former representative of Northumberland, Tory journalist Henry Ruttan, who took over Gilchrist's position as chairman of the Committee on Canals and Internal Improvements.

The committee met in the autumn to consider Stewart's 29 January petition and to hear other witnesses. On 29 November, Ruttan recommended to the legislature "the adoption of the work from the mouth of the Trent to Peterborough."[36] For a start, Ruttan's report recommended that $385,000 (in addition to the $80,000 previously approved for the inland waters) be spent to develop the two lower sections of the Trent in accordance with Baird's plan: "half in 1837 and the other half in 1838."[37]

The reasons given for the recommendations were the oft-repeated ones, mainly political, and based on evidence given by Baird, Myers, Robertson, Manahan, and McDonell. In all, 30 settled townships were dependent on the line of communication: because of the high cost of transportation, produce grown in the inland townships could not compete on the market with produce produced at the front; several gentlemen of very considerable means, who had spent upwards of $50,000 in Fenelon township in the expectation that the Trent system would be developed, would have to abandon their properties; a number of new settlers had left within the last 12 months to find work in the United States; the Marmora Iron Works had suspended operations for want of transportation; the country between Rice Lake and Lake Simcoe was a continuous forest of timber, which would remain locked up until the waterway was completed. The report was debated in the House on 19 December 1836, approved, and eventually incorporated into an act that received royal assent on 4 March 1837.

The earlier act, authorizing the expenditure of $80,000 for improvement of the navigation of the inland waters, had finally received royal assent on 28 November 1836, the day before Ruttan submitted his recommendation for the improvement of the navigation of the Trent River. But there was a quid pro quo. The Reformers in the province had been giving Bond Head a good deal of trouble; he wanted all Reformers removed from the board of commissioners named in the act before he would sign it. George S. Boulton moved an amendment deleting the names of the commissioners, "leaving the appointment of Commissioners to His Excellency."[38] This amendment also received royal assent on 4 March.

And so the bitter struggle over a choice of routes was finally over. At the time, it appeared that the proponents of the Trent River route had won, but their victory was vainglorious. It is true that the Ruttan legislation killed the Cobourg railroad by discouraging private investment, and it removed the last vestige of hope from the proponents of a Port Hope canal, but it did not guarantee development of the Trent River.

An expenditure of $80,000 to improve water communications around Peterborough, as authorized in Gilchrist's legislation, was about as far as the government of 1837 was prepared to commit itself. Neither Gilchrist's act nor Ruttan's act made any commitment to a long-term Trent canal policy: the former was intended purely to provide for a local improvement, the latter provided for no useful transportation purpose at all. Indeed, the former was a facile legislative gesture made to resolve competing demands, to stifle hysterical clamouring for a waterway the province could not afford, and to fulfill partially election promises made by Henry Ruttan. In so acting, the government set a precedent, for similar strategies would be followed many times, making the Trent canal one of the most expensive political boondoggles in Canadian history.

Of the two acts, the earlier (for $80,000), which seems to have been instigated by George S. Boulton for the benefit of the Cobourg railroad, stood the greater chance of being implemented. Funding for this act was to be provided from general provincial revenues; only the lieutenant-governor's warrant was required to release cash to the commissioners. Funds for the Trent River improvements, in contrast, were to be raised by the receiver general by way of loans upon debentures, payable in 20 years. Given the unstable political climate in Upper Canada and the shaky financial position of the government, it is not likely that investors would be anxious to purchase $385,000 worth of government debentures to finance a scheme that did not have wholehearted public support. Moreover, the act imposed no time requirement for completion of the improvements. The sums were "to be raised in such amounts and at such times as may be required."[39] That could have meant years; as it turned out, it meant never.

With the necessary legislation in place, it remained only for the lieutenant-governor to name the commissioners. He had been stalling on the appointments, and the delay was causing George S. Boulton considerable embarrassment and criticism. Implementation of the act had been held up by Boulton's amendment to delete the names of the commissioners, which he made at the lieutenant-governor's request. "Desirous ... that his conduct in that respect should not subject [him] to blame,"[40] Boulton wrote to the lieutenant-governor's private secretary on 7 April, requesting immediate appointment of the commissioners so that work could begin. In response to Boulton's letter, Bond Head named the commissioners in May – true Tories all.

Then, at last, construction of the Trent canal got under way.

CHAPTER FOUR

Improvements on the Inland Waters

The fact that two separate pieces of canal legislation were passed in 1837, each establishing its own board of commissioners, each funded differently, and each authorizing improvements on widely separated portions of the natural waterway, indicates that, from the beginning, there was no settled policy with regard to building a Trent canal. The eventuality of a through waterway from Lake Ontario to Lake Huron existed only in the mind of Nichol Hugh Baird, who recommended it to the lieutenant-governor, and in the aspirations of the residents along the route who were encouraged by Baird's recommendation. But the lieutenant-governor did not accept Baird's recommendation. A through waterway was never, at any time, contemplated by the government in 1837, nor was the proposal ever formally debated or approved, even in principle, by the legislative assembly. Only limited local improvements were agreed to. Because the recommendation for a through system had been made by a government engineer of the calibre of Baird just a few years after the imperial government had shown mild interest in the route for defence purposes, and because, for political reasons, the government of 1837 reluctantly agreed to improve selected portions of the waters, it would always be claimed that a commitment to a canal had been made, and a promise broken; this was the myth that generated the political energy that kept the scheme alive for 90 years and eventually pushed it to completion. But no commitment to built a Trent canal was ever made, in 1837 or in the years following; therefore, no promise was ever broken.

The preamble to the Act to Improve the Navigation of the Inland Waters of the Newcastle District, 1836, made quite clear the limited purpose of the grant of $80,000: "Important accession to the agricultural and mineral products, as well as products of the Forest, would accrue to the Province, and the Inhabitants of a large and fertile section of the Country would be materially benefitted by removing the obstructions to the free navigation of certain parts of the inland waters in the District of Newcastle."[1] No mention was made of through navigation; it was to be purely a local

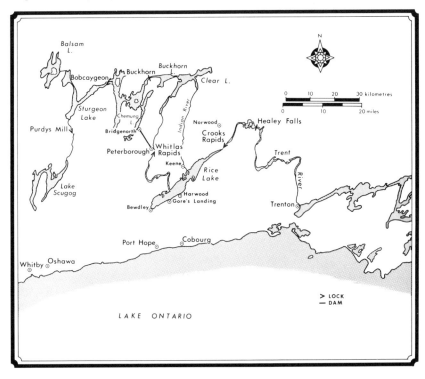

work to serve local transportation needs with some hoped-for provincial economic spin-off.

The act specified six projects that had been culled by Gilchrist from Baird's two survey reports. They were a dam at Healey Falls on the Trent River; a dam, lock, and short canal at Crooks' Rapids; a lock at Whitla's Rapids on the Otonabee River; a dam at Buckhorn Falls; reconstruction of the lock at Bobcaygeon; and a lock at Purdy's Mills. The first three projects, taken from the Trent River survey of 1833, were intended to open navigation from Rice Lake into Peterborough and from Rice Lake into Seymour township as far as Healey Falls; these would facilitate the iron trade. The other three works would complete Bethune's former plan to open navigation from Bridgenorth to the head of Sturgeon and Scugog lakes. These works would assist settlement. State coaches and wagons would continue to provide access to Rice Lake until the Cobourg railroad was built.

The commissioners named by Bond Head to supervise the improvements on inland waters were George S. Boulton (Cobourg), Alexander

McDonell (Peterborough), the Hon. Zaccheus Burnham (Cobourg), Andrew S. Fraser (Sturgeon Lake), and Robert Jameson (Fenelon Falls). Those named to supervise the Trent River construction were Boulton, McDonell, John S. Cartwright (Kingston), Charles Anderson (Otonabee River), and Sheldon Hawley (Trenton). Boulton was elected chairman and Zaccheus Burnham treasurer of the first board; Sheldon Hawley was chairman and Boulton treasurer of the second. Nichol Hugh Baird was hired by both boards as engineer-in-charge of the works and thus became the first superintendent of the Trent Canal. Baird's pay for supervising the Trent River works was $2,500 per year; for supervising the inland waters improvements, he received $1,250. His total salary was extremely generous; labourers earned about $225 per year and skilled tradesmen about $400.

Not surprisingly, work on the inland waters began immediately, as most of the $80,000 was to be spent in Boulton's riding; Boulton had arranged funding for the works in such a way as to ensure that the work would be done. "It is fortunate," he wrote Bond Head, when it appeared that money would not be available for the Trent River works, "that the grant of $80,000 stands on a different footing as ... the Improvement contemplated by it is more urgently desired by the district and moreover is likely to produce more immediate good."[2]

Boulton called the first meeting of the commissioners in Peterborough for 29 – 31 May. Much was accomplished. Tenders for the various works, called earlier by Baird, were opened, and some contracts were awarded. William Purdy was interviewed about the necessity of moving his dam and mills to a new location suitable for the construction of the lock. Because Purdy was in no mood to negotiate, he was asked to name an arbitrator to meet with one to be named by the commissioners who would estimate what damage might be sustained in consequence of the move, for the commissioners intended to expropriate Purdy's property whether he agreed to the move or not. Baird was instructed to prepare detailed specifications for the works and to draft the contracts. Boulton agreed to ask the lieutenant-governor for a first installment of $7,500, so that squared timber then lying on the shore but destined for the Quebec market could be purchased at a reasonable rate and so that other accumulated expenses could be paid.

Euphoria gripped the residents of the district. Land values skyrocketed.

It was impossible for Baird personally to supervise construction and measure the amount of work performed at the various locations scattered over 170 miles of wild and unsettled country, so he employed an administrative staff to assist him. Charles Green was hired as secretary with an annual salary of $500. The man hired to supervise the construction between Healey Falls and Purdy's Mills was Thomas McNeil, a foreman on the Welland Canal construction, recommended to Boulton by John Beverley Robinson, chief justice of Upper Canada. On 5 December 1837, Baird ordered McNeil, who was paid $2 per day, to proceed to Peterborough where he was to establish his headquarters, but even from that central location McNeil found it difficult to supervise the works. "It is my particular wish to conduct the works in a masterly manner, partly for my own credit and also for the benefit of the Department but the works being so far apart it is out of my power to visit them as often as I would wish or as you might require," he complained to Baird, while requesting forage for his horse to permit him to visit the works "as often as might be necessary."[3]

Healey Falls

The work at Healey Falls called for a rock-filled, wooden dam 488 feet long and 12 feet high, to be erected across the river at the top of the falls. The dam's purpose was to raise the level of the river between Healey Falls and Crooks' Rapids, to flood the shallows between, and to back up water over the lower sill in the proposed lock at Crooks' Rapids to a depth of 5 feet. A contract worth $3,750 was awarded to Elijah Parks at a meeting of the commissioners on 11 August. When Parks learned that the dam was to be filled with rock, he reconsidered and resigned the contract in favour of Homer Hecox, a carpenter from Cobourg, who earlier had been awarded the contract for the Scugog River works. Because the dam at Healey Falls could not be built until after the lock at Crooks' Rapids was completed, Hecox's activity was limited to hauling timber and rock to the dam site. By 31 December 1838, he had been paid $650 for material delivered. Then, one after another, he and the other contractors failed, and the dam was never built.

Crooks' Rapids

The contract at Crooks' Rapids (Hastings) was an extensive undertaking. It required a truss-frame wooden dam, rock-filled, 253 feet long, 27 feet high, and 7 1/2 feet wide, a canal 610 feet long, to be cut through the limestone to bypass the rapids, and a masonry lock 134 feet long and 33 feet wide with a 6-foot 9-inch lift to be erected in the middle of the canal. Also, Crooks' mill, which had been erected in 1835, had to be relocated. The firm of Sidey and Craigie was awarded the contract on 11 August.

Of all the contractors engaged on the inland waters, Sidey and Craigie proceeded with the most vigour. By the end of September they had erected shanties and a cook-house for the labourers, cut three-quarters of a mile of road, relocated the mill, and excavated 1,300 cubic yards of rock from the canal. On 15 December, they had 34 men employed quarrying and excavating; they had cut all the timber and lumber for the dam and had commenced hauling it out of the bush before the snow got too deep. But for bad luck, rising costs, and the inability of the commissioners to make regular payments as the work advanced, Sidey and Craigie might well have finished the contract on the assigned completion date of 1 May 1839. As it happened, the contractors went bankrupt and had to abandon the works before they were even half-finished.

One of the most serious problems encountered by the contractors at both Crooks' Rapids and Whitla's Rapids was the lack of a convenient source of suitable building stone. And Baird was very exacting as to both the quality of the stone and the manner in which it was to be cut. The Trenton limestone, through which the lower Otonabee and upper Trent rivers flow, is soft and highly fossiliferous and disintegrates easily. Although readily available at the construction sites, it was totally unfit for lock construction. Baird had been told and so advised Sidey and Craigie when they accepted the contract that deposits of the more massive Black River limestone, suitable for quarrying, were available at Keeler's Mill (now Norwood), just four miles from Crooks' Rapids. The contractors wasted $470 trying to quarry stone in eight different spots around Norwood, but in each case the rock proved unsuitable for ashlar. Eventually they were obliged to draw the heavy stone from a quarry 16 miles from the construction site.

Costs mounted for other reasons. The rebel politician, William Lyon Mackenzie, launched his futile attack on York from Montgomery's Tavern on 7 December. The military skirmish was brief, but it was long enough to ignite the political powder that blew up the province's rotting governmental structure. The brief rebellion also destroyed Baird's construction schedule and eventually forced Sidey and Craigie out of business. The immediate impact of the rebellion as far as the contractors were concerned was the increase in the price of labour, as loyal settlers flocked to join militia units in Peterborough and Cobourg, creating a shortage of workers. Not only did the day rates go up, but because of the unsettled political situation the cost of board increased as well: wheat rose from about $1 to $2 per bushel and oats from 30 to 60 cents in a matter of weeks. The price of other consumables increased in proportion, which "made a very material difference"[4] to the contractors. The increased financial burden associated with feeding the workers was further enlarged when the cook-house accidentally burned down, taking food supplies and equipment with it.

Perhaps the most distressing financial burden borne by the contractors resulted from the inability of the commissioners to advance funds on a regular basis. After the rebellion in December, the Bank of Upper

Canada, on orders from the lieutenant-governor, suspended all cash payments from funds previously voted for public projects. Most of the public funds that the bank held were then diverted by the lieutenant-governor into defence undertakings; large contingents of militia were recruited, trained, and stationed in key locations around the province, especially on the American border, across which several raids by American sympathizers, recruited by the exiled Mackenzie, took place. As a consequence, the commissioners could acquire funds from the $80,000 grant in only small amounts, and these had to be distributed among four contractors at six construction projects. While contractors may have been willing to wait for payment, the workers were not; without payment, they refused to work. Thus the contractors "laboured under great disadvantages, having to run constantly for money for which [they] had to pay a heavy discount,"[5] so that they could pay their workers.

For reasons that were incomprehensible to the contractors, Baird insisted that they complete the dam and raise the water in Rice Lake by seven feet before the lock pit was dug. Baird was probably forced to give the order against his better judgment, even though he knew the consequences of doing so; indeed, on the Trent River construction, he insisted that none of the dams be built before the locks were finished. Zaccheus Burnham was probably responsible for the decision. Burnham was anxious to raise the level of Rice Lake so as to flood the Indian River, to permit the steamers then operating on Rice Lake to reach John Gilchrist's mills at Keene, where he and his brother Mark also owned large tracts of land. Further, John Gilchrist was Mark Burnham's brother-in-law. In its natural state the Indian River, from its mouth to Keene, was barely passable for skiffs, being only about a foot deep and choked with weeds. But "when the water shall be raised to the intended height," Baird reported to the commissioners, perhaps a little ingratiatingly, "this difficulty will be removed and a free Steam Navigation substituted to the village of Keene, destined from its situation and when the navigation is completed to be a place of some consequence."[6]

Naturally, the premature flooding of Rice Lake backed water into the lock pit, causing the contractors much extra expense and inconvenience. They were obliged to employ four men with two pumps, day and night. To reduce the cost, the contractors installed a water wheel to drive the pumps. The wheel cost an additional $120.

Like many Scots, Baird had a stubborn streak. He would not take any of the extra costs into consideration, and he steadfastly refused to admit that his estimate might have been too low. When the contractors tried to convince him to "allow that the valuation of the work may go over his estimation he swore that it shall not."[7] By the summer of 1839, the contractors reckoned that they had accumulated a net loss of $1,750. When they appealed to Baird for redress, he informed them curtly that they "had got too much already."[8] By then Sidey and Craigie had had enough. They abandoned the contract in mid-summer, leaving behind all their equipment and material, an almost completed dam – "a rough piece of work," according to Baird – an almost dug canal, a lock with the sills in place but the walls only partially built, and 1,957 cubic feet of ashlar lying on the ground.

Baird came under pressure from the commissioners to get the Crooks' Rapids work completed, despite the failure of Sidey and Craigie. The work at Whitla's Rapids had also been abandoned, subjecting the commissioners to some ridicule from the steamboat operators and the general public for their failure to execute the works. Further, because the dam at Crooks' Rapids was not completely finished, the water level in Rice Lake dropped in late August, causing "fever and ague to a considerable extent in consequence of the waters receding and leaving the swamps [at Keene] exposed to the Sun's Rays."[9] Being familiar with similar occurrences on the Rideau, Baird assured the commissioners that the fever would be eliminated when the water in Rice Lake could be held to the required height with completion of the dam. He also assured them that when the water was raised in Rice Lake, the shoals at Dangerfield and Yankee Bonnet, on the Otonabee River, would be flooded over and a steamboat drawing no more than 2 feet 9 inches could ascend Whitla's Rapids "without the aid of a lock."[10] The commissioners therefore decided that every effort should be made to finish the works at Crooks' Rapids.

With few works left to oversee, Thomas McNeil had little to do, and so Baird asked him to take over the Sidey and Craigie contract. With a man named Sutherland, McNeil entered into a contract with the commissioners on 16 August 1839, to finish the dam and lock. But McNeil and Company had little more success than Sidey and Craigie. The work was advanced somewhat, but by fall the source of government funds had completely dried up and McNeil, too, was obliged to abandon the work.

Whitla's Rapids

Whitla's Rapids (now Scott's Mills lock) was situated just a mile and a half below the town of Peterborough. A drop in the river of about three feet prevented steamers from ascending the Otonabee all the way to the Little Lake at Peterborough. A wing-and-cross dam of truss-work construction and a masonry lock of the same dimensions as the one at Crooks' Rapids were planned to overcome this natural impediment to navigation. William Hartwell's tender for the lock and dams was accepted by the commissioners at their first meeting, in May, and a contract for $24,565 was later entered into.

Hartwell held the contract for a little over a year, during which time he did very little work. Baird was not surprised. He had been opposed to Hartwell receiving the contract in the first place, because of his inexperience in the kind of construction required. Not only did Hartwell lack experience in lock and dam construction, but he lacked capital to acquire equipment and to carry on the work, as Sidey and Craigie had done, when grant money was slow in coming forth from the commissioners. Because of his inability to pay regularly, he naturally had difficulty in attracting and holding labourers.

By July, Hartwell had done absolutely nothing at Whitla's Rapids, and Baird was disturbed. On 7 July Baird advised the commissioners that Hartwell "should use all diligence this season if he intends to complete the terms of the contract."[11] By mid-August, only 400 cubic yards had been excavated for the canal and lock; seven or eight men were engaged in quarrying, and a couple of carpenters were building a scow and shanties. Again Baird warned the commissioners that because of the "desultory [sic] manner in which the excavation is progressing there is little possibility of it being out this fall."[12] On 22 August, he informed them that "unless very active steps are evinced by the next inspection," he would recommend some "remedial measures."[13] Finally, on 11 November, because the work at Whitla's was still not progressing, the commissioners permitted Baird to order Hartwell to hire more men; 50 were to be constantly engaged at the work "until the engineer recommends a diminution in the number."[14] As a result of the order, Hartwell increased his work-force slightly, but by mid-December he still had only 20 men engaged in excavating at the lock site and a dozen men quarrying.

Hartwell encountered the same difficulty in locating suitable building stone as Sidey and Craigie. Baird had advised him to "look around Hall's mill"[15] near Peterborough or to haul stone all the way from a known location on Pigeon Lake. Hartwell did not take the advice. At first he located a quarry near Gilchrist's mills at Keene, but the stone was of poor quality and not suitable for ashlar; later, a deposit of suitable limestone was found near Burnham's mill at Warsaw. The quality of this stone was good, but the ashlar had to be hauled over 16 miles and Hartwell had "great difficulty in gettin [sic] teams."[16] It seems the teamsters would not haul for him because they were "afread [sic] of not receiving payment."[17] Teams around Peterborough were scarce, and those who did have them wanted the unreasonable price of "3 Dollars per day or [25¢] per cubic foot"[18] for hauling.

The problem of hauling was alleviated somewhat when Baird, annoyed at Hartwell's lack-lustre performance, ordered McNeil to bypass the contractor and hire teams and pay for them directly. When the teamsters learned about this "they came immediately,"[19] and for a time there were

17 teams hauling stone from Warsaw. McNeil was optimistic that he would have all the stone that was needed delivered by the end of the winter, but the recurrent problem of funding intervened; when they were not paid, the teamsters quit.

By 27 June, Hartwell had only 12 men and two horse carts employed in excavating at Whitla's, and he was "still in much difficulty about stone for his lock."[20] Finally, on 6 August, Baird confronted him about his tardiness in executing the contract. Hartwell decided to abandon the contract because, as he put it, he "could not proceed without assistance from the commissioners."[21]

The commissioners met at Peterborough on 11 August to consider what was to be done about the surrendered contracts. (Hartwell had also abandoned the Bobcaygeon works.) It was decided that Baird would take over personal superintendence of the work and finish the construction with day labourers. He was to "ascertain the extent of quarrying and cutting stone for Whitla's Rapids and receive tenders for the same being done."[22] It is doubtful if many tenders were received, but Thomas Choate, a cousin of Zaccheus Burnham and superintendent of Burnham's mill at Warsaw, together with Sutherland, received a contract for cutting stone at the rate of $8 per large stone. McNeil was to engage teams for drawing the stone to Whitla's Rapids "at a rate not to exceed [20 cents] per cubic foot in the rough" and "[18¢] per cubic foot for finished stone or [$3] per day."[23]

McNeil still had difficulty getting teams. It seems that Mackenzie's brief rebellion had created a defiant attitude among workers and tradesmen. Barnabas Bletcher, operator of a stage service from Port Hope, and his partner, Thomas Harper of Peterborough, organized all the teamsters around Peterborough into a combine; consequently all but two teamsters in the area refused to haul stone for less than 25 cents per cubic foot. McNeil was then forced to travel through Smith, Cavan, and Otonabee townships in search of teams. He received a promise from several men to come with horses and oxen, but by 15 January none had made an appearance. Later in the month, teams did come forward, and for a while McNeil had 22 teams on his list, but because of accidents occurring daily he was never able to keep more than 12 teams engaged at one time. And there was always a "great outcry for money."[24] Sutherland complained frequently that if he did not get paid he would have to discontinue quarrying, which is precisely what he did.

The Buckhorn Dam

The Buckhorn dam was built in conjunction with the renovations to the lock at Bobcaygeon, 16 miles upstream. The contract called for the "present dam [built by John Hall in 1830] to be raised sufficient to throw back 5 feet of water over the lower sill at Bobcaygeon at lowest water."[25] This adjustment in the dam was necessary to correct the error made in the Bethune lock of its lower sill being placed too high. Moreover, without some means of regulating the water in Pigeon Lake so as to hold it at a constant level, there would always be problems with the Bobcaygeon lock. Also, by raising the level of the water in Buckhorn, Chemung, and Pigeon lakes by five feet, steamboat and raft navigation would be greatly improved; then the problem that Capt. Nicholls of the *Sturgeon* frequently experienced of piling up on mud banks would be eliminated.

A contract for the dam for $3,300 was signed on 15 August 1837 by George Hall, son of John Hall, owner of the Buckhorn mill; Robert Madge of Harvey township and Samuel Dixon of Monaghan were partners. Like all the other dams designed by Baird, Buckhorn's was a wooden, truss-frame structure, covered with three-inch planks and filled with stone. It was nearly 400 feet long and contained a sluiceway and apron so that logs could be run through. The Halls had plenty of experience in dam construction, having built the original dam as well as one near Peterborough earlier. Work progressed satisfactorily during 1837, but until the Bobcaygeon lock was finished there was no urgency to complete the Buckhorn dam. The spring flood of 1838 carried away about 90 feet of the partially built dam, but this was repaired and the dam completed in the fall.

The Bobcaygeon Works

In addition to the Buckhorn dam, two other corrective measures were necessary to fix the useless lock built at Bobcaygeon in 1834. First, the leaks in the canal had to be staunched. This was to be accomplished by lining the canal with 3-inch planks, chinking the seams with oakum, and pitch and painting the whole structure with tar; the 500-foot-long wooden trough would rest on hemlock sleepers 12 inches square with 3-foot centres. Second, the water level in Sturgeon Lake had to be raised sufficiently to back 5 feet of water over the table rock at the upper entrance to the canal, which was exposed during periods of low water. To achieve this, a dam 6 to 8 feet high had to be constructed to replace the lower dam built by Bethune, and a new dam had to be built between the little island in the centre of the channel and the north shore. In all, 1,185 feet of dams were required across the entrance of the main river. Also, a 5-foot-high dam had to be built across the Little Bob River, because unless this spillway were closed, the dams on the main river would be rendered useless – an obvious fact overlooked by Rubidge and the commissioners when they built the original lock. The small wooden lock was to be left unchanged, except to repair damage wrought by the elements after three years of disuse. Although the original was much smaller than the other locks planned, it was Baird's hope that it would be replaced in five years with a masonry lock of the same dimensions as the others.

Unhappily, the contract for the Bobcaygeon works was let out to William Hartwell, at the same time that he was awarded the Whitla's Rapids contract. During the latter part of 1837, Hartwell progressed more rapidly with the Bobcaygeon works, on which he seems to have concentrated his efforts, than he did at Whitla's Rapids. But Baird was not satisfied. In the spring, he reported to the commissioners that "at Bobcaygeon there is not the progress making I expected to have been ."[26] On 12 July, on Baird's instructions, Charles Green wrote to Hartwell ordering him to meet with the commissioners at Bobcaygeon on the evening of 20 July and to take his sureties with him.

The commissioners heard from Hartwell the same story that they had heard from the others: "The difficulty experienced by the commissioners in procuring funds to fulfil their engagements placed the contractors in a very disadvantageous position, and induced them to be less strenuous in their exertions to proceed with the work, lest they might not be supplied with the means to pay their labourers."[27] Hartwell had no choice but to abandon the Bobcaygeon contract, as well as the one at Whitla's. As with Whitla's, the commissioners ruled that the Bobcaygeon works were to continue under the personal superintendence of Baird, who was instructed to stay at Bobcaygeon until the project was completed.

Baird did not stay at Bobcaygeon permanently, but he did visit the site frequently during the next two months, and McNeil spent a good deal of his time there too. Baird got the work moving more quickly but not without the usual difficulties. On 31 August the foremen, Thomas Carr and Samuel Walles, wrote directly to the commissioners, advising them that unless the back wages owing to the workers by Hartwell were paid the workers would quit and that they, the foremen, would "have to leve [sic] the work as well."[28] The commissioners authorized payment the next day.

Despite the complexity of financial and other problems, the major repairs were completed on schedule during the first week in November. Water was let in to test the canal and lock on Sunday, 4 November. There was trouble. Although the leaks in the canal were effectively plugged with the plank lining, the lock would not fill. The water rose only to within three feet of the top, because the bottom of the lock sank down with the weight of the water, allowing the sills under the gates to sag, creating a gap through which the water escaped almost as quickly as the valves let it in. Upon examination, it was found that the wedges placed under the sills in 1834 "had rot nearly through."[29] The wedges were replaced and additional lining was put in the lock chamber. By Tuesday, the water could be raised to within one foot of the top. The leaky lock then worked, but just barely.

To ensure that the fragile structure would continue to operate, Baird laid down a detailed set of regulations for its use. The lock was not to be used on any pretense whatsoever without the lock keeper being present; no boat or other craft would be allowed to load or unload in the lock or stay in the lock longer than five minutes with pressure on the lower gates; the lower sluice gates were to be raised in degrees to prevent the escaping water from injuring the foundation; and the lock was not to be filled sooner than was necessary. The toll for small boats was set at 30 cents, for large boats and empty scows 60 cents; loaded scows and cribs of timber would cost one dollar. The Trent canal's first lock was ready to do business.

On the night of Monday, 5 November 1838, a barge, the *Sir George Arthur*, arrived at Bobcaygeon from Bridgenorth with the family of the Reverend James Harley Dunsford, who had taken up residence on Sturgeon Lake the previous year. The next morning, in a blinding snowstorm, the barge was locked through into Sturgeon Lake. This lockage of the *Sir George Arthur* was the Trent canal's first. There were, of course, no cameras present to record the event; no reporters, no politicians, none of the hoopla that would mark the opening of locks in the next century. There were just a few workmen looking on as a bewildered and half-frozen immigrant family neared the end of a long and arduous journey that had brought them from the amenities of Tretherne, Gloucestershire, to this snow-shrouded wilderness. Huddled shivering in the barge with Mrs Dunsford and the other children was young Lydia Dunsford, who, seven years later, would become John Langton's bride. No one realized it then, but both John and Lydia Langton would be long dead and their grandchildren would become adults before the Trent Canal's last-built lock would be opened to traffic in 1920.

Purdy's Mills

A decision to build a lock at Purdy's Mills (Lindsay) seems to support the principal thesis advanced throughout this story: that the lock building started in 1837 was not, as has been assumed, the first constructive step along a waterway that would connect Lake Ontario and Lake Huron. The Lindsay lock, located eight miles off the main course of the cherished water route, was built in the first instance to solve a rather local political problem: what to do about William Purdy's enormous mill pond.

In 1830, William Purdy and his sons Jesse and Hazard built a mill at a shallow rapids on the Scugog River at the site of present-day Lindsay, and a village known as Purdy's Mills grew up around it. It was customary in those days for government to grant water power privileges and free land to individuals on condition they provide milling services to settlers. Accordingly, Purdy was granted 400 acres of land and authority to keep one-twelfth of the grist milled. The deed to his property, issued on 9 May 1834, contained a reservation securing him the right to keep the water at its present height without subjecting him to any action for damages. This was the source of the problem.

The Scugog River, a sluggish-flowing stream of low gradient, had few good milling sites. The spot chosen by Purdy for his mill lay between steep banks, where the river dropped three feet to form a slight rapids. To obtain a sufficient head of water for his mill, Purdy built a 14-foot-high dam across the river at the top of the rapids. It took weeks for the mill pond behind the dam to fill, but when it did, it formed what Langton called "the largest mill dam in the world."[30] Even Baird was shocked to see the destructive scale of the flooding caused by the dam and in the prosaic language of the engineer expressed doubt that "a precedent could be found from the construction of similar dimensions of dam anywhere in the Province."[31] The top of the dam having a higher elevation than Lake Scugog, the source of the river, the water was backed up all the way to the head of the lake, creating an immense mill pond 30 miles long. Thousands of acres of land were inundated.

Those who had settled along the banks of the river watched with horror as inch by inch, day by day, the water rose closer to their homes. When the water stopped rising, it had created "one continued scene of drowned lands and decayed timber, with, at intervals, the residences of the settlers, shewing part of their roofs out of the water from which the inmates had made their escape."[32] Hay meadows and cleared land, in crop, had been covered to a depth of nine feet. Baird estimated that at least 1,050 acres of cultivated land on the banks of the river between the dam and the lake had been flooded. He made no attempt to measure the extent of flooding on Lake Scugog, variously estimated at between 11,000 and 60,000 acres. Low, shore-line flats had become deep bays filled with stands of rotting hemlock and tamarack; peninsulas became islands, and large pieces of bog floated from swamps to drift around the lake as islands.

The rising water advanced up the two tributary streams entering the Scugog seven miles above the mill, flooding more land and drowning mill sites. Schools of fish once abundant in the river were destroyed by the noxious gases released from decaying vegetation. A main road running along the bank of the river was submerged under several feet of water, leaving the settlers no alternative but canoes for getting to mill, market, and church. Miasmic conditions produced by the rotting trees and the ideal breeding grounds for mosquitoes caused by the flooding resulted in epidemics of fever and ague. But because of the watertight reservation in his deed, Purdy could not be sued for damages; nor could he be forced to lower the level of his dam. He was not a very popular fellow around the Scugog.

Because of Purdy's apparent disregard for the plight of the settlers, he was thought capable of almost any heinous crime. An ardent Reformer, he frequently spoke out publicly and forcefully against the Family Compact. Thus when William Lyon Mackenzie disappeared after the 1837 rebellion, it was rumoured that he was hiding in Purdy's Mill. A detachment of 300 militia men led by Alexander McDonell – originally on their way to York but not needed there – marched into the village one evening and searched the mill. Mackenzie was hiding in the United States, but Purdy was arrested anyway and dragged off to jail in Cobourg. After a time he was released, sent home, and told to mind his own business, which is what he had been doing all along. In 1838, an epidemic of typhus killed about one-third of the population in the vicinity of Purdy's "pond." The settlers had had enough. A band of men armed with pitchforks, flintlocks, and axes attacked the mill and chopped down part of the dam. Purdy's sons rebuilt them.

What to do? Politically, the dam was Boulton's problem, because it was located in the middle of his riding. Boulton had supported, indeed encouraged, Bethune's plan to build a lock at Purdy's Mills in 1833; when there had not been enough money in the first grant for this lock, Boulton had recommended to the legislature that a second grant of $10,000 be given to Bethune. At that time Purdy had not received his property deed with its unusual protections, and it would have been easy to relocate the dam at a less destructive height. But that plan collapsed with Bethune's bankruptcy. Moreover, not everyone in the area was opposed to Purdy's dam, especially those whose property had not been flooded. For one thing, it was convenient to have a good grist and saw mill nearby. And the dam certainly improved navigation (for heavily laden barges and rafts of timber) on the upper Scugog.

On 15 June 1835, just two days before he started the Rice Lake – Lake Simcoe survey, Baird received an urgent request from Sir John Colborne "to inspect and survey the extent of such overflowings, and probable effect the removing of the dam would have upon navigation of the Scugog River and Lake."[33] Baird carried out the survey in the early summer and as a result of his investigation recommended that Purdy's dam and mill be relocated a quarter of a mile downstream, that the dam be reduced in height by seven feet, and that a wooden lock be built beside the dam. Baird reasoned that the lower dam, located at the bottom of the rapids instead of at the top, would allow most of the flooded land to be drained while still providing sufficient head to operate Purdy's mills. He concluded that the lock would connect the area to the main line of canal between the Bay of Quinte and Lake Huron, which his naïveté led him to believe would soon be built.

This was precisely the recommendation that Boulton was hoping for, and provision for the scheme was included in the act granting $80,000. The proposition was put to Purdy by the commissioners when they met with him in Peterborough on 30 May 1837, at which time he was asked to name an arbitrator. But Purdy was in no hurry to settle. In their annual report to the lieutenant-governor at the end of 1838, the commissioners reported that Purdy "has exhibited no inclination to come to a speedy settlement of any supposed recompense he may claim for the removal of his mill."[34] No wonder! Since the negotiations had begun, Purdy had been carted off to jail by Commissioner McDonell for no reason; the settlers had chopped down his dam and no charges had been laid; and the new dam had not even been started yet. The commissioners did have the power to expropriate, so Purdy eventually had to come to terms, not with the commissioners, but with the board of works that succeeded them. He struck a good bargain. By the terms of the agreement, the government built a new dam and kept it in repair, and Purdy, his heirs, and successors received permission to draw off for milling purposes all surplus water not needed for navigation. Purdy also got $2,000 in cash for the expropriated property.

Specifically, the plan for the Scugog works, ordered by the commissioners and produced by Baird, called for a wooden rock-filled wing dam about 150 feet long and 9 feet high; a lock with the same dimensions as the other locks but made of timber instead of stone was to be erected between the end of the wing dam and the opposite bank of the river; and Purdy's mill was to be relocated below the new dam. A contract for the work was let to Homer Hecox of Cobourg, on 11 August 1837, for $12,500.

Hecox proceeded immediately to cut and draw material out of the bush and to dig an excavation for the lock. The following August Baird reported to the commissioners that the Scugog work was "progressing to satisfaction and [there is] every appearance that Hecox is fulfilling his contract."[35] On 26 January 1839, the commissioners advised the lieutenant-governor that the work was "going on well,"[36] but at the end of the year they were obliged to report that Hecox had "failed and left the country."[37] He failed for the same reason as the others: no regular reimbursement from the commissioners for work done.

Steamers

The purpose of the lock and dam building was, of course, to facilitate steamboat navigation. But it seems that in the 1830s steamboats to navigate the inland lakes were as difficult to produce as the locks to connect them. Written records of such steamers as did exist in the period are spotty and imprecise and conclusions drawn from the records are conflicting; however, it does seem clear that between 1835 and 1840 at least two, possibly three, steamers enjoyed brief but unspectacular commissions on Rice Lake. In 1835, the *Northumberland*, built by a group in Port Hope, replaced Bethune's *Pemedash* on the Peterborough – Rice Lake run. The *Northumberland* passed her first winter on the Otonabee River just below Peterborough; the ice sprung her seams apart, allowing her to fill with water and settle to the bottom in the spring of 1836. Not until July was she raised and refitted. The following year, she was sold to a syndicate from Peterborough that rebuilt her and rechristened her the *Sir Francis Bond Head*, after the lieutenant-governor. It is claimed that a year or two later she was wrecked on the Yankee Bonnet shoal on the Otonabee River and left there to rot.

Because of Bethune's bankruptcy, the *Pemedash*, known also as the *Otonabee*, was put up for auction. She is reported to have been purchased by John Boswell of Cobourg, who refitted her and put her back in service as the *Newcastle*. For a year or two, the *Newcastle* competed with the *Sir Francis Bond Head* for the limited trade on Rice Lake; she outlived the *Bond Head* by a year, and then she, too, ceased to operate. She is supposed to have met her end on the Dangerfield shallows, on the Otonabee River. From 1840 to 1844, when William Weller launched the steamboat *Forester* at Gore's Landing, no steamers operated on Rice Lake.

Since the demise of the short-lived *Sturgeon* in 1834, no steamer had been launched on the Back Lakes either, although a futile attempt was made by a committee to build one. Encouraged by the $80,000 grant and the subsequent letting of contracts for lock construction at Bobcaygeon and Purdy's Mills, a group of residents met in Peterborough during the first week of September 1837 to discuss the possibility of putting a steamer on the Back Lakes. A committee was formed which, while not having a legal charter, was empowered to sell shares, receive plans, and supervise construction of a steamboat. The steamer, estimated to cost $7,500, was to be built at Fenelon Falls; the money was to be raised by the sale of 120 shares at $62.50 each. John Langton and his sister Anne subscribed for two shares each; J.W.D. and Susanna Moodie invested heavily and lost most of their investment. James Wallis of Fenelon Falls was elected secretary and treasurer of the committee. A man named Shea, from Kingston, was commissioned to built the steamer. Baird, who served as consultant, recommended that the steamer be no more than 100 feet long with a 26 foot 6 inch beam, owing to limitations imposed by the dimensions of the Bobcaygeon lock. Baird also advised that the steamer "should not draw more than three feet when laden – flat floor and clean run fore and aft."[38] A 30-horsepower engine was to be built by Messrs. Ward and Co., also of Kingston. Appropriately, the vessel was to be called the *George S. Boulton*.

A poor dividend on the investment, if any, was expected at first, but it was agreed that having regular steamship communication between Fenelon Falls and Peterborough would be "well worth the interest of the money."[39] Alas! Like most of the other dreams founded on the elusive Trent waterway, this scheme, too, turned out to be castle-building. The steamer was never finished. Investments were lost. Not until 1851, 13 years after the Bobcaygeon lock was opened and 7 years after the lock at Lindsay was finished, would a steamer be launched on the Back Lakes – the *Woodman* at Port Perry, on Lake Scugog. Later, in 1853, James Wallis and Robert Jameson built and launched their own small steamer at Fenelon Falls – the *Ogemah*, which was used primarily for towing lumber from their mills at Fenelon Falls to Port Perry; from Port Perry the lumber was hauled, first by wagon and later by railroad, to Whitby.

There was an attempt made, perhaps by the Steamboat Committee, to haul a steamer from the Otonabee River overland to Lake Chemung. In one of his regular reports to Baird – 1 March 1838 – Thomas McNeil described how from 30 to 37 teams of oxen tugged at a steamer for three days but succeeded in moving her only 300 yards. She was then cut in half "with the expectation of getting her to Peterborough."[40] McNeil did not mention the steamer again, and history has not revealed what happened to the severed hull. It certainly did not reach the Back Lakes. Nor is it clear what steamer this was. She may have been the *Northumberland*, in the process of changing ownership about that time. One might speculate that the Steamboat Committee bought the *Northumberland* with the hope of moving her overland to Lake Chemung. The attempt having failed, perhaps the steamer was resold, reassembled, and relaunched as the *Sir Francis Bond Head*. Although this is pure speculation, it offers one possible explanation for the extraordinary spectacle of up to 74 oxen attempting to drag a heavy steamboat through the receding March snow in the direction of Peterborough.

The steamboat business was not successful because there was not enough commerce to support even one steamboat in the 1830s. Most settlers had their own punts, canoes, or sailboats for summer travel. Roads gradually cut through the bush to larger settlements, while not good, were passable except briefly in the spring and fall. Heavy freight was readily moved by sleigh, and passengers by cutter, across the frozen lakes and bush roads in winter. Cleared lots were still small; the production of grain per farm was not all that great. Farmers had large families; labour was cheap, and there was plenty of time. So most farmers found it cheaper to move grain to mills and flour to markets by their own means rather than depend on expensive, unreliable steamer service.

For a time one entrepreneur, J.B. Fortune of Peterborough, operated a barge service from Bridgenorth to Buckhorn and Bobcaygeon, with connecting boats to Fenelon Falls. Barges were easy to build and, being propelled by paddle, pole, and sail, cheap to operate. They were advertised as "possessing every accommodation for passengers, merchandise, cattle, etc."[41] It was claimed that they were even faster than steamboats. Steamboats, in contrast, were expensive to build, hard to maintain, and difficult to winter. Without sufficient regular trade, there was not enough return on investment to make the business attractive.

If there was not enough trade for even one steamer, there was hardly justification for spending hundreds of thousands of dollars for a navigable waterway. Later, perhaps, there would be justification, but not in the 1830s, despite Baird's grand vision and the wild dreams of the "aristocratic" settlers.

CHAPTER FIVE

Improvements on the River Trent

The preambles to the acts authorizing improvements on the Trent River and on the inland waters made clear the limited purpose of the act, and consequently the extent of government policy with respect to a Trent waterway. The Trent River act authorized only a line of communication "between the waters of the Bay of Quinte and Rice Lake," because such communication was alleged to be important to the "agricultural and commercial interests of the Province."[1] There was no mention of a through waterway to Lake Huron; no commitment to a Trent canal. Indeed, although accepting the eventuality of navigable communication from the Bay of Quinte to Rice Lake, all the government actually committed itself to do, in 1837, was to build the first two sections, that is, from the mouth of the Trent River to Percy Landing (now Percy Boom). The amount of money authorized for this purpose was $387,537, based on Baird's estimate for constructing 14 masonry locks and 10 dams and for 2,302 feet of rock excavation. The first section, from the mouth of the Trent to Widow Harris' ferry (Frankford), would be the most difficult and expensive to build, requiring 13 locks and 9 dams to overcome the 9-mile stretch of rapids on this portion of the river; the second section required only 1 lock with a 10-foot lift, a wing dam, and an 1,100-foot rock cut at Chisholm's Rapids (Glen Ross), to open another 21 miles of navigation through Percy Reach to Percy Boom.

The commissioners (members of the board of works) met at Cobourg on 1 June 1837, but because none of the authorized funds had been raised they abstained from adopting steps to proceed with the work. Had Mackenzie's rebellion taken place six months earlier, it is doubtful that the Trent improvements would have been started, as it is improbable under those circumstances that J.H. Dunn, the receiver general, would have attempted to negotiate a loan; he certainly would have had difficulty getting one. Even before the rebellion had taken place, many observers, George S. Boulton included, thought that the receiver general would have difficulty raising the funds to finance the Trent works because of the widespread depression in North America. It was with considerable surprise, therefore, that the commissioners learned in August that the Commercial Bank of Kingston had purchased a portion ($100,000 worth) of the authorized debentures, permitting the work to proceed.

The man largely responsible for ensuring government control of the Trent River, making possible eventual completion of the canal, was John Solomon Cartwright of Kingston: it was he who arranged the partial funding that got the works started in 1837. Cartwright was first elected to the legislative assembly in 1836, one of two representatives for Lennox and Addington. He served on the Standing Committee on Canals and Internal Improvements, which under Ruttan's chairmanship had recommended the Trent River improvements. Cartwright drafted the legislation and later was named by Bond Head one of the five commissioners responsible for implementing it.

Cartwright had long been a supporter of the Trent River route, an interest in part inherited from his father, a leading merchant. Cartwright senior had been one of those merchants in Kingston reported by Simcoe to be "turning their eyes" to the Trent – Lake Simcoe route in 1794. His son, John Solomon, practiced law in Kingston and, more important to our story, was elected president of the Commercial Bank of the Midland District, chartered in 1832, with headquarters in Kingston. As noted earlier, the town of Kingston, still strongly in favour of the Trent – Lake Huron waterway, had prepared a memorial in support of it in 1835. J.S. Cartwright decided that it would be wise for the new bank – one of the first private banks to break the monopoly privilege of the Bank of Upper Canada – to put its money in a project the town supported; accordingly he arranged for the purchase of $100,000 worth of government debentures.

When the other commissioners learned that the Commercial Bank had purchased some of the debentures, they met in Cobourg on 2 September "to adopt measures for commencement of the work forthwith."[2] They decided that the section at Chisholm's Rapids and a lock at Myer's Island, at the mouth of the Trent, should be undertaken without delay, if the engineer and the executive council did not object. Boulton was authorized to write to Baird asking for "his opinion upon the propriety and utility of commencing the work"[3] and requesting his presence at a meeting of the board of commissioners in Cobourg on 15 September.

Baird attended the meeting as requested and presented his estimate of the cost of the proposed works: lock, dam, and excavation at Myer's Island, $30,530; dam at Widow Harris', $1,650; lock, dam, and excavation at Chisholm's Rapids, $69,070. Because Baird had no objection to the plan from an engineering point of view, Boulton was authorized to seek approval to proceed from the lieutenant-governor. Baird was

instructed to place advertisements calling for tenders on the works in newspapers in Toronto, St Catharines, Montreal, Peterborough, and Kingston.

Baird acted quickly. The commissioners had met on Friday, and by Monday morning Baird had the advertisements prepared and sent off to the newspapers. On 29 September, he informed Sheldon Hawley that the necessary plans and specifications were ready, and by mid-October contracts were let.

It is difficult to know why the commissioners decided to spread the money out on two widely separated contracts rather than centring their efforts on the first section only. The reason Boulton gave to Baird was that the commissioners considered it very doubtful whether they could obtain more than the $100,000 for a year or two and therefore thought it advisable "to undertake the Section which under such circumstance they had the means to accomplish,"[4] that is, the Chisholm's Rapids section which, in his 1833 survey, Baird had estimated at $65,000. With the remaining $35,000 the commissioners decided "it expedient to contract for one lock of the other Section [section1] also and go on with the others [locks on section 1] when they could procure the funds."[5]

Unquestionably, short-term social and economic factors influenced their decision as well, for whatever long-term economic effects the waterway might have when completed, there would clearly be an immediate impact on the area in terms of the number of jobs the construction would create. Pouring $100,000 into a pioneering economy in 1837 would be equivalent to injecting millions into a rural economy today, and the commissioners may have thought it wise to spread the largesse over as many communities as possible. Further, Boulton and some of the other commissioners owned land near Chisholm's Rapids. Construction of a lock would increase its value.

The village of Trent Port was also growing up at the mouth of the Trent River. In 1833 James Bethune had secured a grant of $20,000 to build a covered bridge across the Trent to replace the ferry service at Trent Port. Since construction of the bridge, traffic passed through the village daily on the way to and from Kingston and York. Moreover, Trent Port was the mouth of the spout through which timber moving from the interior was disgorged into Lake Ontario in late spring. Rafts of squared timber, booms of saw logs, and pine masts pouring down the Trent were collected there and reassembled for shipment to Quebec. The $39,000 lock contract and anticipated future contracts would be a boon to this developing village as well.

Myer's Island

A contract for the Myer's Island lock and dam was given to the firm of Francis and Hay for the fixed sum of $29,165 on 18 October 1837. The lock was to be the entrance to the waterway and was to be constructed in a dry channel running between Myer's Island and the shore, where it was thought a minimum of excavation would be required. This contract was the smaller of the two contracts and should have been finished without too much difficulty. But there were problems galore, and although upwards of $20,000 was spent on the contract altogether, there was little to show for the money when Francis and Hay, like all the other contractors under the superintendence of the hapless Baird, abandoned the work on 11 January 1839.

As with the contracts on the inland waters, quarrying presented a problem for Francis and Hay. The closest suitable quarrying stone was found at Oxpoint, five miles west of Belleville, on property owned by Anthony Manahan, MLA for Hastings. A camp consisting of "one Store and Dwelling 36 feet by 12 feet framed and covered with boards and seven log Shanties 18 by 12 feet covered with boards" was constructed at Oxpoint to house the "23 Quarry-men and Labourers, one Carpenter and one Blacksmith"[6] employed there. A wharf was made with rubble and waste stone from the quarry for loading barges with the finished stone blocks, which averaged four feet by two feet nine inches and a foot thick. Quarrying continued all winter, but the first stones were not freighted the 12 miles across the Bay of Quinte to the construction site until May. The cost of transporting the stone amounted to about $40 per load.

Despite the distance involved in hauling the stone, the contractors had no dispute with the returns made for quarrying, but there were plenty of arguments over the measurements and the amounts paid for excavating at the lock site. The arguments went on for the best part of a year. Finally the contractors, who had been dissatisfied with the contract from the beginning, asked to be released, claiming that the commissioners had broken the contract by not making regular advances as the work progressed. On these grounds, they entered a protest against the commissioners and asked Baird "to have their works and materials finally measured up and taken off their hands."[7]

There is no question that the commissioners had difficulty obtaining funds from the government and were finally obliged to stop all the works in October 1839, but Baird argued that the stoppage of work at Myer's Island was the contractors' decision and "did not result from the contractors not receiving sufficient advances as the work progressed."[8] In fact, Baird claimed "that in strict terms of the contract, Messrs. Francis and Hay had been overpaid $2,833,10,"[9] because the full 20 per cent for collateral security had been been withheld. He did allow that the commissioners owed the contractors $1,882.82 – the difference between the $4,715.92 that should have been withheld under the terms of the contract and the actual amount advanced to them.

Francis and Hay petitioned the lieutenant-governor, claiming damages for the large sum invested in materials and implements necessary for the work, which they claimed was stopped for want of funds from the commissioners. Their petition (as well as one from the contractors on the Chisholm's Rapids works) was referred to a select committee. The commissioners denied that Francis and Hay had abandoned the work because of a total lack of funds, but they did admit that the contractors had been put to considerable inconvenience in consequence of the irregularity with which payments had been made. The committee therefore recommended that Francis and Hay be paid the withheld $1,882.82 – which seemed to recognize some responsibility on the part of the commissioners for the failure of the contractors to fulfill their obligations. The committee made no recommendation with respect to the claim for damages. The commissioners reconsidered the matter later but "resolved that Francis and Hay were not entitled to any more than the Committee of the Legislature recommended."[10] The contractors continued to petition each new government up until 1855, but without success. Each time they were judged to have been fairly treated ... strictly in terms of the contract!

Chisholm's Rapids

A contract for the Chisholm's Rapids (Glen Ross) section was awarded to Robert Barclay and Company on 17 October 1837, and work was started immediately. This was an extensive contract, requiring a 600-foot dam, a timber slide, an 1,100-foot-long canal, and a masonry lock. The principal difference between this contract and the one at Myer's Island was that the latter was for a fixed amount based on the contractor's tender, whereas the contract at Chisholm's Rapids was "to be done by the yard and foot excavation"[11] based on Baird's estimate and paid in accordance with his measurements. Baird's original estimate for the work, which he submitted to the commissioners on 15 September, had been $69,070, but when the contract was entered into, the agreement called for a maximum of $76,346 for the work.

Barclay and Company "always conducted their work much to the satisfaction of the Commissioners"[12] and, according to Baird, would have fulfilled the contract in terms of the agreement well within the estimate, had "shortness of funds"[13] not interfered. Of the two contractors engaged on the Trent River improvements, Barclay seems to have been more competent and better organized than Francis and Hay. Moreover, he had better luck. Much of the excavation for the canal was through gravel and hardpan and the material therefore could be easily removed. A good supply of quarrying stone was found only three miles upstream from the lock site and was easily and cheaply transported across the ice by sleigh or in summer by barge. In this Barclay and Company were much more fortunate than any of the other contractors, a fact that was pointed out to the commissioners by Sidey and Craigie when they failed to complete their contract at Hastings, largely because of difficulty in finding stone. Apart from difficulties associated with the inability of the commissioners to advance funds regularly, the only major problem that Barclay and Company had was a "turn-out" among a portion of the men "for conditions to which the contractors would very properly not accede."[14] This strike was readily solved when the 40 men involved were fired.

When for want of funds the work was ordered stopped by the commissioners on 31 October 1839, the contract was nearly finished. Already

$57,090 of the $76,346 estimate had been advanced to the contractors for work done. The dam was practically finished; more than 53,000 cubic yards of rock and gravel had been excavated from the canal, and, with the exception of the gates, the lock was built. All that remained to be done was removal of about 1,400 cubic yards of material from the canal, completion of the timber slide, building and hanging of the lock gates, and filling in the embankment behind the lock walls. About $12,500 more would have completed the work.

CHAPTER SIX

Stoppage of the Works

The first indication that the Trent River improvements were running into financial difficulties came on 23 March 1838, the same day the lieutenant-governor, Sir Francis Bond Head, departed from Toronto, leaving a financial mess for his successor, Sir George Arthur, to straighten out. On that day, perhaps at the public farewell arranged for Sir Francis at Toronto Harbour, J.H. Dunn apprised George S. Boulton "of the circumstances and of the difficulties in which the finances of the province [were] involved in connection with this [the Trent River improvements] and other public works."[1] It seems that the commissioners had drawn only $17,500 of the $100,000 debentures as of 16 February 1838, and "to avoid loss from the accumulation of interest on the dormant balance, the residue was paid out for other Public Works then in progress"[2]; consequently, there was no money at the disposal of the receiver general to advance to the commissioners so that they could honour their contractual obligations. The works would have to be stopped.

Boulton called a meeting of the commissioners in Cobourg on 16 April, at which time he informed them of the financial situation and its implications for the Trent River works. The other commissioners were angered. John S. Cartwright was furious. True, only $17,500 had been drawn by 16 February, but it had been assumed that the balance would be available upon demand as the work progressed – a logical assumption, as the $100,000 in debentures had been taken by the Commercial Bank "expressly for the work on the Trent."[3] In the opinion of the commissioners, the government had no right to use the debenture funds for other projects. Under the circumstances, they felt justified in not stopping the works but rather "in proceeding therewith."[4] In a petulant mood, they resolved that it was "impractical to stop the work ... without remunerating the contractors for materials got out, for provisions obtained and for work performed"; they decided that it was "expedient that application be made forthwith for such advances as may be necessary to proceed with the work ... and that Messrs. McDonell and Boulton ... wait on his Excellency the Lieutenant Governor for that purpose."[5] Baird was instructed to prepare an estimate for the loss likely to accrue from stopping the work on both the Trent River and the inland waters.

Punctual and exacting as always, Baird wrote both boards of commissioners the next day, enclosing detailed estimates of the losses that would accrue to the province if the works were stopped in April. He calculated a loss of $50,250 on the Trent works and $40,095 on the inland waters, resulting from work done and materials delivered but not yet paid for and from possible damages that would be sustained on the works under contract, "for which the contractors would seem to have a fair claim."[6] Armed with Baird's report, Boulton and McDonell proceeded to Toronto to plead with the lieutenant-governor for the necessary funds to continue with the works in the Newcastle District.

The improvements to navigation in the District of Newcastle, never held in high esteem by the powers-that-be, were among the first public works projects scrapped by Sir George Arthur as he tried to restore order to the province's finances, thrown into chaos following a constitutional imbroglio that developed between his headstrong predecessor, Sir Francis Bond Head, and a militant legislative assembly. The quarrel had developed over the emerging democratic principle of responsible government.

When Sir Francis refused to appoint men to the executive council acceptable to the Reform-controlled legislature, the legislators took the unprecedented step of voting a stoppage of supplies. This amounted to only about $3,500 and affected primarily the salaries of government employees. Sir Francis had a much more powerful economic weapon at his disposal, which he employed in retaliation and perhaps with some delight, at the prorogation of the legislature on 20 April. He refused to grant any contingencies and reserved royal assent on all money bills that had been passed during the session. This included the act authorizing $80,000 for improvements on the inland waters of the Newcastle District. In contrast to the insignificant amount that the legislature had the power to withhold, the public expenditure stopped by Sir Francis amounted to $810,000, including the money for schools, roads, bridges, and all other public improvements. Public works in the province came to a standstill. Sir Francis waited for the full effect of the unemployment to be felt throughout the province and then dissolved the assembly and called an election for 20 June.

The election took place amid great excitement and turbulence. As Bond Head predicted, the average voter was less influenced by constitutional arguments than by bread and butter issues. Consequently the Reformers were decimated; only 17 were returned to the legislative assembly. Among the prominent Reform candidates defeated were William Mackenzie, Peter

Perry, M.S. Bidwell, who was unseated by John S. Cartwright, and Dr John Gilchrist, who was defeated in Northumberland by Henry Ruttan.

If the Reform Parliament in 1834 – 6, preoccupied by a power struggle with the lieutenant-governor, had done too little for the province, the Tory Parliament of 1836 tried to do too much. Electioneering had concentrated on public works. In pointing out the shortcomings of the Reformers, Tory candidates made rash promises. Now the legislators, summoned to Parliament on 8 November, tried to make good the promises. To every public work that was proposed, a charter was granted and money advanced, till near the end of the session it became apparent to Bond Head that not half the required money could be raised. It was during this spate of public works legislation that Ruttan's bill, authorizing $385,000 for improvements on the Trent River, was passed, Ruttan, Cartwright, and McDonell having campaigned vigorously for the improvements in the election campaign. Reluctant to use the tactic of reserving royal assent which he had employed so effectively against the Reformers, Bond Head devised another method of holding the excesses of the Tory Parliament in check: he insisted that clauses be inserted into all money bills, suspending their implementation until the governor-in-council should authorize commencement of the work. There was danger in this because it gave extraordinary power to the lieutenant-governor, but the alternative was for him to withhold royal assent on the more costly bills, thereby precipitating another constitutional row, with both Tories and Reformers lined up against him.

Chronicler John Langton predicted the consequences of this arrangement in a letter to his brother, written just one week after the act authorizing the improvements on the Trent River was given royal assent: "We for instance have got [$385,000] for the Trent, subject to the above condition; suppose only half the whole sums granted can be raised; what is to hinder Sir Francis from stopping our work altogether and laying out all the sum granted on the Hamilton railway or some other work?" This is precisely what happened. Although Bond Head and his executive council had authorized commencement of the Trent River works in October, they had failed to ensure that the necessary funds were made available to complete the contracts. With total disregard for the needs of the contractors, insensitive to the responsibilities of the commissioners, and heedless of the election promises of the local members, Bond Head and his governing council had diverted the money, loaned by the Commercial Bank expressly for the Trent River improvements, into other public works, the Newcastle improvements having been given low priority by them among the plethora of public projects so recklessly approved by the legislature. Expenses connected with the rebellion and its aftermath created other unanticipated demands on the public purse, leaving Sir

George Arthur, Bond Head's replacement, no alternative but to follow an even more niggardly funding policy for the Trent improvements.

Aware of these political and economic difficulties, Boulton and McDonell went cap in hand to Sir George Arthur in May 1838 to beg for enough money to ensure continuance of the Newcastle works and, inevitably, their own political careers. They seem to have had some success, for in July an additional $40,000 in debentures was issued by the Commercial Bank, of which Boulton was immediately advanced $20,000. But a shortage of public funds seems to have forced Sir George to cut off support for the Trent once more, for when the commissioners requested a warrant for "5 or 10,000 pounds"[8] on 30 October, they were informed by J.H. Dunn, the provincial treasurer, (who was opposed to the Trent), that he had no more funds in his hands that could be spared and that "the works would have to wait for funds to be voted by the next meeting of the Legislature."[9] Despite Dunn's claim that the treasury was empty, Cartwright obtained a warrant from the lieutenant-governor for $10,000 on 6 November, and somehow Boulton got a further $9,000 the following January. Fortunately for Barclay and Company, Francis and Hay panicked and abandoned the Myer's Island contract at that time. All the available funds were then spent on Chisholm's Rapids; otherwise Barclay and Company might have been forced to abandon their contract about that time as well.

The commissioners had great difficulty in obtaining any funds in 1839, the year Governor-General Lord Sydenham arrived to reorganize the government. Boulton petitioned the legislature on 4 April, asking for $60,000 to complete the Trent works and $15,000 for the inland waters improvements. He succeeded in getting an act passed authorizing the funds requested, but despite the generosity of his fellow legislators, Boulton learned from the lieutenant-governor that it was unlikely that the money could be made available. On 27 April, a disconsolate Boulton wrote to Baird from the legislative assembly in Toronto, informing him of the situation and ordering him not to spend "one shilling more on account of the Trent or Inland Waters"[10] until receipt of the money was assured. He also instructed Baird to fire McNeil and, in a confessional mood, confided to Baird that he was sorry that he was a commissioner, as he expected to lose seriously because of it.

On 28 June, the commissioners met at Chisholm's Rapids to see for themselves how the work was going and to apprise Barclay of the seriousness of the financial situation. Thinking it inconceivable that the government would waste the several thousand pounds already expended in the Newcastle District by not completing the works, the commissioners intimated to Barclay that they would probably be in a position "to make further advances on the work performed"[11] in about two weeks. On the strength of this assurance, Barclay and Company "agreed to proceed on their own responsibility until a decision of the governor and council should be ascertained";[12] but by August no decision had been made. No funds had been provided, and Barclay and Company were in serious financial difficulty.

The inability of the commissioners to obtain funds regularly for the prosecution of the several works along the route of the waterway was common knowledge throughout the district. Francis and Hay had left debts when they abandoned their contract in January; so had the contractors on the inland waters. Only a few years had passed since Pierce, Dumble and Hoar had had to petition the legislature for the money due them for constructing the Bobcaygeon lock. Small wonder, then, that no one had confidence that the government would honour its commitments or that the contractors could honour theirs. No one trusted the commissioners, either, and because of this no merchant would advance credit to Barclay. Without cash, which he did not have, he could not purchase provisions for his workers. The situation became so serious that at one point the stores contained only two barrels of pork to feed 60 men; one of the partners had to rush all the way to Toronto to make financial arrangements for the purchase of food. Even Baird was threatened with legal action, when workers at Whitla's Rapids found that merchants in Peterborough would not accept certificates that he had issued, in lieu of cash, on orders of the commissioners.

Frustrated, angry, and apparently suspecting that McDonell and Boulton were not advancing the interests of the Trent vigorously enough, Baird, never averse to speaking his mind, wrote pointedly to the commissioners on 12 August about the future of his cherished waterway. He reiterated his oft-stated claims, economic and military, for "the magnificence of the whole scheme" and added a few current economic and political reasons to justify the completion of the works under contract. "If the Government fully understood the importance of and the advantages of the Trent," Baird challenged, "the matter would immediately be taken up in a different manner than it now is."[13] Whether the commissioners showed Baird's letter to the lieutenant-governor and, if they did, whether it had any influence on the executive council are not known, but two weeks later Boulton did receive another advance of $15,000, just in time to save what was left of the "magnificent scheme" from total collapse. But since most of the $15,000 was committed for contingencies and for work already performed by the contractors, the commissioners were again confronted with a shortage of funds in October.

A little of Baird's impatience seems to have rubbed off on the commissioners, for on 11 October 1839 they wrote to the executive council for a firm commitment, one way or the other, respecting the funding of the

Trent improvements. They asked "if it would be in the power of the Provincial Government to advance them such sums as they may from time to time require to enable them to complete the contracts."[14] One week later they received the answer that would seal the fate of the Trent navigation for the next 60 years: "It was not in the power of the Government to make further advances to the Commissioners."[15] Confronted with this discouraging news, three of the commissioners met at Trenton on 31 October and ordered immediate stoppage of the works at Chisholm's Rapids. A final payment to Barclay and Company was authorized, Baird was instructed to prepare a final estimate and to ensure that the uncompleted construction was made secure from damage, and the contractors were advised "to seek redress if any injury or damage may have been sustained by them at the hands of the Legislature."[16] Secretary Charles Green was asked to organize and index all the accounts, correspondence, and orders-in-council. The commissioners resolved to prepare a report placing blame for stoppage of the works in the lap of the government, where they felt it belonged, "including a statement of the whole facts connected with contracts entered into and the way in which the reasonable Expectations of the Commissioners had been defeated."[17] A final meeting was set for Cobourg on 2 November, at which time, the commissioners agreed, they would resign.

But the commissioners did not resign on 2 November. McDonell and Boulton, who had not attended the 31 October meeting, accepted the decision to stop the works at Chisholm's Rapids, but they were not prepared to abandon a position from which they could be seen to be doing the most good for the district, and perhaps themselves, at the next election. (Boulton retained his seat in Durham, but McDonell was defeated by John Gilchrist in a highly controversial election in Peterborough.) They were still optimistic that something could be done to keep the works going, at least until after the election and the proposed reorganization of the government. Apparently they talked the other commissioners out of resigning and encouraged them to press the legislature of Upper Canada for funds. On 30 January 1840, through a select committee chaired by Henry Ruttan, the commissioners managed to get a recommendation passed on to the legislature for an advance of $40,000 to enable them to complete the work on the Trent. Small sums were subsequently advanced to the commissioners, but only, it seems, in amounts sufficient to allow them to make it appear that the improvements were still being actively pursued. An attempt was made to revive construction, never completely stopped, at Whitla's Rapids, a contract being let to Bletcher and Harper for hauling stone from Dummer. A few pounds were spent at Crooks' Rapids to secure the dam, and an attempt was made to restore the lock walls badly damaged by timber running through the lock in the spring.

A contract was made with Henry Trout, a millwright from Cobourg, to finish the timber slide started by Barclay and Company at Chisholm's Rapids, and Baird and Green were kept on at full salary. But despite the small amounts spent in the next two years, the works had been effectively stopped in October 1839.

Baird did his best to help the commissioners keep the works going, if for no other reason than because his livelihood depended upon them. In early June 1840 he was summoned to Montreal to meet with Governor-General Lord Sydenham, then engaged in the process of reorganizing the political and administrative structures of the colony for union with Lower Canada. Before leaving for Montreal, Baird, in a sanguine mood, wrote to the commissioners: "In all probability I may have an opportunity of forwarding the arrangements for completing improvements in progress in the district which your Board may rest assured I shall make every endeavour to forward."[18] Subsequent events indicate that Baird, the chief proponent of the waterway and up to that time a most outspoken supporter of the works, did indeed make a case for completing the improvements in progress, but one must surmise that he was told what public works were planned for the Newcastle District when the government was reorganized and that if he wanted a job with the proposed board of works he had better keep quiet about a future Lake Ontario – Lake Huron waterway. Never again, after this trip to Montreal, did Baird promote the waterway publicly, and his reports to the commissioners were purely factual accounts, devoid of the canal proselytising that had characterized his earlier submissions.

After the election of March 1841 – the first for the United Provinces – the new board of works, which would have responsibility for administering all public works, was formally established by legislation. At the end of June, Alexander McDonell, who had lost his seat in the spring election but was still a commissioner, learned that no more money would be paid over to the commissioners – a decision not entirely unexpected. Still piqued at having lost the election, McDonell wrote tartly to Charles Green on 2 July, telling him that "if Baird [had] not already gone out to stop the works he had better do so forthwith."[19] Green passed the message on to Baird, and the little activity still under way in the district was immediately halted. On 22 October Thomas Begley, first secretary of the Board of Works, wrote Boulton enclosing an opinion offered by the solicitor general to the effect that with passage of the Board of Works Act "authority of the Commissioners for the improvement of the Navigation of the Trent and Inland Waters of the District had ceased."[20] Boulton was asked to forward the maps, books, and other documents in the possession of the commissioners to the new Public Works office in Kingston.

Thus power and privilege, which had rested in the hands of dozens of commissioners throughout the province, were seized by a centralist fist, the provincial Board of Works. The former system of enacting specific pieces of public works legislation and naming local commissioners to supervise approved construction projects had come to an end. For a pioneering society, which had no form of local government, it had been a good system, since it matched public improvements to local needs; but gradually the system, misused and abused by politicians, had run the province into bankruptcy. In a maturing society, in which local communities were becoming increasingly dependent upon each other for their economic well-being, a more rational method of distributing public resources was needed. A central co-ordinating body was necessary, if the state were to provide the essential services that would enable the colony's economy to develop to its full potential. Politics would continue to play a vital role in the determination of which district got what amount of public funds, and politicians would have to learn how to deal with a central bureaucracy that would set provincial priorities. That would introduce a whole new game of power politics for which the rules had not yet been invented. Thus it was with some misgiving but much relief that the diminutive George S. Boulton, who for over a decade had presided like a colossus over the economic development of the District of Newcastle, handed over the documents on behalf of the commissioners, "happy in being relieved from their responsibilities" and confident that the superintendence of the works was "being placed in better hands."[21]

Earlier, in October, Baird had conducted Hamilton Killaly, first chairman of the Board of Works, on an inspection tour of the works still nominally under his superintendence. Baird could scarcely have been proud of the achievements of five years that he showed to his long-time friend. Upwards of $150,000 had been spent in the district, and all that had been accomplished was the restoration of Bethune's leaking lock at Bobcaygeon; but there was no lock master to tend the lock and there were no steamboats on the Back Lakes to use it. It was not Baird's fault that the other contracts had not been completed. He had done his best. It had been the commissioners who determined where the funds were to be spent, and it had been the government that withheld the funds, forcing the contractors into insolvency. Nevertheless, Baird must have been embarrassed at what they saw.

At Lindsay, the timber that had been hauled out of the bush by Homer Hecox in 1838 was rotting on the ground, and the lock excavation was filling in with mud and silt. The dam at Buckhorn Rapids, completed in 1839, was still standing but leaking badly; no one was in charge of it except John Hall, who regulated it to the advantage of his own mill, frequently flooding out mills upstream at Bobcaygeon and Pigeon Creek. At Whitla's Rapids, quantities of stone and timber were scattered on the ground; the coffer dam had given way, allowing water, mud, and planks to swirl around in the collapsing lock pit. Tools and equipment, available to anyone who wanted to walk off with them, were rusting in a shed. The works at Crooks' Rapids, so nearly completed by Sidey and Craigie and McNeil and Sutherland, were in need of immediate attention to prevent severe damage from spring floods. Maj. Crooks was building a temporary dam to raise the level of the water for his grist and saw mill, flooding from which would further ravage the public works at the rapids, already in a deplorable condition. Water was pouring through the uncompleted section of the dam, gradually washing the rest of it away; the spring flood of 1840 had flushed through the gateless lock, undermining its foundation and allowing the sills to sag and pieces of ashlar to tumble from the disintegrating lock walls into the pit.

Timber, prepared by Hecox for the dam at Healey Falls, had all but disappeared, lumbermen having built shanties with it or having used it for fire wood. Only at Chisholm's Rapids, where Trout was completing the timber slide, was there any semblance of order. But even there the unfinished works were in danger of serious deterioration, if someone were not placed in charge until construction could be resumed. A pier of the dam had already been blasted out by lumbermen to facilitate the passage of large timber rafts.

At the conclusion of the tour, although it then seemed superfluous to do so, the orderly Baird wrote detailed descriptions of the works to each of the boards of commissioners in whose employ he technically still served. He must have known that the commissioners, who had already been stripped of their authority, would be powerless to carry out any recommendations, but Baird made them anyway. Perhaps he had an eye on his own future and was really directing his reports to the Board of Works, to which the reports would eventually go and with which he hoped to be employed should construction resume.

Meanwhile, the "grand work" that had excited "great interest in the country"[22] in 1834 had come to naught. The much-hoped-for line of navigation from the Bay of Quinte through Lake Simcoe to Lake Huron, that would raise the district from obscurity to world prominence, had become a river of sunken dreams laden with leaking dams, flooded marshes, crumbling masonry, and abandoned homesteads. Visions of grand estates were clouded over with shadows of disillusionment. Those who had invested heavily in land speculation prepared to leave the district or to take up occupations other than farming. Romantics like the Traills and Moodies had already left. Need was negotiating for the sale of his mill at Bobcaygeon to Mossom Boyd and making plans to return to England. Jameson had already gone back to Liverpool, leaving his 12,000 acres on Sturgeon Lake for his partner's ravaging axe, there being no settlers' ploughs to work the soil. John Langton, who had concluded early on that "a system of tenantry can never be introduced ... with anything like favourable terms to the landowner,"[23] was forming a lumber partnership with Mossom Boyd and beginning to think about entering the civil service through a career in politics. The Dennistouns, Frasers, and VanSittarts and most of the other large landholders on the Back Lakes were all gone or about to leave. Those who remained to harvest the forests, or to farm on a less grand scale than they had planned, waited for a break in the sullen clouds of misapprehension that had settled over the district and wondered what the new Board of Works might do about the waterway.

PART TWO

The Union Years: 1841–67

Bobcaygeon lock, 1838.
Sketched by Anne Langton.
(Courtesy H. Pammett,
Peterborough)

The Trent-Severn Waterway:
Improvements 1841 – 67

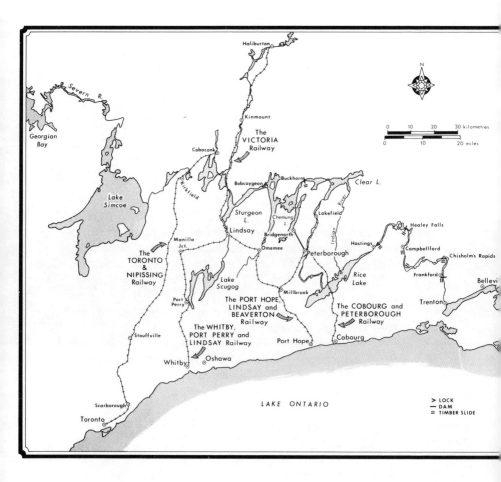

CHAPTER SEVEN

Hamilton Killaly and the Board of Works

Vigorous reform movements culminating in rebellion in both Upper and Lower Canada in 1837 had made clear to the British government the necessity of solving the problems of government in the Canadian provinces. To this end, the British prime minister appointed the Earl of Durham governor-general of all of British North America with responsibility for calming the unrest in the provinces and reporting the causes of the grievances. Upon returning to Britain in 1839, Durham issued his famous report.

The man sent to Canada, succeeding Durham as governor-general and charged with responsibility for implementing as much of Durham's report as the imperial government was then prepared to accept, was Charles Poulett Thompson, soon to be named Lord Sydenham. A bachelor with a charming manner and amiable disposition, a skilled diplomat, and a first-rate administrator, Sydenham was universally admired and respected by both political foes and colleagues. He possessed, to an amazing degree, those qualities of temperament that facilitate the process of political compromise, without which his attempts to introduce constitutional reform would not have been possible.

Sydenham was a member of the British mercantile class, the son of a wealthy London merchant. He began his own mercantile training in a branch of his father's business in St Petersburg, at about the same time that the young Scottish engineer Nichol Hugh Baird was refining his engineering skills in the same city. Upon returning to England, Sydenham entered politics, being elected to represent Dover as a member of the Liberal party. He advanced rapidly in the government, becoming vice-president of the Board of Trade in Earl Grey's ministry and eventually president of the Board of Trade in Lord Melbourne's cabinet. He resigned from the cabinet in 1839 to assume the governorship of British North America and proceeded immediately to Quebec.

Sydenham was faced with three principal tasks upon arriving in Canada: to win acceptance by the two Canadas for a scheme for uniting them; to make Canadians, especially Reformers, content with a form of government that was slightly less than responsible; and to reorganize the financial affairs of the country, then in a state of near-bankruptcy. When he died, just two years later, he had largely succeeded in accomplishing all three.

Sydenham's first step was to bring about the union of Upper and Lower Canada, which was accomplished with the passage by the British Parliament of the Act of Union, 1840. Having subsequently proclaimed the union in February 1841, and carried out the ensuing election, he opened the first Parliament of the United Canadas in Kingston on 4 June 1841. He moved just as quickly and just as skilfully to introduce measures designed to bolster the country's sagging economy. Earlier, Durham had been quick to recognize that the political unrest in Canada had been aggravated by commercial and agricultural depression and pointed out that unless this were righted there would always be discontent accompanied by talk of republicanism or union with the American states, where economic opportunities were decidedly better than in Canada. Influenced by Durham's observations, Sydenham realized that unless the economic advantages of union, which he had promised, were achieved, the union of the two provinces would not last long. The first governor of Canada with a commercial rather than a military background and with experience at the Board of Trade, Sydenham understood more clearly than most the connection between politics and commerce. And so it was to commercial considerations that he gave top priority after the union itself was achieved.

The root cause of Canada's economic difficulties lay in impediments to trade, of which there were several: laws that prohibited the importation of particular articles except from England, monopoly privileges enjoyed but abused by some forwarders, inadequate banking facilities, the colonies' poor credit rating, making it difficult to obtain capital, and heavy import duties that were controlled by Lower Canada, often to the disadvantage of Upper Canadians. These problems were largely political and could be solved by government action, but the principal barrier to trade, especially for Upper Canada, was physical: the lack of an adequate system of transportation for moving products cheaply to and from overseas markets. Durham had recognized the need for, and had urged on the British government, completion of the St Lawrence canal system.

Lt.-Col. Philpotts, of the Royal Engineers, on instructions from Durham, had prepared two comprehensive reports on the subject. Quite perceptively, Philpotts had reasoned that the future prosperity of the St Lawrence River colonies depended upon completion of the chain of canals between Lake Erie and the Atlantic. He recommended that the Welland and Lachine canals be deepened to nine feet and that canals of the same dimensions be built around the other rapids on the St Lawrence River as quickly as possible. Philpotts feared that Canada would lose the chance of securing any portion of the vast trade that he predicted would soon be carried on between the western states and the Atlantic, unless uninterrupted navigation for freighters capable of carrying a cargo of at least 300 tons were opened between Lake Erie and Montreal. Indeed, much of the developing trade was already being siphoned out of the Great Lakes basin to New York through the Erie Canal, opened in 1825.

Baird had argued the case for developing the Trent on the same grounds, but whereas the route he championed wandered cautiously up the Ottawa River, down the Rideau, and up the Trent-Severn drainage system to Lake Huron, skirting the best agricultural land in the country, Philpottss' route made a bold thrust into the heart of the fertile St Lawrence – Great Lakes lowland, where the majority of settlers lived. Baird's vision had grown out of eighteenth-century-military-strategic planning; Philpottss' proposal was based on nineteenth-century commercial necessity. Sydenham, more advanced in his thinking than either engineer and anticipating the age of railroads, did not particularly favour either route, but if water transportation there had to be, it was Philpotts's waterway (which William Merritt had been advocating for years) that Sydenham chose. Anne Langton sensed what Sydenham's decision would be. She wrote: "Lord Sydenham, I understand, does not patronize water communication, expecting railways to supersede everything; and of course our particular claim to be the line of road only rests in our beautiful string of lakes and rivers."[1] Earlier she had observed: "It is thought that the Governor-General is not favourable to us."[2] Sydenham had immediately carried Sir George Arthur's policy of limiting funds for the Trent works one step further, by stopping the funds altogether until transportation priorities could be established by the new government.

Deciding to construct the St Lawrence canals was one thing, but finding the money to finance construction was another matter. At the time of the union Upper Canada was, for all intents and purposes, bankrupt, being burdened with a debt of over $5 million. Lower Canada was in better condition financially because of a much smaller public debt, but it could hardly be expected to shoulder the burden of construction and share responsibility for a large portion of Upper Canada's immense debt, as well. As an inducement to the two Canadas to accept the union, the British government had offered to guarantee the payment of interest on a new Canadian loan of $7.5 million. This would re-establish the credit of Canadian securities in the London money market, by effectively converting the bonds of the Canadian government into gilt-edged securities, equivalent to the bonds of the British government. It was intended that this loan be applied to redemption of the outstanding debt of the two provinces, with the understanding that if new capital were needed to finance public works, further Canadian securities would be issued without the guarantee of the British government. But believing that construction of the St Lawrence canals and enlargement of the Welland were urgently needed to improve the trade on which the economy of the new country was dependent, and expecting that the continuing depression would make it improbable that a new issue of Canadian government securities could be sold at anything close to par value, Sydenham convinced the legislature to use the proceeds from the British loan for public works and to leave the existing debt unredeemed. The British government concurred.

With financing guaranteed, Sydenham's next step was to devise some means of assuring that the money would be spent wisely and not squandered on a myriad of small local projects, as had been done under the old system of appointed commissioners. To this end, he established a Board of Works "for the superintendence, management and control of public works"[3] in the province. As evidence of the high priority Sydenham placed on public works, the legislation establishing the Board of Works was introduced by the solicitor-general, Charles D. Day, on 6 July, just days after the legislature convened; the bill received royal assent on 17 August. The board consisted of five members, one of whom was chairman; all were appointed by the governor. There was also an appointed permanent secretary who was responsible for keeping records and accounts, drafting contracts, writing reports, and conducting general administrative duties connected with the operations of the board. The chairman was a member of the executive council. He and the secretary received annual salaries and travelling expenses. The board was responsible to the governor and was prohibited from spending any funds except those approved by the legislature, and only then with the consent of the governor.

Although future chairmen (later ministers) of the Board of Works would have political rather than engineering skills, Sydenham wanted an experienced engineer as first chairman. Moreover, he seems to have wanted someone who was committed to his own perception of public works priorities for the country – development of the St Lawrence canal system and construction of good roads – and who was courageous and tough enough to resist proposals for smaller local projects that would divert resources from the principal undertaking. It is quite possible that Nicol Hugh Baird, whom Sydenham undoubtedly knew from St Petersburg days, was considered for the position, but Baird's abrasive manner and obtuse personality would have ruled him out, even if he had not been publicly identified with the rival Rideau-Trent system which Sydenham was about to scrap.

The man Sydenham chose to head the Board of Works was Hamilton Hartley Killaly. A moderate Liberal, uncommitted to any political party,

Killaly was more interested in engineering than politics but did allow his name to stand as a candidate in his home riding of London in the March election of 1841. Moved by political fervor instead of being constrained by royal impartiality, and therefore acting more like a prime minister than a governor-general, Sydenham campaigned actively on behalf of those men he wanted in his government. Speaking on behalf of Killaly at London, he is reported to have said: "It is very necessary to secure the services of Mr. Killaly in the new parliament."[4] With Sydenham's endorsement, Killaly won the election handily and, appropriately on 17 March, was named to Sydenham's executive council, where he held office without portfolio, pending the opening of the legislature and the establishment of the Board of Works, when he was named chairman.

Killaly was born in Dublin, Ireland, in 1800. Educated at Trinity College and the Royal Academy of Science, he qualified as a civil engineer and for several years served under his father, who was government engineer for the Irish Board of Works. He emigrated to Canada in 1834 and settled near London, where for a time be combined farming with general contracting and undertook various surveys and commissions for the government of Upper Canada. Sometimes referred to as an "Irish gentleman of the old school," he was also known, especially in his later years, as an eccentric. One observer described him as the "most ill-dressed man on the continent of North America,"[6] a distinction Killaly earned by frequently appearing in public dressed in a dirty, powder-smeared and blood-stained hunting jacket, worn-out trousers, and a buttonless shirt which allowed his brawny and hairy chest to be exposed to public view, while ravelled threads dangled from his sleeves over fat, freckled, and dirty hands. His round purple face, surrounded by a mass of white hair, is said to have had the appearance of "a red cabbage in snow."[7] He aged well; he had a brisk and vigorous step, a hale and hearty laugh, and a "voice like the blast of a clarion."[8] Generally good-natured, he could occasionally be imperious and arbitrary with subordinates; he was cautious, sometimes even obsequious, with superiors or those whose opinions might affect his own interests. And he was a good engineer. He was just the sort of man that Sydenham was looking for to execute his public works program.

Originally (perhaps influenced by Baird, a friend) Killaly had been one of those opposed to the development of the St Lawrence, believing that the Ottawa-Rideau communication between Lake Ontario and tidewater was sufficient for the province's needs. But the rapid developments in Illinois, Indiana, Michigan, and Ohio and growth in southwestern Ontario, almost doubling trade annually, convinced him that a second and more facile outlet to the sea was required. Moreover, he recognized that the navigation of the Rideau Canal depended upon the stability of man-made earthen dams of great height. If one of them should collapse through accident or malice, half the commercial interests of the country would be ruined. Or perhaps Killaly had succumbed to the obsession of his boss, William Merritt, with opening the St Lawrence navigation. Whatever the reason, by the time Sydenham lured him away from his duties as engineer in charge of the Welland to assume the chairmanship of the Board of Works, Killaly was firmly committed to the St Lawrence – Welland development.

During the spring and summer of 1841, Killaly met frequently with Sydenham. Together they created the public works program that would be presented to the legislature after passage of the Board of Works Act, when Killaly would be officially named chairman. Killaly and his principal assistant, Samuel Keefer, worked out the details and estimates of cost and prepared the report, but there is little doubt that the overall plan was Sydenham's. Sydenham himself presented it to the legislature on 20 August.

Killaly's report encompassed one general, all-inclusive plan for the different works that appeared necessary to increase trade and improve the commerce of the new country. The full cost of the program was estimated at $8,697,685. Killaly had prudently divided the works up into three separate classes, based on the degree of national importance and revenue-generating capacity of each work. First, there were projects of a definite national character – mainly canals and timber slides – that were considered indispensable to the advancement of the commercial and agricultural interests of the country at large and from which, it was expected, revenues from tolls would be realized: estimated cost $7,090.910. Second, there were to be roads to connect with the main inland communication routes, necessary to the development of the resources of the country in peace and indispensable for defence in time of war, but that would produce no direct revenue to pay interest on the requisite outlay: estimated cost $1,060.00. The third class of works consisted mainly of roads in Upper Canada, purely local in nature, that had been started before the Union but not completed: estimated cost $546,775.[9]

The two major classes of improvements recommended in Killaly's report were incorporated into a bill, but the third class of works, which contributed little directly to national development, was excluded, the legislature leaving these works for local municipalities to build themselves. The total package included in the bill amounted to $8,298,410. Since the recommendations contained in the report had represented a judicious blending of national economic priorities and local political interests, there was little opposition to the bill, and it passed through the legislature within two weeks, receiving royal assent on 8 September 1841.

The Killaly-Sydenham plan for the Trent must be interpreted against the plan of national priorities outlined above. It will be recalled that the major purposes for developing the Trent route to Lake Huron, expounded by Baird and supported by almost every settler and politician along the proposed waterway, were three. First, the Trent would provide, in conjunction with the Rideau, an uninterrupted line of navigation from lakes Huron and Michigan to the Atlantic. Because it was shorter than the Lake Erie – Lake Ontario – St Lawrence route, it was alleged that it would be a safer and less expensive channel through which produce of the western states could be sent down to tidewater. Moreover, because of its location, the Trent route was thought to be less liable to interruption in time of war than the border route. Second, the Trent's development would offer a facility for transporting agricultural and other products from the inland townships to markets at the front. Third, because the waterway passed through heavily timbered tracts of land, it was argued that removal of obstacles in the rivers would encourage and afford a facility for the growth of an extensive trade in lumber and staves.

The last two reasons motivated residents, especially those of the eastern portion of the route, to seek its development. And there is no doubt that rendering the Otonabee and Trent rivers navigable would have been a tremendous boon to the economic development of that struggling pioneer area. But the cost of construction would be enormous, conservatively estimated by Baird at $3.1 million. In the 1830s there was no possibility that such a large amount of public money could or would be spent on a local improvement for the benefit of a small and sparsely populated district, no matter how beautiful its string of lakes and rivers. And so the grander purpose, the through waterway concept, rationalized on the basis of defence imperatives – of major concern in the aftermath of the War of 1812 – and continental transportation, was put forth as an inducement for government financial support. In other words, an attempt was made to acquire an expensive local improvement by presenting it as a valuable national asset. This same strategy would be employed in future years in an effort to reawaken government interest in the Trent scheme, especially after completion of the Canadian Pacific Railway, when western grain elevators bulged with a backlog of wheat, which the existing transportation facilities did not seem able to handle. Less praiseworthy was the fact that federal politicians capitalized on the strategy; in the name of a vaguely defined canal development policy, which they knew did not really exist, they spent large sums of tax money for nothing more than local political gain.

But in the early 1830s, arguments in favour of the Trent, although unrealistic, were at least sincere. Many prominent citizens and experts, including Killaly and Baird, supported the scheme. But many powerful politicians, especially William Merritt and the directors of the Welland Canal Company, who perceived the St Lawrence as a logical link with the Welland, opposed development of the Trent. Nevertheless, for a time, interest in the Trent canal scheme ran high throughout the province. Regrettably, division and bickering by proponents of the various access routes consumed time, weakened the political front of the canal's promoters, and in the end abetted its opponents. Thus, when legislation was finally passed, only small grants were authorized for construction on portions of the route; these were made more in response to intense public pressure than as a bone fide of the government's commitment to build the waterway.

Killaly and Sydenham never doubted that the Trent canal scheme should be scrapped in favour of the St Lawrence navigation, but, given the strong support for the Trent and the previous governments' initiatives on it, a decision to scrap the project had to be justified. So Killaly examined the alleged advantages of the Trent as a national waterway in comparison with those of the St Lawrence. First, he compared the costs. The $3.1 million estimate for the Trent, made by Baird, he considered too low. Killaly predicted that the Trent system would cost at least another $1.5 million, bringing it close to $4.6 million, a good $850,000 more than the estimated cost of the St Lawrence canals. And what about the advantages? The distance from the upper lakes to tidewater was indisputably shorter by way of the Trent, but that would not necessarily mean a saving of time and expense of transport, Killaly argued. The Trent's 240-mile circuitous course involved 850 feet of lockage to raise a boat from the level of Georgian Bay to Balsam Lake – the high point on the route – and then back down to the Lake Ontario level; this would require upwards of 80 locks, according to Baird's survey. The plan called for locks 133 feet long, bearing only 5 feet of water over the sills, because the shallow waterway could not sustain locks of any greater size without a tremendous increase in costs for dredging. Killaly reasoned that the class of steamer navigating this dimension of canal would be unsuited to the rough water of lakes Michigan and Huron; therefore, trans-shipment would be necessary at the Georgian Bay entrance, increasing costs and eliminating whatever time advantage the route's shorter distance might otherwise provide. Moreover, navigation on the Trent route would be impeded by floods and currents in the rivers, and, further, transportation would be seriously obstructed by ice forming earlier and remaining longer in the several small lakes through which the route passed than was the case in the more southern and broader waters of the St Lawrence River. Defence arguments were not seriously considered. Had the Americans wanted to invade Canada with a view of annexation, they had a golden opportunity during the 1837 rebellion. Such border raids that did take place were not supported by the us government. The threat of war with the Americans no longer seemed to exist. Given the limitations of the Trent as a national waterway, Killaly could not agree that the local wants of the district made necessary or demanded the immense outlay that the undertaking would require. For those reasons, which in retrospect appear sound, he advised Sydenham, who recommended the same to the legislature, that the expenditure contemplated formerly by the Province of Upper Canada on the Trent navigation be suspended.

Once Parliament had decided against spending money on the Trent as a national scheme, a question arose as to how much public support Killaly should recommend be given to the waterway as a local work. After weighing all the economic and political factors very carefully, he recommended that $200,000 be spent in the former Newcastle District for the "formation of cross roads, leading from the Ports on Lake Ontario into the back townships; the construction of some slides for the running down of timber ... and the completion of some detached locks and dams, commenced under the Commissioners, and which were then in different stages of forwardness."[10]

In deciding to spend $200,000 for partial revival of the suspended Trent improvements, Killaly acted both as a far-sighted national architect and a myopic political pragmatist. His mandate as chairman of the Board of Works was to recommend, through the governor-general to the legislature, public works that would contribute to the development of the national economy, not facilities that would bring profit to residents of a local community. But local economies are difficult to isolate from national economies, the latter being the sum total of the former, and there are always the political implications of discrimination against particular localities to be considered, when one tries to differentiate. Killaly's task was not easy. The criterion he seems to have used – probably laid down by Sydenham – in deciding on the merits of spending any of the imperial load in a particular district was the degree to which the district's resource exploitation could contribute to foreign trade. On that score, settlers in the Trent watershed could make a quite convincing claim to a fair share of the country's financial resources. As indicated, the area was richly endowed with fairly accessible stands of timber, and timber had replaced fur as an export staple in the economy of the St Lawrence River basin. Money spent in facilitating the development of the district's lumber industry could easily be justified in terms of national economic development priorities. Killaly was prepared to concede this. But he believed that there was a cheaper and more effective means of accommodating the lumber industry than construction of an expensive canal. Hence he recommended construction of timber slides to move the timber over the more dangerous rapids and falls in the Trent and Otonabee rivers.

Killaly would have been within his rights, following Sydenham's national priorities formula, to stop construction on the locks altogether.

Isolated and unconnected as they were, and with the through waterway proposition dead, the locks' completion would make little direct contribution to the development of the national economy; there was even some question if they were vital to the local economy. By 1841, the government had no legal obligations to the contractors; Robert Barclay had been paid damages for the stoppage of the works at Chisholm's Rapids, and, technically, the others had abandoned their contracts voluntarily. In recommending completion of the four locks, which had reached varying stages of construction before 1839, Killaly was simply "playing politics."

When he was preparing his public works report for Sydenham and the legislature, there was no assurance that his recommendations would be accepted; in fact the Board of Works had not yet been officially established. To ensure adoption of his major recommendations, the national public works priorities had been sugared with local sweeteners to win the widest possible political support. Politically, Killaly had to provide something for the Trent in addition to timber slides, for however advantageous they might be to the national welfare, the slides would be seen as materially benefiting the lumber barons, who had petitioned the governor-general for them. There had to be something of substance in the act for the farmers and merchants along the Trent waterway, who were still represented by some powerful political figures in the new legislature. By not resigning in 1839 when the other commissioners had wanted to, Boulton and McDonell had succeeded in keeping work on the Trent and inland waters improvements active, and public expectations for the waterway alive, right up until the moment the Board of Works had been established and the commissioners' authority had been removed. Killaly knew the political power inherent in public expectations. He knew also the potential risk to the Union experiment if voters' expectations were frustrated, especially an expectation for such as the Trent Waterway, which had been held for so long and which had been partially met by the government of Upper Canada. It was probably this factor, above any economic consideration, that induced him to recommend completion of the "detached locks and dams." The strategy of Boulton and McDonell had forced his hand. Sydenham seems to have agreed.

But there were other considerations. Settlers in the District of Newcastle (now the District of Colborne) had special transportation difficulties, imposed by geography, that other regions did not have. The district was riddled with a mesh of lakes and turbulent rivers, and it was hemmed in on the north by the uninhabited Canadian Shield. No main road, either north-south or east-west, ran through to connect the settled parts of the district to major commercial centres, as was the case with most other settled regions of Upper Canada. It was true that the proposed main highway from Quebec City to Sarnia, skirting the shore of Lake Ontario, would pass through the southern edge of the district, but the road would be far removed and unconnected to the settled back townships. These were isolated and cut off. The Trent Waterway had been seen as providing the necessary link with the "precincts of civilization,"[11] and for this reason a tentative commitment had been made to construct part of it prior to the Union. With the water proposal dead, some reasonable alternative had to take its place. Since it would be years before the municipal government would be in a financial position to provide adequate transportation facilities, the central government would have to provide them.

Killaly recommended a combination of land and water transportation to serve the needs of the settlers in the district. Two plank roads, one leading from Port Hope to Rice Lake, the other from Windsor Harbour (Whitby) to Lake Scugog, were planned. These made good sense and good politics. The Whitby road, connecting with the lock to be completed at Lindsay and the already completed lock at Bobcaygeon, would provide access to Lake Ontario for all the settlements around the Back Lakes from Fenelon Falls to Buckhorn and Bridgenorth. The road from Port Hope to Rice Lake, together with the road from Cobourg to Rice Lake, would, in conjunction with the locks at Whitla's Rapids and Hastings, open up to Lake Ontario several townships bordering on Rice Lake, the Otonabee River, and the upper Trent. The fact that locks had been started in these strategic locations by the previous government suggests that their construction had been planned with the same local transportation needs in mind, and not as part of a through waterway to Lake Huron, as many contemporary residents had thought and some modern writers still believe.

Killaly planned no roads along the lower Trent. The Trent got the slides. Besides, local roads were supposed to be the responsibility of municipal governments. The lock at Chisholm's Rapids was completed purely for political reasons. Killaly admitted that isolated as the Chisholm's Rapids works were, benefits from their completion would be comparatively small. "Only for the advanced stage to which the works had progressed under the Commissioners, it would not have been considered advisable to have undertaken them,"[12] he wrote.

When the settlers living along the route of the Trent Canal learned that Killaly was about to scrap their cherished waterway in favour of the St Lawrence, they did what they had done with a modest degree of success on previous occasions: they held meetings and signed petitions. This time the efforts were co-ordinated. In early June, just days before the legislature convened in Kingston, three public meetings were organized: one in Percy township for settlers on the Trent River, one at Peterborough for residents of Peterborough and the Back Lakes, and one at Barrie for settlers in Simcoe County. Resolutions asking for completion of the internal navigation between Lake Huron and Lake Ontario were drafted and approved unanimously at each meeting, and petitions containing hundreds of names were forwarded through the newly elected MLAs to Lord Sydenham.

The arguments put forward in favour of the waterway were the oft-stated ones and need not be repeated here. The petition from Peterborough, representing the self-styled aristocrats on the Back Lakes, was blatantly self-serving and incompatible with the new national politics. It stated: "Many persons possessed of capital having settled in the back townships and there expended considerable sums of money on the improvement of property induced solely by the prospect of the opening of the navigation, it is in the opinion of your memorialists that success cannot follow their enterprise and they will be compelled to abandon their property and locations at a heavy loss to themselves as well as the province generally unless this outlet be afforded for their marketable produce."[12] Neither Sydenham nor Killaly was moved very far from the principal public works objectives by pleas such as this, although the petitions may have helped produce the cross-roads and a decision to complete the locks.

The district residents never forgave Killaly, whom they blamed for shelving the Trent waterway, accusing him of having sold out to the financial interests in Toronto, where the St Lawrence – Welland was generally favoured, and to the interests of a few lumber barons. So intense was the criticism levelled at him that Killaly felt obliged to defend himself in his report to the legislature in 1845. "I am aware," Killaly wrote, "that much dissatisfaction was felt and still exists throughout that section of the Province at the suspension of the works of general navigation."[14] Many, especially those who advocated the necessity for the uninterrupted navigation, strongly opposed the substitution of timber slides for the locks, claiming that the slides would not pay interest on the outlay as the locks would have done. "Upon me individually, is thrown by them ... the odium of having stopped the works," Killaly protested. "I merely gave my opinion thereon when requested to do so, and that in fact by the legislature was their suspension determined."[15]

Never very interested in political life and apparently lacking the internal fortitude to withstand personal criticism arising therefrom, Killaly had already withdrawn from politics when the above apologia was written. He resigned from the executive council in 1843 and relinquished his seat in the legislature in 1844. But he kept the chairmanship of the Board of Works until 1846, when he resigned to assume charge of the Welland Canal improvements. Later, in 1851, be became assistant commissioner for public works for Canada. This position, in which he was really the technical head of the reorganized Board of Works, allowed him to concentrate on his two principal interests – engineering and fishing. Meanwhile, as first chairman of the Board of Works, he attacked the problem of developing the country's early transportation with much vigour.

On 24 January 1842, Baird was appointed local engineer in charge of "such works as may be proceeded with in the Newcastle District and its vicinity."[16] He received a salary of $2,000 per year plus an annual allowance of $500 to cover expenses. (Killaly's own salary was $4,000 per year.) As local engineer, Baird would be responsible for supervision of repairs to Gull Island lighthouse, construction of Cobourg and Whitby harbours, and building plank roads from Port Hope to Rice Lake and from Whitby to Lake Scugog, in addition to building the timber slides and finishing the locks. By July, the board had received authority from the executive council to proceed with the Newcastle improvements after some prodding from Dr John Gilchrist, who had replaced Alexander McDonell as representative from Peterborough in the new legislature. Then, in true bureaucratic fashion, the board immediately set about the task of establishing a supervising hierarchy. James Lyons was appointed assistant engineer; Thomas McGrath and Thomas Wilson were made superintendents, with Wilson assuming McNeil's former position as overseer of the works from Healey Falls to Lindsay, and McGrath placed in charge of the lower Trent improvements, where most of the slides were built. There were three clerks in the office in Cobourg, and Charles Green, former secretary to the commissioners, became paymaster. A foreman was placed in charge of each construction project. Wilson and McGrath were supposed to submit regular progress reports and fortnightly paylists to Baird, who would forward them to the secretary of the Board of Works, Thomas Begley, along with his own reports. In time Wilson submitted reports directly to Begley, bypassing Baird. This undermined Baird's authority and, as we shall see, rendered him redundant.

Some of the work, mainly provision and delivery of materials, was let out to contract, but all construction was done by the Board of Works, employing day labourers, carpenters, and stone masons under the supervision of the foreman and superintendents. Baird's plans and specifications, most of which had been prepared during his time with the commissioners, were used. In addition to completion of the locks and restorations of the dam started or built before 1841, the following works were carried out: timber slides at Buckhorn, Hastings, Healey Falls, and Ranney Falls; dams at Frankford and Fiddler's Island; timber-collecting booms at Crowe Bay and Percy Landing; bridges at Bobcaygeon, Lindsay, Buckhorn, Peterborough, Hastings, and Campbellford; and some dredging and clearing of obstacles near the locks. Although the original estimate for these works was set at $200,000, by 1843, when they were well under way, the estimate had grown to $272,425. When all the construction was completed in 1846, they had cost the phenomenal sum of $410,395, including over $46,750 for superintendence.[17]

Costs of the Trent works had skyrocketed because of the lax way in which the Board of Works managed its financial affairs. When it was established in 1841, all the members of the board except one were members of the executive council, including Killaly, who was not only chairman but virtually served as chief engineer. While Killaly sat on the executive council and matters relating to the Board of Works were discussed, only verbal approval was given him to proceed with the public works decided upon. Since neither the authorizations nor the approved expenditures were put in written form, there were no records with which to compare actual expenditures. Killaly later claimed that when he requested the executive council to put approvals in writing he was told "such a formality was unnecessary."[18] Even within the board, no regular system of audit was established and no method of checking accounts or controlling the expenditure of funds was set up.[19]

Large sums were paid in wages to day labourers with no check on the rates paid or the number of men employed, other than the certificates of Wilson and McGrath, resulting in the costs of all projects exceeding the estimates. Killaly complained to Wilson, on one occasion, about the high rate he was paying labourers. Wilson replied that when he informed the workers that he would not allow any more than 75 cents per day – Killaly's suggested figure – they picked up their tools and would have left had he not promised to continue the normal $1 per day wage. No more was said about the matter. Later, when the cost of the works had exceeded $300,000, a concerned Killaly asked Wilson about the possibility of suspending the works on the Trent River until the following year. Wilson advised that to leave the works in an unfinished state for a year would result in at least three-quarters of the work done being carried away in the spring freshet, eventually doubling the cost of completing them.

With the Board of Works providing a seemingly inexhaustible supply of funds, work on the locks and dams progressed much more rapidly than it had during the days of the commissioners, when shortage of money had been the principal obstruction to progress. There were a few small personnel problems, in addition to the mild labour dispute referred to above. McGrath caused a minor political flurry when he refused to hire any labourers except Roman Catholics, requiring a certificate of good standing from a local priest; in return for assigning a job he withheld a small retainer from each labourer which was paid into a fund for the priest. Baird, who had recommended McGrath, got into some difficulty with the board because he had not investigated the charges when he learned about them and not provided the board with "the true state of the case"[20] on which it could form an opinion. There was also a problem at a subsidized boarding-house at Hastings, run by a man named Darcey. Because he had, for a time, the only accommodation near the works, Darcey "milked" his monopoly for as much as he could get out of it.

But the most serious problem arose from an outbreak of ague that struck in the late summer and early autumn of 1843. The outbreak was worst at Lindsay, in the vicinity of Purdy's mill pond, still a bone of contention with the settlers and a potential health hazard since the failure of Hecox to complete the lock in 1838. Of the 75 men employed at Lindsay, only 11 were fit to work by the end of September, and 10 men died. There were serious epidemics at Chisholm's Rapids, Hastings, and Healey Falls, too. The situation at Healey Falls "[was] lamentable as not a house or shanty [was] free of sickness."[21] Inconceivably the Board of Works refused Baird's request to "have a medical man occasionally visit Crooks' Rapids," on grounds that "the Government had refused similar applications"[22] elsewhere. Naturally, many men refused to work during the epidemic; those who did wanted excessively high wages and were generally not very competent, albeit most courageous. Despite the temporary setback on account of illness the locks and attached dams were all completed by the spring of 1844.

The locks below Peterborough were immediately put into operation for the exclusive use of William Weller's steamboat *Forester*, the only boat operating on Rice Lake, launched at Gore's Landing in July and put into regular service in September. As pointed out earlier, there was no steamboat to use the isolated Chisholm's Rapids locks and would not be for another 30 years, until a miniature steamer was launched on Percy Reach. Although the wooden lock at Lindsay[23] and the new dam built to replace Purdy's mischievous structure were also ready in the early summer of 1844, it was decided not to open the lock, and thus lower the water in Lake Scugog to the level at which it was to be permanently kept, until cold weather set in. The reason for this was of course to avoid a recurrence of the fever, which, it was feared, would result from exposing the sodden lake bottom to the hot summer sun. There was no urgency to put the lock into operation anyway because there was still no steamboat anywhere on the Back Lakes to use it, and there would not be until 7 years later, when the *Woodman* was built in Port Perry on Lake Scugog.

CHAPTER EIGHT

The Timber Slides

The timber slides were enormous structures that took longer to build than the locks. They were used in the spring timber run of 1845 but were not finally finished until 1846. It was much later before the lumbermen and the inexperienced slide masters learned how to use them properly. Consequently the slides were for many years a subject of much contention, not only among the dissatisfied lumbermen, but also among those who had advocated locks and resented the construction of slides instead.

The Trent timber slides were originally Baird's idea. Realizing that there was little chance of full financial support forthcoming for the Trent-Simcoe scheme and always showing a willingness to compromise to ensure continuation of the works, Baird had recommended that timber slides be constructed at the major falls on the Trent River. He estimated the cost of these at about $20,000. Even earlier, in his final report to Sir John Colborne in December 1835, he had suggested the construction of slides at the most difficult falls "which cost comparatively little and much *better* suit the purpose for heavy lumber, than lockage."[1] Killaly lifted this statement out of the context of Baird's report and quoted it in his own report to the legislature in 1841, to justify slides rather than locks on the Trent. Baird's recommendation, used somewhat unfairly by Killaly, and the fact that he had surveyed the route of the Cobourg railway and, indeed, had purchased shares in the Cobourg Rail Road company at the same time that he was forcefully promoting the Trent scheme, have cast some doubt on Baird's integrity. It has even been suggested that Baird was not fully committed to the development of the Trent at all but, hoping to capitalize on local political agitation, had promoted the Trent waterway for personal employment. In fairness, it should be pointed out that Baird recommended the slides both in 1835 and 1839 as temporary measures, "as an expedient only," until an increase in trade "should be such as to warrant the putting the whole in full operation."[2] There is no evidence to show Baird to have been other than a firm supporter of the Trent waterway until 1841, when

Sydenham and Killaly conspired to scrap the scheme. In any event it was to be slides for the Trent and not locks.

Timber slides were a unique Canadian invention. Developed to facilitate the movement of squared timber down the turbulent rivers that cascaded off the Canadian Shield, they had been used with happy results on the Ottawa and its tributaries for several years before being introduced to the Trent. Until the 1880s, large pine logs were squared with adzes in the bush to form what were known as timbers – timber-making this process was called. The timbers were hauled out to Montreal and Quebec City, where they were exported mainly to Britain for the construction industry to be used principally as beams for large buildings. Initially, when a good supply of pine was available on the shores of the St Lawrence and its major tributaries, transportation of timber was not a problem. The timbers were assembled into rafts about 50 feet wide and 100 feet long, bound together with withes or straps of wood, and floated down the St Lawrence to overseas ports. When large trees suitable for timbering were used up in the areas accessible to the St Lawrence, lumberers had to retreat up the secondary rivers, further into the wilderness. Transportation to Montreal then became more difficult, time-consuming, and expensive. To facilitate the passage of timber over the falls and rapids and to speed up delivery before the spring freshets receded, timber slides were invented. Designed to accommodate whole rafts of timber rather than individual pieces, the slides had to be very large and substantially built. They were quite different in structure from the sinuous, trough-like chutes that were used to move saw logs and pulpwood around narrow rapids and shallow places in streams and rivers, until trucking rendered water transportation of logs obsolete in the mid-twentieth century. Timber slides could be used only on major rivers because of the great volume of water required to flush the timber rafts through them.

The slides built on the Trent rested on massive timber foundations, bolted securely to the bedrock. The bottoms and sides were lined with two-inch planks. They were all 33 feet wide, corresponding to the width of the locks through which some of the rafts would also pass. The lengths of the slides were determined by the height of the falls and the length of the rapids. The slides built at Healey and Ranney falls were very long: the upper slide at Healey Falls was 713 feet long, and the lower slide was 360 feet; at Ranney Falls the upper slide was 1,102 feet long, and the lower one 390 feet. The slides at Hastings and Buckhorn were fairly short, being 79 and 65 feet long, respectively. Substantial rock-filled wooden dams were built at the upper entrances to the slides, both to control the level of water in the river and to divert the flow into the slides. Booms were strung across the river below Crowe Bay and Percy Landing to collect the rafts for reassembly and counting for toll purposes. Glance booms were installed at the entrances to some slides and at narrow places in the river to prevent the rafts from being caught up on rocks.

Because of the irregular way the Board of Works kept its books, figures reported annually to the legislature are confusing and conflicting; hence it is impossible to determine exactly how much the slides and dams cost. A statement of expenditure published in 1848 reports the cost of the Healey Falls slide at $46,780, the Middle Falls slide at $26,115, and the one at Ranney Falls at $61,045. The cost of the other slides, being included in the cost for locks, dams, and bridges built at the same places, is impossible to identify separately.

Prior to construction of the slides, lumbermen ran timber down the Trent in individual pieces. Rafting took place at the mouth of the river. There were no tolls. Running timber down the turbulent river was both dangerous and expensive, and so lumber merchants generally contracted for running their timber from Healey Falls to Trenton, at a cost of about $25 per 1,000 feet of timber for rivermen's wages, the purchase of floats and withes, and labour for rafting on Lake Ontario. It was hoped the slides would eliminate the danger, save time, and reduce costs, for the timber could be rafted at the place where they were hauled out to the river, with the cutting of withes and rafting done by the lumberers' own men. Tolls were set at $1.50 per raft per slide for squared timber, masts, staves, and sawed lumber; rafts of saw logs cost $1 per slide; the toll for loose pieces was set at 15 cents per piece per slide. The government hoped that revenue from the tolls would pay interest charges on the capital and for maintenance and repairs.

Because of the inexperience of the lumbermen in the use of slides, there were plenty of problems at first. The builders' unfamiliarity with slide construction resulted in errors, and the inexperience of slide masters added to the difficulties. Natural obstacles in the river created more problems.

The first rafts passed over the slides at Hastings and Healey Falls in early April 1845 without any difficulty, according to Thomas Wilson, who reported to Killaly: "The owner of the crib that passed Healey Falls is Mr. Thompson from Grand River. He is quite satisfied with the slide and says that he can run with [the] greatest ease; himself and five men were upon the crib and not any of them had been on the river before."[3] But trouble started when Wilson ran Thompson's lead raft down the Middle Falls slide. The raft stuck on a shoal 200 feet below the slide, the water in the river being only two feet deep at that spot. This was a portent of the disaster that was soon to follow.

Within two weeks, timber rafts by the hundreds and saw logs by the thousands descended the river in droves, as the whole winter's timber harvest was launched along the river at the same time. The rafts cleared Hastings and Healey Falls with comparative ease, but, propelled by the relentless rush of the river, the wood piled up at the entrance to Middle Falls slide, which could not handle the vast quantity of timber approaching all at once. Cribs of squared timber, rafts of pine masts, and loose logs burrowed beneath each other, creating a log-jam of unimaginable proportions and complexity. Water backed up behind the jam, creating enormous pressure. A boom placed in front of the dam broke, and then the whole mass gave way. Rafts disintegrated. Pieces of timber, masts, and saw logs were hurled over, through, and under the dam, much of it bypassing the slide altogether. The dam and slide were in danger of being swept away in an avalanche of bouncing logs and boiling water. The logs piled up on the shore, on shoals, on islands, and on the Campbellford bridge. Wilson placed a gang of men on the bridge to break up the jams as they formed; otherwise the bridge would have been toppled over. When the wood reached Ranney Falls, there was more trouble. The open water between the two slides was not deep enough to float the heavier cribs. More jams formed. The mounting pressure of logs and cribs collecting at Percy Landing broke the retaining boom there. The uncontrolled timber then drifted down the Reach and crashed into the dam at Chisholm's Rapids. Only the great exertions of the lumbermen, funnelling the logs through the timber slide, prevented the works there from being severely damaged.

Meanwhile Wilson, his foreman, and men worked with the lumbermen in a desperate attempt to keep the wood moving. While trying to remove a log-jam from the pier at the foot of Middle Falls, John White, foreman for the Board of Works, had his leg badly crushed when a crib of timber rushed down the slide and, catching him unawares, squashed him against the pier. For a week two doctors treated White day and night during which time it was feared he would "either lose his leg or his life."[4] This incident launched a spate of rumours in the district, denied by Wilson, that there were many accidents on the slides with loss of life.[5]

By the end of May, the logs and timber were cleared out of the river. All the wood managed somehow to get to Trenton, where the owners had to sort it out and re-raft it. Having seen their timber run down the river with comparative ease for years, the lumbermen were not very happy with the Board of Works' expensive improvements. They refused to pay tolls. Under the circumstances, it would have been impossible to count logs and cribs for fixing tolls anyway.

Although difficulties encountered in the run of 1846 were not as great, there were still problems in working the slides. Some arose because the lumbermen did not crib the timber properly or made the rafts too long. In time regulations governing the cribbing of timber were laid down. The dams were heightened; more booms were built; some of the slides were extended. The open space between the slides at Ranney Falls was completely planked over, creating one continuous slide 2,203 feet long. George Ranney, who became superintendent of the Trent works upon the death of Thomas Wilson on 24 September 1846, soon learned how to regulate the water in the river and to conserve it for the annual timber run. With experience, the problems were gradually overcome, and for the next 30 years the timber slides would be a valuable asset to the district's timber and logging industry.

But the unhappy experiences of the first couple of years left an unpleasant memory that never completely disappeared. The English journalist Sir Richard Bonnycastle, who visited the Trent in 1845 and whose perceptions were undoubtedly manipulated by the slides' critics, later wrote: "Had the Trent canal been finished, instead of the miserable and decaying timber-slides which now encumber that noble river, another million of inhabitants would, in two years more, have filled up the forests which are now only penetrated by the Indians and seekers after timber."[6] Bonnycastle did not indicate where the million inhabitants might come from, or how they could be settled in such a short time without at least clearing the forests first, or what would become of the Indians. But his hyperbolic calculation helped keep alive the myth of the Trent canal's commercial importance.

Long before the slides were finished, Nichol Hugh Baird was gone, the first of many Trent canal superintendents to become a victim of a capricious government. Around mid-November 1843, Baird received a copy of a letter, allegedly sent to him on 13 October, informing him that his services as local engineer in the Newcastle District would no longer be needed after 1 November. He was stunned and hurt. The date on which his services were to terminate had already passed, and he had just spent the previous week inspecting the works at Whitby harbour. He immediately wrote to Killaly: "I have scarcely yet brought myself to the reality that you would ever order such a letter to be written to me."[7] He declared, upon his honour, that the original letter had never reached him; he claimed that his contract with the Board of Works permitted him to remain until the works were finished; he expressed the opinion that it would not be possible to finish the works without the services of an engineer; he pointed out that terminating his services so precipitously would place him in "much jeopardy and predicament," ruin his reputation, and give some of his enemies the satisfaction of seeing him and his family "reduced to penury."[8] Finally, he begged Killaly to reconsider, to let him see the completion of a work that had cost him so much labour for 10 years.

There is no record of Killaly having replied to Baird directly, but Thomas Begley wrote on behalf of the Board of Works, informing Baird that he was being released because the board found it necessary to reduce the establishment in the Newcastle District and that the works had advanced to the stage at which they could be completed with the local foremen reporting directly to the board; a local engineer was no longer needed. The board rejected Baird's claim that his contract must extend to the completion of the works. A board policy provided that "an Engineer or Superintendent of a work was supposed to be engaged only for so long a period as his services were required or useful upon that particular work."[9] The policy applied to Baird. The termination decision was final. To his credit, Killaly did apply to the board to have Baird's salary continued to the end of December. The board concurred.

Baird then petitioned Governor-General Sir Charles Metcalfe, requesting that he either be reinstated in his position or be paid a severance allowance to 1 May 1844. Sheldon Hawley, former chairman of the board of commissioners, wrote a letter testifying to "the high opinion of Mr. Baird's qualifications as an Engineer" and expressing the hope that Baird's "long service and superior skill in his profession … not be forgotten by the government."[10] Baird enclosed a medical certificate verifying the fact that surgery resulting from an accident sustained at Whitby, in the course of his duties there, had incapacitated him. But all to no avail. Sir Dominick Daly, provincial secretary and constitutional adviser to the governor-general, replied: "His Excellency learned on enquiry of the Board of Works that you were notified repeatedly during last summer, that the establishment in the Newcastle District was to be broken up at the end of the working season; and that you were not taken unawares; but on the contrary had full intimation and were accordingly paid up to the 31ST December last."[11] The petition was denied.

And so, after 16 years of faithful service in the development of most of the major public works in upper Canada – the Rideau, the Welland, the St Lawrence, and the Trent – Baird was ungraciously cast aside before seeing his carefully designed plans for the Trent fully completed. It is not precisely clear why Baird was dismissed. It is doubtful that Killaly, a close friend, fired him; more likely he dismissed Baird on behalf of others. Baird had plenty of enemies. "I am too blunt,"[12] he confessed to Killaly. Certainly his caustic tongue did not win him many friends. If he had been informed repeatedly the previous summer that the establishment was to be broken up, it appears not to have dawned on him that he would be the first to go, since there were others less qualified and less senior than he. His shock at being told was genuine enough.

Just as Superintending Engineer Tom S. Rubidge would crack under similar pressures some 40 years later, Baird seems to have suffered some sort of mental collapse in 1843. First drafts of his letters and petitions to the Board of Works and the governor-general, written after his dismissal and preserved in his papers, are scribbled, with words crossed out and other words substituted; in places the syntax is incoherent, suggesting, understandably, a mind that was tormented. Even the finished drafts lack the precision of expression and confident style so characteristic of his earlier reports and letters. And there is further evidence of a confused state of mind. After the rejection of his petition for reinstatement and of follow-ups to it, he began petitioning the Board of Works for expenses alleged to have been incurred and never paid. The Board of Works had already awarded him $520, admittedly due him by the late board of commissioners, but despite the fact that Baird had given the board a receipt for this money, he submitted another claim for the same debt. He also submitted claims for other very large expenses alleged to have been incurred for office rental and travel. All of these were turned down by the Board of Works because there was no evidence that they had ever been incurred.[13] This was certainly atypical behaviour for Baird, who was normally precise and orderly in business matters.

After his dismissal Baird moved back to Montreal. In 1847 his wife died, leaving him with eight young children. Two years later Baird died of unknown causes in Prattleboro, Vermont. His children were placed under the tutelage of their uncle, Andrew White, of Montreal.

James Lyons was given Baird's job as superintending engineer for a time; then Thomas Wilson became superintendent of the Trent works until his sudden death in September 1846. George Ranney, who operated a mill at Ranney Falls, became superintendent in 1847 and held the position for 25 years. Then he too was dumped, by the Macdonald government, just prior to the election of 1872.

Of Nichol Hugh Baird, it may be said that he contributed more to the early development of the Trent canal than any other person. In fact he created the canal. Despite all the proposals for canalizing the route, and despite all the surveys, it was basically Baird's plan and Baird's route that were eventually followed. Without his exertions and exhortations the beautiful waterway, which has given pleasure and recreation to millions during the last 60-odd years, might never have been. For without Baird's strong recommendations and support, the first Trent canal promoters would not have had the leverage to force a start on the canal, and subsequent promoters would have had no foundation on which to build. The only tangible evidence remaining on the waterway of Baird's efforts is the limestone lock below Peterborough, now known as Scott's Mills lock; thousands pass through the lock every year, unaware of Baird's one-time existence. Like many of Canada's other fine engineers, who designed and built the canals, the railways, the bridges, the public buildings, the whole physical fabric of the country, Baird has been ignored by history. Generally, it was the politicians, who cut the ribbons, carved their names on public buildings, and captured the limelight, who denied engineers their proper and lasting recognition. Baird was no exception.

CHAPTER NINE

The Lumbermen's Committee

On 1 October 1850, an advertisement appeared in local newspapers offering for sale the locks, dams, slides, roads, and water powers – all the improvements recently completed in the Newcastle District. Previously, the Board of Works had offered to sell the works, including the bridges on the Trent River and the Port Hope and Whitby toll roads, to the county council of Peterborough and other municipal governments. They refused to buy them. Having failed to sell the works to the municipalities, the board was now offering them for sale to any corporation, private or public, that was willing to buy them. Had the sale of the locks been achieved, the Trent canal story would probably have ended in 1850. The five locks, which slipped innocently enough under the control of the federal Department of Public Works in 1867, would instead have been distributed among several municipalities or private companies. At worst, the sale of the locks would have resulted in their disintegrating or being torn down, because in the 1850s and 1860s they produced no financial return and the cost of maintenance and repair was high. At best, the locks would have come under the jurisdiction of the province of Ontario in 1867, in which case they might well have met the same fate: the government of Ontario, with limited resources, probably could not have maintained the locks, and definitely would not have been charmed by local politicians into constructing the canal, as the federal government was. Having failed to sell the locks, the government of Canada did the next best thing: for 30 years it practically ignored them, hoping no doubt that they would simply disappear because of almost total neglect. The period 1850 – 80 was bleak for Trent canal promoters.

There were many reasons the government tried to sell the Trent works in 1850. First, there was William Merritt's private reason. He had opposed the development of the Trent canal from the very beginning; in 1841 he had argued that any improvements necessary in the Newcastle District should be undertaken by municipal governments. Now, as chief commissioner of public works, he was in a position to implement his personal conviction, and he wasted no time in recommending to the cabinet the sale of the public works on the Trent.

Second, political support for the Trent canal had all but disappeared as a consequence of the constitutional and political changes of the recent past. The principle of responsible government, so vigorously pursued for so long by the Reform party of Canada, was firmly established in 1849, when Lord Elgin signed the controversial Rebellion Losses Bill, despite strong opposition from the Tory minority in Parliament. Gone were the days when an autocratic governor, supported by a loyal oligarchy, could "produce the happiest results" in a district, as Colborne had done in 1834, and, to a lesser degree, as Sydenham had done when he approved Killaly's limited support for the Trent. The fortunes of the Trent canal were now at the mercy of the legislature. In 1849 the legislature was controlled by the Reform ministry of Robert Baldwin and Louis Lafontaine, in which Francis Hincks and William Merritt were two of the principal ministers. Even Peterborough county was represented in the legislature by a Reformer, James Hall, who seems not to have opposed the government's policy of selling the public works.

Politically, Canadian Reformers believed in responsible parliamentary democracy. Economically they espoused, to a greater or lesser degree, the laissez-faire doctrines of Adam Smith and the free trade policies recently introduced by the governing Liberal party in Britain. Reformers believed that governments had no place in the board rooms of the nation and that they should interfere as little as possible in the economic life of a country, permitting the forces of the market to regulate business. Whenever possible, this philosophy was applied to political action in Canada in the mid-nineteenth century.

Hincks and Merritt were middle-of-the-road Reformers. In truth, they were what successful Canadian politicians have always been – political pragmatists. They fully realized that a pure laissez-faire doctrine, with its corollary, free trade, would not work in a capital-poor, agricultural-commercial economy such as Canada's; clearly not in transportation at any rate. This had been demonstrated in 1820 when an attempt to build the Lachine canal by private enterprise failed miserably. Even Merritt's own Welland canal had to be taken over by the government. And the St Lawrence canals and Welland enlargement could have been built and financed only by the government in the 1840s. As inspector-general in the second Baldwin-Lafontaine ministry, and after 1851 as prime minister, Hincks developed the finance policy that launched the railway-building era in Canada. Typically, his railway policy was a compromise between outright free enterprise on the one hand and full government control and ownership on the other. The railways were owned and built by private companies, but with massive government financial assistance. Although laissez-faire principles could not be applied to the St Lawrence canals at all, and only partially to railway construction, there was no reason why they could not be applied to less important public works such as those on the Trent River and inland waters of the Newcastle District. The government should sell these works, it was decided; let them be turned over to municipal or private corporations, to whomever would take them.

A third and perhaps more compelling reason that led the central government to try to divest itself of the Trent works was an economic one. The Canadian economy entered a difficult period of adjustment in the late 1840s and early 1850s. Ironically, the country's economic difficulties had their roots in the laissez-faire, free trade movement born in Britain and supported by Canadian Liberals. For many years Canadian wheat and flour had been granted tariff preferences in British markets by the Corn Laws of 1815, 1822, and 1828. The whole economic and political framework of the empire had been based on this policy of preferential tariff treatment of the colonies. Indeed, the hopes and fortunes for the St Lawrence commercial system, of which the St Lawrence canal was the corner-stone, were staked on the advantages of the trading privileges that this policy ensured.

Canadian timber received preferential treatment similar to that of agricultural products. As a maritime trading nation, Britain was completely dependent upon its merchant ships and naval forces. Since ships were made of wood – the hulls of oak, the masts and spars of white pine – Britain could not hope to retain the status of a first-class power without an assured supply of oak timber and pine masts, in times of peace as well as war. With the disappearance of native English wood after 1500, Britain depended upon foreign timber to an increasing degree. From the end of the fifteenth century to the beginning of the nineteenth, Britain had imported timber for naval and domestic needs from countries surrounding the Baltic Sea. But those sources were cut off during the Napoleonic Wars, and Britain was obliged to turn to the colonies in North America to satisfy its timber requirements, especially for pine masts. As a sizeable investment in capital was needed for cutting the large trees and transporting them all the way to England, the trade could not be carried on profitably in masts alone, and so the navy had encouraged the development of a general timber trade with the colonies. With the cessation of hostilities in Europe there was a strong possibility that British shipbuilders would once more look to the Baltic for a cheaper and more readily accessible supply of timber, to the disadvantage of Canadian producers. To protect the colonial trade from European competition, a tariff wall, through which Canadian timber could pass duty-free, was erected, and from 1821 to 1842 Canadian timber entered Britain free. The cost to the British economy of maintaining artificially high prices for an essential construction material during a period of rapid development was very high indeed. A consoling feature of this cost was the fact that Canadian timber relieved Britain of complete dependence on the Baltic.

All the tariff preferences for Canadian products were swept aside by the free trade movement that gripped Britain in the 1840s. Cheap food and raw materials became indispensable to Britain's developing industrial system, and to get them it was willing to cancel the trading privileges that its overseas colonies had enjoyed. Moreover, the increasing volume of goods that flowed from Britain's factories required world-wide markets, not just markets confined to the overseas colonies. Foreign countries could acquire the sterling to buy British manufactured goods only if they were allowed to sell their natural products in Britain. High tariffs, which benefited only the colonies, would therefore have to go. In 1846 the Corn Laws were repealed, and all tariffs on foreign timber were removed as well.

The long-term result of this double blow to the Canadian economy was two-fold: North American colonies sought closer trading relationships with each other, a move that led eventually to Confederation; and Canadian producers sought alternative markets for their raw materials in the United States, a move that culminated in Canada's economic dependence upon the United States in the twentieth century. But the immediate shock of the repeal of the Corn Laws and the simultaneous removal of the timber preferences was felt in Canada in the years between 1847 and 1849 – before the St Lawrence canal system was even completed.[1] Severe economic depression set in. Political disturbances occurred, and a strong movement developed, fostered by disconsolate Montreal merchants, for annexation to the United States. All of this had serious implications for the immediate and longer-term fortunes of the Trent. Merritt's personal conviction, encouraged by a popular economic-political philosophy now put to the test by a severe depression with every prospect of worse yet to come, led logically to the government's desire to apply Smith's principles of an unerring market-place to public works. Consequently, the government adopted a policy of "transferring to the Municipalities certain unproductive works on which public expenditure had been incurred."[2] If the municipalities would not take the works, they would be offered to private companies. The only consideration for disposing of a public work was its direct economic utility; that is, whether it brought the government a profit or a loss. The Trent works, being unproductive in terms of revenue, were clearly covered by the policy.

Merritt soon discovered that it was not easy to sell a public work. First, the municipalities were just as anxious to avoid assuming the heavy financial liability that maintenance of the works entailed as Merritt was to get rid of it. And there was the question of whether the locks would truly contribute very much to the development of the district. James

Lyons, superintending engineer for the Trent, claimed in his report of 1845 "that no section of the Province has been more essentially benefited by its Public Works than this [Newcastle District] nor is there any other District that can take precedence in advancement of Wealth and Prosperity."[3] But engineers of the Trent canal from Baird to Rogers (with the exception of Tom S. Rubidge) had a tendency to exaggerate the importance and advantages of the canal. While there is no doubt that an expenditure of several thousand dollars during the two years the works were being built brought a measure of wealth and prosperity to the district, there was no reason to believe that the completed locks would make long-term contributions to the district's economy. Had that been thought likely, the municipalities might have been more anxious to take them over.

In the same year that Lyons submitted his opinion, Thomas Wilson reported "no trade whatever on the Trent excepting lumber."[4] In 1845, only 325 tons of freight and 480 passengers went through the lock at Whitla's Rapids, principally on Weller's steamboat *Forester*. If the records are correct, this was not as much freight as Bethune's *Pemedash* carried into Peterborough in 1833. (See chapter 1.) In 1847, the engineer reported that the lock at Hastings "has hitherto been of little use"[5]; and he reported that the lock at Whitla's "affords some facilities for trade between the flourishing town of Peterborough and the Cobourg and Port Hope landing places but yields no revenue worth mentioning."[6] The isolated and unused lock at Glen Ross (Chisholm's Rapids) was an embarrassment and an obstacle that created flooding. Many were demanding that it be removed. The lock at Lindsay was not used at all, except for the passage of timber and small boats, until the *Woodman* was launched in 1851, and its 32-foot beam prevented it from using the 26-foot-wide Bobcaygeon lock, which was now rotting and leaking badly. The only public works in the district that were being used extensively were the roads and the timber slides, but they were not paying for themselves.

Merritt also learned that selling locks, dams, and water power privileges on a public waterway was much more complex than he had realized. John Langton, who was now warden of Peterborough County, raised some of the problems in a letter to Merritt on 28 November 1850. What quantity of land adjoining the works would the government convey to the purchaser? Where the works and the land conveyed with them were surrounded by private property, would the government provide an access road to the purchaser? What protection would the proprietors of mills, operating at spots such as Bobcaygeon, Lindsay, Buckhorn, and Hastings, have if the water powers at these places were sold? What limitations would be placed on the purchasers of locks and slides with respect to tolls? What stipulation if any, would be made with regard to repairs? (Repairs at

Bobcaygeon were tantamount to building a new lock, and the works at Lindsay and Whitla's had never been totally finished.) Would a purchaser of water power privileges at a falls be authorized to build slides at the falls and charge tolls? What terms of payment were being proposed? These questions raised many legal complexities that apparently the government had not even considered.

A standing committee on county property for the county of Peterborough examined the proposal and, dissatisfied with answers to Langton's questions, advised that the "council should decline having anything to say to the said works."[7] Later the council informed the government that it would decline the offer of purchase of the public works; other municipalities did the same thing. Having declined to purchase the works itself, the council was concerned lest the works fall into the hands of individuals and urged that the sale of the works not be permitted but be retained under the control of the Board of Works. Merritt retired from the cabinet in 1851, and the board reconsidered its decision to sell. Typically, a compromise emerged.

By 1854, the public works commissioners had grouped the works in the Newcastle District into two distinct classes: "those whose improvement and maintenance were indispensable if the necessity for keeping open the existing inland navigation was admitted" and "those which were solely required for assisting in the passing of timber."[8] The first group of works consisted of the various locks and their associated dams; theoretically, they benefited everyone. The second group comprised the timber slides and booms on the Trent River; they were of benefit to those engaged in the lumber trade. Since it was "generally acknowledged that the navigation should be kept up" to facilitate settlement in the townships bordering the waterways, the commissioners recommended an appropriation of $63,000 to render the "navigation really and permanently effective."[9] The money was never appropriated, but the locks at least were saved from imminent destruction. The commissioners admitted that the earlier decision to sell all the works had been reassessed because of "several difficulties ... which prevented this course from being carried out."[10] They were probably influenced by the persuasive arguments of John Langton, who was elected to represent Peterborough county in 1851 and re-elected in 1854. As for the sale of the slides, however, the commissioners remained adamant; they recommended that they "be handed over to the respective Municipalities or to such other Corporations as would be willing to take charge of them; but that, in any case, public expenditure on them should cease."[11]

The principal reason for getting rid of the slides was that they were costing money. Unlike the locks, which were seldom used, the slides had to be maintained. In 1833 Baird had optimistically predicted that canalization of the Trent would yield $30,000 in timber tolls in the first year alone. Killaly had assured the legislature that tolls from timber would pay the interest on the outlay for the slides. In the winter of 1844 – 5, Thomas Wilson had enthusiastically estimated that tolls from the passage of timber down the soon-to-be-completed slides would amount to $45,000. His estimate was based on the knowledge that 800 men were engaged in timber-making in the woods between Campbellford and Peterborough: using his own unique production formula, he calculated that that many men would produce 6 million feet of timber, all of which would have to move down the Trent.

But at no time did the revenue from timber tolls come anywhere near the various predictions. The disastrous timber run of 1845 produced no revenue at all, but plenty of damage to repair. In 1846 tolls amounted to only $11,635; in 1849 and 1850, only $5,870 and $6,600 respectively were collected, but management and repairs consumed most of the revenue, leaving only a small surplus each year. For 1852 – 4 the aggregate revenue was $19,935, but the outlay was $29,725. Tolls were not meeting routine maintenance and administrative costs, let alone interest charges. Apart from the fact that the engineers had grossly overestimated the optimum revenue that the slides would produce, the decrease in toll revenue was a function of the abolition of Britain's timber tariffs. The Canadian timber trade slumped badly as Baltic timber found its way again into British markets.[12]

By 1855 there were indications that the timber trade would pick up in Canada. In the 1840s and 1850s industrialization began to take root in the United States and great cities began growing up, not only on the eastern seaboard but also in the Midwest, in places like Chicago. The spread of industry and the growth of cities produced heavy demands for lumber and general building materials. As forests near the growing metropolitan centres rapidly dwindled, builders inevitably looked northward for Canadian lumber. Export of Canadian lumber to the United States was encouraged in 1854 when the British North American colonies, with the support of Britain, negotiated a ten-year Reciprocity Treaty with the United States. By the terms of this treaty, import duties were abolished on a wide range of natural products entering Canada from the United States and vice versa; timber and lumber were included. Heavy demands in the United States, coupled with the abolition of import duties, would have a phenomenal impact on the growth of the Canadian forest industry, especially in saw logs and lumber. For the first time it was possible to develop within North America a large-scale market for a Canadian staple. The Canadian timber trade would soon be revived and flourishing.

Individuals engaged in the lumber trade along the Trent became alarmed on being informed that the policy of the government was to abandon all unproductive works – of which the Trent slides were clearly one – just at a time when they would be most needed. A deputation named by the lumberers met with Hincks, "pointing out to him that to abandon these Works would be quick ruination to all in the Trade on the River."[13] After hearing several appeals asking the government to retain the works and to maintain them for the purpose for which they were constructed, Hincks informed the lumbermen that "the Government have made up their minds that these Works are to be abandoned so far as the Government is concerned. They have been offered to the Countys Council [sic] in which they lay, who refuse to have anything to do with them. The Government will hand them over to the Trade to be managed for their use, and will give the required Authority to collect tolls and to manage the Works. If the Trade would not undertake this the whole Works would be abandoned."[14]

Subsequently all the lumbermen in the district met and decided that they had no alternative but to accept the works and to manage them themselves. In an industry that was often competitive – sometimes marked with open hostility – this was not a pleasing prospect. Nevertheless, they had no other option. A management committee of six leading lumbermen [15] was appointed, headed by James Cumming of Trenton. In December 1854 Cumming informed the chief commissioner of public works, Francis Lemieux, that the lumbermen were prepared to take over the works. Accordingly an order-in-council was passed on 20 February 1855, authorizing the transfer of the timber slides at Healey Falls, Middle Falls, Ranney Falls, and Chisholm's Rapids to the committee of the lumbermen, on condition that the slides be maintained. Typically, the transfer of the slides was as poorly handled as any previous government decision respecting the Trent. The order-in-council did not make clear what, precisely, was being transferred to the lumbermen, nor did it outline the authority and responsibility that the lumbermen would have. On 10 April George Ranney was instructed to hand management of the works over to the lumbermen's committee, with the provision that "no other property besides the slides is included."[16] He was also advised that the slide at Hastings, omitted from the order-in-council, was included. On 10 May Ranney was informed that the dams, locks, and lockmasters' houses at Hastings and Chisholm's Rapids, being directly connected with navigation, were to remain under the management of the Department of Public Works. Only the five slides, booms, and piers on the Trent River, it seems, were transferred to the committee, but none of the dams, not even those connected with the slides.

At first the authority of the lumbermen's committee for managing the slides and collecting tolls was not disputed, but during the run of 1856 some lumbermen, especially those new to the district, challenged this authority. Some refused to pay tolls; some injured the works by cutting holes in the dams and would not repair the damage; some built dams for milling purposes across the river beside the slides, raising the water over the slides and dams and rendering them unmanageable. Cumming wrote to Lemieux for clarification of the committee's authority. An order-in-council approved on 22 April 1857 clarified the position somewhat: "By the conditions of the transfer the committee assuming the works was bound to maintain them in a state of good and sufficient repair, but was not to be liable for their renewal in case of their failure from decay of their material, or their destruction by fire, flood or any other cause; with power to continue the levying of tolls at rates not exceeding those already exacted by the Government."[17] Then, to complicate matters, the Department of Public Works was informed by the solicitor-general's office that "the whole proceedings [were] irregular, the Order-in-Council [was] wrong, the transfer invalid."[18] All members of the lumbermen's committee, except James Cumming, resigned in disgust, and the transfer process had to be carried out all over again. On 14 September 1859, John Rose, minister of public works in the Cartier-Macdonald government, turned the works over to a new committee consisting of Mossom Boyd of Bobcaygeon, Alex Dennistoun of Fenelon Falls, and James Cumming, under the same conditions as before.

This committee, represented as it was by reliable, profit-minded businessmen, managed the slides most effectively for the benefit of all the lumbermen for many years.[19] George Ranney was hired by the committee as superintendent of slides at around $2,000 per year, the salary varying with the changing fortunes of the lumber trade. Ranney held this job in addition to his departmental job of superintendent of the Trent works, with responsibility for the management of the locks and dams. The slides were so well managed that the lumbermen discovered that they were accumulating a surplus each year, and so in 1859 they asked the government to remove the tolls charged for the shorter slides at Hastings and Chisholm's Rapids, as the revenue generated by the other three was sufficient to maintain those two slides. In 1861 they requested that the tolls be reduced to one cent per saw log and one dollar per crib for square timber, per slide. An account submitted to the government by James Cumming in 1866, just before Confederation, indicated that the aggregate revenue from the slides, over the ten-year period during which the lumbermen's committee had managed them, was about $52,000; expenditures were in the neighbourhood of $48,000. In 1867, the new federal Department of Public Works assumed control of all the works on the Trent system, but the lumbermen continued to manage the slides under the existing conditions.

In the spring of 1870 disaster struck. Excessive stripping away of the forest cover in the Trent watershed, followed by extensive settlement, reduced the water-holding capacity of the ground. Spring floods were frequent, but an unusually heavy snow fall in the winter of 1869 – 70, followed by a rapid spring thaw, caused a flood of unprecedented proportions. The level of Rice Lake rose four feet above any previously known high. As the water poured out through the Trent, the lake's only outlet, severe damage was inflicted on public and private property. So great was the rush of water that the course of the river was permanently changed in places. Although badly damaged, the locks and most of the dams held, but the slides were decimated. All the booms and piers were swept away; most of the planking on the floors and sides of the slides was washed off. Ranney Falls was hardest hit. Both the grist and sawmills, including the one owned by George Ranney, were carried away. The lower slide disappeared completely; the upper one was left only partially standing. None of the slides was usable for the run of 1870.The logs above Healey Falls were towed across Rice Lake and shipped to Lake Ontario on the Cobourg and Peterborough Railroad.

The lumbermen gathered in Caise's Hotel in Peterborough on 11 August to discuss the possibility of rebuilding the slides and how best to accomplish this. Ranney estimated that it would cost at least $60,000 to restore the slides. Since the manufacture of square timber had been reduced to a small quantity, and since most of the logs cut above Peterborough were being sawed in local mills, it was agreed that it was "not advisable to expend the large sum of money that would be required to reconstruct the Trent Slides for the running of Cribs of Timber, even if available."[20] It was decided instead to renew the slides only to the extent that they would permit the running of single sticks of square timber and saw logs. Ranney estimated the cost of this at $11,000.

By the terms of the transfer agreement, the lumbermen were not obliged to rebuild the slides, but they realized that if they depended upon the government to restore them, they might wait a long time. So they decided to rebuilt them themselves. They did ask permission of the minister of public works for the use of such material as still existed from the damaged works. Construction funds would come from three sources: the surplus funds in the hands of the lumber trust; a grant from the Ontario government, which obtained substantial revenue from timber licences; and an assessment on those lumbermen who most frequently used the Trent slides, to be repaid by remission of slide dues except for the minimum needed to keep up the works.

The Trent slides began to diminish in importance in the years following. One of the effects of the Reciprocity Treaty and the coming of the railroads was the establishment of many lumber mills in the district. The square timber trade declined and disappeared in the 1880s. As lumber produced in local mills – millions of feet of it – was shipped to markets on district railroads, a decreasing number of logs went down the Trent every year. The last year in which lumbermen are known to have used the remaining slides was 1906. When the Trent was at last canalized, the slides rotted away to mingle with the dust of history.

Including money spent on the slides before 1841, their construction and reconstruction had cost $317,195. Revenues were adjusted from time to time by changes in tolls, so as to acquire the minimum needed for repairs and maintenance. In terms of William Merritt's nineteenth-century profit-based definition, the slides were not "productive." They certainly did not make any money for the government. But in terms of the prosperity they contributed to the district during the heyday of lumbering, they were very productive. And in terms of the number of wealthy lumbermen they helped to create, the slides were exceedingly productive.

Chisholm's Rapids lock, built by Robert Barclay in 1838. (PAC/ACC 14390-12)

CHAPTER TEN

The Union Locks

Having completed the five locks in 1844, more for political reasons than for navigation purposes, the Board of Works proceeded to neglect them – but not before the residents of the district tried one more time to induce the government to complete the Trent River navigation. Many argued that it had been unreasonable to cancel the Trent improvements on the basis of Baird's plans and estimates alone. It was claimed that there were cheaper and safer routes than the one following the course of the river that Baird had recommended. In fact, some attributed blame for cancellation of the scheme to Baird, for designing and insisting upon a plan of canalization that involved unwarranted expense. This may have been part of the reason why the Board of Works thought it prudent to discharge Baird before the works were fully completed. In any event, during the years 1844 and 1845, Killaly came under intense pressure to reconsider the Trent River scheme. Being assured that if a survey should reveal that a cheaper and more practical route did not exist, those who advocated it would be mollified, Killaly recommended to the legislature that a survey be made "in order to set the question fully at rest."[1] Accordingly, James Lyons was ordered to conduct a survey in the autumn of 1846.

Baird's plan for canalizing the Trent by a series of dams and locks was considered no longer safe or suitable after the construction of the timber slides, as it was thought that the immense quantity of timber descending the river might damage the locks, or that one of the dams upon which the locks would depend might give way in a spring flood, causing destruction of the whole system. Consequently, Lyons was asked to make his survey on the principle of an "inland Canal," paralleling the river but beyond the influence of the floods. He made a careful survey, following, where possible, gullies and ravines pointed out by local residents. His estimate for a canal, largely inland but incorporating the navigable reaches of the river, came to $1,276,520. Before submitting Lyon's survey report to Killaly, Samuel Keefer, Killaly's assistant, revised the estimate upwards, concluding that $2 million, excluding land damages, was a more realistic estimate.[2] Since this was $825,000 more than Baird's estimate for the all-river route, clearly a cheaper and more practical route did not exist, and so the question of canalizing the Trent was set "fully at rest" as far as the government was concerned.

If there was a policy after 1846 with respect to water regulation and control, it was aimed at guarding against injury to existing water powers and mills and preventing the flooding of private lands along the margins of the rivers and lakes. Anyone who operated a steamboat did so on his own account with no water rights or guarantees. Officially, the Trent system was no longer considered a navigable waterway. Maintenance costs were kept to a minimum. No buoys, markers, or other aids to navigation were provided. No engineer was placed directly in charge of the works. If there were disputes or difficulties, an engineer made an ad hoc examination; his recommendations might or might not be implemented. No lockmasters were placed in charge of the locks, and no tolls were charged. Owners of batteaux and other small boats operated the locks themselves. Vandalism was widespread.

Without proper supervision, the works soon deteriorated. Lumbermen cut holes in the dams when it suited them. Millers took as much or as little water as they wished, heedless of the needs of those mills above or below their own. Saw mill operators dumped large quantities of sawdust and slabs into the river, obstructing navigation for such steamboats as did exist. Nature played havoc with the works too. As the water receded in the summer, planking on the dams was exposed to the sun, dried out, cracked, and became loose; the loose pieces were washed away by the spring freshets, allowing the gravel and rock fill to escape, weakening the structures, and creating permanent leaks. Lock gates rotted and leaked; gears rusted and broke. Each year, Ranney requisitioned funds for repairs, but the deterioration advanced beyond the capacity of the small government grants to keep abreast of it. Finally, as noted earlier, the government decided to dispose of the works.

Then came the railways. Although the government insisted on handing the management of the timber slides over to a committee of lumbermen, it was persuaded by individuals with vested interest, such as John Langton, MLA for Peterborough county, to retain control of the locks. Langton, who, in partnership with Mossom Boyd, had bought Need's mill at Bobcaygeon, could see that the locks would be vital for connecting the isolated townships with the railheads, especially for the transportation of lumber. For the next 25 years, therefore, the fortunes of the locks would wax and wane with the fortunes of the railways.

Between 1855 and 1872 five railways were built into the Trent watershed: the Cobourg and Peterborough Railway, the Port Hope, Lindsay and Beaverton Railway (later called the Midland Railway of Canada), the Whitby, Port Perry and Lindsay Railway, the Toronto and Nipissing Railway, and the Victoria Railway. These were essentially portage roads, built to haul the natural wealth out of the Trent watershed to ports on Lake Ontario. While the railways existed and while the resources lasted, the district prospered. The town of Peterborough is a good example. The railway era, which commenced for Peterborough in 1854, produced an increase in the trade of the town and the development of manufacturing in a variety of industries: flour mills, woollen factories, foundries, breweries, and carriage and sleigh works. In 1860, imports to Peterborough amounted to $600,000, but exports invariable exceeded imports, leaving, on average for the next five years, a balance of half a million dollars per year in favour of the town.

The principal export commodity, providing the major revenue for the district, was lumber; it was also the trade on which the railways depended for their existence and the means of keeping freight rates for other commodities at a minimum. Consequently, the assault on the forests of the Newcastle District was devastating, the capacity of lumbermen unquenchable. The *Directory of the United Counties of Peterborough and Victoria* for 1858 listed 43 saw mills with a combined cutting capacity of 535,000 feet per day. Fortunately, the mills did not run at anything like full capacity, nor did they run all year round; nevertheless they buzzed up a staggering quantity of lumber each year. In 1865, 31 million board feet were exported from the town of Peterborough: 19 million on the Cobourg and Peterborough Railway and 12 million by steamer and rail to Cobourg. This figure does not include the immense quantity of sawlogs and square timber that went down the Trent for export or consumption by mills at Trenton and other mills along the river; nor does it take into account the great quantity of lumber that was shipped from mills at Buckhorn, Bobcaygeon, and Fenelon Falls through Lindsay and Whitby. The production of lumber increased every year. In 1870, the Midland Railway hauled 71,225,600 feet from its various stations to Port Hope. In 1872, the peak year before the onset of the depression of 1873, an estimated 117 million board feet of pine lumber was produced in the Trent Valley by 19 large operators. In addition, some 10 million feet of square timber was shipped to the Quebec market, and small operators took out 100,000 to 400,000 feet each.

By its very nature, the lumbering industry was inextricably linked to the waterway: to the falls for milling, and to the lakes and rivers for transporting logs to the mills and sawed lumber to the railway depots. Thus the railways encouraged lock building and renovation, because without locks to make the interlocking water navigable neither the railways nor the lumbering concerns would have prospered. Such locks as were built or rebuilt during the railway era were intended only for local trade, the through canal being temporarily forgotten. Later, when the forests were depleted, when lumber traffic declined, railways were obliged to increase rates on general merchandise – easily achieved because of the Grand Trunk monopoly – and business stagnated. Then interest in the Trent canal was revived. It was thought that a canal running from Georgian Bay to Lake Ontario through the heartland of this now developing industrial area, providing a cheaper means of transportation than the railways, would force the railways to reduce freight rates. Pressure for the canal's completion, principally from businessmen in Peterborough, was resumed.

The Whitlas Lock

As early as 1847, William Weller complained that the dam at Whitlas (the apostrophe was dropped in the 1850s) was not high enough to contain the River Otonabee during the spring freshet. So intense was the current caused by water pouring over the dam that Weller, risking a smash-up, was forced to run his steamer into the lock at full steam to avoid being swept over the dam. He requested additional stop-logs for the dam, but these seem not to have been provided, as Samuel Keefer reported in 1851 that the *Forester* had been swept over the Whitlas dam no less than five times.

Timber and sawlogs inflicted greater damage than usual on the lock and dam during the timber run of 1852; consequently $4,110 was spent installing a 1,400-foot boom for the protection of the lock and for collecting logs for rafting. By then, there were four steamers operating on Rice Lake, freighting goods from Peterborough to Gore's Landing and Bewdley for trans-shipment to Cobourg and Port Hope. Navigation was hazardous, not only because of problems associated with the lock but also because of sunken logs, flood wood, and silt accumulating in the shallows at Yankee Bonnet and Robinson's Island on the lower Otonabee. Despite frequent requests and petitions to have these obstacles removed, nothing was done, because there were no regulations to force lumbermen to clean up after the annual run or to stop millers from dumping refuse into the river.

After the opening of the Cobourg and later the Port Hope railways, the Whitlas lock was seldom used and eventually fell into disrepair. In 1862, George Ranney reported a breach of 60 to 70 feet in the dam and a large accumulation of sawmill litter on the upper lock gates: "The works are of no public benefit at present."[3] Peterborough county council was allowed to build a fixed bridge across the Otonabee 300 feet above the lock, on condition it be converted into a swing bridge or removed should the lock ever be restored.

Petitioning for restoration of the lock began in 1865. Businessmen in Peterborough and Ashburnham asked that the lock be reopened to re-establish communication with the Cobourg railway at Harwood, cut off after the collapse of the Cobourg and Peterborough Railway bridge across Rice Lake. Ranney estimated the cost of repairing the lock at $5,325. Owing to the uncertain future of the works on the eve of Confederation, nothing was done, although $200 was authorized for removal of some of the obstacles in the river. Following Confederation, district MLAs and MPs added their names to a petition addressed to the Ontario government, asking for the same renovation. The new Ontario government, still unsure of its role in the Trent watershed, chose to do nothing. Finally, in 1870, after the Cobourg, Peterborough and Marmora Mining and Railway Company decided to build a line from Ashburnham to Lake Chemung, the mayor of Cobourg, the superintendent of the company, and 50 residents of Cobourg petitioned the federal government for restoration of the Whitlas lock. As there were by then several steamers operating on Rice Lake, hauling ore, lumber, and general merchandise to Harwood, the government agreed to restore the lock. A contract for $7,500 was given to Thomas Walters of Lindsay on 8 October 1870. On 1 June 1872, the restored lock was opened for traffic. Barring temporary closure for repairs, the lock has been used continuously from that day to this.

The Bobcaygeon and Lindsay Locks

Other than for the passage of scows, row-boats, and sawlogs, the wooden locks at Bobcaygeon and Lindsay were never used until 1851, when the steamboat *Woodman* was launched at Port Perry, but she was unable to use the Bobcaygeon lock because of the lock's small size. In the mean time, the lock had deteriorated badly. In 1852 the Bobcaygeon lock, basically the structure built by Pierce, Dumble and Hoar in 1834, was in such a state of decay as to make it impracticable to repair it. The lock at Lindsay leaked so badly that it was almost impossible to fill the chamber. The swing bridge, built over the Lindsay lock in 1843, had become so rotten that it was unsafe for loaded teams, yet it was the only crossing on the Scugog River.

As with the locks below Peterborough, no settled policy was ever adopted respecting the locks on the Back Lakes; consequently they were never fully completed or rendered efficient and only imperfectly answered the purpose of opening up and developing the resources of the back townships as intended. Because of the temporary depression following repeal of the Corn Laws in 1847, and because of the Baldwin-Lafontaine objective of disposing of unproductive works, these locks had been totally ignored. But after the coming of the railways and prodding by local residents and politicians, the government was forced to do something about them.

The Trent canal, always a secondary priority of the Canadian government, had funds spent on it only when they were in plentiful supply. "When the resources of the country permit" was the usual answer given to canal promoters when tax dollars were scarce. When money was abundant, however, local politicians invariably managed to obtain some for the Trent. Thus the canal's history reads like an electrograph of the country's economic health: periods of lock construction identify national economic highs, and intervals of purposeful neglect mark the lows. The second Bobcaygeon lock owed its creation to one brief period of economic advancement in the 1850s.

The influx of British capital for railroad construction provided the foundation for a remarkable period of prosperity in the early and mid-1850s. The establishment of railway depots, maintenance sheds, foundries, and engineering shops introduced Canada to its first taste of industrial technology. Employment opportunities were good. Speculation in land, building, and general construction was encouraged by the world trend towards rising prices and falling interest rates, which followed gold discoveries in Australia and California. The resulting investment boom created an atmosphere of heady optimism and free spending in Canada. Canadian farmers benefited when world food prices rose as a consequence of the Crimean War, which had interrupted the export of Russian wheat, and bad harvests in Britain. Montreal's import trade, principally in iron, coal, and textiles, expanded rapidly between 1849 and 1854, reflecting the prosperity in Canada. Since the Reciprocity Treaty had created tariff-free markets for Canadian lumber and flour in the United States, the Trent waterfalls, once a barrier to trade, now became valuable power sources; grist and saw mills sprang up everywhere, visible signs of the economic revolution that the railways had brought to Canada. As the citizenry prospered, so did the government. Government revenue increased as import tariffs, the principal source of government income, rose. Thus when Langton, Wallis, and others petitioned for new locks at Bobcaygeon and Lindsay in 1853, the government was in a mood to listen.

Wallis and Langton were two of the original "aristocratic" settlers on Sturgeon Lake. When the dream of establishing tenantry estates perished with the collapse of the canal scheme in 1841, they quite sensibly went into the lumber business: Langton at Bobcaygeon and Wallis at Fenelon Falls, where he built extensive saw and grist mills. In 1853, Wallis launched the steamboat *Omegah* to haul his lumber and flour to market. But the only access to markets from Fenelon Falls was through the Lindsay lock to Port Perry and on to Whitby, or through Bobcaygeon via Pigeon and Chemung lakes to Peterborough. The two railways then being planned, one from Cobourg, the other from Port Hope, both headed for Peterborough, made restoration of the Bobcaygeon lock imperative.

There was good reason to rebuild the Lindsay lock too. Canada's economic boom attracted many immigrants in the 1850s. To encourage settlement, the government provided grants of 100 acres of land under the authority of the Public Lands Act, passed by the legislature in 1853. Since most of the arable land in the southern portion of the province had long since been taken up, tracts were set aside for settlers in the north, mainly in Muskoka and Haliburton. The most direct route into Haliburton and the unsettled townships north of Fenelon Falls and Bobcaygeon was through Whitby and Lake Scugog. A restored Lindsay lock was, therefore, consistent with the government's immigration policy. Thus in 1854 a decision was taken to replace the decrepit wooden locks at both Bobcaygeon and Lindsay with masonry structures, of the same dimensions as the other locks below Peterborough. A contract was let for the Bobcaygeon lock in 1855, and work started immediately.

Typically, construction difficulties were encountered at Bobcaygeon, and the lock was nearly three years in the making. The contractors had hoped to get by with the canal lining of plank and timber put down by Baird in 1837 to staunch the leaks in the rock, but it was found to be rotten and warped and had to be replaced. In order to lay the foundation for the new lock chamber, the contractors planned to lower the water in Pigeon Lake, but when the inhabitants learned about this, fearing health problems from the miasmic conditions that would arise from decaying vegetable matter, they picketed the works. So intense were the feelings that the contractor was assaulted. Warnings by the superintendent that delay of the work would add substantially to the cost of the lock and result in claims for compensation by the contractor were not heeded. In the end the level of Pigeon Lake was left unaltered. Coffer-dams were built around the lock, and continuous pumping was done. Naturally, this added to the expense and held up completion of the lock by two years.

The new lock at Lindsay never did get built. A recession in 1857 brought the economic boom to a close. A collapse of the stock market in Britain made it virtually impossible to raise any capital for construction, placing the railways, especially the Grand Trunk, in imminent danger of bankruptcy, as funds could not be found to complete tracks, bridges, and other projects under construction. To make matters worse, a number of municipalities that had incurred debts under the Municipal Load Fund found it impossible to meet their interest payments, and the government, to protect the country's credit rating, had to make large advances to enable the fund to meet its obligations. The loan guarantees for railways made under the Guarantee Act added another $37.5 million, on which 6 per cent interest was due annually, to the public debt. Prior to 1857, the interest had been a charge on the revenues of the railway companies, but with the depression, most of the interest had to be paid from the revenues of the country. Further, as the financial obligations of the government increased, its revenues from customs duties dropped, as imports declined. The government was no longer in a position to undertake an "unimportant" project such as a Lindsay lock. Yet political pressure – more incessant following completion of the Bobcaygeon lock – for restoration of the Lindsay lock continued. In the fall of 1859 John Rose, commissioner of public works, sent John Page to investigate.

Page found that about $5,800 had been spent under a contract let in 1857 for furnishing a portion of the material for the proposed lock. Some ashlar quarried at the Bobcaygeon site was still sitting there. About 60,000 feet of pine planking and oak timber, which had been delivered, was deteriorating in piles on the roads and streets of Lindsay. Page's estimate of $60,000 to restore the lock, rebuild the swing bridge, and dredge and straighten the Scugog River brought Samuel Keefer, Killaly's successor as deputy commissioner of public works, to the scene in July 1860.

Keefer, like his mentor Killaly, had always been opposed to the Trent waterway. He had killed the last hope for a canalized Trent in 1846 by recommending against Lyon's survey; now he was about to kill the Lindsay lock. Referring to the Trent and inland waters improvements generally, Keefer reported: "Whatever may have been the policy adopted in reference to these improvements in former years, there is now no longer any doubt that construction of railways ... has materially neutralized their effect and rendered some of them, at least, all but useless."[4] Keefer considered the Lindsay lock one of the useless ones. The Port Hope, Lindsay and Beaverton Railway, having reached Lindsay in 1857, had diverted or changed the course of trade to such an extent that the portion of trade southwest of Lindsay was entirely abandoned by the steamer *Woodman*. She had been bought by George Crandell and moved out of Lake Scugog; with the *Ogemah* she was now engaged in freighting lumber and general merchandise from the Back Lakes to the Lindsay railway station, situated north of the lock. "For all purposes of steamboat navigation, the Lindsay Lock is in reality no longer needed,"[5] Keefer concluded. In his opinion, timber produced around Lake Scugog could be better accommodated by a slide than a lock; therefore he recommended that the Lindsay lock be converted into a timber slide, using the material previously delivered. He estimated the cost at $1,500. This recommendation was immediately accepted by a cost-conscious government; an order for conversion was given, and appropriation of the necessary funds was made in August.

The conversion was made the following summer. Thus, although railways had caused the regeneration of the Bobcaygeon lock, they were responsible for the expiration of the one at Lindsay, at least until Whitby decided to build a railway.

The Hastings Lock

The experience at Hastings[6] illustrates the consequences of the government's commitment to milling and lumber interests and the absence of any navigation policy in the 1850s and 1860s. The Hastings lock was finished in 1844 but, other than for passage of lumbermen's batteaux, was never used; consequently it deteriorated badly. Weller's *Forester* and later Fould's *Forest City*, launched at Hastings in 1858, regularly hauled flour and lumber from mills at Hastings to Harwood, but these boats seldom, if ever, descended the river below the locks. For one thing, there was no trade below Hastings; moreover, because the dam at Healey Falls was never properly staunched, the water level between Healey Falls and Hastings was not maintained at navigation depth.

Indeed, but for the shallow drafts of the *Forest City* and *Forester*, the river above Hastings would not have been navigable in the summer months either. Constant leakage through the dam, augmented by the water drawn off for milling, lowered the water in the river and Rice Lake well below the navigation level determined by Baird when the works were planned. Unfortunately Baird, one of the few who understood the requirements of navigation, was not there when the works were finished. Foulds frequently complained about the low water in the upper Trent, but little was done about it. According to Ranney, the slide-master at Hastings could have maintained the water at a navigable level without creating flood damage, but he was "an old fogy ... good for nothing but hunting muskrats"[7] and did nothing. It was not until 1866 that an order-in-council was finally passed, authorizing the expenditure of $800 for the removal of boulders in the channel between Hastings and Rice Lake.

The absence of any navigation policy had serious consequences in 1867, when the Cobourg, Peterborough and Marmora Mining and Railway Company began transporting ore from Blairton to Harwood. Because of the low water in the river, the heavily laden barges had difficulty entering the lock and the company's steamer *Otonabee* had trouble in navigating the river. The company repeatedly asked Ranney to staunch the dam and insert bracket boards to raise the water to navigable depth, but Ranney would do nothing, constrained as he was by a departmental order "not to interfere with the levels of Rice Lake [lest] complaints be made by mill and land holders and [because of] damages that would be incurred to parties taking timber and logs down the River."[8] The company rejected

Ranney's excuse outright, holding that the "river [was] a public navigable water and that private or individual rights and privileges should be subordinate to the public therein";[9] otherwise, what was the good of a lock at Hastings? J.H. Dumble, managing director of the company, wrote to the minister of public works about the problem but got no results. By September, the water levels were so low that transportation of ore had to be suspended. Then the company took matters into its own hands.

Dumble invited Alex Campbell and Alex Cockburn, MLAs for Hastings and Victoria North, respectively, to examine the situation. The politicians advised the company "to go ahead" and put the bracket boards on themselves. Dumble instructed Dr John Beatty, mayor of Cobourg, who happened also to be the company's paymaster, to proceed. Beatty ordered Fred Boseville, the company's agent at Hastings, to hire men and put the brackets and boards in "no matter who says no to you."[10] Beatty told Boseville not to worry about it because Campbell, Cockburn, and Burnham had supported the action. But George Ranney had other ideas. He arrived just as the brackets were going on, stopped the work, and threatened to lay charges under the public works regulations. He then wrote to F. Braun, secretary of the Department of Public Works, complaining about political interference with the management of the works. The department sent trouble-shooter John Page to investigate the cause of the dispute.

Page's investigation disclosed the irony in government-owned locks with no accompanying water regulation policies. Although the Hastings lock had been approved by the legislature in 1836, primarily for transporting ore from Blairton to Cobourg, Page found no evidence of government assurance that the depth of the water would be maintained for navigation when the lock was finished in 1844. Thus ore, eventually produced in 1867, could not be moved through the lock originally built for that purpose. The only reference Page found in the records to the depth of water for navigation at Hastings was in Baird's preliminary report of 1833, in which he stated that his estimate of cost was based on rendering the river navigable for steamboats drawing five feet of water. But Page could find no official approval or rejection of that depth. Indeed, subsequent decisions had ignored Baird's report altogether. For example, when flood damages had been paid to James Crooks and others in 1850, Baird's navigation levels were not used as a reference point. Instead the provincial arbitrator, for reasons unknown, awarded damages on the basis of a water level determined by a depth of eight feet six inches of water over the base of the dam. This depth assured an adequate supply of water for milling and logging, but not for navigation. By paying damages on the basis of this measure, the government had tacitly accepted it. To raise the water above this level for navigation would now bring new claims for land damages on the river and for the destruction of water powers at the head of Rice Lake, hence Ranney's earlier instructions not to interfere with the level of the lake. The arbitrator's decision had effectively changed the raison d'être of the public works at Hastings: they now existed for the benefit of millers and loggers, not for navigation, the purpose for which they were originally intended.

Page recommended against bracketing the dam: "If this line which may be termed local navigation should have a fixed minimum depth, it would be better to effect this object by cleaning out the channel and staunching the dam than by raising the water and thereby rendering the Government liable for damages."[11] Page's recommendation was not acted upon until early April, when Dumble petitioned the minister of public works, once more requesting improvements to the lock and dam; then an expenditure of $1,200 was authorized. The subsequent improvements raised the water level to six feet on the lock sill. This level established a precedent that was used as a standard for the other locks until a serious commitment was made to finish the canal in the early twentieth century and a navigable depth of eight feet was formally established. Thus by deed, if not by word, the government at last recognized the rights of boat owners. A navigation policy began to emerge.

The experience at the Hastings lock was typical and demonstrated how difficult it was for the government to begin regulating the water in the Trent system for navigational purposes, after allowing the waterway to exist for many years without any comprehensive water use policies at all. As indicated earlier, after the canalization scheme was formally shelved in 1841 (confirmed in 1846), the chain of lakes and rivers ceased to be recognized officially as a navigable waterway, if indeed it ever was. Such regulations as did exist for the use of water applied only to running timber, and these referred mainly to toll charges. Water power licences were gradually given out at many falls and rapids where private dams were erected. The water level at each dam was regulated by the mill owner, who drew off as much or as little water as he pleased; as long as water levels were not raised to the point of flooding out river properties, no one in officialdom interfered with the operation of the mill dams. There was generally enough surplus water in the spring freshets to facilitate the passage of timber, and so the water powers of the mills were rarely interfered with. Thus, for several years an uneasy peace existed among millers, loggers, and landowners. But with the rise of steamer traffic, following the advance of railways into the district and the growth of the lumber trade, disputes over water privileges became common.

The number of steamers increased rapidly as the lumber trade flourished. In 1851, there was only 1 steamer operating on the Back Lakes; in 1853 there were 2; in 1867 there were 7. By 1870, 11 steamers and 40 scows were freighting lumber to the Midland Railway station at Lindsay, and, by 1873, 13 steamers and 60 scows were engaged in the lumber trade on the Kawartha Lakes. In the absence of any water regulation, it was most difficult for the steamers to operate. There was usually not enough water for the combined needs of the steamboat operators, who wanted the natural discharge of water dammed up in order to maintain navigation levels, and of the loggers and millers, whose trades depended upon a constant flow. Steamers had become much larger, with deeper drafts than the district's first primitive steamboats such as the *Sturgeon* and the *Pemadash*, but no adequate or even consistent navigation levels were maintained in the channels or on the lock sills, where water levels could vary several feet from one season to the next. The dams leaked so badly most of the time that surplus run-off water, which should have been stored for navigation and lockage, was wasted. Nor was there any systematic method of regulating the flow of water down the whole drainage system.

The main course of the Trent drainage, fed by numerous streams and rivers, falls down a water stairway 158 miles long with a drop of 600 feet, between Balsam Lake and Lake Ontario. Interfering with the flow of water on one of the steps of this water course almost certainly affects the flow of water over the others, and this is exactly what the haphazard construction of locks and dams at irregular intervals did. The solution to the problem of maintaining consistent water levels throughout the waterway was to create a network of dams and auxiliary storage basins adjacent to the main stream, so that water could be fed into or out of the system where and when needed. Eventually hydraulic engineers would design such a system, but in the 1860s and 1870s, given the absence of government policy, a shortage of funds, and division of ownership and control of the dams and tributaries, nothing could be done.

Without adequate controls, everyone on the entire waterway lay victim to the vagaries of nature: with no way of conserving water in dry seasons or regulating the run off in unusually wet seasons, periods of drought and flood resulted. Ranney recommended that navigation be turned over to the municipalities or a committee of management similar to that which managed the timber slides so well, but the recommendation was ignored.

With no regulations and no co-ordinating body, millers, loggers, and steamboat operators tried to regulate the water levels to suit their own needs. When the water became too low for the safe navigation of steamers, boat owners installed brackets and planks on the top of the stop-logs to raise the water over stumps, rocks, and shallow places above the dams. Millers often did the same thing to increase water power. While this practice might produce enough water for local needs, it tended to reduce water heads and sometimes even flooded out mills operating upstream, and it reduced the depth of water for navigation and power needed to operate mills downstream. During the timber drives in late spring, lumbermen opened the slide dams wide open, often forgetting or deliberately refusing to close them afterwards, allowing valuable water to be wasted. Through the years there were constant complaints addressed to the government about the unilateral control of water levels by one interest group or another to the disadvantage of everyone else.

There was always the question of who had the right to the use of surplus water. Millers argued that their water leases gave them the prior right to draw off as much as they needed, even if this meant lowering the water below navigable depth. Steamboat operators argued that water levels should be maintained for public navigation. And lumbermen asserted the paramountcy of their rights to the water over the other two. Actually, all three groups had equal dependence upon the waterway, and the economy of the district depended upon a co-operative relationship among them. Regrettably, conflict most often outweighed the co-operation that was vital to the success of the district's lumber economy. George Ranney, who did his best to maintain harmony among the groups, frequently found himself in the centre of conflict over water rights without any government policy to guide or protect him.

In addition to the recurring shortage of water, there were other impediments to steamboat navigation. Booms of logs blocked narrow channels and entrances to the locks, sometimes tying up steamboats for days. Sunken logs and "deadheads" infested the navigation channels in ever-increasing numbers, creating considerable damage to the hulls and paddle-wheels of the steamboats. Shallow rivers were constantly in need of dredging. The situation was so bad in the Scugog River that during excessively dry seasons steamer traffic from Sturgeon Lake to Lindsay was stopped completely, and rarely could barges be loaded to full capacity. Yet, despite numerous petitions from steamboat operators and regular requisitions for funds by Ranney, never enough money was provided to dredge the rivers properly.

Another serious hazard that caused considerable inconvenience to the steamers and even threatened to suspend the lumber trade permanently was the accumulating refuse from saw mills. Tons of sawdust, slabs, board edgings, bark, and wood chips were dumped into the mill races every day. The waste drifted downstream and settled in rotting layers on the bottom of quiet bays, promising to convert the lovely chain of Kawartha Lakes into an oozy morass of decaying wood fibres. Ironically, the millers themselves were in danger of becoming the principal victims of the practice. The production of sawed lumber was increasing enormously, but the most economical channels of export for this lumber were gradually but surely being destroyed by the millers' refusal to desist from dumping waste into the water, although they were frequently admonished by Ranney for doing so.

In complaining to Ranney about the refuse, a group of steamboat captains reported that at Lindsay "the accumulation is such that it will soon be impossible to approach the wharf"; at Fenelon Falls, "what was once a deep eddy and the only landing is now so filled up that boats cannot land and other landing places have to be sought"; at Bobcaygeon, "the lower entrance to the lock is so much filled that boats and loaded scows stick now and soon will not be able to pass up and down loaded."[12] Fish died by the thousands; Atlantic salmon, once abundant, were totally obliterated from the streams. Residents everywhere complained about the odours released from decaying wood and rotting fish. Little Lake, below Peterborough, was so polluted that residents were forced to move away from the vicinity of the lake to escape the noxious smells and unhealthy living conditions.

Finally, in 1859, canal regulations applicable to the Trent waterway were approved by order-in-council, under section 18 of the Public Works Act. There was then de jure recognition of navigation rights. The regulations provided for stiff fines for obstructing navigation. The method of collecting fines permitted the seizure and sale of property, and while this system encouraged the lumbermen to be more responsible with respect to the movement of timber, it did little to stop the odious habit of polluting. As Ranney observed, "I fear the sawdust would not sell."[13] Also, millers seemed quite prepared to undergo a civil suit rather than incur the expense of removing the refuse from the water or of disposing of the waste by conveyor or other means. It was only after the Ontario legislature in the 1870s required saw mills to burn sawdust that pollution was brought under control.

Meanwhile, enforcement of the canal regulations did much to improve navigation in the Trent watershed, but the problem of controlling water levels remained. The task became even more difficult after 1870 because the Ontario government began building locks and dams on the waterway as well.

Hastings lŏck, built by
Board of Works in 1844.
(PAC/ACC 14390-215)

PART THREE

The Macdonald Years: 1867–96

Steamers in Burleigh locks.
(Courtesy Roy Studio,
Peterborough)

Cottagers assembling at
Juniper Island, Stony Lake.
(TSWO)

Original Fenelon Falls locks,
c. 1890. (PAC/ACC 14390-17)

Original Burleigh Falls locks, 1890. Note cordwood for steamers. (PAC/ACC 14390-132)

Locking logs through
Fenelon Falls lock, c. 1890.
(PAC/c8577)

Trent valley woollen mill and
old log dam at
Campbellford, c. 1910.
(TSWO)

Covered bridge at Trenton,
built by Baird in 1833.
(Courtesy Peter Johnston,
Trenton)

Square timber rafts at
Bobcaygeon, c. 1890.
(Courtesy H. Pammett,
Peterborough)

The Trent-Severn Waterway:
Improvements 1867 – 96

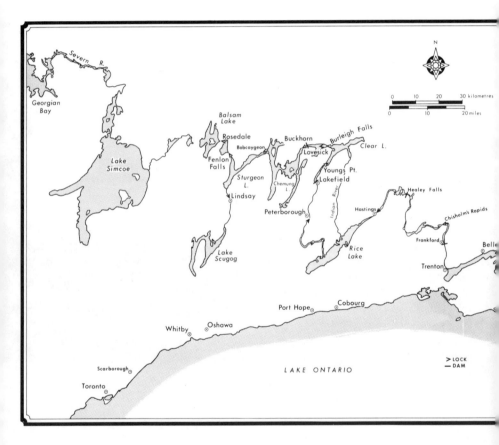

CHAPTER ELEVEN

The Ontario Locks

It was logical that after 1867 the new government of Ontario would direct its attention to the Trent watershed, and it was natural that the residents of the area would turn to the provincial government for transportation facilities that the previous Union government had been reluctant to provide. Ontario's interest in the waterway was an outcome of its settlement policy and timber regulation.

One of the first major policy decisions taken by the Ontario government, headed by Sandfield Macdonald, was to increase the population of the province. To this end the Free Grant and Homesteads Act was passed in 1868, primarily to attract British settlers to Ontario, but also to counteract the American Homestead Act, which was not only attracting British settlers to the United States but was even encouraging emigration from Ontario. It was hoped, moreover, that the act would speed settlement of the sparsely populated northern part of the province with hardy pioneers, capable of developing the north's rich resources, needed by Ontario to lay the foundation for a prosperous future. A large tract of land lying between the upper Ottawa River and Georgian Bay – the Ottawa-Huron Tract – was set aside for settlement. The first townships selected for free grants were located in Parry Sound, Muskoka, and Haliburton districts.

To build up revenue in anticipation of the enormous expenditure of public funds for roads and public buildings in the new settlements, the Ontario government substantially increased timber dues (the principal source of provincial revenue) and put new timber regulations into effect. To ensure the collection of vital forest revenue, the commissioner of crown lands employed travelling inspectors or "woods rangers," whose duties consisted of visiting lumber camps to verify the measurement of timber cut and the amount of dues payable. So great was the increase in revenue under the new system that Commissioner Richards was able to report to the legislature in 1869 that government revenue from Ontario forests was as much as that yielded by all forests of Upper and Lower Canada combined in the best pre-Confederation years. Since a good deal of the timber revenue was being collected in the counties of Victoria and Peterborough, the residents sought to have a fair share of it spent for improvements in their district. Moreover, since the most direct route for settlers into the free grant lands in Haliburton was through the Trent watershed, a rationale could be provided to justify the expenditure of provincial funds for the improvement of water transportation in the district. Consequently, the ink was barely dry on the Free Grant and Homesteads Act when a shower of petitions began descending on the Ontario Department of Public Works for dams, slides, locks, bridges, roads, and dredging.

The newly created dominion government was anxious to divest itself of responsibility for the public works on the Trent and inland waters, which had been a source of aggravation and expense for so long. It had no more intention of completing the Trent waterway than the previous Union government had. A transfer to the province had been anticipated. Prior to Confederation the Board of Works, which would become the new dominion Department of Public Works, had been refusing requests from municipalities for bridges, roads, and other improvements. The provincial government had not only been given direct control over the lumber industry and the management of streams and rivers by the British North America Act, 1867, but under the local works provision of section 92 of the act, had also acquired responsibility for railways in the district; therefore, there was no longer any reason for the dominion government to maintain a presence on the waterway. Besides, since the provincial government was now reaping the financial benefits of the timber trade, it was thought fair that the province, not the dominion, should bear the cost of maintaining the works already in existence, which benefited primarily the timber trade. Although the locks, dams, and slides on the Trent Waterway had been acquired by the dominion Department of Public Works at Confederation, it had never been the intention of the dominion government to keep these works.

The dominion government was encouraged by the first annual report of John Carling, Ontario's commissioner of public works, in 1868. Carling indicated the likelihood of Ontario building locks at Young's Point, near Peterborough, and Rosedale, on the Balsam River, in response to petitions presented to the legislature for improving navigation on the inland waters. The report of 1869 revealed that detailed plans and specifications for construction of these locks had already been drawn up. The dominion government saw in this action of the province an opportunity for freeing itself from the burden of maintaining the Trent works.

Section 54 of the dominion Public Works Act, 1867, gave authority for the transfer of dominion works to provincial or municipal governments, provided certain conditions were met. Thus on 15 March 1870 an order-in-council was passed authorizing the dominion government to enter into negotiations with the government of Ontario, with a view to effecting a transfer of all public works "connected with the navigation and the descent of timber on the River Trent and in the Newcastle District."[1] Anticipating an immediate transfer, dominion engineers began to co-operate with their provincial counterparts: maps, plans, and specifications for all the works in existence and those previously planned were turned over to provincial authorities. Through the influence of Thomas Paxton, Liberal MPP for Ontario North, J.B. Campbell of Port Perry was appointed by John Carling to look after the dominion-owned dam and timber slide at Bobcaygeon at a salary of $1.50 per day, the dominion government having already laid off its dam keepers and slide-masters. Because his services would be no longer needed, George Ranney was let go after 26 years of service. At the request of John Carling, James Cummings, chairman of the Committee of Management of the Trent Slides, sent a copy of his 1870 report and financial statement for the Trent River slides to Toronto.

The governments must, indeed, have come close to reaching formal agreement, because on 25 October 1872 a dominion order-in-council was passed, authorizing transfer of all the dominion works to the province. But when John A. Macdonald's government was voted out of office in 1873 on a non-confidence motion, no agreement had been signed, despite the de facto transfer at the operational level. The provincial cabinet would not approve an accepting order-in-council at the last minute, because the dominion would transfer the works only on condition that the province maintain them. This condition the province was not prepared to accept.

The Ontario coalition government of Sandfield Macdonald had stalled on the negotiations; then his government, with which the dominion Conservatives might eventually have been able to reach agreement, was defeated in the legislature by the Liberals under Edward Blake. Blake, who also held a seat in the House of Commons, became prime minister of Ontario. Blake and John A. Macdonald, opposed politically, also had long-standing personal dislikes for each other. Neither Blake nor his successor, Oliver Mowat, who also disliked John A. Macdonald, was willing to spend scarce provincial resources to relieve their arch-enemy of financial responsibility for the several dominion public works, which had been permitted to disintegrate badly and which would require a considerable amount of money to restore, let alone maintain.

The Lindsay Lock

The Lindsay Lock was rebuilt at the request of the Port Whitby and Port Perry Railway Company because unless the lock, which had been converted into a timber slide in 1859, were restored Whitby's plan to build a railway to Port Perry to recapture the lumber trade lost to Port Hope on the Midland Railway would come to nought. Accordingly, on 15 April 1868, just a month after the railway charter was granted, Joseph Bigelow, provisional president of the railway company, wrote to William McDougall, first commissioner of public works in the dominion government, seeking assistance in getting the Lindsay lock rebuilt. It seems that the cautious Sandfield Macdonald, who had been approached earlier, had informed the company that the question of which government was to have control over the inland waters "had not yet been settled,"[2] but should the Ontario government acquire control over the waters the company had Sandfield Macdonald's assurance that the Lindsay works would proceed. "Our special desire," Bigelow wrote McDougall, "is that this question should be settled or if not at present settled that some provision will be made for completing these improvements as soon as possible."[3] McDougall did not respond, and, having heard nothing further from the provincial government, the railway company petitioned the governor-general, requesting "that the Government of the Dominion of Canada take Immediate steps to Rebuild and Complete the Lock on the Scugog River at Lindsay."[4] As a result of the petition, McDougall summoned Bigelow, Sandfield Macdonald, and Thomas Paxton, MPP for Ontario North and director of the railway company, to an interview in Ottawa, to outline the dominion government's position with respect to the proposed improvements at Lindsay. Regardless of which government had control over the inland waters, the dominion government would not build the Lindsay lock for two reasons: first, because McDougall believed that the "object to be attained was entirely local and ought therefore to be undertaken by the Ontario Government or the Company or local municipalities"; and, second, "because the country north of the proposed lock already had railway communication with Lake Ontario via the Port Hope and Lindsay Railway that the whole question was therefore reduced to a proposal to grant $20,000 or $30,000 to enable lumberers north of Lindsay to secure an additional outlet by rail and possibly thereby save a few cents per thousand in freight."[5] McDougall did promise that if the site of the lock were proved to be the property of the dominion government, he would recommend that it be given over to the Ontario government.

There was a good deal of public support for the Port Whitby and Port Perry Railway, and thus for the rebuilding of the lock. Ontario Public Works was in favour, because the lock would "extend navigation through Sturgeon, Pigeon, Chemung and Buckhorn Lakes connecting Port Perry with Lindsay, Fenelon Falls, Bobcaygeon, Bridgenorth, Buckhorn and other points of importance, for the manufacture of sawn lumber, and as being places from whence main lines of travel lead northwards to the new settlements."[6] This was the same motivation that earlier had induced the Union government to contemplate reconstruction of the lock after passage of the Public Lands Act in 1853. The lumbermen, who formed a powerful lobby in Toronto, wanted the lock rebuilt for the reasons stated by McDougall. Business interests in Toronto, especially contractors, favoured the scheme for much the same reason. It would be much cheaper to freight lumber and cordwood to Toronto on a railway connecting with the Grant Trunk at Whitby than on the existing route, which required hauling the wood from Lindsay all the way east to Port Hope and then west to Toronto, increasing the distance by 90 miles.

But Sandfield Macdonald had to move slowly. Because of the vulnerability of his coalition government, he was forced always to manage the affairs of the province with great prudence and economy. McDougall's promise notwithstanding, the Lindsay works still belonged to the dominion government; the province could not simply move in and begin erecting a lock on dominion property. To complicate matters, McDougall gave up the Public Works portfolio in 1869, and a new minister had to be consulted. Further, the directors of the Midland Railway opposed reconstruction of the Lindsay lock and were campaigning against it. In fact, in extending its line to Beaverton in 1869 the company endeavoured to build a fixed bridge over the Scugog River, purposefully, it was said, "to interfere with the Navigation of the River to prevent the passage of Lumber and other freight through to the proposed Port Whitby and Port Perry Railway."[7] Naturally, this brought a petition from the directors of the Port Perry and Port Whitby Railway Company, who desired "that their interest should be protected in the free and uninterrupted Navigation of the River."[8]

While Sandfield Macdonald weighed the political pros and cons of rebuilding the lock, Whitby was becoming anxious about the future of its railway. The charter required $100,000 in capital stock to be subscribed, before the provisional directors could call an organizational meeting and elect a board of permanent directors to get the railway under way. After a whole year, only $62,000 of stock had been subscribed. The company had promises of $97,000 in municipal bonuses, but these could not be accepted until the company was formally organized. Some lumbermen were prepared to subscribe for the balance of the stock needed, but only after the matter of rebuilding the lock was settled. The directors located an American capitalist who was willing to take up a substantial amount of stock, but only on condition that "the construction of the lock at Lindsay was beyond a doubt."[9] The directors were becoming extremely frustrated.

Taking a cue from a suggestion made by McDougall at the meeting with Bigelow and Paxton in Ottawa, the company decided to rebuild the lock itself. The governor-general was petitioned in May 1869 for "the power to construct the lock and collect tolls subject to the right of resumption by the Crown at any time on payment of compensation."[10] The petition was forwarded to the Department of Justice, where lawyers poured over their law books in search of any possible legal obstacle that might prevent transfer of a public water course to a private corporation. Meanwhile, the company, the municipalities, and sympathetic lumbermen continued to bombard the Ontario legislature with petitions for action on the lock.

Finally, Sandfield Macdonald decided to act. T.B. Molesworth, assistant engineer for the Ontario Department of Public Works, was sent to Lindsay on 14 September to examine the controversial lock site and to estimate the cost of reconstruction. He estimated the cost for restoring the lock and dredging the river at $21,000. On instructions from John Carling, Kivas Tully, architect and chief engineer for the department, applied to the secretary of the dominion Department of Public Works for the plans of the lock and the river and for permission to proceed with reconstruction. Permission having been granted (pending transfer of all the works in the district), an expenditure of $21,000 was approved by the legislature for rebuilding the lock, improving the Scugog River, and building a swing bridge. Tenders were then called.

In February 1870, two contracts were let to Thomas Walters, a master shipbuilder from Lindsay: $14,400 for the lock and swing bridge and a separate contract for excavation and removal of material from the bed of the river at fixed rates per cubic yard. After the work was begun, it was found necessary to build a new fish run, the former one having been made inside the wall of the old lock, and part of the old dam was found to be decaying and required rebuilding. An additional contract for $1,597.63 for these repairs was let to Walters as well.

The lock was built on the foundation of the former lock; consequently the dimensions of the new lock were the same as the earlier one: 131 feet by 32½ feet, with a 7.70-foot lift. The plan of construction was similar to the lock built in 1844: walls of timber crib work, lock chamber sheeted inside with a double lining of one-and-a-half-inch pine plank. One span of the permanent bridge, located north of the lock, was removed and reconstructed as a swing bridge with an opening of 49 feet and a roadway 18 feet wide. By the end of December 1870, well ahead of schedule, the lock and swing bridge were "finished and well executed"[11] and required only the removal of coffer-dams to make the lock available for navigation in the spring. The total cost of the works was $20,985.15. A lockmaster was appointed in June. By the close of navigation in November, 36 steamers, 122 scows, 145 cribs of logs, and 26 cribs of boom timber had passed through the lock.

The matter of the lock having been settled, Whitby was able to raise the necessary funds for its railway. The first train entered Port Perry in the spring of 1872. A large increase in the trade on the Scugog River, after the completion of the Port Whitby and Port Perry Railway, led each year to demands for additional improvements along the navigable channel.

In 1872, $5,221 was spent for dredging between Lindsay and Lake Scugog and for cutting a new channel 60 feet wide through the "Devil's Elbow," one and a half miles above Lindsay. A further $6,000 was spent in 1873, for dredging and removing roots, snags, and other debris from the river between Lindsay and Sturgeon Lake. In September 1874, on the recommendation of the new federal prime minister, Alexander Mackenzie (who served as minister of public works as well), a dominion order-in-council transferred the dam at Lindsay and the leases of water power to the province, the negotiations with John A. Macdonald's government, as noted earlier, having collapsed and the transfer to the Ontario government never having formally taken place.

Traffic through the lock increased steadily in the next few years. During the peak year of 1876, 465 steamers, 867 scows, 521 cribs of timber, and 4,055,200 feet of lumber passed through the lock. But after 1877, when the Port Whitby and Port Perry Extension Railway reached Lindsay to connect up with the Victoria Railway, lock usage declined sharply. The lock was rebuilt in 1886. In 1906 it was transferred, along with all the other provincial works in the Kawartha Lakes, back to the federal government. In 1910 the present concrete lock was built.

The Young's Point Lock

The Young's Point lock was built to compensate the Midland Railway for the freight lost to the Port Whitby and Port Perry Railway as a consequence of the construction of the Lindsay Lock and because Kivas Tully's brother-in-law, Roland Strickland, planned to enter the transportation business. In 1868 the Millbrook branch of the Midland Railway had been extended nine miles north of Peterborough to Lakefield, making it possible for lumber, timber, and agricultural products to be shipped out of Lakefield by rail, rather than down the treacherous Otonabee River, or by wagon over unreliable roads. It was alleged that the construction of a lock at Young's Point, at the south end of Clear Lake, would extend the transportation network of the Midland Railway by permitting a small steamer to pass from Lakefield to the north-west and north-east extremities of Stony Lake, a distance of about 30 miles. By connecting with the Burleigh Road, a steamer would facilitate the settlement of the free grant townships north and west of Stony Lake and tend to improve the timber trade carried on, principally by the Stricklands, in the surrounding townships. Roland C. Strickland, a square timber manufacturer, justice of the peace, and son of pioneer settler Samuel Strickland, intended to operate, with his brother George, the proposed steamer.

In 1865, when the railway had reached Nassau, Samuel Strickland, his many sons and daughters, and their friends in Duoro and Smith townships had petitioned the Board of Works for a lock at Young's Point, but the petition, like all the others received on the eve of Confederation, was ignored. Samuel Strickland died in the year of Confederation, but as luck would have it, his son-in-law Kivas Tully[12] was appointed architect and chief engineer for the newly organized Ontario Department of Public Works; a son, Walter Strickland, was employed as an engineer by the same department. Construction of a lock for the Stricklands' steamer was then assured. Given the pressure being exerted by the railway companies, lumbermen, and others in the district for improved water transportation, and given the Ontario government's commitment to spend some of the surplus revenue of the province for the construction of public works to induce and promote settlement, Tully had no difficulty convincing his boss, John Carling, and ultimately the Ontario legislature that a lock at Young's Point would be desirable. An appropriation for the lock was included in the estimates for 1869.

There was a question of what kind of lock to build for the Strickland steamer. The Stricklands had been impressed by the masonry lock built by the Board of Works at Whitla's Rapids in 1844. Samuel Strickland claimed that it was "the best constructed one in the country."[13] Perhaps for this reason, Kivas Tully decided to duplicate it at Young's Point. Specifications called for the new lock to be built on precisely the same dimensions as the Whitla's lock: 133 feet long by 33 feet wide, and a lift of 6 feet with 5 feet of water over the sills. The hollow quoins and the recess and breast walls were to be constructed of ashlar masonry, and the wing walls were to be of the best-quality coarse rubble laid in hydraulic cement mortar. The gates were to be built of oak and pine timber bolted together, forming leaves 16 inches thick at the quoins and 14 inches at the mitre sills. The valves, two in each gate, were to be made of cast iron and oak, each 30 inches by 48 inches and worked by wrought iron levers attached to balance beams. The lock was to rest on a foundation of oak timbers, filled between with concrete, and planked over. The lock would be situated in a canal 600 feet long and 60 feet wide cut across the point to connect the river above and below Young's dam. A contract for $26,950 for construction of the lock, canal, and swing bridge was let to Messrs McDonnell and McDonald of Hamilton on 16 May 1870. Kivas Tully supervised much of the construction himself.

Work commenced in June and progressed smoothly through the summer. Stone for the lock was quarried on the south shore of Clear Lake, about a mile from the site. Large derricks were erected at the quarry and on the river bank above the lock, permitting the stone to be loaded and unloaded from a large scow of about 60 tons. Conditions had changed a good deal since Hartwell first tried to construct a masonry lock at Whitla's Rapids 30 years earlier. By September, the lock pit and most of the canal had been excavated, coffer-dams had been built, and the foundation and part of the lock walls had been laid. In early September, the contractors encountered labour problems. Several of the workers left the works to engage in harvesting because, curiously, farmers paid higher wages than the contractors were willing to offer. Labour shortages notwithstanding, Tully was able to report in December 1870 that the lock was finished, well within the contract price. Only removal of the coffer-dams was needed to make the lock available for navigation in the spring. The lock was, in fact, finished well ahead of Roland's steamer.

The *Colonel Strickland* was built by Francis Beamish, a master shipbuilder from Port Hope. Construction was delayed because the oak timber for the hull, cut in the forests bordering Stony Lake, could not be rafted to Lakefield until the lock was finished. There was a further delay because the coffer-dams left in place through the winter of 1870 – 1 had been washed out by the spring currents and lodged against the lock gates, preventing their opening until the material was removed. Once this difficulty was overcome, Beamish was able to raft the already seasoned oak to Lakefield and the *Colonel Strickland* was hastily assembled. She was a paddle-wheeler, 60 feet long, with a 19-horsepower engine. She made her maiden voyage in September 1871.

For the next five or six years, other than for the passage of rafts of timber, the lock was used solely and exclusively by the *Colonel Strickland*, renamed the *Chippewa* in 1872. Locked through twice a day on her return run from Lakefield to Mount Julian, the steamer carried passengers and small quantities of freight destined for settlements struggling to gain a foothold in the rocky soil bordering the Burleigh Road in the northern townships of Peterborough county. After 1874, tourists heading for the new summer resort hotel, the Mount Julian, travelled on the steamer, and in season she towed rafts of timber and occasionally a scowful of lumber, hardwood timber, and cordwood.

In 1876 a second small steamer, the *Tiger*, was launched at Lakefield, and in 1878 a third steamer, the 24-ton *Cruiser*, was competing for the limited trade, principally passengers.

The Rosedale Lock

A lock was constructed near Rosedale on the Balsam River, in response to pressure from the directors of the Toronto and Nipissing Railway and the saw mill operators at Fenelon Falls. A lock on the Balsam River would open up steam navigation from Fenelon Falls, through Cameron and Balsam lakes, to Coboconk on the Gull River – the proposed terminus of the Toronto and Nipissing Railway – thus providing an alternative outlet to Toronto markets for settlers on the two lakes and for the lumber mills at Fenelon Falls. An appropriation for construction of the lock was included in the provincial Public Works estimates for 1869; a contract for the work was let to William Whiteside of Toronto on 14 September, for the sum of $19,800.

The contract called for a 350-foot-long frame and earth-filled dam, located about half-way between Balsam and Cameron lakes, to raise the level of the water at the head of the lock about five feet. This would flood the shallow Balsam River to a depth suitable for the navigation of small steamers. The dam was to contain a short timber slide. The wooden lock, located at the north end of the dam, was to be constructed on the same design as the one later built at Lindsay, but it was to be much smaller – only 100 feet by 30 feet – it being assumed that the two small lakes that it connected would never require a steamboat longer than 100 feet.

Work on the lock started in October. The contract stipulated a completion date of 1 September 1870, but because of inexperience in lock construction, Whiteside had difficulty, and by the end of December 1870 only $2,720 of the contract price had been spent. Molesworth constantly pressed Whiteside to get on with the work, with little success. Finally, on 23 February 1871, he advised Carling to cancel Whiteside's contract and to "relet to some more reliable and competent person."[14] This seems to have spurred Whiteside to greater effort, because by the close of 1871 about three-quarters of the contract had been completed. However, by the end of 1872 the lock still was not available for service, Whiteside having encountered considerable difficulty with defective coffer-dams and unusually high water conditions. A frustrated Molesworth then took the work off Whiteside's hands; he finished the lock with a party of men employed under the immediate supervision of the provincial Department of Public Works.

The Reservoir Dams

As discussed in the previous chapter, seasonal regulation of the water in the Trent drainage basin had always been a problem. In the early 1870s the problem had become critical, but also by then the solution had become both apparent and possible. It was the lumbermen who created the problem, but it was also they who discovered the key to the water's regulation.

By 1870, practically all the pine, hemlock, and spruce had been cleared from the lower Trent and the land bordering Rice Lake. Lumbermen were then forced to move their operations north and west into the northern townships of Victoria and Peterborough counties and the southern edges of Haliburton, where pine and spruce were still abundant. The main avenues for floating logs from the northern timber berths down to the 20 or more mills operating between Minden and Rice Lake were the Gull and Burnt rivers, which drained a vast region of lakes and marshes on the Canadian Shield and flowed respectively into Balsam and Cameron lakes. In former years, when the distance from the forests to the mills had not been great, lumbermen could bring their logs down to the mills on the crest of the spring freshet, but now, because of the distance the logs had to travel, and because of the tremendous number of logs (estimated at over 500,000 in 1872) descending the same narrow channels, the logs did not reach the mills until late summer or early fall, when the natural water supplies were exhausted. In fact, sometimes saw logs were not able to get to the mills around Peterborough in the same season, and it nearly always took two years to run logs the 300 miles from Haliburton to Trenton. When the logs did reach the mills, the water was often so low that there was scarcely enough power to run the saws. When the millers tried to regulate the scarce water, they came into conflict with steamboat captains or interfered with riparian rights of property owners and risked damage suits. No one was very happy, the lumbermen least of all, because the cost of lumber production was higher in the Trent watershed than in any other region of the province. The solution lay in being able to maintain a steady supply of water in the system, even after the spring freshet had passed. This is what the lumbermen discovered was possible.

To facilitate the passage of timber down the Burnt and Gull rivers and their tributary streams, some of the big lumber operators had built dams and slides. The dams created large reservoirs of water that could be released gradually, when the lumbermen were ready to run their timber. Mossom Boyd, for example, had constructed reserve dams on several lakes in the Canadian Land and Emigration Company's property in Haliburton, which raised a head of water to an average of seven feet over an area of 80 square miles. So great was the amount of water stored in the reservoirs that it was possible, even after the logs had been brought down, to feed enough water into the system through Balsam and Cameron lakes to support navigation and mill operation in the late summer.

But the cost of constructing and maintaining the dams was high, and those who built them had no protection against their reckless and indiscriminate use by others and occasionally their wanton destruction. Nor was there any method of co-ordinating the operation of the dams. To resolve this difficulty a group of the major lumbermen, led by Mossom Boyd, petitioned the legislature in 1871 for the formation of a joint stock company "for the purpose of erecting dams and slides, and of improving and increasing the supply of water in the Gull and Otonabee Rivers."[15] A charter for a company – the Gull Waters Improvement Company – was granted in 1872. The company was empowered to charge tolls for the use of its dams and slides, but because of pressure exerted on the legislature by some of the smaller operators, so many restrictions were imposed on the company that the act was rendered inoperable. The lumbermen did not proceed with the scheme.

Although the joint stock company had collapsed, the importance of maintaining a network of reservoir dams in the Haliburton Highlands was by then well recognized. A group of 28 lumbermen, millers, and steamboat owners, in an unusual display of co-operation, then petitioned the commissioner of public works asking for provincial management of the dams. An appropriation of $10,000 was asked for to purchase the existing dams and build others. The petitioners argued that "the works being one of public and widespread utility naturally devolves upon the Government, who have derived a very large revenue from the sale of timber limits."[16] The $10,000 asked for seemed to be a stumbling block, and nothing came of the petition. Finally, on 25 January 1873, Mossom Boyd, a Conservative respected by all politicians, wrote personal letters to each of the four Liberal MPPs representing Peterborough and Victoria counties (Paxton, Wood, Fairbairn, and Read), urging them to "use their influence and endeavour for the furtherance of the object."[17] The MPPs, who were oblivious to the political significance of the dams until Boyd tactfully pointed it out to them individually, then intervened on behalf of the petitioners. An agreement was signed on 10 September 1873 by the provincial government, the dam owners, and the Canadian Land and Emigration Company, on the lands of which most of the dams were located. By the terms of the agreement, the lumbermen turned their dams over to the government for the nominal sum of one dollar, the government agreed to maintain the dams and slides, and the lumbermen agreed to pay tolls on timber.

For the next 30 years, the province built and maintained a network of dams on the major streams and rivers that drained into the Kawartha Lakes. These dams converted several northern lakes into important reservoirs for the storage of water which, when released into the Trent system, greatly facilitated navigation, milling, and the movement of timber. Management of the dams sometimes lacked co-ordination, and occasionally some of the crude log structures gave way in the spring floods, but gradually they ensured that the earlier problems associated with a shortage of water were alleviated. In 1906, with the logging industry almost at an end but with water conservation and regulation even more necessary for the burgeoning hydroelectric generating plants, the reservoir dams were handed over to the federal government. The primitive log structures have long since been replaced by concrete dams, but the web of reservoirs that they sustain are just as essential today for maintaining a consistent flow of water in the canal as they were in 1873.

CHAPTER TWELVE

A Crucial Debate

In July 1881, Mossom Boyd wrote enthusiastically to his old friend and neighbour Thomas Need, then retired and living in Nottingham, England: "The most important event as effects us is the resumption of the old scheme which was at one time so dear to you. The Canadian government have earnestly taken in hand the construction of the Trent Valley Navigation and engineers are at work. About three years will probably see it completed."[1]

That Mossom Boyd,[2] who had lived and lumbered on the Trent waterway since 1834 and now owned a fleet of steamers, was so thoroughly convinced of the government's earnestness shows how completely misled the public was with respect to the dominion government's true intentions, when the Trent canal scheme was revived in 1881. In actual fact, the government had not the slightest intention of building the canal, let alone completing it in three years. There was no firm policy, no construction plan, no time horizon, and no commitment. The scheme was partially revived solely for political reasons. Here is how it came about.

On 20 February 1879, Joseph Keeler[3] of Colborne, Ontario, a Conservative recently re-elected after one Parliament out of office in the federal riding of Northumberland East, was reading a summary in the Toronto *Globe* of the previous day's debate in the provincial legislature. He was surprised to see reference to a notice of question to the Ontario minister of public works to be put by James Ferris,[4] Liberal MLA from his riding: "Inquiring ... whether it is the intention of the government to put a sum in the supplementary estimates for the purpose of removing such dams or works on the River Trent as may on investigation be found to be no longer of public utility."[5]

Wondering what lay behind Ferris's question, Keeler made an inquiry and learned that the Trent works had been transferred to the provincial government. That was news to him. At the next opportunity, which came 24 February, Keeler moved a return in the dominion Parliament "for all Orders-in-Council relating to the transfer by the Dominion to the Ontario

Government of the Trent and Newcastle District Navigation and Canal Works,"[6] as well as all correspondence, statements of sales, water leases, and covenants binding on the government.

The return was brought down on 11 March. Although the record was incomplete, Keeler did not like what the documents revealed. He learned that a dominion order-in-council, transferring all dominion works on the River Trent to the Ontario government, had been passed on 8 October 1878. There were several aspects of the transfer that bothered him. First, Alexander Mackenzie had recommended the transfer on the terms spelled out in an Ontario order-in-council, approved just four days before passage of the dominion one: Ontario agreed to accept the Trent works "provided that such transfer is made free from all conditions and stipulations as to any future maintenance of or expenditure on account of said works."[7] In other words, after the transfer, the Ontario government could do as it wished with the works, including dismantling them. This was apparently what it intended to do with some of them, as a sum of $3,000 was placed in the supplementary estimates for this purpose, a few days after Ferris's question in the legislature. Keeler wondered if the transfer might not be illegal, since the Public Works Act empowered the dominion government to transfer public works only on condition such works "be kept in thorough repair."[8] It had been this statutory condition that prevented transfer of the works to the province on the several attempts made since 1870. Second, Keeler noted that although the Public Works Act required orders-in-council related to such transfers to be "published in the *Canada Gazette*,"[9] this had not been done. But what aroused his suspicion and anger more than the possible illegality of the transfer was the way it had been made. The transfer had been made secretly, three weeks after Mackenzie had lost the 1878 election, and just two days before his government resigned. It seemed obvious to Keeler that there had been collusion between the two Liberal governments and that the transfer had been "accomplished for some secret purpose or motive, and that it was in some way mixed up with politics, and connected with the approaching local elections in Ontario"[10] (held on 5 June 1879).

What the Ontario government was being pressured to do was to remove the dam at Chisholm's Rapids and possibly the one at Healey Falls as well. It was alleged that these dams were no longer useful for either navigation or the descent of timber but were overflowing and damaging large quantities of valuable land, portions of which belonged to the province. The Chisholm's Rapids dam had been a bone of contention with local residents and lumbermen ever since Barclay had built it in 1839, in connection with the never-used lock. After Killaly had cancelled the Trent canal scheme, lumbermen petitioned to have the dam removed, claiming that it was a hindrance to the lumber trade. Residents in the vicinity of the dam believed that the swampy conditions caused by it were responsible for the severe sickness that had prevailed in the summers of 1846 and 1847; they supported the lumbermen in their bid to have the dam taken down. But Thomas Keefer, who was sent to investigate the complaints, advised against the dam's destruction. Keefer deduced (quite correctly) that the dam's presence had little to do with the sickness, although he did not know exactly what caused the epidemics. Keefer also reasoned that in a few years the dam would be needed to facilitate the passage of timber through the rapids, predicting (again quite correctly) that as the timber trade inevitably moved further west, logs would not reach Chisholm's Rapids until late summer, when the river levels would be at their lowest. But his principal reason for recommending against the dam's removal was that he believed that if it were removed in response to public pressure, a most dangerous precedent would be established that would threaten the existence of the most important dams and water powers in the province. Instead of removing the dam, the government, as a concession to the lumbermen, discontinued the collection of slide dues at Crooks' and Chisholm's Rapids in 1851. Next, in 1865, hundreds of settlers in Rowdon, Seymour, Murray, and Percy townships petitioned to have Chisholm's Rapids dam taken down, because "by it, hundreds of acres of very valuable land was [sic] totally destroyed ... making it appear to immigration and others like one great sea of water also spreading disease and death over the country by the stench and stagnant waters caused by said dam."[11] Nothing was done. Finally, in July 1877, James Ferris wrote to Alexander Mackenzie on behalf of his constituents, asking one more time that the dam be removed. Ferris claimed that the dam was no longer needed for either navigation or the timber trade and that with its removal 20,000 to 25,000 acres of flooded farm land, valued at $12 to $15 per acre (some valued the land at $30 to $40 per acre) could be reclaimed.

Alexander Mackenzie was anxious to get rid of the Trent River works. As a tight-fisted Scot, he had always been opposed to public works schemes initiated by the Conservatives; he thought these were designed more often for political profit through patronage than for any real economic value. As a Liberal, he stood for retrenchment in government spending; like his predecessors Hincks and Merritt, he believed that the government should abandon non-productive public works. And the Trent locks were certainly non-productive: it took $5,000 to $6,000 a year to maintain them, but income generated by them amounted to less than $40 annually. The great continental depression, which strapped Mackenzie's government financially throughout the period of his ministry, made it even more imperative that unproductive works like those on the Trent be scrapped. Also, as a federalist, Mackenzie thought that the dominion government had no business maintaining works that fell within provincial jurisdiction, as the Trent works clearly did. Like Macdonald before him, he would have transferred the works to Ontario long before had it not been for the maintenance provision in the Public Works Act, which had dissuaded the provincial government from taking them over. So when pressed by the Ontario Liberal government of Oliver Mowat, which in the summer of 1878 now wanted the works, and having been assured that they were no longer needed and could, if necessary, be removed without repercussion, Mackenzie happily agreed to finalize a transfer agreement with no strings attached. It was typical that this Scots stonemason, with a self-righteous sense of public purpose, did not see that in handing the Trent works to the province he was throwing away a potential political asset for his federal party. Perhaps it was because of his persistent political myopia, as typified by the Trent transfer, that he had just passed Macdonald in the revolving door of public preference, as Sir John was returning to the office from which Mackenzie had been evicted by the electorate after a residence of only one Parliament.

The Ontario Liberals saw clearly what Mackenzie had not been able to see: the political importance of the Trent River. The six provincial members from the Trent watershed were alarmed when nearly all their dominion counterparts had been voted out of power in the 1878 dominion election.[12] Fearful lest the swing to the Conservatives be carried over to the upcoming provincial election, the Ontario Liberals were looking for a campaign advantage. What better one than thousands of acres of good farm land, not in the inaccessible north, but in the very centre of their constituencies and readily available but for the existence of a couple of rotting old dams that had long outlasted their usefulness? All land claims for flooding and property damage had been paid in 1851. Now those residents whose land had been flooded and paid for and their descendants or successors expected to get the land back free of charge. Also speculators, anticipating that the dams would some day come down, had bought up swampy land adjacent to the flooded sections, hoping to make substantial profits when the water receded. And the provincial government assumed that the reclaimed land, valued at $525,000 (some placed the value at $1 million) would revert to the province to be disposed of as the government saw fit. Any way one looked at it, this was a sweet pre-election plum and one that Keeler was determined should not fall into the hands of Ontario Liberals. Keeler wanted the dams back.

As a first step in ensuring return of the Trent works to the dominion, Keeler moved on 2 April 1879 for the appointment of a select committee, composed of himself and six other members, to investigate the transfer. His motion touched off the first of many major debates in Parliament on the subject of the Trent canal. The debate also set in train a sequence of political moves that forced the central government to make a volte-face in its former policy of making no improvements on the Trent system. This particular debate was acrimonious, one-sided, and directed mainly against Alexander Mackenzie, there being few Liberals from the 16-odd constituencies that bordered on the potential route of the Trent waterway to share with him the burden of the verbal assault.

It was obvious from the outset of the debate that the Conservative members who rose, one after another, to speak in favour of the motion not only wanted the dams, locks, and slides back but wanted them returned soaked in Mackenzie's blood. They did their utmost to convince the House that Mackenzie had betrayed the public trust by transferring valuable dominion property to his friends in Toronto for purely political purposes on the eve of his departure from office. Each speaker explained, in detail, why the transfer was unconstitutional, illegal, immoral, or just plain stupid.

Hector Cameron (Victoria North), who had seconded the motion, claimed that the transfer was unconstitutional because Mackenzie had handed over $1 million worth of dominion property to one of the provinces, "doing an act for which there was no immediate urgency, and which was not in accordance with the settled policy of the country as established by parliament."[13] Not only was the act unconstitutional, but, according to Cameron, it was immoral because it had been done by a defunct government that did not even have the support of the electorate.

John Burnham (Peterborough West) said the late government had acted improperly in disposing of works a few days before quitting office, because there was no authority for the action and the motive was clearly outside the government's legal and official duties.

James Cockburn (Northumberland West) reminded the House of commitments the government had made to two private companies with interest in the Trent River, commitments that were effectively broken by the transfer of navigation to Ontario. One was the Huron Trent Valley Canal Company,[14] incorporated in 1874 by several businessmen and politicians (including James Cockburn himself) for the purpose of completing the Trent canal. Cockburn claimed that the government agreed to transfer the public works on the Trent to the company as soon as a certain amount of stock had been subscribed. Financial difficulties had prevented the enterprise from being carried on and the scheme had been laid aside, but there was no intention of abandoning it. "It still remains a favourite scheme in that part of the country," Cockburn said. "Indeed," he added, "the merchants of Chicago had taken so much interest in the scheme that they had agreed to take up a very large share of the capital stock of the company as it was found that the canal would shorten the route to the extent of 200 miles from Chicago to Montreal."[15] Then the company found that, without notice, an order-in-council had been passed sweeping away any chance of renewing the charter, which had lapsed only four months before Mackenzie had given away the Trent.

The other firm that had a commitment from the government was the Cobourg, Peterborough and Marmora Mining and Railway Company, which freighted its ore from Blairton to Cobourg by way of the Hastings lock and Rice Lake. The company's investment of over $1 million would be lost, if the internal line of navigation were destroyed, as allegedly proposed by the province of Ontario. Cockburn maintained that the dominion government was morally, if not legally, responsible for any loss that might be sustained by the company, and he ventured to predict that a serious course of litigation would come out of the transfer in which a question would arise as to how far the crown could go in transferring its obligations by order-in-council. He deplored the fact that none of the eight area MPS had been informed or consulted before the action was taken. He challenged James Brown (Hastings West), the only Liberal member from the district left in the House, to state whether he had been informed of the transfer. "I trust that the motion will be granted so that there will be a further searching enquiry into the matter,"[16] Cockburn concluded.

Alexander Mackenzie withstood about half an hour of this verbal abuse before jumping up to defend himself. Characteristically, he saw the issue as simply a matter of saving public dollars and accused the government members of creating a bogus political issue out of the transfer. "The honourable gentlemen who have spoken on this subject have evidently spoken with a view to the local advantages derived from expenditure of public money on this work,"[17] Mackenzie began. Then he pointed out that, despite Cockburn's glowing picture of the Trent canal as projected before the Union of Upper and Lower Canada, the work had long ago been given up as utterly impracticable; every practical man knew that there was not the slightest intention to build a canal or a possibility of it being made through to Georgian Bay. The project had been denounced by every engineering authority of both the provincial and dominion governments. It had been nothing but a source of expense to the dominion since Confederation and threatened to become a matter of even more serious expense in the future. He reminded the House that two years previously he had mentioned in connection with the estimates for river improvements – for slides and booms – the desirability of giving up the Trent works altogether, because they imposed a heavy burden on the taxpayers but yielded no corresponding advantage whatever. No one had objected then. With typical sarcasm, he dismissed Cameron's charge of political chicanery by stating that "Cameron sees in this as he sees in everything else some political reason."[18] He denied hearing of any political disadvantage to be suffered by his opponents from the transfer. As far as he was concerned, the works were only a great disadvantage to the government. In transferring them to the province, he had adhered to the principle that the government should get rid of such works as were not only unprofitable now but showed no prospect of ever becoming profitable in the future. He cited the case of the Dundas Canal, which had been given to the Dundas town council without opposition because that canal was unprofitable.

The Trent navigation was not one of the great lines of navigation, he said; it was purely one of provincial concern and properly belonged within the domain of Ontario. Slyly seeking the support of members from the Atlantic region and the west, he argued that other parts of the dominion should not now be compelled to pay for the maintenance of public works that had belonged to the old Province of Canada, either in Quebec or Ontario. He offered the opinion that all the slides and booms on the Ottawa, St Maurice, and Saguenay rivers, as well as those on the Trent, should be given over to provincial authorities. With a characteristic Mackenzie broadside, he demolished both Cockburn and his legal argument by suggesting that if asked as a lawyer, rather than as a politician, Cockburn would have given a different opinion regarding the legality of the transfer.

Then transfixing his accusers with his icy blue eyes, he dared them to question his integrity further: "My sole motive in transferring these works was to save an expenditure utterly useless to the Dominion at large. Instead of censuring me for this, you ought to give credit for having cut off the expenditure on these works from the annual taxation."[19] Finally, to show his sincerity, he promised to support the present government in getting rid of similar works.

James Brown was not very much help to his leader. He avoided Cockburn's challenge to say whether or not he had been advised of the transfer; Brown, like everyone else on the river, had not been aware of the transfer until the $3,000 for demolition of the dams appeared in the supplementary estimates of the Ontario government. Like Cockburn, Brown had a vested interest in the works, being a charter founder of the now dormant Huron and Trent Valley Canal Company. Moreover, he represented the lumbermen at Trenton who now discovered, as predicted by Keefer 30 years earlier, that the dam and slide at Chisholm's Rapids were necessary for bringing logs down to Trenton from Haliburton in the late summer. The lumbermen now wanted the dam maintained. The best Brown could do in Mackenzie's defence, therefore, was to state that it was a matter of indifference to him whether the works belonged to the dominion or the province but that, in either case, the works should be maintained in the interests of steamboat proprietors and lumbermen.

Several other speakers, including Mackenzie Bowell, Macdonald's customs minister and a future prime minister, attacked Mackenzie for a while. Then John A. Macdonald, his big nose as usual sniffing upwind for signs of a political opportunity and having detected one, joined the debate. "The discussion has evolved on two points on which I should like to say a few words," this craftiest of all political strategists began. "The first is whether the late government had the power to do what it did; the second is whether, if it had that power it was wise to use it."[20] Shrewdly avoiding the charges of political impropriety, he concentrated on the procedural irregularities of the transfer. "It seemed quite clear the Government had no right to pass this Order-in-Council, that there had been no legal transfer of this property ... that, at this moment, that property belongs to the Dominion Government,"[21] he contended. He had arrived at this conclusion after a "fair reading" of the statute, which required publication of the order to make the transfer legal and required further that the property so transferred be maintained. "Since neither condition had been met," he went on, "I have no doubt the conveyance will be found illegal, and, if so, the Minister of Public Works will be guilty of dereliction of duty if he does not immediately get possession of this property."[22]

As for the wisdom of the transfer, he believed that "it was unjust, it was wrong, it was unconstitutional"[23] for the following reasons. The property was one of immense value – prior to 1870, $670,403[24] had been spent on it, and, in addition, there were all the expenditures made between that year and 1878. Instead of waiting for the responsible men who came after them to deal with this great property, the late government had made an absolute and unconditional transfer without considering the liabilities assumed by the government when the works were constructed. Even if there had been an absolute necessity for the transfer, or if it had been an everyday transfer, the government still should have waited until its successors were appointed. But instead, the government had passed an order-in-council, when it knew that its existence was measured not by days but by hours. Then, allowing his anger to rise, preventing him from finding the proper words to express his indignation and disgust, Macdonald stammered: "I will say to the honourable gentlemen opposite, this was one of the most, one of the most inexcusable acts ever perpetrated – that is the word – one of the most inexcusable acts ever perpetrated by any government."[25]

Cooling down somewhat, he outlined the legal difficulty in which Mackenzie's irresponsible act had placed his own government. The gist of his argument was that anyone owning a lease on the waterway would have a claim for damages against the dominion government and not the province, should the province destroy the water powers. This was because all the obligations and responsibilities entered into with the old Province of Canada had been assumed by the dominion government and had not been transferred to the province; indeed, by the terms of the order-in-council, the province had refused to accept any obligations.

While Macdonald's arguments appeared credible, they were sheer bunkum, and he must have known this. He found out about the transfer after taking office in October and had not questioned it. In fact, it was Macdonald's secretary of state who had finalized the transfer arrangements with Ontario, by sending a copy of the order-in-council authorizing the transfer to the provincial secretary's office. Mackenzie's law officers had investigated the liability risks in transferring the works to Ontario. So had Macdonald's lawyers. There was no risk. The only water power lease ever issued on the Trent River had been to James Cummings in 1853, for surplus water at Chisholm's Rapids (the only dam Ontario intended to remove), but the 21-year lease had not been renewed when it expired in 1874. The Hon. James Cockburn and his partners had been given a licence "for ever" to erect a dam across the Trent River at Campbellford, in 1869. This dam was private property, not included in the transfer, and the Ontario government had no intention of touching it. All other mills on the Trent, none of which would be affected by the removal of the Chisholm's Rapids dam, operated without leases; their owners had no claims against any government.

As for the constitutionality of the transfer, typically Sir John A. Macdonald was far ahead of everyone else in being informed about the legal ramifications of such a sensitive political issue. Three days after Keeler moved for the return in the House, Macdonald had his Department of Justice examine the legality of the transfer. The department advised him that nothing further than the publication of the order-in-council in the *Canada Gazette* was needed to conform to the requirements of the Public Works Act. Since no time limit on the publication of the order was required, Sir John A. could have legalized the transfer at any time by simply doing what Mackenzie had neglected to do; that is publish the order-in-council.

But Macdonald had no intention of doing that. Although he had been anxious to get rid of the Trent works in 1870 and still believed that they logically belonged to the province, he now wanted them back. The only way he could justify repossessing them was on legal grounds, and that is why he had stressed the legal arguments in his statement. But this was not a legal issue or a constitutional one. It was a political matter. The only crime Mackenzie had committed was one of political stupidity for not recognizing it as such.

Sir John A. Macdonald had raised the practice of opportunism almost to the level of political principle, and here was a political opportunity if ever he saw one. Every one of his Conservative supporters from Trenton to Lake Simcoe saw some value in the retention of these works by the dominion government. That was reason enough for retaining them. Nor was Sir John unfamiliar with the political history of this waterway. As a young man in the 1830s, he had served for a time in the law office of George S. Boulton in Cobourg, when Boulton had been steering the first pieces of canal legislation through the legislative assembly of Upper Canada. First elected to the legislative assembly of Canada in 1844, Macdonald had sat in parliament ever since. One of his first parliamentary responsibilities was to serve on a special committee, appointed in January 1845, to examine a claim made by Nichol Hugh Baird, for $385 in expenses alleged to have been incurred while appearing before the committee of the legislature that had drafted the 1836 canal legislation. Since then, Macdonald had either observed or participated in all the parliamentary wrangles associated with the major decisions affecting the Trent. He had been in Parliament when Killaly came under attack for having cancelled the Trent navigation. He had seen Merritt's plans for disposing of the Trent works frustrated in 1851. He understood the political liability attached to this troublesome waterway, but he was aware of its vote-getting potential as well. Since the transfer issue had arisen he had been plagued by petitions and letters about it. David Gilmour, chairman of the committee of lumbermen that managed the Trent slides, had written: "We are anxious that the works should remain under the control of the Dominion if it can possibly be so arranged and as the Works do not cost the Government anything it will be no burden for them."[26] Mossom Boyd and 74 steamboat owners, millers, shippers, and others engaged in navigation on the inland waters petitioned Macdonald "to take the necessary course to have the order-in-council cancelled as all their interests would suffer by having these expensive works under control of a Local Government."[27]

"Two things only the people anxiously desire – bread and circuses," the Roman satirist Juvenal had written in AD 315. This political aphorism was as valid in the petitionary society of nineteenth-century Canada as it was in the days of imperial Rome. Macdonald understood this. Often during election campaigns he had played the role of circus clown, as he teetered on the edge of public platforms engaged in good-humoured banter with partisan audiences. But these antics, which he enjoyed, were only a minor part of the political game. Macdonald the serious-minded statesman had a railway to build to British Columbia and a National Policy of protectionism to put in place. To achieve these goals and realize his "national dream" of a Canada extending from sea to sea, he had to stay in power. The 16 seats aligned through central Ontario were crucial to him. If casting a little bread on the Trent waters would ensure the return of most of these seats in the next election, then so be it. He must maintain control of the Trent.

In winding up his speech, Macdonald made his intentions quite clear to the House and to the nation. "It would be well for a Committee to be struck for the purpose of enquiring into the disastrous consequences to the country by the transfer of this property,"[28] he said. And then, in a devilish frame of mind, he could not resist the temptation to out-moralize Mackenzie. He concluded: "I hope the Committee will address themselves with all speed to this question, for I believe a more unjustifiable, a more improper, a more unwise – I was almost going to say" (one can visualize him looking directly as Mackenzie) "a more wicked act – could not have been committed than the transfer of this property the day before the honourable gentlemen ceased to administer the country."[29]

After the Master had spoken, the rest of the debate was anticlimactic. The motion was agreed to. The select committee was established. It met in early May. Except for James Brown, its members were Conservatives. Since, in addition to Keeler, four of them were from the Trent watershed (Burnham, Cameron, Cockburn, and Hilliard), the committee's recommendation was a foregone conclusion. Despite finding no evidence of a settled provincial policy to remove any of the dams on the Trent, the committee nevertheless recommended that the dominion government cancel the transfer of property to the province "and take all such legal proceedings as may be deemed necessary to re-vest ... in Parliament the full control of the works and properties in question."[30] The recommendation was based on evidence taken from George Ranney, D.W. Dinwoodie (who operated a saw and grist mill above Campbellford), David Gilmour, R.R. Pringle (manager of the iron mine at Blairton), Thomas Belcher (superintendent of the dominion works), E.S. Caddy (provincial land surveyor), and James Ferris. Not surprisingly, all the witnesses except Ferris recommended against removal of the dams at Chisholm's Rapids and Healey Falls, as the "commercial, mining and agricultural interests of that whole line of country would suffer."[31] As for the land question, the committee noted that "a grave misapprehension existed in the mind of the public as to the quantity of land fit for agriculture which would be available"[32] if the dams were removed. Caddy estimated that no more than 2,000 acres would be available for sale and settlement.

The committee[33] reported on 10 May 1879. On 13 June, an order-in-council was passed rescinding the previous transfer. All the works on the River Trent and on the inland waters (except the lock at Lindsay which had been transferred separately in 1874 and was not included in the 1878 transfer) were once again brought under the control of the dominion. The timber slides were put back under the jurisdiction of the Department of

Public Works, but control of navigation, including the locks, was taken over by the new Department of Railways and Canals. Thus, although the dominion government did not really want it, the Trent system, then known officially as the Trent Valley Canal, became once again a dominion works. And it remains so to this day.

Request for tenders for improvement of River Trent, 1837. (PAC/Baird Papers)

TO

EXPERIENCED CONTRAC' FORS,

FOR THE

Improvement of the Navigatio n of the

RIVER TREN'T,

NEWCASTLE DISTRICT.

SEALED TENDERS

Will be received for the executio n of the whole, or a portion, of the underm entioned Works, (for the due performance of which good and sufficient security will be required) till Tuesday, the 16th of October next.

Plans and Specifications of the works may be seen, after the 1st of October next, at the Office of *Sheldon Hawley, Esq.*, Trent Port, or of *G. S. Boulton, Esq.*, Cobourg; and necessary information had, on application to N. H. Baird, Esq., *Civil Engineer.*

Tenders to be addressed (*post paid*) to Sheldon Hawley, *Esq.*, *Trent Port*, and marked, *"Tenders for the Improvement of the River Trent."*

ON SECTION 1st.

A Dam, Stone Lock and excavation at Meyers' Island, Mouth of the River Trent, and a Dam at Widow Harris's.

ON SECTION 2d.

Stone Lock, Excavation and Dam at Chisholm's Rapids.

Cobourg, Sept. 18, 1837.

[STAR OFFICE, COBOURG]

CHAPTER THIRTEEN

A Barge Canal

While admitting that the question of preservation of the internal line of navigation as public policy was not within the scope of its inquiry, the Commons committee that examined the transfer of property to Ontario craftily wrote a statement into its report of May 1874 suggesting that such a policy was worthy of consideration. Although reviving the Trent canal scheme was the furthest thing from Sir John A. Macdonald's mind, the fact that he had accepted the committee's report and rescinded the transfer order led many to believe that he might be induced to consider such a policy. Thus interest in the decades-old dream of a Lake Ontario – Lake Huron water communication through the Trent watershed was revived. Encouraged by local Conservative politicians, pressure on the government to resume construction began to grow.

Sir Charles Tupper, first minister of railways and canals, wanted to know just what Parliament had repossessed and how the works might best serve the interests of the government. On 25 June, he ordered engineer David Stark to survey the Trent navigation from Fenelon Falls to the Bay of Quinte. Stark was instructed to make an inventory of the works in existence and to ascertain what additional improvements would be needed to open local navigation from Sturgeon Lake to Lake Ontario. That was all. After spending a few pleasant weeks on the waterway in the company of Thomas Belcher, who convinced him of the importance of a through canal, Stark submitted a report in August that was singularly lacking in engineering detail and grossly misleading in terms of its cost estimate; further, it included recommendations that went far beyond the terms of reference included in his instructions. His report was, in fact, a promotional document for a through canal from Lake Ontario to Georgian Bay. Stark wrote: "Finding that the general desire throughout the whole of this section of the country is not merely a local opening of the Navigation to the St. Lawrence (great as such a boon would be held) but that the 'Trent Navigation' is with integrity, regarded as the forming of a barge route for the produce of the great North West, from Georgian Bay to the Bay of Quinte, I resolved upon examining the ground to Lake Simcoe."[1]

From observations made in his unauthorized survey to Lake Simcoe and with information gleaned from lumbermen who were acquainted with the Severn River, Stark was convinced that there was little to fear from the canal's ultimate extension to Lake Huron, "because to get it there was too easy a task to call forth fear"[2]; and because once it were built the "results would prove of transcendent benefit to the entire Dominion."[3]

From a technical point of view, Stark's report was little more than an update of Baird's survey. His proposed canal route followed almost exactly the route recommended by Baird, with the exception of two canal cuts to shorten the distance and the cost: one cut extended from Crowe Bay to Chisholm's Rapids, avoiding the stretch of rapids between Crowe Bay and Percy Reach (the route Lyons surveyed in 1846); the other cut would join Katchewanooka Lake to Chemung Lake, bypassing Buckhorn and Burleigh Falls. Together the two short-cuts would decrease the length of the navigation recommended by Baird by about 32 miles. Stark estimated a need for 65 locks in addition to the 5 in existence to complete the canal from Trenton to Port Severn. The cost he set at $2.5 million, which, incredibly, was less than Baird's estimate made 45 years earlier.

Stark's reference to a "general desire" for a barge route from Georgian Bay to Lake Ontario reflected primarily the aspirations of the many steamboat operators on Rice Lake and the isolated (in terms of navigation) Kawartha Lakes. Millers, merchants, and manufacturers supported the steamboat owners, and Conservative politicians supported and encouraged everybody in the pursuit of such a canal. In 1879, 23 steamboats were operating on the lakes: 13 steamers were engaged in towing barges of grain, lumber, iron ore, sawlogs, square timber, and general freight; 10 steamers were engaged exclusively in passenger traffic. Although several men were engaged in the steamboat trade, there were three principal boat owners – George Crandell of Port Perry, Mossom Boyd and his son, Mossom Martin, of Bobcaygeon, and Henry Calcutt, a brewer in Ashburnham. These three were anxious to expand their shipping interests and were about to charter navigation companies.

The tourist trade, which would soon replace the rapidly diminishing timber business and would eventually justify the existence of the Trent Canal, was already beginning to develop. The Boyds, Crandell, and Calcutt had recognized the importance and potential of tourism and were already operating regular excursions for tourists from Peterborough, Lakefield, and Lindsay. To stimulate the tourist trade, Crandell built the Sturgeon Point Hotel on Sturgeon Lake in 1876; Calcutt built Idyl Wild Hunting Lodge near Harwood on Rice Lake in 1878; earlier, in 1874, the first summer hotel on the Kawartha Lakes – the Mount Julian – had been built on Stony Lake. Passengers for day excursions and those destined for holidays at the hotels came by special train from Port Hope or Toronto to Lindsay and Peterborough, where connections were made with the handsome steamers that conducted the enthralled passengers on tours through the varied and picturesque scenery of the Kawartha Lakes. Stops were made for picnics and swims; in the evening day passengers were delivered back to the railway terminals for the return journey to the city. Occasionally rowing regattas were organized. Then tourists came to the Kawarthas in the thousands, and every steamer on the lakes would be pressed into service. Tourism was becoming a lucrative business.

But whether engaged in the passenger trade or the barge business, the steamers had limited runs. The steamer on Balsam and Cameron lakes was restricted to the Fenelon Falls – Coboconk run. Steamers operating out of Lindsay and Bobcaygeon could go no further than Bridgenorth and Buckhorn to the east and Fenelon Falls or Port Perry to the west. Peterborough steamers were confined to the lower Otonabee and Rice Lake. And the steamers at Lakefield could not get past Burleigh Falls. Clearly, if locks were built at the various falls and rapids that separated the lakes, the steamer routes could be extended, and if Rice Lake were opened up to Lake Ontario by way of Port Hope or Trenton, the steamers could capture some of the railway traffic to Lake Ontario ports.

A direct water communication between Fenelon Falls and the Bay of Quinte was really all the steamboat operators wanted in 1879. That is what they petitioned for. That is what Stark had been sent to investigate. The Ontario government had refused to build the waterway. The Huron and Trent Valley Canal Company had not been able to raise the capital, and its charter had expired. The only hope lay with the dominion government. If Mackenzie would not consider building any part of the waterway, perhaps Macdonald, who was more sympathetic to public works, might be persuaded to act. But before Macdonald could be persuaded, the expense would have to be justified. And therein lay the problem that had confronted the Trent canal promoters since the earliest days: how to justify a large national expense on a purely local work?

The value of the canal as a national enterprise could be argued on the same grounds that were argued 50 years earlier: it would reduce the shipping distance from the upper Great Lakes to tidewater by at least 400 miles over the Lake Erie – Welland Canal route. It could be claimed that a greater urgency for a Trent canal existed now than formerly, because the increase in trade from the west, predicted by Baird and others, was a reality. The American Midwest was rapidly becoming one of the major agricultural regions of the world. Tons of grain were being shipped annually through the port of Chicago; shippers there were pressing for a shorter and cheaper transportation route to the sea. The Canadian west was growing, too. The population of Manitoba had increased from 18,995 to 65,954 in just 10 years. When the CPR was completed, the far west would be opened up for settlement, too. Soon a veritable river of wheat would be flowing out of the prairie granaries. The cheapest way of moving the wheat east would be by water from the Lakehead, and the shortest, most direct route to Montreal was through the Trent. These were irrefutable facts. But the criticism that the shallow Trent waterway, with a limited supply of water, could not accommodate the large class of steamers already navigating the Great Lakes and getting increasingly larger, was also irrefutable. This limitation would have to be dealt with before a convincing case could be made for the development of the Trent as a viable national route.

The criticism was met by presenting the Trent's apparent limitation as the route's principal asset. A still water navigation, through the cool lakes and rivers to Trenton and thence across the tranquil water of the Bay of Quinte to the St Lawrence, was admirably suited for the conveyance of wheat, the canal's promoters argued. Further, the protected route would render insurance costs almost nominal. The wheat could be transported not in grain-carrying steamers but in barges.

It was natural that the idea of using barges should occur to steamboat operators on the Kawarthas. They had learned that the most practical and efficient way of freighting lumber, cordwood, railway ties, iron ore, etc on the shallow lakes was in barges towed by their tiny steamers. They had become experts in barge-towing. Steamboat captains competed with one another in the quantity of goods towed. In fact, the measure of a Kawartha steamer was not how much it could carry, but how much it could pull. The *Victoria* once hauled five barges, laden with half a million feet of lumber plus two large cribs of square timber, from Fenelon Falls to Lindsay. The *Ogemah* was known to have towed five barges of lumber and railway ties. The *Anglo-Saxon* held the record for 1874, having hauled one barge load of stave-bolts, three barges of lumber, and three cribs of logs. If barges were suitable for hauling wood, why not wheat?

The plan was naïvely simple. Wheat would be brought from western ports to the land-locked harbour of Midland on Georgian Bay, just being developed and capable of receiving the largest vessels navigating the Great Lakes. The wheat would be stored in elevators in Midland and later transferred to barges, towed through the Trent canal to the Bay of Quinte, and moved on to Montreal without trans-shipment. Captains reckoned that the steamers could pull up to 15 or 20 barges, each holding 25,000 bushels of wheat. A train of barges could accommodate 30 or 40 boxcars of grain.

Having convinced themselves that a barge canal was feasible, the promoters set out to demonstrate to Macdonald that it was not only feasible but highly desirable from the standpoint of the national economy. The first step was to convince Stark of the merits of the scheme and to encourage him to support it in his survey report. He obliged. The next step was the establishment of a pressure group to promote the canal, both locally and in government circles. In September 1879, the Trent Valley Canal Association was formed.

Originally consisting of Conservative politicians and businessmen from Trenton, Peterborough, and Lindsay, the association was later expanded to include Liberals and neutrals; it would gain the support of nearly everyone from Trenton to Midland. More than to anything else, the Trent canal owes its existence to the ceaseless pressure exerted by this association. The Toronto *Tribune* observed, just two months after the group was formed: "Their activity shows an amount of energy that betokens a spirit determined to deserve success."[4] Not once in the next 30 years would this association let the governments of Macdonald, Abbott, Thompson, Bowell, Tupper, Laurier, Borden, and Meighen renege on alleged commitments to build the canal. Other groups would emulate the association, but few would be as successful in achieving their goals and in demonstrating that politics truly is the "art of the possible." The first chairman of the association was Roland C. Strickland of Lakefield; Henry H. Smith, a Peterborough lawyer, alderman, and future mayor, was made secretary.

The Trent Valley Canal Association decided on a strategy at its first meeting that would be followed with only minor variations until the canal was finished in 1920. First, a general meeting would be called in Peterborough, to which representatives of the dozens of municipalities along the route would be invited. The municipal leaders would be asked to collect names for petitions, write letters, and lobby MPs. Next a delegation would be sent to Ottawa to present proposals to the government. Finally, support for the scheme would be sought from other parts of the country, particularly Montreal, which stood to regain some of the trade diverted to American ports by the railways, if the canal were built. Later, sophisticated brochures and even (decades later) a movie enumerating the several advantages of the canal would be prepared and distributed throughout the continent.

The first meeting with municipal heads was held in late October. It was decided at this meeting that a delegation of representatives from the municipalities would go to Ottawa in December to advocate the merits of the barge scheme to Tupper and Macdonald. Henry Smith was asked to arrange the meeting. An astute politician, Smith also wrote a private letter to Macdonald, outlining a canal policy that Macdonald might consider following. Typically, it was more a political blueprint than a canal plan. "You may have observed from reports in the papers a very strong feeling has been aroused in favour of the scheme and something of this belief is shared by parties of all shades of politics," Smith wrote. "Can you see your way to undertake the work?" he asked. He assured Macdonald that "it would be a masterly stroke of policy" if he did, as "all the counties in that part of the province would be safe for his government for many years to come."[5] Smith argued that the cost of the scheme was a trifle compared to the benefits that would be conferred on the country at large, and by extending the work over several years, Macdonald could be assured of continuing support in the district. This strategy of extending work over many years was the one that Macdonald eventually adopted and, indeed, that was later copied by Laurier's government. Although many had their hearts set on an immediate canal, it appears that the more realistic politicians were content to use prolonged canal construction as a means of assuring their continued existence in office.

The delegation met with Tupper in mid-December but received no commitment from him other than a promise to visit the waterway. On the 18th of the month, Joseph Keeler and John Carnegie, a former Conservative member of the Ontario legislature from Peterborough, met with the Montreal city council; on the 19th they met with the Montreal board of trade. The deputation must have been fairly successful in convincing the city officials of the trade advantages to Montreal, because Mayor Rivard and Alderman Nelson "were appointed to proceed to Ottawa ... to urge upon the government to undertake the work."[6]

Meanwhile, petitions from the district began to arrive in Ottawa. In October, the counties of Peterborough and Northumberland petitioned for improvements to navigation on the Otonabee and Trent rivers. Six steamers were operating on the reach between Peterborough and Healey Falls. Because the average depth of water over the shoals in seasons of low water was only four feet, the larger steamers, drawing five feet, were laid up after mid-September, losing the fall trade. The old problem of boulders and sediment at Yankee Bonnet and Dangerfield shoals, which had obstructed navigation on the Otonabee since the time of the *Pemedash*, still existed. At Tupper's request, Belcher estimated the cost of dredging the Otonabee and Trent rivers and making repairs to the Hastings dam – $3,300 – but nothing was done.

In November 1880, A. McQuade of Omemee, Conservative MP for Victoria South, sent Tupper a petition signed by the inhabitants of Bobcaygeon and parts of Victoria and Peterborough counties, asking for repairs to the Bobcaygeon lock. McQuade asked Tupper to give consideration to the request as soon as possible, as the petitioners were "all jolly good followers"[7] The fact that the malfunctioning lock was interfering with public transportation seems to have been only a secondary reason for government action. Tupper also received many requests for water power leases at Buckhorn, Hastings, Healey Falls, Campbellford, and Chisholm's Rapids. Macdonald's decision to repossess the Trent works was raising expectations everywhere, and the Conservative party was acquiring many "jolly good followers."

Tupper made his promised visit to the district in June 1880, just a few weeks before leaving on a trip to England. Accompanied by Mackenzie Bowell, he advanced up the Trent valley by carriage, examining the river at various spots were the roads came into contact with it. The party was met at Chisholm's Rapids by Joseph Keeler and Thomas Belcher. After inspecting the decrepit lock and dam that had precipitated the angry debate in Parliament a year earlier, Tupper promised to have the lock gates repaired, so that navigation could be extended 16 miles from Percy Landing to the village of Frankford, even though there was, at the time, only one "small toy steamer ... capable of carrying three men"[8] navigating the reach. From Chisholm's Rapids the party moved on to Healey Falls and finally to Hastings.

The next day, the ministerial party was met at Hastings by a delegation of the Trent Valley Canal Association, headed by Maj. Lundy of Peterborough and including H.H. Smith, George Hilliard, and several other prominent citizens. Henry Calcutt donated the steamer *Golden Eye* for the trip. She was freshly painted, her bar was well stocked with champagne and whisky, and there was plenty of food on board. Wearing "quite a festive appearance" and thronged with a "merry party bent upon the triple object of enjoying the scenery, seeing the Ministers and promoting the interests of the canal,"[9] the steamer left the landing at the foot of Sherbrooke Street in Peterborough at 7a.m. and headed for Hastings.

Tupper and Bowell were taken on board in the forenoon, and after a pleasant day cruising Rice Lake and shooting wildfowl with pistols and rifles, the party was brought to Peterborough in the evening. The ministers were greeted by a blunt editorial in the Peterborough *Examiner*, the organ of the Liberal party in Peterborough county, published weekly and by coincidence on the day of the ministers' visit. Referring to the Trent valley canal, the *Examiner* cautioned:

It now lies in the power of the Minister of Railways and Canals to reassure the public mind by asserting definitely and officially that the government is prepared to undertake and prosecute this work ... We don't want any of those vague promises calculated to mislead the public without pledging the government to any responsibility ... If Sir Charles is prepared to come forward and say that the government intends to build the Trent Valley Canal we shall be compelled to lend him our loyal support, but if he merely comes here to say that the government will next year make a vote for a "further survey" or anything of that kind, the public will understand exactly what is meant.[10]

Despite its admonition, the *Examiner* was obliged to report a week later that "Sir Charles was non-committal about the government's prospect for building the canal,"[11] but, as predicted, Tupper did promise to arrange for a location survey.

The Trent Valley Canal Association was determined not to let Sir Charles forget the promised survey. On 3 July, H.H. Smith wrote asking Tupper to make the necessary arrangements for the survey prior to his departure for England. But Tupper went off to England without making the arrangements – or giving approval for repairs to the Chisholm's Rapids lock as promised. The following February, the citizens of Bobcaygeon submitted their second memorial to Tupper, this time requesting that a government survey be made of the Trent valley canal and that a reliable estimate of cost be made. There was no response from Ottawa.

By the spring of 1881, the Trent Valley Canal Association was growing impatient with Tupper's indifference to the canal, and Conservative MPs were getting especially angry, because of no tangible evidence of government commitment to the scheme. In promoting the canal the MPs had made rash promises, thinking they had the support of the government, especially after Stark's survey which was initiated by Tupper. Tupper's inability (or unwillingness) to fund even the small amount of funds to repair the lock at Chisholm's Rapids resulted in Keeler's "friends about Chisholm's ... poking fun at [him] all summer."[12] In desperation, Keeler wrote to Mackenzie Bowell to "remind Sir Charles of the promise and to see if he would not redeem his promises in some way and relieve [Keeler] of the heap of odium that [his] revilers were pouring over [him]."[13] The Peterborough *Examiner* was not helping the cause of the Conservative MPs much with such provocative statements as: "We believe we are justified in saying that nothing would more effectively secure construction of this important work than the placing of Mr. Edward Blake in power"[14] and "If the Government do not build the work at once, Mr. Blake and his party will."[15]

Edward Blake and his Liberal opposition had no intention of ever building the Trent canal, if elected, but such utterances from the *Examiner* made the Conservatives nervous. In late March a delegation of 12 leading Conservatives journied to Ottawa to plead with Macdonald for some action on the canal. Sir John was having one of his periodic bouts with the bottle and was unavailable for an interview. The delegation left him a sobering message: "If the government does not proceed vigorously in parliament with the Trent Works in the next session, no government supporter will be elected in the constituencies interested in the work."[16]

This was language that Sir John understood. Accordingly, on 31 May at Tupper's request, the secretary of the Department of Railways and Canals instructed John Page, chief canal engineer, to "take the necessary steps to obtain, during the ensuing summer, surveys for a system of canals etc. whereby connection may be made between the Bay of Quinte and Georgian Bay."[17] Page chose Tom S. Rubidge, currently engaged in the enlargement of the Cornwall canal, to make the survey. Rubidge's presence on the Trent in July with sextant, level, and rodman did much to placate the Trent Valley Canal Association and allay the fears of the MPS. And it led residents like Mossom Boyd to think construction of the canal was being "earnestly taken in hand" by the government.

But Macdonald was not convinced that the course his government was being urged to follow was wise. Despite support for the barge canal along the Trent, there was plenty of opposition to it in other parts of the country. The Liberal opposition, now under the leadership of Edward Blake but with the sharp-tongued Alexander Mackenzie acting as railways and canals critic, was still adamantly opposed to the development of the Trent despite the *Examiner*'s bold claim to the contrary. Chief engineer John Page was vehemently opposed to the Trent canal, from both an engineering and an economic point of view. He was convinced that there was not enough water in the system to support frequent lockages. Page's views were well known. Reactions of the press were mixed but generally opposed. The Toronto *Globe*, reflecting the stand of the Liberal opposition, was opposed to the canal. The Barrie *Gazette* was negative, claiming that the municipal councils that spent money supporting the scheme "allowed their hopes and imagination to run away with their reason and judgment."[18] The Toronto *Tribune* advocated building the Trent "even if it can be made nothing better than a respectable ditch."[19] The *Tribune*'s support grew out of self-interest, the publishers Carroll and Larkin hoping to secure lock contracts.

Plagued by doubt, Macdonald wrote to H.H. Smith in mid-December, raising several points about the proposed canal, one of which was "whether the undertaking should really be a dominion or a provincial work."[20] Smith turned Macdonald's letter over to John Carnegie, who answered it the day after Christmas. "Your government has already practically assured this question by refusing to carry out Mr. Mackenzie's order-in-council and by the surveys already and now being made," Carnegie wrote. If Macdonald had any doubts about it being a dominion work, why expend money on surveys that could only have to do with the feasibility of the undertaking? It was too late now for the government to take the position that the Trent valley canal should be taken up by the Ontario government, because, as Carnegie cautioned, if such a line of argument should be made public, it would be seized upon by Macdonald's opponents as evidence that he was only "playing with the matter for the purpose of catching votes."

"There is no good reason why you should not do this," Carnegie continued to lecture. "You have the resources to do it and you may depend that the people will think far more of such expenditures than any paltry reduction in the custom duties which they will never either feel or see." He gave Macdonald some advice that he knew Macdonald wanted to hear: "Keep up the present tariff and expend it on public works and let the Grits cry out as much as they like about increased expenditures and high taxation because it would amount to nothing." Finally, he cunningly tied the Trent canal to Macdonald's two major policies: "Let your friends hereabouts be able to point to the Trent Valley Canal under construction and it will be more than an answer to all your opponents can say about the N[ational] P[olicy] or the Pacific Railway."[21] This was encouraging advice, but still Macdonald vacillated.

Macdonald earned the sobriquet "Old Tomorrow" because of his tendency to procrastinate. True to form, he had put off making a decision about the Trent canal for nearly three years, but some decision would have to be made very soon. Parliament opened on 9 February 1882. It was an open secret that this session would be the last before a general election took place, probably in the spring. Loose bits of government business would have to be tidied up before the session ended. What to do about the damnable Trent? If he ignored it, Macdonald would undoubtedly lose seats in the Newcastle District. He would also lose many loyal and faithful friends, which would cause him more distress than the loss of a few seats which he probably did not need to carry the election anyway. Or did he? Although he was 67 years of age, tired and often ill, Macdonald wanted desperately to win the election of 1882, as he needed five more years in office to complete the work of nation-building he had set out to do. True, the contract for the CPR was made with the government of Canada, and therefore any successor government would have to honour it, but the national railway was only one of the measures to which his government was committed. Macdonald's whole program of national development had now been laid before the Canadian people. What he wanted more than anything at this early stage in its implementation was confirmation of his national policy by an overwhelming vote of confidence from the electorate. A mere majority would not do. He wanted to win handsomely in 1882. So the seats along the Trent were important.

But should the government embark on an expensive construction project against which all reason and logic advised? Carnegie and Smith were, of course, right: the government could afford to at least start the work. Money was rolling into the national treasury. The country was prosperous and growing again. Suppose he followed Smith's advice and extended the work over a number of years. Where should the work begin? How much money should his government commit? Before he could decide, he needed more time and he needed more information. Where was the engineer's report?

Rubidge was asked for a preliminary report of his summer survey; it was submitted on 20 February. The report said nothing about the waterway that had not already been said by Baird, Stark, and two generations of politicians, although Rubidge did report on a number of alternatives to the main line recommended by Baird. He actually did a survey of the Severn River, the first one made since Portlock's in 1819. On the basis of this survey, Rubidge recommended against choosing the Severn as a western outlet to the canal because of the river's circuitous route, contracted channels, and rocky banks. He added further to a future controversy over the question of an appropriate route by suggesting a line for the western outlet running between Orillia and Matchedash Bay by way of North River. This was one of the routes surveyed by Kivas Tully in 1856 for the Huron and Ontario ship canal.

Rubidge advised that it would require another season in the field before the all-important question of a sufficient supply of water could be determined. "I trust my preliminary examination and surveys ... will be considered as having been conducted in accordance with the tenor of the instructions to me,"[22] he concluded his report. Judging from the vagueness of the report, one suspects that the tenor of the instructions implied that Rubidge should make only a perfunctory survey, to mollify the canal's promoters in the summer of 1881. There is little question, as this history will later reveal, that Rubidge was chosen to make the survey because, unlike Stark, he was as much opposed to construction of a Trent canal as Page was.

And still the political pressure continued. In mid-February, Tupper received yet another memorial from the county of Victoria, praying that "a sufficient amount be placed in the Estimates of the present year to construct locks at Fenelon Falls and to construct a canal between Chemung Lake and the town of Peterborough."[23] Since this petition asked only for completion of the central portion of the waterway, it seems to have given Macdonald the option he was looking for: to spend some money on lock construction so as to solve, at least temporarily, the political problem but without committing the government to construction of the whole canal. On 11 March, Rubidge was asked for his opinion "relating to the selection of the most favourable point whereat to commence the work of construction."[24] Rubidge suggested that Baird's original proposal be adopted: locks at Fenelon Falls, Buckhorn, and Burleigh Chute, thus connecting all the Kawartha Lakes and opening up, in conjunction with the Ontario locks, about 80 miles of navigation from Lakefield to Coboconk and Port Perry. He estimated the cost of the locks at $290,000.

Rubidge's recommendation was accepted and an order-in-council passed on 17 April, authorizing the government to place $290,000 in the supplementary estimates for 1882 – 3, to be brought before Parliament in the current session. The order-in-council was cautiously worded. The works approved were "best calculated to meet immediate requirements while being at the same time of use in any further development."[25] But there was no commitment to a further development by Macdonald's government, only a hint of a "greater scheme of through communication which may hereafter be carried out."[26] The estimate was tabled and approved on 10 May, only one week before Parliament was prorogued. Old Tormorrow had put off a decision on the Trent Valley canal until the last possible moment.

After prorogation on 17 May, Macdonald asked for a dissolution of Parliament and called a general election for 20 June. The election gave him the strong mandate he was seeking: 130 seats to 72. He gained a majority of seats in every province expect Manitoba. He lost some seats in Ontario but still maintained a substantial majority there. And he captured, as predicted by Smith, every one of the 10 Trent canal seats between Balsam Lake and Trenton.

After an interlude of 40 years, the Trent canal scheme was resurrected. Only time would prove if it was to become more than a "respectable ditch."

CHAPTER FOURTEEN

Buckhorn, Burleigh, and Fenelon Falls

A few days after the 1882 election was called, Rubidge was instructed to make detailed surveys at Burleigh Chute, Buckhorn Rapids, and Fenelon Falls and to prepare plans and specifications for the works before 10 August. Then, on the eve of the election, a call for tenders was posted, signalling a wish by the government to enter a pact with the voters: canal construction in exchange for votes. Rubidge having completed the surveys and the works having been located on time, albeit "with much difficulty,"[1] and the electorate having kept its side of the bargain by returning Conservatives in all the Trent ridings, the tenders were duly opened on 24 August; but there was a month's delay before any contracts were awarded.

The contracts were held up while Macdonald investigated a proposition for using the Trent canal contracts to assist the provincial Conservatives in the forthcoming election and in the long run to serve the wider interests of the federal Conservatives as well. In mid-August, he received a letter from Toronto barrister and prominent Tory Edward Meek, acting as an intermediary between Macdonald and John Carroll, co-owner and publisher of the Toronto *Tribune* and initiator of the proposition. Ontario Conservatives had been searching for years for some way of dividing the Roman Catholic vote, which under the management of Christopher Fraser, Ontario's minister of public works and recognized political leader of the Roman Catholics, had solidly supported Mowat's Liberals. A disenchanted Carroll offered Macdonald a way of splitting this vote. Had it been accepted, it would have made Alexander Mackenzie's transfer of the Trent to the province appear like an act of piety by comparison. An unscrupulous but sharp and clear-headed Irish Catholic politician, Carroll had become disillusioned with Mowat's government, which his paper had consistently supported since its founding in 1874. He and his partner, Larkin of St Catharines, were railway and canal contractors. They had built a section of the new Welland Canal for the dominion government but had not received any favours at all from the Ontario Liberals and therefore no longer felt any obligation to Fraser or any of the other cabinet minister. Through Meek, they informed Macdonald that they were now willing to go over to the side of the Conservatives and to use their newspaper to help overthrow Mowat's government. In return, they wanted contracts for some of the locks about to be built on the Kawartha Lakes. If necessary, they would take out the contracts under assumed names. Meek would have an interest in them, too.

Macdonald found this a tempting offer. There were two Catholic newspapers in Toronto: the *Irish Canadian* and the *Tribune*. Both supported the Liberals, provincially and federally. The *Tribune*, with a circulation almost as large as the *Irish Canadian*'s, was considered even more influential with the Catholic voters because it had always been consistent. Gaining the *Tribune*'s support would be a stroke of good luck for the Conservatives. Macdonald looked into the matter. He sent a hasty note to Hector Langevin, minister of public works, inquiring if the awarding of the contracts could be held up until his investigation was completed. Langevin forwarded the request to John Henry Pope, acting minister of railways and canals, under whose jurisdiction the Trent locks now fell. Pope assured Macdonald that the contracts could "be kept over."[2] But Carroll did not get any. Macdonald discovered that the *Tribune* was having financial difficulty. For months the paper had been asking its readers to pay outstanding subscription accounts. Apparently convinced that the paper would soon be neutralized through its demise, Macdonald ignored Carroll's offer.

On 27 October, contracts for the Burleigh and Buckhorn works were awarded to George Goodwin, a contractor from Grenville, Quebec. The contract for the Fenelon Falls locks was given to Alexander Manning, a former mayor of Toronto and a personal friend of Macdonald; he and his partner, Angus Mcdonald, operated under the name of A.F. Manning and Company. Contracts to rebuild the Lakefield and Young's Point dams were awarded to Charles Wynn of Peterborough.

Fenelon Falls

The village of Fenelon Falls commemorates the name of François de Salignac de Fénelon, a Suplician missionary, who established the first mission among the Iroquois on the Bay of Quinte in 1668. It is not clear how the name of a priest who spent only seven years in Canada became attached to the township (and later the village) of Fenelon, surveyed 194 years after he was censured by Governor Frontenac for behaviour unbecoming a priest and sent home to France. Originally the village was called Cameron Falls, after the Hon. Duncan Cameron, a Family Company stalwart and provincial secretary of Upper Canada between 1817 and 1838. In the 1820s Cameron received the patent, probably as a surveying grant, for a large piece of property that included both the falls and land that now comprises the heart of the modern village of Fenelon Falls. Cameron died in 1838, having done nothing with the property; his sister and sole heir, Janet, sold it to James Wallis and Robert Jameson, who thus receive the credit for being the founders of the present village.

Wallis and Jameson settled first on Sturgeon Lake in 1833 and later on 12,000 acres bought from Janet Cameron, with the object, like many of the "aristocratic" settlers in those days, of establishing tenant farms. With the collapse of the first Trent waterway in 1841, their dream of setting up a system of tenantry was quashed. Jameson returned to England, and Wallis went into the lumber business. In line with his new business objectives, Wallis demolished the original combined saw and grist mill and constructed separate mills; the saw mill had the capacity to operate 48 saws. Stimulated by the lumber industry, the village prospered, especially after the coming of the Victoria Railway in 1876. When the Fenelon Falls locks were completed in 1886, the population of the village had reached 1,312, a peak that would not be equalled again until 1961, by which time tourism had created a second wave of prosperity in the village.

In 1871, the Wallis mill property was bought by R.C. Smith or Port Hope and Robert Waddell of Trenton. By 1882, three large mills were operating at the falls with a total annual cut of pine lumber averaging 18 million feet. Attached works consisted of a mill dam, in very bad repair, and a timber slide on the the south end of the dam, with the necessary booms and piers.

For several years Fenelon Falls marked the northern terminus of navigation in the Kawartha Lakes; but the locks, when completed, would extend navigation through Cameron Lake and by way of the Ontario lock at Rosedale to Balsam Lake. The contract, awarded to A.F. Manning and Company on the basis of Manning's lowest tender for $105,701, included a canal 60 feet wide, 12 feet deep, and about a third of a mile long that would run through the village, bypassing the 26-foot-high falls and connecting Cameron Lake with the Fenelon River. A flight of two locks, each with a lift of 14 feet and the same dimension as the other locks in the system, was inserted in the east end of the canal. Entrance and landing piers above and below the locks, pivot piers, and two swing bridges, one in the centre span of the Victoria Railway bridge, the other across the upper lock, were also included in the contract price. The government paid R.C. Smith $14,200 for the small amount of canal property required and also agreed to strengthen and repair the badly leaking dam with rock taken from the canal excavation.

Two days after the contract was awarded, the aggressive Angus McDonald arrived in the village to make preparation for the work. Construction started "with a bang" nine days later, when the first rock was blasted from the lock pits. Apparently McDonald's excavators were not yet familiar with the capability of dynamite, the new explosive that had recently replaced the less stable nitroglycerin as a blasting agent. Too much dynamite was placed in the first charge, creating a tremendous explosion that sent pieces of limestone crashing through the roofs of buildings hundreds of yards away. Trent canal construction had, indeed, received an auspicious revival. Fortunately, no one was hurt.

McDonald reduced the quantity of dynamite used in future blasting but not the amount of energy expended in executing the contract. Had the contractors not encountered difficulty in unwatering the 36-foot-deep lower lock pit, because of strong currents from the mill races and timber slide, they would undoubtedly have completed the contract by the assigned date of 1 July 1885. But because of the delay caused by the unwatering problem it was not until 30 September that McDonald was able to report that the contract was finished; he asked that "the labour due ... and percentage retained during progress of the work be paid with the engineer's September estimate."[3] Rubidge reported that the work had been "conducted and completed in a highly satisfactory manner, and reflected the greatest credit on the contractor"[4]; but, as was customary, the contractors disagreed with the engineer's final estimate and submitted a claim for "extras."

Disputes in government contracts generally arose over the engineers' measurements of quantities of earth and rock taken from excavations, the amount of masonry used in lock walls, and the quantities of timber, rock fill, and the like. The contract rates per cubic yard for excavation varied according to the quality and texture of the rock and earth excavated and whether or not it was taken from above or below the surface of the water. There was plenty of scope in this system for graft and corruption if the engineers were dishonest and room for controversy if engineers were meticulously scrupulous, as Baird and Rubidge were. Aylmer's calculation of the actual cost of the Fenelon Falls canal and lock, based on contract prices, was $62,864.68.[5] The contractors' claim for an extra $34,000, based on their own measurements, was arbitrated by John Page, who awarded them only $7,855. But the actual amount paid to Manning and Company over the three-year life of the contract, for basic work plus extras, was $108,642.84.

William McArthur was appointed lock-master, with an annual salary of $250, on 26 November 1887. His duties commenced with the opening of navigation the following spring, but it is difficult to know just what he did most of the time, as it would be years before the lock was put into regular service. The old mill dam leaked so badly that water levels in the canal could not be held above three foot six inches; it needed to be replaced. Extensive dredging was needed to remove a sand bar that lay across the entrance to Cameron Lake, before any but the smallest steamer could enter the canal. A system of booms and piers was needed on the Fenelon River to separate the log run from the navigation channel; when logs were running free, the river was so jammed that steamers could not pass up. The timber slide, located on the south side of the dam and facing the entrance to the lock, would have to be removed to the north side to permit the logs to run out into the main channel and away from the lock. Because of the location of the slide, during the timber run logs filled the strong eddy at the foot of the locks, threatened to damage the gates, and barred boats from entering the lock. But even with these improvements, the Fenelon Falls locks would still have been all but useless because of the fixed low railway bridge across the Fenelon River, which allowed only barges to run through the canal. In September 1887, Aylmer reported a "great deal of dissatisfaction ... being expressed at Fenelon Falls that nothing had been done towards building the piers and abutments for the swing bridge."[6] The Midland Railway Company (which by then had taken over the Victoria Railway) was in no hurry to replace the bridge, a satisfactory financial arrangement with the dominion government being difficult to achieve. Incredibly, it was not until 1894 that the railway line was at last rerouted and a swing bridge built, permitting access by steamers into Cameron Lake. This confirms that the underlying motive for reviving the Trent canal was pork-barrel politics, not any urgent necessity for transportation facilities.

Buckhorn

Buckhorn was originally known as Hall's Bridge, after John Hall, who in 1830 built a dam across the rapids, erected a saw and grist mill, and constructed the bridge that gave the settlement its first name. The village's second and permanent name derived from Hall's quaint practice of mounting prime specimens of bucks' horns on the side of the mill.

In 1858, the dam built by the Halls in 1838 was rebuilt by the Board of Works. A restructured bridge 642 feet long was framed into the new dam, and a timber slide, piers, and booms were built. For many years Buckhorn was the eastern terminus of navigation on the Kawartha Lakes. During the summer months steamers plied between Buckhorn and the railheads at Lindsay or Port Perry hauling barges loaded with lumber, square timber, shingles, and staves from Hall's mills. Until a bridge was built at Burleigh Falls, Buckhorn provided the only means of land communication between Peterborough and the lumbering operations in the northern townships. In 1866, a colonization road was started with the intention of linking Buckhorn to land belonging to the Canadian Land

and Emigration Company in Haliburton. Although 34 miles of road were completed, failure of the road to reach Haliburton and the availability of free crown land further south resulted in the demise of the company in the mid-1870s.

George Goodwin's tender of $67,280 on the Buckhorn works was accepted and a contract awarded on 27 September 1882. The completion date was 1 September 1884. The contract called for a 500-foot canal on the north side of the upper rapids between Deer Bay and Buckhorn Lake, a masonry lock (excluding gates), and the removal of some rocks, boulders, and debris in the channel leading to the canal. Construction began in March 1883. The contract was completed in late November 1884 "in a very satisfactory manner,"[7] but not without considerable difficulty, extra cost, and much haggling over the estimates.

Goodwin was an experienced lock contractor, having built locks at Grenville and Carillon on the Ottawa River, but, being unfamiliar with conditions on the Trent canal, he underbid on both the Buckhorn and Burleigh contracts. It is questionable if, as he claimed, he lost money on the Buckhorn contract, but he certainly encountered construction difficulties that increased his costs considerably and reduced his profit. Even Rubidge was forced to admit that his original estimate of $50,000 was much too low, and John Page allowed that the rates were inadequate. The principal difficulty lay in the nature of the Laurentian granite in which the canal and lock pit were excavated. The seven locks previously built on the Trent waterway (including the Fenelon Falls lock in the process of being constructed) had been situated in limestone; so had the locks on the Welland, St Lawrence, Rideau, Ottawa, and Chambly canals. The Buckhorn canal was the first in Canada [8] to be hacked through the tough granite of the pre-Cambrian shield. Even the engineers had not anticipated the difficulty. Having no previous experience in the excavation of granite, they had no basis for setting an accurate rate.

Goodwin found that his drilling equipment was barely up to the task. He had eight steam drills, "but the rock proved so very hard that it was impossible to keep a drill in working order, the percussion being so severe that the machines could not stand it for any reasonable length of time."[9] Consequently, he could rarely keep more than two drills operating at one time, the others being constantly in the repair shops or in Peterborough being rebuilt. As many men were kept busy in the shops repairing drills as were engaged in the excavation. Moreover, the soft iron bits, although suitable for drilling limestone, were scarcely adequate for boring through hard granite; they had to be changed frequently. Consequently excavation costs were much higher than anticipated.

Labour costs were higher than expected, too, Goodwin being forced to pay labourers $1.50 per day, much higher than the normal rate for labour. Most of the labourers who were willing to work at the higher rate were unsuitable, taking much longer to do jobs than experienced workers. Finding it impossible to procure local workers, Goodwin had to import a number of Italian labourers. He claimed that for the first year or two that Italians spent in the country, so far as excavation of granite was concerned, they could not "do more than half as much work as good quarry men could do"[10] (good quarry men presumably being Irish and Scots stonemasons).

The contract rate for surface excavation was $1.50 per cubic yard. Although Goodwin accepted this rate when he signed the contract, he found from actual experience that it was too low. At first he tried to recover his higher than expected excavation costs by claiming a greater quantity of material excavated from below the "water surface line," for which the contract rate was $5 per cubic yard. When this ploy failed, he asked that "a uniform rate of $3.50 per c.y. [cubic yard] be allowed as a fair and equitable remuneration"[11] for excavation. On this basis he claimed an additional $31,704 for the 24,946 cubic yards of rock and earth excavated for the canal. He claimed further payment for other parts of the contract as well. For example, he had submitted a tender for a bulk sum of $500 for the removal of sunken logs and sawdust, which Rubidge estimated covered a distance of 75 feet to a depth of about 1 foot. It turned out that Rubidge's estimate was far too low. The Halls had been dumping refuse into the river for more than 50 years. The accumulation on the bottom was immense. Goodwin actually had to remove about 24 times the quantity of material for which the bulk sum was originally fixed, the debris having settled on the bottom to an average depth of 4 feet 4 inches and extending 425 feet down river. This fluid, formless ooze was difficult to lift. It could not be raked and could not be scooped up in buckets but had to be screened out of the water. Goodwin originally asked for 24 times the contract price, or $12,000, for this item but on reflection reduced the claim to $3,000.

Goodwin submitted claims amounting to $59,296 more than what Rubidge allowed for the work. Because Rubidge refused to reconsider his final estimate, the claims were arbitrated by John Page, who accepted many of Goodwin's arguments and awarded him $26,638. Thus the Buckhorn contract, like all the others, cost considerably more than the original estimate.

Burleigh Falls

In its natural state, Burleigh Falls (formerly called Peninsula Falls) was one of the most picturesque spots on the entire waterway, "The Burleigh Falls are worth seeing," Samuel Strickland wrote in 1849. "Viewed from

Stony Lake, the landscape is one of remarkable beauty. The four cascades foaming and tumbling into the bay through lofty walls of granite, over-arched by the rich foliage of dwarf oak, the more lofty pine, and gnarled branches or red cedar, whose roots are seen firmly fixed in deep fissures of the overhanging rocks present a picture whose varied features are not easily described."[12] Nichol Hugh Baird was impressed not at all with the beauty of Burleigh Falls, only with the challenge they presented to lock building. "The falls disgorge themselves with boisterous rapidity from the several ragged and iron-bound outlets,"[13] this laconic Scottish engineer wrote in his survey report to Sir John Colborne in 1835. To Baird, the 26-foot falls with "dreaded iron-bound nature of the rock" were "a mass of adament [sic] obstruction ... an obstacle ... of somewhat a serious nature"[14] to be overcome if the inland waters of the Newcastle District were to be canalized. Fifty years later, George Goodwin would have endorsed Baird's description.

For many years after Baird's visit, the falls existed in solitary splendour, their remarkable beauty unmolested. No mills were built there; no settlement grew up nearby, the surrounding terrain, strewn with "Burleigh Rocks," not being conducive to agriculture. In 1856, lumbermen built a dam and timber slide at the falls, and some shanties were put up to house the lumbermen during the annual log drives, but no permanent settlers took up residence.

After 1874, tourists staying at the Mount Julian Hotel anchored their row-boats at the foot of the falls or cast their lines from the rocks to enjoy what Strickland called the "best fishing in Stony Lake."[15] But for most of the year, Burleigh Falls was a lonely and isolated place when Goodwin moved his derricks and steam drills there in 1884.

Tom Rubidge planned to overcome the falls with a 600-foot canal cut north of the falls between Burleigh Bay and Stony Lake and to insert two combined locks, each with a lift of 13 feet with 6 feet of water over the sills, after the fashion of the Fenelon Falls locks. Lock technology had not yet reached the stage that permitted locks to be built with a lift of more than 14 or 15 feet. Single locks at Burleigh and Fenelon Falls would have had lifts of 26 to 28 feet, requiring the lower gates to be 34 to 36 feet tall. Pressure exerted on gates of such dimension, combined with the weight of the heavy structures themselves, would have made it difficult, if not impossible, to open and close them with existing, crude, hand-operated equipment; hence the combined or flight of locks, one opening into the other, like a set of marine steps.[16]

A new regulating dam to replace the old loggers' dam was to be built across the Burleigh River, just below the head of the chute. A series of dams with regulating weirs was to be built on the west side of the upper lock to shut off Perry's Creek, an alternate outlet from the Burleigh River into Stony Lake; another dam across the low ground between the canal and the north end of the main dam would also be required. These dams would raise the water in the Burleigh River by seven feet at the main dam, and the level would taper-off to zero at the foot of Lovesick Lake a half-mile upstream, drowning out a succession of rapids that lay in between. At Lovesick Rapids, another lock, with a three-and-a-half-foot lift, a regulating dam with a timber slide, and four minor dams connecting the islands and the mainland were to be built. The Lovesick works would raise the water in Deer Bay one foot eight inches above normal, drowning out little Buckhorn Rapids. The whole improvement, which covered a distance of about two-and-a-quarter miles and included also some sub-marine excavation, wharfing, piers and booms, and a pier for a swing bridge on the colonization road at the Burleigh lock, was to be let out in one contract.

In April 1884, when the contract at Buckhorn was nearly finished, Goodwin began moving plant and equipment downstream to Burleigh Falls. A quarry was opened up about a mile south of Burleigh, and a small work-force was engaged, preparing stone for the locks and cutting timber for the lock foundation and the dams. By July, Goodwin had built a workshop, stables, storeroom, and cook-house at the construction site; the drills and derricks had been moved into place, but he did not start excavating right away. In fact, in August he suspended work at Burleigh Falls altogether, and he did not resume construction until June the follow-ing year.

There were several features of the contract that bothered Goodwin and that he wanted corrected before investing money in a work on which he might sustain a loss. He was not satisfied with the contract rates, especially those for excavation. Experience at Buckhorn had shown that the rates were too low, given the nature of the rock. A second concern related to the unwatering of Burleigh Chute. This item had not been included in the contract but was to be done by the Department of Railways and Canals under Rubidge's supervision. Rubidge had not unwatered the site to Goodwin's satisfaction; until all the leaks were staunched in the coffer-dams, he refused to begin work on the permanent dam. To make matters worse, Goodwin did not get along with Rubidge, whom he found unco-operative, arbitrary, and at times abrasive. Rubidge, for example, had refused to give him a copy of the general plan of the work, although he had been promised one when the contract had been signed. Without the plan, Goodwin would not proceed, because without it he could not lay out the work properly and would be, in effect, at the mercy of the govern-ment engineer.

In April 1885, with no changes having been made in the rates, with the unwatering problem still not resolved, and with Rubidge threatening to cancel the contract and impose penalties, Goodwin came up with a proposal to revise the nature of the whole Burleigh project. He suggested that instead of cutting a difficult and costly canal, with two locks and three permanent dams at Burleigh Falls, and building one lock and five permanent dams at Lovesick, an alternate route through Perry's Creek be adopted. The Perry's Creek route would require only one canal instead of two and would reduce the number of dams needed.

There is no question that the Perry's Creek route, which was probably suggested to Goodwin by some of the lumbermen, had merit. It was, in fact, the method of overcoming the Burleigh Falls suggested by Baird in 1835. It required only two dams instead of eight. Both plans called for three locks, but in Perry's Creek route the locks would be located in one place instead of two miles apart. With only one short canal to equip and maintain, future maintenance costs would be considerably reduced. By placing the locks in the natural ravine, much expensive excavation could be avoided, reducing construction time and cost. Further, the change would be advantageous to the lumbermen, as it would require them to disband their drives of timber and saw logs only once; Rubidge's proposal called for two disbandments, which led some of them to observe that this canal "was not properly placed."[17] Because Rubidge was adamantly opposed to the change, Goodwin wrote directly to the secretary of the Department of Railways and Canals, requesting the minister to refer the matter to John Page for consideration. If Page thought it proper to send for Rubidge to hear his opinion, Goodwin asked that he be called, too, so that he might "have an opportunity to reply to any objection [Rubidge] may raise."[18]

In the mean time, Rubidge corrected the unwatering problem and advised Bradley by telegram that if Goodwin intended going on with the work "he should be required to go up at once."[19] Goodwin sent a small gang back to Burleigh, but its activity was limited to "quarrying stone for the contemplated locks pending adjustments of [the] matters"[20] outstanding between Goodwin and the department. In mid-June, at the request of the minister, John Page met Rubidge and Goodwin at Burleigh Falls. He examined the Perry's Creek proposal and the one on which the contract was based and listened to "the explanations of both gentlemen at the respective places." Having no correct information about the Perry's Creek line of which to make a decision, Page ordered Rubidge to have the line surveyed and a cost estimate prepared. Rubidge reluctantly complied.

On 18 July, Rubidge submitted the results of his survey. Following the contract prices, the original plan would cost $152,710.50; the Perry's Creek route would cost $193,683. If the rates were adjusted upward, in line with Goodwin's request, the original plan would cost $177,557, and the Perry's Creek route $238,433. On the basis of cost, therefore, the Perry's Creek route was unacceptable, whatever engineering merits it might have. But what worried Rubidge more than the basic construction cost was the additional cost that would arise from claims for flooding of property.

Flood damages paid because of the new dams at Lakefield and Young's Point had set the standard of values for such claims. They were extremely high. Because of the 1879 ruling of the Ontario Court of Chancery, which had established the water level in Lake Katchewanooka, the dominion government was obliged to buy nearly all the 12-mile shoreline at inflated values when the Lakefield dam was rebuilt, raising the water to a level suitable for navigation. This cost thousands of dollars.

Rubidge was strongly opposed to the government paying "the excessive claims of riparian owners for damages."[22] It irked him that inhabitants like the Stricklands,[23] Smiths, Dinwoodies, Hilliards, Halls, Youngs, and Chalmers, [24] who had pressed for the improvements, and for whose benefit they were designed, were demanding compensation for harmless damage to shorefront property, much of it useless. Rubidge argued that if the projected canal possessed even a fraction of the importance its promoters alleged, it "should be readily conceded that the bed and waters of the rivers and immediate lakes ... [were] public and belonged to the State, and that ... manufacturers, steamboat owners and other private persons [had] no right to encroachment upon them."[25] He believed that riparian claims to damaged hydraulic powers should be disallowed as well. He recommended that the minister take the steps necessary to clarify the whole subject of riparian rights in order to determine the position of the government, before proceeding with the works on the canal. This suggestion did not endear Rubidge to the local inhabitants, but the government ignored it anyway. To have denied riparian claims would have destroyed the pork-barrel character of the canal, which was one of its more attractive features. So the government continued paying excessive riparian claims (a few of them justified), which by 1923 would add hundreds of thousands of dollars to the final cost of the canal.

Meanwhile, residents were wondering what was going on at Burleigh Falls. Many thought the government itself was causing the delay, a point of view propounded by the Peterborough *Examiner*. Purporting to speak the "plain truth," The *Examiner* attributed the delay to the government for employing "an engineer whose plans and specifications were so misleading that the contractor would not go on with the work"[26] and claimed that the government was glad of any excuse to put a stop to it. This bungling was understandable because of the way the Department of Railways and Canals was managed, sneered the *Examiner*. During his 10 years in the portfolio, Sir Charles Tupper had been "more intent on drawing his salary of $7,000 as Minister, and feathering his nest ... than looking after the interests of the country and the district."²⁷ As for John Henry Pope, Tupper's successor, he had "neither the ability nor inclination"²⁸ to do anything about the Trent, the *Examiner* said.

Talk such as that worried George Hilliard, MP for Peterborough West. The next election was rapidly approaching, and the delay at Burleigh was "creating intense disatisfaction throughout the counties adjacent to the route of the canal."²⁹ Since he had been taking "a great deal of badgering from both friends and foes of the government,"³⁰ Hilliard decided on 1 August to take a ride up to Burleigh Falls on the steamer *Cruiser* to see for himself what was happening. He was shocked to discover that Goodwin had only 10 or 12 men working. He concluded (correctly) that Goodwin did not intend to "make anything immediately otherwise he would not allow the fine weather to pass without availing himself of its advantages."³¹ Hilliard wrote immediately to Pope, urging him to insist that Goodwin get on with the work.

Earlier, after being informed that there would be no change in the rates, Goodwin had gone to see Pope and asked to be relieved of the contract, since he could not complete the work at the contract prices "without a great loss."³² Pope asked him to put his terms for withdrawal in writing, which he did on 12 August. He wanted the government to release his security (5 per cent of the contract price), pay him for the work already done and materials delivered, pay for the stables, shed, etc, and take his plant at a fair evaluation. In the mean time, having received Hilliard's letter pointing out the political implications of the delay, Pope seems to have panicked: he ordered Goodwin either to proceed with the contract immediately or to forfeit the security and take the risk of being sued by the crown for damages for not completing the work by 1 July 1885, the date agreed upon in the contract.

Goodwin had no choice but to comply with the order. He had expended a large sum of money procuring plant and materials, most of which would be lost or disposed of at great loss, if he gave up the contract. More serious would be the damage to his reputation as a contractor to have it placed on record that he had failed to finish a contract even though there were sufficient reasons, in his opinion, to justify his retirement. All in all, he reasoned that the loss in finishing the work would be less than the loss sustained if he surrendered the contract. On 24 August, he informed the Department of Railways and Canals that he had taken steps to increase the work-force at Burleigh Falls and that "the operations [would] be conducted with satisfactory dispatch."³³

From then on Goodwin's principal objective seems to have been to get the job done, so that he could move his half-frozen Italians away from Burleigh Falls as soon as possible. During the fall and winter of 1885, they blasted 18,000 cubic yards of rock and rubble out of Burleigh and Lovesick canals, and by April the masons had begun to lay the masonry in the lock walls. But it was not a happy experience for the contractor.

Irascible at the best of times, Rubidge's behaviour became totally irrational, his treatment of Goodwin downright vindictive. Through 1886 and 1887, Rubidge was under tremendous stress. The press, the politicians, and the public were criticizing him. They accused him of trying to scuttle their beloved Trent valley canal, opposition to which he frequently and openly expressed. Even his own engineers were conspiring against him. He soon became suspicious of everyone. He trusted nobody, least of all Goodwin, who had maligned him to his superiors in Ottawa, challenged his engineering judgment, and even succeeded in getting a survey made of the preposterous Perry's Creek route. Eventually, Rubidge cracked under the strain. He lashed out at everyone, becoming especially abrasive with Goodwin.

Suspecting that Goodwin would try to reduce construction costs by cutting corners, Rubidge had the work watched closely. The only two men on his staff in whom he had any confidence were J.H. Ramsay, a masonry inspector, and H.S. Greenwood, a rodman, both of whom Rubidge had brought with him from Cornwall. Bypassing his own engineers, Rubidge gave these men almost complete authority for supervising the Burleigh and Lovesick works. They operated "by the book." Inspector Ramsay was "so exacting that [Goodwin could not] perform the work according to his directions without entailing a large expenditure over and above the amount that would be required under supervision of a fair and practical inspector,"[34] Goodwin complained. Ramsay and Greenwood harassed and embarrassed the contractor at every opportunity and always, according to Goodwin, with Rubidge's knowledge and consent. They ordered the work stopped from time to time, keeping a gang of men idle for days until minor corrections were made. They ordered Goodwin to replace foremen without reasons given; indeed, they assumed "all the authority of the government so that it [was] difficult to know in whom the proper authority [was] vested."[35] Goodwin complained constantly to the secretary of the department about the harassment and finally, in desperation, requested that John Page "visit the work at an early date as ... his personal observation [was] necessary."[36] Because he had become a political liability, Rubidge was replaced; his job was given to David Stark, then superintending engineer of the Ottawa River canals. Through J.A. Aylmer, Rubidge's former assistant, Stark supervised the finishing up of the Trent canal contracts from Ottawa.

Despite Rubidge's refusal to "give a fair and liberal interpretation of the contract,"[37] and despite the injustice of the alleged embarrassment, Goodwin endeavoured to "do first class work and to complete the contract with the utmost possible dispatch."[38] By mid-summer 1887, the locks and dams were practically finished. Mr Power installed the gates in the Buckhorn, Lovesick, and Burleigh Falls locks in the autumn. On 26 October, the first steamer (probably the *Fairy* from Young's point) passed through the new locks. David Stark, who was on hand for the occasion, sent on the happy news to A.P. Bradley the next day. There is no record of Rubidge being present at the opening of the new section of the canal.

Timber slide at Hastings
(Crook's Rapids), designed
by Baird in 1842. (TSWO)

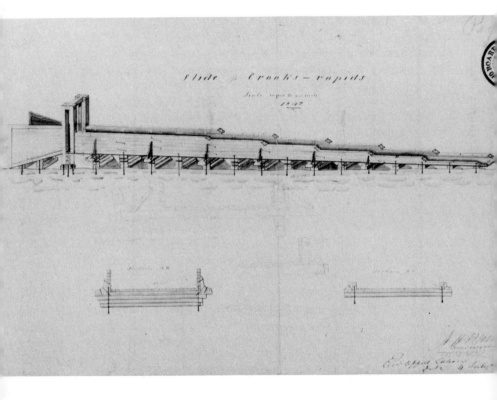

CHAPTER FIFTEEN

Tom S. Rubidge

Between 1878 and the outbreak of the First World War, two main issues dominated federal politics in the Peterborough area: the National Policy of protection for secondary industry and completion of the Trent Canal. During John A. Macdonald's years in office (and in opposition), Peterborough had begun to develop many small industries which demanded protection against cheap manufactured goods coming from the United States; the Trent canal, offering the possibility of cheap transportation, was seen as a corollary to protectionism. Both were needed, it was thought, if Peterborough's industries were to survive. Although Macdonald received support from Peterborough's business community for his tariff policy, there were many, led by the Peterborough *Examiner*, who suspected that his vague policy for the Trent canal was nothing more than an ill-disguised ploy to get votes, especially from those who opposed his National Policy. Time after time the Trent Valley Canal Association, dominated by Conservative businessmen, tried to point out to Macdonald the political risk in vacillating on a firm commitment to the Trent, but Macdonald always turned a deaf ear to pleas for a firm decision to complete the canal until the eve of elections, when he would feign a Trent canal policy by appropriating funds for construction.

Macdonald's vote-getting strategy did not go unnoticed by the *Examiner*. "Whatever expenditure there had been on the scheme is properly chargeable to capital (political) account and this is the explanation of all the delay and trifling with this important work,"[1] The *Examiner* charged in 1883. "The government is using the undertaking as a political engine,"[2] it accused in 1884. "The scheme has been made the tool of party politicians. On the strength of it, the government has secured the support of a dozen representatives from the district,"[3] the paper reminded the electorate in 1885. Commenting on a trip by a delegation from the Trent Valley Canal Association to Ottawa in 1886, the *Examiner* warned: "The deputation ... will submit to being put off with no evasive excuses and will be satisfied only with an expressed and definite declaration of immediate action."[4] But Macdonald continued to waffle on a firm commitment to the Trent, despite the exhortation of politicians and the battering that his government was receiving from the *Examiner*.

By 1887, the proposed Trent valley canal had become more than just a perceived economic necessity. It was an obsession. Money and effort had been expended in promoting it. Investments in steamers, industries, and property had been made on the promise of it. Futures of politicians rested on its completion. But impatience and frustration were growing because of government stalling. And a few political souls were being searched because of the government's inaction. "I have long been a supporter of the Dominion Government, but I no longer have any confidence in the Minister of Railways and Canals,"[5] long-time Tory and defeated provincial candidate John Carnegie proclaimed publicly. George Hilliard vowed: "If the Government does not push on with the work, I will give up my politics and support the party that will build the canal."[6] The Reverend J. Logan of Fenelon Falls, a lifelong worshipper of Macdonald but with his faith in his idol now shattered, confessed: "Henceforth I have only one politic and that is the Trent Valley Canal."[7]

Into this coterie of canal promoters, plotters, and propagandists strode a hostile Tom S. Rubidge like an angry Christ come to cleanse the temple. Rubidge criticized, he ridiculed, he denounced, and he condemned. Unlike his predecessors Baird, Ranney, and Belcher and his successors Stark, Rogers, Grant and Killaly,[8] all of whom were ardent promoters of the Trent waterway, Rubidge opposed development of the canal with a passion that was unrelenting. His opposition was not because of an alleged government suspension stratagem in which he was supposed to be a leading conspirator; rather, he denounced the Trent primarily because, as a young engineer with the Board of Works, he had become a convert to the Sydenham-Killaly – sponsored St Lawrence canal system, on the development of which he had spent much of his professional life. Now, with trade from the west growing rapidly, requiring an enlargement of the St Lawrence canals, he saw that money was being squandered on a useless alternate route that had been proved long before to be impracticable. While work on the St Lawrence demanded his attention, he was frittering away his time and talents on a political canal that the country did not need. He was angry and bitter. His bitterness was increased when, on Good Friday 1883, his infant daughter Mary died in Cornwall while he was engaged on the Trent survey. No wonder he did not hesitate to express to anyone who would listen his low opinion of both the canal and its promoters.

Tom Rubidge was born in Oxford, England, on 6 February 1827. He was the only son of the celebrated English portraitist and miniaturist Joseph William Rubidge, who exhibited his work in the Royal Academy in 1823 and 1824. Tom was orphaned at a young age and sent out to Canada to the care of his father's half-brother, Capt. Charles Rubidge, a retired naval officer living in Peterborough. Another uncle was land surveyor Frederick P. Rubidge, who, it will be recalled, designed the first Bobcaygeon lock for Bethune and assisted Baird with the Trent canal and Cobourg railway surveys in 1835. Encouraged by his uncle, young Tom studied engineering and in 1844, at the age of 17, joined the Board of Works as a member of the engineering staff of the Williamsburg canal, becoming resident engineer at Iroquois. Thus began a distinguished 60-year career, principally with the government of Canada, as hydraulic and railway engineer. When he was sent to survey the Trent and supervise construction of the locks Rubidge had been, for 10 years, engineer in charge of enlargement of the St Lawrence canals for a 14-foot navigation.

Rubidge not only possessed great engineering skill, but he also tried to keep abreast of the times; he was always ready to discard old engineering methods and techniques the moment he found that modern ones were better. Because he made civil engineering a progressive science, he enjoyed both the respect of his superiors in Canada and the admiration of the international engineering fraternity. When John Page died in 1890, Sir John A. Macdonald offered Rubidge the position of chief engineer of the Department of Railways and Canals, but he declined the offer, preferring to devote his remaining years to the improvement of the St Lawrence River canals. He was also offered an appointment by the Panama Canal Company as one of its consulting engineers, and in 1903 he was invited to accept the position of consulting engineer for construction of the New York barge canals. Rubidge declined both offers. A Conservative, he was one of the few superintending engineers to hold his job after the defeat of Tupper's government by the Liberals in 1896 – a clear indication of the high regard in which he was held by both parties. In recognition of faithful service, the Canadian government presented him with a special medal, and the Ontario government made him a grant of land in northern Ontario.

On 21 June 1904, at the age of 77 and while still in active service with the Department of Railways and Canals, Rubidge died of sclerosis. He was buried in Woodlawn Cemetery in Cornwall, Ontario. His widow, Emma (née Carman), survived him by 12 years; she had borne him two daughters, one of whom died in infancy.

Engineering prowess and long and loyal service to the nation notwithstanding, Rubidge had a personality aberration that landed him in serious trouble on the Trent, where, because of the politically sensitive nature of the superintendency, his duties required more tact and diplomacy than engineering expertise. His political naïveté cost him the

Trent superintendency and put a black mark on his record, but his engineering ability saved his career.

It is not clear why Rubidge persistently displayed poor public relations, particularly in his home town of Peterborough. Whether his erratic behaviour was an early symptom of the diseased nervous system that eventually brought on the sclerosis, or whether his "cussedness" was simply a function of unhealed emotional scars of a young orphan, will probably never be known. Whatever the cause, Rubidge rarely enjoyed close relationships, a posture he seemed determined to maintain even after death. It was probably not by chance that his remains and those of his wife, Emma, and daughter Mary occupy only three grave sites in the centre of a 32-grave plot purchased by Rubidge in 1833. Their tombstone stands apart, surrounded by a sea of grass that separates it from the thousands of other closely positioned grave markers in the now filled-to-capacity Woodlawn Cemetery, ensuring that Rubidge lies in death as he moved in life – with a good deal of distance between him and his nearest neighbour.

Tom S. Rubidge had been given three responsibilities on the Trent valley canal between 1881 and 1888: to superintend construction of the works at Burleigh, Buckhorn, and Fenelon Falls, to supervise the digging of the Murray Canal,[9] and to undertake a thorough survey of the proposed Trent canal. Many believed that Rubidge had a fourth responsibility: as an agent appointed by the government to kill the canal scheme. This canard – the suggestion that Rubidge was an agent provocateur planted by Macdonald to arouse opposition to the canal – was repeated frequently during the five years between 1882 and the publication of his survey report. Rubidge's personal unpopularity, coupled with his constant ridicule of the proposed canal, added credibility to the rumour. When the survey was finally released with its astronomical – some claimed deliberately inflated – estimate of cost, people were convinced that the rumour had been true.

The dominion election of 1887 produced one of the most vicious campaigns in Peterborough's history. The main issue became Rubidge. As the election approached, the Trent Valley Canal Association, never entirely idle, increased the tempo of its efforts. In 1885, memorials seeking parliamentary appropriation for the prosecution of more works on the canal were forwarded to Ottawa from every municipality along the route. The association also sent a deputation to Ottawa in March to urge the government to place a sufficient sum in the estimates to begin active operation on three new sections of the canal: Balsam Lake to Lake Simcoe, Lakefield to Peterborough, and Glen Ross to Trenton. But nothing was done.

The resumption of work at Burleigh Falls in the autumn of 1885 eased the pressure on local politicians somewhat, and for a time the activity of the association subsided. Then, on 10 February 1886, taunted by a deriding *Examiner* – "They [the local members] sat dumb in the House while the government submitted and the House voted half a million dollars for deepening the Welland Canal"[10] – and encouraged by support from communities at the west end of the route – the Barrie *Northern Advance* now strongly supported the canal, and the towns of Barrie and Orillia and the village of Midland had added memorials to the flood of petitions descending on Ottawa – the association called another meeting in Peterborough, attended by over 60 delegates from 22 municipalities between Trenton and Midland, to prepare for yet another apostolic journey to Ottawa. Armed with a resolution, unanimously approved at the meeting, and inspired by the considerable rhetoric of the politicians present, a large deputation headed by the association's chairman, Roland C. Strickland, went to Ottawa on 10 March "to impress upon the government in the strongest manner the necessity of entering upon the work of the completion of the new sections of the Trent Valley Canal."[11] Although advised in advance that his presence at the meeting with the minister "would carry prestige, the deputation being a strong mix of political texture,"[12] Macdonald, suffering from one of his frequent illnesses, declined to attend. Those members of the government who did meet the group gave it a full and sympathetic hearing, and Pope promised that $350,000 would be placed in the estimates in the next session of Parliament. But this promise was a sham, the "sum" representing no more than the amount needed to pay for the works already under construction; however, an ecstatic Strickland reckoned that it "would result beneficially from a party point of view."[13]

Despite Strickland's apparent optimism, it was becoming increasingly clear that the government was not going to make a commitment to extend the work before the upcoming election. Rubidge was blamed for this. The more antagonistic towards the canal he became, the more suspect his motives. Conservative canal promoters now saw Rubidge as the villain in the piece, a subversive, a traitor in their midst. It was not the government, not the minister, not Macdonald, but Rubidge, who was engineering the canal's delay. The suspicions were not entirely groundless. Cutting from the Peterborough *Review* a copy of the resolution that had emanated from the 10 February meeting of the Trent Valley Canal Association, Rubidge scribbled a sarcastic refutation beside every point made and sent it to John Page just before the arrival of the deputation in Ottawa in March. So great was the antipathy towards Rubidge that businessmen throughout the district condemned him, the press vilified him, and politicians sought his dismissal.

The first person to try to get Rubidge was Roland C. Strickland, the most conniving of all the canal promoters. Not daring to challenge

Rubidge's suitability for the superintendency with a charge of technical incompetence, he sought to undermine the government's confidence in him on partisan political grounds. To this end, he wrote an incriminating letter privately to Sir John A. Macdonald just three days after the 10 February meeting of the association, at which time Rubidge's alleged transgressions were undoubtedly discussed. "I trust you will excuse my troubling you but as I occupy the position of President of the Liberal-Conservative Association in this district and up to the present time have always succeeded in giving the Conservative candidate a large majority,"an ingratiating Strickland began his letter. Then, slithering up to an indictment of Rubidge, he wrote: "I think it would only be right and due to myself and the party to point out to you the difficulties I have to contend with and I am satisfied if they are not removed that the result of the next election will not be very satisfactory." Finally, the charge: "They arise from the course pursued by the Chief Engineer on the Trent Valley Works in employing all reformers on those works and it would appear systematically refusing appointment to conservatives." "Conservatives have not received their share of the patronage," he charged. "There are many other acts of the Chief Engineer that compel us to think that he is opposed to the Conservative Party and which would tell very much against the party at the next election,"[14] Strickland concluded. A list of names of employees alleged to be Reformers hired since the work began was appended to the letter. But it was all a fabrication.

A concerned Macdonald turned the letter over to John Henry Pope, who sent his spies to investigate. They found none of the names on Strickland's list in any government records. "I do not know where Mr. Strickland got his information or where he finds his men, [as] none of the names mentioned appear on our paylist," Pope informed Macdonald. Rubidge was a "dyed-in-the-wool tory ... unlikely to strain a point to oblige the opposite party," and Mr Rogers, who employed a gang of men on booms, slides, and repairs under the Department of Public Works, "was recommended to all our friends not only in Peterborough but elsewhere," Pope assured Macdonald. Not one of the names appeared on Roger's paylist, either. "We know nothing of these men or who hired them," Pope reiterated. But one thing was certain: "Neither Mr. Rogers nor Mr. Rubidge [was] likely to have employed the men to whom [Strickland] referred."[15]

Macdonald pointed out the discrepancy to Strickland, who confessed that his "reformers" had really been hired by the contractors Goodwin and Charles Wynn, over whom, he admitted, Rubidge had no control. But some of the men had been engaged in building houses for Rubidge and Aylmer at Burleigh. Conservatives had been complaining to Strickland that preferences on government work were being given to Reformers. "I thought ... that if Mr. Rubidge had been a true friend of the party he would have acted differently,"[16] a sulking Strickland terminated the correspondence.

Strickland and his cronies tried a different tack to get rid of Rubidge, who by now was a definite political liability, as the Liberals in the district were not only blaming Rubidge for the absence of government policy on the Trent but, encouraged by the *Examiner*, were claiming that a Liberal government, if elected, would build the canal. Strickland and his friends concocted a bizarre strategy to link Rubidge with the provincial election held on 26 December 1886, even though construction of the Trent canal had absolutely nothing to do with provincial politics. It was hoped that if provincial Conservatives lost some ground because of Rubidge, other people would join the crusade to get rid of him, and Macdonald might be forced to listen to reason. Accordingly, one week before the provincial election a petition, signed by 40 Conservatives at Lakefield and 30 supporters in North Smith and seeking the immediate removal of Rubidge, was sent to the Department of Railways and Canals. As expected, the petition was not granted. In protest, none of the signatories voted in the provincial election; they made public their reasons for abstaining.

The strategy worked, perhaps even better than the strategists had intended. The provincial Conservative organizers in Peterborough West had predicted a slim margin of victory for their candidate, John Carnegie, even conceding all the Catholic votes in the riding to the Liberals. But *Examiner* publisher James Stratton defeated Carnegie with a small majority. The 70 Conservative abstentions in Lakefield and North Smith had made the difference. As hoped for, the defeat of Carnegie made dominion Tories nervous. Rubidge was blamed for the defeat, and dislike for him grew more intense. The feeling spread. It was worked up in Peterborough, Hastings, and Victoria, gaining ground daily. Letter after letter and petition after petition, asking for Rubidge's dismissal, were sent to Macdonald and other members of the government. A number of the best Conservative workers and strongest supporters vowed not to vote for the party unless Rubidge were removed. A panicky C.S. Malers, political hack in Peterborough, wrote directly to the national party predicting a catastrophe in the coming dominion contest if Rubidge were not removed at once. While admitting to a liking for Rubidge's family, Malers nevertheless pointed out that there was "no disguising the fact that his retention in office may mean the loss of 2 or 3 perhaps more seats to the party."[17] "What with the post-office and the Temperance business, we have quite enough to fight about without having Rubidge's sins to answer for,"[18] Malers lamented.

The message, which was passed on to Macdonald, was clear: if he hoped to hold the seats along the Trent in the election now set for 22 February, Rubidge would have to go. Reluctantly, despite a generous intervention made on Rubidge's behalf by D.R. Murphy of Trenton, Macdonald relieved him of the Trent superintendency on 9 February. The position was given to David Stark, which pleased the Trent canal promoters very much, especially a jubilant Roland Strickland.

In the mean time, Rubidge, a sensitive man despite his blustering ways, had cracked under the relentless diatribe and bolted. Not even his wife knew where he had gone. She wrote a touching letter to Macdonald, "so excited over the injustice of the whole thing,"[19] pleading with Macdonald to use his "acknowledged kindly and considerate disposition" to ensure that her husband be "fairly and justly dealt with and restored to his position which he had hitherto so faithfully filled."[20] Macdonald promised Mrs Rubidge that he would speak to Pope about the matter.

Strickland's spirits were dampened somewhat when Greenwood began circulating a report that Stark's appointment was only a blind and that Rubidge would return as chief engineer after the 22nd. Strickland wired Macdonald on the 19th, asking for confirmation of Stark's appointment as "Burnham's and Stevenson's elections largely hing[ed] on this."[21] Macdonald wired back: "Stark's appointment is permanent."[22] But it was too late, at least for John Burnham.

Macdonald won the 1887 election with a solid majority – 128 to 87 – but his Trent canal policy lost him seats in the Midland District. James Stevenson, who replaced retiring George Hilliard as the Conservative candidate in Peterborough West, managed to hold the riding with a majority of only 16 votes, but Liberal John Lang defeated John Burnham in Peterborough East. Victoria North (which included Fenelon Falls and Bobcaygeon), Northumberland East, and Hastings East all fell to Liberals.

After the election, John Page sent Rubidge back to Peterborough in mid-March to complete his survey. Feeling somewhat vindicated, Rubidge informed a perplexed Mr Wade, Goodwin's foreman at the Burleigh works, that "reports circulated to the effect that he had been removed from the works ... were utterly false,"[23] that he had left Peterborough the previous winter on private business, but now that he was back he was in full charge and Greenwood would be looking after things at Burleigh on his behalf. As for Belcher and Aylmer, since they had moved out of his office, they had no further connection with the work; Wade was to pay no attention to them. None of this was true. Stark was officially in charge. But because he was busily engaged in superintending construction on the Ottawa River canals, he was not able to move to Peterborough at once. Moreover, since the work at Burleigh was winding down and since no other construction was planned for the Trent system there was no call for his presence in Peterborough; he relied a good deal on the judgment of Aylmer, who kept him posted almost daily on the progress of the work as well as on the activities of Rubidge who, on his own initiative, gradually assumed full control of the work. If Page knew about this, he seems not to have cared.

Rubidge's behaviour became even more obnoxious after his return. His vengeance was now directed primarily against Aylmer, Belcher, and Fuller, whom he considered to have betrayed him during the election vendetta. He locked up government canoes and tents, so that these engineers had difficulty getting around the works. He removed the surveying equipment from the construction sites, permitting only Greenwood to have access to it. When at Stark's request Aylmer moved out of Rubidge's office in February, to establish a new headquarters on George Street, he broke into Rubidge's desk, seized the plans and working drawings for the locks that Rubidge had guarded so carefully, and took them with him. When Rubidge returned, he charged Aylmer with break and entry. Aylmer countered with a libel suit against Rubidge. Next Rubidge precipitated a fist fight with Fuller over a property boundary dispute. Being the older man, Rubidge came off second best, receiving severe blows about the head. He pressed a charge of assault against Fuller, who was convicted and later fired. The "respectable ditch" had taken on an aura of disrespectability, particularly because of the engineering staff, whose brawling made the politicians' battles over the canal seem mild by comparison.

Meanwhile, the Trent Valley Canal Association continued its relentless pressure on Macdonald for extension of the canal. Hoping to influence Macdonald because of recent Conservative election losses, former MP George Hilliard and others sent a petition to the government in the wake of the election, asking that the Trent valley works be continued. Page sent the petition to Rubidge for his opinion. After meticulously and expertly refuting every argument put forward by the petitioners, Rubidge not surprisingly wrote: "This enormous expenditure involved in perfecting even our local navigation throughout and its more than doubtful advantage as a Dominion work deter me from recommending the expediency of undertaking the completion of the Trent Valley Water Route."[24]

The association became truly alarmed when John Henry Pope announced in the House on 1 June that the government was intending to appoint a commission to examine the Trent valley canal proposal. Determined to prevent the appointment of the commission, the association sent a deputation to Ottawa on 15 June with the strongest-worded petition yet. Comprised of both Liberals and Conservatives, the deputation met with Sir John A. Macdonald and some of his ministers in the Railway Committee Room.

Regarding the commission, the deputation registered its protest: "All who appear before you to-day feel that this great scheme will be jeopardized or at least thrown back by the appointment of the proposed commission, leaving new works in abeyance until a report is made." After further chastising Macdonald and his ministers for reneging on "past assurances," the delegation concluded with the customary urging "to place a substantial sum in the supplementary estimates ... for placing under contract a new section of the canal."[25]

After the election of 1887, Macdonald's attitude towards the Trent canal had hardened. Having made no promises and voted no new funds for further construction before the election, he felt no obligation to the canal promoters after 22 February. Neglecting the Trent had cost him some Trent canal seats, and the Conservative majority had been reduced in others, but support for his National Policy had held most of the seats in the Midland District and had given him a strong mandate nationally. Now, God willing, he would be in office for the next four years. He did not need the Trent. Yet the canal was obviously an important issue in central Ontario. It had been useful in the election of 1882. It might be needed again. Therefore it must be preserved, put on ice, not buried. The proposed Trent valley canal commission offered the best way to accomplish this. He would push on with the commission despite the objections of the Trent Valley Canal Association, but he needed a reason for doing so. The most obvious reason was cost, which Rubidge had intimated would be enormous, much more than Baird and more than Stark had recently estimated. But where was Rubidge's damned survey? It was promised for 20 August.

John Page telegraphed Rubidge about the report on 1 September: "Minister pressing for report ... When will it be here?"[26] Rubidge wired back: "Have been beaten and my head injured by Fuller ... may be some time before I can continue office work."[27] By 5 November he was still unable to work steadily in his office but was doing all he possibly could to complete the maps and graphs for his report. Finally, on 15 November he submitted the report to Page. It was a shocker. It produced, in fact, the reaction the government wanted.

"THOMAS S. RUBIDGE'S DISCOURAGING REPORT – A DOCUMENTARY DAMPER ON THE SCHEME,"[28] the *Examiner* headlined its criticism of the report. "When we consider that Mr. Rubidge was practically verifying Mr. Baird's report as to a great portion of the route, the public, I think will agree with me that some years of labour and a good deal of money have been wasted,"[29] John Burnham, still smarting over his election defeat which he attributed to Rubidge, wrote in a letter to the editor. Other provincial newspapers commented on the report, condemning or supporting it depending upon the paper's political leaning. Thus the report created the controversy that Macdonald needed to justify the commission that had been appointed even before the report was finished.

The most controversial aspect of Rubidge's report was, of course, the estimate of cost. Based on a route that closely followed Baird's recommended route, with the exception of the western outlet (Rubidge proposed an outlet from Lake Couchiching by way of the North River to Waubaushene on Matchedash Bay), the cost was estimated to be $8,684,650. This figure did not include claims for land damages and riparian rights, buoying, and dredging or the amount already spent on the works nearing completion on the Kawartha Lakes. Rubidge's plan called for 83 locks – 71 in addition to the 12 already built or under construction – and 58.69 miles of dug canal to supplement the natural waterways. The total lockage would be 850.50 feet. The scale of navigation would be adapted to barges not exceeding 250 tons when loaded, that is, for locks 134 feet long by 33 feet wide with a 5-foot depth of water over the mitre sills. The prism of the canals would be 50 feet wide on the bottom and 6 feet deep.

In transmitting Rubidge's report to the secretary of the Department of Railways and Canals, John Page added the following estimates: for isolated works consisting of partial improvements of the intermediate stretches, $200,000, for land damages and claims for riparian rights, based on recent claims, $450,000; for the works nearing completion on the Kawartha Lakes, $650,000. The real cost was therefore estimated to be $9,984,500 – a far cry from Baird's estimate of $2.5 million, confirmed by Stark in 1880 and the figure to which the canal promoters were still referring.

As for the alleged advantages of the Trent route over the Welland, there were none, according to Rubidge. True, the distance from Waubaushene to Kingston by way of the Trent was 235 miles shorter than the distance from Sarnia to Kingston through the Welland, but the time of transit was estimated to be eight hours less by the latter route, the necessity of reduced cruising speed and additional time consumed by the great number of lockages on the Trent working to its disadvantage. John Page added a further consideration to Rubidge's calculations: a vessel travelling by the Welland route could carry a cargo six or seven times larger than could be carried by vessels suited to the Trent canal. All told, if Rubidge's calculations and cost estimates were accurate, it was hard to justify the Trent route over the Welland in terms of transportation advantages.

David Stark added fuel to the controversy by entering the debate, although as a government engineer he might have been advised to keep his mouth shut. Perhaps because Rubidge's estimate was so different from his own that it implied criticism of his professional competence (there was a good deal of jealousy among the engineers in the Department of Railways and Canals), or perhaps because he feared that the report would ruin the Trent canal scheme, over which he was still superintending engineering – a job he no doubt wanted to keep – Stark rejected Rubidge's estimate and submitted a new report of his own. Following the Severn River route (which he had never seen), using a slightly different style of construction and basing his report on data provided by Aylmer, Stark came up with a canal plan that would require nine fewer locks than Rubidge's plan and only 28 ¾ miles of dug canal. Allowing an average of $32,250 per lock and $10,000 per dam and a total of $640,000 for canal excavation, $42,000 for waste and supply weirs, and $218,000 for contingencies, Stark estimated the cost of construction at $3 million. Adding 15 per cent for engineering and $550,00 for "Riparian Rights and all the rest of it,"[30] he arrived at a total cost of no more than $4 million.

Whatever Stark's motives for challenging Rubidge's figures, he gave the government a second set of estimates vastly different from Rubidge's; yet both reports were made by engineers in the same department. Under the circumstances, who could criticize the government's decision to appoint a commission of inquiry?

Healey Falls before
construction of the locks,
showing remains of timber
slide, c. 1900.
(PAC/ACC 14390-17)

CHAPTER SIXTEEN

The Trent Valley Canal Commission

The idea for the Trent Valley Canal Commission originated with James Stevenson. An old friend of Macdonald's and one of the shrewdest politicians to serve Peterborough West, Stevenson, following his election victory in 1887, served simultaneously as mayor of Peterborough, chairman of the board of education, and member of Parliament. Although a supporter of the canal, Stevenson had a realistic appreciation of the dilemma confronting the government because of it: local politicians, in both parties all along the line, were vigorously promoting the scheme, but the rest of the country, including most of the government's own engineers, was opposed. Stevenson was also well aware of the unreliability of the canal as a local political issue: Burnham had lost his seat and Stevenson had barely squeaked past George A. Cox by only 16 votes, because of Macdonald's lack of policy for the Trent. A commission, Stevenson reasoned, would serve two purposes: it would cool the issue for a time (the disgraceful performance of the engineering staff during the spring and summer was keeping the political pot boiling), and a commission would give the government an independent opinion on the merits of the canal, in place of the impassioned arguments of politicians and the equally emotional opposition of the government engineers. After the election, Stevenson had discussed the possibility of a commission with John Henry Pope, who expressed a keen interest; then in September, sensing that "the season was now sufficiently advanced for such a commission to make an intelligent examination of the route," he wrote to Pope recommending its early appointment, "to enable it to get to work without delay."[1]

Macdonald liked the idea of a commission and indeed had been working on it, having written in July to those men whom he wished to appoint. He selected the commissioners carefully. There were two engineers – Frank Turner of Toronto and John Kennedy of Montreal – and Judge Clark of Cobourg. Turner, a hydraulic engineer, had formerly acted as consulting engineer to the Huron and Ontario Ship Canal Company, and John Kennedy was chief engineer of the Montreal Harbour Commission and a frequent appointee to royal commissions dealing with waterways and water powers. Judge Clark was not able to serve; he was replaced by Judge Weller of Peterborough, who "was appointed chairman [so] that he, as a legal man, might marshall the evidence."[2] Dr Oliver was named secretary. The commissioners were paid $20 per day plus expenses. Stevenson's September letter jogged Macdonald's memory, and the commission was established by order-in-council on 8 October 1887.

The announcement of the commission aroused bitter resentment along the Trent. Many thought the government had established it "to give them an opportunity to get out of the work."[3] Individually the commissioners were perceived as being antagonistic towards the Trent canal, and so even before the commission met, the Liberal opposition was predicting that it would report against going on with the canal. This was a natural assumption given the government's reluctance to commit itself to more construction during the election campaign of 1887 and because the commission had been given virtually no power, it not being a royal commission in the truest sense. Its terms of reference were extremely vague: "to consider the question of further extending the line of water communication between Lake Huron and Lake Ontario, and to determine whether any other local works are necessary and whether it is advisable that an extension of the main work should be undertaken.[4] The power of the commissioners was strengthened somewhat in January 1888, with an order-in-council authorizing them "to hear evidence under oath,"[5] but a suggestion that the government pay a per diem and travelling expenses for witnesses was rejected, because "it would open the door to a great many frauds."[6]

Disappointment over the establishment of the commission notwithstanding, the Trent Valley Canal Association readied itself to meet the issue head-on. Forty representatives from municipalities along the route of the canal met in the council chambers in Peterborough on 15 December, "for the purpose of devising the best method of placing before the commission ... undeniable evidence of the canal's usefulness and comparatively small cost."[7] A committee consisting of the mayors of the towns and wardens of the counties was set up "to place the required evidence before the commission."[8] John Carnegie was named secretary and convenor. Subsequently, the committee asked the municipalities to make an appropriation to defer the cost of collecting and presenting the evidence: Peterborough and Victoria counties were each asked to contribute $1,000; Simcoe county was asked for $500, and the smaller counties of Hastings, Northumberland, and Durham combined were asked for a total of $500. Richard B. Rogers, now superintending engineer of the Trent canal, having been asked to provide evidence of a sufficient supply of water, submitted a detailed calculation that rebutted the long-time criticism that there was not sufficient water in the system to sustain the dimension of canal contemplated. Rogers estimated that the 50 square miles of reservoir lakes in Haliburton could store 8.4 billion cubic feet of water per year. Allowing 44,000 cubic feet of water per lockage and 100 lockages per day over a 200-day navigation season, the maximum annual consumption of water would be 880 million cubic feet, leaving 7.5 billion cubic feet in the storage reservoirs – a surplus greater by millions of times than what was required for the canal and that still left plenty for all the water power that would ever be needed. "The canal's supply [of water] is assured,"[9] Rogers stated emphatically.

The Trent Valley Canal Association had plenty of time to muster its evidence, the commission being in no hurry to hold hearings, and it certainly was not being pressured by Macdonald, who did not want a report any sooner than necessary, preferably not until after the next election. Not until 1 April 1888 was the first meeting held in Montreal, at which time the commissioners laid out their plans for the study and took the first evidence from forwarders in Montreal. The Barrie *Northern Advance*, naïvely expecting a report in the 1888 session of Parliament, complained about the commission being "so slow to move on this important matter."[10] But the *Northern Advance*, along with everyone else, would have to be patient; it was not until nearly two years after the Montreal meeting – 26 March 1890 – that the commission got around to taking evidence in Barrie. Persistently, during every session of Parliament for the next three years, John Barron, Liberal member from Victoria North, asked if the commission had yet made a report to the government, and each time Sir John A. Macdonald, who, after the death of John Henry Pope in November 1889, assumed the Railways and Canals portfolio, replied that no report had yet been received.

The continued tardiness of the commission precipitated some angry exchanges in Parliament. On one occasion, Macdonald was obliged to intervene to defend the reputations of the commissioners (and the government), who were accused by Barron of participating in a conspiracy to permit the government to back out of election pledges to complete the canal. Conservative members Stevenson and Hudspeth, who seemed to be wearying of the canal, consistently supported the government's decision to appoint the commission.

One of the reasons for the commission's delay in making its investigation was that John Kennedy became inflicted with a serious eye ailment and went to England for several months of treatment. Macdonald did not consider it prudent to replace him. When they were finally able to get to work, the commissioners had an enjoyable time. They went over the whole route of the canal, travelling by steamer from Peterborough to

Healey Falls and from Lakefield to Fenelon Falls and Lindsay. They also visited the Erie Canal and talked to authorities there. Testimony was taken in Montreal, Kingston, Toronto, Collingwood, Midland, Barrie, Orillia, Lindsay, Peterborough, Trenton, and Desoronto. A 24-item questionnaire, soliciting opinions on the merits of the proposed canal in relation to its cost and the effect it would have, if any, on the traffic in the St Lawrence River canal system and the railways, was circulated widely throughout the country. The few responses to the questionnaire were interpreted by the commissioners as lack of interest in the canal by the general populace. Most of the information that the commissioners did receive came from the delegations who met with them at the several places visited along the route, much of it compiled by the Trent Valley Canal Association. It was hardly unbiased data.

Macdonald had mixed feelings about the not too strongly worded recommendations made in the commissioners' report. "Some further enquiry is necessary,"[11] he wrote in the report of the minister of railways and canals for 1890. By recommending that "an extension of the main work should be undertaken by completion, as soon as convenient and practicable, of the work necessary to give continuous navigation from Balsam Lake to the Bay of Quinte,"[12] the commissioners gave the lie to the accusation that they had been appointed to kill the scheme, but this recommendation would give encouragement to those who were persistent in their efforts to secure the entire canal. Pressure on the government would likely continue. The commissioners were non-committal about the desirability of extending the line through to Georgian Bay and, indeed, avoided any reference to the question of national advantage to be derived from the canal, although a strong case had been made for the national character of the work in the 1,700 pages of testimony that the commissioners recorded. The recommendation to complete the Balsam Lake – Bay of Quinte section was made purely on the basis of local benefits: it would "increase the value of the works already constructed ... assist and develop the industries along its route and open up the resources of the country through which it would pass."[13] This being the case, it could be argued that the waterway was more properly a provincial work than a dominion one; Ottawa could have been justified in refusing to continue construction on those grounds.

Only an oblique reference was made to the western outlet. Probably reflecting Turner's earlier interest in the Huron and Ontario ship canal, and the possibility that Barrie and Collingwood made stronger representation than Orillia and Midland, the Lake Simcoe – Nottawasaga River route was suggested as more satisfactory and judicious than the Lake Couchiching – Matchedash Bay route proposed by Rubidge. A survey of the former was recommended, in order to determine the respective merits of the two routes – "should that section be built."[14] The Severn River outlet was not mentioned.

The commissioners accepted Rogers's calculations of water supply, offering the opinion "that this has been established beyond question."[15] It was suggested that a saving in construction cost could be realized by reducing the width of the locks from 33 feet to 23. The practice of building 33-foot-wide locks on the Trent was started by Nichol Hugh Baird, who adopted the standard set for the Rideau Canal, where locks had been planned to accommodate side-wheel steamers; they were now no longer needed. The commissioners suggested that further savings might be made by constructing hydraulic "lift locks" and recommended that the possibility be investigated. This recommendation probably originated with Turner also, as he had recommended hydraulic lift locks as the best means of building a canal through the Oak Ridges moraine in a report to the Huron and Ontario Ship Canal Company in 1879. (It was probably this recommendation that later gave Rogers the idea for the Peterborough lift lock.)

All told, the commissioners' brief report was a masterpiece of obfuscation, giving plenty of leverage to the canal's promoters, but also providing the government with enough loopholes through which to escape further commitment to the scheme, if it so wished. The report was submitted to Macdonald on 17 December 1890, while Parliament was prorogued. He kept it until a more propitious moment for its release, being fully aware that in politics, as in telling a joke, timing is all important.

The election in the winter of 1891 was Macdonald's last. When presenting the election writ for the governor-general's signature on Monday, 2 February, Macdonald had many more important national problems on his mind than the Trent valley canal. But on 3 March, just two days before polling day, the report of the commissioners would be uppermost in his thoughts, prompting him to send a telegram from his sick-bed in Kingston which, while securing the election of his followers along the Trent, would also commit his successors to an extension of the canal. With the sending of the telegram – one of Macdonald's last partisan political acts – the eventual completion of the Trent canal would be assured.

The main issue of the election was unrestricted reciprocity with the United States. The Liberals supported it; Macdonald opposed it, believing, as he always had, that reciprocity presented a fundamental threat to Canada's economic autonomy and political independence.

On the same night that the governor-general signed the election writ, Macdonald began to draft his election theme – the now-famous "A British subject I was born, a British subject I will die" oration that was delivered at a Conservative rally in Toronto on 17 February. "The question which you will shortly be called upon to determine," he told his audience, "resolves into this: shall we endanger our possession of the great heritage bequeathed to us by our fathers, and submit ourselves to direct taxation for the privilege of having our tariff fixed at Washington, with a prospect of ultimately becoming a portion of the American Union? ... As for myself, my course is clear. A British subject I was born, a British subject I will die."[16]

Two pieces of good fortune assisted Macdonald in the election campaign. First, his arch-enemy Edward Blake, who had resigned the leadership of the Liberal party in favour of Wilfrid Laurier in 1887, agreed with Macdonald; Blake, too, opposed unrestricted reciprocity as being dangerous to Canada. Many other leading Liberals sided with Blake, thus dividing the Liberal troops. Then, on the eve of the Toronto address, by a stroke of good luck, Macdonald had delivered into his hands a pamphlet written in secret by Edward Farrer, an ardent annexationist and editor of the Toronto *Globe*, the leading opposition newspaper in the country. The pamphlet, directed towards an American audience, suggested several methods of economic retaliation by which the United States could bring the citizens of Canada to their knees: tactics such as the imposition of tonnage duties on Canadian vessels, suspension of bonding privileges in the United States, and the cutting of connections with the CPR at Sault Ste Marie. "The document points out every possible way in which Canada and its trade can be injured, and its people impoverished with the view of eventually bringing about annexation,"[17] Macdonald told the Toronto audience. Waving the incriminating document in front of his stunned listeners, he charged Farrer with participating in a deliberate and treacherous conspiracy in which some members of the opposition were more or less compromised.

Through the twin appeal of anti-American sentiment and British loyalties, Macdonald was able to win the election. He wrote his own analysis of the victory in a letter to George Stephen on 31 March: "I have of course pointed out that unrestricted reciprocity meant annexation, and the movements of Cartwright, Farer and Wiman[18] enabled us to raise the loyalty cry, which had considerable effect."[19] But on 3 March, when a letter arrived from Conservative organizer D.R. Murphy of Trenton, asking Macdonald for assistance in the election of the Conservative candidates along the Trent, the outcome of the election was by no means certain.

Macdonald was 76 years old. Exhausted by the vigorous winter campaign, he had succumbed to a bronchial infection on 24 February and was confined to his bed in Kingston where, for the last two hectic weeks, he was out of touch with the electorate and had no feel for how the campaign was going. He was apprehensive above the effect of the new US McKinley tariff. Farmers in southern Ontario, where the barley trade was in danger of being ruined because of the tariff, were deserting the Conservative cause, "unrestricted reciprocity," as Macdonald put it, "having got hold of them."[20] He had no knowledge of what effect the tariff was having in the Atlantic region either, or the appeal of reciprocity, but he feared the worst. "The effect of the McKinley tariff is so disastrous that if our election had been postponed until another harvest, we should have been swept out of office,"[21] he told George Stephen. There was no way of knowing what influence the popular Wilfrid Laurier was having on the rural voters of Quebec, in this, his first contest as Liberal leader. Nor was Macdonald convinced that his government, now composed of ageing ministers, would be strong enough to carry the election: "I am a good deal discouraged as to our future," he had written to Sir Charles Tupper in early June. "Not that the country has gone or is going against us, but because our ministry is too old and too long in office."[22] Illness, idleness, and frustration had clouded the old man's vision and dampened his spirits as election day approached. And so it was to an apprehensive, bedridden old campaigner that secretary Joseph Pope handed Murphy's letter on the morning of 3 March. Murphy had written:

I see the Trent Valley Canal Commission have reported favourably to the project and recommend work commence. Now if you can telegraph me that the work will be commenced this year at this end of the route and at Peterborough and that a sum will be put in the estimates for that purpose, I know of nothing that will assist more to secure Cochran and Corby's election. Please telegraph me here a favourable reply ...

If favourable, I will report telegram to Stevenson and Burnham and request them to repeat northward to Georgian Bay, all along the line. I think a favourable telegram will be of great assistance all along the route.[23]

Macdonald thought back to the election of 1872; it had been extremely close. He had crept back into office then with a majority of only 6 seats. Ten or 12 seats along the Trent could easily determine the outcome of this unpredictable election, the most important of his long career. The grant for the Trent construction had delivered nearly all the Trent seats in 1882, but he had lost many of them in 1887. He could not afford to lose any more, and, if possible, he needed the lost seats back. It was time for another grant. He dictated the following telegram to Murphy: "Trent Valley Canal Commission have reported favourably on the completion of the scheme. Parliament will be asked next session for a grant for the purpose."[24]

The next day Macdonald's health was sufficiently improved to allow him to return to Ottawa to await the election results. He did much better than he expected: 123 seats to the Liberals' 92. Congratulations poured in from all over the country. "Your telegram to me re Trent Canal did first class work," a grateful Murphy reported to him. "I ... repeated the telegram to Stevenson and Burnham and no doubt it did good service there."[25] Nine of the 13 seats bordering the Trent canal had gone to the Conservatives. Apart from York North, which touched the south shore of Lake Simcoe and was solid Mulock territory, only Victoria North, Simcoe East, and Northumberland East voted Liberal. The elections in the latter three ridings were close; they were later contested and negated, and all three were won by Conservatives in by-elections held early in 1892. Until the next election, at least, the Trent canal route was a Conservative stronghold. Ill or not, Macdonald made his considerable political instinct pay off, although, as events proved, he would still have been returned without the block of Trent seats.

"During the session no doubt a larger deputation favourable for the construction of the Trent Valley Canal will visit you,"[26] Murphy warned Macdonald. But it did not wait for the session to start. Thrilled with Macdonald's telegram and encouraged by the strong political support along the route (even Liberal members who won seats temporarily had campaigned in support of the canal) but still somewhat sceptical of the government's intentions as a result of past experiences, the Trent Valley Canal Association called a large meeting in Peterborough on 8 April, at which time another deputation "to wait on the government in reference to the Trent Canal"[27] was appointed. Since the deputation was anxious to meet with Macdonald before the opening of Parliament, James Stevenson arranged for a meeting with him and his ministers at three o'clock on 21 April. But Macdonald was not able to meet the group personally. Still not recovered completely from his illness, he spent much of his time at home in bed preparing for the opening of Parliament, called for 29 April. In fact, he was dying. Although he jested with Laurier in the debate on the speech from the throne, everyone could see how feeble he had become. On 12 May, he suffered a mild stroke from which he recovered well enough to allow him to make a brief visit to Parliament a week later. But on 29 May, he suffered another major stroke from which he did not recover. He died peacefully on the evening of 6 June 1891.

It was Hector Langevin, the minister of public works, Postmaster-General John Haggart, and Customs Minister Mackenzie Bowell who met the Trent canal deputation on 21 April. The ministers listened politely to the dreary incantation that they had heard often before and that now was supposed to charm the government into somehow finding, in the midst of a severe depression, the millions of dollars needed to extend this wondrous national work. "Yes, the government is committed to this great undertaking! Yes, the government will put a sum in the estimates to extend the canal," the weary ministers assured the deputation. Confronted with Macdonald's telegram, which had been published in every newspaper along the Trent canal route, they really had no other choice. So it was a gratified deputation that left Ottawa that night to carry the good news to its several constituencies along the route. But it would have to wait a long time yet before there was any government action on the canal.

Macdonald died without having named a successor. In the five years following his death four prime ministers – John Joseph Caldwell Abbott, John S.D. Thompson, Mackenzie Bowell, and Charles Tupper – led the badly disorganized Conservative party through one political disaster after another. Because of the prolonged period of unrest in the government, coupled with complications arising from the financial stringency of the depression and the American tariff, nothing was done about the Trent canal despite annual visits from the association to remind the government of Macdonald's promise. John Haggart, who held the Railways and Canals portfolio throughout the government's five years in office, assured the association (and Parliament) "that the policy of the Government is entirely unchanged in reference to the building of that great work."[28] The policy, of course, was that adopted by Macdonald on the recommendation of Smith in 1879 – to extend the work over several years. Haggart had already promised the Trent canal MPs that the "interlake communication" – that is, the stretch of waterway connecting Rice Lake and Lake Simcoe – would be completed first and that the work would be started at the appropriate moment. Naturally, the appropriate moment would come just before the next election.

True to a now well-established tradition, the Conservative government, in an attempt to hold the Trent canal seats, began early in 1895 to signal an intention to proceed with the canal. In the spring, surveyors swarmed over the route. At the Lake Ontario end, surveys were made through Trenton and Port Hope to create the impression that each of these towns was a possible lake terminus of the canal. Also, highly visible and much publicized surveys were made between Balsam Lake and Lake Simcoe and Lakefield and Peterborough. Rogers was instructed to prepare detailed plans for locks and canals based on these surveys, as a decision had already been made to proceed with construction on these two division at the appropriate moment. On 22 April 1895, the appropriate moment having come, a contract for $475,000 was let to Andrew Onderdonk for the first section of the Simcoe – Balsam Lake division, consisting of a canal from Balsam Lake to Kirkfield. Then on 27 August another contract was let to Messrs Brown, Love, and Aylmer for section 1 of the Peterborough-Lakefield division. This 6½-mile stretch of canal, to run between Lakefield and Nassau, was estimated to cost about $780,000. Also, arrangements were made to purchase rights of way for the two canals.

In contrast to the behaviour of Rubidge during the previous election, Rogers's activities on the local scene were carefully orchestrated to correspond to the political decisions being made in Ottawa. In addition to the surveys conducted, Rogers spoke at a meeting of the board of trade in Peterborough and at various public meetings in communities along the route, extolling the virtues of the canal and outlining government plans for it; he went to Europe to examine the hydraulic lift-locks in England, Belgium, and France to determine the suitability of this type of construction on the Trent, and he set up a laboratory in the basement of the Trent canal office for testing cement, as his plans called for concrete locks in place of the traditional limestone masonry ones. All his movements were advertised and of course were intended to demonstrate to the electorate the advantages to be gained by voting for the Conservative government. It was the same old political canal game that had been played prior to every election since 1836. But as usual the government's play-acting did not go uncriticized by the Peterborough *Examiner*: "If the canal is what it has claimed to be at every general election for the past twenty years, why has it not been completed years ago? ... Why have five years, singularly coincident with the general election, been allowed to elapse between the spurts of activity that mark the survey and construction of portions of the canal? Why ... has it been degraded into a vote-catching machine? ... Two generations have passed away since the work began and unless we can bring on a general election every six months, two more generations will pass away before the canal will be completed."[29]

The Conservative government had no intention of finishing the canal, at least not in the lifetime of the current generation, despite the surveys, the letting of expensive contracts, and the considerable pre-election rhetoric. Fellow Conservatives in Parliament continually chaffed Stephenson and Burnham about the large sums being voted for construction of what many of them called a "Frogpond." According to the *Examiner* the reason was obvious; it was because the government was using the canal "not to catch 'frogs' but votes."[30] Perhaps the clearest evidence that the *Examiner*'s perception was correct can be seen in the actions of the American Deep Waterways Commission, established by resolution of the US Congress in 1895. This commission, which included three Canadians – two engineers (O.A. Howland and T.C. Keefer) and a politician (T. Monro) – was charged with examining the feasibility of building a system of canals between the Great Lakes and the Atlantic Ocean. The commission examined the several proposed routes in both Canada and the United States, including the Ottawa River – Lake Nipissing route and the Toronto – Georgian Bay canal. Despite the Canadian government's alleged commitment to built it, the Trent was not examined and not even mentioned in the commissioners' report published in early 1896.

In the mean time, while Onderdonk and Messrs Brown, Love, and Aylmer had been proceeding slowly with the execution of their contracts, the resignation of John Haggart on 6 January 1896, with the six other ministers in Bowell's "nest of traitors," held up plans for spending the maintenance funds especially voted by Parliament for election purposes. "Things are a little mixed at Ottawa but I hope in a few days everything will be lovely again."[31] R.B. Rogers wrote to his good friend Mossom M. Boyd on 11 January. Money had been set aside for reconstruction of the Bobcaygeon lock and other major repairs on the canal every year since 1892, and the time had now come to spend it, but chief engineer Collingwood Schreiber (John Page's successor) had told Rogers not to start the work until he telegraphed him, which would be after a new minister was appointed. Rogers was also instructed to hurry up with the plans for section 2 of the Peterborough-Lakefield division, including the hydraulic lift-lock, as the government intended to award a contract for this section before the election expected in the spring. On 9 January, Sir Charles Tupper was brought back into the cabinet as secretary of state; his presence healed the rift between Bowell and his cabinet, the renegade ministers resumed their portfolios, and everything in Ottawa was soon "lovely again." On 6 February tenders were called for section 2, and on 7 May a hastily drafted contract for this section was awarded to Messrs Corry and Laverdure. Rogers was permitted to proceed with the maintenance repairs. The election campaign along the Trent canal was well under way.

But it was all in vain. Laurier won the election with 122 seats to 88 for Tupper, only recently sworn in as prime minister. Surprisingly, Laurier swept Quebec despite his stand on the controversial separate school question in Manitoba; he gained ground in Ontario and Manitoba and won increased support across the rest of the country. Although most of the Trent canal ridings remained solidly Conservative, the Liberals won two crucial seats: Peterborough East, which elected John Lang over incumbent John Burnham, and the traditional Tory stronghold of Victoria South, which returned Liberal George McHugh.

By 1 July, Laurier had named his cabinet. Parliament convened on 19 August. It was not long before the new government had visitors from along the Trent.

Collapse of the canal wall
at Peterborough that sealed
Rogers's fate, 26 January
1906. (Courtesy Roy
Studio, Peterborough)

PART FOUR

The Laurier Years: 1896–1911

CHAPTER SEVENTEEN

The Conversion of Wilfrid Laurier

Liberal politicians had been waiting for years for an opportunity to mine the rich vein of political patronage that was the Trent canal but that for a generation had been staked out by Conservatives. Laurier's victory in 1896 gave the Liberals their big chance, although only two were elected in Trent canal ridings: George McHugh, a farmer from Ops township, who won Victoria South, and John Lang, another farmer, who captured Peterborough East. Since Lang sat as an Independent-Liberal, it was into the hands of party stalwart George McHugh that the privilege of dispensing patronage fell. McHugh's immediate objective was to replace Conservative canal workers with Liberal supporters and to shift priority for government spending on maintenance and repair projects to locations and suppliers with Liberal party sanction. The sums that the Conservatives had authorized for repairs prior to the election were, therefore, immediately cut off, and work was suspended.

Superintendent Rogers soon found that he "could not get a cent to spend on anything,"[1] until the work was approved by McHugh. When repairs were authorized, Rogers was forbidden to hire anyone until "McHugh had seen them."[2] Those on Roger's engineering staff who were known to be Conservative supporters were discharged and replaced by Liberals – a common practice on most public works when governments changed, but as it had not happened in Canada at the dominion level for nearly 20 years, it was a great shock to those who suddenly found themselves out of work. The matter was raised in the House of Commons, as a consequence of which engineers were requested to report the names and positions of people who were laid off after the election. Rogers reported four: a cement tester, a timber inspector, a rodman, and a foreman – all Conservatives and all but one replaced by Liberals. The men, ranging in age from 17 to 62, were given only two or three days' notice, received no gratuity or superannuation, and were given no reasons for their dismissal. Nor did Rogers have an opportunity to select or even interview their replacements. They were hired by McHugh. Many Liberals in the district even wanted to replace Rogers, a Macdonald appointee and a strong supporter of the Conservative cause, but it would be another 10 years before the Liberals would be able to dispose of him.

As dispensing a few part-time jobs and shifting patronage to Liberal suppliers for the small amount of material and equipment consumed annually on canal maintenance provided only minimal political pay-off, it was far more important – but far more difficult – to convince Laurier and his cabinet to reverse the Liberal party's long-held antipathy to the Trent canal and to commit itself to the canal's completion. It was, after all, in the massive construction projects that the richest political profits lay. Further, the *Daily Examiner* and local Liberals had claimed for years that a Liberal government would complete the canal. The credibility of local Liberals rested, therefore, on some commitment on the part of the new government to go on with the work. Paradoxically, the local Liberals had the support of their Conservative counterparts because, as the reader must by now be fully aware, practically everyone in the Trent watershed saw himself as a potential benefactor of a through canal and was, consequently, an ardent promoter of it. During a debate in the House of Commons in June 1914, J.H. Burnham revealed how canal politics, at least in Peterborough, had for years transcended party loyalties: "It is true that there are some people amongst them [canal promoters] who belong to the Conservative party, or say they do, for political purposes or financial purposes, who transfer their allegiance when necessary to the Liberal party, and that there are members of the Liberal party who, when necessary, will transfer their apparent allegiance to the Conservative party. The two sets of men acting together, by reason of their political influence, turn the keys in the door of favouritism on the part of the leaders of both parties. That is the way the thing is worked."[3]

During the Laurier years, the mechanism by which "the two sets of men acted together" was the same Trent Valley Canal Association that had so consistently and successfully pressured the Macdonald government into reviving the canal, for, although the association's leadership was taken over by Liberals after 1896, its membership remained bi-partisan.

A large delegation from the association made a first visit to Ottawa in early October to impress upon the minister of railways and canals, Andrew George Blair, the desirability of actively pushing forward the work of the canal. But the most a not-too-enthusiastic Blair would promise was that "he would inquire well into the matter";[4] in the mean time, the work "would go no further than the present contracts."[5]

The always persuasive Trent Valley Canal Association did obtain from Blair a promise to visit the waterway, which he did soon after Parliament prorogued on 5 October. His visit was planned to the last detail, W.H. Moore being in charge of arrangements. Just as Tupper had been met 16 years earlier at Hastings and brought to Peterborough on the *Golden Eye,* so Blair was picked up there on a sunny October morning and, accompanied by a large contingent of enthusiastic citizens, was escorted to Peterborough on the steamer *City of Peterborough.* And just as Tupper had been lavishly feasted, so Blair, a former premier of New Brunswick, was also fêted with fine food and excellent wines at a grand public banquet. After dinner he was assailed by a spate of canal propaganda delivered by a host of speakers, each of whom exhorted the minister to encourage the goverment to commit itself to completing the canal. Regardless of party affiliation, each also pledged his support to the government if it would continue the work. The display of solidarity was overwhelming, especially to a New Brunswick politician who was not used to seeing strong bipartisan support for anything.

The next day Blair was taken by carriage to Lakefield, examining en route the works under construction by Brown and Aylmer. R.B. Rogers showed him the location of the hydraulic lift lock, excavation for the foundation of which was just being started by Corry and Laverdure's workmen. From Lakefield, Blair was conveyed to Bobcaygeon by Mossom Boyd and a large committee of canal promoters in Victoria county on Boyd's new steamer, the *Esturian.* The trip took them through the Ontario government's locks at Young's Point and the substantial locks built by Goodwin at Burleigh Falls and Buckhorn in the 1880's, a direct result of Tupper's visit. At Bobcaygeon, the party was elegantly entertained in Boyd's recently built mansion, situated just below the canal's first functional lock, which, although rebuilt by the Board of Works in 1857, was now in a dilapidated state, repairs authorized for it by the previous Conservative government having been cancelled by Blair's own order.

The following day the party proceeded to Balsam Lake, inspecting on the way the locks at Fenelon Falls and Rosedale. Then, following in the footsteps of Lt.-Gov. Sir John Colborne, who walked the route in 1834, having been taken there for precisely the same reason Blair had been invited, the minister was hauled by wagon as far as Gamebridge on the Talbot River. Whereas Colborne had walked along the Indian portage trail to examine the route of what was little more than a wide-eyed canal dream, Blair was able to inspect the work of Onderdonk's steam shovels as they dug their way from Balsam Lake westwards to Kirkfield on the first section of the Balsam Lake – Lake Simcoe division. The canal dream was growing much nearer to reality.

Blair boarded the Toronto and Nipissing Railway – then part of the Grand Trunk system – at Kirkfield and returned to Ottawa by way of Toronto. He was much impressed by what he had seen and heard. The natural beauty of the Trent waterway is spectacular at most times of the year, but in mid-October, when Blair saw it with its hardwoods ablaze with autumn colours, the scenery was especially appealing. The Cannington *Echo* reported Blair as saying that "he was amazed with the vastness of the water stretches over which he passed and which form the natural portion of the Trent Canal system."[6] But what Blair's conclusion would be as to extension of the work he kept to himself.

What probably impressed Blair most was the total commitment, the zealous determination to have a canal, that he witnessed in the "large number of prominent men from all points along the route"[7] who spoke to him. If there was a dissenting voice in the district, it was certainly kept well beyond earshot of Blair. Although the Liberal government's intention and as yet unannounced policy were to abandon the Trent, Blair's own objection to the canal began to weaken somewhat as a result of his tour of the waterway. Upon his return to Ottawa, he wrote to Mossom Boyd to thank him for the hospitality extended and to invite him to Ottawa for the purpose of "talking over the subject of the Trent Valley project and to get [Boyd's] views upon it."[8] But even if Blair were beginning, for obvious political reasons, to favour an extension of the Trent, promoting the merits of the scheme to Laurier and the rest of the cabinet would be another matter.

For over 60 years Liberal-Reformers, adhering to a laissez-faire political philosophy, had consistently opposed large public work schemes in general and the Trent canal project in particular. Reformers in 1836 had preferred the privately owned Cobourg Railway to a government-funded canalized Trent River; Sydenham and Killaly had killed the canal scheme in 1841; Merritt and Hincks had tried to sell the existing works to the municipalities in 1850. Liberals had encouraged the formation of the Huron-Trent Valley Canal Company in 1874, but when this private company failed to raise the necessary funds to build a canal, Alexander Mackenzie turned the works over to the province of Ontario; now Wilfrid Laurier was inclined to abandon the project, revived by Macdonald, and let the Ontario government take it up if it wished. He would have had plenty of support for this course of action because there was a good deal of opposition to the Trent development in the rest of the country. When, for example, it was learned that the Trent Valley Canal Association was soliciting the favour of the new Liberal government, Toronto newspapers launched their customary jeremiad against the Trent canal, proclaiming it to be a purely local work and exhorting the government to desist from wasting more money on it.

But the Trent canal promoters had a valid argument for their barge canal, to which the government had to at least listen. Wheat from the expanding prairie farms was piling up in western granaries for want of an adequate transportation system. It was argued that this grain could be transported more cheaply and quickly through a Trent barge canal than by any other method; this belief formed the basis of the promoters' case.

Laurier personally favoured the movement of western grain by railway and was sympathetic to railway promoters, who proposed enlargement of the railway network as the best solution to the country's transportation problems. Indeed, Laurier was already beginning to think about duplicating John A. Macdonald's achievement by constructing yet another transcontinental railroad – the Grand Trunk Pacific. Another group, headed by Laurier's minister of public works, J. Israel Tarte, and supported by the Toronto board of trade, favoured the movement of grain from the Lakehead to Montreal by water, indisputably the cheapest and, for Toronto financiers perhaps, the most profitable method. This group held the view that the country's wheat transportation problem could be solved with bigger steamships – designs for which were already on the drafting boards at Collingwood – moving through an enlarged Welland and St Lawrence canal system, but definitely not by barges through a minuscule Trent canal. Blair sided with this group.

On 22 March, Blair informed the secretary of the Toronto board of trade that the cabinet had arrived at the conclusion that the work of enlarging the St Lawrence canals should be pushed forward with utmost dispatch: "Our present expectation is that a 14-foot waterway will be available for traffic in the spring of 1899,"[9] Blair wrote to the secretary. When Parliament opened five days later and the speech from the throne committed the government to deepening the St Lawrence and Welland canals but no mention was made of the Trent, the Trent Valley Canal Association decided it was time for another trip to Ottawa.

A deputation was assembled in less than a week – a formidable task for most groups, but not for the experienced Trent canallers. The association, now under the chairmanship of J.R. Stratton, had a permanent mechanism in place for arranging such deputations quickly. The deputation that would descend on Ottawa on 5 April was, up to that time, the largest assemblage ever to converge on the capital. Representatives came from places all along the route between Trenton and Midland: reeves and mayors of dozens of municipalities, scores of councillors, dozens of businessmen and politicians – Liberals and Conservatives – including present, former, and aspiring members of Parliament. There were former Prime Minister Mackenzie Bowell from Belleville and Senator George Cox of Toronto, one of the country's leading financiers; Col. Sam Hughes and George McHugh from Lindsay, and William H. Bennett, newly elected member from Midland. The city of Peterborough sent 56 delegates, the village of Ashburnham 12; the town of Orillia sent the whole town council. There were over 270 delegates altogether, most of whom took their wives. McHugh made a special point of personally inviting Mossom M. Boyd to accompany the Victoria delegation because Boyd, although not a member of the council, was a leading citizen and had, moreover, favourably impressed Blair with his sincerity and wisdom. The Grand

Trunk Railway, although standing to lose considerable revenue if the deputation's objective were realized, co-operated by providing reduced rail fares.

Although the capital was accustomed to accommodating large crowds, the immensity of this deputation "brought consternation to the hearts of the Ottawa bonifices,"[10] the *Examiner* reported. All the reputable hotels – Russell House, the Grand Union, the Windsor, and the Brunswick – were filled to overflowing with delegates, for most of whom it was a first trip to Ottawa. They enjoyed the sightseeing, and many took advantage of the occasion to attend an evening sitting of the House of Commons where, from the visitor's gallery, they observed a debate on the merits of the proposed – and 90 years later still controversial – Crow's Nest Pass freight rates.

On the morning of 6 April, members of the deputation assembled in the rotunda of the Russell House, on the corner of Sparks and Elgin streets, where arrangements were made as to who should address the minister and the order of speaking. At half-past ten, they marched in a body from the hotel to the House of Commons. By the time the first delegates had reached the Parliament Buildings, the last of the procession were still falling into line at the Russell House door.

No mob of rowdy, placard-carrying protesters these, but serious-minded professionals and businessmen – the starched-collared, pin-striped, morning-coated crowd. They were the political élite of municipal, provincial, and dominion law-making bodies, brokers of several thousand voters in the Midland District, all, regardless of political affiliation, united in one resolve – to have the Trent valley canal. And, more important, these men held the power to deliver 16 members for any leader's parliamentary caucus.

The railway committee room, where such deputations were usually received, could not accommodate more than half of them, and so they were led into the Commons chamber, where they soon occupied all the seats; the overflow spilled into the visitors' gallery. The delegation was received by Postmaster-General Sir William Mulock and, of course, Andrew G. Blair. Conservative member William H. Bennett introduced the deputation by stating that if the government needed endorsation by the people for the Trent scheme, surely it had it in the large deputation present.

As Bennett was speaking, Wilfrid Laurier, tall and magisterial, his entrance dramatically timed, took his place beside his two ministers. No political leader in Canada ever received such a spontaneous and thunderous bipartisan ovation as this prime minister received that morning. Whether it was at that precise moment that Laurier travelled his private road to Damascus, whether it was after hearing over 30 speakers pleading for an extension of the Trent and pledging support for his government, whether it was the discovery that George A. Cox (a director of the Grand Trunk and Laurier's first senatorial appointee) and even his own postmaster-general (who was supposed to be a neutral observer but who had his own reason, soon to be revealed, for wanting the Trent continued) both supported the scheme; whether it was something he saw in the face of his incredulous minister of railways and canals, who wore a constant smile; whether it was an illusion of power felt by a novice prime minister in that sacred chamber filled to capacity that day, with all the "members"solidly united behind him on a most controversial political issue; or whether he was only pursuing the same alluring vision that had beckoned Macdonald for 20 years (a vision of 16 seats in central Ontario, all occupied by men of his own party) – whatever the reason – by the time the last speaker, ex-MP John Burnham, had finished, Laurier's conversion to the Trent canal scheme had taken place. The congregation had converted the pastor. Sixty years of official Liberal persecution of Trent canallers would come to an end.

"The government has," Laurier assured the expectant audience, "adopted the completion of the Trent Valley route as part of their policy."[11] But missed in the euphoria of the moment, probably because it was unheard over the roar of ecstacy that swept through the chamber, was Laurier's caveat: "The work will go on as rapidly as the finances of the country will permit,"[12] almost verbatim the same condition that Macdonald had offered Trent canal promoters many times in the past. And when, two days later, $650,000 was included in the estimates brought down in Parliament, Trent canal history had, indeed, begun to repeat itself. Just as the $350,000 placed in the estimates by the Conservatives a few days after a visit by the canal deputation headed by Roland Strickland in 1886 was a sham, so the Liberals' $650,000 was a deception. It, too, represented no more than the funds needed to pay for the work already under construction. Like the Conservative government's estimates a decade earlier, the $650,000 included not one cent for new contracts.

Because the Liberals adopted the same disingenous policy for the Trent canal that the Conservative government had pursued, the record of the canal's development during the Laurier years is marked by the same kind of promises, stalling devices, pressure tactics, and election-eve decisions that characterized the Macdonald era. The Liberals' policy for the Trent was, if anything, even more insidious. Certainly the architects of the policy were more mendacious than their Conserative predecessors, so that under Laurier's government Trent canal management tumbled to an all-time low in corruption and skulduggery.

When a year had passed after Laurier's policy announcement and there was still no sign of extending the canal beyond the two divisions under contract, Trent canallers did what they had always done: they drafted petitions and wrote letters. In March 1898 a shower of petitions asking for completion of the canal, sponsored by dozens of municipalities and signed by thousands of citizens, fell on Blair's desk. To supplement the petitions, the Trent Valley Canal Association published a slick, 29-page pamphlet entitled "The Trent Valley Route – The Waterway of Canada," in which 14 reasons were given why the government of Canada should push on with the immediate construction of the canal. In addition to the traditional and oft-quoted advantages that the canal was alleged to offer, a new justification, reflecting nineteenth-century Liberal entrepreneurial philosphy with a hint of twentieth-century democratic equity, was added. The canal was now billed as the "poor man's route," implying that lines of deep water navigation such as the Welland – Great Lakes route required large and costly vessels beyond the ownership of men of moderate means, whereas, on a line of barge navigation such as the Trent, anyone possessing a few thousand dollars could engage in the transportation business and compete with the carrying trade that was tributary to it. However commendable this line of argument might have been, it did not recommend itself to the business community of Toronto.

When the Toronto board of trade saw what the Trent canal promoters were up to again, it assigned its Railway and Transportation Committee the task of preparing a report to counter the arguments put forth by the Trent Valley Canal Association. A committee report was submitted to the council of the board of trade on 1 April 1898 and approved by that body on 3 April, and a copy, together with a resolution protesting against any further expenditure on the Trent, was sent to Laurier the next day.

Peterborough and other area newspapers reacted angrily to Toronto's interference. The *Daily Examiner*, in publishing the Toronto report in its entirety, editorialized: "Such a report is hardly worthy of serious consideration,"[13] In the same edition, the paper published a letter under the caption "Hog Town and the Trent." The author had written: "The Toronto Board of Trade had just discovered that this canal does not pass through Toronto and consequently it is undertaking to instruct the Dominion Government that the scheme is folly."[14] Clearly, passions had become inflamed. One whose anger was especially aroused by the board of trade's report was John Carnegie, now president of the Peterborough board of trade. Carnegie called a meeting in Peterborough in early May, to which representatives of other boards of trade in the district were invited, to devise a strategy for countering attacks by the canal's opponents and to furnish "proof that the people of the district are a unit in demanding [the canal's] early completion."[15]

As a result of the pressure that emanated from the Peterborough meeting, the government performed another hollow gesture: $600,000 for construction on the Trent canal was included in the Railways and Canals estimates tabled on 31 May. When the item came up for debate, the first critic to jump to his feet was Edmond B. Osler, a stockbroker representing Toronto West, a Conservative, a director of the CPR, and, as it happened, president of the Toronto board of trade. "Apparently this government has money to burn,"[16] Osler charged. While admitting that in opposing the canal he was going against the wishes of many of his Conservative friends, he nonetheless proceeded to lambaste the government for "spending the country's money on building a six-foot ditch ... an absolutely useless piece of public work ... that will never be of any use."[17] Then, to the amusement of the Liberal members of the House, there followed a heated exchange over the merits of the Trent canal between Osler, who spoke for the four Toronto members, and W.H. Bennett and Col. Sam Hughes, who represented all the Trent canal members. Andrew Blair was especially amused at the fiery exchange in the opposition's camp because the $600,000, some of which was a re-vote, would be spent only on the works already under construction on the Peterborough and Lakefield section, which had been let out of contract by Conservatives. Again, no money was included for new sections of the canal.

As 1898 gave way to 1899, with still no sign of government commitment to an extension of the canal, Liberal politicians began to feel uneasy. On 31 March, Richard Hall, J.R. Stratton, and Peter Hamilton wrote to Wilfrid Laurier to express their concern, Their letter was a carbon copy of the sentiment, if not the syntax, of the letter written by John Carnegie to Sir John A. Macdonald in December 1881, when Conservative politicians were concerned about the lack of action on the canal by Macdonald's government. "What can your friends say to justify this apathy?" the Liberal politicians wrote. "There is an enormous political vote along this waterway," they reminded Laurier. "If once the hue and cry is raised that you have repudiated the policy of your predecessors and that you are hostile to the scheme, what can your friends do?" they complained. "Why court trouble with hostility?" And finally, a warning: "The people have been very patient and we have all assumed your friendliness, but this condition of affairs cannot last; and as ardent supporters of the government we tell you frankly that nothing can do more service than an energetic prosecution of this work, and we as frankly tell you that we cannot justify or excuse the apparent indifference which now seems to prevail."[18]

The truth was that Laurier's "conversion" as witnessed by the huge deputation in 1897 was one more of convenience than of conviction. If he was seriously committed to the Trent valley route as part of the government's transportation policy as he claimed that day, he had certainly done a good deal of backsliding during the next two years – probably because of the malign influence of the Toronto financial community, the support of which he needed to finance his railway ventures. The best that could be done to allay the anxieties of Messrs Hall, Stratton, and Hamilton was to place another $850,000 in the estimates in July.

The $850,000, as Blair pointed out, was largely to pay government bills accumulating from the work on the existing contracts, but a small amount was for the final section of the Balsam Lake – Lake Simcoe division connecting Onderdonk's canal at Kirkfield with Lake Simcoe. No contract for this section had previously been let, but unless it were built the money already spent on the division would be wasted. There was still no indication of the government's intention to proceed with either the eastern or western outlets, even though without their construction the soon-to-be-completed 160-mile stretch of inter-lake navigation would be practically useless as well. Indeed, it appears that the government had no intention of building the expensive outlet divisions at all. In replying to a question from William Pettet, and independent MP from Prince Edward county, who asked "if the canal would be of use to the country when constructed,"[19] Andrew Blair said: "I should be sorry to say that it would not be of any use to the country."[20] Then why spend any money on it? A long debate ensued, in which Blair half-heartedly defended the action of the government in completing contracts for the letting of which it was not responsible. "The Liberal government did not initiate the enterprise but inherited it," Blair complained. The only reason the government was completing the stretch between Balsam Lake and Lake Simcoe was because there was no alternative, since the government would quite properly be reproached if it left the canal half-way finished between the two lakes. William Gibson, a hard-nosed Liberal free-trader from Hamilton, suggested that since the canal was "only a ditch at the very best"[21] the parliamentary estimate be cut in half. But the sum was approved unaltered.

The year 1900 was to see an election. As the campaign approached, without any tangible evidence of the bona fide of the government towards an extension of the canal, Liberal candidates and party supporters along the canal became despondent. It was back to business as usual, as party leaders in the several Trent constituencies prepared to square off against each other in the forthcoming contest. Conservatives and Liberals exchanged long-standing positions on the contentious Trent canal debate; it was now the Conservatives' turn to deride the Liberals for inaction. Laurier was a liar, the Conservatives charged; he had no intention of finishing the canal as he promised. The only thing he had done in four years was to continue the contracts let by the Conservatives before the election of 1896. Clearly the only hope that the canal would ever be finished lay in the return of the Conservatives to power. The ice and snow of late November 1899 that descended on the waterway, closing navigation and stopping construction, seemed to add credibility to the Conservative charges. Moreover, Ottawa had given local Liberals virtually no ammunition, not even a promise with which to counter the Conservatives' attack.

Still, it was not too late, and if the campaign were handled properly there was a good chance that the Liberals might win some Trent seats, particularly Hastings West, which included Trenton, the proposed eastern outlet of the canal. The riding had been held by the Conservatives since 1882, the incumbent being Henry Corby, a gin distiller and wine importer in Belleville, who had managed to seize the seat with a fairly substantial majority in 1891, thanks to Macdonald's famous telegram. But Corby's popularity had slipped. He had never been a strong supporter of the Trent canal and rarely spoke in favour of it in parliamentary debates. His majority had dropped to a mere 245 votes in the election of 1896, a decline that the Liberals hoped would continue in 1900. If the Liberals in Hastings West could convince Laurier to take action on the Trenton end of the canal, the opposition building up against Corby would grow and there was a good chance the voters would choose Liberal hopeful S.J. Young. The Conservatives in the riding were clearly worried about their candidate. Not being in a postion to make any promises about the Trent, the best they could do was try to buy off Liberal party workers with generous quantities of Corby's gin, "wine suppers and the best girls that is [sic] on the canal."[22]

Laurier seems to have had a miraculous reconversion about this time, for despite Blair's assertion in July that the Trent canal would be of no use to the country if constructed, Rogers was ordered to Trenton in December to survey the nine-mile section of river between Trenton and Frankford. The locations of the locks and dams were laid out, plans and specifications were prepared, and the work was advertised for tendering. It was hoped that this dramatic, last-minute decision would not only win Hastings West for the Liberals but also send a signal to all the other constituencies along the route that the Liberal government was indeed committed to the Trent valley route as part of its policy.

Six tenders were received for the Trenton section, but to everyone's consternation, especially that of the local Liberals, no contracts were let. "The tenders were held for consideration by the government," Blair admitted when asked about it in Parliament in February. But he was "not free to state to the House just what the matters [were] which [were] being considered by the government."[23]

It soon became apparent that the matter that the government was considering was the Rice Lake – Port Hope canal which, although shelved in favour of the Trent in 1836, had never been entirely forgotten by the people of Port Hope. When word got around that another survey was being made of the Trent River route by Rogers, the residents of Port Hope did what their ancestors had done in 1833, when it became known that Baird was conducting the first Trent survey: they called a public meeting, out of which grew a demand that the government consider the Port Hope route, which was alleged to be cheaper to construct than the Trent River outlet. As a result, on 11 January Chief Superintendent Collingwood Schreiber wrote to R.B. Rogers, instructing him to make a survey of the Port Hope route. "You will, of course, undertake this sevice with an unprejudiced mind,"[24] Schreiber cautioned, knowing full well that Rogers was opposed to the Port Hope route and that he, along with just about everyone else in Peterborough, was anxious to see the completion of the canal speedily accomplished.

Despite Schreiber's instructions, Rogers seems to have undertaken the survey with a prejudiced mind, for he made only a cursory examination of the route laid out by Maigny in 1834. In a report to Schreiber on 31 January 1900, Rogers, while admitting that "from an engineering point of view there did not appear to be any serious difficulties in adopting [the Port Hope] route"[25] and that it might even be found, after a proper survey, to be a little cheaper than the Trent River route, nevertheless recommended against choosing the Port Hope outlet; first, because the distance through Port Hope to Montreal would be 59 miles longer and, second, because barges travelling that route would have to pass through about 36 miles of open water on Lake Ontario. The latter was the more serious objection because, in Roger's opinion, the class of barges that was intended to navigate the Trent canal would not be able to weather storms on this open stretch of water, necessitating the transferring of grain into larger vessels at Port Hope; thus any advantage that the Trent canal might have for transporting grain would be lost. Rogers's advice made good sense if the government had any serious intention of constructing the canal as a grain route. But it had not. The Trent canal was still what it had always been – a political canal. And good sense and good politics do not necessarily mix. So Rogers was ordered to make a "proper survey" of the Port Hope route, and the contracts for the Trenton section were held up.

While Rogers surveyed, the government stalled, and the election grew nearer, Liberals in Trenton became restless. They did what Trentonians had done in 1834 when Maigny was conducting his Port Hope survey: they sent a petition – to Blair, on 16 March. They asked that the original plan for building the canal from Hastings through Trenton be adhered to. On 31 March, the Liberal-dominated Trent Valley Canal Association, fearing that the Port Hope survey would cause an unnecessary and, from a political standpoint, harmful delay, sent a report of its own to Blair. The report contained a comparison of the costs of the Port Hope and Trenton routes which definitely favoured Trenton, construction costs of the two routes being determined as $5,564,500 and $4,400,500 respectively. The association did not make clear where it obtained its figures or what basis was used for their calculation. Obviously, Blair ignored the report.

Summer came, with still no decision on the Trent River contracts. Conservatives in Trenton naturally derided the local Liberals, claiming that the calling of tenders six months earlier was only a pre-election dodge, not to be taken seriously. In July, a discouraged Joseph Bigalow, president of the Reform Club of Trenton, endeavoured to emulate D.R. Murphy's telegram strategy of 1891; he wrote to Sir Wilfrid Laurier seeking help. "If work can be started within the next two months, it will bring friends in large numbers to the support of the government that will relieve the House of Mr. Corby's presence in the next parliament,"[26] Bigalow wrote. Laurier responded immediately. He had placed Bigalow's letter in the hands of James Sutherland, acting minister in the temporary absence of Andrew Blair. "I have asked him to push the work on the Trent Canal with all possible speed. I have no doubt that he will make every effort to meet your views,"[27] Laurier promised. Unlike Macdonald's succinct telegram, Laurier's chatty letter was hardly the kind one could publish. So all the Trenton Liberals could do was wait patiently for the contracts to be let and assure the electorate that the work would soon begin. But nothing was done.

Despite Laurier's promise, Liberal election strategists decided against letting the contracts. Rogers had submitted his detailed survey report on 22 September. It showed a saving in cost of $1,032,957 in favour of the Trenton route. Several other advantages of the Trent River route over Port Hope were also listed in the report, giving the government the hard evidence it needed to justify choosing the Trent River. Contracts could have been let in plenty of time before the election set for 7 November. But the government decided not to act. Rogers's report was suppressed. No decision was announced. The choice of route was still open.

The objective, of course, was to try to win two seats: Hastings West and Durham East, in which the proposed Port Hope canal was located. It was hoped that the electors in both ridings would attempt to outvote each other to gain Liberal representation in Parliament and thus acquire a canal. But the strategy backfired. Liberals won neither seat.

Corby was returned in Hastings West with a larger majority than ever, a tribute to his splendid gin and the charms of the filles de joie in Trenton. H.A. Ward, a newcomer, captured Durham East for the Conservatives. Indeed, because of the obvious duplicity in their Trent canal policy, the Liberals lost heavily all along the waterway. George McHugh lost Victoria South to Conservative Dr A.E. Vrooman and was appointed to the Senate. Even Durham West, Edward Blake's old riding and a Liberal stronghold since before Confederation, fell to a Conservative. William Mulock kept

York North, a seat he had held for the Liberals since 1882. Strictly speaking, although the riding touched the south shore of Lake Simcoe, it was not a Trent canal seat, at least not until 1905, when an attempt was made to build a branch of the Trent canal right through the centre of the riding. Independent-Liberal John Lang managed to hold Peterborough East, but his majority fell from 615 to 174 votes. Conservatives won all the other seats.

With the election over, talk of a Trent River outlet subsided, Corby not being anxious to push it; nor did the Liberal government promote it, not wanting to spend any more money on the Trent canal than was necessary. But the citizens of Port Hope continued to press for their canal; in fact, they made the choice of the Port Hope route a major issue in the dominion election of 1904. But it would not be until 1907, 10 years after Laurier's conversion, that a decision was finally made to begin construction on the Trent River. That decision, when made, had nothing at all to do with barges or the transportation of wheat. In the mean time, work on the two divisions let out to contracts by the Conservatives in 1896 continued at a snail's pace.

CHAPTER EIGHTEEN

The Peterborough-Lakefield Division

The Peterborough-Lakefield division, when finished, would provide a navigable stretch of waterway from Little Lake to Lakefield, thus opening up a continuous line of navigation for 126 miles, from Healey Falls to Balsam Lake. Construction on the division involved canalizing a 9-mile stretch of the Otonabee River, which formed what Baird described as the "the most serious obstruction on the whole route."[1]

Engineers had long disagreed on the best method to overcome the series of rapids and falls over which the Otonabee River tumbled as it dropped 144 feet between Lake Katchewanooka and Little Lake. Baird had observed that the "high and well defined banks"[2] of the river afforded the possibility of constructing dams placed suitably far apart to create calm reaches between the rapids, the rises of which could be overcome by locks. It was a system similar to that which he advocated for canalizing the rapids between Trenton and Frankford and that had been suitably tested on the Rideau Canal. Nevertheless, Baird proposed that his canal leave the river at the upper end of Little Lake and, paralleling the west bank of the river, pass through the village of Peterborough by way of a natural ravine and a two-and-a-half-mile collateral cut to enter the river again at a spot just below the present location of Trent University. "Thus," Baird assured the lieutenant-governor, "all the mill operations would be left undisturbed, and the wicked chain of rapids avoided."[3] His plan called for following the river, on which a succession of locks and dams would be built, on the remaining five miles to Lakefield (then called Harriot's Rapids), where another cut about one-eighth of a mile long would be necessary to carry the line past the mill and rapids into Lake Katchewanooka. His proposal required six dams and 14 locks. The cost was estimated at $330,000.

Stark recommended a route almost identical to Baird's, but his plan called for 10 dams and 12 locks and was estimated to cost $550,000. Rubidge's plan called for a nine-and-a-half-mile dug canal from Ashburnham to Lakefield, leaving the river entirely so as to "avoid interference and conflict with the owners of mills and other valuable property."[4]

Rubidge's canal would have contained 13 locks but no dams. The cost was set at $1,437,814.

The route chosen by Rogers – and eventually built – was a combination of both plans. Section 1 of Rogers's plan followed Baird's proposal, requiring a series of locks and dams between Lakefield and Nassau. Four dams, five locks, considerable excavation of the river bottom, five short cuts across points of land at the bends of the river, culverts, diversion roads, and abutments for a swing bridge at Lakefield were included in the contract. Section 2 incorporated part of Rubidge's plan. The route left the river on the east side at Nassau and followed a four-mile stretch of excavated canal to Little Lake. In addition to requiring considerable excavation for the canal, the contract called for construction of a standard-type lock at the lower end of the canal, a hydraulic lift lock at Peterborough, one dam across the Otonabee River below Nassau, abutments for three highway bridges, and one high-level bridge at Nassau for the Grand Trunk Railway. Contracts for the two sections were let by the Conservatives on the eve of the 1896 election: section 1 to Messrs Brown and Aylmer of Toronto on 25 August 1895, and a hastily prepared and incomplete contract for section 2 to Corry and Laverdure on 7 May 1896.

Several innovations in lock construction, revealing the engineering genious of R.B. Rogers, were introduced on this division. First, the locks were built of concrete, replacing the limestone or wooden structures previously built on the Trent canal; second, an improved method of opening and closing the lock gates was designed; finally, the first hydraulic lift lock in North America was erected, a massive structure, also built of concrete and to this day the only one of its kind in the world.

The Romans are credited with the discovery of concrete, a composite material formed from mixing gravel, sand cement, and water. Concrete was used by the Romans in the construction of such notable buildings as the Pantheon and the Coliseum and also in aqueducts and on parts of the Appian Way. That these structures are still in existence indicates the high quality and durability of the concrete made by the Romans.

The quality of a concrete mixture depends upon the careful selection of the cement, the cleanliness of the aggregates, the purity of the water, the correct proportioning of the ingredients, and the proper mixing and laying methods. If any of these particulars is neglected, failure will probably follow, resulting in crumbled sidewalks or collapsed bridges. Ignorance of mixing methods led to many failures, causing an early prejudice against the use of concrete in engineering works. Moreover, craftsmen in the traditional building trades resisted its use; consequently the potential of concrete as a building material was slow to be recognized in the nineteenth century.

Its poor reputation notwithstanding, Rogers reckoned that locks built with concrete might be cheaper than the traditional limestone ones; thus the high cost of construction, one of the objections to the Trent canal, would be removed. And if the Roman example could be emulated, concrete locks might prove just as durable as limestone masonry structures. Rogers endeavoured to solve the mystery of concrete mixing, which seemed to have been commonplace among the ingenious Romans. Having solved the mystery, he became one of North America's leading authorities on the use of concrete in construction projects. To facilitate his research, he obtained permission from the minister of railways and canals to build a laboratory in the basement of the Trent canal office in which he tested various types of cement and different combinations of constituents.

The system of concrete mixing that Rogers adopted is known as a "dry" mix; that is, as little water as possible is used in conjunction with as much cement as is necessary. He discovered, through his testing, that a low water-cement ratio produces concrete that is reasonably watertight and abrasion-resistant and therefore more durable than concrete made with a "wet" or high water-cement ratio. Watertight concrete is absolutely necessary for lock construction, especially in Canada because of its cold winters. The absorption of water by permeable concrete will cause it to reach the critical saturation point for freezing and thawing actions that will deteriorate it. Moreover, harmful acids and salts will penetrate a porous surface, erode the cement, and further weaken the structure. Also, if the concrete is porous, pure water from rain and melting snow will slowly dissolve the soluble elements of hydrated Portland cement and weaken the structure even more.

Rogers quite accurately deduced that a dry mix concrete would minimize the risk of damage from these hazards. But a dry mix is more difficult to work with; it requires more tamping, takes longer to lay, and is therefore more costly from a construction point of view than a wet mix. Consequently, in the days before automatic mixers, contractors had a tendency to add more water to produce greater fluidity in the mass for greater speed and ease in laying. If that was done, more cement had to be used to balance the additional water so that the cement-water ratio remained the same – a fact that cost-conscious contractors often overlooked, with dire consequences.

In recommending the construction of concrete locks – never attempted in Canada before – Rogers was taking a great risk, not the least of which was the risk to his own engineering reputation if the locks crumbled. He therefore insisted that the contractors meticulously follow his prescription for mixing. To ensure that they did not scrimp on the quantity of cement in order to cut costs, Rogers arranged for the government to purchase the Portland cement under separate contracts, directly from the manufacturers, who delivered it in wooden barrels or sacks to the nearest railway siding. The contractors were responsible for hauling the cement to the construction sites, for storage and mixing, and for laying the concrete, the costs of which were included in the contract. To ensure that only suitable aggregates were used and that proper mixing and laying methods were followed, Rogers employed on his own staff a number of cement testers and sand and concrete inspectors who maintained a close watch over the concrete mixing. At least they were supposed to.

Section 1

Messrs Brown, Love, and Aylmer began work on section 1 on 19 August 1895, six days before the contract was signed. The construction plan called for cutting short canals across the bends in the river at the location of the rapids. Locks were placed in each cut, and dams to control the water levels in the reaches above the locks were built between the islands formed by the cuts and the opposite bank, slightly above each rapids. The canal cuts, which have not been changed since they were dug, range in length from about 2,000 feet at Lakefield to 500 feet at lock 22 (Nassau Mills lock). The lifts of the five locks range from 16 feet to 10 feet, overcoming 66 feet in the total drop of 144 feet in the Otonabee River. The sill depth in each lock is 6 feet. Although the locks were built wholly of concrete, Rogers seems to have been unwilling to risk building the dams of concrete. He designed ordinary timber dams with stop-log openings, but each of the dams did have walls of concrete, built along the upper face of the foundations for their entire length.[5] The substantial dam built at Lakefield by Charles Wynn 10 years earlier obviated the need for a new dam there.

In the spring of 1896, excavation for the canal and lock pit for the Otonabee lock (22) was finished. As Rogers was anxious to test his design for concrete locks, work began on this lock immediately. First, forms were built in the bottom of the pit and a floor of concrete about one foot thick was laid; the lift in the bottom of the lock was then boxed in and a concrete base laid for the upper sill. When the foundation had hardened, the false work for the lock walls was built, using two-by-eight-inch scantling with two-foot centres, covered by three-inch planed planks joined with a ship joint. The whole structure was adequately braced at both the top and bottom, so there would be absolutely no "give" in the forms when the heavy concrete was poured in. The lock walls were poured 10 feet thick at the bottom and 4 feet thick at the copings; at the lower end of the lock, the walls were 25 feet high and on the upper end about 13 feet. In all, about 5,400 cubic yards of concrete were poured into the forms, at a cost of $14,850. The concrete was poured in layers 8 to 10 inches thick and thoroughly rammed, forcing the excess water to rise to the surface. This being the first lock constructed, extreme care was taken in the selection and screening of materials, and the work was closely supervised by

Rogers's inspectors. The concrete laying was finished in mid-autumn, but the falsework was not removed until early December, allowing plenty of time for the concrete to set. Rogers was pleased with the result, but the real test lay in how well the structure would hold up over the winter.

No water was let into the canal, the lock gates not having been installed; thus the bare walls were left exposed to the harsh elements of a Peterborough winter. The following September, a jubilant Rogers reported to Collingwood Schreiber that Canada's first concrete lock "had gone through winter showing no defects whatever."[6] But this report was not quite accurate. Rogers had neglected to make provision for one important feature of concrete in his design and specifications for solid 225-foot-long lock walls: no allowance was made for the contraction and expansion of the concrete. Consequently, as Rogers himself put it in an address to the Canadian Society of Civil Engineers in January 1899, "it [the expansion] made provision for itself, and two cracks were found ... at the greatest line of weakness of each wall."[7] But the cracks were thin, only one thirty-second to one sixty-fourth of an inch wide, and no further cracks developed, the expansion and contraction always taking place at these points.

Experience with the first lock produced some changes in the method of constructing the remaining four. About one-tenth of a barrel of cement per cubic yard was added to the mix, and provision was made for the expansion and contraction of the concrete. This was accomplished by building the lock walls in sections about 40 feet in length, one section being carried up 4 or 5 feet ahead of the adjoining section by placing a plank bulkhead at the end of it. The next section was poured against the dry surface of the first section after the bulkhead had been removed. A more rapid method of constructing the falsework was also devised. The planed three-inch ship-lapped planks were spiked to six-by-six-inch posts, placed 5 feet apart and well braced. This less ponderous formation was found quite adequate for withstanding the weight of the concrete.

When a three-inch coat of mortar (in the proportion of two parts sand to one part cement) was put on all exposed surfaces, when the lock gates were hung and painted white, when the railing and other metal parts were painted black, when the ground around the locks was graded and sodded, and when the water was let into the canals, the locks proved to be not only attractive but highly functional and, time would show, quite durable.

Opening and closing heavy lock gates had always presented a problem for engineers. The first locks built on the Trent were pulled open and shut with ropes (see p. 105). The system used by the Ontario government engineers for the locks built in the 1870s was to extend the top beam of the gate some 20 feet beyond the pivot. Rudder-like, the gates were easily swung open and shut by pushing on the beam. This system was also used on the Hastings lock (p. 121). The lock gates designed by Tom S. Rubidge and built by Goodwin and Manning at Burleigh, Buckhorn, and Fenelon Falls, in the 1880s, were worked with cables fastened to each side of the outer end of the top beams of the gates. The cables were attached to winches bolted to the coping of the lock; eight sets of winches – two for each gate – were required (p. 126). Although functional, the winches were unsightly and constantly in the way. Rogers placed the winches in a recess under the coping of the lock. The wire cables were passed around a corrugated drum attached to a capstan placed in the recess. The capstans were turned by hand, with bars attached horizontally to a vertical shaft extending upwards from the capstan through an opening in the coping. Rogers intended to work the capstans with electric motors when the canal was finished. On lock 20 (Ashburnham lock), built by Corry and Laverdure in 1900, the wire cables were replaced with oak beams attached to the end of the gate and worked out and through a set of gears. Later, iron beams would replace oak beams, resulting in the system used on the Trent today. But more than half a century would pass before Rogers's vision of electrically operated gates would be realized. Indeed, many of the gates on the Trent-Severn locks are still operated by hand.

Brown, Love, and Aylmer had the contract practically completed in the summer of 1899, but they were in no hurry to finish the work totally. Until section 2 was opened, there was no urgency to open the locks on section 1. Further, the contractors, like all their predecessors dating back to 1838, were claiming underpayment for extra work done outside the specifications of the contract and were reluctant to turn the works over to the government until their claims were settled.

Rogers's gamble to construct with concrete paid rich dividends. Concrete proved to be an ideal material for lock construction, there being no joints to leak or require constant filling as in limestone masonry construction. Cement had the further advantage of costing about half as much as stone masonry. But perhaps the greatest outcome was the stimulus the Trent construction – especially the massive concrete structure for the hydraulic lift lock – gave to the cement industry in Ontario. Rogers demonstrated that concrete construction was not only cheap but, if done properly, highly functional, and his success with the material did much to overcome the prejudice against its use in engineering projects.

Section 2

The route of section 2 cut across country for about four miles, from Nassau to Little Lake at Peterborough. The rise of 78 feet in the river was overcome with two locks: one standard-type lock with a lift of 13 feet at the outlet of the canal at Little Lake and one hydraulic balance lock with an unprecedented lift of 65 feet. The contract required earth cutting and the laying of embankments for about two miles, the dredging of a two-mile flooded reach between the Warsaw Road and Nassau, and a shallow rock cutting of about 2,000 feet through Nassau, to connect the flooded reach with the river. A seven-sluice-way timber dam was constructed across the Otonabee River below Nassau to back the water up into the canal. The contract also included the abutments and guards for three highway swing bridges, one high-level bridge, and a pipe culvert to carry a small creek under the canal; as with the contract on section 1, the cement and superstructures of the bridges were excluded. Corry and Laverdure commenced work on 21 May 1896 – one month before the general election.

For Rogers, the construction on this section was a constant source of irritation and frustration. From the beginning, work progressed slowly. Corry and Laverdure were inexperienced in canal construction, and they knew very little about concrete work; nor would they, at least at the beginning, employ a superintendent with the necessary knowledge and experience to direct work of the kind required. With proper supervision lacking, gangs of men were frequently seen idling over their tools; consequently the excavation and embankment took twice as long as, and cost the contractors a great deal more than, they should. Although the material to be excavated in the canal and lock pits was of a most favourable nature – sand and clay mixed with small stones and boulders and a small amount of hardpan underlain with thin layers of shaly limestone – it was removed painfully slowly. One steam shovel dug up the material and dumped it into cars, which were supposed of be hauled away with two small steam locomotives running at regular intervals. But because of poor management, rarely were the two locomotives in operation at the same time, and occasionally both were out of service. Thus, instead of the steam shovel being kept constantly working, it was idle a good deal of the time, and excavation costs to the contractors – for which they were paid a flat rate of 16 cents per cubic yard – mounted, consuming much of their profits. Six or seven gangs of men were employed to lay stone pitching for protection lining, adjoining the entrance piers to the Ashburnham lock and guard piers to the bridges. The work of these gangs also lacked supervision by competent foremen and cost the contractors many times more than their contract price ($1.75 per cubic yard) allowed. Year after year, Rogers informed his superiors in Ottawa about the slowness of the work, but because Corry and Laverdure were strong supporters of the Liberal party nothing was done. Besides, the government, not being anxious to commit itself to any further contracts, was satisfied to have the work on the sections already under contract stretched out as long as possible. Consequently construction on section 2 lasted for eight years: four years before and four years after the 1900 election.

When they began laying the tons of concrete for the substructure of the hydraulic lock, the contractors, instead of making money as anticipated, found that they were losing even more than they lost on the excavation. But, as will be shown, the fault was not entirely their own.

Concrete pouring nears
completion, Peterborough
lift lock, 1903. (TSWO)

CHAPTER NINETEEN

The Hydraulic Lift Lock

Ever since the beginning of the nineteenth century, canal engineers had been attempting to create a device for lifting a vessel from one level to another without consuming the large quantity of water required to operate the standard locks invented by Leonardo da Vinci in the fifteenth century. The trouble with ordinary locks is that a whole lock-full of water, whether used to raise or lower a vessel, flows in one direction only and is lost forever. If the supply of water at the summit of a canal is limited, the water will eventually be used up and navigation will cease. What was needed to solve this problem was some sort of balance system that would permit a boat or barge to be lifted out of a lower reach and deposited in an upper reach, without wasting water.

Early in the nineteenth century, an English inventor made a gated tank, mounted it on wheels, and pulled it up an inclined track. Another engineer hung a tank on cables running over sheaves, or grooved pulley wheels, and counterbalanced it. These were the first known counterbalance locks built, and, although they worked, they did not have enough merit to put them into general use. In 1874, an inclined plane lock was built on the Chesapeake and Ohio Canal in the District of Columbia about two miles above Washington, but it was a failure. In the same year, the English engineer Edwin Clark designed a system of mounting lock chambers, in balance, on hydraulic rams. Clark built the world's first hydraulic balance lock to use this system at Anderton on the River Weaver, in Cheshire. Later, similar locks were built at La Louvrière in Belgium and Les Fontonettes in France.

The principle of operation is very simple. The locks may be likened to two large hydraulic elevators of a simple plunger type. In place of an ordinary elevator platform, a watertight box or caisson, closed at each end by a gate, is mounted on top of each ram. The rams slide up and down in two oil-filled presses[1] connected with a pipe, so that the descent of one ram forces oil into the other, causing that ram and its attached caisson to rise. A lockage is performed by running a vessel into one of the caissons and closing the gates so that the caisson becomes independent of the reach and is free to move vertically. The caisson with the floating vessel is raised or lowered to the other reach by opening the valve in the pipe connecting the two presses. The descending chamber is filled with a few more inches of water than the ascending one, giving it the necessary additional weight to force the oil (or water) into the press of the ascending ram. Since boats displace their own weight in water, the weight of the vessel is irrelevant to the operation of the locks; a rowboat can descend in one chamber while a 100 foot yacht is ascending in the other.

While acting as a witness before a select committee of the Ontario legislature, appointed in 1879 to study a petition by the Huron and Ontario Ship Canal Company for a government grant to build hydraulic locks, engineer Frank Turner spoke very favourably about them. The success of the Anderton lock had led engineers to believe that such locks were "capable of lifting ships of any size."[2] Turner's evidence, supported by written submissions from other competent engineers, convinced the select committee that hydraulic locks would solve the problems long associated with construction of the proposed Lake Huron – Lake Ontario canal: the quantity of excavation through the Oak Ridges moraine would be reduced by three-quarters; fewer locks would be required; there would be no waste of water, except from evaporation; and the cost of the canal would be reduced from $40 million to $20 million. But even the advantages of hydraulic lift locks did not save the ill-fated Huron and Ontario ship canal; like many other Canadian canal schemes of the nineteenth century, it too became a shattered dream.

As a member of the Trent Valley Canal Commission, Turner recommended hydraulic locks for the Trent. The possibility of their use captured Rogers's imagination. An ardent promoter of the Trent barge canal, Rogers saw the hydraulic lift lock as a means of overcoming many of the objections to the Trent. One of the major arguments against the canal was the time required for lockages. Rogers reasoned that since hydraulic locks could raise or lower a vessel 60 or 70 feet in the same length of time as it takes to lock through an ordinary lock with a lift of 6 or 7 feet, they would not only reduce the number of locks required but would also lessen considerably overall lockage time in the Trent. If Turner were right, construction costs could also be reduced. Although Rogers was convinced that there was an ample quantity of water in the highlands of Haliburton to supply standard locks working at full capacity, hydraulic locks would have the added advantage of being useful to counter the arguments of those who claimed a shortage of water in the Trent drainage system. Further, since hydraulic lift locks had a limit in size (some engineers estimated caissons no more than 225 feet long), they would work to the advantage of the Trent barge canal by discounting some of the factors that favoured the rival Welland-St Lawrence route, where hydraulic lift locks were out of the question. Soon after the Trent Valley Canal Commission's report was released, Rogers, being quite familiar with the principle, began sketching models of hydraulic locks that might be built on the Trent. He envisioned three in all: at Peterborough, Kirkfield, and Healey Falls.

The Hon. John Haggart was impressed with Rogers's plans and agreed to include one hydraulic lock in the contract about to be let for section 2 of the Peterborough-Lakefield division. But since Rogers had never actually seen a hydraulic lock in operation, Haggart sent him to Europe to examine the locks there. Upon his return, he assured Haggart that on the basis of what he had learned in Europe his own design for the Peterborough lock would work. Thus the contract signed by Corry and Laverdure on 7 May included a clause committing them to build a hydraulic lift lock, although they had never seen Rogers's plan – still in a rough stage – and, incredibly, no details related to its construction were included in the contract.

Perhaps the most remarkable aspect of this most bizarre construction achievement is the fact that Rogers designed the complicated structure without having previously seen one; even more remarkable is the fact that Corry and Laverdure built the whole structure without once having seen the full plans and specifications. In sworn testimony 10 years later, Rogers admitted that the plans for the lock had been completed before he went to Europe and that the trip was ordered by the government as a precaution against possible failure before committing itself to Rogers's unique design. No one, not even the contractors, was allowed to see the plans, for reasons that will be revealed shortly.

Rogers's lock design was, and still is, unique in several respects. First, it was much larger than the locks in Europe; the caissons are 33 feet in width and 140 feet long, with a normal depth of water of 8 feet. The weight of the water in each chamber, when full, is 1,700 tons. The lift is 65 feet. The locks in Europe were only half that size, the Anderton lock being only 70 feet by 14 feet with a lift of 50 feet. The Belgian lock was 140 feet long but had a width of only 19 feet; the French lock was similar in size. But the most unusual feature of the Peterborough lock was the method by which it was constructed. Whereas the European locks had steel and brick substructures, the Peterborough lock was built entirely of concrete – a daring undertaking given the poor reputation of concrete as a building material and Rogers's inexperience with it.[3]

Of all the hastily prepared and controversial contracts for construction on the Trent canal, none was more remarkable than the one signed by Corry and Laverdure on 7 May 1896, for section 2 of the Peterborough-Lakefield division. The specifications, signed by R.B. Rogers and Collingwood Schreiber on 24 January, were 20 pages long. They covered, in endless detail, the work required on the canal excavation and the dam and the standard lock to be built at the Little Lake entrance, but regarding the hydraulic lift lock – then one of the most ambitious engineering projects ever undertaken in Canada – the contract was singularly silent. The specifications consisted of only three sentences: "Hydraulic Lift Locks will be constructed at about Station No. 175. The iron work in connection with the locks and aqueduct and the excavation of the piston wells will not be included in this contract. The contractor shall make all necessary excavation, embankment, build all required works of concrete such as wells, floors, foundations, drive all piles, if any, in connection with these works."[4]

One other paragraph dealt briefly with the embankment leading into the lock. An exhibited plan, which gave "a general idea of what is required," was referred to, and "detailed plans [which were] to be furninshed as the work progresses"[5] were mentioned. No other provisions were included for the lock, and no prices were fixed for the difficult work needed to be done to construct it.

There is a simple explanation for the omission of contruction particulars in the contract – there were not any when the contract was drafted in January. The successive governments of Abbott, Thompson, and Bowell had procrastinated on a commitment to the Trent canal for five years; then, on the eve of the 1896 election, with the possibility that power might slip from their dithering fingers, the Conservatives made a belated decision to proceed with the Peterborough-Lakefield division. It was hoped that construction of a massive hydraulic lock would provide the dramatic impact needed to lure enough Conservative votes to save the Trent ridings. Thus, at the last moment, a hydraulic lock was included in the contract for section 2. But detailed plans and specifications for the kind of experimental design that Rogers had in mind, to make the Trent "an up to date canal,"[6] would take months, if not years, to prepare. They were not ready when the general specifications were drawn up – or when the contract was signed.

Corry and Laverdure interpreted the absence of any detailed specifications or schedule of rates for construction of the hydraulic lock to mean that the whole structure would be treated as an "extra." Experience had shown that it was in performing extras that the most profitable work was done; hence their willingness to sign the incomplete contract. They would have reason to regret making that assumption before the contract was completed.

On 23 May 1899, with the excavation at last completed, Collingwood Schreiber, on the advice of Rogers and under the authority of a provision in the original contract for extras, ordered Corry and Laverdure to start the concrete work "required for and connected with construction of

Section No. 2."[7] Schreiber set the rates, probably also on the advice of Rogers: "Three dollars and twenty-five cents ($3.25) per cubic yard for all concrete contained in the masonry of the main retaining wall and wing walls and five dollars ($5) per cubic yard for all concrete in the towers."[8] The contractors considered these rates too low and asked for $5 per cubic yard for the main walls and $10 per cubic yard for the concrete in the towers. They refused to do any work until 4 August, when they were obliged to sign a supplementary agreement confirming the rates set earlier by Schreiber. The only reason the contractors signed the supplementary contract (they claimed later) was because Rogers assured them that the "prices were fixed more on an experimental basis" and that if they found they could not do the work at those rates, "the government would see that they did not Loose [sic] money."[9] But there was no guarantee of this in writing.

The contractors certainly placed themselves at the mercy of Rogers and Schreiber when they signed the supplementary agreement. Lacking construction experience with concrete, they had no way of ascertaining a fair and proper price for the work. Only limited plans, numbered 1 to 10, were available for inspection in 1899; there were still no detailed specifications on which they could base an opinion. There were no comparable works in Canada or the United States, an examination of which might have provided data to enable the contractors to form their own estimate. It was a matter of astonishment to many engineers in Canada that the contractors began pouring concrete for the hydraulic lock without being furnished with proper specifications by the government engineers. And it soon became apparent to the contractors, as the concrete pouring began, that there was a strong possibility that they would lose money at Schreiber's rate; before the contract was finished, they were definitely losing money and asked for redress.

The contractors claimed a construction loss for several reasons. First, as a consequence of the Boer War, prices for material and labour had increased substantially since 1896: lumber and iron by 35 per cent; labour by 50 per cent. Second, being unfamiliar with concrete construction themselves, they had brought in skilled men from Montreal, Toronto, and Buffalo. These experts commanded high salaries, and, to make matters worse, the concreting operations were frequently stopped because of the non-delivery of cement from the manufacturers, leaving the high-priced experts idle. Third, and more seriously, the pouring of concrete in the high walls and tall towers proved more difficult and costly than the contractors were led to believe when the contract was signed.

The contractors found out about the peculiar and expensive moulding for the pilasters, cornices, and string courses, which Rogers added to the design to avoid a stark appearance of so large a formation, only when the remaining 22 plans were made available to them at irregular intervals. Gradually they learned, too, about elliptical forming in the passageways, the hundreds of square yards of face work to be mortared, the number of voids to be built into the solid structure, and the difficult forming in the walls between the upper and lower recesses. Had they known about all these, they would never have signed the supplementary contract.

They were incensed at Rogers for not making the full plans available to them. They wrote him frequently (in order to maintain a written record, as they saw him nearly every day) between June 1900 and October 1901, demanding the "necessary information and drawings to proceed with the work."[10] Unsatisfied with Rogers's indifference, the contractors asked Collingwood Schreiber if in his long experience he had ever seen "a structure of the importance, size and cost of the Hydraulic Lock, erected without specifications describing the work."[11] If Schreiber knew the reason for the absence of specifications, he kept the information to himself.

Rogers withheld the plans and specifications deliberately, giving the contractors only what they needed to build one phase of the structure at a time. He did this to protect his job. Being a Conservative sympathizer, Rogers had long known that his position as superintending engineer of the Trent canal under a Liberal government was tenuous. Indeed, there had been a good deal of political agitation in the district aimed at getting rid of him. Not least among the agitators were Corry and Laverdure, and Rogers was aware of this. As long as he held in his own possession the plans and specifications for the complex structure that he had personally designed, his position would be secure. Without him and the plans, the lock could not be finished. So he kept the plans to himself, releasing them to his assistants and the contractors only when necessary. Even as late as 30 July 1904, weeks after the lock was finished, officially opened, and in daily use, Rogers was still unable to provide a full set of plans and drawings requested by Schreiber, as "no finished drawings of the lock [were] as yet made."[12]

Corry and Laverdure tried to cut the cost of construction by increasing the water content in the mix to facilitate pouring. Local Liberals supported them and tried to get Rogers to relax his standard for mixing. "Grit Water Cement," Rogers privately called the proposal. But he insisted that his dry mix method, which had proved so successful in the locks built by Brown, Love, and Aylmer, be adhered to.

Convinced that they were being ill-used and that they had become victims of engineering experimentation, the contractors appealed directly to Schreiber for an increase in the rates. He refused. Finally, at their own expense, they contracted five prominent engineers, including Charles Keefer and Frank Turner, to examine the concrete work and to give an opinion about the rates. The engineers, who inspected the works individually, reported unanimously that the prices set by the government were too low. Then, in November 1900, at the request of the contractors, Schreiber visited the works. He was convinced that the prices paid were fair, but, confronted with the written opinions of the prestigious consultants employed by Corry and Laverdure, he referred the matter to the minister of railways and canals. The minister ordered an arbitration.

After careful consideration of the facts, including personal inspection of the lock, the arbitrators recommended changes in the prices that would net the contractors an additional $126,000. The price for the concrete was increased from $3.25 to $4.70 per cubic yard for the retaining and wing walls and from $5 to $6.65 for the towers. Excavation rates for the lock pit were increased from 44 cents and 19 cents per cubic yard to $1.10 and 65 cents per cubic yard, respectively. The price for building up the embankment leading into the lock was increased from 25 cents to 70 cents per cubic yard.

Initially Schreiber refused to accept any of the arbitrators' recommendations. Later, under pressure from the government, he accepted the increased price for excavation, but he absolutely refused to accept the recommended increase in the price for concrete, which he himself had set. So Corry and Laverdure were never paid the additional $31,850.02 that the recommended increase rate would have netted them, although they continued for months to press Laurier for payment of the arbitrators' full award, which they in good faith had agreed to accept in advance. The government made up for this by paying the contractors interest of $26,533, at 5 per cent per year, on the principal sum of the award. The government also paid, although it did not have to, one-half of the contractors' cost of the arbitration ($2,209.50) as well as the interest on it ($159.20).

A contract for the superstructure and installation of the rams and presses was awarded to the Dominion Bridge Company of Montreal in 1899, for a tendered price of $244,000. The contract was to have been completed on 1 May 1900, but because of the delay on the concrete substructure work could not even begin until 1902. Other than this unavoidable delay, there were no difficulties or disputes with the contractors, who designed the specifications for the superstructure largely by themselves. As the work progressed, Rogers presented the contractors with rough drafts of what was required; they make their own shop drawings and submitted the prints to him for approval. Rogers approved or altered the specifications as required and returned them to the contractors. Thus he was able to keep plans and specifications for the superstructure as well protected as the plans for the concrete.

On 21 May 1904, Rogers reported to Schreiber that "everything in connection with the construction of the hydraulic lock at Peterborough [was] ready for testing by the Dominion Bridge Company"; [13] on 21 June, he reported that all the tests had "proved most satisfactory, and that the lock could be opened at any time."[14] Opening day was set for Saturday, 9 July 1904.

People came in thousands to witness the opening of this engineering wonder. The Trent Valley Canal Association saw an opportunity for getting national attention and possible support for their scheme through the publicity for a gala opening ceremony that was planned. The town of Peterborough prepared for the event for weeks. A joint committee of the town and county made arrangements to entertain the scores of official visitors invited: press representatives, boards of trade and town councils, distinguished engineers, and numberless politicians. Merchants were quick to take advantage of the occasion; with the dominion election only a few months away, so were the politicians.

Robert Fair and Company offered "Lift Lock Bargains" and "Hydraulic Prices" in their Golden Lion dry goods store. Schneider, the watchmaker and jeweller, sold "Lift Lock Souvenirs": sterling silver and gold-plated spoons with an engraving of the lock in the bowls, maple leaf and coat-of-arms brooches, hat pins, and souvenir cups. The railways gave single-fare return rates from Friday to Monday from all points within 100 miles of Peterborough. A special train from Ottawa brought an immense parliamentary delegation with representatives from almost every part of Canada, including some who had opposed the canal. There were over 100 altogether: cabinet ministers, back-benchers, senators, senior civil servants, and railway commissioners. The Hon. J.R. Stratton and the Hon. F.R. Latchford represented the Ontario government.

Thousands of ordinary citizens came, too, travelling for miles in carriages, steamers, and by train. A multitude gathered on the hillside to the west of the lock, proud Canadians who stood "with stoical heroism"[15] in the pouring rain to see the first lockage of this Canadian-designed, Canadian-built engineering miracle. There were old people, the pioneers who as children had come to the county when it was still a wilderness, in canoes, barges, or primitive steamboats. They had seen the first stone locks built on the canal, they had witnessed the coming of the railroads and macadamized highways, and they had lived to see construction of this greatest marvel of all. There were the business and professional men who had striven all their adult lives for a Trent canal. Now it seemed to be nearing reality. There were hundreds of children who, like children of every age, born with the latest technological advances, took this one for granted.

This was the greatest day in Peterborough's history. From this day onwards every schoolchild in Canada would know about Peterborough, with its "highest lift lock in the world." To mark the occasion, everyone wore his or her finest clothes.

The official party was given lunch at the Nassau Mills lock, on P.P.

Young's new steamer *Stoney Lake*. Afterwards, followed by Boyd's steamer *Express* and a flotilla of other steamboats, the *Stoney Lake* sailed down the canal towards the lift lock. At 2:50 p.m., as if according to plan, the rain stopped as the *Stoney Lake* was guided into the overhanging lock chamber perched precariously atop its slender ram. Sensing that something might go wrong, the thousands on the hillside were gripped by silence and those on board the *Stoney Lake* stood in muted expectation. Through the silence one could hear the gurgle of the chamber gates as they were raised into place. The valve in the pipe connecting the presses was opened, and, as the water slowly flowed from one press to the other, the *Stoney Lake* began its gradual descent. The band of the 57th Regiment began to play, cheers broke from the thousands of relieved throats, and the whistles on the lock's auxiliary engine, and the nearby steamers, shrieked congratulations. In five minutes it was all over.

The *Stoney Lake* steamed up to the lower landing pier. The lock was declared officially opened by the Hon. Henry R. Emmerson, who had recently replaced Blair as minister of railways and canals. Then, from the deck of the *Stoney Lake*, with Maj. Rogers acting as master of ceremonies, the politicians delivered their speeches.

Emmerson was first. He very graciously extended, on behalf of all Canadians, congratulations to Collingwood Schreiber and the engineering staff "on the success which had attended their efforts."[16] Most eloquently, he described the lock as a product of "engineering skill which while inspiring, almost commands everyone … to stand in silence before it. All those present had witnessed," Emmerson said, "an event that will stand out in the history of Canada. Such events mark the progress of a country," he went on, "and no event which had transpired in Canada so clearly illustrated the advances we had made. Not only were all Canadians to be complimented, but the Empire itself, because of the accomplishment in Canada of a work that was the first of its kind in North America and the largest of its kind in the world." To the loud applause of those on the bank who could hear him, he stated that the lock illustrated the commercial energy and pluck of the people and demonstrated the skill with which Canadians could carry out such works without any outside assistance. He assured the audience that this fact would give Canadians greater faith in themselves and enable them to create greater and grander works in the future. In declaring the lock open, he dedicated it "as a public utility in the interest of trade and commerce and in the business of the country." He paid tribute to his predecessor, Andrew George Blair, whom he incorrectly credited with the initiation of the work.

Emmerson's was an inspiring speech, remarkably free of partisan political rhetoric and capturing the essence of Canadian nationalism, which was beginning to emerge during the Laurier years. His reference to Canadians doing things for themselves without outside assistance may have reflected the government's concern over the entry of American trade unionism into Canada, especially the attempt by the radical United Brotherhood of Railroad Employees to organize CPR employees in Alberta. But this experienced Baptist politician from New Brunswick was careful not to mention any government intention to complete the rest of the canal.

Postmaster-General Sir William Mulock, who spoke next, was not so constrained. Mulock was hatching a private scheme by which the Trent canal could benefit his constituents in Newmarket. He wanted the canal finished. With this in mind, he congratulated the people of Peterborough who "in season and out of season for the best part of three generations ... had assumed the responsibility of educating the people of Canada to supply the capital to develop these waters" – perhaps the understatement of the century. With Newmarket foremost in his mind, Mulock encouraged the people of the Trent to continue to bring pressure to bear upon the government and upon succeeding governments until vessels that entered the lift lock might "discharge alongside ... the ocean ships of Montreal carrying to the world the produce of the industry of the people of Canada."[17]

Mulock was followed by Dr James Mills, for 25 years president of the Royal Agricultural College at Guelph and recently named to the newly created Board of Railway Commissioners. A long-time supporter of the Trent, Mills interpreted Mulock's comments to mean that " the government intended to complete the canal system."[18]

The affable Sen. William Kerr of Cobourg promised that he would "never give the Ministers peace, day or night, until they complete the canal." Emmerson pleaded, "Leave us alone at night"[19] – with irony that would not have been missed by officials from Ottawa, where Emmerson, a widower since 1901, had the reputation of being one of the most active womanizers in town.

Sen. George Cox, the Peterborough telegrapher who had become rich and famous from railroads, banking, and insurance, also expressed a desire to see the canal finished. He was convinced, he said, that "the people of the country had become sufficiently impressed with the importance of the enterprise to push forward its completion."[20]

To the accompaniment of enthusiastic cheers, Jim Stratton, provincial secretary in George Ross's Liberal government in Toronto, assured the dominion ministers that, "irrespective of political views, it would be the intention of the people of that community to hold the ministers to their statements."[21]

Speech-making concluded, the visitors were taken for a cruise down the Otonabee River, the Peterborough-Lakefield division now being fully completed and open for traffic. At six o'clock, the official party returned to Peterborough to be entertained at dinner at the Oriental Hotel and the

Snowden House. These were happy events, the gaiety punctuated with impromptu speeches and frequent toasts. At 8 p.m., hundreds of townspeople gathered at the railway station to bid farewell to the Ottawa contingent; its special train bore it away amid loud cheers and the strains of the regimental band playing *Auld Lang Syne*.

Given Mulock's comments, the inspiring address by Emmerson, and the declarations of assorted senators, there was sanguine optimism in Peterborough that night about the future of the Trent canal, even among the most disillusioned cynics. But another generation of Peterborough residents would grow to maturity before the canal would be finished, and no vessel going through the Peterborough lift locks would ever discharge cargo alongside any ocean ship in Montreal from any industry in Canada. Nor would one kernel of wheat ever pass down this now very "respectable ditch."

Emmerson proclaiming
Peterborough lift lock
officially open from deck of
the *Stoney Lake*. (Courtesy
Roy Studio, Peterborough)

The Hydraulic Lift Lock   239

CHAPTER TWENTY

The Simcoe – Balsam Lake Division

The Simcoe – Balsam Lake division was built concurrent with the Peterborough-Lakefield division but, because of construction delays and political skulduggery, was not completed until three years after Peterborough-Lakefield. The 17-mile-long division required joining the two drainage systems in the natural waterway that became the Trent canal: the Trent drainage, which has its headwaters in the highlands of Haliburton and flows eastwards into Lake Ontario, and the Severn River, which drains the water of Lake Simcoe and Lake Couchiching into Georgian Bay to the west. Originally all of post-glacial Lake Algonquin (of which Lake Simcoe is an isolated remnant) drained through the Trent system, the base of the spout being located near Kirkfield. After the retreat of the Wisconsin glacier, the land in the vicinity of Kirkfield rose slightly to form a watershed, separating Balsam Lake from the Lake Simcoe basin and creating two distinct drainage networks.

To connect the drainage systems, some means had to be designed by engineers to move the crest of the watershed a few miles east into Balsam Lake, allowing its waters to feed both systems and thereby permit lockage of boats in both directions. To do this, a trench through the height of land would have to be dug for a few miles west of Balsam Lake to connect up with the Talbot River, which flows into Lake Simcoe. A series of locks and small dams could then be built along the Talbot to control the flow of water as it poured out of Balsam Lake. Although it was technically not difficult to create another outlet from Balsam Lake, the cost of doing so would be enormous and the commercial advantages to the country not very great, or so it was argued. Moreover, many claimed that the perennial shortage of water for milling and logging in the Trent watershed demonstrated, beyond question, that there was not enough water in Balsam Lake to feed both halves of a navigable waterway. Through the years, engineers were divided on the question of water supply and therefore on the merits of the scheme. Thus, like all other decisions connected with the Trent canal, the decision to construct this link became strictly political, the determining factor being votes, not transportation.

Although politically motivated, construction of all the locks on the waterway prior to 1895 – with the exception of the Chisholm's Rapids lock – could be justified on grounds of local transportation needs, if not national ones. The Simcoe-Balsam locks, however, could not. There never had been any historic trading relationship between settlements around Lake Simcoe and those on the Trent drainage system. The principal market for Lake Simcoe communities was Toronto, and there were now numerous railroads and highways connecting the Lake Simcoe communities to the city. The division had only one justification: it was the keystone of the whole throughway concept. A government decision to build the division would, therefore, be tantamount to accepting the concept, and the division's construction would represent a major commitment towards completing the canal. Succeeding governments were reluctant to take that step. Had it not been for the relentless energy of the Trent Valley Canal Association in pressing the case, supported by scheming local politicians, the decision never would have been made. As it was, it took 117 years from the time the linkage canal was first proposed until the division was finally completed in 1907.

The first survey of the land between Lake Simcoe and Balsam Lake for determining the feasibility of canalizing the ancient Indian canoe portage was made by John Collins in 1790, as part of his overall examination of the Trent route, ordered by Lord Dorchester for defence purposes in 1788. Collins found the sluggish-flowing Talbot River blocked with "Trees and Rubbish."[1] Because of this, the Indians avoided the river, preferring to portage their canoes 17 miles overland from Lake Simcoe to Balsam Lake – the so-called Talbot Portage. Collins did reckon, however, that with "a very small Expense [the river] might be made Commodious and good."[2] No action was taken of his report, because John Graves Simcoe subsequently selected the Toronto Carrying-Place as a more appropriate route for communication between Lake Ontario and the upper Great Lakes, and for a time interest in the Trent route waned.

The War of 1812 removed all doubt about American expanionist designs on Canada, and interest in discovering a protected defence route to the upper lakes was revived. It was at this time that a decision to proceed with the Rideau Canal was taken. Wellington ordered further surveys with the object of discovering a potential route between Lake Simcoe and the Ottawa River which the Iron Duke, although never having been in Canada, was convinced must exist. Thus, in 1819 Lt. J.P. Catty examined the Talbot Portage once more, in connection with his survey of the Madawaska – Ottawa River route. Catty reported the Talbot River navigable for about two miles from its mouth, beyond which it was completely choked with fallen trees. He followed the river to its source in a cedar swamp some two and a half miles nothwest of Balsam Lake and concluded that the narrow and shallow river, which for a mile and a half flowed underground, while perhaps navigable for a time in the spring, "scarcely [afforded] water enough for a Canal."[3] Subsequently, the British government abandoned its plan for creating a protected water communication inland from the Great Lakes, the need for one having diminished as relations with the United States returned to normal. The Trent proposal, and along with it the proposal to canalize the Talbot Portage, were shelved.

But settlers who moved into the Trent watershed after 1820 did not forget the Trent waterway proposal. Hoping to obtain an improved water transportation system for getting products to market, the Trent valley settlers, as well as those who settled around Lake Simcoe and who sought a direct water communication with Toronto by way of the Kawartha lakes and Lake Scugog, induced Sir John Colborne to have yet another survey made of the upper Trent drainage system. This resulted in Nichol Hugh Baird's survey of the route between Rice Lake and Lake Simcoe, in 1835.

Baird, who favoured construction of the Trent waterway, was much more optimistic about the feasibility of a water connection between Lake Simcoe and Balsam Lake than Collins or Catty had been. He and F.P. Rubidge conducted systematic surveys of the Talbot River in June and October and concluded that canalization of the river was possible. Baird proposed two alternative routes: a two-and-a-half-mile cut from the north end of Balsam Lake to the headwaters of the Talbot and thence down the river to its mouth, and a thirteen-and-a-half-mile cut from West Bay on Balsam Lake to a point on the Talbot River, two and a half miles upstream from its mouth. Baird favoured the latter plan, because it avoided the numerous serpentine bends in the Talbot. Further, the section of country through which the proposed canal would run was very favourable for excavation, with the exception of a portion of bedded limestone on the edge of Balsam Lake, which would have to be intersected. But this rock excavation, while expensive, would not impose a severe burden on construction cost because, as the canny Scot pointed out, the limestone removed would "meet well the purpose of lock building."[4] Baird envisioned the construction of 12 locks with average lifts of 10 feet, to overcome the 121-foot difference in elevation between the two lakes. He estimated the cost at slightly over $600,000.

The publication of Baird's report precipitated a tremedous amount of political agitation for the canal. Indeed, hopes ran high all along the route when, in response to intense public pressure, the legislature of Upper Canada finally authorized two grants for construction to begin on the eastern extremity of the waterway. The prospect of a canal, running through what became the northern part of Victoria and Ontario counties, brought settlers, and in a short time the northern townships were converted from a wilderness into a thinly populated community. The villages of Balsover, Kirkfield, and Gamebridge were established, and trade began to develop. But alas! hopes for the waterway were dashed in 1844, when the Board of Works cancelled the Trent scheme in favour of developing the St Lawrence River canals. In the 1850s, Lake Simcoe settlers directed their attention to the proposed canal from Toronto to Georgian Bay. Then in 1862 the Victoria Road, running north from Lindsay to connect up with the Peterson Road, was started, and in 1872, the Toronto and Nipissing Railroad was built through the Talbot River country to Coboconk. Their transportation needs thus being well provided for, the settlers in north Victoria contented themselves with working their marginal farm land, securing part-time employment in the timber trade, and cutting cordwood for the hungry furnaces of Toronto. Visions of muddy Talbot River converted into a national canal were pushed aside by the reality of eking out a living from the shallow acidic soil.

When John A. Macdonald cancelled Alexander Mackenzie's transfer of the Trent works to the Ontario government, the accompanying fanfare led the bush farmers in north Victoria to fantasize once more about lucrative canal construction jobs to bolster their income, diminishing with the decline of pine and hardwood forests. The machinations of the Ottawa government did little to dispel the fantasy.

In August 1879, David Stark, on his own initiative, examined the Talbot River, accompanied by canal superintendent Thomas Belcher. Stark sought out lumbermen, asked them detailed questions about the flow of water in the Severn River, and generally left the impression that the government was seriously considering reviving the Trent canal scheme. In June 1880 Sir Charles Tupper, ever the political opportunist, visited the Talbot Portage, having been invited by the newly formed Trent Valley Canal Association to inspect the proposed waterway. At a meeting in Collingwood a few days later, Sir Charles "expressed himself most favourable disposed to the canal from his personal observations"[5] and promised that a thorough survey would immediately be undertaken. A year later Tom S. Rubidge began his survey of the Trent route, and the effect on the region was resuscitating.

The Woodville *Advocate* noted: "The Trent Canal is agitating the people of the north counties."[6] On 6 June 1882, the Beaverton *Express* informed its readers that houses vacated by those who had left Balsover a year earlier were being occupied by others, induced there by the prospect of the Trent valley canal. It was natural for the residents to anticipate construction, for prior to the election of 1882 there was plenty of surveying activity on the portage; the surveys were conducted under Rubidge's supervision by A. Belcher, but they were instigated by Toronto lawyer Hector Cameron, who represented Victoria North in Parliament.

An unsuccessful candidate on two previous occasions – once in Victoria South and once in Victoria North – Cameron was finally chosen in a by-election in 1874. Long having seen the political potential in the Trent canal, he was one of those who convinced Macdonald of the wisdom of rescinding Mackenzie's transfer. In fact, it was Cameron who seconded Keeler's motion for the appointment of a select committee to investigate the transfer. In the subsequent debate, he spoke in favour of the dominion keeping the canal works, and he later served on the select committee which, predictably, recommended that the dominion recover the Trent works from Ontario. Cameron was also an active member of the Trent Valley Canal Association. Having been instrumental in the recovery of the canal, he intended to take full advantage of it to muster support in the 1882 election to impede the shift in popular support to his Liberal opponent, G.G. Gibbs: this accounts for the considerable surveying activity in the neighbourhood of Kirkfield and Balsover.

Through the influence of Cameron, an order-in-council was passed on 17 April 1882 authorizing the expenditure of $290,000 for locks at Fenelon Falls, Buckhorn, and Burleigh Falls, and construction of the Trent canal was under way after a hiatus of 42 years. Cameron was elected, with a solid majority over Gibbs, in June. In October, the *Express* reported: "Every person in Balsover is anticipating the revival of business in this locality when the canal is put through."[7] In November the grateful citizens of Victoria North gave a banquet at Fenelon Falls to honour Hector Cameron for his contribution "in the inauguration of work on the Trent Valley Canal."[8]

These were heady days for residents around the Talbot Portage. The *Express*, which had "heretofore been somewhat dubious as to the intentions of the Government in the work, and regarded the matter simply as an election dodge," admitted that it had been mistaken "and agreeable so."[9] Thus, for the next few years, while the locks at Fenelon Falls were being constructed and the Trent Valley Canal Association was making its annual pilgrimages to Ottawa, the people between Beaverton and Balsam Lake were optimistic about the prospects of a canal through their townships. But as the election of 1887 approached, with no sign of the government moving on a canal beyond Fenelon Falls, their ardour began to cool. In the February election, the now ungrateful citizens of Victoria North threw Hector Cameron out of office in favour of Liberal John Barron. And when Rubidge's long-awaited report was finally released in November, showing an estimate for the Simcoe-Balsam division of $2.067,134, the citizens began to suspect that they had been tricked. Reacting to Macdonald's decision to appoint the Trent Valley Canal Commission, a disillusioned Beaverton *Express*, giving vent to a general feeling, predicted that "the Government do not intend ... to keep the project alive and about the time of the next election we will no doubt learn that a report has been made and that [the canal], is found impracticable."[10] This would not be a bad thing, the *Express* consoled its readers, because it would "put an end to the tomfoolery which the various municipal councils have for several years been indulging in, of spending deputations to Ottawa to urge forward a scheme which is already condemned."[11]

But the *Express* was wrong. As has already been pointed out, the commission, while not overly enthusiastic about the canal, did not condemn it. The unpredictable Macdonald sent his famous telegram to Murphy two days before the 1891 election, and the on-again, off-again Trent canal was very much on again.

The man who ensured that the government honoured Macdonald's promise to Murphy, and who pushed it into action on the Simcoe – Balsam Lake division, was the bumptious Sam Hughes, Orangeman, former Fenian-fighter, former school teacher, and since 1885 publisher of the Lindsay *Warder*. In his second attempt at seeking political office, Hughes edged Liberal John Barron out of Victoria North in a by-election in 1892. For the next 29 years, this handsome but headstrong politician dominated the political scene, sitting as Conservative MP first for Victoria North, and after 1904 for the combined riding of Victoria and Haliburton. In 1899, Hughes took a contingent of Canadian troops to the Boer War. In 1911, in the Borden government, he became Canada's first minister of militia and defence, in which capacity he organized and dispatched the Canadian Expeditionary Force to France in 1915. For his military contribution, he received a knighthood (KGB) and was promoted lieutenant-general. Unfortunately, although an administrator with great drive, Hughes lacked discretion and good judgment. He became a liability in the Borden cabinet because of his insensitive handling of the opposition to the war effort in Quebec, and Borden asked for his resignation in November 1916. He continued to sit in the House of Commons, an outspoken critic of everyone – Liberal or Conservative – with whom he did not agree, until his death in 1921.

Initially, Hughes gained the support of the people in the riding because of his contribution to the development of the Trent canal. He convinced John Haggart to finish the inter-lake communication before giving any consideration to the terminal links, if the Conservative government's policy of building the canal over a period of years were to be followed. By the inter-lake communication Hughes meant the Peterborough-Lakefield division and, more particularly, the Simcoe – Balsam Lake division, which would pass in part through his riding. With his eye on the next election, which could come at any time during the shaky post-Macdonald ministries, Hughes inveigled Haggart into putting $73,000 into the departmental estimates for the Simcoe-Balsam division in June 1894 and a further $130,000 in the supplementary estimates in July. As if the route had not been surveyed enough, Rogers was asked on 1 August to send yet another survey team to the portage – always the first step in a pre-election propaganda campaign. Naturally, Hughes's *Warder* kept its reader well informed about the surveying activities. On 3 August, it reported: "Several splendid young men have secured employment on the survey party now locating the canal across Eldon. Next spring when regular work begins, chief engineer Rogers will require all the good men in the locality."[12] The Liberal Beaverton *Express*, which reprinted the article, could not resist adding: "That is, provided they are all good Tories."[13] Almost every farmer in the area had his own notion about where the canal should run, generally through his own unproductive farm. Dutifully, Rogers had all the proposals examined. On 17 August the *Express* reported: "The survey of possible routes for the Trent Valley Canal is being pushed with vigour and already several lines have been surveyed."[14] The following week, yet another proposal – a direct line from the south end of South Bay on Balsam Lake to Beaverton – was surveyed. By November, the surveyors were running lines between Gamebridge and Lake Simcoe. Although Rogers already knew where the canal was going to run, he was obliged to act out the surveying charade for the benefit of the voters.

But this time, thanks to Hughes's efforts, action would follow the frenetic pre-election surveying activity. Using his newspaper as a vehicle and his own ebullient personality as the engine, Hughes bulldozed the government into a firm commitment to begin construction on this keystone division of the canal. Consequently, on 19 October tenders were invited for the first section of the Simcoe – Balsam Lake division. On 19 November, 12 tenders ranging from $492,059.15 to $915,468.05 having been received, a contract was awarded to Andrew Onderdonk of Chicago, his bid being the lowest. On 21 December a still sceptical *Express* announced: "Yes, the canal is coming!"[15] In early April, Onderdonk's agent spent a few days around Kirkfield inspecting the proposed route of the canal. By 15 May Onderdonk was erecting two enormous boarding-houses in Kirkfield to accommodate his large staff and a siding was being built for the contractors from the Grand Trunk Railway line to the site of the canal. Excavation began in July.

In October, the village of Victoria Road boasted: "Business is booming in this village. Just now every line of industry is working to its full capacity, especially the blacksmiths. The Trent Valley Canal has done wonders for this village."[16] Hughes kept the enthusiasm running high. Surveyors were busy surveying a line for the canal from Kirkfield west, and there were rumours that further sections would soon be placed under contract. Land evaluators were engaged in placing values on the property expropriated for section 1. (Altogether, 2,188.3 acres of land, valued at $21,830.80, were expropriated for the section.) Parliament was agonizing over the controversial Manitoba school question. Bowell's cabinet was badly divided. The government could fall and an election be called any day. When it did, the aggressive Hughes would be well prepared for an election campaign, which finally came in the spring of 1896.

Typically, when the politicians had finished playing pre-election games with the electorate, the engineers had to plan how best to build the sections of canal that were eventually decided upon. Had the politicians left the engineers alone, had they allowed them to hire their own staff, choose their own routes, and follow their own time schedules, the canal would have been built much more quickly and much more cheaply than it was, but it is doubtful if it would have been built any better. For one of the elements redeeming the long, shameful saga of political intrigue that chronicles the Trent canal is the skill with which the engineers built it. Ever since the days of Baird, the Trent canal had been blessed with highly competent superintending engineers. Rogers was one of the best. The Simcoe – Balsam Lake division, like the Peterborough-Lakefield division, also designed by Rogers, is an example of Canadian hydraulic engineering at its finest.

The plan adopted by Rogers, similar to the one previously surveyed by Rubidge, was in principle not unlike the second alternative proposed by Baird: a canal was cut from the end of West Bay on Balsam Lake to connect with the Talbot River. The difference between the Rubidge and Rogers plan and Baird's was that their canal was much shorter, being only six and a half miles in length. In the Rubidge-Rogers plan, the amount of excavation was reduced, as greater use was made of the natural course of the river. The principal difference between Rogers's design and Rubidge's was in the lock construction. Whereas Rubidge planned for 11 masonry locks of the standard type, Rogers's plan called for concrete locks. Moreover, his system required only five standard locks, the planned 50-foot lift hydraulic lock at Kirkfield eliminating the need for six locks.

The work on section 1 consisted mainly of earth and rock excavation. In all, 424,618 cubic yards of earth, for a total cost of $97,662.14, and 406,143 cubic yards of rock, costing the government $304,607.25, were excavated. Additional works consisted of concrete abutments for three bridges, two entrance piers on Balsam Lake, two guard gates used for draining the canal, two regulating wiers, and one small dam. The final amount paid to Onderdonk was $483,874.70, $8,184.45 less than his contract price. The only American to be awarded a contract on the Trent canal, Onderdonk was also the only contractor to complete the work under estimate.

Most of the excavation for the canal was completed in 1899, but since sections 2 and 3 had not yet been let out to contract, Onderdonk was not pushed to finish the final touches until early 1900. Another reason for the delay in completing the work was because the water in Balsam lake, controlled by the Ontario government through its dam and lock at Rosedale, was kept unusually high, preventing construction of the canal's concrete entrance piers. Not being responsible for the Rosedale dam, Rogers had no way of controlling the level of water in the lake to expedite construction.

Had the Conservative government not awarded the contracts for section 1 of the Simcoe – Balsam Lake division and both sections of a Peterborough-Lakefield division just prior to the election of 1896, it is unlikely that the Liberals, opposed as they were to the canal for so long, would have let them. Indeed, they would probably have cancelled the canal scheme permanently, railways having higher priority with them. But the Liberals were obliged to honour the contracts entered into by their predecessors. Between 1896 and 1904, the Liberal government concentrated its efforts on the Peterborough-Lakefield division, not only because the whole division was under contract but because the Liberals' political influence was strongest in the area: Peterborough East was held by Independent-Liberal John Lang from 1896 to 1904 and Liberal John Finlay from 1904 to 1908; Peterborough West was held by Liberals R.R. Hall and J.R. Stratton from 1904 to 1911. The Simcoe – Balsam Lake division crossed staunch Tory country and was given lower priority.

For contract purposes, the Simcoe-Balsam division was divided into three sections. The reason sections 2 and 3 had not been let out to contract when Hughes secured the contract for section 1 was that they were not located in his riding, and the member in whose riding they were located did not press for them. Part of section 2 and all of section 3 were in Ontario North, held from 1887 to 1896 by Frank Madill, a lawyer in Beaverton. Although he was a Conservative, for some strange reason the Trent canal was not a priority with him. During eight years in Parliament, he did not speak once on behalf of the Trent canal, and he rarely even so much as asked a question about it. Neither did he participate in any of the intensive lobbying that went on in Ottawa, or join any of the delegations. Nor did his successors, J.A. McGillivray and Angus MacLeod, who held the seat successively from 1896 to 1904, promote the canal. No one from this riding, not even representatives of the municipalities, took part in the massive rally in Ottawa in 1897 at which Laurier made public a commitment to the Trent. It was the Liberal government, therefore, that finally let the contracts for the remaining two sections, just months before the 1900 election, in the vain hope that in doing so the indifferent Conservative member in Ontario North might be displaced. In announcing his intention to tender the contracts, Andrew Blair confessed that while his canal division would have no value to the country, the government could be reproached for leaving the division unfinished half-way between the two lakes. So it was a consequence of the Conservatives letting a contract to Onderdonk that forced the completion of the division, not pressure from the Ontario North riding and certainly not a commitment by the Liberals to any definite canal policy.

A contract for section 3 was awarded to Brown and Aylmer on 6 September 1900 and one for section 2 to Larkin and Sangster of St Catharines on 7 September. It will be recalled that it was Larkin and his partner, John Carroll, who endeavoured, without success, to sell their newspaper and their souls to John A. Macdonald for lock contracts on the Kawartha Lakes. With their Liberal patrons now in office, they were at last able to obtain two of the more lucrative contracts on the canal without compromising their virtue. (The other contract was for section 1 on the Ontario – Rice Lake division.)

Section 2 extended from the site of the hydraulic lift lock for seven and a half miles down the Talbot River to the Balsover lock. The major construction in this section included excavation for the hydraulic lock pit, construction of the lock foundation, excavation for and construction of the entrance walls for the lock, excavation of a short stretch of canal from the base of the hydraulic lock to the Talbot River, construction of abutments and piers for road bridges and one railway bridge, and a dam on the Talbot River at Balsover lock. The Balsover dam backs up the water in the river, creating a reach for the full seven and a half miles to the Kirkfield lock. The numerous serpentine bends in the original river, which concerned Baird, were flooded out, and a new lake – Canal Lake – was the result. Canal Lake is about five miles long and nearly a mile wide at its widest point. The channel of the canal is dredged out and buoyed along the south side of the lake. This man-made lake serves two purposes: it creates a navigable reach in the canal, and it serves as a reservoir, providing a supply of water for lockages through the five standard locks between Balsover and Lake Simcoe. The reservoir lake is necessary because little water from Balsam Lake passes through the hydraulic lift lock, the lock consuming as much water from the lower reach as it does from the upper. The lake can be replenished, especially in dry seasons, through the dam on Grass Creek which, when opened, allows water to flow from Balsam Lake through Mitchell Lake into the upper Talbot River and thence downstream to Canal Lake, bypassing the lock at Kirkfield altogether. Since there are no mills or power plants on this division of canal, water is consumed only in lockages (and evaporation);

consequently, there has rarely been a shortage of water in this division as there has been, from time to time, on the waterway east of Balsam Lake.

Section 3 extended the remaining five and a half miles from the end of section 2 to Lake Simcoe. The canal follows the river for two miles, then leaves the river and, by way of an excavated prism, runs for three and a half miles in a straight line to Lake Simcoe, crossing the river again near its mouth. The section contains five concrete locks, two in the river proper and three in the excavated canal. These five locks, following one another in direct succession, serve as a set of steps to overcome the 75-foot rise between Lake Simcoe and Canal Lake.

Both contractors made construction preparations in the fall of 1900, providing visible signs of government intent prior to the November election, but it was not until the spring of 1901 that serious excavation began. Because the Liberal government had adopted the same Trent canal policy as its predecessors – voting only enough money each year to keep the contracts going – it took seven years to finish work that could easily have been done in two seasons.

The entrance walls for the Kirkfield lock were poured in sections 50 feet long with pine stops between each section, using the same mixing ingredients and pouring techniques as were used on the Peterborough lock. The pit for the lock was excavated entirely in the rock, the sides having been cut with a Sullivan channeller. The press wells for the hydraulic rams are 50 feet deep, lined with concrete and floored with blocks of granite as in the Peterborough lock. The principal difference in design between the two locks is that at Kirkfield three steel towers guide the caissons instead of concrete towers, and a steel aqueduct rather than a concrete one leads to the upper gateways. The excavation and concrete work were done by Larkin and Sangster, but the steel structures, including the towers, caissons, and presses, were made by the now experienced Dominion Bridge Company of Montreal for the bulk sum of $297,300.

The excavation for the upper entrance walls having been completed in the fall of 1901, concrete pouring began on 8 November but had to be discontinued on 26 November because of frost. Pouring was resumed on 5 April 1902 and from then until the concrete work was completed in 1905 took place only in the spring and summer months. Because Larkin and Sangster's contract, unlike Corry and Laverdure's, specified the rates ($3 per cubic yard for concrete, 75 cents per cubic yard for rock excavation, and 18 cents per cubic yard for earth), no conflict over prices, as was experienced on the Peterborough contract, developed. In fact, the contractors did not even submit a claim for extras.

But there was plenty of controversy over pouring the concrete. Defects developed in the walls, not so much from any fault of the contractor, but through neglect on the part of the government supervisors, which can be directly attributed to the system of political appointment of government employees. The divisional engineer in charge of sections 2 and 3 was R. Adams Davy, appointed in August 1901. Davy arrived at the work in September, just before the concrete pouring began. A competent enough engineer, he was appointed because of his political affiliation, not because of any special knowledge or experience in concrete construction. It took him some time to familiarize himself with construction details, and because he was responsible for the work on both sections, he could not always be at Kirkfield to supervise the work there. That was one reason for the problem. But the main reason for defects in the concrete walls was the negligence of D.E. Bethune, the concrete inspector, who was directly responsible for supervising the pouring. Bethune was appointed through the influence of R.J. McLaughlin, a Liberal party stalwart from Lindsay who was defeated by the indomitable Sam Hughes in the 1896 election.

Bethune was a drifter. Since 1873 he had rarely spent more than two years in any one place, having worked for a host of contractors, mainly on railroad construction in Ontario, Minnesota, Nova Scotia, Maine, and New York. He went to the Trent as a foremen for a small subcontractor to Onderdonk in July 1895. He claimed to have been a superintendent or foreman of construction in all his previous positions, and if that were true, his career was definitely on a downward slide when he arrived on the Simcoe – Balsam Lake division, for the only work he did for Onderdonk was to supervise the digging of a drainage ditch from the prism of the canal to Mitchell Lake. He joined the government staff after the Liberal victory in 1896, first as a blaster, or "dynamite man," on the Rosedale channel excavation at $3 per day, and later as a concrete and sand inspector on the Peterborough-Lakefield division, at the same wage. In 1901 he was sent to inspect the concrete pouring at Kirkfield.

The truth of the matter is that Bethune was a drunk. He was frequently seen during working hours in an inebriated condition in the hotels of Kirkfield, or he could often be found somewhere, sleeping off a hangover. Even when on the job, he was seldom in a fit condition to supervise the work properly, and there is some evidence that he did not know much about concrete work to begin with. Both Davy and Rogers knew about Bethune's drinking problem but seemed powerless to do anything about it, Rogers not being able to hire or fire his own staff. To avoid confrontation with Bethune over his drinking, Davy, whose office was in Beaverton, and Rogers, who was, of course, based in Peterborough, always phoned ahead to advise of intended inspection visits. This was the signal for Bethune's friends to drag him out of a hotel, sober him up, and get him to the construction site. When the engineers arrived, the concrete pouring would be running smoothly under Bethune's apparent supervision, the defects caused by his negligence hidden behind the forming or buried several feet under the visible surface.

The specifications detailed clearly how the concrete was to be mixed and poured, but in Bethune's absence, or because of lax supervision when he was there, the labourers did not always bother to follow the specifications. Sometimes the concrete was not tamped down sufficiently, with the result that when it hardened, sections of the walls were porous. Nor was the four-inch thick, hard mortar face put on the first nine sections, as was clearly called for in the specifications. It was not until May 1902 that Rogers noticed the absence of the mortar face. He then instructed Davy to have a mortar face put on all remaining sections, an order that should not have been necessary if Davy had supervised Bethune properly. Because the first nine sections, which happened to be at the low end of the canal, were left with a rough open face, the concrete leaked so badly when water was let in to test the lock in August 1905 that the reach could not be filled to more than 11 feet below the required level. Water poured through the walls at the rate of about 1 million gallons an hour.

Rogers was summoned at once. After inspecting the defect, he wired M.J. Butler, the deputy minister, asking for permission to hire some of the Dominion Bridge Company's men, who had been temporarily thrown out of work because of the leaks, to repair the damage. Rogers estimated the cost of the repairs at $1,000, which amount he recommended be taken from his own budget. The message was received by L.K. Jones, secretary of the department, who forwarded it to Butler, then in Moncton, New Brunswick, on railway business. Butler wired Jones back and told him to refer the matter of the Kirkfield walls to Collingwood Schreiber and to "do as he directs, as he is familiar with all the circumstances."[17] Through Jones, Schreiber, who was then a private consultant, instructed Rogers to take the necessary steps to stop the leaks and to give the work his personal attention.

On 6 September Rogers wired back, advising that the leaks had been staunched. The error had been easy enough to correct. Under Rogers's supervision, the Dominion Bridge workers, "a superior class of men,"[18] using plasterer's trowels, covered the rough walls with a thin cement grout. This treatment with cement paste stopped nearly all the leakage, the few small holes remaining being gradually plugged with silt as water percolated through them. It took only four days to do the work. The cost was $204 for labour and $50 for cement – a trifle on a $717,000 project.

In October Butler, who was desirous of amassing evidence to get rid of Rogers, wrote directly to Davy, asking for a full report. Davy's report was a deliberate distortion of the truth and most damaging to Rogers. He blamed Rogers for the defects. Quoting Bethune, of all people, and the contractor, who was guilty of not following the specifications, Davy claimed that the nine sections of wall had been built according to Rogers's instructions. But he did not explain what he, as supervising engineer, had been doing and why the contract specifications had not been followed. Moreover, Davy took credit for having plugged the leaks.

Rogers would eventually lose his job over the matter, but nothing would happen to Davy or Bethune. The Liberal party took care of the engineer, and God took care of the drunk. When the division was finished, Bethune drifted off to another job. Davy was kept on as divisional engineer, working out of the Peterborough office.

Meanwhile, work was progressing satisfactorily, if slowly, on section 3 under the experienced contractors Brown and Aylmer, who had built the first concrete locks in North America on section 1 of the Peterborough-Lakefield division. Although it took nearly four years to build the five locks, the dams, and the abutments for bridges, the concrete was properly laid under the close supervision of inspectors Joseph T. McCabe and James Doyle. Today (1987), the locks, except for some erosion by ice at the water level, are still in as sound condition as when they were built 80 years ago.

The principal difficulty encountered on this section was in the excavation of the three-mile-long prism, which had to be dug through the heavy clay that was deposited on the bottom of post-glacial Lake Algonquin. Hard enough to dig at any time, the clay was almost impossible to remove during periods of wet weather. Horses and men could not stand up in the slippery stuff, steam shovels could barely penetrate it, and wagons bogged down in it. When the weather was hot and dry, the clay hardened like cement and was equally difficult to remove.

When human and natural impediments were eventually overcome, construction on both sections was finally finished, in June 1907. A gala opening of the division was arranged. The locus of the formalities, naturally, was the hydraulic locks at Kirkfield. The day was 6 July. Because of its isolated location, fewer attended the Kirkfield opening than the Peterborough ceremony, but a few thousand spectators braved the blistering July heat to witness the festivities. The honour of opening the lock was given to Postmaster-General Rudolphe Lemieux, H.E. Emmerson having been asked to resign as minister of railways and canals three months earlier and no replacement having yet been appointed. Conspicuously absent was the lock's designer, R.B. Rogers, forced to resign from his position through the pressure of a vengeful Liberal party machine a year earlier. P.P. Young's steamer *Stoney Lake* once again had the privilege of conveying the official party through the division and was therefore the first steamer to pass through the Kirkfield lock. Three other steamers were in the procession: The *Sovereign*, a narrow, top-heavy steamer from Peterborough, under charter to the government for canal work, which brought the press corps from Peterborough; the *Bob Hall*, another government steamer, named after the local MP, which brought a group of dignitaries from the Peterborough area; and Boyd's *Manita*, which brought local sightseers from Bobcaygeon and intermediate points. Some small, privately owned steamers and even one or two of the canal's first gasoline-powered motor launches followed behind.

The official party, wives, and friends had travelled from Ottawa to Lindsay by train, where they were picked up by the *Stoney Lake* and taken to Kirkfield. After the opening ceremonies, the steamers cruised through the canal to Lake Simcoe. The *Stoney Lake* deposited the official party at Beaverton, whence it returned to Ottawa by train. The others retraced their steps to Peterborough. There were no banquets, no toasts, and no canal promises.

A kaleidoscope of unfamiliar images passed before the eyes of the deck passengers as the steamers nosed their way along this newest link in the Trent water chain. There was the silent descent in the hydraulic lock, its massive steel superstructure glistening in the summer sun – an awe-inspiring experience, especially for those who had not previously seen the Peterborough lock in operation. There were the five newest Canadian locks, their timber gates freshly painted and recently stepped, their concrete walls still silver-grey and clean, models of modern hydraulic technology. There were the six lock-masters, just appointed, unsure of their duties, but looking smart in their new Railways and Canals uniforms, proudly recording the first lockages in their journals and issuing the division's very first let-passes. There were the miles of rock lining the sides of the canal prism, the neat rows of freshly cut blocks of limestone not yet stained with slime or buckled by frost action, conveying an illusion of order and efficiency. There were the brand new bridges – nine in all – some rotating gently on their pivots to let the steamers pass, others stretched across the canal high above the heads of the passengers, signs of an expanding transportation network in a burgeoning Canadian economy.

The politicians were pleased. The engineers were ecstatic with this array of achievement stretched out across 19 miles of northern bush. But any naturalists on board must have been appalled at the evidence of devastation and destruction everywhere. Mitchell and Canal lakes were no more than flooded forests. The steamers followed a watery pathway carved out through depressing acres of dead and dying trees standing motionless, their roots suffocating under six feet of murky water, their limbs stretched stark and stiff in the hot air, a grim reminder that human progress usually comes at a frightful cost to the natural environment. Such sights were typical during construction of all the Trent canal divisions as water levels were raised to create navigable reaches, but tree destruction on the Simcoe-Balsam division, where whole new lakes were created, was enormous.

Perhaps it was this unsightly spectacle that prompted an order to canal superintendent J.H. McClellan to clean up the mess. When navigation closed for the season, the canal was unwatered and the dead trees were harvested. Cedar posts for canal fencing, 60,000 feet of hemlock, pine, and elm for bridge planking, and joists and rafters for lock-masters' houses were salvaged. Today Canal and Mitchell lakes are surrounded by trim summer cottages, but the shallow lakes are little more than deep swamps. The well-preserved stumps of what were once verdant forests remain scattered about on the bottom, ready to wreak revenge on the hull of any boat that dares stray from the buoyed channel.

Richard B. Rogers inspects
first concrete lock, December
1896. (PAC/ACC 14390-101)

CHAPTER TWENTY-ONE

R.B. Rogers

Few public servants have ever been treated more disgracefully by a government than R.B. Rogers was in 1906. A civil engineer who served the departments of Public Works and Railways and Canals faithfully for nearly 25 years, Rogers was known and respected by his professional colleagues in many parts of the world for his unique and historic contribution to civil engineering, especially in concrete construction. His innovative concrete lock was the admiration of engineers who came to examine it from nearly every developed country in the world, including the designer of the prototype lock at Anderton. This unique structure gave his home town of Peterborough a landmark that made it famous throughout North America. Indeed, after 80 years of continuous operation, the solidly built lock still impresses engineers and thousands of tourists every year.

During his 25 years of service to the government Rogers designed and built many works and had the responsibility of spending millions of dollars of public funds, without once having had a charge of dishonesty or negligence levelled against him. Not until 1906 that is, when, his faithful service notwithstanding, he was summarily dismissed by the minister with only one month's notice, no retirement gratuity, and not even so much as a letter of commendation. At the age of 49, he saw his brilliant career terminated and his professional reputation badly tarnished by malicious and unsubstantiated charges of gross negligence against which he was given no opportunity to vindicate himself, merely to satisfy the whims of a few petty politicians and to advance the ambitions of a handful of electric power developers.

Richard Birdsall Rogers was born in the village of Ashburnham on 16 January 1857, a product of United Empire Loyalist stock on both sides of his family. His mother was Elizabeth Birdsall, eldest daughter of Richard Birdsall of Asphodel, a public land surveyor who laid out the town of Peterborough in 1825. Her maternal grandfather was the Hon. Zaccheus Burnham, who had played such a prominent role in the early development of the Trent. R.B.'s father was Robert David Rogers, who in 1842 settled in Ashburnham, where he built flour and saw mills and carried on a successful mercantile business for many years.

Robert David Rogers inherited a love of military life from his illustrious grandfather and grand uncle, founders of the famous Rogers Rangers – later Queen's Rangers – which participated both in the capture of Quebec and on the British side in the American Revolution. Robert saw service during the rebellion of 1837, taking an active part in capturing and destroying the steamer *Caroline*, used by William Lyon Mackenzie to strengthen his position on Navy Island in the Niagara River. It was said that young Robert was one of the last to abandon the burning vessel before it plummetted over Niagara Falls. In 1863, he organized a volunteer company that saw active service, under his command, against the Fenians. Later, he relinquished command of the company – the 57th Regiment – to his oldest son, James Z. Rogers, brother of R.B. It was the band of this famous family-led company that performed at the opening of the Peterborough lift lock in 1904.

Unlike his father and brother, R.B. was not interested in following the family's military tradition. After graduating from the Union School in Peterborough and Trinity College School in Port Hope, Rogers entered McGill University, graduating in 1878 with a bachelor of arts in science and a major in civil and mechanical engineering. His first job, 1878 – 81, was as assistant engineer in charge of the Trent River slides and booms. In 1881 and 1882, he served briefly as assistant engineer on the Midland division of the Grand Trunk Railway, before returning to the Trent as assistant engineer on the survey for the Trent valley canal under Tom S. Rubidge. On 8 September 1886, following the retirement of Thomas D. Belcher, he was made superintending engineer of the Trent canal. In this position, he had responsibility for superintending the routine maintenance and management of the works and, after 1896, new construction. In May 1905 his responsibility was divided, J.H. McClellan, defeated Liberal candidate in Peterborough West, being made superintendent of maintenance. Thus, practically all of Rogers's professional experience was acquired on the Trent canal, a fact that the commissioners who investigated leaks in the lift locks would hold against him.

Rogers was elected a member of the Canadian Society of Civil Engineers in 1887, and in the following year a member of the Institute of Civil Engineers of England. In 1881, he married Clara Mina Calcutt, second daughter of Henry Calcutt, an Ashburnham brewer and proprietor of the Calcutt Steamboat Line. They had five children: two sons and three daughters.

Trent canal promoters usually criticized one another more savagely because of canal politics than they did outsiders opposed to its construction. The treatment of R.B. Rogers was a case in point. Although he managed to defend himself from Peterborough's political barbarism for 10 years – he did not even vote in provincial or dominion elections – he eventually fell victim to it. Knowing that he was a Conservative – an appointee of Macdonald's government – many Liberals in the district had clamoured for his dismissal since the election of 1896. Officers of some Liberal riding associations, especially angry after the election of 1900, blamed Rogers for the Liberals' not winning more Trent canal seats. They believed that if a Liberal engineer had been in charge of the canal, they would have had better access to patronage, "to the many ways [they] could be consulted regarding changes in staff and little jobs that could come through the local committees."[1] "Could it be too much for us to ask you to assist us in seeking to have Mr. Rogers replaced by an engineer more friendly to the party?,"[2] E. Musgrove, secretary of the Liberal association of Victoria North, asked Laurier. But through the intervention of Willie Boyd, who spoke to Sen. George McHugh, Rogers's position was made at least temporarily secure. Despite his political background Rogers had the confidence of McHugh, who found him "courteous and obliging;"[3] also, Andrew Blair was "favourably disposed to Mr. Rogers"[4] and could see no reason to have him replaced.

Actually, inaccessibility to political patronage because of the presence of Rogers was more imagined than real. As was pointed out earlier, Rogers had no control over staff appointments after the Liberals came to power in 1896; these were made by Liberal party stalwarts such as George McHugh, R.J. McLaughlin of Lindsay, and R.R. Hall and J.R. Stratton of Peterborough. After May 1905, when J.H. McClellan was made superintendent of canal operations, the Liberal organization had unlimited access to patronage and used it in abundance, as a commission investigation revealed in 1914.[5] Nevertheless, although from a patronage point of view there was nothing to be gained by Rogers's dismissal, a group of Peterborough Liberals wanted him out of office, if for no other reason than that his presence on the canal was an embarrassment. As long as Rogers was around, the canal was identified as a Conservative achievement. Rogers claimed privately that Stratton's *Examiner* "was always antagonistic to [his] retaining the position of Superintending Engineer of the Canal after the change of government in 1896."[6]

Although Rogers was well aware of his many minor political opponents, he and his family may not have been aware of his more powerful and influential enemies. After 1904, the men most anxious to get him out of the way were a small group of electric power developers, most of whom were Liberals, including his friend R.R. Hall, although a few of them were Conservatives. Two groups, both with strong connections to the Liberal governments in Toronto and Ottawa, competed for water power leases on the Trent River, and Rogers became a victim in the power struggle between them.

One group was headed by J.A. Culverwell, a financial promoter from Toronto who had taken up residence in Peterborough and later in Port Hope. He was president, managing director, and principal shareholder of the Central Ontario Power Company, founded in 1900 to develop water power at Burleigh Falls. In 1905 this group formed another firm, the Northumberland and Durham Power Company, to develop water power on the Trent River. The other group was headed by the firm of Smith, Kerry and Chace, water power engineers with headquarters in Toronto. The president of this company and driving force behind the group of capitalists whom the company represented was J.G.G. Kerry, formerly an assistant professor of engineering at McGill University.

Culverwell and his group had been antagonistic to Rogers for quite some time, as they perceived him to be an obstacle to their power development plans. First, there was the matter of the Port Hope outlet for the canal, which Culverwell and H.A. Ward vigorously promoted in the elections of 1900 and 1904, but which Rogers opposed. Culverwell's desire for the Port Hope outlet was tied to his water power scheme and had little to do with transportation.

Although he had strong connections with the Liberal government in Ottawa through R.J. McLaughlin, Culverwell's main sphere of influence prior to 1905 was with the Ross government in Toronto, through Richard Harcourt and J.R. Stratton. If water power leases were to be obtained on the Trent, Culverwell and his group stood a better chance of getting them from Toronto than from Ottawa. But it was not clear which government had jurisdiction over the Trent River and therefore had the power to grant leases. Although it was generally conceded that the dominion government had jurisdiction over the Trent for navigation, many believed that surplus water not needed for navigation belonged to the province and that the provincial government, not the dominion, should have control over granting water power leases. The situation was so vague that Culverwell, to be on the safe side, had obtained water power leases from both the dominion and provincial governments for Burleigh Falls. Settlement of the argument about ownership of the water would require a ruling by the court, but, in the meantime, if the Trent canal passed through Port Hope, ownership of the Trent would be clarified. The province, not the dominion, would have complete and uncontestable control of the water if the Trent were no longer classed as a navigable river. It was for this reason that Culverwell and Ward campaigned so vigorously for the Port Hope outlet during the elections.

But Rogers, having surveyed the Port Hope outlet in 1900, had recommended against Port Hope in favour of the Trent, which Ward and

Culverwell considered "unfair and biased."[7] They circulated this point of view widely in Port Hope and environs, asserting that Rogers's attraction to the Trent was related to water power development and had nothing to do with a barge canal as he claimed. Rogers had planned a third hydraulic lift lock at Healey Falls, which would have been higher than the Peterborough lock and would, unlike the Peterborough and Kirkfield locks, have created an immense head of water for electric power generation. This immense water power potential at Healey Falls was the greatest prize on the Trent, a lease for which both Culverwell's and Kerry's groups were anxious to obtain. Culverwell had bought some property at Healey Falls, on the basis of which he claimed water privileges as a riparian owner, and had applied for a lease from both the provincial and dominion governments in the name of the Northumberland and Durham Power Company.

Culverwell was convinced that Rogers was also interested in the lease and was using his position as superintendent of the Trent canal both to develop the water power and to obtain the lease. There may indeed have been some grounds for Culverwell's suspicion. An application for a Healey Falls lease had been made by Albert A. Mulholland, owner of the Northumberland Paper Mill at Cambellford, and J. Kilbourn of Owen Sound, who also owned some property at Healey Falls. Willie Boyd of Bobcaygeon and Rogers, who was a friend of Mulholland, were considering going into business with Mulholland and Kilgour and, according to Culverwell, had joined with them as silent partners in the lease application. But actually (as will be discussed later), Smith, Kerry, and Chace would soon be the significant partners. They had been operating sub rosa on the Trent, buying up property, and were then negotiating with Mulholland to purchase his mill and water power rights at Campbellford.

When he got wind of Rogers's alleged involvement with Mulholland and Kilbourn at Healey Falls, Culverwell wired Laurier: "Charges of malfeasance made against Trent Valley Canal Engineer Rogers with Partner regarding their purchase of parts of Healey Falls and regarding canal outlet. Have documentary proof."[8] It was not entirely clear what Culverwell expected the prime minister to do with this confusing bit of information. When Laurier received the telegram he wrote to A.B. Aylesworth, the Liberal condidate in Durham, to find out just who J.A. Culverwell was (see chapter 25).

Culverwell, still unaware of the covert activities of Messrs Smith, Kerry, and Chace, had grossly overestimated Rogers's involvement with Mulholland and Kilbourn. Culverwell had, in fact, very little evidence to substantiate a charge of malfeasance against Rogers, but that did not stop him from maligning Rogers in a letter to Toronto, Hamilton, and Port Hope newspapers. Later he brought the matter up publicly at a meeting of the Port Hope town council on 5 July 1905, when he was seeking support for his power scheme. Again, he accused Rogers and boasted that Rogers had not dared to reply to his charge of malfeasance. "Mr. Rogers had purchased parts of this water power [Healey Falls] for himself and partner Kilbourn," Culverwell charged at the meeting. "But [I] forced him to transfer it to the Department of Railways and Canals."[9] This was nonsense. Rogers, on instructions from Ottawa, had bought right of way for the canal at Healey Falls; the purchase had nothing to do with power development. Nevertheless, thanks to Culverwell's vicious campaign, Rogers became persona non grata in the counties of Northumberland and Durham. By the time a deputation from these counties arrived in Toronto in early November to press J.P. Whitney, recently elected Conservative premier of Ontario, for a water power lease at Healey Falls, Rogers had become, at least in the minds of the deputation, head of a power syndicate "who proposed to carry off the power to the growing young city of Peterborough."[10]

R.R. Hall, MP for Peterborough East, played an ambivalent role in the piece. He had no connection with Culverwell's group other than a political one, but he, too, was in the water power development game, sharing a lease with W.H. Meldrum and William A. Stratton for surplus water at dam 5 on the Otonabee River and being a major shareholder in the Otonabee Power Company, which planned to build a power plant at the dam. Hall was also suspicious of Rogers's motives, but had the politician's unique ability to compartmentalize relationships. Rogers had reason to believe that he and Hall had "always been good friends";[11] in fact, after his election in 1904, Hall had used his influence to get Rogers a $600 per year raise in pay. But at the same time that Hall, the friend, had been obtaining the pay raise, Hall, the politician, had been conspiring behind Rogers's back. On 30 October, when allegations of engineering incompetence on the part of Rogers were being circulated around Peterborough, and when Culverwell was conducting his malfeasance campaign, Hall, who was opposed to hydraulic lift locks, considering them to be "an expensive and fantastic luxury,"[12] wrote an incriminating letter to Laurier impugning Rogers's motives for proposing a hydraulic lock at Healey Falls:

It is in contemplation of the local engineer Rogers to have a lift lock erected at Healey Falls ... Mr. J. Kilbourn of Owen Sound and Mr. Mulholland of Campbellford have an application in for a lease of water power pending before the railway department now, with view of getting the surplus water power in consideration of their building a dam which would involve the construction of a lift lock. If ordinary masonry locks were installed, there would be no necessity for the dam; therefore, they stand to win in the matter and particularly to win if ordinary masonry locks are not adopted. I would suggest that this lease be held up and not granted ... I have a very shrewd suspicion that Mr. Rogers, the chief engineer, is interested in the lease with them. I will not state it as a fact but every fact points to it.[13]

Laurier assured Hall that he would "watch for the application for water power" and advised him "to write to Emmerson and caution him."[14]

Although Rogers would later become a shareholder in Mulholland's paper company, as a consequence of which he would be associated with Kerry's power syndicate, there is no evidence that this took place before his resignation in February 1906. When Hall and Culverwell were conspiring against him in 1905, Rogers had no direct involvement with any of the power developers.

There were other powerful Liberal supporters who were anxious to see Rogers cast aside. These were the leaders of the Irish Catholics, who for many years had been denied an appropriate share of government patronage, primarily because their arch-enemies, the Orange Irish, had strong connections with the Conservative goverment of Sir John A. Macdonald. When Laurier came to power the Irish Catholic establish-ment, which favoured the Liberals, sought to win the support of the average Catholic voter for the Liberal cause. To this end, it endeavoured to ensure that there was adequate Catholic representation in both the Ontario and the dominion cabinets, on the court benches (especially in the Ontario Supreme Court), and, of course, on the patronage lists, where it counted most. One of the more influential members of this group was Michael J. Haney, éminence grise of the Ontario Liberal party.

Born in Galway, Ireland, in 1854, Haney had immigrated to Canada in 1873, having studied engineering at Watertown, New York. Like many of his countrymen, he showed an aptitude for railway construction, and in 1882, while only 27 years of age, he had become manager of construc-tion for Andrew Onderdonk when he built 360 miles of cpr track in British Columbia. After working for several other railway contractors in Canada and the United States, Haney formed his own company, which received many lucrative government contracts after the Liberals come to power in 1896. These contracts made Haney an extremely rich man. In 1904, Haney was elected president of the Toronto Liberal Club, a position of power he used both to advance the cause of Irish Catholics in Ontario and to ensure the maintenance of the Liberal presence in Ottawa, so that his own business interests would be protected.

Then, as now, Ontario represented the key to electoral success in Canada. Except in 1896, when the Liberals had outpolled the Conser-vatives, Orange Ontario with its developing industries had consistently voted Tory in national elections. If Laurier were to stay in power, he had to have strong support in Ontario; the Roman Catholic vote was crucial. For this reason he seems to have been willing, almost to the point of sycophancy, to allow Irish Catholics like Haney to influence his political judgment. Haney, who claimed "some knowledge of the temper of the Catholics on the question and also [with] the interests of the Liberal party at heart,"[14] took it upon himself to advise Laurier on deserving Catholics for appointment to the bench or the cabinet. He demanded Laurier's presence at political rallies in Toronto on the eve of elections. He thought nothing of instructing Laurier to order Blair to purchase 25 locomotives for the Intercolonial Railway from the Canadian Locomotive Company in Kingston, of which Haney was vice-president, and he even bothered Laurier with such mundane personal requests as reserving seats for him and his friends at the ceremonies in Regina marking Saskatchewan's entry into Confederation, in September 1905. Since the key to political and business success lay in the patronage system of the Department of Railways and Canals, Haney used his influence over Laurier to secure the appointment of another Irish Catholic, M.J. Butler, a friend and former employee, as deputy minister and chief engineer, when Collingwood Schreiber retired in 1905.

It is quite clear that this Irish connection had been working to undermine Rogers's influence. In 1904, he was relieved of responsibility for the Trent surveys, largely because of the controversy over the Port Hope outlet; the surveys were given to another Irish Catholic, Edmond J. Walsh, who operated an engineering consulting firm in Ottawa. As was pointed out earlier, Rogers was also relieved, in 1905, of responsibility for maintenance of the canal works, the job being given to yet another Irish Catholic, J.H. McClellan. If Rogers could be completely replaced by a Catholic superintending engineer loyal to Butler and Haney, so much the better, especially with more contracts about to be let on the canal.

Thus in the autumn of 1905 Rogers had an array of powerful men lined up against him, all of whom wanted him out of office for one reason or another. The problem was, how could this be done? There had to be some reason for having Rogers fired, and there was none. Better if he could be induced to resign voluntarily, and so a trap was set for him: J.H. McClellan set it, the Peterborough *Examiner* baited it, and Rogers, who had always been somewhat naïve politically, walked right into it. Here is how it was done.

McClellan had personal reasons for wanting Rogers out. A coal dealer who knew absolutely nothing about hydraulic engineering or water management, McClellan had been appointed to the superintendency in May 1905, as a reward for his long contribution to the Liberal party, being the defeated candidate in Peterborough West in 1900. Lacking the technical skills necessary to manage such complex structures as the

Peterborough lift lock, McClellan naturally felt insecure with Rogers looking on. And Rogers resented the fact that a man with no experience or qualifications had been placed in charge of costly canal works that he had managed for 20 years and many of which he had designed and built. To make matters worse, Rogers had been instructed to devote his whole time and attention to construction and not to interfere with McClellan unless McClellan appealed to him for advice, which, according to Rogers, had happened only once. Also, McClellan unquestionably felt constrained in his ability to use the canal for political shenanigans – the reason for his appointment – with the high-principled Rogers looking over his shoulder. Consequently, there was constant tension and a strained relationship between the two men.

Whether at the suggestion of his political patrons, who unquestionably wanted to build a case against Rogers, or whether on his own initiative, perhaps to offset his own sense of inadequacy, McClellan used his position as superintendent of maintenance to conduct a campaign of vilification against Rogers. Hints of gross negligence in the construction of the two lift locks, charges of faulty engineering and lax supervision in the construction of these expensive and controversial works, were spread throughout the district soon after McClellan was appointed. We have only Rogers's assertion that the "malicious and absurd reports were written in McClellan's office and published in the Liberal organ, the Peterborough Examiner,"[16] but given that Peterborough was a small town in 1905, where everyone knew everyone else and there were few secrets, there may indeed be a good deal of truth to the allegation. Moreover, some of the employees on McClellan's staff remained loyal to Rogers and kept him posted.

The innuendo, which cast doubt on Rogers's engineering competence, began when the leaks were discovered in the entrance walls to the Kirkfield lock. On 1 September 1905, the Examiner carried a lead story that grossly exaggerated the extent of the leaks and the conditions that caused them and demanded an investigation to fix the blame. A week later, the paper published a bare-bones statement by Rogers, advising that the leaks had been stopped, explaining the cause, and giving the cost of $250 for repairing them, but the paper did not retract its allegation of mismanagement.

Then leaks were discovered in the aqueduct leading to the Peterborough lift lock. Rogers had anticipated leaks, expecting them to develop at the juncture of the breast wall, which rested on solid rock, and the concrete aqueduct, which rested on the built-up earth embankment, when settlement of the earth occurred. The European engineers had experienced leaks at this same point. Rogers had a plan to cope with the anticipated leaks. He intended to draw the water out of the canal every month to examine the floor of the aqueduct and, as the cracks developed, to place movable stopwaters over them until the settling had stopped, when the leaks would be permanently plugged. When the leaks did develop in the summer of 1905, Rogers was no longer responsible for the maintenance of the lock, and he was debarred by his instructions from advising McClellan on the appropriate procedure for dealing with them. The lock-master reported the leaks to McClellan when they first appeared and advised him to have the water drawn off and the canal floor examined, but McClellan refused to have this done. The fact that McClellan did not once, over a period of several months, take the logical step of draining the canal to see what was causing the leaks indicates either that he was extremely inept or that Rogers's charge, that "his whole desire was to have something happen that would throw discredit on me,"[17] was valid. By November, the water was percolating noisily through the terraces on both sides of the aqueduct, making it obvious to everyone that the banks would soon cave in. Still McClellan did not drain the canal, even though navigation was closed for the season. He reported the leaks to the *Examiner*, instead.

On Saturday 4 November, a reporter from the *Examiner* visited the locks and apparently discussed the leaks with McClellan, certainly not with Rogers, for it was McClellan's estimate of $20,000 for repairs, not Rogers's more realistic estimate of $300, that was published in the paper Monday evening. "A SERIOUS DEFECT HAS BEEN DETECTED IN THE PETER-BOROUGH LIFT LOCK," the *Examiner* headlined Monday's story. Once again charges of faulty construction requiring expensive repairs, dramatized now by the stream of water gushing through the banks, were leveled. Again the *Examiner* demanded that an investigation be conducted by the minister of railways and canals "to clear up these statements that are constantly being made as to the defective construction of the lock."[18] This call for an investigation was the trap into which Rogers would soon be lured.

Other newspapers picked up the story, and soon everyone, from one end of the canal to the other, was discussing the alleged defects. Rogers's engineering reputation was gradually being destroyed. To what end? As Rogers himself said: "Never was there a truer exemplification of the old adage, 'Making a mountain out of a mole hill.'"[19] The leaks at Kirkfield had been caused by two factors: Bethune had not ensured that the hard mortar face was put on the first nine sections of the wall, and the pine stopwaters placed between the sections of wall had dried out and shrunk during the three years that had elapsed between the time they had been put there and when the water was let into the canal. The mortar face had been put on at a cost of $250, and the pine stopwaters soon absorbed water and swelled up, filling the joints. The leaks at Peterborough were anticipated and could have been corrected for about $300. The rest of the construction at Kirkfield and Peterborough was sound and, as one European engineer put it, "well conceived and splendidly carried out and to be a really monumental and in the front rank with any canal work of the world ... Any serious criticism of it is unjust."[20] But serious criticism there was. Finally Rogers, in frustration following the suggestion of the *Examiner*, asked Butler for an investigation. The request led to his undoing.

Within a week, Butler requested Emmerson to commission a competent engineer to proceed with the investigation under oath, "either to clear Rogers of the charges, or, if guilty to let him go."[21] Butler recommended Henry Holgate, a civil engineer with the firm of Ross and Holgate of Montreal. Emmerson accepted the recommendation. Then Rogers's enemies had a mechanism, requested by Rogers himself, for mustering the evidence that could "prove" his incompetence and bring about his downfall. And it would all be legal.

Holgate wasted no time in conducting the hearing. He had received his commission on 8 December and by 14 December had summoned the first witness to Peterborough. The hearing lasted nine days, 14 to 20 December and 28 and 29 December. Twenty-three witnesses were heard altogether, all but one hostile to Rogers. Rogers was the first witness called.

He was surprised to find two lawyers present at the hearing: D. O'Donnel, a Liberal barrister from Peterborough, and none other than R.J. McLaughlin of Lindsay, secretary and lawyer for Culverwell's two power companies and twice-defeated Liberal candidate in Victoria North. Rogers was told that the lawyers represented the government. They had been appointed, Mclaughlin said, "to assist the commissioner in every way to get the facts for the interest of the crown."[22] But he really meant for the interests of the Liberal party. Rogers had been authorized by the deputy minister to engage counsel but had decided against it, considering the issue to be an engineering, rather than a legal, question. He would soon regret the decision. It had not occurred to him that the hearing was politically inspired and had little to do with either engineering or the law. Another mistake Rogers made was to trust to the professional knowledge of Holgate, whom he considered a friend, to draw out the technical information necessary to form an unbiased judgment. The two lawyers present would see that that did not happen.

Holgate had been given 20 questions, 10 for each lock, that Butler wanted answered. The questions were designed to prejudice the case; they dealt with the molehill and not the mountain. That is to say, they concentrated on the two small defects that would cost a pittance to correct and ignored the rest of the construction, valued at about $1.5 million.

The report that Holgate submitted to Emmerson on 8 January 1906 was damning to Rogers and some of the other engineers and does little credit to its author. Read 80 years after it was written, compared with the verbatim testimony recorded, and judged by subsequent events, it becomes quite clear that the conclusions reached by Holgate were those sought by Rogers's enemies and not those that the facts demanded. There is no evidence to justify such wild generalizations as "Preparation of the bottom of the walls and ... the omitting of mortar facing shows a lack of serious or intelligent appreciation of the importance of the work in hand and the results are the natural outcome of lax supervision"; "The plans and specifications were not followed faithfully"; or "Mr. Rogers' personal attention was not aggressive enough"; or "Owing to the lack of proper system and of good organization, he [Rogers] had not that control over the contractors or his staff that is necessary in the carrying on of heavy works, and he had not the sympathy and fair cooperation of the men under him."[23] And much more that was both critical and untrue.

It is not entirely clear why Holgate wrote such a derogatory report about a friend and colleague. Certainly it was not true, as Rogers reported in 1912, that "Holgate had recently admitted to the present Minister of Railways and Canals [Frank Cochrane] that for party purposes, when acting as commissioner for the late Government, he had made dishonest and unjustifiable reports";[24] in fact, Holgate defended his conclusions when asked about them by Cochrane. What does seem clear, though, is that Holgate was influenced more by the current speculation that surrounded the case than by the facts or lack of facts that the testimony produced. For example, although he was not asked for an opinion on the matter, he condemned the construction of hydraulic lift locks, asserting that locks of ordinary design would have been cheaper and would have better served the purpose of the canal. Coincidentally, this was the position taken by R.R. Hall and other electric power developers and seems to have been inserted into the report to kill Rogers's plan for a third hydraulic lock at Healey Falls. The motive for including the statement aside, the contract for the Peterborough lock had been approved by the previous Conservative government and the contract for the Kirkfield lock by the Liberals, and so although Rogers recommended the locks he could hardly be held responsible for government policy.

The report may have been a classic example of an investigator telling a client what the client wanted to hear. Holgate operated a private consulting firm; the government was one of his principal clients. Clearly, he had a vested interest in writing the negative report that some in the government wanted. Later, Holgate would be asked to serve as chief commissioner on two other Trent canal investigations and each time would support the position of the government. And in 1907, he would clear Butler of charges of criminal negligence in the Quebec bridge disaster.

There is also some question whether Holgate was technically qualified to investigate the case. He had, after all, never designed or built a lift lock, and he did not have much experience in concrete construction. Col. Sam

Hughes claimed that the forebay wall built by Holgate in 1904 for the Canadian General Electric Company's power plant at Nassau "gave way as soon as the water was let in."[25] There is other evidence to suggest a lack of technical competence. Holgate claimed that Rogers's plans for constructing the entrance walls at Kirkfield "were not such plans as would secure first class work."[26] He based this conclusion on the opinion that the entrance walls should have been bonded to the bedrock by means of trenches filled with concrete; this, in his view, would have prevented the leaks. Rogers had built the walls directly on the rock and connected them with a concrete floor, creating in effect a concrete trough resting on, but independent of, the bedrock. Time would prove that Rogers's plan was the only logical one to follow. Bonding trenches, normally used in the construction of dams, would have been not only unnecessary but useless because of the deep fissures in the limestone at Kirkfield. Blasting the rock for trenches would only have further shattered the rock and increased the fissures. Had Holgate's plan been adopted and not Rogers's, the same situation would have obtained in the Kirkfield canal as obtained at Bobcaygeon in 1834. When Charles Keefer examined the Kirkfield lock in 1914, he concluded that Rogers's plan was the only appropriate one. According to Keefer, Holgate's conclusion, based on his own proposal that "there was shown lack of serious or intelligent appreciation of the importance of the work in hand,"[27] applied to no one but Holgate. Holgate also claimed that the change of location of the Peterborough lift lock from the original plan added substantially to its cost. Actually, the figures that Rogers gave Holgate at the hearing proved beyond doubt that the change in location saved the government thousands of dollars in excavation costs, but Holgate ignored the evidence.

Finally, there is no question that Holgate was influenced, if not manipulated, by the two government lawyers, especially McLaughlin, who, as secretary of Culverwell's power companies, was not neutral regarding the outcome of the hearings. Moreover, McLaughlin not only acted as counsel for the government but also was retained by Bethune, his own political appointee to the canal works. McLaughlin ensured that any evidence damaging to Bethune was suppressed. Bethune's drinking had been the principal cause of the leaks at Kirkfield. He even showed up drunk to give testimony under oath at the hearing, but when Rogers asked McLaughlin if he were going to go into the question of Bethune's drinking habits, McLaughlin answered, "No. That is a personal matter."[28]

False and misleading testimony given by Bethune and Andrew Johnson, Larkin and Sangster's foremen, was accepted to build up a case for poor organization and lack of supervision against Rogers, even though both of these men were mainly responsible for the defects in the walls. Both diverted blame from themselves by claiming that there had not been enough concrete inspectors on the job to supervise the work properly. Bethune claimed that the concrete pouring was done on both walls simultaneously and that he could not be present on both walls at the same time. This was untrue. The concrete was laid alternately, the forms being built up on one wall while concrete was being poured on the other. It could not have been done any other way without stopping the concrete pouring for several days at a time, which had not happened. But it was Bethune's testimony, not Rogers's, that was accepted. Johnson blamed the Italian labourers for the defects. He claimed that they "had to be closely watched"[29] and that not enough supervisors had been provided for the purpose. Using the evidence of these two unreliable witnesses – evidence that would never have stood up in any court of law – Holgate concluded that the defects were "the natural outcome of lax supervision"[30] on the part of Rogers.

Emmerson was not sure at first what he should do with the Holgate report; it was condemnatory, but were the accusations strong enough or accurate enough to warrant asking for Rogers's resignation? Emmerson had no animosity towards Rogers; for that matter, neither did Butler, although he clearly wanted him out of the superintendency. Finally, on 26 January, Emmerson did what politicans frequently do: he "leaked" a summary of the report to the press so that public reaction to it might be assessed and perhaps, too, so that the alleged seriousness of the situation would be planted in the public mind well in advance of any strong action the cabinet, which was scheduled to discuss the report on 1 February, might take. An article that appeared in the Toronto *Globe* hinted at "a most serious condition of affairs" and "blunders which would involve a considerable sum of money to repair."[31] This was the first indication Rogers had of the damaging tenor of the report. Although several newspapers were soon discussing it, another two weeks would pass before Rogers would actually see the report. Then it would be too late for him to do anything about it.

The day before the *Globe* article appeared, fate, as though responding to a cue, intervened to close the case against Rogers. In the early morning hours of 26 January, a section 40 feet wide broke away from the west bank of the canal near the Warsaw Road bridge, permitting 500,000 gallons of water to pour into East Peterborough. Trees were uprooted, basements were flooded, a brick works was inundated, horses and cows found themselves standing in three or four feet of water, and squeeling pigs and squawking hens were swept away by the sudden deluge, many of them to drown. Ironically, Rogers's own basement was filled with water. Had the guard gate a few feet above the break not been forced into position by the rush of water, all of the canal as far as Nassau would have been drained into the town and the damage would have been catastrophic. As it was, about 2,000 feet of the canal were emptied.

An old farm drain over which the canal was built had given way, allowing the canal wall to sag and eventually collapse as water seeped through the cracks. (McClellan claimed that the breach was caused by faulty construction of the bank.) Rogers immediately wired the news to Butler. A few hours later, a summary of the Holgate report was leaked. Thus the *Globe* article entered Peterborough on the evening of 27 January, just 24 hours after the dramatic flood. It was the juxtaposition of the two, coming after a year of rumour and innuendo, that finally determined the outcome of the case. After the flood, the *Examiner* openly demanded that Rogers resign. Those whose property had been damaged agreed. Events then moved rapidly.

On 2 February, Emmerson and Butler went to Peterborough to inspect the damage. They met with the Liberal MPs in the Oriental Hotel to discuss "departmental business."[32] No record of the discussion survives, but it is quite clear that as a result of the meeting Rogers's fate was sealed, for a few days later the departmental secretary, Jones, wrote Rogers on behalf of Emmerson: "I am directed to furnish you with a copy of the Commissioner's report on the perusal of which you may deem it in your interest to place your resignation in the hands of the department at an early date."[33]

The message was clear: Rogers must resign or be fired. He replied on the 16th, asking for "a reasonable time to consider the matter before any action is taken," but Jones responded:[34] "The question is not a subject of contention or further correspondence ... Your decision must be immediate."[35] And so, on the evening of 19 February 1906, realizing that the game was finally up, Rogers penned a simple letter of resignation on plain stationery: "In compliance with the instruction contained in your letter of the 14th instant, I hereby tender my resignation as Superintending Engineer of the Trent Canal."[36] The resignation was accepted effective 31 March. Two days before leaving office, Rogers wrote Emmerson asking that he might be "granted a gratuity of one year's salary," in view of his "many years of employment in the Department of Railways and Canal."[37] Hall, acting as a friend again, supported the request, but Emmerson denied it.

Three Liberal-appointed engineers – Davy, Sawyer, and Francis – received similar letters asking for resignations, but it was really Rogers the party was after. Within a month, Davy and Sawyer were back on the job; W.J. Francis, despite having been censured by the report, was immediately hired by Henry Holgate to supervise the construction of a 32,000-horsepower hydroelectric power plant being built by the firm of Ross and Holgate for a British Columbia power company; and Butler hired

Francis as engineer for the Royal Commission of Inquiry into the Quebec bridge disaster in 1907. So much for Francis's alleged incompetence.

Surveyor E.J. Walsh was offered the superintendency, but he turned it down because of the salary. Although not really qualified, Roman Catholic and Liberal supporter Alex J. Grant, resident engineer at Port Colborne on the Welland Canal, was sent to Peterborough as Rogers's replacement. Ironically, Grant did not get along with McClellan either.

What distressed Rogers most was not the loss of his job, serious as that was, but the way the dismissal had been done. He understood the game of canal politics well enough to know that he had always been vulnerable. Had he become simply a victim of the political changeover in 1896, he would have understood and perhaps accepted it. After all, he too had been a political appointee. But that his professional reputation, of which he was justifiably proud, should be destroyed in order that his enemies achieve their purpose was an outrage from which he and his family would never fully recover. Indeed, 70 years after the fact, a surviving daughter in Peterborough still bore the pain of her father's humiliation. It would have been of some comfort to Rogers had he known that, at the very moment Emmerson was demanding his resignation, Sir Wilfrid Laurier had in his desk a signed but undated letter of resignation from Emmerson as a pledge of his word to give up intoxicating drink and to refrain from visiting whorehouses – a curious pledge by a minister of the crown and a former president of the Baptist Congress of Canada.[38] In any event, Rogers had now to find some other means of earning a living.

In May 1906 he accepted a position as superintendent of Mulholland's paper mill in Campbellford, a position that lasted for two years. For the next year, he pursued other job leads: a position in Detroit with a firm developing a new system of reinforced concrete, an unsuccessful tender for section 1 of the Ontario – Rice Lake division of the Trent canal, and a promise of a job with L.P. Nott, an English contractor who won the contract for section 1 – subsequently, Nott backed out of the contract, and the position fell through. Then in February 1908 "the tide turned." He "landed in the position that [he had] been covetting [sic] for the last ten years, namely in a contract on the Trent Canal."[39] He and William Dennon, manager of the American Cereal Company, received a contract for section 2 of the Ontario – Rice Lake division, having submitted the lowest tender.

The Conservative government of Robert Borden did not treat Rogers much more fairly than its Liberal predecessor had. Soon after the government took office, Rogers endeavoured to have the Holgate report reviewed. He approached Frank Cochrane, Borden's minister of railways and canals, who promised to have a department expert examine the case; if the report of the expert warranted further action, he would select a commissioner to make an official investigation. Instead, Cochrane wrote to Holgate for his opinion. Naturally Holgate was opposed to opening the case. "You will understand, " Holgate wrote Cochrane, "that Mr. Rogers and several of his staff were personal friends of mine and that it was rather painful for me at the time to have to make such a report against them, but at this date ... I feel justified in saying to you that Mr. Rogers was quite incapable of handling the position that he was placed in on the canal."[40] Consequently, Cochrane let the matter drop. When nearly two years had gone by and Rogers had not heard from Cochrane, he contacted the Conservative MPs on the canal, in consequence of which Cochrane was bombarded with letters asking for a review of the Rogers case. Then Cochrane went ahead with it.

The man Cochrane appointed was Charles Keefer, former president of the Canadian Society of Engineers and oldest son of the renowned engineer Thomas C. Keefer, who was prominent in railway, canal, and harbour construction in the nineteenth century. Keefer examined the locks at Kirkfield and Peterborough and studied Holgate's report and Rogers's reply to it. On all issues, Keefer sided with Rogers. His report, submitted to Cochrane on 19 November 1914, completely vindicated Rogers. Cochrane sat on it for nearly three months, after which time Rogers somehow obtained a copy and had it published without having, as Cochrane put it, "the decency to pay the bill."[41]

There was a dispute over who should pay Keefer's fee of $1,150. Rogers was under the impression that the government, having appointed the commissioner and having received his report, should bear the cost of the investigation. Cochrane, however, expected Rogers, by prior agreement, "to settle the bill."[42] Finally, his bitterness now complete, Rogers paid up, but not without expressing his disgust with the Conservative government: "The honourable vindication of my record by Commissioner Keefer had been degraded into a personal or professional favour by imposing upon me the cost of an offical enquiry affecting a government work and a public servant. An official vindication at the private expense of the person vindicated forms a precedent that does little credit to the administration."[43]

Holgate was furious at the publication of Keefer's report. "I have been more or less discredited by having my report on the Trent Valley matter reversed," he complained to Cochrane. But with his eye now on lucrative Conservative government contracts he went on to plead, "I would like from you an assurance that the recent enquiry and report in no way prejudices me, and that you have full confidence in my judgment."[44] That Rogers's career and reputation had been destroyed by Holgate's own irresponsible report seems not to have been a matter of remorse with him, nor, apparently, was it a matter of concern to Cochrane.

There was no question of Rogers's reinstatement in the Department of Railways and Canals following Keefer's review. Rogers did not ask for a job. Even though Cochrane made no public comment on the Keefer report, Rogers was content to let it restore, at least in part, his professional reputation, so severly damaged by the Holgate study. Meanwhile, he continued to execute his government contract on the Trent River.

The contract was finally finished in 1918, and Rogers retired to "Beechwood," his farm on the outskirts of Peterborough, where he participated in community farming organizations but took no active part in the public life of the city. Taking a page from the book of former contractors with whom he had dealt as superintending engineer, Rogers submitted a claim for extras on his contract early in 1919. Typically, the case dragged on for years through departmental committees and the Exchequer Court, so that it was not until May 1926 that the cabinet finally approved a sum of $11,547.14 to be paid in Rogers's favour. Even then there was a delay in the payment. When Rogers suffered a near-fatal heart attack in the spring of 1927 the money still had not been paid. An urgent telegram from his lawyer to the deputy minister finally produced the cheque on 11 June.

The Department of Railways and Canals hounded Rogers to the brink of the grave. In August 1927 a Roman Catholic priest, S.A. Corrigan of Frankford, complained about material lying in an unsightly pile on government property opposite the church. An investigation revealed the material had been left there by Dennon and Rogers in 1918. On 15 September, the chief engineer of the Department of Railways and Canals instructed canal superintendent A.L. Killaly to order Dennon and Rogers to remove the material within 10 days of receipt of the order. But William Dennon had died in 1924, and Rogers was dying in Peterborough and was incapable of taking any action on the matter. Dennon's son, William Jr, was tracked down in Mobile, Alabama, where he managed a paper mill. He arranged by telegram to have a local Jewish junk dealer remove the material, before the 10-day period had expired. The bulk of the material was removed on 26 September, but 27 and 28 September being Yom Kippur, clean-up was suspended until the 29th. Finally, on 1 October the material was entirely removed. The next day, his last dealings with the Department of Railways and Canals completed, Rogers died.

In the summer of 1928, the Peterborough branch of the Engineering Institute of Canada, believing that Rogers had not received proper recognition for his contribution to the canal, sought and received permission from Charles Dunning, Mackenzie King's minister of railways and canals, to place a commemorative plaque on the Peterborough lift lock. The simple inscription reads: IN MEMORY OF RICHARD BIRDSALL ROGERS C.E., M.E.I.C., O.L.S. WHO WAS SUPERINTENDING ENGINEER ON THE TRENT CANAL DURING THE CONSTRUCTION OF THIS LIFT LOCK – BORN PETERBOROUGH, JANUARY 16, 1857 DIED OCTOBER 2, 1927. The gracious memorial does not say enough. It does not, for example, give Rogers credit as the true designer of the lock.

This omission probably reflected a doubt about Rogers's contribution that was created in 1917, when *Who's Who and Why* falsely credited Walter J. Francis as the man who "designed and had charge of construction of the two hydraulic lift locks on the Trent Canal."

It is an irrefutable fact that Rogers, not Francis, designed the Peterborough and Kirkfield locks and that history should give him undisputed credit for it. The closing comments of Commissioner Keefer in his 1914 report were these: "The work of the Trent Canal, done under the direction of Mr. Rogers, is the best evidence that it has been properly designed and constructed and is a work that any Engineer might be proud to have been connected with."[45] As for the efficiency of Rogers's design and the quality of the workmanship done under his supervision, not Keefer, not Holgate, not the contemporary batch of politicians, and not even Rogers himself, but Time has been the final judge. Eighty years have passed since the Peterborough lift lock was finished, yet its concrete substructure is as solid as it was the day it was poured. And anyone who has ridden his or her boat through the lock will know that the mechanism functions as smoothly now as it did when the *Stoney Lake* first passed through on 9 July 1904, despite the hundreds of thousands of lockages made in the intervening years.

The time has come for Parks Canada to commemorate the names of the individuals who were responsible for the building of the Trent Canal by naming some of the locks after them. Naming the Peterborough lift lock the R.B. Rogers Lock would be an appropriate place to begin.

CHAPTER TWENTY-TWO

Mulock's Madness

At the same time as Rogers was being asked to resign in 1906 because of alleged responsibility for the small repair bills for the hydraulic lift locks at Peterborough, the Liberal government was planning to waste over a million dollars to build what the Hon. A.B. Aylesworth would later call a "perpetual monument to government folly."[1] Known officially as the Holland River division, a proposed extension of the Trent canal from Lake Simcoe to Aurora by way of the east branch of the Holland River had many names: the Newmarket canal, the Holland River canal, Aylesworth's canal, Our Ditch, the Famous Ditch, and a Scheme Conceived in Iniquity and Born in Shame, but perhaps its most appropriate pseudonym was Mulock's Madness, after the man who conceived the crazy idea.

Born in Bond Head in 1844, William Mulock (later Sir William) had been a lawyer and law professor in Toronto before being elected in 1882 as Liberal MP for York North. Laurier made him postmaster-general in 1896, and the first minister of labour in 1900. The son of a Reform member of the legislative assembly, Mulock was initially considered a conservative Liberal; as such he had the confidence of the business and financial community in Toronto and soon became the party's political boss and Laurier's right-hand man in Ontario. But in 1905 his political philosophy began to move to the left. Finding himself at odds with his cabinet colleagues, he resigned from active politics to become chief justice of the Exchequer Court. In 1923 he was made chief justice of the Supreme Court of Ontario. The following year, he was elected chancellor of the University of Toronto (he had been a very active vice-chancellor 1881 – 1900) and held the position until his death at the age of 100 in 1944. His evolving proclivity to what some called socialist ideas led him to inaugurate a scheme for the Newmarket canal, which became the one serious blemish on an otherwise flawless parliamentary career.

The northern part of York county and, more particularly, the market town of Newmarket, 30 miles north of Toronto, prospered during

Mulock's years in office. When the Liberals came to power in 1896, there was but one major industry in Newmarket: Willian Cane and Sons, manufacturers of wooden wares such as pails, tubs, washboards, snow shovels, and butter churns. Known for a time as the United Factories, it was operated in 1904 by the three Cane brothers. The company was an outgrowth of a lumber mill, established at Newmarket by their father in 1875. When the pine had been harvested in the land south of Lake Simcoe, the firm switched from sawing logs to manufacturing wood products. The Canes prospered, despite increasing reliance on hardwoods that had to be brought down from the north at great cost. The Canes were staunch Liberals. In 1905, H.S. Cane was mayor of the town.

Mulock brought other industries to Newmarket. In 1897, he brought a branch of the Office Specialty company from Rochester, New York. The company made both wooden and steel office furniture. When the Davis Leather Company's plant at King burned down in 1903, Mulock convinced the company to rebuild in Newmarket.

Thanks to government patronage – furniture and office equipment for government offices, postmen's boots and bags, materials and equipment for post offices all over Canada, most of it purchased by Mulock without tender – Newmarket's industries flourished and, with them, the town. But in 1904 the Grand Trunk, which had a virtual monopoly on transportation in the province, increased its freight rates by 50 per cent and Newmarket's industries and Mulock's political base were threatened. It was then that Mulock proposed the Newmarket canal.

He had never been a supporter of Laurier's railway policy. He was particularly opposed to the government-sponsored Grand Trunk National and to railway subsidies generally, which he considered beneficial mainly to the railway barons. Gradually, like many in Ontario, he became a strong advocate of outright government ownership of railways and other public utilities such as electric light plants. As indicated, he eventually resigned from the cabinet and the House of Commons because he found himself increasingly isolated in a government dominated by men who purused the ideal of private ownership of utilities and were opposed to his desire for an increasing role for the state in public affairs. Mulock was one of the first modern-day Liberals. His proposal for a government-built Newmarket canal was consistent with his political philosophy, local partisan politics notwithstanding.

Mulock had always been a supporter of the Trent canal. He sympathized with those who saw a completed canal as a lever in the hands of the public to force railways to keep freight rates in line. He had been impressed ever since 1882 at the achievement of successive representatives of the Trent Valley Canal Association who had gone to Ottawa and acquired extension after extension of the Trent canal system. He saw, in this kind of response to the sustained and legitimate demands of the people, government functioning at its best. If group pressure worked for the people of Peterborough, why not for the residents of York North? All he needed to do was awaken the people of the riding to the possibility of a canal, help them organize a pressure group, and then offer what assistance he could in Ottawa.

For many months, perhaps even years, Mulock had contemplated the possibility of an extension of the Trent canal up the east branch of the Holland River to Aurora. Water transportation through Newmarket was not a new idea. Ever since 1796, the town site had been on the canoe route of the Toronto Carrying-Place, over which travellers destined for the far west had journeyed. After 1812, Indians paddled their canoes up the east branch of the Holland River to trade at Borland's trading post. Soon trappers and settlers came to the "new market" that grew up around the trading post, instead of travelling all the way to the old market at York. Thus the town acquired its name. When Thomas Need visited the Lake Simcoe region in 1832 in search of land, settlers were already talking about the possibility of a canal to Lake Ontario by way of Lake Scugog. And then came the proposal for the Toronto and Georgian Bay canal, later called the Huron and Ontario Ship Canal. Mulock had been a boy of 11 when Kivas Tully's surveyors passed through Bond Head in search of a route for the canal. Thereafter he had witnessed the ups and downs of this canal, which had been supported by many of the world's leading engineers. In 1900, the Huron and Ontario Ship Canal Company's charter was still active.

But whereas the Huron and Ontario Ship Canal would drain the water of Lake Simcoe south through a cut in the Oak Ridges Moraine into the Humber River, Mulock's partial canal would run the other way and would depend on the water that could be collected in the dry hills south of Newmarket. The technical problem notwithstanding, Mulock thought the idea made good sense, although he kept it to himself until the propitious moment, which seemed to have arrived in September 1904.

Several factors determined the timing of his initiative. First, the Peterborough – Lakefield division had just been finished and the Balsam – Lake Simcoe division was under contract and would be completed soon. Second, the Transportation Commission had recommended completing the canal, and so Mulock believed that the Trent and Severn rivers divisions would be let to contract in the near future. Third, since the Grand Trunk had increased its rates, water transportation would be all the more appealing to the manufacturers in Newmarket, on whose support the success of the scheme ultimately depended. Fourth, and most important, a dominion election was coming in November.

As Mulock saw it, a water communication with Lake Simcoe would be advantageous to the towns of Aurora and Newmarket and the surrounding country. The Canes' factory, Davis's tannery, and the Office

Specialty Company could import lumber, logs, and tan bark more cheaply by water than by rail. Oats could be transported from farms in York North to the American Cereal Company's mills in Peterborough. When the Severn River division was opened, wheat could be brought from the Lakehead to the large flour mill in Newmarket directly and more cheaply by water than by rail, as was then required. Finally as the public-spirited Mulock reminded Laurier, "The tourist traffic [could] not be overlooked."[2] Most of the vessels plying the Trent were engaged in the passenger trade, taking thousands and thousands of people from the south on day outings or to summer camps and hotels along the inland waters. "This custom is not a waste," Mulock pointed out, "but is of much public benefit, such outings being ... healthful and thus in the public interest."[3] A Newmarket canal would capture some of this trade. Mulock had a vision of tourists by the hundreds coming to Newmarket from Toronto on the Metropolitan Street Railway and taking boats from the town "to spend a day cruising in Lake Simcoe, visiting some of the islands there, fishing, etc."[4]

It was a politician's vision, not an economist's forecast, and certainly not an engineer's brain-child. True, the town of Newmarket was prospering, but in 1904 it was still little more than a rural hamlet with a population of 2,125, postal revenue of just $5,297, and real estate assessment of only $555,125. The village of Holland Landing had a population of only 446, living in 79 houses, with a total assessed value of $66,249. The cost of constructing a canal through these towns would exceed the assessed value of both of them. As for commercial traffic, only about 60 tons of freight per day moved in and out of Newmarket, half of which was exchanged with Toronto. So a canal running north would carry at most about 20 tons of freight per day, providing it had somewhere to go when it reached Lake Simcoe. Nevertheless, in the first week of September 1904 Mulock initiated a chain of events that would culminate in one of the most disgraceful wastes of public funds in Canadian history.

While riding on the train from Newmarket to Toronto during the first week in September, he chanced to meet Mayor H.S. Cane. "How are you getting along with the railways regarding their freight rates?,"[5] he asked Cane. Cane was depressed. He had just made a personal but unsuccessful appeal to the Board of Railway Commissioners for a reduction in the rates. The recent increase in freight rates for raw materials was hurting not only his factory but the other industries in Newmarket as well. Moreover, Newmarket was discriminated against on lumber and other heavy freight coming from the north, as the rates to Newmarket were the same as those to Toronto. Newmarket industries were further penalized by paying higher transportation costs on manufactured goods because they had to be shipped through Toronto, adding to the shipping distance. Consequently, Newmarket industries were having difficulty competing with Toronto firms and would have either to close or to relocate. Canes were contemplating moving to a location on Georgian Bay, where they would have access to cheap water transportation. It was on that train in early September that Mulock outlined his canal scheme and suggested to Cane how one might proceed to muster popular support for it. Cane was enthusiastic. Events then moved quickly.

On 9 September, a notice was placed in the Newmarket *Era* and the *Express-Herald* calling attention to a public meeting in the town hall in Newmarket on the afternoon of 10 September, "to discuss freight rates and the extension of the Trent Valley Canal to Newmarket, Aurora, Schomberg, etc."[6] Despite the short notice, the meeting was attended by about 300 people. Mayor Cane acted as chairman. Mulock outlined his canal scheme, enumerated its advantages, and proposed that an organization be formed in order "that the matter be presented to the Government."[7] Two motions emerged from the discussion; one stated "that the meeting was of the opinion that the public interest demands the deepening of the east branch of the Holland River via Holland Landing, Newmarket and Aurora"[9] and, while building canals on paper, added: "the west branch via King township, the Black River via Sutton with such improvements thereon as will make them available for commercial highways."[10] The other motion set up a temporary organization with authority to prepare a constitution and elect officers and "to prosecute the object of the association with all energy."[11]

Two weeks after the meeting, E.J. Walsh, chief of the Trent surveys, arrived in Newmarket upon the invitation of Mulock, to determine the feasibility of the plan. With the help of local workers, Walsh spent 10 days on the east branch of the river taking levels and making preliminary sketches. Meanwhile, the Trent Valley Canal Extension Association was formally organized, with H.S. Cane as president, E.T. Daville, mayor of Aurora, as vice-president, and T.H. Burton of Newmarket as secretary. Neighbouring town councils were encouraged to endorse formal resolutions of support, and a petition circulated by the Extension Association was signed by nearly everyone in northern York county. Under Mulock's expert coaching, the residents of York North were playing the same game that mainstream Trent canallers had perfected over a period of 80 years. By mid-January the delegates from the county who would wait on the prime minister had been selected and their expenses authorized. Cane then informed Mulock that the delegation was ready to present its case for the Newmarket canal to the government. But there was hitch in Ottawa.

The cabinet had discussed the scheme on 11 January and was opposed to it. The engineers in the Department of Railways and Canals, resenting Mulock's interference in their affairs, had advised against the scheme.

After the meeting Mulock wrote privately to Laurier, advising that the situation "called for very delicate treatment." Because the people of York North felt so strongly about the canal, "it would be inexpedient on the part of the Government to appear indifferent or deaf to their proposal,"[12] he told Laurier. And because he was committed to arrange for the delegation to present its case, he cunningly suggested: "It is possible that if a deputation of reasonable men came to Ottawa, laid their views before the Government, and received a patient hearing, they might be sent home with pleasant words and with the feeling that their petition would at least receive the most careful consideration with a view to being dealt with on its merits."[13]

Because, as usual, Laurier could find no flaws in Mulock's political logic, he accepted the suggestion and told Mulock "to arrange for the delegation to come here any time that it may be convenient."[14] Mulock arranged for the deputation – 59 leading citizens of York North – to meet with Laurier on 22 February. Like all other Trent canal delegations, this one was non-partisan, consisting of municipal leaders, businessmen, and leading provincial and dominion politicians, both Liberal and Conservative. After listening to the petition presented and numerous speeches, Laurier promised that a survey would be made, after which the government would look closely into the proposal. A group photograph was taken on the steps of the Parliament Buildings, providing an embarrassing record for those Conservatives in the deputation who would later deny ever having supported the scheme.

Sir William Mulock ensured that the plans and estimates, when completed, would place the canal scheme in the most favourable light. E.J. Walsh was sent back to Newmarket to make a comprehensive study of the canal, taking his preliminary instructions from Mulock, who "very strongly impressed upon [him] that everything possible was to be done to have the work designed so that it could be carried out with a minimum of expenditure."[15] Walsh seems to have been one of those government engineers who believed that if a proposal were politically desirable, it had to be technically possible. He advised Mulock that the scheme was feasible and proceeded to get out his plans and specifications "based on the most economic principles and expenditure."[16]

Walsh planned the canal in three sections. Section 1 extended from the south end of Cook Bay on Lake Simcoe to Holland Landing, a stretch of about five miles that required only dredging. He estimated the cost at $46,000. Section 2 covered the four-and-half-mile stretch of river from Holland Landing to Newmarket. The 43-foot difference in elevation between the two towns would be overcome by four locks: a flight of two locks, each with a lift of 10 feet, at Holland Landing and two other locks with lifts of about 11 feet. The locks were to be the same dimension as those on the mainstream of the Trent canal. In addition there were to be three dams, swing bridges, retaining walls, pipe culverts, and a dock in Newmarket. The estimated cost of this section was $314,220. Section 3, the plans for which were not completed until 1908, comprised the improvements from Newmarket to Aurora. Two alternate routes were proposed. One followed the river right into the town of Aurora and required six locks. There would be five dams and a dock, 250 feet long and 150 feet wide, in the centre of town. The cost would be $822,498. The other route would leave the river two miles above Newmarket and follow the bed of Hartman's Stream. It required five locks and would cost only $634,602, but it would terminate some 1,000 feet outside the town limits. Walsh's plans were excellent. Consistent with Mulock's instructions, the improvements required the cheapest yet adequate type of material and methods of construction. There was only one thing lacking: water.

The source of the east branch of the Holland River is a marshy area on the Oak Ridges Moraine, about six miles east of Aurora. The stream emanating from the marsh wanders westwards among the sand hills to a point about two miles south of Aurora, where it turns north and then, flowing through Aurora, Newmarket, and Holland Landing, joins up with the west branch about two miles from Lake Simcoe. A number of small streams feed into the river above Newmarket. The average precipitation in the drainage area is only 30 inches per year. Walsh's weir measurements revealed that while there would be sufficient water in the system to operate the locks during the spring freshet, the minimum quantity of water flowing in the river in the summer was not adequate. Since each lockage would require from 52,000 to 62,000 cubic feet of water, storage reservoirs to conserve the spring floods would have to be built for navigational purposes in the summer months.

Two possibilities were available: two reservoir dams on the supply streams east of Newmarket, with a storage capacity of 24,422,400 cubic feet and a combined cost of slightly more than $50,000, could be built, or a diversion of the water in Lake Wilcocks, the headwater of the Humber River, could be made through a mile-and-a-half conduit into Hartman's Creek, a tributary of the Holland River. This would cost $40,315. But even with a reversal of the drainage of Lake Wilcocks, an additional storage dam would have to be built on White Rose Stream at a cost of $114,246 to ensure a sufficient supply of water to operate the locks over a seven-month navigation period.

Walsh's water supply calculations were highly speculative; his cost estimates were tentative; there was no allowance for flood damage and land purchase and no consideration of the ecological effect of the reservoirs or of the diversion of Lake Wilcocks on the environment. The canal was a foolish proposal made for political purposes and ought to have been rejected out of hand. But the hydra head of York North politics had emerged from the marshes of the Holland River to panic the government into taking an immediate and, as it turned out, indefensible decision to build the canal.

York North had been a Reformer-Liberal stronghold since its very beginning. The first secret meeting of the insurrectionists who planned William Lyon Mackenzie's ill-fated march on Toronto took place in Newmarket on 3 August 1837. Afterwards, many of the rebels were incarcerated in the Old Scottish Kirk on Trinity Street. Prior to Confederation, York North had been represented in the legislative assembly usually by Reformers, most notably Robert Baldwin, Henry Widdifield, and Thomas Mulock. Since Confederation, the riding had returned Conservatives only twice: in 1878 – 82 and briefly in 1873, when the American lumberman A.G.P. Dodge double-crossed the electorate by running as an Independent, claiming to be a Reform sympathizer but supporting Macdonald when he took his seat in Parliament. As noted earlier, Mulock had held the seat for the Liberals since 1882, but by the turn of the century political sentiment in the riding had begun to shift towards the Conservatives.

Mulock initiated the canal scheme in September 1904 to check the shift and to improve his chances of keeping the seat in the November election. Having won the election, he ought to have abandoned the scheme on economic grounds, but there were definite indications that the riding was still moving inexorably to the Tories, his own popularity notwithstanding, and so the canal proposal was kept active. Evidence of a swing towards the Conservatives came on 26 January 1905, the very day Laurier authorized the visit of the Newmarket canal delegation. A provincial election took place that day. Not only was the Ross government defeated by the Conservatives under James Whitney, but York North elected the Conservative Thomas H. Lennox over Liberal A.E. Widdifield. By the spring of 1905, Mulock had decided to exchange his seat in Parliament for a seat on the bench. The man chosen to replace him was Allen B. Aylesworth, a prominent Toronto lawyer whom Laurier wanted as minister of justice. When Mulock resigned in October, Aylesworth was immediately given the postmaster-general's portfolio and a by-election was called in York North for November.

Aylesworth had run and been defeated in Durham in 1904, largely because of the Liberals' handling of the Port Hope outlet of the Trent canal. To ensure that the Trent canal would not defeat Aylesworth a second time,

Mulock encouraged Emmerson to push a supplementary estimate of $100,000 for the Holland River division through Parliament in July, even though there was only a preliminary report from Walsh (dated, appropriatly, 17 March) and Walsh's verbal assurance that the canal scheme was feasible.

Aylesworth won the by-election and was appointed minister of justice. Again the canal scheme should have been dropped, but Aylesworth's majority had been only 149, a considerable reduction from Mulock's majority of 962 a year earlier. The drift towards the Conservatives seemed to be accelerating; it was essential, looking down the road to the next election, to arrest that drift. The Newmarket canal scheme was, therefore, pursued vigorously.

Although Walsh did not submit his final report with the plans and specifications until 29 September 1906, tenders had been called the previous March for dredging section 1 on the Holland River. A contract for $46,497.10 was let to Liberal supporter E.S. Cane, co-proprieter of the United Factories, who, with Dr Spohn of the Penetang mental hospital, had formed the Lake Simcoe Dredging Company and built a dredge and barge especially for the contract. By then, M.J. Butler had replaced Collingwood Schreiber as chief engineer and deputy minister, Rogers had been dismissed, and Alex J. Grant was superintending engineer of the Trent canal and would be responsible for supervising construction on the Holland River. But the man influencing decisions in the Department of Railways and Canals was Michael John Haney, who had been responsible for the appointment of Butler and whom Butler kept posted on developments in the department. These Irish engineers, using their own unique style of operation, succeeded in converting the Newmarket canal scheme from burlesque into complete farce. Through their shenanigans the government was victimized.

It has already been implied that E.J. Walsh, in endorsing the canal, came close to compromising his engineering integrity to ingratiate himself with the politicians, especially Mulock. Butler and Grant, with the connivance of Haney, set out to stop the scheme and, while they were at it, to embarrass Mulock and put their colleague Walsh in the pillory. Butler and Haney disliked Mulock personally. They were particularly resentful of his interference in the affairs of the Department of Railways and Canals and, being "railway men," did not trust his negative attitude towards railways. According to Walsh, just after taking office Butler spoke "in a contemptuous manner of Sir William Mulock and the Holland River improvements and expressed himself as thoroughly opposed."[17] As Walsh had endorsed the scheme, Emmerson had approved it, and Mulock had been pushing for it, there was only one way in which Butler could have it stopped: change the plans and increase the cost to a level that would discourage the government from undertaking Walsh's plans, even if this meant discrediting Walsh.

Consequently, when Butler received Walsh's plans and specifications for section 2, he sent them to Grant with instructions "to go over them carefully and make any notes"[18] that occurred to him. Thereupon Grant, according to Walsh, "from the confines of his office and with the connivance of Butler undertook and did within a few days mutilate the plans and proposals"[19] that Walsh had carefully considered over a period of several months. According to Walsh, moreover, Butler and Grant, neither of whom knew anything about hydraulic engineering, never mind the situation on the Holland River, copied the plans of the Soulanges Canal on which Grant had once been employed in a subordinate capacity and applied them to the Holland River improvements. Whatever their motivation, the record shows that Walsh's plans were indeed changed drastically, the alterations being most extravagant and calling for a much larger expenditure than required by the original plans. For instance, the dimensions of the locks were increased from 142 feet in length to 175 feet; the proposed flight of locks at Holland Landing was replaced with a single lock with a 20-foot lift, necessitating a very large additional expenditure for an artificial foundation of piles; the cheaper system of gate valves was changed to the more expensive installation of culverts in the side walls of the lock, requiring much thicker and, therefore, more expensive lock walls; the river channel was made wider and deeper; and concrete cores were substituted for puddle cores in the dams, concrete piers for timber piers in the bridges, and concrete culverts for cedar culverts. The changes made increased the cost to almost three times Walsh's estimate. The politicians knew nothing about the changes, as it was Grant's revised report that was submitted to the minister.

The strategy of dissuading the government from undertaking the work by increasing the cost of the canal through elaborate changes in the plans did not work. Despite the increased estimate, the government went ahead with the tenders anyway. As the winter session of the 1908 Parliament dragged on, it became quite evident that there would be an election in the spring or late summer. Aylesworth was in trouble in York North. Not known personally in the riding, he had to be seen to be doing something for his constituents, and so it was decided to go ahead with section 2, construction of which would generate plenty of pre-election jobs. Tenders were called, and a contract for $652,009.50 was let to Liberal supporter John Riley of St Catharines on 12 February. Riley, who was only a "front man," assigned the contract to W.B. Russel, C.W. Dill, and A. Lothian on 19 February; they in turn assigned it to the York Construction Company of Toronto, of which they were the principal partners. The contract included only the locks, dams, and dredging of the river bed. As was customary, separate contracts were let for the cement ($8,000 to the Lakefield Portland Cement Company) and three bridges ($17,792 to the Hamilton Bridge Company).

The equipment of the inexperienced Cane dredging company had proved unsuitable for dredging, and so that firm had allowed its contract to lapse. Consequently, new tenders were called for dredging section 1, based on Grant's ridiculously high estimate of $131,000. The same John Riley submitted the lowest tender, by coincidence only $150 under Grant's estimate, but in the end it was decided not to let a contract because there was no need for the dredging to be done until section 2 was completed.

Work on section 2 started at the end of April. All summer long, gangs of men, most of them locals, were engaged in excavating and building forms for the concrete. During the last week of October – the week of the election – 250 hands were working on the canal. About 25 per cent of the contract was completed when work terminated for the winter. The letting of the contract definitely contributed to Aylesworth's re-election. He squeaked by his opponent with a majority of 306 votes, even though it had been patently obvious to all in Newmarket that the canal was being built for purely political reasons, everyone knowing that under normal circumstances no attempt would ever be made to canalize the shallow Holland River.

Many citizens who knew nothing of the political manoeuvring behind the scenes, or even that a canal was contemplated, were surprised when gazing out the windows of Grand Trunk passenger trains as they glided along the bank of the river to see two giant steam shovels and an army of men with horses and scrapers digging huge holes in the river bank. "What on earth are they doing to the peaceful scenery?" some asked. Upon being told that locks were being constructed, the immediate response was: "Where will the water come from?" Where indeed the water would come from to canalize this muddy stream was the question on many minds, for construction had been started before the crucial question of water supply had been determined. Soon people were discussing the enterprise with levity, and Tory newspapers were having a field-day with it. "People who know nothing about engineering should not presume to discuss in this fashion a great public work and in order to prevent this flippant discussion a screen should be built to shut away the view from passing trains until the election is over,"[20] *Saturday Night* chuckled. "Even with storage reservoirs, the mud-cat might find the going rather hard,"[21] scoffed the Orillia *Packet*. "Those people who have been saying there is no water in our ditch ought to come and see it now,"[22] the *Express-Herald* derided, after a flash flood on 24 November 1909 washed away a coffer-dam and flooded out the excavation.

Even before construction started it had been decided that Walsh's plan to build conservation reservoirs would be too expensive. The Wilcocks

Lake diversion was ruled out, too, not only because of the expense but also because of legal suits that would result from cutting off the natural flow of water in the Humber River. It was then that someone in the Department of Railways and Canals came up with the improbable idea of pumping water from Lake Simcoe to Newmarket to solve the water supply problem. The newspapers had more fun with that suggestion. The Toronto *News* and *Telegram* carried cartoons depicting Aylesworth and Graham pumping water with a hand pump into a dry ditch. The *Mail and Empire* complained that "in the end the country may have to pay for pumping water from Lake Simcoe to Newmarket in order that the same water may run again into Lake Simcoe by way of the canal."[23] Even the new minister of railways and canals, George P. Graham, could not resist joking about the canal: "There is plenty of water in it for all the commerce there will ever be on it,"[24] he told a mirthful audience in Newmarket. But not all the criticism was flippant. When it dawned on newspaper editors how much money was being wasted on the farce in York North – Butler and Grant were quoting a figure of $1.1 million to complete section 2 – editorials became quite strident.

Stirred by the newspaper stories, Opposition members were already anxious to confront the government about the money being wasted on the Newmarket canal when the Trent canal estimates were tabled in February 1909. The Opposition had been tricked when the estimates were introduced in 1908. The $200,000 spent on the Newmarket canal had been buried in the $1 million voted for all construction on the Trent canal, the Opposition having been led to believe that all the money was to be spent on the Trent River contracts let at the same time as the Newmarket contract. They were determined not to be tricked this time.

Ever since 1882, when the Macdonald government voted funds to revive the Trent canal scheme, the Opposition, whether Liberal or Conservative, had been content to challenge the estimates and to score a political point or two against the government of the day, but the estimates were always allowed to stand without much serious objection. Not so the estimates of 1909. So incensed was the Conservative opposition at the waste of public funds on this ridiculous undertaking that it determined, if at all possible, to stop the work. The first Opposition barrage was fired on 25 February, when another $1 million estimate was tabled for work on the Trent canal. Once again the government had cleverly concealed the amount for the Holland River improvements by tabling a total sum for all the Trent works. Graham denied the Opposition's request that the amounts for each section be tabled separately, because he claimed that it was impossible to make the separation. Consequently, the Opposition refused the consent to the Trent estimates that day. It attacked the Newmarket canal again briefly on 2 March, but it was not until 23 March, the last day for approving the estimates, that the full fury of the Opposition's assault was launched.

The fight started shortly after the House of Commons convened at 2 p.m. When the question period was finished, the minister of finance moved that the House go into Committee of Supply, normally a routine motion, but Thomas G. Wallace, representative from York Centre, rose to move an amendment to the supply motion that came just short of being a motion of non-confidence in the government.

The motion called for cancelling the Newmarket canal, because the project, when completed, would be useless and the expenditure on it was "wholly improvident and unwarranted" and constituted "a wanton misuse and waste of public money."[25] One after another, Conservative members rose to condemn the government. The Toronto members, who could see absolutely no economic advantage in the canal, and the members from the Trent constituencies, miffed that money was being spent on the Holland River extenion before the main canal was finished, spearheaded the attack. The minister was ridiculed (he could not give an estimate even of tonnage likely to pass through the canal); the engineers were censured (the estimate had risen from $324,000 to over a million dollars in a couple of months); Aylesworth and the departed Mulock were vilified (all the dirty political linen in York North was hung out to air on the parliamentary clothes-line). J.A. Currie of Collingwood, a Conservative representing North Simcoe, summarized the gist of the thousands of words uttered that day when he said: "A political job costing $5,000 or $6,000 is wrong in principle but when the cost runs into millions ... it is a political crime."[26] After a few hours, the speaker intervened to remind the House that the discussion was "irregular," but no one paid any attention to him. When the House recessed for dinner at 6 p.m., the Opposition was just getting warmed up. The debate continued for another two hours in the evening before – mercifully for the government – the division bells rang. The government was then able to round up a majority to negate the amendment.

The government's defence of the canal had been pathetically weak. Only Graham, Aylesworth, and Laurier had defended the government's actions; no other Liberal in the House would touch the subject. The best Graham, who privately made fun of the canal, could do was justify the use of reservoirs and pumping because they were used on some European canals. As he had on previous occasions, Aylesworth disclaimed any responsibility for the canal because it was started before he was elected. His repeated proclamations of innocence were not entirely justified. True, the Newmarket delegation had gone to Ottawa nine months before his election and the first $100,000 for the improvements had been voted the July prior to his taking a seat in Parliament, but not one penny had been spent until after he took office. The contract to the York Construction Company had been let to ensure his re-election in 1908, and even earlier, in March 1906, he had ordered Butler to use some of the $100,000 parliamentary vote to build a $20,000 bridge across the Holland River, where no bridge or road had previously existed. Nevertheless, Aylesworth continued to plead innocence of the whole affair, even later, after he had left Parliament. On this occasion, he argued that the question to answer was not why the canal had been started but rather "ought we to discontinue it?"[27] He answered his own question by observing that he could see no reason why, of all the public works going on in Canada, the Holland River improvements "should be singled out as one to be condemned and abandoned, when the reports of scientific men showed there was no question about a sufficiency of water, and because the canal would be a great benefit to the people of the locality"[28] – a remark that prompted the *Weekly Sun* to ask "whether a canal begun in folly should be completed in iniquity."[29] Perhaps the weakest defence was that put up by Laurier himself. He tried to neutralize the Opposition's attack by pointing out that the delegation that appeared before him in 1905 had contained many Conservatives and, therefore, the Opposition must share with the government the burden of responsibility for the canal.

On 6 April, when the estimates appeared before the House for final approval, Currie tried one more time to scupper the canal by moving that the item of $1 million for Trent construction "be reduced by whatever amount is contained therein for expenditure upon the Newmarket canal."[30] Once again the government used its majority to quash the amendment, and the full estimate was approved. Consequently, during the construction season of 1909, several more thousand dollars were poured into lock construction on the Holland River.

Because Walsh had borne the brunt of the criticism and blame for the fiasco over the increase in cost instigated by Butler and Grant, he complained privately to Graham after the session. As a result of the meeting with Walsh, Graham ordered the dimension of the locks reduced to the original length of 142 feet, the gate valves were put back in the plans, and the design of the dams was returned to the original, cheaper type of construction. Consequently, the estimate for section 2 was reduced by about $80,000.

When the estimates for 1910 came before the House, the Opposition continued to attack the government for the waste of public funds at Newmarket. Because he could think of no better defence than a petty political one, Laurier wrote to Sir William Mulock for background information on the delegation that met with him in 1905, because he thought "there would be in the representations which were made to us good material for defence."[31] Mulock contacted H.S. Cane, who provided him with the names and political affiliations of all the delegates, a summary of the presentations made to Laurier, and copies of various newspaper accounts of the events leading up to the initiation of the canal. Mulock forwarded the material to Laurier. It showed beyond question that leading Conservatives, including Haughton Lennox, representative of South Simcoe and now one of the canal's most ardent critics, had supported the original petition.

Mulock's letter reiterated the advantages of the canal and exhorted Laurier not to discontinue the work, because it was benefiting the town of Newmarket, "which [was] growing rapidly and [was] a most thriving and prosperous place."[32] The wily Supreme Court justice took it upon himself further to advise his former leader on a tactic for outwitting the Tories at the next election. At Mulock's request, J.W. Wildman, manager of the Office Specialty Company, had written to Laurier supporting the canal scheme. Mulock advised Laurier to make public use of Wildman's letter because "the Opposition will doubtless say that the letter was given because of the patronage which the government gives the Co." and "if the Opposition should cast reflections upon [Wildman] or make insinuations because of his letter, he will naturally resent it, at the first opportunity – namely the next election. If however, "the old war-horse continued, unfolding his diabolical strategy, "Mr. Wildman should be attacked and you were to defend him you would be sure to win the sympathy of the whole factory. There are several hundred votes there now and it may be very important for your candidate to get them at the next election."[33]

Mulock's intelligence came too late for Laurier to make use of it in 1910, because on 16 March the estimates had already passed the House after another futile attempt by the Opposition to reduce the Trent canal estimates by the amount of intended expenditure for the Newmarket canal. The finance minister did make some use of the newspaper articles sent by Mulock, in the last debate on the Newmarket canal in 1911, but, to Laurier's credit, Mulock's suggestion to use Wildman's letter was not followed. William Fielding, the finance minister, did try to bait a hook for the Conservatives by singling out Wildman's name as one of the supporters of the scheme. "He's a Liberal, isn't he?," Fielding asked, sotto voce. But the Conservatives did not rise to the bait.

Meanwhile the Liberals, who seemed to think that elections were won by buying votes, continued to spend money like water on the Newmarket works. By the end of the construction season of 1910, another $114,574 had been spent and about 60 per cent of the contract was complete. Opposition members continued to fume and newspapers to satirize. One wag penned a limerick:

A dear little maiden named Sal
Strolled along the Newmarket Canal.
She fell in with a thud,
And stuck fast in the mud.
That smothered the life out of Sal.[34]

The Newmarket canal was no laughing matter for engineer E.J. Walsh; in fact he was fighting mad about it. During the bitter debates of 1909 and 1910, he had been blamed by the parliamentarians for the whole Holland River misadventure. He had been accused of submitting a misleading cost estimate. He was charged with misleading the minister regarding the water supply, and he was accused of overstating the canal's commercial advantages. A stigma had been cast upon his professional reputation, but neither Graham nor Aylesworth had said one word in his defence. All of that was hard enough to take, but when Graham, in the course of the debate, referred to Grant as "one of the most efficient engineers in the whole department,"[35] and Aylesworth described Butler as "an engineer of eminence and experience,"[36] it was more than the jealous Walsh could bear. When he learned "beyond peradventure" that Butler had convinced Graham that he (Walsh) was "solely responsible for the unwarranted cost of the Holland River improvements and Canal to Newmarket,"[37] Walsh was livid. When it became clear why Butler had falsely accused him of responsibility for the unwarranted costs, which Butler and Grant had engineered, Walsh got his Irish up and began to blab.

The private fight between the Irishmen involved a competition for the position of chief engineer in the Department of Railways and Canals. Butler had resigned as deputy minister and chief engineer in January 1910 to become general manager of the Dominion Iron and Steel Company in Sydney, Nova Scotia. Graham divided the dual position into two offices, immediately appointing Archibald W. Campbell, former deputy minister of public works for Ontario, as deputy minister, but he left the chief engineership open for competition. Walsh became an applicant. His friends in the department informed him that Butler and Haney were lobbying to have Alex J. Grant, another applicant, appointed. In order to have Walsh, the superior engineer, eliminated from the competition, they had convinced Graham that Walsh was responsible for the excessive cost of the Holland River works, the result of which had brought the government so much public abuse. And even worse, they had convinced Graham that Walsh was a Conservative. Formerly a flagman on Walsh's engineering staff, Grant had no formal professional training and was not a particularly competent practical engineer, despite his patrons' claim. His first work in the Trent superintendency was designing and supervising the construction of a new dam at Buckhorn Rapids which, although costing $54,443.51, required an additional expenditure of $4,229 three years later to make it "conform to the requirements for which it was originally constructed."[38] Not very impressive qualifications for the nation's top engineering position. But Grant did have one important qualification. He was Haney's and Butler's man, "subject to their dictation – like clay in the hands of the potter,"[39] as Walsh put it, and a useful person for private entrepreneurs to have in this key government patronage position.

On 5 April 1910, his patience at an end and not knowing where else to turn, Walsh wrote to H.S. Cane to tell him the real reason for the excessive cost of the canal and how the government had been "knifed by Butler and coterie," who had engineered the whole thing "to damn Sir William Mulock, the Engineer [Walsh] who reported favourably thereon, and the contractor of the Section No. 1 [E.S. Cane and Co.]."[40] Walsh asked Cane to show his letter to Sir William Mulock, who would undoubtedly inform Laurier and the cabinet of the truth. It was quite clear that Walsh's real reason for writing the letter was to blackmail the government into giving him the chief engineership.[41] He ended his letter with a clear threat: "Whether or not I get the appointment ... the truth must be told and the stigma cast on my professional reputation removed – otherwise I shall consider myself absolved from futher silence in the matter."[42] An alarmed Mulock passed a copy of Walsh's letter on to Laurier, cautioning him to alert Graham "so that he may be prepared to answer any attack Mr. Walsh may instigate."[43]

Walsh initiated his attack on 20 January 1911, when he wrote a long letter to Graham "to place on record in the Department some observations and explanations concerning the Holland River improvements so that they would be available for parliamentary enquiry."[44] They were interesting observations. He told how, in January 1905, he had been compelled by Schreiber, Mulock, and Emmerson to prepare an estimate for the Holland River canal before the data were all available, even though he protested that the estimate would not be accurate. He revealed how Butler and Grant had mutilated his plans, thereby increasing the cost threefold. He complained that the minister, through subtle suggestion and implications in Parliament, had allowed the whole blame for the unpopular expenditure to fall upon him. He accused Aylesworth of "contributing his 'mite' of expense to the lofty offspring"[45] by arranging for the construction of a township bridge at dominion expense. He objected to having been falsely accused of being a Conservative, especially because he had never directly or indirectly allowed politics to interfere with the way he worked. But he did remind Graham that he had been instructed, when organizing the survey for the Trent River, to apply to Graham, then the Liberal party organizer in eastern Ontario, for the names of appropriate staff and that Graham had given him the names of the two defeated Liberal candidates in West Hastings and Northumberland East, both of whom were hired on the survey.

Nor was M.J. Butler,[46] "a parvenu whose previous authority was exercised chiefly over navvies and shanty-man,"[47] spared from the acid sting of Walsh's caustic pen. He revealed how Butler had secured an award for Haney whereby extras amounting to a very large amount of money were paid for the Hillsborough bridge built by Haney on Prince Edward Island, even though the bridge had already cost about three times the amount of the estimate. He accused Butler of a cover up in the Quebec bridge disaster, claiming he diverted blame from himself to an invalid engineer in New York. He claimed that Butler's mismanagement of an Intercolonial Railway contract at Moncton resulted in an Exchequer Court award to the contractor valued at more than the contract was worth. Finally, he pointed out that the cost of the famous Aylesworth bridge at Holland Landing had been increased because of the need to correct construction errors resulting from faulty plans made by Grant but approved by Butler.

It was a most scurrilous letter, notable if for no other reason than to illustrate the depths of degradation into which the Laurier ministry had fallen, especially the Department of Railways and Canals, which Walsh, in his concluding words, suggested should have engraved over its entrance the inscription: "Abandon principle, and unman yourselves all engineers who take employment here."[48]

To prevent his report from being buried in the department's files, Walsh advised T.C. Wallace of its existence. Wallace requested a copy of the report in January, but it was not until six months later, on the last day of the session, that Graham gave it to him. Wallace read every offensive word into the record of Hansard, in support of yet another motion censuring the government for "using moneys for purposes that were not in the public interest."[49]

Walsh undoubtedly wrote his report out of anger and to clear his own name, but if he thought his startling revelations would precipitate a parliamentary inquiry he was sadly mistaken. Neither Aylesworth nor Fielding, in defending once again the Newmarket canal expenditures, answered any of the charges made by Walsh in the letter so dramatically read to the House by Wallace. Currie half-heartedly retracted the harsh statements he had previously made about Walsh's engineering competence, but by and large the Opposition ignored the letter and its revelations, too. The House seemed embarrassed and even resentful that a public servant had broken his oath of allegiance by revealing confidential government information. Although it was technically an internal document addressed to the minister, it had clearly been written for the parliamentary record.

Although Fielding and Aylesworth were severly censured for the wastage of public money, specifically in Newmarket, the Opposition chose to concentrate its attack on the generality of Wallace's motion; consequently, the debate spread out to include other instances of government wrong-doing. Neither Graham nor Pugsley, the minister of public works, was in the House, and so Laurier was obliged to sit silently with no one to share the criticism as speaker after speaker described the "crookedness, malfeasance and incapacity of his administration in dealing with the money of the Canadian people."[50] There had been a public clock built by Mackenzie King for his constituents in Berlin (later Kitchener), Ontario; $5,000 had been wasted on a wharf on Lake Simcoe; $25,000 was spent on a useless wharf on Lake Manitoba; illegal dredging contracts worth thousands of dollars had been given out to friends of the government; public works projects started before the last election had been abandoned in ridings when Conservative candidates won. But the Newmarket canal had been the grossest and most expensive boondoggle of them all.

After several hours of acrimionious debate had petered out, the House finally divided for the vote on Wallace's motion. The government had enough members present to defeat it. Not that it mattered very much, because the next day, Saturday, 29 July, Parliament was dissolved and a national election was called for 21 September.

The principal issue of the election was reciprocity with the United States, a long-standing Liberal policy, which, despite having beaten the party in 1891, was dragged out again in 1911. The unofficial election issue was the Liberal government's record of scandal and corruption. The local issue in York North was the Newmarket canal. Lloydtown farmer J.A.M. Armstrong, running for the Conservatives, campaigned against the canal. A young criminal lawyer, R.C. Robinette, brought into the riding from Toronto by the Liberals to take the place of the retiring Aylesworth, campaigned for it. Borden and his Conservatives soundly trounced Laurier, taking 72 of the 86 seats in Ontario, but the election in York North was very close. Armstrong won with a majority of only 49 votes. The Newmarket canal was doomed.

Borden appointed Frank Cochrane, a Sudbury hardware merchant and former Ontario minister of lands, forests, and mines, to Railways and Canals. One of Cochrane's first acts was to suspend work on the Newmarket canal, which had accelerated during the election campaign.

Meanwhile, chief engineer W.A. Bowden was asked for a full report on the amount of work done and for an estimate of the cost of completion. Bowden reported on 3 January 1912.

On section 2, the right of way had been purchased, the locks (excluding gates) had been finished, about 80 per cent of the excavation was completed, three swing bridges had been built, and the turning basin in Newmarket, with most of its stone protection lining, was done. On section 1, the right of way had been purchased but very little dredging had been done. A dredge had been purchased by the government, which intended to carry out the work with day labourers. This would probably cost $41,000. An estimated capital expenditure of $17,000 would be required for the controversial pumping system, and the annual cost of operating the pumps was put at $4,000.

As for the question of probable traffic, it was predicted that apart from a few gasoline pleasure launches, the only use to be made of the canal would be by the occasional holiday excursion steamer and a scow or two, loaded with hardwood for the factories in Newmarket. Bowden pointed out that for this light traffic the locks and the swing bridges would have to be constantly manned, at a further annual cost of $4,000. Against this expenditure, he estimated a possible saving of $393,000 if the works were abandoned. This was enough evidence to convince Cochrane to cancel the scheme. Typically, he wasted no time. On his recommendation, an order-in-council authorizing the minister to enter into an agreement with York Construction for surrender of the contract was signed by Borden two days after Bowden's report was received.

Under the terms of the agreement, the contractors were paid in full for all the materials delivered and the work done and were given $1,000 in compensation for the shut-down of their plant. Claims for damages by the subcontractors were also paid by the government. A separate agreement was entered into with the contractors, for finishing the approaches to the bridges and doing other small jobs to render the abandoned works safe. For this they were paid the full cost plus 15 per cent. But they received still more. They were promised the contract for the Port Severn lock on the Severn River, which was to start the following year.

Newmarket prospered, despite the abandonment of the canal project. Today its population is about 30,000. The town's directory list 127 industrial, commercial, and service industries. The principal centre of the region's trade is, as it always has been, the city of Toronto, with the Canadian National Railway and number 11 highway affording easy and fast communication. A goverment of Ontario (GO) bus line has replaced the Metropolitan Street Railway; buses provide regular half-hour service between Newmarket and the Toronto subway terminus at Finch Avenue.

The east branch of the Holland River is now an extension of the Trent-Severn Waterway. Parks Canada keeps the river dredged and buoyed as far as Holland Landing.

The three gateless locks, stained to the colour of the muddy water that trickles through them, stand sturdily amid weeds and vines, offering mute testimony to the skill of the workmen who put them there. As Aylesworth predicted long ago, their very durability has made them "perpetual monuments to government folly."

The press pokes fun at the Newmarket Canal. (Toronto *News*, 12 February 1909)

CHAPTER TWENTY-THREE

Hydroelectric Power and the Port Hope Canal

While Sir William Mulock was "playing politics" with the Trent canal at Newmarket, the Port Hope outlet was becoming a major political issue at the eastern end. Ostensibly the issue was the decades-old one of whether a canal through Port Hope was cheaper, and therefore more desirable, than a canal down the Trent River. But beneath the canal question was a much larger issue: hydroelectric generation and who was going to control it.

By 1904 there was a growing movement in energy-starved Ontario for public ownership and control of hydroelectric power generation, by then seen clearly as the solution to the province's energy needs. Generally, Ontario Conservatives supported public control, while dominion Liberals (Mulock notwithstanding) favoured private development of electric power. The battle, which would eventually be won by the advocates of public ownership, was fought out on the waters of the Trent canal. The first volley was fired in the dominion election of 1904. Port Hope was the battleground, although, at the time, few people understood what the fight was all about.

We now return to where we left the Port Hope story in chapter 17, with Rogers's 1899 survey. It will be recalled that, after making a cursory examination of the route, Rogers had concluded that a Port Hope outlet for the proposed barge canal might cost somewhat less than the Trent River route but had recommended against choosing the Port Hope route, because it was considered less favourable for barge transportation. This recommendation did not sit well with the merchants in Port Hope who, in June 1900, formed the Port Hope Canal Association with the primary objective of promoting and acquiring government support for the Port Hope outlet. The association published an illustrated pamphlet extolling the merits of the canal, and it exerted pressure on the government to have a proper cost survey made. With an election imminent, the government readily agreed. Rogers carried out the detailed survey in the summer of

1900 and submitted his plan and estimate on 22 September. This time he determined a saving in cost of \$1,032,957 in favour of the Trenton route. The comparison probably was not fair, because Rogers compared his own cost estimate of the Port Hope route, which included two proposed hydraulic lift locks and came to \$3,861,520, with Rubidge's 1887 estimate of \$2,828,563 for the Trent River route. It was this fact, when it later became known, that led Culverwell to charge Rogers with having made an unfair and biased report against the Port Hope route and led him, along with several others, to seek Rogers's release. The government made no immediate decision on the choice of route; it suppressed Rogers's report until after the election, hoping that at least one of the critical ridings, Hasting West (Trenton) and Durham East (Port Hope), if not both, would be won by Liberals. But they won neither. Corby held Hastings West for the Conservatives, and Col. H.A. Ward won the traditionally Conservative riding of Durham East. Subsequently, the government was content to leave the question of route in abeyance until the next election. Meanwhile, it proceeded to complete construction on the Peterborough-Lakefield and Balsam – Lake Simcoe divisions.

The people of Port Hope were determined to have their canal. To this end, the Port Hope Canal Association adopted a strategy as aggressive as the one pursued by the main Trent Canal Association with its headquarters in Peterborough. A deputation sent from Port Hope to Ottawa managed to secure another comparative survey in 1903. This one was conducted by Railways and Canals engineer Henry Macleod, who did not conduct a full field survey but simply made a cost update of the Rubidge and Rogers reports. He arrived at a cost difference of \$144,537 in favour of the Port Hope route, but it was not a conclusive differential, given the historic gaps between estimates and actual costs of construction on the Trent canal.

Then in June 1904, with another election coming up, the Port Hope Canal Association developed a whole new strategy. It proposed an entirely different purpose for the Trent canal, particularly the eastern end of it, which, it was hoped, would render the Port Hope route indisputably superior to and cheaper than the Trent River route. The barge canal concept was rejected. A deep-water canal with a draft of at least 10 feet was proposed, instead; this would make Peterborough a deep-water port. Not Montreal, but Toronto and other Lake Ontario ports, including the coal docks at Oak Orchard on the American side of the lake, would become supply ports for an exchange of trade with Peterborough and the other inland towns in the Midland District.

Politically, the proposal had considerable appeal in Toronto and Peterborough, both of which would benefit more from a deep-water canal than from a shallow barge canal. The argument about the hazards of open-water communication on Lake Ontario, which had always been used to Port Hope's disadvantage, could be refuted because deep-water freighters, not shallow barges, would emerge from the canal into Lake Ontario. Moreover, Port Hope had a modern deep-water port, whereas Trenton had a shallow port which, although suitable for barge traffic, would require considerable expensive excavation for the accommodation of deep-draft freighters. But the greater advantage, from Port Hope's point of view, would be in the cost of construction. The ten-mile stretch of land between Rice Lake and Port Hope consisted of glacial till, relatively cheap to excavate, whereas the cost of excavating a 10-foot-deep canal through the rock on the Trent River, most of it submarine, would be extremely expensive. If Port Hope could sell the deep-water concept, it stood a good chance of winning the 70-year competition with Trenton, because the government had intimated that the comparative costs of the two proposals would be a major factor in the final choice of route. Consequently, the Port Hope Canal Association demanded cost surveys based on a 10-foot, rather than a 6-foot-draft canal.

The association's literature now promoted the new concept, and during the summer of 1904 political pressure for the surveys was intensified. Tactics similar to those used by the citizens of Port Hope in 1834 were adopted: the townships, villages, and towns on Lake Ontario to the west of Port Hope were encouraged to draft memorials and prepare petitions for submission to Ottawa, all demanding a deep-water survey. The strategy was successful. When Toronto saw it, not Montreal, would be the prime beneficiary of a deep-water canal through Port Hope, its long-time antipathy to the Trent canal vanished. A petition favouring the Port Hope route, and asking that reports "by mutual and independent engineers"[1] be prepared for both routes before the matter was finally settled, was forwarded by Mayor Thomas Urquhart of Toronto to the governor-general. Peterborough, by and large, adopted the same indifference to the choice of outlets as it had in 1836. In response to an inquiry by H.R. Emmerson for Peterborough's point of view, R.R. Hall wrote: "The majority of people are indifferent as to the outlet, whether it is Port Hope or Trenton,"[2] but, probably reflecting the wishes of the American Cereal Company, Hall did advise Emmerson that the large importers were "quite concerned to see that a route is given which would be feasible to barge navigation on the open lake."[3] This was really an endorsement of the Trent River route. Because it was more a political issue than a departmental matter, Sir William Mulock intervened, asking Emmerson to ensure that the surveys requested by Port Hope be undertaken. Emmerson consented, and in July $11,000 was placed in the supplementary estimates for the surveys. In August, he announced that E.J. Walsh, who was then engaged in private practice, had been hired to conduct the next round of surveys, but he did not indicate what depth of canal would be surveyed.

Enter Allen Bristol Aylesworth. He first appeared in our story in the last chapter without a proper introduction. It was during the election campaign of 1904 that Aylesworth had his first unhappy encounter with Trent canal politics. Born of United Empire Loyalist stock in 1854, he was raised on a farm near Newburgh, Ontario. A brilliant student, he graduated from the University of Toronto in 1874 with a BA and the Prince of Wales medal. In 1875 he received an MA, and in 1878 he was called to the bar, following three years of study at Osgoode Hall. He was created a queen's counsel (QC) in 1889 and a bencher of the Law Society of Upper Canada in 1891. In 1903 he declined an appointment as a justice of the Supreme Court of Canada. Although long well known in the legal profession, Aylesworth first came to public prominence that year, having been appointed a member of the Imperial Alaska Boundary Tribunal. His refusal to sign the tribunal's award, which in his opinion represented a betrayal of Canada's interests, caught Laurier's attention, because Aylesworth's stand, although symbolic, typified the kind of Canadian independence from Great Britain that Laurier, the Canadian nationalist, was trying to achieve. On 5 October, he asked Aylesworth to join the cabinet as minister without portfolio until a seat could be found for him in the forthcoming election. The riding chosen for him by Sir William Mulock was Durham, through the centre of which the proposed Port Hope canal would run.

The twin ridings of Durham East and Durham West had been combined into one riding by the electoral boundary changes made in 1903. This new riding seemed to be a safe place for the 50-year-old novice to test his political wings. Although Durham East had traditionally voted Tory, Durham West was a long-time Liberal stronghold. The great Reformer Edward Blake had held the riding from 1867 until his retirement in 1891, and for the next two Parliaments the seat had been occupied by Robert Beith, Blake's anointed successor. Although Conservative C.J. Thornton had captured the riding in 1900, Mulock believed that his victory, with a margin of only 40 votes, was an aberration and that there would be enough Grits in the new combined ridings to elect his prestigious candidate. Aylesworth's opponent was Col. H.A. Ward, incumbent in Durham East.

Aylesworth and Mulock went to Port Hope on 12 October to prepare for Aylesworth's nomination meeting and his first-ever political address, which would take place the next night. They found the town in an uproar over the canal surveys. Col. Ward had been circulating a rumour in the town that Walsh "had received instructions from the government what to report and that it was intended there should be no honest examination."[4] The Liberals were naturally upset, and Aylesworth was bombarded with questions even before he was nominated. Was Walsh going to conduct surveys based on a 6-foot or a 10-foot-draft canal? Had the government already made up its mind about the route? What was Aylesworth's stand on the Port Hope outlet?

Knowing little about the Trent canal and even less about the government's policy for it, but sensing that the question of route was critical to his election success, Aylesworth telephoned Laurier, who was campaigning in Toronto at the time, for advice. A seasoned Trent canal politician would have known instinctively what to promise without guidance from his leader, but it was the measure of Aylesworth, a jurist with unshakeable integrity, not to promise anything that he could not deliver. His action was also an indication of his political naïveté. A letter that required considerable editing and rewriting was drafted for Laurier's signature and sent to Port Hope by special delivery. Aylesworth read it out at the nomination meeting. In part, the letter said: "It is ... intended to have such survey and report made with reference not only to work at the depth and capacity of the completed portion of the Trent Valley Canal, but, also, of a work of greater depths and capacities, and, therefore, the instructions to the engineers will be given in accordance with such intention."[5]

The letter was received with much relief by the Liberals in Port Hope, but Mulock did not think it specific enough. He told Laurier this when he met him in Toronto the next day, and so a supplementary letter was sent to Aylesworth, assuring him "that a survey will be made for each southern outlet of a canal eight and one third feet on lock sills, nine and one half feet in canal cuttings, and ten and one half feet in lake and river channels."[6] Laurier promised, in addition to the surveys, that the government would have "a report of detailed costs of each route made."

The campaign was a frustrating experience for Aylesworth. While he wanted to talk to the electorate about social reforms, economic growth, and prosperity under the Liberals, and Canada's emerging status in the international community, all the people of Port Hope wanted to talk about was the canal outlet. Regrettably, Laurier's assurances about the surveys were to no avail. Aylesworth lost the election to Ward, but the outcome was close: 149 votes out of 5,495 cast separated the contestants. It is not clear what effect the canal debate had on the result – probably very little. Ward, as president of the Port Hope Canal Association, was a strong advocate of the canal too. Also, while speaking in Peterborough on 8 October, Conservative leader Robert Borden had promised that, if elected, the Conservatives would complete both the eastern and western outlets of the canal immediately. Since Port Hope's chances of acquiring the canal seemed as good under a Conservative government as under the Liberals, the residents of Durham stood by the local candidate rather than take a chance on the unknown Aylesworth brought into the riding by Mulock. Mulock resigned his seat in York North the following summer. As we learned in the last chapter, Aylesworth won the riding by a by-election, only to be harassed by Trent canal politics in Newmarket. With the 1904 election over, there was little more to be said about the choice of routes until Walsh completed his surveys. This took the greater part of two years.

Walsh conducted three comprehensive new surveys, ostensibly for the purpose of determining which of the contending routes leading from Rice Lake into Lake Ontario it would be advisable to adopt on the basis of cost: the Port Hope route, the Trent River route, or an overland route by way of Cobourg. Two detailed cost estimates were worked out for each route: one on the basis of six-foot navigation; the other on the basis of eight feet four inches on the lock sills. The costs of the routes compared as follows: for six-foot navigation via Port Hope, $3,541,917; via Cobourg, $7,906,401; via Trenton, $3,118,811. For eight-foot-four-inch navigation the amounts were $3,958,051, $8,236,040, and $3,997,482 respectively.

Solely on the basis of estimated construction cost, the Port Hope outlet should have been chosen, but the government had never had any intention of building a Port Hope canal. Walsh's surveys, which cost $36,515.27, had been conducted for purely political purposes and perhaps to demonstrate the principle that justice must appear to be done. Ward's contention that the government had already made up its mind before the surveys were made was accurate, as we shall see presently.

Walsh submitted his report to M.J. Butler on 20 December 1906. Butler considered the findings for a month and then, after consulting several other "transportation experts," submitted his recommendation to Emmerson on 26 January 1907. Emmerson forwarded Butler's recommendation, without alteration, to the clerk of the Privy Council on 7 February, and on 19 February an order-in-council adopting the route was approved. After 75 years of wrangling, the route finally selected was the one nature had carved out: the Trent River route through Trenton. "After a careful consideration of all circumstances, and resulting consequences, I am of the opinion that the interests of the country will be best served by the adoption of the Trenton 'all river route,' with 8'4" on sills of lock gates, as such depth of water will enormously reduce the cost of transportation, and may be had for $455,565 over and above the cost of six foot navigation,"[7] was the recommendation that Butler made.

Because so much had been made of construction costs in the debates preceding the surveys, Butler still had to justify the choice of the Trent, which all the surveys had demonstrated would be more expensive than a Port Hope route. He did this by adding a cost to the Port Hope route which, until that time, no one had considered. A choice of either the Port Hope or Cobourg route would have resulted in diversion of water from the Trent River. A well-established principle in English common law ensures that if water is diverted from a natural channel into another watershed riparian owners on the natural channel are entitled to damages; and it is not even necessary for the riparian owner to operate a mill to qualify for such damages. According to Butler, Gould's Law of Water had formalized the principle in the following way: "A riparian owner may maintain an action for the diversion of a stream without proof that he has an ancient mill thereon or that he has appropriated the water to any special use."[8] Clearly, there would be damage suits resulting from diversion of the Trent, and the cost of these suits would have to be added to the cost of the Port Hope and Cobourg outlets if a full and fair comparison of the routes were to be arrived at. Butler estimated the quantity of water that would be diverted from the Trent to be 103 cubic feet per second which, running for a full 24 hours, would equal 4,083 horsepower, calculated on the basis of a fall of 350 feet between Rice Lake and Lake Ontario. At the current departmental rental fee of $2 per horsepower, the diversion would cost the dominion government $8,166 per year, being the full amount riparian owners could claim for damages. Capitalized over 25 years, this would amount to $204,150, which, when added to the construction cost of the Port Hope outlet, made it a more expensive route. But the cost factor was only a red herring.

Had the eighteenth-century Italian physicist Alessandro Volta not developed a method for producing a continuous electric current, the Trent canal might not have been completed. And had the Serbian-American Nicola Tesla not invented the split-phase electric motor in 1883 and had he not also discovered a revolutionary new way of generating and transmitting electric power over long distances, the Trent River outlet would not have been chosen. For it was only after the realization that the Trent River could be converted into a power canal capable of producing thousands of horsepower of electric energy that the decision was taken to complete the canal. The power could have been developed without the accompanying locks, but, in that case, control of the water, along with the revenue and political advantages, would have gone to the province of Ontario. That is primarily the reason, although transportation of wheat by barge was no longer a priority, that Ottawa decided to ignore the cheaper Port Hope route and canalize the Trent River. In his concluding remarks in the recommendation to Emmerson, Butler stated almost as an afterthought the true reason for recommending that route: "The Trenton outlet, if adopted, ensures the development of an immense quantity of power alongside of an excellent transportation route. The Port Hope and Cobourg outlets will not admit of any power development."[9]

Industries in towns adjacent to the Trent River valley were waiting for electric power, which was readily available at the undeveloped falls on the Trent River. The delay in developing the water powers caused by the controversy over the choice of routes was causing frustration. On the same day that Butler submitted his recommendation to Emmerson, Laurier received a nasty letter from W.J. Doxsee, mayor of Campbellford, complaining about the decision delay and criticizing W.H. McColl, Liberal MP for Northumberland West, who had been responsible for the ridiculous survey of the Cobourg route, which only further delayed the choice of canal outlet. The town of Campbellford owned a water privilege at Crowe Bay, on the proposed route of the Trent River canal. The town operated a small electric plant at the old government dam there, but the dam was in very poor condition and the electric power plant was not large enough to serve the growing needs of the town. The town council was anxious to build a new dam and to enlarge its plant, but nothing could be done until a decision on the canal route had been made.

Nor was the town of Campbellford the only potential power developer being hindered by the delay. Culverwell's Northumberland and Durham Power Company was anxious to develop power at Healey Falls. The Northumberland Paper and Electric Company at Campbellford, now controlled by Kerry, Smith, and Chace, was anxious to expand its power plant, and the Seymour Power and Electric Company (also controlled by Kerry and company) wanted to develop the falls above Campbellford. The Trent Valley Woolen Mill in Campbellford was desirous of converting from water power to electric power, and development in the towns of Trenton, Belleville, Cobourg, Port Hope, and Bowmanville was also being held up for want of electric power. "I am sure the Honourable Ministers do not wish to keep this whole section tied up much longer,"[10] Doxsee pleaded with Laurier.

Butler was as frustrated over the delay as the mayor of Campbellford, but he had to move cautiously on his recommendation. As pointed out in chapter 21, two potential power developers – Kerry, Smith, and Chace and J.A. Culverwell and his backers – were competing for Trent River water leases. Culverwell had been moving towards his goal through political channels and was stirring up controversy and confusion throughout the district; Kerry, in contrast, had been trying to get leases privately and secretly through Butler. As will be shown later, Butler definitely favoured the Kerry group. "They [Kerry, Smith, and Chace] seem to stand in with Butler and what arrangements they have made with the department, I don't know,"[11] R.B. Rogers – who was then superintendent of the Northumberland Paper and Electric Company – confided to Willie Boyd, when informing him about the "big power scheme" that Kerry, Smith, and Chace were forming. But however desirous Butler might have been to help Kerry, he had to move slowly on his recommendation because of the powerful forces operating on behalf of Port Hope and, to a lesser extent, of Cobourg. Doxsee's letter to Laurier forced the matter of the choice of route before the question of power leases was settled, and even before the government's policy for developing the Trent River water powers had been formed.

There was another political consideration, more fundamental than the self-interest of local politicians and the avarice of power developers, that clinched a dominion commitment to the Trent River route and forced the government to move quickly on canal construction once the route had been decided upon. Simply put, it was a question of who was going to control the Trent water powers and reap the political reward from electric power development: the dominion Liberal government, or the Ontario Conservative government, through its fledgling agency, the Hydro Electric Power Commission of Ontario. Underlying this question of which government should control the Trent River was the polemic of private versus public development of hydro power – a public controversy rooted in the basic differences in nineteenth-century Liberal and Conservative philosophies. By 1906, this issue was tearing the province apart. On one side, the dominion Liberal party, illustrating one of those paradoxes that are the stuff of history, championed private development of hydroelectric power; on the other side stood the Ontario Conservative party, which was attracting an increasing number of small businessmen and municipal leaders – it favoured a more socialistic solution to the provision of cheap energy, through public ownership and development of the province's water power resources.

L.B. Powers, president of the Port Hope Liberal Association and candidate for Durham in the dominion election of 1911, put his finger on this two-pronged political issue in a private letter to George P. Graham in 1910. Complaining about the delay in issuing a water power lease for dam 3 on the Trent River to one of the private power companies, Powers wrote: "If this lease is not granted forthwith to the Central Canada Power Company, the Hydro Electric Power Commission will undoubtedly secure control of the electric power question in this and adjoining ridings ... It is simply a question of whether the Dominion government and the Central Canada Power Company will control the district and secure the credit and benefits of the Trent canal expenditure or whether it will go to the Ontario Hydro Electric Power Commission."[12]

So accustomed now are Canadians to having government agencies, crown corporations, and other public bodies managing the affairs of daily life that it is difficult to imagine the alarm that the Hydro Electric Power Commission (HEPC) – the administrative organ of the world's first publicly owned power system – produced when it appeared. Now called Ontario Hydro, this body, established by legislation in 1906, has long since allayed the fears of its most vocal opponents and has more than fulfilled the expectations of its creators by providing the province with cheap electric power, without which Ontario's vast industrial base could not have been built. But in May 1906, when the lieutenant-governor signed the bill that created a three-member commission responsible only to the cabinet, but with powers equal to or greater than those enjoyed by a minister of public works, there was no general consensus that such an experiment in public ownership was desirable, even if it should work – which many doubted.

Establishment of this most powerful public body, over which the public had very little control, was welcomed by the proponents of public ownership. For years they had been engaged in an ideological crusade against what they perceived to be the evil powers of monopolistic capitalists such as the Mackenzie-Pellatt-Nicholls syndicate of Toronto. This group, through its federally chartered Electric Development Company, had been given a franchise to generate 125,000 horsepower at Niagara Falls and was charging its customers double what the customers of municipally owned plants at Orillia, Campbellford, and Fort William were paying for power. (The Electric Development Company was, for example, charging the Toronto Electric Light Company and the Toronto Street Railway Company $35 per horsepower, while the municipally owned plants were delivering power at a cost of $15 – $16 per horsepower.)

Opponents of the HEPC, consisting of the private developers and many Liberal politicians, saw the commission not only as a threat to their personal interests but also as a danger to the free enterprise system to which they were also passionately and ideologically committed. They predicted that public ownership and control of water power would lead to political patronage, graft, inefficiency, and, eventually, provincial bankruptcy.

It was in the midst of the polemical debate that accompanied the preparation of the Hydro legislation that Walsh conducted his surveys of the Trent River and Port Hope canal routes. By the time he had submitted his report to Butler and Butler had made his recommendation to the dominion cabinet, the HEPC had become reality. Then, water power development – not transportation and certainly not costs – became the critical factor determining the choice of routes. The dominion Liberal cabinet and its free enterprise supporters were anxious to check the invidious march towards socialism in which the HEPC was seen to be an advanced guard. (Not all Liberals shared this belief. A Philosophical dichotomy over the matter was splitting both the Conservative and Liberal parties. The commitment of the Liberal government to private development of hydro power forced Sir William Mulock, a strong advocate of public ownership, to leave the cabinet.) If the provincial Liberals, now in opposition, had been powerless to abort the birth of the HEPC by political means, the dominion Liberals could at least stunt its growth through administrative action. By limiting the HEPC's sphere of influence, they hoped to check the erosion of the free enterprise system. The Trent River would become the barricade.

There was an immense quantity of water power on the Trent River (by 1906 standards), over which the dominion government claimed control by virtue of the British North America Act, 1867, which assigned jurisdiction over canals and navigable waters to Parliament. But the redoubtable Adam Beck, drafter and sponsor of the Hydro legislation and the commission's first chairman, had fastened his sharp eyes on this water power, which he considered a provincial resource. Indeed, the HEPC had already sent engineers to survey the water and was considering means by which it could be developed. Ontario's transfer of its dams and locks in the Trent watershed to the dominion a year prior to passage of the Hydro legislation seemed to confirm the province's acceptance of Ottawa control. But there were many, led by Adam Beck, who, with the emergence of the importance of water power, began to challenge the dominion's claim to jurisdiction. With one leaking lock at Hastings, a decrepit and rarely used lock at Glen Ross, and a few rotting timber dams and slides, the Trent River could hardly be classed a navigable river. The only sure way the dominion government could maintain control over the Trent and thereby keep Beck's grasping fingers off its water power was to canalize it fully. Therefore, Butler's recommendation that the Trent River route be adopted as the canal's outlet was accepted by the cabinet with alacrity, even though the Port Hope route may well have been cheaper, probably easier to build, and more efficacious from a transportation point of view. Transportation was the public rationale, but control of electric power development was the real motive behind the order-in-council approving the Trent River construction in February 1907.

And so the choice of the Trent River outlet served two purposes. First, it ensured that the Trent River's water power remained under dominion control and therefore could be leased to private developers, of whom there were plenty who were anxious to obtain these leases. Kerry and company and Culverwell and company were the two principal contenders, but there were others. Even Max Aitken, later Lord Beaverbrook, would soon be inquiring about leases for one of his firms, the Montreal Engineering Company. Second, the concomitant power development would add a new ingredient to the canal pork barrel: the delivery of electric power to municipalities would pay rich political dividends, as L.B. Power so crassly reminded George P. Graham in 1910. Had the canal gone through Port Hope, the Trent water powers would have reverted to provincial control and, ultimately, into the imperious clutches of the Hydro Electric Power Commission. The dominion cabinet was determined not to let that happen.

CHAPTER TWENTY-FOUR

The Ontario – Rice Lake Division

One of the ironies associated with the protracted public works project known as the Trent valley canal was the quickness with which plans were executed, once the interminable political problems that separated construction periods were solved. Engineers moved quickly when the green light was given by the politicians, which usually happened just before elections. Thus the ink was barely dry on Wilfrid Laurier's signature authorizing the Trent River route when A.J. Grant was ordered to get his engineers and draftsmen busy on construction plans and specifications so that tenders could be called. The Hydro Electric Power Commission was by then well established and under Beck's vigorous leadership was moving quickly. The horses of free enterprise had to be spurred on, the evil forces of socialism cut off at the passes – in this instance the ravines through which the Trent water cascaded on its way to Lake Ontario. And, predictably, another national election was due in 1908.

The engineering staff at Peterborough was increased several-fold in 1908, and axemen, rodmen, timekeepers, carpenters, cooks, and labourers were hired by the dozens. Between 1906 and 1908, engineering costs increased from $13,629 to $60,682; by 1911 these costs had grown to $128,660. Payments to contractors increased from $466,049 in 1908, when the first Trent construction accounts were paid, to $1,083,640 three years later, as the momentum of activity picked up for the 1911 election.

For tendering purposes, Grant divided the river into seven sections. The order in which the sections were let to contract was determined by the electric power potential on the sections and by the date on which controversies over routes were resolved or the issuance of power leases finalized. Consequently, section 5 was let out to contract first, and the adjacent section 4 was last. In most cases, contracts were let to "friends" of the Liberal party. Typically, the main contracts covered only excavation and construction of the locks, dams, entrance walls, piers, and abutments for bridges; as on previous occasions, the lock gates, bridges, and cement were covered by separate contracts.

One of the mysteries connected with the construction of the Ontario – Rice Lake division is why longer and more expensive locks were designed than those existing on the older sections of the canal, especially when it was already clear that the customers who would use the canal were "chiefly tourists and pleasure seekers."[1] The Trent River locks are 175 feet long, while the locks found on the rest of the waterway are only 142 feet long. Instead of having cheaper sluice valves built into the gates, the Trent locks contain the more expensive wagon valves, which permit water to enter the chamber along the side walls. Not only were the valves themselves more expensive – $6,300, installed – but they required thicker and more expensive lock walls with built-in conduits. Consequently, large locks, which can accommodate a great number of small boats per lockage, are located on the Trent River, where the traffic is very light, whereas on the Peterborough – Lake Simcoe portion of the system, where pleasure boat traffic is extremely heavy, shorter and slow-filling locks exist, and delays are common. From a historical point of view, the building of large locks on the Trent required that the original quaint but quite sound limestone locks, built at Hastings and Glen Ross in the 1830s and 1840s, be torn out and replaced with the less durable and less attractive concrete locks. Today the only lock remaining from the first construction phase, 1833 – 44, is the limestone one at Scott's Mills, no. 19.

The only explanation for the longer Trent River locks is the one offered by Walsh in his vindictive letter to H.S. Cane of Newmarket in 1910. Walsh claimed that Grant, knowing little about lock construction, copied from the elaborate and costly Soulanges Canal, where a type of lock was required for the large class of steamer on the St Lawrence River different from the type needed for the protected traffic on the Trent canal. Whatever the reason, Butler approved the more expensive locks, and thus they were built, but not because they were needed for power development and certainly not because they were necessary for the boat traffic. Only the contractors benefited by them.

Section 5

The first section let out to contract was no. 5, a short stretch of river three miles long, extending from the railway bridge in Campbellford to Crowe Bay, on which two dams and two locks were to be built. This section, located in a series of rapids roughly in the centre of the division, would be irrelevant for transportation until the other sections were completed. That no. 5 was tendered first supports the thesis that water power development, not barge transportation, was the primary motive for opening up the Trent River. The decision also reveals the close collaboration between J.G.G. Kerry and M.J. Butler.

In April, following approval of the order-in-council adopting the Trent outlet, Parliament voted $450,000 for the Trent construction. In late June and early July, much pressure through letters, telegrams, and long-distance telephone calls was exerted on Grant to speed up preparation of the specifications and plans for section 5 for tendering purposes. The department showed particular interest in the specifications for lock and dam 1 (now the Campbellford lock and dam), which were to be built at the rapids where, coincidentally, Kerry had purchased the Stephens mill property with the intention of building an electric power plant. A mile further up river, where dam 2 was to be built (now Crowe Bay lock and dam), was the Campbellford municipal power plant that needed rebuilding. Grant rushed the specifications to Butler on 11 July, and tenders were called immediately. Brown and Aylmer, having submitted the lowest tender ($551,688.50), were awarded the contract on 28 August.

The previous day, 27 August, the Quebec bridge had collapsed. Its construction, over the St Lawrence River, seven miles above the city of Quebec, was started in 1903. It was to have been the longest cantilever bridge in the world. The south anchor, the cantilever arms, and four panels of the suspension span had been erected. But on 27 August 1907 the structure collapsed, carrying 75 workmen to their deaths in the tangled wreckage. In his long diatribe against Butler, read out in Parliament in 1911, E.J. Walsh claimed that it was on Butler's certificate testifying to the substantiality of the bridge specifications that millions of dollars worth of bonds issued by the Quebec Bridge and Railway Company were guaranteed by the government. "The subsequent collapse of the bridge was a national disgrace," Walsh wrote, and he added, "the chief engineer of the day [Butler] cannot evade his share of responsibility."[2]

Walsh's accusation notwithstanding, the collapse of the bridge placed the government in an embarassing position because of the bond guarantee, to say nothing of the loss of life. A royal commission was appointed only four days after this greatest construction disaster in Canadian history. By 4 September the commissioners were in Quebec, undertaking a preliminary survey of the wreckage, and on 9 September they began to hear testimony. Because of the government's involvement in the case, it was important to appoint commissioners whom the government – and especially Butler – could "trust." Not surprisingly, Henry Holgate, who had performed splendidly in the Peterborough lift lock investigation the year before, was named chairman. Professor John Galbraith, dean of engineering at the University of Toronto, was one of the other two commissioners named. The third was none other than J.G.G. Kerry, the private power developer who had been negotiating with Butler for water power leases on the Trent River. As mentioned earlier, W.J. Francis, who had been asked to resign along with Rogers because of alleged incompetence in constructing the Peterborough lift lock, was hired as research engineer.

Butler must have felt a strong sense of relief when the commissioners' report was received on 20 February 1908. Both he and his predecessor, Collingwood Schreiber, were absolved of any responsibility for the disaster, even though evidence brought out at the hearing revealed beyond question that the chief engineer of the Department of Railways and Canals was required, both by the terms of the agreement with the Quebec Bridge and Railway Company and by subsequent orders-in-council, to approve the bridge specifications and any changes therein before they could be adopted for the work. Theodore Cooper, consulting engineer for the Quebec Bridge and Railway Company, objected strenuously to this requirement because, as he phrased it, "This puts me in a position of a subordinate which I cannot accept."[3] To appease Cooper, an ageing and infirm but highly respected engineer, Collingwood Schreiber, and his successor, M.J. Butler, more or less ignored the requirements of the orders-in-council, "the government approval being a mere formality,"[4] and accepted Cooper's judgment without question. As a result, Butler routinely signed the certificates on which the bonds were guaranteed by the government. Holgate glossed over the evidence, which clearly placed legal responsibility for the design and specification errors that caused the collapse of the bridge on the shoulders of Butler. Full blame for the disaster was attributed to "errors in judgment" on the part of Theodore Cooper and P.L. Szlapka, design engineer for the Phoenix Bridge Company which built the superstructure under subcontract. "The ability [of the two Americans] proved to be insufficient for the task,"[5] Holgate wrote. And to ensure complete absolution of Canadian government officials, Holgate stated: "The professional record of Mr. Cooper [before the disaster] was such that ... the complete confidence that was placed in his judgment by the officials of the Dominion government ... was deserved."[6]

It is quite clear that Kerry, and to a lesser extent Holgate, had a vested interest in writing a report favourable to the government. Butler's recommendation was needed if Kerry were to obtain the water power leases on the Trent. Had Butler been condemned and discharged, Kerry's influence in the department would have been severed, and the leases would probably have gone to his rival, Culverwell.

When the tenders for section 5 of the Ontario – Rice Lake division had been advertised, in July, Grant sent Kerry a copy of the plans. Kerry was concerned about the proposed location of dam 1, which, although generally suitable for the purposes of his Seymour Power and Electric Company, would have necessitated a considerable amount of excavation for the power plant's tail race before a contract was let; he asked if the dam could not be moved 900 feet down river. Grant later asked Kerry for a formal proposal, which Kerry submitted on 27 August, by coincidence the day the Quebec bridge fell. On 9 September, the day the Quebec bridge commissioners began hearing testimony, Grant informed Butler of Kerry's request for a new location for the dam. Butler immediatly wrote to Kerry, who was staying in the Château Frontenac Hotel in Quebec City during the commission's hearings, asking precisely what he wanted. Kerry replied on 16 September (while the hearings were in progress), suggesting that the dam could probably be relocated without additional cost to the government but that the relocation would save the power company considerable expense of excavation. Kerry also informed Butler that his lawyer, A.B. Colville of Campbellford, would visit the department in Ottawa at an early date to discuss the terms on which Kerry would transfer the property he owned at the dam site for canal purposes, in return for which the government should grant the power company a water power lease. Butler appeared most anxious to accommodate. On 20 September he met with Grant and Colville, and tentative arrangements for relocation of the dam were agreed to.

In the mean time, Brown and Aylmer had signed the contract and quite properly demanded more money, as the proposed relocation of the dam and lock would involve costlier excavation than work on the site on which they had submitted their tender. Given the breadth of the authority of the chief engineer over government contracts, this problem could easily have been resolved by Butler to the satisfaction of both Kerry and the contractors, had the ever-watchful Culverwell not heard about the proposed change in plan.

On 26 September, Culverwell wrote a letter of complaint directly to the recently appointed minister of railways and canals, George P. Graham. Culverwell, it seems, had purchased property near Kerry's property at the proposed location of dam 1, on the basis of which he hoped to acquire the lease that Kerry was seeking. He suspected that the proposal to relocate the dam was intended to place Kerry, Smith, and Chace "in a more strategic position when dealing with the government with respect to their water power rights to the disadvantage of [Culverwell's] water power property."[7] "If the attempt of these parties is successful," he warned Graham, "it will show that the construction of this section of canal is being manipulated in the interests of these power owners who are endeavouring to change the established route and survey."[8] He ended his letter with a subtle threat, reminding Graham that one of the water power owners was "Mr. Kerry ... who [was] also employed as one of the commissioners of the Dominion Government in connection with the Quebec bridge disaster."[9] There is no record of the discussion that took place between Graham and Butler as a consequence of Culverwell's letter, but Butler prudently decided to let the matter of relocating the dam drop. Departmental secretary Jones informed Grant a few days later "that the department had decided to adhere to the original location as shown on the original plans."[10]

The matter of the dam location having been resolved, Brown and Aylmer began construction in early October 1907. In the fall of 1908, work was started on the Seymour Power and Electric Company's power plant. On 31 December 1908, on Butler's recommendation (the royal commission's report having been submitted long before), the cabinet approved an order-in-council granting Kerry the surplus water at the Campbellford dam, at an annual rental of $2 per horsepower – the first dominion water power lease for electric power generation issued on the Trent River. On 30 November 1909, the dam and lock having been completed, the coffer-dam was removed, the stoplogs were inserted, and the water in the reach above was allowed to rise to navigation depth. On 2 December, the power company tested its turbines, and on 4 December a switch was thrown, sending a current of 44,000 volts over the transmission line to Kerry's first customer, the Delora Mining Company, located 22 miles north-east of Campbellford – the first long-distance transmission of elctricity from a source on the Trent River. The Hydro Electric Power Commission had been checkmated. But it would be nine years before boats would move through the Campbellford and Crowe Bay locks. By then, ironically, the Ontario government would own Kerry's power plant.

Section 1

Section 1 extended from Trenton to Glen Miller, a distance of about four and a half miles. Three locks, three dams, and five bridges were to be built. The section contained considerable electric power potential. J.G.G. Kerry had acquired the water privileges where dam 2 was to be built and was anxious to develop electric power in the name of the Sidney Electric Power Company, one of several power companies he had established anonymously, but with Butler's knowledge, for the purpose of developing the Trent River water powers. Tenders were called for the section on 5 November 1907, while the Quebec bridge commission was preparing its report.

It seems that the contract was to have been let to Larkin and Sangster, Irish contractors from St Catharines, Ontario, and long-time supporters of the Liberal party. It will be recalled that these contractors had built the hydraulic lift lock at Kirkfield and had given testimony detrimental to Rogers at the Holgate hearings. Moreover, Larkin was a shareholder in Culverwell's Central Ontario Power Company, which was hoping to get a government water power lease at dam 3.

Government contracts were awarded to the lowest bidders, a traditional policy from which it was difficult for the government to deviate, as the tenders soon became public knowledge after they were opened. There was a way, however, of ensuring that "friends" had a good chance of submitting the lowest bid. Departmental engineers made their own detailed estimate of costs, which were generally quite accurate. The deparmental estimates could then be given out to friendly contractors, so that their tenders could be set close to, and generally a little lower than, the departmental figure. Grant's estimate of the cost of the section was $1,074,313. Larkin and Sangster's tender, one of six, was $969,237.45. But Larkin and Sangster did not get the contract, at least not immediately. An English contractor named Lewis P. Nott had submitted a tender for the ridiculously low figure of $866,679, and the government was obliged to accept it. Nott was awarded the contract but, upon reading the document, refused to sign it. In 1900, through the efforts of William Lyon Mackenzie King, Canada's first deputy minister of labour, Ottawa adopted a policy of including a minimum-wage clause in all government contracts. The minumum wage rates in 1907 were not very high: labourers were to receive $1.75 for a 10-hour day or $17\frac{1}{2}$ cents per hour; foremen received 25 cents, carpenters 22 cents, a driver with a team and wagon 35 cents; steam shovel operators were the privileged members of the work gangs, receiving $100 per month plus room and board. Nott had not been aware of these rates when he submitted his tender and, thinking them too high, refused to sign the contract with the rates included. The government, not wanting to irritate Nott and discourage British capital for Canadian industry by creating bad feeling among British contractors and financiers, returned Nott's security deposit, although it was not obliged to do so. On Butler's recommendation, a contract was then awarded to Larkin and Sangster.

Larkin and Sangster were experienced contractors with plenty of plant and equipment and a good deal of capital behind them, and they had a cadre of seasoned supervisors. They had carried out contracts on the Welland Canal and had only recently completed the Kirkfield lift lock. Their aggressive firm was now anxious to get to work at Trenton; indeed, it was ready to start before the government was prepared. When the partners visited Trenton on 24 February 1908, they found men already lining up for work. Wanting to be helpful, they hired a gang of men to begin clearing trees at Glen Miller. The Miller brothers, who owned a paper mill at the rapids, chased the workmen off their land, for, incredibly, although a year had passed since the decision to canalize the Trent, the government had not yet expropriated the necessary property.

Through the month of March, the contractors had a small force at Trenton unloading plant: two small locomotives, cars and trucks, steam drills, steam shovels, hoists and derricks, concrete mixers, stone crushers, timber for coffer-dams, carts, and dozens of horses. Storage sheds, bunkhouses, store buildings, blacksmith shops, and offices were erected at various points along the section. By 16 April, the problem of land claims being settled, work began in earnest.

The locks and entrance walls were built first, the dams last. This was because the dams required the construction of coffer-dams and unwatering, whereas the locks could be built in dry canal prism and the contractor wanted a fast return on investment. Also, the start of construction on dams 1 and 2 was held up pending settlement of water leases and expropriation agreements. In the summer of 1910, Kerry was successful in obtaining a water lease for dam 2 and began building his second power plant on the Trent River. Because this power house – now known as Sidney no. 2 – was to be built into the west end of the dam, occupying two spill-ways, Larkin and Sangster were contracted to build it when they built the dam. The dam and plant were completed in the summer of 1911. The power plant began operating on 1 September, just three weeks before the dominion election.

For all intents and purposes the contract, which had been rushed faster than most Trent River contracts, was finished in 1912. All that remained to be done was some dredging between lock 1 and the Bay of Quinte, sodding around the locks, installation of hand rails, and the like. Because the dredging, much of it blasting in submarine rock, required specialized equipment and experience, the work was subcontracted to the firm of R. Waddell and Company of Trenton. On 9 January 1914, the entire work embraced by the contract having been completed, the Department of Railways and Canals accepted the works.

As for the quality and durability of the construction, it was not good. In 1924, two departmental engineers, T.S. Lazier and F.C. Jewett, reported on the condition of all the concrete structures on the Ontario – Rice Lake division. The works built by Larkin and Sangster had stood up least well of any. Dam 1 was found "rotten," dam 2 was "in poor shape," and the condition of dam 3 was rated "very poor." In each case the defects were attributed to poorly graded and dirty aggregate, with too little cement and too much water. The locks and entrance piers were in slightly better condition, but considerable flaking of the concrete had taken place. Expensive repairs were required to arrest the erosion. Concrete inspectors had been employed by the government on section 1, but obviously they did not do a very good job, nor, apparently, did Grant insist on as close supervision as Rogers had. Ironically, it was Rogers, not Grant, who was fired for alleged supervisory lapses over the same contractors. Such is the uneven quality of political justice.

As for the electoral gain to the Liberals from the construction at Trenton, there was none. Conservative Gus Porter won the riding in the election of 1908 with a greater majority than he had in 1904; and in 1911, when

Borden swept Laurier's decadent government out of office, Porter again won, polling 1,771 votes more than his Liberal opponent.

Section 2

While construction on section 1 progressed rapidly, work on section 2 proceeded with the measured pace of a funeral march. The section, which extended from Glen Miller to Frankford, a distance of about four and a half miles, called for three dams, three locks, one bridge, and considerable dredging. There is every indication that someone in the Department of Railways and Canals wished Larkin and Sangster to obtain this contract as well; as with the tender for section 1, theirs was too close to the superintending engineer's estimate to have been arrived at by coincidence: the departmental estimate was $733,482; Larkin and Sangster's was $756,455. But they did not win. They were beaten out by former Trent canal superintendent R.B. Rogers, who knew the tendering game on the canal as well as anyone. He knew that the lowest tender won the contract but that in the final analysis the amount paid out was usually much greater than the amount tendered for, and there was always the possibility of picking up "extras." Rogers and his partner, William Dennon, tendered for $618,804, by far the lowest tender of the eight submitted. There was, of course, some risk in submitting such a low tender, because the amount actually paid per cubic yard for excavating and laying concrete – the major components of the contracts – was the rate tendered for. Rogers's tender for solid rock excavation was only $1.43 per cubic yard, the lowest rate for excavation in any of the tenders for the seven contracts on the Ontario – Rice Lake division. He gambled that he could easily remove the rock, about 60 per cent of it submarine, at this low rate; besides, he was willing to make a minimum profit to be assured of the contract, being desperate for work and not having had a steady job for over a year. The Rogers and Dennon tender was accepted, and a contract was awarded by order-in-council, dated 24 March 1908. Rogers moved his family to Frankford in mid-April, making that village his base of operations. From the day he took up residence in Frankford until the contract was completed in the fall of 1918, he had nothing but trouble.

Rogers's principal problems stemmed from shortage of funds and lack of contracting experience. Although a superb engineer, he had never been a contractor and therefore had no plant and equipment, no capital with which to purchase them, and no organization of experienced supervisors and foremen; nor did he, with his easy-going nature, possess the toughness and drive needed to get maximum effort from immigrant workers on temporary employment. His own time was taken up with engineering matters, leaving no one competent to manage the workers; consequently the work was sometimes done in "a haphazard and slipshod manner."[11] But because Rogers was a man of high principles, he insisted on errors being corrected. Everything had to be built correctly, even if it meant taking longer.

A.J. Grant complained constantly to Butler and Butler's successor, A.W. Bowden, about the slowness of progress on section 2. His monthly progress reports were studded with comments on this. "Progress on this section is very slow and there does not seem to be much prospect of it getting better."[12] "The work on this section is very much delayed for want of men ... and also the want of plant."[13] "The work on this section is as usual greatly delayed for want of men."[14] At the present rate of progress the contractors will take several years to finish the section."[15] Grant attributed the slow progress to poor organization, which was partly true, but the major cause of the problem was lack of funds.

Rogers had little money to buy plant even to get the work started, and what he could afford was barely adequate. William Dennon went to Montreal to buy a steam shovel and other plant in late April, but Dennon was the manager of an oatmeal mill: he knew little about construction equipment. The steam shovel he purchased was small, probably second-hand; it frequently broke down. While Larkin and Sangster used small locomotives to haul away excavated material, Rogers had to rely on horses and carts. He was short of mixers, pumps, derricks, and hoists. He had, in fact, only enough equipment to work on one structure at a time, be it dam or lock. He could not attract and hold labourers for long, because of his inability to pay them regularly, nor did he have comfortable bunkhouses and the like for them. Consequently, workers no sooner arrived than they left again, keeping the work gangs disorganized.

At the end of the first construction season, while Larkin and Sangster's mammoth machine operating down river had churned through about 30 per cent of the contract, Rogers, with a handful of Italian workers and a score of teams, had barely started his. At the end of December, less than 10 per cent of the contract, valued at $71,709, had been finished.

For the next three or four years, Grant exerted tremendous pressure on Rogers to accelerate construction, either directly through the divisional engineers or indirectly through his progress reports to the chief engineer. The urgency to complete the contract had very little to do with completing the canal for transportation. The contracts for sections 4 and 6 were not even let until the late spring of 1910; it would be years before they would be finished. The urgency to complete dams 4 and 5 on the Rogers contract was connected with power development, and most of the pressure to get them built was coming from J.G.G. Kerry. Through 1909 and 1910 Kerry had been competing with Culverwell's group for a water power lease at Glen Miller (dam 3), but development at dam 3 could not take place until lock and dam 4 were built; otherwise, the water levels at dam 4 would be raised six feet, rendering the unwatering of the pits for the lock and dam a serious matter. In February 1910, Rogers had not so much as cleared the land at the site of dam 4, let alone done any excavating. In June, the dispute between Kerry and Culverwell was resolved, and a request was made to the Department of Railways and Canals for permission to proceed with the development, but Rogers still had not started work on these structures. Further, Kerry had obtained clear title to the water power privileges at dam 5 and was desirous of proceeding with construction of a power plant there. He was being frustrated in that development by Rogers who, because of shortage of labour and equipment, had done no more than a modest amount of excavation by the summer of 1910. Hence the incessant criticism and condemnation of Rogers from both Peterborough and Ottawa.

As for the quality of the work, not surprisingly, Rogers's locks and dams were among the best of all those built on the Trent River. The Lazier and Jewett survey in 1924 rated the condition of the concrete as "good" or "very good." In 1982 I found locks 5 and 6 to be in the original and still excellent state; lock 4 had been resurfaced. Not a bad record for 66-year-old concrete, exposed to extreme annual climatic changes.

Section 3

Extending from Frankford to three miles west of Glen Ross, section 3 was the smallest contract on the Ontario – Rice Lake division. The work to be done consisted of rebuilding the old lock at Glen Ross (formerly Chisholm's Rapids), construction of a new dam across the rapids, and considerable dredging in the river channel. A contract for $289,520 was let to the Canadian General Development Company on 24 April 1908, that firm's tender being the lowest of five submitted. Work began immediately on the construction at Glen Ross.

Canadian General Development widened and deepened the old canal to bring it up to the standard of the new canal design – 80 feet wide on the bottom and 9 feet deep; it tore out the masonry lock, replacing it with the present concrete one, and built a concrete dam some distance further down river from the site of the old one. This work, which cost $177,940, was finished in 1911, but until the locks and dams on sections 1 and 2 were completed, dredges and drill barges could not be brought up river from Trenton to complete the contract, and so work was suspended. Canadian General Development subsequently went bankrupt and in February 1914 assigned its Trent canal contract, with the approval of the government, to Fred A. Robertson and Company for $10,000.

The locks on Rogers's section still being some time away from completion, Robertson decided to build and launch a dredging fleet at Glen Ross and to proceed with his contract. His fleet consisted of a dredge 22 feet by 65 feet, a tug with a 37-foot keel, two dump scows each with a 35-cubic-yard capacity, one drill scow 16 feet by 40 feet, and one coal scow 14 feet by 36 feet. In addition, he built a boat-house and a blacksmith's shop on the point below the lock. The fleet was crude, intended to be of a temporary nature, but it did the job, albeit slowly; in fact, it took Robertson five years to complete the dredging on this 10-mile stretch of canal. The most difficult and time-consuming part of the contract was the removal of solid submarine rock, for which purposes the drill scow was used.

Robertson's drill scow was typical of those used on the Trent canal construction. It was equipped with adjustable pylons – one on each corner – that were lowered and raised with gear devices. The first step in the removal of submarine rock from the marked-out channel was to float the drill scow into place above the shoal and to lower the pylons until they stood on the bottom. A firm platform thus being created, steam drills bored into the underwater rock, using a technique similar in principle to that used today on offshore oil-drilling rigs, but on a much smaller scale. When a sufficient number of holes was drilled, dynamite was inserted by a diver, whose support system also operated from the drill scow. Once dynamite was in place and the diver had been safely retrieved from the water, the drill scow was floated away and the charge was ignited, fracturing the drilled section of rock. Next, a dredge was brought in to suck up the shattered pieces, or, if the chunks were large, as when granite was being removed, the diver placed the pieces of rock on a submerged platform in a sling by which they were hoisted to the surface and either dumped on the shore or dropped in deep sections of the river, away from the main channel. The procedure was repeated until the submarine rock was stripped down to the desired depth of navigation. It was slow, moderately dangerous work that usually exacted a heavy toll on fish. Sand, gravel, and loose sediments were, of course, picked up by the dredge, deposited in the dump scows, and hauled away from the channel by the tug. The dredging on section 3 was finally finished in the late spring of 1918, in time for the official opening of the Ontario – Rice Lake division.

Section 4

The letting of a contract for section 4, which extended from Adam's Landing, three miles above Glen Ross, to Campbellford, was delayed until 22 June 1910. Typically, the hold-up resulted from power politics; specifically a controversy over the choice of canal routes through the town of Campbellford.

In its natural state, the 11-mile stretch of the Trent River from Percy

Boom to Healey Falls was one long series of rapids and falls which, while creating an obstacle to water transportation, provided valuable power for pioneer industries such as saw and grist mills and, later, woollen, shoe, and paper factories and the like. Mills were established at Myersberg, Ranney Falls, and Middle Falls (Crowe Bay), and hamlets grew up around them. But it was at the site of a natural ford in the river about a half-mile above Ranney Falls, where half-pay army officers Col. Campbell and Maj. Campbell erected a log hut on their 1,800-acre land grant – at Campbell's ford – that the major centre of population in the township of Seymour developed. In 1840, a wooden bridge was built across the river just south of the ford, and in 1846 a power dam was constructed by James Cockburn, brother of the local MLA. The 14-foot head of water created by the dam powered several industries, which provided the impetus for Campbellford's rapid growth in the second half of the nineteenth century. In 1908, when A.J. Grant was developing plans for canalizing the Trent, five major industries were powered from the dam: the Trent Valley Woollen Manufacturing Company, the Campbellford Flour Mills, Dickson's Foundry and Machine Shop, the Weston Shoe Company, and James Benor and Sons' planing mill. Also, the town of Campbellford powered the pumps for its recently installed water system from the dam.

The problem confronting Grant was how to run the canal through Campbellford without interfering with the power dam, situated now in the heart of the town. Ranney Falls would have to be overcome by excavating a canal parallel to the gorge and building a flight of two locks at the lower end of the canal, and a new dam would have to be built across the falls. How high should the new dam be? Should it be high enough to flood out the existing dam at Campbellford, destroying the water power on which the industries were dependent, or should the water power at Campbellford be maintained with a lower dam at Ranney Falls? How much would it cost the government in damages to obliterate the existing dam, the whole basis of the town's economy?

On Valentine's Day, 1908, Grant submitted no less than eight route proposals to Butler. Seven of the proposals were calculated to preserve the existing water power. Two of them would leave the river on the west side a few hundred feet above the existing dam, run through the town, and connect with the collateral cut at Ranney Falls. Two others would bypass the existing power development in a similar way, but on the east side of the river. The disadvantage of these four routes was that they would divide the town, already cut in half by the river, require several swing bridges for street and road crossings, and require the expropriation of much expensive town property. They would also require a 14-foot lock to be built in the town. The other three routes would follow the river to Ranney Falls but would preserve the existing water power with a new dam and an attached lock. The difference in these routes was in the way they would bypass Ranney Falls, one on the east side, the other two on the west side of the falls.

The eighth proposal was one Grant referred to as the "Kerry proposition,"[16] because it was proposed by Kerry. It was the only route that made sense, and , understandably, it provided substantial advantages to Kerry. Kerry's proposition was an all-river route through Campbellford. It called for drowning out the existing hydraulic power in Campbellford with one high dam at Ranney Falls and building retaining walls on each side of the river in front of the mills and other waterfront properties. A collateral cut would leave the river at the bend below the Grand Trunk Railway bridge and run behind the Northumberland Paper and Electric Company (of which Kerry was president), in effect creating a power canal for the paper company. One flight of two locks, each with a lift of 25 feet, would be built at the south end of the canal. This proposition, the one eventually adopted, was favoured by almost everyone in Campbellford. Indeed, Kerry had done a good deal of lobbying for it among the power users, even before Grant submitted his proposals to Butler. It did not make sense to maintain water-powered machinery in the factories in Campbellford, when most factories in Ontario were switching to the more dependable electric power. Nor did it make sense to cut up the town with a canal bypassing an existing dam or to replace a magnificent 50-foot head for power development at Ranney Falls with two lower heads (36 feet and 14 feet) spread out over a mile of river. The factory owners were desirous, indeed anxious, to switch to electric power and were willing to support Kerry's proposition – but for a price.

The water power users thought that they had a watertight case against the government and could, therefore, practically dictate their own terms. As compensation for the loss of existing water rights and privileges, they wanted the government to pay for installing electric motors in their factories and to provide them with free electricity equal to the amount of power lost at the dam (estimated to be about 700 horsepower). In addition, they wanted the guarantee of an additional 750 horsepower of electricity held in reserve for them, to be delivered at any time they should require it.

When Grant learned about the exorbitant demands of the power users, most of whom he suspected of being Conservative supporters, he proposed yet another canal route that would have avoided the town altogether, thereby freeing the government from any claim for damages by the mill owners. His ninth proposal called for digging a three-mile canal from a spot on the river just below the Campbellford lock, to connect with the river just above the paper mill. Swinging to the west of the town, the canal would pass through low swampy ground where the buildings were "of an inferior class,"[17] thus avoiding cutting up the town, reducing expropriation costs because of the low value of the property, and leaving the power users in possession of their ancient log dam and antiquated water wheels. If the mill owners chose to convert to electricity, it would be no concern of the government's.

The ninth proposal had one serious drawback. The inferior class of buildings on the route belonged to labouring men, most of whom were Liberal supporters and most of whom would be isolated from the town by Grant's proposed canal. They wrote to Butler, appealing to him not to adopt the route, for, as they said, "the only ones who would suffer by it were Reformers who would be turned out of their homes by their own party."[18] When the power users perceived that route 9, if adopted, would deny them an opportunity of modernizing their plants at government expense, they too objected. A spate of petitions supporting Kerry's proposition, organized by the power users, but signed by almost everyone in Campbellford, descended on the minister. The power users asked for a meeting with the minister to discuss a compensation package. Meanwhile, construction plans and specifications for section 4 were being held up.

Graham met with the mill owners on 15 December but made no promises. In the mean time, the Department of Justice had been examining the extent of government liability in the event the dam at Campbellford was removed. There was none. The dam had been built originally by Cockburn without authority, but it had been allowed to remain because it was a valuable resource in the village and because the sluice-way built into its centre permitted passage of the annual timber drive. In 1869, the government had issued a licence to the contemporary power users, revocable by the government at will and under its terms and expressly precluding licensees from making claims. The government could, therefore, in the opinion of the Justice Department, remove the dam without paying compensation. When this was learned, Kerry's route was selected.

In November 1909, Butler advised Grant to prepare plans for section 4 for tendering. These were ready in March 1910, and tenders were called. On 24 August 1911, just before the dominion election, an order-in-council revoking the 1869 licence was passed; the mill owners were individually advised that the old dam would be removed, that expropriation proceedings would not be taken (the Justice Department considered this unnecessary), and that the government would not assume liability for the loss of water power. The dam was blown up on 10 August 1912.

The outgoing Liberal government had made no promises of compensation to the mill owners. In fact, on the advice of the Justice Department, the minister of railways and canals advised the mill owners that their alleged claims for damages would have to be ruled on by the court. The owners, however, knowing that political settlements were generally more generous than adjudicated ones, pressed their claims with the new Conservative government. The inexperienced Conservatives proved much more accommodating than a court would have been. Dickson's Foundry received $7,000 in cash for loss of its water power; the town of Campbellford was paid $12,000 in compensation for the loss of water power and the destruction of a section of its water supply pipe, even though it was given a free water lease at the Crowe Bay dam. But it was the Trent Valley Woollen Manufacturing Company, which had used about half of the water power at the old dam, that won the best agreement. Of all the political settlements made because of the Trent canal through the years, this one was the most contentious, certainly the most expensive. The cost of it is being borne by the taxpayers even today.

The deal was this: the government would compensate the woollen company with $21,477.86 in cash (the cost of converting its factory from hydraulic to electric power), and it would supply and deliver to the company, its successors, and its assignees, in perpetuity, 350 horsepower of electrical energy per year. Also, the government would construct and maintain a power line from the Seymour Power Company's plant to the woollen mills. An order-in-council authorizing the minister of railways and canals to enter into an agreement with the company on these terms was passed on 25 August 1913. But it was over a year later that the agreement was finally signed.

There was much opposition within the government to the terms of the agreement. The Justice Department was strongly opposed for the reasons previously given. Auditor-General J. Fraser objected to payment of the cash portion of the agreement until it was approved by Parliament; he advised the deputy minister of railways and canals to reconsider the arrangement. Nevertheless, Frank Cochrane executed the agreement on 25 September 1914.

The immediate cost of the agreement was insignificant. It is in the accumulative obligation assumed by the government under the agreement, still in force, that the cost to the taxpayers becomes outrageous. The government entered into a subagreement with J.G.G. Kerry to provide 350 horsepower of electricity at a cost of $4,200 per year ($12 per horsepower). When Kerry sold his interests to the Ontario government in 1916, the government and eventually Ontario Hydro assumed responsibility for delivering the power.

In 1923, the Trent Valley Woollen Company sold and assigned its power agreement to Campbellford Cloth, a right the company had under the original agreement with the government. In 1975, Campbellford Cloth offered to terminate the power agreement for a cash settlement of

$320,000. The maximum cost to the federal government was still $4,200 per year, but the actual cost to Ontario Hydro for delivering the power was by then $13,300 per year. The federal government, which had already paid over $252,000 through the years, was prepared to put up $42,000 towards a cash settlement, but Ontario Hydro was unable to find the money needed for its share of a counter-proposal to Campbellford Cloth, and so the power agreement continued in force.

Campbellford Cloth was subsequently closed down, and the parent company, Barrymore Carpets, put the factory up for sale. By then the annual value of the power agreement was $18,885, which added substantially to the value of the old unused stone factory. Barrymore sold the property to the town of Campbellford for $202,000 and assigned the power agreement to the town. In January 1978, the town asked if the agreement could be amended, permitting the 350 horsepower to be delivered into the town's power grid rather than to the transformers at the vacant factory. Parks Canada (which by then had assumed administrative responsibility for the Trent-Severn Waterway) seemed amenable to this suggestion, and some power was delivered under the new arrangement. Consequently the town demolished the old factory and converted the property into a park.

In February 1979, the austerity-minded Conservative government of Joe Clark re-examined the 1914 agreement and concluded that the government's obligation to deliver power had come to an end, and so it unilaterally terminated the agreement. The town of Campbellford sued. Judge Patrick M. Mahoney, who heard the case in September 1981, ruled in favour of the town. "This agreement does use the phrase 'in perpetuity'," the judge stated. "I see no reason not to give it its ordinary meaning: forever. The company gave up something forever and it got something forever, and what it got was freely assignable by it."[19]

And so the 1914 agreement continues. Parks Canada still pays Ontario Hydro $4,200 for 261 kilowatts at $16.08 per kilowatt per year (the billing basis since 1949). Ontario Hydro delivers the power into the Campbellford power grid. The current value of the power delivered is in excess of $51,000 per year. With the cash surrender value of the agreement increasing every year, the federal government and Ontario Hydro will have to come forward with a substantial amount of cash to induce the town of Campbellford to terminate the agreement. If they do not, the accumulated cost will, in time, exceed the original cost of constructing the whole Trent canal. And except for the expediency of politics, the agreement was not even necessary.

To return to 1910, it is perhaps not surprising that Michael John Haney should receive the contract for section 4, the most lucrative of all the contracts on the Trent River. Tendering under the name of Haney, Quinlan and Robertson, Haney submitted a bid of $1,428,466.50, which, being the lowest, was accepted. A contract was signed on 22 June. The 14-mile section included three single-chamber locks (now Percy Reach, Myers, and Haigues Reach locks), one flight of two locks (Ranney Falls locks), about three miles of excavated canal, three dams, bridge abutments, retaining core and river walls, and a supply weir for power development at the Northumberland Paper and Electric Company (now the Breithaupt Leather Company). Clearing for the Ranney Falls bypass started on 15 July. The first construction was the forebay and control sluices at the head of the power canal leading to Kerry's Northumberland Paper and Electric Company plant!

Haney proved to be as competent a canal builder as he was a railway contractor. The concrete work on this contract, finished in 1918, was generally of good quality except for the flight of locks at Ranney Falls, where considerable scaling later took place and repairs were necessary. After coming into office in 1911, the Conservative government pared down some items in the contract, with the result that Haney received only $1,262,733 for the work, some $165,733 less than his tender.

Section 6

The three-mile stretch of canal in section 6 extended from Crowe Bay dam to 1,000 feet above the Healey Falls bridge. To overcome the 76-foot rise at the falls, one single-chamber lock and a flight of two locks (Healey Falls) were constructed in a mile-long canal excavated on the west side of the river. The longest concrete dam on the Trent River was built across the head of the falls, replacing the old log dam built in 1844 to maintain navigation levels for the Hastings lock.

Although Grant submitted four alternate plans for the Healey Falls contract in June 1908, it was not until 23 May 1910 that the route was selected and a contract finally awarded. The hold-up was caused by a controversy over who should receive the water power lease for electric power development at this highest and most valuable head of water on the whole Trent system. The government faced a dilemma largely of its own making. It had established a policy on the Trent of expropriating land at the site of falls and rapids, in exchange for which water power leases were given to the principal riparian owner. J.A. Culverwell, in the name of the Northumberland and Durham Power Company, had bought several parcels of land bordering Healey Falls and under the policy was logically entitled to the water lease; indeed, in 1906 the Ontario government had granted Culverwell a lease for the water at Healey Falls, but this lease had no validity after the decision of the dominion government to initiate canalization of the Trent River. Ottawa was committed to an alternative power development policy, which it adopted following a recommendation made by the Hydro Electric Power Commission in 1906: "that the only way to get power at the best price for the public was through one strong company getting control of the power and distributing it through Central Ontario."[20] Clearly, the strongest company operating on the Trent was Electric Power, founded by J.G.G. Kerry, who, with the encouragement of the government, had quietly bought the riparian rights at most of the other power sites on the Trent River and had already been granted one power lease and was actually operating another power plant. To give a water power lease at Healey Falls to Culverwell would violate the monopoly policy, a commitment that Graham had already placed on public record. To complicate matters the competitors were both Liberals, and each had strong backing in his party. It required a little time for Graham, through subtle manipulation, to force an amalgamation of the two power companies, thus clearing the way for construction of the locks and dam to begin and the concomitant development of the hydroelectric power to take place.

M.J. Haney and his associates, Quinlan and Robertson, were awarded the contract – their second on the Trent River – their bid being the lowest of 13 tenders submitted. Work began in July 1910.

Healey Falls was a difficult place to which to haul heavy equipment and material in 1910. No railway passed the falls. There was access by dirt road, but automobiles were still in their infancy, and trucks large enough to haul freight had not yet been developed. Logically, access to the construction site was by water over which there were three possible routes: down river from Hastings, up river from Campbellford, or down the Crowe River from the railway depot of Blairton. Reconstruction of the lock at Hastings rendered delivery of materials from that source difficult, and material could not be delivered easily from the railway station at Campbellford, locks 13 and 14 on section 5 not yet being completed. And so it was from the mining village of Blairton on the Grand Trunk Railway that the dozens of pounds of dynamite and the thousands of barrels of cement, for the 73,718 cubic yards of concrete that went into the dam, locks, and retaining walls, were hauled: by teams in winter and down the Crowe River by scow in the summer. A supply of good gravel and sand was found on Rowe's farm, near the dam.

By June 1911, despite an acute shortage of labour, the dam was practically finished; the pits for locks 16 and 17 were excavated, and construction of the long retaining wall between the dam and lock 17 had been started. At about this time, Kerry let a contract for construction of his power plant to Haney. When construction of the plant was started, it was found that the positioning of the supply weir required a considerable increase in the height of the retaining wall, which added about $30,000 to the cost. Grant, ever the frugal Scot, suggested that Kerry pay the difference, but the government ended up covering the additional cost.

In the fall of 1913 the contract was, for all intents and purposes, completed, except for some dredging at the lock entrances. This could not be done until the locks down river were finished, allowing dredges to be brought up river from Lake Ontario. The electric power plant was put into operation in the summer of 1914 but was immediately shut down, the other hydroelectric plants in the Electric Power Company's system being sufficient to carry the load until demand picked up.

Section 7

Section 7 comprised the 20-mile stretch of river from Healey Falls to Rice Lake. The principal work on the section consisted of a considerable amount of earth and rock dredging in the river and construction of a new lock and dam at Hastings, a new swing bridge at Trent River, and new guide piers for the Grand Trunk bridge above Hastings. A contract for $429,097.25 was entered into with the Randolph Macdonald Company of Toronto, on 9 January 1909. The old wooden dam built at Hastings in 1844 was in bad shape and needed replacing, but there would have been no need to replace the perfectly sound limestone lock had A.J. Grant not designed 175-foot-long locks on the Ontario – Rice Lake division. As the Hastings lock, like the limestone one at Glen Ross designed by Nichol Hugh Baird, was only 134 feet long, it was felt that it should be replaced with a lock built to the same dimension as the other locks. So, although no boat longer than 134 feet has ever passed through the Ontario – Rice Lake division, the historic old lock was torn out, and a new concrete lock was placed in commission on 30 March 1911. Remains of the original limestone structure can be seen today, forming part of the upper entrance to the lock.

The Conservative government of Robert Borden, which came to power in September 1911, honoured the contracts on the Trent that had been let by its Liberal predecessor. But the Conservatives also continued the traditional practice of spreading construction over many years. Indeed, the Conservatives extended construction even longer, if possible, than the Liberals had. By 1912, most of the electric power needs of the district had been met by the Electric Power Company's three plants and Campbellford's plant at Crowe Bay dam, and since there was no pressing need for transportation facilities there was no urgency to complete the locks. The First World War created a shortage not only of government funds but also of labourers, and so construction dragged on through the war years. It was not until 3 June 1918 that the Ontario – Rice Lake division was formally opened. But no through traffic came.

Opening of the division had created a through navigation system from Lake Ontario to Lake Couchiching. Ironically, despite the 90 years of lobbying for the canal, now that nine-tenths of it was completed no one seemed anxious to use it. To encourage traffic, the Department of Marine and Fisheries put up a silk flag as a prize for the first boat carrying six passengers or more to make the trip from Trenton to Washago. There were no immediate takers. Then the Orillia board of trade, hoping to attract tourists, offered a flag to the owner of a boat of 10 horsepower to be the first through from Lake Ontario. The people of Midland, long accustomed to hosting large grain and passenger freighters, sneered at Orillia's aspiration to "measure up among the big ocean and lake port towns,"[21] by virtue of its location on the canal. "Unhappily the Cunarders and the c.p.r. ocean going vessels are all very busy on war work or there might be a procession of ships after that flag,"[22] the Midland *Free Press* chuckled.

On 26 July 1918, the first boat from Lake Ontario finally arrived at Orillia to claim the flags. It was the *Kitchener*, and it came all the way from Belleville. On board were E.G. Porter, Belleville MP for Hastings West and long-time promoter of the canal; Belleville city assessor Kerr; Hastings county engineer L. Allen; and two other passengers, V. Hyman and Sandy Burrows. The *Kitchener* had a captain, a pilot, and, of all things, a steward. After spending a day sightseeing around Lake Couchiching and being entertained by the town, the party had photographs taken at the park dock before leaving for Trenton. Tourism, the final and lasting raison d'être of the Trent canal, had been inaugurated in grand style.

CHAPTER TWENTY-FIVE

Kerry and Culverwell

Messrs Kerry and Culverwell have been standing off stage, prompting the raconteur of this Trent canal story since chapter 21. It is now time for them to come out to tell the behind-the-scenes story of how hydroelectric power was developed on the Trent River and to reveal how they became two of the first victims – but not losers – in Canada's twentieth-century shift from a free market to a mixed economy. At first fierce competitors for water power rights on the Trent, Kerry and Culverwell were forced by the dominion government to join forces and later, coerced by the politicians, had to sell all their assets to the state. But they did not do this without putting up a stiff fight, and not without making a huge profit.

John Alexander Culverwell entered the district in 1898, nine years before Kerry. With his head start, Culverwell ought to have been able to win the race for power leases, the legal instruments on which the generation and marketing of electricity depended. His company ought to have been "the one strong company to get control of the power on the Trent"[1] for which the government was looking. But, unfortunately, he chose the wrong tactics and, having aligned himself with local politicians – often unreliable partners of dubious value in any game – lacked the right sponsors. In pursuing his goals, Culverwell relied on the once effective but declining practice of nineteenth-century society – the public petition to government. In this regard he sought the support of municipal councils, industrialists, financiers, politicians, and ordinary citizens, but, alas, despite the public furor he created, and despite the efforts of numerous political figures on his behalf, he had to settle, in 1910, for becoming a minor shareholder in an $8 million company that acquired a monopoly over hydroelectric power development in central Ontario.

The head of that company was John George Gale Kerry, who, although not entering the contest until 1907, nine years after the energetic Culverwell, demonstrated that the race is not always won by the swift. Kerry was an engineer and an academic, involved in two fields of endeavour that gave him an edge in the emerging politics of electric power development. With an engineer's precision, he carefully plotted his course, cultivated the right people in government, and made all the proper moves. A pioneer in the new field of electrical engineering, he became one of the leading experts in North America, acting as a consultant to many major power developers in Canada and the United States. Realizing that he had more knowledge and greater ability than any of the engineers in the Department of Railways and Canals, the government depended upon him for advice and direction. It was he who worked out the policies and principles for power development on the Trent – which, while furthering his own goals, also served the interests of the Liberal dominion government, too.

With an academic's penchant for circumspection, Kerry operated secretly along the Trent, quietly buying riparian rights at power sites, setting up power companies headed by interim and little-known boards of directors, and arranging his financing so that there would be no public quotation of securities – all with the knowledge and consent of Ottawa. The public would one day "simply find itself amply served throughout the district and before the time of the next election [would] realize that the Dominion Government had permitted the creation of a private company giving just as efficient service to the people as [would] be given by the Hydro Electric [Power] Commission and without involving the public credit in any way."[2] That was the way Kerry described the unwritten affiance that he, an industrialist, worked out with George P. Graham, a politician, through intermediary M.J. Butler. Thanks to the clumsy and somewhat noisy persistence of J.A. Culverwell, the marriage nearly collapsed. Only because Kerry was willing to share the pleasures of the bridal chamber with his opponent did the plan succeed, and then only for a while.

First, Culverwell's story. John Alexander Culverwell was born of English parents in Peterborough in the 1870s. While still a boy, he moved with his parents to Toronto, where he attended Upper Canada College. His first job was selling insurance for the Royal Victoria Life Assurance Company, and he eventually rose to become general agent for the Toronto area. Later he joined the Edison General Electric Company as a salesman. When he arrived back in Peterborough in 1899, as a potential developer of hydroelectric power, he called himself an electrical and mechanical broker. In later years he referred to himself as a hydraulic electric engineer, but this title was merely an affectation, as Culverwell had no training in either hydraulics or engineering. Actually, he was a promoter, hydroelectric power development being the commodity he endeavoured to sell.

Although he knew next to nothing about the technology of hydroelectric development, he was shrewd enough to realize that this was a promising field of investment for the future. His years at Edison Electric had taught him that. Where to begin? He needed a source of water power, before he could raise capital for its development and sale. Since water power leases had already been assigned for the major power sites on the Otonabee River, and since the town of Peterborough was about to be supplied with electric power from the Otonabee Power Company's plant and by the Peterborough Light and Power Company, Culverwell looked to Lindsay, which seemed a more promising place. Street lighting in Lindsay was being provided by the Light, Heat and Power Company of Lindsay, founded in 1895 by the amalgamation of two competing and unprofitable steam-powered electric companies. Because electrical energy provided by the new company was exclusively steam generated, it was very expensive, and the town was looking for an alternate source of supply. It was then that Culverwell arrived on the scene.

He bought from J.B. McWilliams the land on both sides of Perry's Creek, on the basis of which he claimed the rights to the water power created by the dam and lock at Burleigh Falls. On the strength of this, he applied for and was granted a water power lease by the Ontario government, for which he was required to pay a nominal rental of one dollar per year.[3] Then he proceeded to promote a hydroelectric power scheme in Lindsay. He managed to obtain a long-term franchise for street lighting from the town, and he secured a commitment from many merchants and manufacturers in Lindsay to buy power from him. He also obtained the necessary pole-line right from the municipalities through which the power would have to be transmitted from Perry's Creek to Lindsay. Meanwhile, he had begun to organize a joint-stock company to be known as the Lindsay – Burleigh Falls Electrical Transmission Company.

But before Culverwell could proceed with the development of the power, he needed the permission of the dominion government to remove the log dam at the head of Perry's Creek, which he planned to replace with a new concrete dam to be built further downstream. On 20 January 1899, he wrote a request to the minister of railways and canals, with supporting letters from J.W. Walters, mayor of Lindsay, George McHugh, MP, and J.B. McWilliams. Typically, the government stalled on the request; it was not until February 1900, and only after the intervention of Sir William Mulock and the Hon. Richard Harcourt, Ontario's minister of education (and a principal shareholder and president of Culverwell's company), that a dominion water lease, with permission to remove the dam, was issued. Culverwell assigned the lease to the company, now called the Central Ontario Power Company, for $70,500 worth of stock. Unfortunately for Culverwell, by this time the Light, Heat and Power Company of Lindsay had acquired the power rights at Fenelon Falls from the estate of R.C. Smith, those rights having been assigned to the estate when the Smith property was expropriated for lock construction in 1883. The Lindsay company built a small generating station at Fenelon Falls for $75,000 and began delivering electric power to Lindsay on 31 May 1900. With no available market for the Burleigh Falls power, Culverwell's company lay dormant, and he began looking for another power source.

Culverwell surfaced again in 1904, this time in Port Hope, where he took an active part in the election campaign on behalf of Allen B. Aylesworth. Aylesworth wrote his impressions of Culverwell in a private letter to Laurier on 11 August 1905:

I really know ... very little about Mr. Culverwell, whom I never met till October last. He is a very energetic gentlemen, and his business, I think , is that of a promoter of one sort and another of financial schemes. During the general election campaign in Durham last Fall, he bustled about a great deal as though he was very active, his whole politics being the Trent Canal and the Port Hope outlet for it ... I do not think he had any vote in Durham, but he was continually talking "canal" and "Port Hope outlet" on the streets and, I think, also at occasional public meetings and by letters to the newspapers. He professed to be of the opinion that my election would have contributed materially to Port Hope being chosen as the place for the canal outlet, and in that view stated himself to be a warm supporter of mine, but if this was really his preference in the matter it was, I am persuaded, entirely due to his idea that his wishes in regard to the Canal would have been furthered by my being elected.[4]

Culverwell's wishes regarding the Trent canal were that its outlet to Lake Ontario be by way of Port Hope, leaving, as discussed earlier, the province in undisputed control of the Trent River water. Culverwell already had his eye on the water power at Healey Falls; he believed his chances were greater for obtaining a lease for the water from the provincial than from the dominion government. A second wish was to have canal superintendent R.B. Rogers, whom he perceived to be hostile to the Port Hope outlet and, even worse, a competitor for Healey Falls power, removed from office.

The net result of Culverwell's "bustling about a great deal" during the election campaign was the commitment forced from Laurier to order further comparative-cost surveys of the Port Hope and Trenton outlets, the results of which Culverwell hoped would favour Port Hope. In the mean time, having purchased property at Healey Falls on the basis of which he assumed a right to water privileges, Culverwell formed another power company backed by business and political leaders, principally in Cobourg and Port Hope. Northumberland and Durham Power Company Ltd was chartered by letters patent on 7 November 1905, with share capital of $750,000; its head office was in Cobourg. Culverwell then applied to both the provincial and dominion governments for water leases at Healey Falls. Encouraged by Culverwell and an associate, William J. Crossan, president of the Crossan Car Manufacturing Company of Cobourg, both of whom devoted a good deal of their time to selling the advantages of hydroelectric power, the neighbouring municipalities petitioned the two governments in support of Culverwell's lease application. It was this deluge of memorials and petitions descending on Laurier's desk that prompted him to inquire of Allen B. Aylesworth just who Culverwell was.

The new provincial Conservative government of James Whitney, which fathered the Hydro Electric Power Commission and laid claim to the surplus water in the Trent, regardless of the route of the Trent canal, responded to the pressure and granted a lease on 3 January 1906. The annual rental for water was set at 75 cents per horsepower. With Walsh's surveys not yet completed and no decision yet made with regard to canalizing the Trent, the dominion government ignored Culverwell's request.

Passage in February 1907 of the order-in-council authorizing development of the Trent River made clear that the dominion would maintain control over the water of the Trent River. It was anticipated that with the canal's development, water power leases would soon be issued by the dominion government, and so Culverwell and his associates, a group known as the Culverwell Trent Power Syndicate, began taking options on parcels of land at or near anticipated dam sites. By 1909, they had acquired small parcels with some riparian rights at or near six of the existing or future dams, representing control, in aggregate, of about 38 feet of the total fall of 234 feet from Ranney Falls to Lake Ontario. Meanwhile, Culverwell mustered immense political support for his application for a dominion water power lease at Healey Falls.

In April 1909 a delegation, representing some 20 area municipalities, met with the minister of railways and canals to convince him of the importance of issuing a Healey Falls lease to Culverwell. The advantages of hydroelectric power were now manifest. Other municipalities in the province had acquired or were acquiring cheap electricity, and their industries were prospering: Peterborough from the Otonabee River, Lindsay from Fenelon Falls, Ottawa (and Montreal) from the Ottawa (and St Lawrence) rivers; even Campbellford was getting cheap power from its own plant at Crowe Bay dam. But the lakefront municipalities between Bowmanville and Belleville and smaller communities to the north of the lake were too far removed from the existing sources to benefit. The urgency for power was great, but nothing was being done to develop the Trent River with its magnificent heads of water, flowing right through the centre of the district. The Northumberland and Durham Power Company had the capital and was ready to build. It had applied for a lease three years earlier, but no decision had been made. What was the delay?, the delegation wanted to know.

Graham was faced with a dilemma. He wanted the power on the Trent developed by a monopoly company and had already, through the intercession of Butler, made a gentleman's agreement with Kerry's group, about whose existence few people yet knew. But, faced with the groundswell of municipal support for Culverwell, who was backed by such Liberal politicians as Stratton and McLaughlin, Graham's only choice was to comply with Culverwell's request. On 22 May, he recommended to cabinet that an order-in-council be drafted, granting a 21-year lease to the Northumberland and Durham Power Company for an annual rental of two dollars per horsepower. A lease was not immediately issued, but the order-in-council authorizing it, passed on 29 May, was taken by Culverwell as a bona fide of the government's intention in the matter. It should be noted that in making the recommendation to cabinet, Graham bypassed his deputy minister, Butler, who normally submitted reports to the minister on which such recommendations for orders-in-council were drafted. This was probably because Butler opposed issuance of a lease to Culverwell, favouring Kerry, to whom he believed the government was already committed.

With two leases (Burleigh Falls and Healey Falls), and the possibility of acquiring additional leases as construction of the canal advanced, Culverwell next sought a source of development capital. With such valuable assets as water power leases in his possession, the capital soon found him. It came from Max Aitken, the future Lord Beaverbrook.

In his autobiography, *My Early Life*, Beaverbrook recalls that in 1909 two hydroelectric developments were occupying his attention: Calgary Power, in Alberta, and Western Canada Power, in British Columbia. Actually, there were three, and the third was the Trent River power, which seems to have been forgotten by the great man, perhaps because failure to gain control of it was one of his few failures. Trent canal politics, it seems, was too tough a nut for even Aitken's financial might and political clout to crack.

In 1902, as a young man of 22, Aitken had established the Royal Securities Corporation of Montreal, a bond and shares distributing organization which, through the years, prospered mightily. One of its subsidiaries was the Montreal Engineering Company, a firm engaged in the management and control of public utility undertakings created by the parent company. Montreal Engineering became interested in developing electric power on the Trent, for which purpose Aitken contemplated establishing yet another utility company. But, first, he needed power leases. On 15 July 1909 he wrote to Graham, asking how Montreal Engineering might go about securing water leases on the Trent canal.

Graham turned the letter over to Butler, who ignored it. Aitken then wrote to Butler, asking him "to kindly advise ... what powers have already been disposed of and to whom and also what powers were still available and under what conditions these could be secured."[5] Butler's cryptic reply informed Aitken that "it is not the policy of the Department to send out information of this kind."[6] Undaunted, Aitken, who by his own admission "struggled against arrogance and ... was impatient of opposition and resistance of [his] schemes,"[7] next wrote to A.J. Grant, applying for such water power leases as were still available on the Trent River between Healey Falls and Trenton. Grant refused to give any information without an order from Butler. An annoyed Butler then terminated the exchange with Aitken by telling him that until he addressed a communication to the department advising what his company proposed to do on the Trent, he could not get the information he wanted. In the mean time, Aitken discovered Culverwell, which was not difficult, given the public posturing that had been going on.

Aitken and Culverwell worked out a deal, negotiated by R.J. McLaughlin, lawyer for Culverwell's companies. Royal Securities would establish the Central Canada Power Company, to be federally chartered and capitalized at $10 million; Central Canada Power would merge the Central Ontario Power Company (Burleigh Falls lease), the Northumberland and Durham Power Company (Healey Falls lease), and several small river properties owned by the Culverwell Trent Power Syndicate. Royal Securities would sell stock in the new company and issue bonds for construction. Montreal Engineering would build and manage the works. But there was a condition. Culverwell and his associates had to obtain at least one more water power lease on the Trent River before the arrangements would be finalized. An application was immediately made for a water power lease for dam 3, to be built at Glen Miller.

There was good reason for applying for the Glen Miller lease. Construction could not start at Healey Falls because the contracts for the canal works there had not yet been let, but Larkin and Sangster were already at work on section 1, and construction of an electric power plant, to provide badly needed power for the towns and cities along the lakefront, could begin at dam 3 almost at once. It was thought that this would have political appeal to the government. The Culverwell Trent Power Syndicate had aquired parcels of land on both sides of the river, part of the original Myers land grant, which included riparian rights. Engineers employed by Montreal Engineering examined the property and reckoned that Culverwell owned about nine-tenths of the water power at the proposed location of the new dam and, therefore, was legally entitled to a water power lease in exchange for the property which the government would have to expropriate from him for canal purposes. On the strength of this, McLaughlin made application for the lease on 26 October 1909. This brought the Trent Power Syndicate and Aitken into indirect confrontation with Kerry and his group. The minister of railways and canals was caught in the middle of the row.

John George Gale Kerry was born in Montreal in August 1867. He attended McGill University, graduating in 1886 with a BASC in civil engineering, and was recipient of the British Engineering Association's gold medal. In 1894, he obtained a master of engineering degree. After graduating, he was engaged for a number of years in surveying and engineering with various railway companies in Canada and the United States. In 1893, he returned to McGill to lecture in surveying and railway engineering, rising in the next 14 years from lecturer to assistant professor. In 1907, he left the university to establish a firm of consulting and construction engineers in Toronto in partnership with W.G. Chace, a former assistant engineer with the Hydro Electric Power Commission (HEPC), and Cecil B. Smith, former chief engineer for the HEPC and one of its first commissioners. The firm bought Mulholland's Northumberland Paper and Power Company in Campbellford that year. Also in 1907, Kerry was appointed to the royal commission investigating the Quebec bridge disaster.

The partners' interest in Northumberland Paper was aroused because its mill, established in 1886 and later purchased by Mulholland, was one of the first to generate its own electric power for the operation of its machines. Moreover, the company held the water rights at Ranney Falls, and hydroelectric development was a goal to which Kerry's firm had become committed. Interest in hydro development was probably inspired by Smith and Chace, because of their knowledge of electrical development gained during the short time they had spent with the HEPC. Smith, having conducted the provincial power survey for the HEPC in 1906, knew that approximately 70,000 horsepower of electricity could be developed from the Trent waters. The cost of generating electricity in 1907 ranged from $12 to $14 per horsepower, but electric power could be sold for at least $20, leaving a profit of at least $6 per horsepower, or about $420,000 – a large sum – per year for the Trent River water. So the engineers began working out a scheme for developing the power.

Kerry's simultaneous appointment to the royal commission provided him with an opportunity of manoeuvring the government, especially Butler, into a position of indebtedness by ensuring that the commission's report absolved government officials of any culpability in the bridge disaster. Moreover, Smith knew Adam Beck's long-range plans for the Trent River water power, information that Graham no doubt considered useful to achieve the dominion government's objective of preventing the HEPC from gaining entrance into the district served by the Trent River.

Kerry convinced Butler, who advised Graham, that the several water power sites on the Trent should be developed as one undertaking, by one strong company. This, he argued, was the best way to make available, to the municipalities and residents of the adjacent area, access to the enormous source of power at reasonable rates. Indeed, this had been a recommendation made in the 1906 report of the HEPC, which, in large part, had been written by Smith while still employed by the commission but already contemplating leaving to enter private business. The monopoly concept became dominion government policy, and Graham privately agreed, on Butler's recommendation, that Kerry, Smith, and Chace, not Culverwell's group, should form the monopoly company.

Apart from reasons of personal preference, there was a practical purpose for favouring Kerry's group over the Culverwell Syndicate. The political reward from hydroelectric development on the Trent would be great, much greater than from the development of the now obsolete barge canal concept. Also at stake was the dominion government's conviction that private ownership and development of water power resources were preferable to public ownership; therefore, it was imperative that the private Trent power development scheme succeed. Graham seems to have had greater faith in Kerry's ability to carry off the scheme than in Culverwell's. Culverwell was perceived as merely a promoter and speculator, a fast operator. Building a network of electric plants and transmission lines and tying these into a system of water transportation had never been attempted in Canada before, indeed, never anywhere in the world on the scale contemplated for the Trent. This kind of power development required a high degree of technical knowledge and skill and a good deal of engineering innovation, which Graham was convinced Kerry and his associates possessed – as, indeed, they did.

One problem that troubled Graham was the question of rates that a monopoly company might charge its customers. To protect the public's interest (and the government's credibility), Graham introduced a bill in 1909 to amend the Railway Act, giving the Board of Railway Commissioners power to regulate rates charged by crown lessees of water powers. In introducing the bill, which was later passed into legislation, Graham declared that it had particular reference to the Trent valley canal. The policy he outlined to the Commons confirmed the long-standing Liberal principle of public control, but private ownership, of resource development. By contrast, the idea underlying the creation of the HEPC was public ownership of natural resources, clearly enunciated in the commission's motto, "Dona natura pro popula sunt" – Nature's gifts belong to the people.

It was generally conceded that the primacy of one principle would soon be determined on the Trent River.

It having been determined by the dominion government that public policy required the development of the water powers by one company, or a series of companies controlling one transmission system, the question arose as to the rights of existing riparian owners. The Expropriation Act gave the minister of any department charged with construction and maintenance of any public work the right to take lands and waters necessary for the work, and the act provided that all hydraulic powers created through construction be vested in the crown and that any portion of these hydraulic powers not required for the public work could be sold or leased. But the act provided further that no such sale or lease of hydraulic powers could prejudice any right or privilege of any existing riparian owner.

It was obvious that, from an engineering point of view, the only feasible method of developing the Trent water power was by means of government dams, which would be constructed in the course of completing the canal. Under common law, riparian owners owned the bed of a river to the centre thread of the stream and, therefore, the water thereon. This created a problem for the government. The government was under no legal obligation to grant leases for the created water powers at the dams to the present landowners, but neither could it grant leases to anyone else, if rights of existing owners were prejudiced. To get around the problem, Graham advised Kerry, who already owned the riparian rights of the Northumberland Paper and Electric Company, that he "should acquire all other riparian rights which would be affected by the construction of the canal, so that the Department would not have a multiplicity of interests to deal with."[8] Graham then promised (but not in writing) that, if the rights were acquired, leases to the surplus water at the dams would be granted to Kerry's companies when the dams were constructed. In summary, the arrangement that Graham made with Kerry, mediated by Butler, was this: Kerry had to acquire the riparian rights at all dam sites; he had to contribute his share of the cost of the development by paying rental for the use of the dams; he had to develop power when the government required him to do so; he had to set reasonable rates, and submit them for review to the Board of Railway Commissioners if the rates were challenged; he had to convey to the crown any lands or rights he owned that would be required for the construction of the canal; and, because he would get the leases for the dams, he would make no claim against the crown for compensation for any lands taken or water rights that the canal might destroy or otherwise affect. It was a good bargain. The government would get the land it needed for the canal without paying for it and considerable annual rental for the water. Kerry would have use of the water, with which he could make a handsome profit. The communities would get cheap electric power, the dominion government would get political credit, and the HEPC would be contained.

With this understanding, Kerry, Smith, and Chace proceeded to carry out their plans "all with the full knowledge and consent of the Minister."[9] First came the task of acquiring existing riparian rights. The partners had arrived too late to purchase riparian rights at Healey Falls; these had been bought up by Culverwell while Kerry was still at McGill and Smith and Chace were with the HEPC. But they moved quickly to acquire as many of the remaining rights as they could, either through outright purchase or through merger with companies that already controlled the rights. They operated secretly because the rather noisy Culverwell Trent Power Syndicate was trying to acquire the same rights and because Graham did not want the government's plan for Trent development revealed until the appropriate time.

For the purpose of acquiring land and water rights, Kerry established the Campbellford Water Power Syndicate, a group of capitalists who were interested in investing in water power development. Mulholland, R.B. Rogers, and Willie Boyd were original members of this syndicate. The group first bought the former Stephens mill property above Campbellford, where Kerry obtained the first lease and built the first power plant in 1909. Next it acquired, by outright purchase, riparian rights at the 80-year-old Myersberg dam at the foot of Myers Island. The riparian rights at dam 5, below Frankford, were acquired through a merger with a syndicate consisting of Messrs Grass, Donnell, and Willis. Title to the water rights at dams 1 and 2, above Trenton, was owned by the Trent Power Company and the Trenton Electric and Water Company, by virtue of a decree of the High Court of Justice of Ontario, issued in 1888. Both these companies were experiencing financial difficulties and agreed to merge with Kerry's group. Kerry was negotiating with the Miller brothers for control of the water at Glen Miller dam, when Culverwell's group made application for a lease at the same dam. Then Kerry's plans and Graham's policy nearly went down the drain.

The Trent Valley Paper Mill Company, owned by the Miller brothers of Montreal, had erected a dam for the operation of a paper mill at Glen Miller in 1881, with the permission of Sir Charles Tupper. Erection of the dam had been permitted on the advice of Tom S. Rubidge, who inspected the proposed site in June 1881 while he was conducting the Trent survey. Rubidge advised that the dam would "in no ways interfere injuriously with the prospective construction of the Trent Valley Canal";[10] on the strength of this, Tupper allowed the Millers to proceed. When plans for section 1 of the Trent canal were made public, it was quite obvious to the Millers that dam 2, located downstream from their mill, would flood out their water-wheels. The government would undoubtedly pay damages, but the Millers decided that it was time to switch to electrification, and so, thinking that they were entitled to the surplus water power created when dam 3 was built, they requested the right to develop the power without rental to the crown and the right to use the canal above the dam as a headrace for a future power plant.

The Millers had operated their mill for 30 years under the misapprehension that they actually held a water lease at the dam. But they did not have a lease, as an exhaustive search of departmental files in 1909 revealed; unlike the mill owners at Campbellford, who had a licence, the Millers had only Tupper's permission to build a dam. The Millers did own the riparian rights, having purchased property that was part of the original land grant made to Capt. John W. Myers in 1803. When Kerry learned that the Millers had no lease, he advised them to apply for one at once. They submitted their application in April 1909, six months before McLaughlin applied for the same lease.

Anxious to get control of the water at dam 3, Kerry had approached the Millers with a suggestion that they join the merger of power companies he was putting together. Dam 3 would generate more power than the Millers would require for their mills; the surplus could be fed into Kerry's power grid. The Millers were definitely interested in the proposition, hired Kerry, Smith, and Chace as consulting engineers, and asked them to prepare plans for the development of the power. But other than acting as consultant, Kerry had no formal agreement with the Millers when McLaughlin applied on behalf of Culverwell for the same lease. The Millers' application was then held up, even though Butler knew that granting a lease to the Millers was tantamount to granting it to Kerry. Soon after McLaughlin made application for the lease, Culverwell entered into the agreement with Max Aitken and the Royal Securities Company. The matter of the Glen Miller lease then became inexorably bound up in the political power struggle between the two large developers for control of the Trent River water; Butler had no choice but to hold up the Glen Miller lease.

On 12 January 1910, at the request of McLaughlin, Graham met with him, Culverwell, Aitken, and Carl C. Gillies, president of Montreal Engineering, to discuss the matter of the lease. Aitken advised that he had initiated the legal process for establishing the Central Canada Power Company. Royal Securities had the funds, and Montreal Engineering was prepared to start construction on 1 February. In a few months, electricity could be delivered to the power-starved industries in the communities along the shore of Lake Ontario, if a lease were granted immediately. Graham, as was so often the case, was faced with another dilemma. If he granted the lease to Culverwell, two companies would share water power on the Trent, and his policy for its development would probably fail. So he stalled for time. He asked McLaughlin to put the chief features of the proposition in writing, which McLaughlin did the next day. And Culverwell proceeded to do what he always done so superbly: he recruited local investors for the Central Canada Power Company and mustered political support for the lease application. A good number of businessmen and municipal leaders, many of them Liberals, subscribed for stock in the company. Subsequently, Graham's office was inundated with letters, petitions, and telegrams urging immediate action on the issuance of the power lease.

In early February, M.J. Butler resigned unexpectedly, and with him went Kerry's principal means of influence in the Department of Railways and Canals. Butler's replacement, W.A. Campbell, knew practically nothing about the background of the issue at Glen Miller and was not familiar with the private understanding between Kerry and Graham concerning the overall development of the Trent River water powers. Campbell seemed to favour granting the lease to Culverwell, for on 17 February, just days after assuming office, he sent a request to the Justice Department for interpretation of his department's legal rights over the water at dam 3 and for an assessment of what claims, if any, the Millers would have when the dam was constructed. On the same day, he wrote to the Millers asking them for any objection they might have if the lease were issued to another party – a strange request, given the Millers' earlier application for the lease and their rationale for applying.

E.L. Newcombe, deputy minister of justice, responded to Campbell's request the next day. He offered the opinion that the department could construct such works in the bed of the river as were necessary for canal purposes and that it could lease surplus water or water power created by the dam; the Millers, he concluded, had no legal claim to compensation for any resulting loss of water power at their existing dam, standing slightly downstream from the proposed location of the new dam. On 22 February, the Millers submitted arguments again supporting their claim to the water power which they had actually been using for 30 years and on which they had built a substantial business. They would develop the full water power at dam 3, they promised, and they were willing to sell all power that was surplus to their own needs. But they did not mention any connection with Kerry's group.

On 3 March, McLaughlin submitted another detailed and convincing argument in support of the Central Canada Power Company's lease application. Meanwhile, Campbell instructed A.J. Grant "to prepare and file expropriation plans and descriptions at once," but to make no reference to a power house, which was "a matter incidental."[11] Graham apparently told Campbell to take no action on the lease, because, in response to a letter from McLaughlin asking him to get "this matter [of a lease] in shape,"[12] Campbell replied: "With regard to the Culverwell claim, I am not in a position to advise ... as the case is one that when last before me was in the hands of the Minister and I have not been informed of what action is to be taken."[13] Meanwhile, letters from local Liberals supporting Culverwell's application continued to arrive in Ottawa.

Despite the political pressure being exerted upon him, Graham remained reluctant to grant a lease to Culverwell. If he did, Montreal Engineering would start building a power plant immediately. (Larkin and Sangster, who were shareholders in the company, advised that $15,000 could be saved if the power plant were built simultaneously with the dam, construction of which would begin in a few weeks.) But Kerry also had a plant in operation above Campbellford and, since he had clear title to other power sites, would undoubtedly build more plants. Eventually, Montreal Engineering would develop the power at Burleigh Falls and Healey Falls; there would then be two companies, building transmission lines and competing for customers. Since the market was not large enough to support two companies, either both would have to charge exorbitant rates for power, which would be politically untenable for the government, or both would go bankrupt and the HEPC would move into the district. Either way, Graham's policy would fail. Clearly, there had to be only one company. One would have to buy out the other. But who should buy out whom? When it was merely Culverwell against Kerry, there was no question about the outcome, but now that Montreal Engineering had entered the picture, with its technical know-how and the vast resources of Royal Securities behind it, the situation had changed.

Kerry had advised Graham privately that he was "prepared at any time to buy out opposing claims,"[14] but at reasonable rates. Indeed, in the beginning, when Culverwell was buying small parcels of land, he had boasted that Kerry and his associates would have to purchase his holdings. But that was before Culverwell obtained a promise of the Healey Falls lease and before he acquired the backing of Aitken. Now Culverwell believed that he had as good a chance and, indeed, as much right to get control of all the water power on the Trent as Kerry had. To that end, he suggested a scheme that would not only extricate Graham from the horns of the dilemma but might serve his own interests as well. He proposed that the government expropriate all the land needed for the Trent canal from whomever owned it and then put all water leases up for public tender. Officials in the Department of Railways and Canals were amenable to the idea and promoted it within the government.

When Kerry heard about the proposal, he was naturally alarmed, because if this process were adopted he stood to lose not just the Glen

Miller lease but everything. "Such action on the part of the government would result in taking from us, possibly without compensation, the results of all our forethought, work and expenditure,"[15] he complained in a private letter to the Millers' lawyer. R.C. Smith. With Campbell and Bowden now in charge of the department, Kerry did not know where to turn. He had built his power scheme on the private assurances of Graham and Butler. Now Butler was gone, and Graham was keeping quiet. Knowing that Smith had a personal relationship with Campbell, Kerry wrote to him, revealing the whole situation with regard to the water powers on the Trent: "I do not think that any of the responsible officers in Ottawa yet realize that we control in Peterborough 3 out of the 4 companies serving the town; that we control in Campbellford both the Seymour Power and the Northumberland Paper and Electric; that we control in Trenton both the Trenton Electric and Water Company and the Trent Power Company; and that we are working voluntarily in conjunction with the established rights of Messrs. Miller Bros. and of the Grass Syndicate."[16]

On 27 July 1909, two young, unknown lawyers and three accountants had petitioned for, and had received on behalf of Kerry and his associates, a charter for a holding company known as Electric Smelting and Power Company Ltd. Unbeknown to the public but not to the government, this outfit, later renamed the Electric Power Company, controlled all of Kerry's properties and power companies "as one large whole."[17] It would be impossible for the goverment "to expropriate any part of that whole [as Culverwell proposed] without materially affecting the value of the entire proposition," Kerry wrote. "The basis of damages would not be the value of certain isolated water rights but the value of these rights as affecting a proposition whose expenditures are already in the millions."[18] Regarding Culverwell's proposal for expropriation and public tender, Kerry asserted: "In sporting parlance, having lost the fight, they are endeavouring to get the referee to give a decision which will in effect, reverse the outcome of the result."[19]

Smith sent a copy of Kerry's letter to W.A. Campbell, who showed it to Graham. Kerry's letter reached Graham just after the letter from L.B. Powers of the Port Hope Liberal Association, referred to in chapter 27, in which Powers pointed out to Graham the consequences of delaying a decision on the Central Canada Power Company lease application much longer. It was clear then that time on the political clock had almost run out. Graham would have to act at once. Quite correctly, he had ascertained that the potential power users in the district did not really care who developed power on the Trent, as long as it was developed and delivered soon. If the lease were given to Culverwell, the value of his holdings would be increased substantially, making it difficult for Kerry to buy him out. The two companies would destroy each other, and the HEPC would move in. So the lease would go not to Culverwell, as Powers and others had requested, but to the Millers, who clearly had a moral, if not a legal, claim to the water anyway. By denying Culverwell the lease, the government would force Montreal Engineering to drop out of the picture, not an unhappy consequence as far as Graham was concerned, Aitken being a staunch Tory. With his financial backing gone, Culverwell would have no option but to make a deal with Kerry, and because Kerry could not develop the full Trent River power potential without Culverwell's properties, he would have to listen.

Typically, once the political knot was untangled, a string of events then unravelled rapidly. On 7 June, R.C. Smith informed Campbell that "Mr. Kerry and his Associates [had] paid to the Culverwell syndicate a very large sum for their rights,"[20] the harmonious arrangements having been mediated by McLaughlin. On 12 July, the dominion government formally issued the Healey Falls lease to the Northumberland and Durham Power Company which, on the same day, assigned it to the Eastern Power Company, a subsidiary of the Electric Power Company created by Kerry to develop Healey Falls power. The Northumberland and Durham Power Company then ceased to exist, and Culverwell dropped out of the picture. Aitken continued to devote his attention to Calgary Power and Western Canada Power, two successful ventures that later provided him with the capital to purchase the newspaper chain in Britain that launched him on the road to a peerage.

With the purchase of Culverwell's interests, the Electric Power Company then controlled all the major water powers on the Trent system from Fenelon Falls to Trenton, although it did not yet have leases for them. It did not, however, have control over the water power at Glen Miller, the dispute over which had, ironically, brought about the merger of the two principal companies. Graham let it be known that he desired "that a settlement should be made between Kerry and Miller,"[21] so that all the power on the Trent would come under the control of the Electric Power Company. Because, in Smith's opinion, Kerry, who all along had been acting as the Millers' engineer, now represented "adverse interests," Smith advised the Millers to consult an independent engineer to "examine [their] property thoroughly to determine just what [their] rights were worth."[22] The Millers hired Henry Carre of Belleville, who estimated that the water power owned by the Millers was worth considerably more than Kerry had offered. The Millers refused to sell. There the matter stood. No lease was ever issued for dam 3. Eventually the Millers built a small plant in connection with their paper mill and converted their machines to electric power. The plant continues to serve the mill today.

Development of the water power took place rapidly after ownership of the riparian rights was settled. In July 1910, construction began on the

Sidney Electric Power Company's plant at dam 2; the plant began distributing power in September 1911. Soon afterwards, construction started on the second Sidney plant, at dam 5. This plant was finished in the summer of 1912. Also in the summer of 1911, construction began on the Healey Falls power plant, and, further up the system, the Auburn Power Company began building a small plant at Auburn Mills near Peterborough. Kerry soon had five plants on the Trent system. These plants, when developed to full capacity, were capable of generating some 28,000 horsepower of electricity. In addition, the Electric Power Company owned another estimated 18,500 horsepower potential that needed only completion of the Trent canal works and the issuance of leases to make possible its development.

Under Kerry's aggressive and capable leadership, the Electric Power Company expanded rapidly. The Sun Life Assurance Company of Montreal financed the scheme. For financial reasons, it was deemed advisable to have a series of companies making separate bond issues but essentially constituting a single entity. The holding company soon owned, through purchase or merger or by its own creation, 22 subsidiaries. By 1912, 5 per cent interest bonds to the extent of $4 million were issued by Sun Life; these were secured by mortgages covering all the assets of the different companies, including undeveloped water rights. The company was spending about $200,000 a month building plants, transmission lines, substations, and distribution systems in towns and villages, as it tried to keep up with the ever-increasing demand for hydroelectric power. In addition to purchasing small hydroelectric firms such as Lindsay Light, Heat and Power (1912) and the Otonabee Power Company (1910), it bought out steam-generating plants and distribution systems in Cobourg, Port Hope, Oshawa, Napanee, Trenton, and Peterborough, the intention being to connect these systems to the hydroelectric network as soon as power was available from the company's growing number of generating stations. In conformity with a provision in a statute of the Ontario government, public votes were held in the municipalities on the question of granting a franchise to the company. Referendums passed almost unanimously in the municipalities of Whitby, Bowmanville, Newcastle, Orono, Port Hope, Millbrook, Colborne, Brighton, Napanee, Desoronto, Stirling, Lindsay, Peterborough, Trenton, and Belleville. No municipality was refused a franchise. And no municipality complained about the service or about the rates charged, which varied between $15 and $20 per horsepower.

Electric Power was a good company, able to provide a valuable service to central Ontario, because it united into one energetic corporate whole a number of small companies, none of which had the financial resources, the technical skill, or the breadth of outlook to operate successfully on its own. By providing cheap power, the company had awakened a more or less stagnant area of Ontario into realizing its commercial and industrial possibilities. The unification had been carried out with a minimum of expense and without the overvaluation that commonly results with the merging of a large number of diverse interests. The promoters of the company and its principal shareholders had so much faith in it that they turned over water rights for stock considerations only, so that the company possessed valuable water rights unencumbered with heavy first charges (Culverwell's holdings being an exception). The company had the business know-how, the technical expertise, and the capital to develop these water rights into a highly efficient and profitable power system.

The *Canadian Electrical News* reported regularly on the activities of the Electric Power Company. The magazine was most favourably impressed with the company's facilities. All its plants were interconnected by high-tension transmission lines, enabling its customers, scattered over a wide area, to obtain continuous power and light, guaranteed against almost any contingency. Graham's policy of private ownership with public control seemed to be working out well.

Everyone was favourably disposed towards the Electric Power Company except one man: Adam Beck. He saw the company as a cancer in the stomach of the evolving, provincially owned hydroelectric power system; he wanted it removed. From the day Kerry and his associates took over official direction of the company and made the extent of its holdings known to the public, Beck vowed to destroy it. The fact that the company was highly successful only strengthened his resolve.

Beck discovered that although Electric Power owned the riparian rights at all the major power sites, the leases had not all been granted, it being the policy of the dominion government to grant leases only when dams were actually under construction; construction on some of the dams had not started when the Conservatives came to power in 1911. Beck was determined to prevent the outstanding leases from falling into the hands of the Electric Power Company. His HEPC would acquire the leases, build its own power plants, undersell Electric Power, and force it to sell out to the provincial system. In November 1911, he made application on behalf of the HEPC for water leases at dam 8 (Myers Island) on the Trent River and dam 4 (Otonabee) on the Otonabee River, leases that the Electric Power Company claimed the previous government had promised to it.

Beck was fortunate in Borden's choice for minister of railways and canals, Frank Cochrane, formerly Ontario's minister of lands, forests, and mines. Cochrane believed that the province was the rightful owner of the surplus water in the Trent. He had, in fact, fathered an act in the Ontario legislature that in essence set aside the principle of English common law that vested ownership of the bed of a navigable stream or river in riparian owners and in effect vested ownership of the water in the province. There was some question as to whether this act applied to the Trent River, but it did reveal where Cochrane's sentiments lay. Moreover, Cochrane believed that the dominion government should not be involved in the electric power business, which he thought a purely provincial matter. But Cochrane was now in the dominion cabinet and was the inheritor of commitments, whether he agreed with them or not, made by his predecessors.

Cochrane called a meeting of all the power interests at his office in Ottawa, to hear their arguments over the various claims for the leases. Beck and the Ontario government's lawyer, George Lynch-Staunton, put forth the case of the HEPC. Strachan Johnston, formerly a lawyer for Beaverbrook's Central Canada Power Company, but now representing Electric Power, argued the case of the latter, especially the interests of those who had purchased some $4 million worth of company bonds. Johnston pointed out to Cochrane that while the Expropriation Act permitted the minister to grant the leases to the HEPC, it prevented him from doing so if such leases affected the rights of present riparian owners, currently the Electric Power Company. If the government gave the leases to the HEPC, there would be damage suits. They would not be small, because the effect would not be limited to specific sites but would be directed to a large company, which would be substantially damaged if it could not carry out its full plan of development. Lynch-Staunton countered with the argument that the dominion had granted leases on the Trent under the assumption that the dominion owned the water, but the province disputed that contention. Ontario believed that it owned the water in the Trent and that the dominion had no right to give it away. Ontario wanted the leases now on the same terms as anyone else, subject to ownership of the water being determined by the court.

Cochrane faced a dilemma: there was no question in his mind that the leases should go to the HEPC, but there was the real question of damages, which he did not intend to pay. Two weeks after the meeting, he wrote Beck, offering the disputed leases to the HEPC but on condition that the HEPC or the province of Ontario pay for any future damages won by the Electric Power Company. Beck would not accept the terms. In the mean time, Cochrane refused to grant the leases to anyone; construction on the Trent canal's dams and locks proceeded, but no new power plants were built.

The Electric Power Company presented a compromise that Cochrane thought fair and reasonable. If it obtained the leases and could develop its power system, it would sell its distribution system to the HEPC, at a price to be determined by an arbitrator, and it would sell all its power to the commission. Beck would not accept this arrangement. To him there was only one solution: Electric Power would have to sell out totally to the HEPC. The company finally agreed to sell, but Beck would not accept the price. He considered the asking price of $8,350,000 about two times the actual value of the property. A stalemate lasted for four years during which time no additional power was being developed, and both the dominion and provincial Conservative governments were coming under intense public criticism. Finally, in 1916, an exasperated Cochrane bypassed Beck altogether and arranged through Howard Ferguson, the provincial minister of lands and forests, for the Ontario government – not the HEPC – to buy the Electric Power Company. The provincial government paid the company's asking price. Initially Beck would have nothing to do with the plants; however, he eventually relented, and the HEPC managed the Trent system for the Ontario government. But it was not until 1928, after Adam Beck had died, that the HEPC took over the Trent River power plants as an integral part of its system.

As for J.G.G. Kerry, the man primarily responsible for the Trent power system, history has ignored him as it has most of the engineers connected with the Trent canal. In 1914, Kerry resigned the presidency of the Electric Power Company in favour of Strachan Johnston; it was Johnston who signed the agreement of sale with the Ontario government on 9 March 1916. Meanwhile, following Cecil B. Smith's death in 1912, Kerry reorganized the partnership with Chace, Kerry becoming president of the revised consulting firm of Kerry and Chace. After 1914 it moved on to other things, principally designing and building electric plants all over North America. Kerry's old adversary on the Trent, Montreal Engineering, hired him to design and superintend the construction of power plants for Calgary Power. He built other plants in Manitoba, Oregon, Idaho, northern Ontario, and Newfoundland. Ironically, one of his last major projects was construction of the Canada Cement Company's hydroelectric plant at Lakefield in 1927, the last private power plant built on the Trent canal. Kerry rebuilt the Northumberland Paper and Electric Company plant at Campbellford in 1917, but he lost the company through bankruptcy in 1922. In 1947 he was awarded the Gzowski Medal, the highest engineering award given in Canada. He retired to Port Hope in the 1940s and died in 1957. He was buried in the Kerry family plot in Mount Royal Cemetery in Montreal.

Pouring concrete entrance
walls to Kirkfield lift lock,
1901. (TSWO)

PART FIVE

The Borden Years: 1911–20

Stoney Lake being locked
down Kirkfield lift lock on
opening day, 6 July 1906.
(PAC/C10956)

Uncompleted lock at
Holland Landing, 1912.
(TSWO)

4.

Orillia power plant and dam
at Ragged Rapids, 10
November 1917. (TSWO)

York Construction camp,
Big Chute, 1919.

Construction of main core
wall at Big Chute, May
1920. (TSWO)

First marine railway at Big
Chute, November 1917.
(TSWO)

Blowing the last obstacle to
through navigation on the
Trent canal, 23 June 1920.
(TSWO)

Dredging fleet removing
final obstacle in the
Couchiching canal, 23 June
1920. (TSWO)

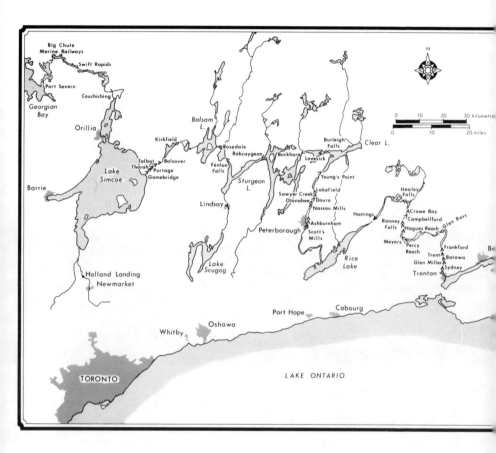

CHAPTER TWENTY-SIX

The Western Outlet

It was fitting that the Conservative and Unionist governments of Sir Robert Borden (1911 – 20) should complete the canal that had been revived and pursued by the Conservatives under Sir John A. Macdonald but toyed with for 15 years by the Liberals, who did not want it in the first place. Within days of taking office in 1911, Frank Cochrane, Borden's minister of railways and canals, stopped construction of the Holland River extension, committed his government to completion of the contracts let by the Liberals on the Trent River, and initiated work on the Severn River division, the final link that would connect the chain of navigable lakes and rivers between Georgian Bay and Lake Ontario.

The reason for completing the final division had more to do with Cochrane's character than any national economic value that would accrue from the work. Electric power development certainly was not a factor, as it had been in the decision to canalize the Trent River, since all the major hydroelectric sites on the Severn River had been developed long before construction began. The barge canal proposal for moving wheat from Georgian Bay to Montreal, although still occasionally talked about, was an all but dead issue. There was some limited demand by a few lumbermen on Georgian Bay for better water transportation on the Severn, and there was some pressure from hydroelectric developers to provide water access to their isolated power plants, but these localized demands could probably have been ignored. Politics and patronage would determine the awarding of contracts and influence construction details, as they always had on the Trent canal, but, basically, Cochrane decided to proceed with the division simply because he was the sort of person who could not tolerate an uncompleted task. Until the western outlet was opened, the millions of dollars of expenditure were wasted, and the years of endless debate and controversy that surrounded the canal were in vain. And so the Trent canal was finished only because it had been started, and Frank Cochrane was the man most singly responsible for its completion. On 11 December 1911, he ordered a complete survey of the Severn River with the object of preparing plans and specifications for the work of canalizing it. In September 1913, the first contract was let. Thus Cochrane ended decades of speculation about which route the western outlet should take, and thus he terminated seven years of political game-playing with the western route by the previous Liberal government.

Feasibility studies for canalizing the Severn River had actually been carried out long before Baird's survey of the Trent River in 1833. But because no settlers took up residence along the Severn, its pre-Cambrian granite shores being unsuitable for farming, no politicians were encouraged to champion the cause of the Severn as they had the Trent, after the earlier proposition for a defence network was abandoned. Proposals for an outlet from Lake Simcoe to Georgian Bay came from where the settlers were, and that meant support for a route either by way of Barrie and the Nottawasaga River or by way of Orillia and the North River. Pressured by settlers, politicians convinced successive engineers and surveyors to recommend selection of one or the other of these southern routes, and for many years the Severn River route was ignored, even though it, like the Trent River, was the natural drainage outlet from the system and therefore the logical route for a canal.

The 33-mile-long Severn River, which drains Lake Simcoe through Lake Couchiching into Georgian Bay, was known to white men from the earliest days of exploration and colonization in North America. One of the major avenues of commerce for the enterprising Huron Indians, the river appears on early French maps under its Indian name, Kiondacharia, a word with obscure meaning but that probably refers to the granite rock formation through which the river flows. Unquestionably, the first European to have seen the Severn was the French youth Etienne Brulé, who spent 17 years among the Hurons, from 1610 to 1627; he was murdered and cannibalized by Indians near Penetang. It is doubtful if Champlain actually travelled on the Severn during his visit to the Hurons in 1615, but he assuredly crossed its mouth while following the shore of Georgian Bay from the mouth of the French River to Huronia. The river was well known to the Recollet missionaries and later to the Jesuit fathers who established missions among the Hurons between 1625 and 1649. In 1669, the French fur trader Jean Peré descended the Severn, and a few years later La Salle navigated it at least three, and possibly four times.

At the beginning of the British period, in 1760, Maj. Robert Rogers (great great uncle of R.B. Rogers) heard about the Severn River from Indians living near the site of Toronto, when he was on his way to take possession of the French lake forts for the British. In 1764 Alexander Henry passed down the Severn on his way from the upper lakes to Fort Niagara.

The first recorded description of the Severn was written by the French soldier-explorer Baron de Lahontan, who examined the river in 1683. The river "forms several cataracts that are equally impracticable both upon the ascent and descent,"[1] the baron wrote in his memoirs. In 1819, surveyor-engineer Joseph Portlock described the Severn as "a river which displays scenery of the most picturesque description and is indeed a noble stream."[2] The first drawings of the Severn River were made on birchbark by Lady Simcoe, wife of Upper Canada's first lieutenant-governor, who presented them to King George III in 1796. Lady Simcoe's charming pictures were taken from sketches made by Lt. Pilkington, one of a party who accompanied Lt.-Gov. Simcoe on a trip down the Severn in 1793. Today Lady Simcoe's originals are found in the British Museum, London, where they form part of the King's Topographical Collection, but reproductions may be seen in the Ontario Archives in Toronto.

One of the first to recognize the stragegic importance of the Severn River for defence purposes was Lahontan, who served in the French-Indian wars. Lahontan proposed that a series of forts be built – one at Sarnia, one at Fort Erie, and one at the mouth of the Severn river – (for defence against the Iroquois). By the time Lahontan's report was published, the power of the Iroquois had been broken and the forts were no longer needed by the French, but the strategic importance of the Severn River and the Toronto Carrying-Place remained and was soon recognized by the British.

On 19 May 1780 Gen. Haldimand, governor-in-chief of Quebec, issued an order to "open a Communication with Michilimakinac from Niagara by way of Toronto."[3] Haldimand was, of course, concerned about the defence of Canada against the new republic emerging in the south. As a result of his instructions, a party of Indians and white men went up to Toronto from Niagara (then the capital of Upper Canada), crossed the portage from Toronto to Lake Simcoe, and descended the Severn River to Little Go Home Bay, through which it entered Georgian Bay at present-day Honey Harbour. The party then turned south, entered the Severn again at its main mouth, and, following the river, retraced its steps back to Toronto and Niagara. An incomplete copy of a journal of this expedition survives, notable only because it contains a first detailed description of the Severn with its seven original falls.

The difficulty of using the Severn River to transport men and heavy material in sufficient quantities to maintain an adequate defence network was pointed out by fur trader Benjamin Frobisher. In a letter dated 2 May 1785, he described the problem to Henry Hamilton, lieutenant-governor of Quebec: "There is no want of Water in the River ... but it seems there is in it several Falls of Water, which with other obstacles occasion Six or Seven Carrying Places, all of them short ones – large canoes have gone up and down it at different times, but [I] am told it is not practicable for Boats until some of the carrying places are levelled so as to get them over upon rollers."[4]

In 1788, Gother Mann was sent out by Lord Dorchester, Haldimand's successor, to "examine the mouth of the French River, and that of the River Matchedosh [Severn] ... to give every information how far they will answer for shipping and of what size."[5] As directed, Mann examined the mouth of the Severn but did not proceed upstream more than a mile. His discouraging report contained only what his Indian guides told him: "The banks of the river are rock, and continue so as I am informed the greater part of its course ... It is impracticable to pass with large Canoes on account of the Rapids and difficult carrying places."[6]

John Graves Simcoe was as concerned about the safety of the young province of Upper Canada as Haldimand, Hamilton, and Dorchester had been. He too was interested in the possibility of using the Severn River as a safe avenue for transporting military supplies to the upper Great Lakes, but unlike the other three, who relied upon the reports of Indians and others for information about the river, Simcoe decided to examine it himself. In the summer of 1793, he travelled down the Severn as far as Matchedash Bay to see if the river was indeed impracticable for transportation, as all previous reports had indicated. When he saw the several falls on the river, especially the Big Chute and Ragged Rapids, he apparently decided that it was not, for he chose alternate routes from Georgian Bay to Lake Simcoe: the Nottawasaga River, Willow Creek, and the Nine Mile Portage into Kempenfelt Bay and a winter road from Penetang to Atherley.

The route chosen by Simcoe was used consistently for the next 50 years. Not surprisingly, the route chosen for the Toronto – Georgian Bay canal in the 1850s was the same Kempenfelt – Nottawasaga River route. Significantly, Ontario's first railway, the Northern, built between 1853 and 1855 in lieu of the proposed canal, was really a portage that followed the same route: from Toronto to Barrie and then west to Collingwood on Lake Huron. Clearly, Simcoe's choice of routes had set a precedent that affected future thinking about avenues of transportation, including the route of the western outlet for the Trent canal, and for years the Severn River route was ignored, but not entirely forgotten.

Attention was once again directed towards the Severn River following the near disastrous outcome of the War of 1812. The fact that the Americans acquired control of the Great Lakes, and almost succeeded in their attempt to capture Canada, re-emphasized the need for a secure waterway capable of accommodating large boats, far removed from the American border. Accordingly, Joseph Portlock was sent by the colonial government in 1819 to determine the feasibility of canalizing the Severn and to estimate the cost thereof. Like the previous reports, Portlock's was not encouraging. Although he considered the engineering necessary to make the Severn navigable "not beyond the reach of science," he pointed that the river "offers the greatest obstacles to improvement." He estimated that an expenditure of 20,000 pounds sterling would "remove all but two great Falls"[7] – Big Chute and Ragged Rapids.

In 1825 the Duke of Wellington, then master-general of ordnance, sent Maj. Gen. Sir James Carmichael Smyth to inspect fortifications in Canada. Water communication in the colony was uppermost in the duke's mind. Reporting on this matter to the duke, Smyth pointed out the two possible means of connecting Penetang with Lake Simcoe: one was "by cutting a canal from the head of Kempenfelt Bay into Nottawasaga Creek";[8] the other was by way of the Severn River. Smyth's report alluded to the difficulty of canalizing the Severn, which he estimated "would require 30,024 pounds to make navigable";[9] nevertheless, he did recommend the Severn River over the Nottawasaga River route.

At Wellington's urging, several more surveys were conducted in the late 1820s, through the territory between Georgian Bay and the Ottawa River, in what is now Haliburton and Muskoka districts. The surveyors were looking for an alternative to the Severn, and possibly more navigable, and a water-course more accessible than the ancient Lake Nipissing – French River route. There was none. The only natural and therefore logical water communication between Lake Ontario and Lake Huron was the historic Trent valley waterway, known to the Indians for centuries. And the Severn River was the only feasible outlet at the western end of it.

Peace with the United States and the enormous cost of the Rideau Canal discouraged the imperial government from pursuing further the idea of an inland water communication. Simcoe's choice of the Toronto Carrying-Place shelved official consideration of the Trent as an access route to Lake Simcoe, until settlers moved into the area in the 1820s. Then, as discussed earlier, the scheme was revived and pushed through to completion, but the choice of an appropriate western outlet still remained as elusive as ever. Baird's two commissions, in 1833 and 1835, instructed him to survey the route between Trenton and Lake Simcoe only. Consequently, he did not examine either of the proposed outlets from Lake Simcoe to Georgian Bay, but he did "hazard the opinion that either by the Severn or Nottawasaga Rivers must be the line of communication."[10] Having read the earlier reports on the Severn, he judged quite correctly that it would be no more difficult to canalize than the lower Trent. Tom S. Rubidge did examine the Severn in the 1880s but was dissuaded from recommending that route by the massive amount of granite through which excavation would have to take place. Perhaps thinking about the difficulty Goodwin was encountering with the granite excavation at Buckhorn and Burleigh Falls, Rubidge recommended a third alternative: a route from Orillia by way of North River to Matchedash Bay with a terminus at Waubaushene, in which excavation would be largely through clay and boulder till. This route was originally surveyed by Kivas Tully in 1856, as an alternative route for the Toronto and Georgian Bay canal, but was rejected in favour of the Nottawasaga River route. The Trent Valley Canal Commission, appointed by John A. Macdonald, was apparently persuaded by the representations made by Collingwood and Barrie, because it suggested that "the route from Lake Simcoe to Nottawasaga Bay would be more satisfactory and judicious one"[11] than the overland route from Lake Couchiching to Matchedash Bay, proposed by Rubidge and Tully. The commission recommended that surveys be made of both routes "in order to determine the respective merits of the two."[12] R.B. Rogers, motivated by engineering common sense, not politics, put a survey team on the Severn River prior to the election of 1896, but the surveyors were removed after the election. Finally, Laurier's Transportation Commission of 1903, also more interested in the movement of wheat than local politics, recommended that the outlet of the Trent canal be by way of the Severn.

Not until 1904, as the Balsam – Lake Simcoe division neared completion and serious pressure began to mount for a western outlet, did the Liberals make the choice of route a major political issue, as they had with the Trenton and Port Hope outlets. By ordering three surveys at the western end, and postponing a decision on the choice, they were able to keep the question alive through three dominion elections. But in the end, they lost all the seats they hoped the surveys would win or keep for them, as had happened to them at the eastern end of the canal.

In August 1904 E.J. Walsh, who was already charged with responsibility for the Trent River and Port Hope surveys as well as the Holland River extension, was asked to make yet another survey of the country between Lake Simcoe and Georgian Bay, to determine a suitable route and the cost for a canal. M.J. Butler, deputy minister of railways and canals, informed him verbally that "there were two possible routes over which the surveys were to be made, viz: one via the Severn River, and the other by way of a "cut-off" across country, leaving Lake Couchiching at the most suitable point north of Orillia."[12]

The cut-off route, impractical though it was, was ordered to assist Barrie lawyer Leighton McCarthy, MP for Simcoe North, through the centre of which the cut-off route would run. McCarthy had won Simcoe North in a by-election in 1898, taking over from his uncle, the notorious D'Alton McCarthy, who had held the seat since 1878. Originally a staunch Tory and supporter of Macdonald, the elder McCarthy left the Conservative party in 1889 in a split with Macdonald over the Roman Catholic question and henceforth sat in Parliament as an Independent. After 1896, he gave partial support to Laurier. The nephew also sat as an Independent, but he too tended to support the Liberals. The so-called cut-off route survey was made to court favour with McCarthy, by giving him an assist with the September election. It is doubtful if Walsh would have surveyed the route on his own initiative without verbal instruction from Butler, because, despite Rubidge's recommendation in 1887, most engineers had rejected the route. So this survey which Walsh started on 29 August, would, like so many previous Trent canal surveys, be purely political. Walsh's men were in the field, taking levels, buying supplies, and holding out promises of jobs for the farmers of the stony soil of North Simcoe, during the election campaign.

The route Walsh chose left Lake Couchiching about two miles north of Orillia, at the South end of Wood's Bay. It crossed the Muskoka Road (now no. 11 highway), entering a boggy area about a mile west of the lake. From there the route followed the bed of Silver Creek, a small stream that drained the bog and flowed into North River. The survey left the stream bed in the vicinity of Uhthoff and, paralleling the Midland branch of the Grand Trunk Railway, extended north-west to the village of Foxmead. It turned west at Foxmead and ran for about a mile through the township of Medonte, where it again veered north-west, skirting the village of Coldwater, and it finally entered Matchedash Bay at the confluence of the North and Coldwater rivers. A longer alternate route, the one originally proposed by Rubidge by way of Silver Creek and the North River, was surveyed but rejected by Walsh because of the cost and, presumably, because it did not touch as many centres of population with potential voters. The route Walsh selected would have required dry land excavation for its entire 14-mile length, creating in fact a man-made ditch. All the water necessary to fill the ditch would have to be drawn out of Lake Couchiching. Walsh planned to overcome the 139-foot difference in level between Lake Couchiching and Matchedash Bay with 12 locks, with lifts varying from 8 to 17 feet. The cost he placed conservatively at $1,999,197 for six-foot navigation and $2,396,466 for a nine-foot-draft canal. Apart from the high cost of both construction and maintenance, the principal objection to the Coldwater route was the necessity to divert water from Lake Couchiching by building dams at the mouth of the Severn River, thus destroying the natural water powers on that river. Walsh estimated that the diversion of water through Wood's Bay outlet would destroy 1,343 horsepower and 1,580 horsepower for six- and nine-foot-draft canals, respectively. On the basis of two dollars per horsepower this would add $66,150 and $79,000 respectively to the cost of the canal, such amounts being the water power income lost on the Severn over a 20-year period. When the town of Orillia, which had favoured the cut-off route in the days of Rubidge, learned that the proposal would reduce power production at the hydroelectric plant at Ragged Rapids, built in 1901 at considerable cost to the town, it naturally opposed the route.

If the Coldwater cut-off route was impractical, except for political purposes (McCarthy won the seat with a majority of 41 over Conservative candidate J.A. Currie), a third survey, which Walsh was ordered to make in December 1905, was even more foolish. This was a survey of the historic Kempenfelt Bay – Nottawasaga River route, long since rejected by engineers because of the extensive excavation it would require. Nevertheless, impractical and costly as it would be, this route was vigorously defended until 1911 because of political considerations.

Conservative MP Haughton Lennox (Simcoe South), another Barrie lawyer, both a supporter and a critic of the controversial Holland River extension, had for months been pressing H.R. Emmerson, the minister of railways and canals, for a survey of the Nottawasaga River route. Emmerson ignored the request, Simcoe South being a Conservative stronghold since 1867. Prior to the electoral boundary changes of 1903, the town of Barrie, through which the Nottawasaga River route would run, was in Leighton McCarthy's riding of Simcoe North, but in the 1904 election the people of Barrie voted in Simcoe South. McCarthy had not pressed for a Barrie survey, even when he represented the town, because he needed help in the northern part of the riding, where his opponent, journalist-soldier John A. Currie, was very popular. Now, of course, a survey through Barrie would help only Lennox.

Recognizing the political advantages of a canal through Barrie, Lennox continued to campaign for a Nottawasaga survey even after the election, which he won handily. Animated by Lennox's fervor for a canal and visualizing large wharfs and grain elevators in the town, the Barrie town council then took up the cause. The mayor wrote Emmerson, asking "to have a survey and examination of the route by the Nottawasaga River made before a decision [on the choice of the route] is arrived at."[14] Although McCarthy no longer represented Barrie, neither he nor Emmerson could ignore the wishes of the people of Barrie, and, with the election over and nothing to lose, McCarthy came out in favour of the survey, too. Consequently on 28 December Walsh was instructed "to have a reconnaisance survey made of the said route shortly after the first of the New Year."[15] The Barrie *Northern Advance* and *Gazette* rejoiced at the good news, but the Orillia *Packet* lamented over the delay and, knowing full well that the Severn River, Orillia's preferred route, was supported by Walsh, argued: "The Question of route should be left to the engineers, to be decided on its merits in the best interest of the Canal and of the whole country."[16]

Walsh put aside his other work and made the reconnaisance in January 1906. The report that he submitted on 8 February, although noncommittal, was not very encouraging. No firm cost estimates were included, as these would have required a careful instrumental survey which had not been asked for, but it was clear from his report that the cost of the 29-mile-long canal would be substantial. The stretch between Lake Simcoe and the Nottawasaga River would require a five-and-a-half-mile-long excavation some 40 feet deep. Even a novice could see how costly that would be. Having submitted his somewhat vague report, Walsh let the politicians ponder it while he went back to work converting the raw data collected on the Severn River and the Coldwater surveys into firm plans and cost calculations.

The Severn River survey – the only sensible one – had not been started until March 1905, there being no urgency to make it before the 1904 election. If there were ever to be an outlet for the Trent canal, it would undoubtedly be by way of the Severn River, with Midland as the terminus. But there had been no more desire to help Simcoe East's Conservative incumbent, W.H. Bennett – who had been advocating the Severn River route since 1891 – with a pre-election survey than there was to help Haughton Lennox with a survey in Simcoe South. The election over, and the Coldwater survey having done its job for McCarthy, Walsh then carefully examined the Severn.

Although his plan for canalizing the Severn called for considerable solid rock excavation, especially at Big Chute and Ragged Rapids, Walsh's cost estimates for nine locks and nine dams favoured the Severn outlet over the Coldwater route by differences of $852,467.29 and $1,024,159.70 for six- and nine-foot-draft canals respectively. He pointed out other advantages of the Severn route, in addition to the cheaper costs. Instead of destroying water powers, a Severn canal would in fact develop them. There would be no appreciable damage to forests from flooding or destruction of farm land, as there would be on the Coldwater route. Because of the high granite banks on the Severn, constant dredging and other maintenance costs would be avoided. And then Walsh mentioned, almost as an afterthought, what was beginning to emerge as the most valid reason for canalizing the Severn, and indeed for justifying the whole Trent canal: tourism.

The hauntingly beautiful Severn River had inspired poetic outpourings from the prosaic pens of engineers since the earliest days of survey. Pilkington had made sketches of the river, not because they were of any engineering value, but simply because the wild magnificence of the falls aroused his artistic instincts. And Portlock, in taking levels and measuring the water flow at Big Chute in 1819, had been moved by the natural beauty of the rapids to describe them in most unscientific terms: "The river endeavouring to burst from restraint, covered with foam and hurled with violence from one rock to another, the Pines throwing an air of Solemnity over the whole, form a scene too beautiful for description."[17] Nor did Walsh escape capture by the river's natural charm. By the time he arrived on the Severn, most of the primeval forests had been destoyed by lumbermen and forest fires, but enough of the river's beauty remained to impress him too. He saw the Severn's loveliness in practical terms:

"Much of the pristine beauty of the district remains, and here, on the very threshold of intense commercial activity, lies dormant that wild natural grandeur, with the great opportunties for restful recreation, consisting of bathing, canoeing, and fishing, so much sought after by the holiday tourist during the fetid heat of the summer."[18] Continuing in more banal language, Walsh estimated that in the summer of 1905 at least 1,700 tourists "had camped or sojourneyed along the Severn River for periods of from one to several weeks."[19] He reported three steamers plying regularly between Severn Bridge and the foot of Sparrow Lake, all of them carrying tourists to and from summer hotels. For tourism, if for no other reason, Walsh reckoned the Severn should be developed.

Needless to say, when he submitted his report of the two surveys with maps, profiles, plans, and estimates to Butler on 28 February 1906, Walsh recommended the adoption of the Severn River route because, as he put it, the Severn outlet appeared "to be the logical and proper one."[20]

On the basis of Walsh's survey data and recommendation, Butler drafted an order-in-council authorizing selection of the Severn River route and submitted it to the cabinet through H.R. Emmerson. Unlike the order-in-council that authorized construction on the Trent River and was approved by a month earlier, this one ran into trouble. Because of the intense lobbying done by Haughton Lennox, and to a lesser extent by Leighton McCarthy, seeking a full survey of the Nottawasaga route before the final decision was made, cabinet referred the matter back to Emmerson. He had no choice but to order the perambulating Walsh to make the required survey. And so a week later Walsh and a party of engineers arrived at Barrie and, amid much rejoicing in the town, began taking soundings in Kempenfelt Bay through the spring ice, while preparations were made for the instrumental survey which, by Walsh's reckoning, would take several months.

When Orillia learned about the new survey, the whole town rose up in anger, not so much because the citizens had any doubts that eventually the superiority of the Severn over the Nottawasaga route would be demonstrated, but because of the delay in construction that the new survey would cause. Moreover, they felt betrayed by the minister. In the summer of 1906, Emmerson had been taken on a promotional trip, later known as "that famous cruise" down Lake Couchiching to the mouth of the Severn River and then down the river in a war canoe as far as Ragged Rapids. Despite Laurier's admonition to leave liquor alone, Emmerson had imbibed freely of the champagne on board and while inebriated had assured the town officials that the Severn River outlet would be the one chosen. Drunk or sober, the minister of railways and canals had been taken at his word, and so it was only natural that the Orillians should feel peeved when they learned that Emmerson had backed down on his commitment and had ordered what was obviously another politically motivated survey. The town clerk and the secretary of the board of trade wrote letters of concern to Emmerson, and the *Packet* editorialized against the survey, but all to no avail. The survey was already under way and would continue throughout the summer.

Meanwhile, encouraged by the survey, inspired by Lennox, and egged on by the Barrie newspapers, the municipalities along the route of the proposed canal mounted pressure on the government for a Nottawasaga outlet. In mid-July, the leaders of all the municipalities west of Barrie met in the Barrie council chambers to form the last of dozens of such Trent canal pressure groups and to determine how best to force the government into selecting "their" route. Haughton Lennox addressed the group at length, "pointing out the advantages of the proposed route and giving it as his opinion that no physical obstacle would prevent its selection."[21] A committee was formed to solicit the support of other municipalities, and Messrs Lennox and McCarthy "were asked to arrange with the government in regard to hearing a deputation at an early date."[22]

The principal obstacle to the route's selection was of course the enormous cost, as Walsh's report would eventually reveal. For lock construction, excavation, bank lining, and dredging, he estimated costs of $3,818,345 and $4,465,854 for six-foot and nine-foot-draft canals. Since a draft of nine feet would probably be chosen for the western outlet, conforming to the dimensions of the canal being planned on the Trent River, where construction was just getting under way, the cost of the Nottawasaga route would exceed the cost of the Coldwater route by $1,984,249 and the cost of the Severn River canal by more than $3 million. Also, the Nottawasaga route would enter Georgian Bay in the shallow water of Wasaga Beach. Considerable expense would be required to build breakwaters, and the entrance would require steady dredging to keep it free of the constantly shifting beach sand. And even if the entrance problem could be overcome, there was still the difficulty of towing barges across the nine miles of open water to Collingwood, the only harbour available where cargo transfer to and from barges could be made. With a strong north-west wind blowing, barge towing across the exposed stretch of water would be extremely hazardous, if not impossible. A logical solution would be to dig a deep-water harbour at the entrance to the canal, but this would be a costly and difficult task.

Under normal circumstances, Walsh should have submitted his Nottawasaga survey report in the fall of 1907 or early 1908 at the latest; then, on the basis of information in it and the previous two surveys, a final decision on the choice of route should have been made. But decisions with respect to the Trent canal – this most political of all public works projects – were never, in its 80-year history, made under normal decision rules.

The government did not want Walsh's report in 1907 or even in 1908. The minister did not want to make a route decision just yet. There were more politics to be played with the western outlet and, if the game were played properly, more votes to be collected in the route auction. Or so George Graham, the new minister, who replaced the disgraced Emmerson in August, believed.

As 1908 advanced it became clear that there would be an election before the end of the year. The Nottawasaga route would be held out as tantalizing bait to the voters in Simcoe South, to lure enough of them away from Haughton Lennox to elect Liberal candidate Dr J. Campbell. The survey that Lennox had worked so hard to obtain would be used to the advantage of his opponent, just as the Coldwater survey had worked to McCarthy's advantage in 1904. If the results of the survey were released before the election, the survey would have no electoral appeal whatever because Walsh's estimates would obviously rule out the route; therefore the results had to be kept hidden. Walsh was asked to hold up his report. The final draft was not submitted to Butler until 28 November, a full month after the election.

In the mean time Graham and Campbell hinted that if the report were reasonable the Nottawasaga route would be chosen. Speaking in Stayner on 21 February, Graham promised: "If I stay where I am as Minister of Railways and Canals, I am going to build the Trent Valley Canal through to the Georgian Bay."[23] He made no specific promise about the route, but, given the proximity of Stayner to the Nottawasaga River – four miles away – the implications of his statement were clear: the canal would be built if the Liberals stayed in power, and the Nottawasaga route stood a better chance of being selected if a Liberal were elected locally.

Alas! The strategy backfired. Lennox held Simcoe South with a comfortable majority, and Currie won Simcoe North for the Conservatives, McCarthy having decided not to run. A curious power shift took place in Simcoe East. Lumberman Manley Chew, running for the Liberals, convinced enough voters in the Midland area that if elected he would acquire the Severn River outlet, which opposition member W.H. Bennett had not been able to deliver in 17 years of trying. Chew beat Bennett by 264 votes.

In his final report Walsh had stated emphatically, after taking into consideration the economy in construction, the small annual maintenance cost, the saving in travel time between Lake Simcoe and Georgian Bay, the prospective water power revenue, and the minimum hazard in barge towing, that "as an outlet for the Trent Canal from Lake Simcoe to Georgian Bay, the Severn River is incomparably superior to that of any other possible route."[24] So there it was. The Severn River was, as many had known for some time, the preferable route. Logically, with the Liberal Chew now representing the route that the engineering data confirmed and with his continued support in the riding dependent upon action on the Severn, and with Conservatives now representing the ridings through which the competing, but demonstrably inferior routes ran, the Severn River route should have been immediately selected, and the uncertainty over the choice removed. That was the politically logical course to follow. But whatever it was that determined Graham's policy for the Trent canal, logic was not part of it. He did not make an immediate decision in favour of the Severn, nor did he even make the results of the three surveys public. In fact, for months after the submission of Walsh's report, Graham denied that it was available. It was not until 25 November 1909 that he finally admitted to Lennox that the report had been received, but he refused to table it in Parliament. He did, however, show it to Lennox. For the next two years Graham left the question of route unresolved while proponents of the three different proposals continued to lobby for the respective routes.

It is difficult to determine after nearly 80 years exactly why Graham refused to publish Walsh's survey results, but it does seem clear that he did not want to give Chew and the Midland Liberals, or, indeed, the citizens of Orillia of both political persuasions, the ammunition to force him to start construction on the Severn division. Apparently he did not want to commit the funds. The government was already spending a lot of money on the Ontario – Rice Lake division, and there was the costly and controversial Holland River extension, a commitment from which the government seemed unable to extricate itself. There was no urgency to develop power on the Severn. Orillia's Ragged Rapids plant had been producing electricity for eight years, and on 18 April 1909 the Midland Railway and Power Company had received a charter of incorporation with authority to build electric plants at Big Chute and Port Severn. In the summer of 1909 work on the Big Chute plant was already under way. With power development on the Severn River safe in the hands of private enterprise, there was no need for the dominion to move in to thwart the advances of the Hydro Electric Power Commission, as was deemed necessary on the Trent River.

And so by the time the 1911 election took place, it had not been decided where or when the western outlet would be opened. By then everyone in Simcoe county realized that all along the Liberal government had been trifling with their political affections. There was also considerable anger in the county over wastage of public money on the ridiculous Newmarket canal while a decision on the western outlet of the main line was held in abeyance. Not unsurprisingly, voters in all three ridings expressed their displeasure at the polls. Lennox was returned with a larger majority than ever in Simcoe South. McCarthy,[24] shedding all pretense of being Independent, had contested Simcoe North as a full-fledged Liberal, but was soundly defeated by Currie. Chew was defeated by Bennett, who regained Simcoe East with a majority of nearly 500 votes.

Then, as was so often the case on the Trent canal, once the political road blocks were cleared away, action soon followed. Frank Cochrane was in office less than a month when he announced that contracts for work on the Severn River division would be let in the spring, so that the western outlet of the canal would be ready at the same time as the eastern end. On 27 December 1911 A.J. Grant and E.B. Jost, who would have direct responsibility for getting out the plans and specifications, arrived in Orillia and made immediate preparation for the ninth, and what proved to be the last, engineering survey of the Severn River.

Official opening of Port
Severn lock, 26 July 1915.
(Angus collection)

CHAPTER TWENTY-SEVEN

The Port Severn Lock

E.J. Walsh chose the historic village of Port Severn, at the mouth of the Severn River, as the outlet for the canal. There he planned to build a 1,605-foot-long dam across the four channels that emptied into Georgian Bay. This dam would create a navigable reach extending eight miles up river, through Little Lake and Gloucester Pool to the Big Chute. The dammed-up water would drown out the natural four-foot fall at the Little Chute and, with the removal of some large boulders, would make this section fully navigable. A lock with a lift of 14 feet would be built into the dam at Port Severn, allowing boats and barges to pass out of the reach into Georgian Bay. At the Big Chute end of the reach, a small chute and rapids that then exisited at the west side of the main chute would be excavated, creating a channel into a pool some 600 by 400 feet that existed at the top of this small rapids. This pool, which is still there at the foot of the power plant and forms the lower entrance to the two marine railways, would have been lowered by three feet as a consequence of removing the rapids; thus a difference in elevation of 57 feet, from the surface of the pool to the upper level of the river, would have resulted. This difference would have been overcome with a sequence of three locks, each with a lift of 19 feet, situated in a 500-foot-long rock cutting between the upper river and the pool, to be made roughly in the location of the present power plant and forebay.

When the Simcoe Railway and Power Company built the plant in 1909 the rock obstruction that created the little rapids was removed, creating what for many years was known as "the gap." When the new enlarged marine railway was built in 1976 the gap was widened and deepened and a six-foot-high wall was built across the depression in the side of the main chute, preventing any overflow from entering the pool when the dam above is open. Thus all trace has been removed of a picturesque little falls that so enthralled John Graves Simcoe that he had his men paddle him across to the west side of the river to have a better view of it. The falls was sketched for posterity by Lt. Pilkington and later copied by Lady Simcoe for the king.

Walsh planned to build a 680-foot-long dam across the river and low ground to the west of the entrance to the Big Chute. This would raise the level of the river 5.8 feet, creating the second navigable reach extending another nine miles to the foot of Ragged Rapids where the Orillia power plant was then located. Three shallows – Dinner Time, Flat, and Wallace rapids – would be flooded out in this reach.

Ragged Rapids and the Orillia power plant would be bypassed with a 2,820-foot-long canal cut in the south side of the river. Three locks in the canal, two with lifts of 16 feet and the third with a lift of 14.35 feet, would overcome the rise of 46.35 feet at this point. A 90-foot-long dam erected at a point 1,050 feet above the power plant would raise the water level 8 feet, drowning out McDonald Rapids and Sparrow Lake Chute in the third navigable stretch of river. The route would then leave the river about 2 miles above the summer resort of Hamlet and, by way of a two-and- a-half-mile cut across land, would enter the north end of Lake Couchiching, thus avoiding the several falls and bends in the river between Hamlet and Washago. Two locks, one of 11 feet, the other 10.65 feet, would be placed in the excavated canal to overcome the 21.65-foot difference in elevation between the level of the third reach and Lake Couchiching.

When Jost began his engineering survey in the winter of 1912 he found many changes on the Severn that rendered Walsh's canalization plan obsolete. Two new railways crossed the river: the Canadian Pacific at Severn Falls and the Canadian Northern Ontario Railway (now the CNR) at Ragged Rapids, both built in 1907. These railways, in making the Severn less isolated, would assist construction by facilitating the delivery of men and materials to construction sites. A more significant change, which rendered Walsh's plan obsolete, was the power dam and electric plant built at the Big Chute in 1910. The power company had built, in addition to the main dam and plant, a dam at Six Mile Channel to lower the level of the river below the power plant and a dam at Pretty Channel which, in conjunction with the main dam at Big Chute, controlled the level of the river above the power plant. These structures forced Jost to find an entirely different method of bypassing the Big Chute than that proposed by Walsh. In fact he was obliged to reject most of Walsh's proposal and to design an entirely new scheme for canalizing the Severn River. Both engineers had adopted the Baird plan for canalizing rivers, that is, the construction of dams to create navigable reaches along the river, the differences in level between the reaches to be overcome by locks. But Jost came up with a more economical plan requiring the construction of only five locks instead of the nine required in Walsh's plan. Jost's plan also required much less sold rock excavation than Walsh's. However, as will be shown presently, Jost's plan was not followed either, an even cheaper – if somewhat less efficient – scheme being finally adopted to render the Severn navigable.

Instead of following the Severn to its mouth, Jost's plan called for cutting a channel across the short portage between Little Go Home Bay and Baxter Lake, making Honey Harbour and not Port Severn the entrance point of the canal. Whereas Walsh's plan called for a dam and lock at Port Severn, with a controlling dam at Little Go Home Bay, Jost's plan was the reverse: a lock and canal at Little Go Home Bay and a controlling dam at Port Severn.

Jost's choice of Honey Harbour, which in retrospect seems an unlikely entrance point for the Severn River, indicates the presence then of a still-lingering dream that the Trent route would become a barge canal for the movement of wheat. It also shows the political influence of the CPR. The CPR had been searching for some time for a shorter route to the Atlantic seaboard for its rail and Great Lakes steamship operations, which before 1912 had been centred in Owen Sound. It eventually chose a natural harbour at a spot on Georgian Bay some three miles east of Midland. The harbour was called Port McNicoll after David McNicoll, a vice-president of the company. Between 1907 and 1911 the Georgian Bay and Seaboard Railway Company built a line from Orillia to Port McNicoll and leased it to the CPR. In 1908 construction of a grain elevator was commenced, and in 1912, just before Jost started his survey, the CPR moved its steamship fleet – *Assiniboia, Keewatin, Manitoba, Alberta,* and *Athabaska* – from Owen Sound to the new port. If the completed Trent canal were to be capable of transporting wheat economically by barge, as its supporters had for so long claimed, the CPR concluded that the barges might just as well carry CPR wheat, trans-shipped from its new elevator at Port McNicoll. Jost was willing to co-operate and for this reason proposed Honey Harbour as the canal outlet. The advantages of the Honey Harbour outlet over Port Severn, from the CPR's point of view, were that the distance to Port McNicoll would be reduced, the shallow rocky channel leading into Port Severn would be avoided, and vessels would be able to run under shelter fo Beausoliel Island to within two or three miles of the elevator. If the canal were to be for barges, this route made good sense.

Jost proposed bypassing both the Big and Little chutes with a mile-long canal from the upper end of Big Chute to the south-west corner of Gloucester Pool. Two locks, each with a lift of 29 feet, would be built at each end of the canal. This would be the most costly section to build, but it would avoid interference with the power plant at Big Chute.

Jost was forced to redesign completely the Big Chute – Ragged Rapids reach proposed by Walsh. The power dam built at Big Chute in the interim was not high enough to extend the reach all the way to Ragged Rapids, and so Jost's plan called for the reach to end at Swift Rapids, a shallows in the river a mile and a half below Ragged Rapids. Here a 47-foot-high dam with a correspondingly high lock would be built. The advantage of this plan was that the Swift Rapids dam would create a navigable reach extending all the way to the Couchiching cut-off, avoiding the necessity for a half-mile-long rock cut, a dam, and three locks at Ragged Rapids. The disadvantage would be the elimination of the power site and, with it, of Orillia's power plant. It was proposed that this problem be solved by the government's building, free of charge, a new and better power house at Swift Rapids for the town.

From Hamlet to Lake Couchiching, Jost's plan was the same as Walsh's, except for proposing one lock in the Couchiching cut-off, instead of two. Both plans called for regulating dams at White's Falls and in Pretty and Lost channels (to control the water in Six Mile Lake) and for dams on the tributaries of the river near Washago (to control water levels in Lake Couchiching). Both plans also required some submarine excavation at the several flooded rapids, to provide the required eight feet for navigation.

When the spring of 1912 passed into summer, and summer into fall, without the letting of contacts on the Severn River promised by Cochrane a year earlier, Trent canal promoters began to suspect that they had been duped again by promises from yet another government. Once more they did what they had always done. A deputation representing the principal cities, towns, and villages along the canal was assembled under the leadership of W.H. Bennett and sent to Ottawa on 3 December to meet with the new prime minister, Robert Borden, and press for an early letting of contracts on the Severn River outlet. A.A. Armstrong, Peterborough's city clerk, urged the completion of the canal for the same old and oft-repeated reasons: the rapid and cheap transportation of wheat from Midland to Montreal and the alleged deposits of minerals in Haliburton, which wanted only cheap transportation to make possible their exploitation. Orillia alderman J.R. Tudhome saw the value of the canal from the standpoint of general manufacturing. Cheap coal could be delivered to manufacturing centres along the route of the canal; this was of special interest to manufacturers in Orillia, where coal was more expensive than in the rival town of Midland. There, it was delivered much cheaper by water from the coal fields of Pennsylvania. McTavish of Midland deplored the grain congestion in Midland and Port McNicoll, caused by a lack of grain cars to carry away the wheat. As many as five grain boats had been sighted lying off Port McNicoll, waiting for an opportunity to unload in the bulging new elevator. A completed barge canal would relieve the situation, McTavish claimed.

But it was C.H. Hale, publisher of the Orillia *Packet*, and Col. Sam Hughes of Lindsay who presented the most realistic economic arguments for completing the canal. They saw the Severn's development in terms of enlargement of the tourist trade, which "would bring a large amount of money into the district."[1] Conveniently located as it was between the chief summer resorts on Georgian Bay and the St Lawrence River, this beautiful chain of lakes and rivers "was bound to become one of th most popular tourist routes on the continent,"[2] Hale prediced. He also prophesied, quite accurately as it turned out, that the beautiful Severn River "would be one of the chief charms of the waterway".[3] The pragmatic Sam Hughes backed up Hale's predictions by pointing out that the state of Maine was already receiving twice as much money from its tourists business as it was from its declining lumber trade.

Robert Borden listened courteously to what this delegation had to say, just as all previous prime ministers had listened to similar delegations. Since he was not responsible for any of the previous Trent canal decisions, he could indulge in a little wry humour at the expense of his predecessors: "If it was true that the canal had been begun in 1832, it would certainly appear that there had been some delay," he remarked. In a more serious vein, he said that he was not convinced that a completed Trent canal would have as great an effect on overcoming the grain blockage as many claimed, but he did recognize (reflecting Cochrane's position) that the work already done was relatively valueless as long as the canal were not opened throughout its entire length. He promised that the government would give careful consideration to the representation, and he asked that the information given be put in written form for presentation to the cabinet. Thus concluded the visit of what proved to be the last Trent canal deputation to descend on Ottawa, marking the end of an almost annual ritual that had commenced with the first junket of the Trent Valley Canal Association in 1881.

There is no question, as time has shown, that in 1912 Hale and Hughes put their fingers on the only legitimate reason for canalizing the Severn and completing the waterway. But no one raised the constitutional nicety, then or later, as to whether the construction of tourist facilities, which the Severn locks would almost exclusively become, was a legitimate undertaking for the dominion government. When the canal was completed, it would be people, not grain, that would move through it, and primarily for pleasure. The only beneficiary, apart from the tourists themselves, would be the province of Ontario. Therefore, it should have been a provincial public work and not a dominion one.

It was not true that the Conservative government, which recognized the vote-getting potential of the canal as finely as any of its predecessors, was backing down on a commitment to complete it, as the delegation that went to Ottawa believed. Contracts had not been let because Jost's survey and plans, which were needed for the calling of tenders, were not yet finished. Further, a controversy had developed over where the entrance to the canal ought to be: at Honey Harbour, as proposed by the engineers on behalf of the CPR, or at Port Severn, as advocated by W.H. Bennett on behalf of the Simcoe Railway and Power Company and his own constituents.

In 1909 a group of lumbermen in Midland and Waubaushene formed the Simcoe Railway and Power Company and obtained a charter from the provincial legislature, authorizing the construction of an electric railway to connect the towns and villages between Penetang and Coldwater. Hotels and sanitoriums were to be constructed in the major centres along the line. The whole enterprise was to be powered from electric power plants to be built at the Big Chute and Port Severn. Construction of the dams and plant at the Big Chute started in the fall of 1909, and on 22 June 1911, to celebrate the coronation of King George v, Big Chute power was turned on to light the streets of Midland for the first time. The company never did build the railway or the hotels and sanitoriums, but by 1912 the Big Chute plant was producing 4,200 horsepower of electricity, which was sold to the Hydro Electric Power Commission for distribution to the villages in the area.

There was a problem of access to the Big Chute. Construction materials for the generating plant had been delivered to the flag station of Severn Falls on the CPR and freighted downstream to the construction site in barges. With the plant now in operation there was still a problem of delivering food and supplies to the boarding-house and of supplying material for routine maintenance. A seven-mile winter road had been cut through the bush from Big Chute to Buckskin station on the CPR but, because there was no direct rail connection between Midland, headquarters of the company, and the CPR main line, delivery of goods by that route was time-consuming and costly. In the summer months, goods and materials were delivered to Port Severn by boat, portaged around the rapids, and transported up the river to the foot of the Little Chute; from the Little Chute the goods were hauled to the community over a mile-long "tote" road by horse-drawn "jumper." A lock and dam at Port Severn would connect Big Chute directly with Waubaushene and Midland for at least six months of the year. Moreover a dam at Port Severn would lessen the cost of developing the company's power rights there. So Simcoe Railway and Power definitely wanted the Port Severn lock. Its secretary-treasurer and vice-president was William Finlayson, former mayor of Midland, future minister of lands and forests in the Ferguson government, and, by coincidence, law partner of W.H. Bennett. The logic of placing the lock at Port Severn notwithstanding, the company was in a strong position to exert pressure on the government, through Bennett, to have it built.

A further reason for Bennett to favour a lock at Port Severn was the prospect of jobs for the French Canadians who lived there and who had suffered prolonged economic hardship ever since the Georgian Bay Lumber Company's mill burned down in 1896. Construction of a lock at Port Severn would create jobs in the short term and would improve the economy of the area in the long run by enlarging the tourist trade. A lock at Honey Harbour would be located in Muskoka riding and would do little for Bennett's cause in East Simcoe.

Cochrane agreed to a compromise on the canal outlet. Little Go Home Bay, where a standard-sized Trent canal lock was later to be built, would eventually be the main outlet of the canal, but, in the mean time, a dam and small lock – 100 feet by 25 feet – would be built at Port Severn to facilitate access to Simcoe Railway and Power plant at Big Chute and to meet Bennett's political commitments. Tenders for the Port Severn contract were called in the summer of 1913, and a contract was let to York Construction Company of Toronto on 24 September.

It is not surprising that York Construction won the contract. This company, which had close connections with both political parties, was chartered by letters patent on 3 March 1908 for the specific purpose of taking over the contract for the Newmarket canal works, awarded originally by the Laurier government to Liberal supporter John Riley of St Catharines. The principal shareholders in the company were William B. Russell, a civil engineer in Toronto, and Charles W. Dill and Archibald Lothian, contractors from Maxville, Ontario. Reginald Parmenter and Strachan Johnston, with the Toronto firm of Thomson, Tilley and Johnston, were directors and lawyers for the company – and staunch Tories. Johnston was a close friend of Dr J.D. Reid, acting minister of railways and canals. It seems quite clear that York construction was awarded the Port Severn contract in compensation for the loss of the Newmarket contract, which was cancelled by Cochrane before the work was finished. Of the six tenders submitted, York Construction was the lowest, being a mere $1,800 more than the government engineer's own estimate.

The contract was a small one, worth only $130,000. It called for construction of the main dam, lock, and swing bridge at the principal outlet of the river and two smaller control dams, one at the Little Chute near the Bayview Hotel, the other on the back channel, one mile west of the main dam. Retaining walls were to be built on the low ground on both ends of the main dam, and considerable rock excavation was required at the lower entrance to the lock. Work began in the second week of October, when the contractors built an office, store-house, boarding-house, and stables. A boiler for operating steam drills and a derrick to excavate rock were delivered to the site in November. During the winter months some work was started on the coffer-dams and some excavation was carried out.

Two coffer-dams were used at Port Severn. One was built across the river below the site of the dam to hold back the water of Georgian Bay and to serve as a temporary bridge when the old one was torn down. The other coffer-dam was the Georgian Bay Lumber Company's mill dam which, although unused since 1896, was still in fairly good repair. This timber-and-stone dam had been built in two sections. The first section, some 240 feet long, was located about 700 feet up river from the location of the present dam. It extended from the east side of the river to Saw Mill Island; it contained sluice-ways for water control and the flume for the mill. The other section, about 300 feet long, crossed the channel between the south side of Saw Mill Island and the north end of the main island of Port Severn, formed by the two mouths of the river. The sluice-ways in the old dams were filled in, the crib work was repaired by divers, and the dams were made watertight with a layer of two-inch planks covered with painted canvas, held in place with sheeting. The whole discharge of the river was then diverted, temporarily, through the Little Chute. A pool of dead water, about four acres in area, was created between the two coffer-dams.

In late June, the coffer-dams having been completed, the water between them was pumped out and the bed of the river laid bare. The exposed bottom, littered with decades of accumulated mill refuse, looked like the suburbs of hell. The bottom of the main channel had been swept bare by the current, but in the backwater between the two mill dams an immense quantity of waterlogged material had collected: timber, trees, roots, slabs, bark, chips, hulls of discarded batteaux and scows, and numerous pieces of scrap iron. The bottom beneath this jumbled mass of slimy material was covered with several inches of black oozy sawdust that had accumulated from the mill. As the lowering water contracted into pools, hundreds of trapped fish flapped and gasped among the logs and branches, adding an element of the macabre to the already grotesque spectacle that seemed to rise out of the water before the eyes of the astonished residents of Port Severn, who lined the shore to watch the unwatering of the pool.

Partly as a concession to conservation, but mainly to prevent the inevitable stench of rotting fish, the contractors hired young boys to save the larger fish. The boys waded through the shallow pools scooping up pickerel, bass, pike, maskinonge, and sturgeon, which they hurled over the coffer-dam into the clear water above. One 145-pound female sturgeon, its belly distended with several pounds of roe, was too heavy for the boys to toss over the dam and was carried to the cook-house to end up that night on the dinner plates of the construction workers. Never again after the construction of the dam and lock at Port Severn would spawning sturgeon, once a common sight, be seen in the Severn River.

In the fall, A.J. Grant had the good sense to order the debris piled up and burned. Having been exposed to the sun and air all summer, the logs and sawdust had dried out and would have floated to the surface when the pool was filled, causing endless trouble in the lock gates and valves.

Consequently, huge clouds of black smoke hung over Port Severn by day and flames from the massive bonfires illuminated the sky at night.

Immediately after the water was drained from the pool, excavation for the lock pit began. Carpenters built forms for the lock walls, dam footings, and pivot piers for the swing bridge. On 1 August concrete pouring began. Gravel for the concrete was hauled by barge from Beausoleil Island, there being no suitable gravel in the vicinity of the lock. Cement and dynamite, delivered to the Grand Trunk station at Waubaushene, were also brought to Port Severn by barge. Early in July a barge full of gravel was caught in high winds on Georgian Bay, swamped and sunk, confirming the hazardous conditions grain barges would have encountered had the barge canal idea been carried through.

There is little doubt that the contractors would have finished the work by the contract date of 31 March 1915 had they not been held up by changes to the design of the main dam. As a result the contract was extended to 30 November. The changes were requested by the Hydro Electric Power Commission (HEPC). In June 1914 the commission purchased from Simcoe Railway and Power the Big Chute power plant (the first electric plant to be owned and operated by the commission), together with the water rights and land owned by the company at Port Severn. The HEPC decided to develop the Port Severn power. On 17 July, just as construction of the dam was getting under way, A.J. Grant received a request from the HEPC's chief engineer, Fred Gaby, for design changes in the dam to accommodate the proposed power plant. The HEPC's proposal required nine sluice-ways instead of the original five and called for raising the height of the dam and consequently of the swing bridge. Negotiations between the HEPC and the Department of Railways and Canals lasted most of the summer, during which time work on the dam was suspended. The changes were eventually approved and carried out by the contractor, the additional cost being paid by the commission, which never did build the electric plant. Nevertheless the changes in the design of the works proved to be beneficial in the long run. The original plan had called for the dam and swing bridge to be about five feet lower than those actually built. The elevated bridge has permitted all but sail boats and the tallest yachts to enter and leave the lock, without the necessity of swinging the bridge. Given the amount of present-day boat traffic and the number of automobiles that take the road to Honey Harbour, frequent traffic jams, with the possibility of accidents, have thus been prevented.

Despite the delay, the contract was nearly completed by mid-July 1915. Only some concrete work needed to be done to the spillway on the east end of the dam, and more excavation was required below the lock. A temporary road bridge of stop logs and planks had been erected over the lower end of the lock, pending installation of a steel swing bridge by the

Hamilton Bridge Company. It was decided that the work was sufficiently advanced to allow the coffer-dams to be breached and water let into the lock for an official opening on 26 July. The request was made by W.H. Bennett. The occasion was the annual picnic of the Retail Merchants' Association of Midland. To add colour to the ceremonies planned to recognize this historic opening of the western outlet of the canal, a large Canadian ensign and a giant banner welcoming visitors to Port Severn were stretched across the lock. A flotilla of boats, carrying hundreds of Midlanders and people from surrounding communities, crossed over to Port Severn in the morning. Following an appropriate speech by Bennett, the launches were locked through in bunches as several hundred people stood on the temporary bridge and lock walls, looking on. The party spent a pleasant afternoon cruising on Gloucester Pool before returning through the lock to Midland in the evening. Tourism had been inaugurated on the lower Severn River in an auspicious manner.

Construction of the lock did much economically for the people of Port Severn, as Bennett had predicted. Many of the local men received temporary employment as teamsters, labourers, boiler tenders, and kitchen hands, resulting in a substantial amount of the contract money being distributed through the village. But not all the workers were locals. The contractor was obliged to import skilled workers such as carpenters, divers, mechanics, and construction foremen. The presence of these outsiders caused a certain amount of resentment and some social upheaval in this isolated French-Canadian community, especially after the introduction of alcohol. The Georgian Bay Lumber Company had banned liquor from its lumber camps and mill villages. Port Severn had traditionally been a "dry" community, until the contractors arrived with a more tolerant attitude towards the consumption of alcohol in the construction camp. Drinking bouts became common. When these included local men, considerable anguish was felt by the local women. On one occasion, anguish turned into terror. One Saturday night in July 1914 some of the construction workers, having secured a quantity of liquor, started a drinking bout that lasted well into Sunday morning. An altercation arose, during the course of which one W.J. Campbell from Thorold drew a revolver and commenced shooting into the crowd of revellers. Three men were wounded, fortunately none seriously. Realizing what he had done, Campbell beat a hasty retreat down the road towards Waubaushene and, to the relief of the community, was never seen at Port Severn again.

By 1915, the First World War was already creating a serious manpower shortage in Canada. There not being enough labourers around Port Severn to finish the work, the contractor was forced to import Bulgarian and Italian immigrants from the Toronto area. The presence of these foreigners, especially the Bulgarians, whose homeland had just entered the war on the side of Germany, caused even more resentment and suspicion in this close-knit French-Canadian society than the English-speaking tradesmen had caused. The English and the French at Port Severn had existed side by side with a symbiotic tolerance, if not grudging repect, for each other for decades, each group being dependent on the other: the French needed the English Canadians' political connections, economic power, and administrative know-how, and the English speakers depended upon the French Canadians' bush skills, which were second to none anywhere on the continent. "The English were all right as clerks and store keepers," Billy St Amand mused, in recalling his days as a lumberer at Port Severn. "But you'd never put an Englishman in a bush gang or on a lumber drive, where a man was expected to carry his end," the 94-year-old resident of Port Severn confided to me. The English were one thing; the foreigners were something else. During the few months they spent at Port Severn, they did not receive even grudging approval from the paysans.

On one occasion a local carpenter, David Ouellette, wrote to the minister of railways and canals complaining about the hourly rate paid to immigrant workers. It seems that the contract rate for labourers was 17½ cents per hour for a 10-hour work day, but, according to Ouellette, the immigrants were working for 15 cents, threatening, it was feared, the wages paid to local workers. In answering the charge, works superintendent Bill Monroe confessed to having five foreigners working at 15 cents per hour. He claimed that because they had been found "not to be up to the mark,"[5] they were to have been let go; the men, however, had asked to stay on at the reduced rate, which the contractor allowed them to do. All the other labourers were paid 17½ cents per hour, the better ones received 20 to 22 cents, and carpenters were paid 30 to 35 cents per hour. "We now have not nor have we had a white man employed on our contract here at less than 17½ cents per hour,"[6] Monroe wrote the minister. Even to Monroe, Bulgarians and Italians were not considered "white men."

Legend still persists around Port Severn that the lock walls and core walls built near the Big Chute contain the bodies of Bulgarian, Romanian, and Italian labourers who either fell or were pushed into the forms and were left to be buried beneath the descending concrete. "Behind every joke is a grievance," Sigmund Freud once wrote. Apocryphal stories of entombed foreign workers, told with good-humoured bravado by old-timers who were there, reveal the racial resentment from which even the residents of a small, out-of-the-way place like Port Severn were not immune.

By 1916 the foreigners and the contractors were gone. But life at Port Severn would never be the same again. Joe White, eldest son of an English settler who received a large tract of land on Gloucester Pool for services rendered in the Northwest Rebellion, and who was to give White's Falls its name, was appointed lock-master, a position he held for 32 years. White understood, and frequently remarked to the author, that it was the construction of Bennett's lock at Port Severn that saved the community, for had the lock not been built, the village would unquestionably have disappeared when the lumber trade around Georgian Bay finally expired. The lock brought thousands of tourists every summer. Port Severn became the service centre for the dozens of summer cottages and tourist resorts that sprang up on Gloucester Pool and on the Georgian Bay side. Summer hotels, marinas, boat engine repair shops, garages, guiding services, bait dealers, grocery stores, restaurants, coffee shops, and beer parlours took the place of the once-whining saw mill as the economic base of the community. For a time, Port Severn's lock was the busiest in Canada, putting through an average of 75 boats per day. Had this lock been built in Little Go Home Bay, as the engineers recommended, no one would have gone to Port Severn. Honey Harbour, or some new village in the vicinity of Go Home Bay lock, would have flourished, and Port Severn would have ceased to be. Permanent residents of Port Severn owe a debt of gratitude, of which fact they are probably unaware, to a young Barrie-born lawyer-politician who established a law practice in the rail head town of Midland in 1890. For without the intervention of W.H. Bennett in the political process in Ottawa, the Port Severn lock and the present-day community would not exist.

The Marine Railways

For contract purposes the Severn River division was divided into three sections. A contract for section 2 was awarded to the Inland Construction Company on 23 April 1914, and a contract for the work on section 3 was signed by the Randolph Macdonald Company on 4 August. A few hours after the latter document was executed, Britain's 24-hour ultimatum to Germany to stop the invasion of Belgium had expired. At 6 p.m. Ottawa time, the British Empire was at war. Had the Canadian government anticipated the extent of the country's involvement in the conflagration that started that evening, it is doubtful if the contract for section 3 would have been executed; indeed, had the events of August been predicted in April, the contract for section 2 probably would not have been signed either. Had Britain gone to war a few months earlier, the Trent canal might never have been finished. It was only because nearly half the work on the Severn River had been completed before the works were shut down in 1917 that construction was resumed after the war.

Section 2

Section 2 extended from Big Chute to a point one-half mile above Macdonald's Rapids, a distance of about 11½ miles. The contract included construction of concrete dams at Pretty and Lost channels and of a 70-foot-high dam, a single lock with a lift of 47 feet, and a power house at Swift Rapids; reconstruction of the CNR bridge at Hydro Glen; and considerable granite rock excavation.

Like nearly all the contracts on the Trent canal, this one was awarded through the patronage system rather than by strict adherence to the tendering process. The beneficiaries were the relatives of Haughton Lennox, former MP for Simcoe South, who, as we learned in the last chapter, was mainly responsible for the Nottawasaga River survey. In 1912, Robert Borden rewarded Lennox for 12 years as a Conservative MP by appointing him to the Supreme Court of Ontario. But in 1914, he still exercised considerable political influence in Ottawa.

When tenders were called for section 2, Haughton's cousin, T. Herbert Lennox, the Conservative MLA for York North, decided to bid for the contract, in the name of the Inland Construction Company. On 30 March an order-in-council was passed authorizing acceptance of the company's tender, although technically on 30 March there was no Inland Construction Company. With the contract assured, an application for letters patent was then hastily prepared and submitted to the provincial secretary on 31 March; the letters patent were issued the same day. To ensure the anonymity of the real tenderers (the Toronto press had already announced the awarding of the contract), the application for incorporation was made by Malcolm Keith Lennox, a relative who was junior partner in T. Herbert's law office, a law student named B.F. Fisher, and three stenographers, all of whom were named in the application as provisional directors. It was their names that were published in the Ontario *Gazette*. On 3 April the real directors of the company took over. A second application was submitted to the provincial secretary for reincorporation of the company as the Inland Construction Company, Limited; John F. Lennox, T. Herbert Lennox, Lewis P. Burns, and F.H. Dickenson were the sole members of the company. Dickenson was president, and John F. Lennox was secretary-treasurer. This application was not made public. On 8 April the contract was assigned to the new company. Dickenson and Burns were railway contractors in Hamilton. They owned the plant and possessed the technical know-how to carry out the contract. They also put up the $36,000 security deposit. The Lennoxes merely provided the legal work and, more important, had the political connections in Ottawa.

Inland Construction's tender was $712,258. This ridiculously low bid was actually $165,188 less than the estimate of the engineer of the Department of Railways and Canals but was submitted probably to ensure acceptance of the tender, the Lennoxes knowing full well that the actual cost of construction would eventually be paid. Work started in the early summer.

To facilitate delivery of materials to the construction sites, the CPR built a short siding at the flag station of Severn Falls. Soon afterwards, the station building at Buckskin was moved to the new location. In the summer of 1914, and for several seasons thereafter, Severn Falls was a busy place. Inland Construction built an office and warehouse there. Tugs hauled barges loaded with construction materials daily from the railway depot to the construction camps at Swift Rapids and Pretty Channel.

Pretty Channel and Lost Channel dams were completed first. At Pretty Channel a large concrete structure with seven spillways, each 20 feet wide and 9 feet deep, replaced the old wooden dam built originally by the Georgian Bay Lumber Company for running logs around the Big Chute by way of Six Mile Lake and Six Mile Channel. The rock formation at Big Chute proved to be an formidable log trap, and lumbermen avoided running logs that way as often as possible. Hence the Pretty Channel dam. Simcoe Railway and Power had restored the old log dam in 1910 and would undoubtedly have replaced it with a concrete structure, had the decision to complete the canal not been made. By the fall of 1915, Pretty Channel dam and Lost Channel dam – a small dam with one spillway located about two miles down Lost Channel – and a blind dam at the bottom of Copps Bay were finished. Pretty Channel and Big Chute dams were used to regulate the water in the Big Chute – Ragged Rapids reach, consistent with the needs of construction at Swift Rapids and power production at Big Chute.

But the main work of the contract was done at Swift Rapids, where the main dam and lock were to be built. In the summer of 1915, 200 men were working at the Swift, taking out the massive excavation for the lock and building concrete piers for the dam. The construction camp included a sawmill, blacksmith shop, store, library, stables, and "a whole settlement of shanties"[1] for the workers. The first structure built was a brick house for the future lock-master; it was occupied in the interim by John Boyd, government inspector of the work.

The reason for building the dam and lock at Swift Rapids was to flood Ragged Rapids, thereby averting the need for expensive rock excavation there. But as was indicated earlier, a dam at the Swift would destroy the power development at Ragged Rapids and the town of Orillia would have to be compensated. Jost estimated that, even allowing for the cost of building the town a new power house at Swift Rapids, and paying compensation for relocation, the government could still save $150,000 by the Swift Rapids development, compared to the original scheme proposed by Walsh for a long rock cut at the Ragged. The minister accepted Jost's plan, and on 24 February 1914 an order-in-council was passed authorizing the Department of Railways and Canals to enter into negotiations with the Orillia Water, Light and Power Commission for acquisition of its power development at Ragged Rapids.

Even though the somewhat primitive plant at Ragged Rapids, which generated about 1,600 horsepower, was a source of much pride to the citizens of Orillia, the town was happy to negotiate a change of location of its power plant. The plant that had been producing electricity for Orillia since January 1902 had always been vulnerable to the vagaries of the current in Ragged Rapids. A coffer-dam had been swept away in the fall of 1899, setting back the construction schedule by a year, and in the spring of 1904 the main dam was washed away, destroying the power house and forcing the town to rely on its old steam plant to supply power for the water system and street lighting. Power generation at Ragged Rapids had been restored in the winter of 1905, but there was no assurance that another wash-out would not occur. Far better for the town to rely on a substantial dam, built and maintained by the Department of Railways and Canals, than to operate its own. Further, it had become apparent in 1914 that the small Ragged Rapids plant could not meet the increasing industrial and domestic demand for electricity. The proposed plant at Swift Rapids would more than triple the production of the Ragged Rapids plant.

Adam Beck, as was his wont, intervened during the negotiation. He was then engaged in a bitter dispute with the dominion government over his takeover bid for the Electric Power Company operating on the Trent River. He tried to talk the town out of entering into an agreement with the dominion government by inviting it instead to join the provincial system and to buy power from the commission's newly acquired plant at Big Chute. Beck had his own eyes fixed on the Swift Rapids power. To his dismay the Orillia ratepayers turned down a hydro by-law by a vote of 517 to 79. Obviously the town preferred to own and operate its own plant.

As a result of Beck's interference, negotiations with the dominion representatives were held up for nearly two years. But in the end it was agreed that the dominion government would build a new power house for the town large enough to hold equipment capable of generating 5,000 horsepower. Orillia would be responsible for installing the new machinery, for extending its power line from Ragged Rapids to the new plant, for cutting a "tote" road from the new location to Hydro Glen station (built in 1907), and for moving the community. The dominion would pay the town a lump sum of $25,000 as compensation for inconvenience, and it agreed to pay for electricity delivered from the Big Chute plant during the interval between the closing of the old plant and operation of the new one. Orillia agreed to supply electricity for the government works at Swift Rapids at the regular rate for power. And the town contracted to pay the dominion government a water rental of 50 cents per horsepower, with a minimum of $800 per year. This latter arrangement was most distressing to Adam Beck, who considered that the surplus water belonged to the province. Orillia had in fact been paying water rental to the province before the dominion government intervened.

By October 1917 construction of the dam and power house at Swift Rapids was sufficiently advanced to permit installation of the new equipment and for the task of dismantling the old plant to begin. Once this was done, on 10 November the Ragged Rapids dam and the power plant were blown into oblivion with a substantial charge of dynamite. The reach above the Swift was filled, the new generators were tested, and on 17 November the first electric current from the new plant reached Orillia.

A settlement of about 30 people, principally plant operators, maintenance men, and their families, had grown up at Ragged Rapids, by then called Hydro Glen. The whole community, including the houses and the small school operated by the Orillia Water, Light and Power Commission for the children of its employees, was moved to the new location, and the village was reconstructed on the land set aside under the dominion water lease. All that remained at Hydro Glen were the railway station, the post office, and a small store. Later, even these would disappear.

The work of excavating a rock cut across the Indian portage at Macdonald Chute, eliminating a dog-leg in the river there, was subcontracted by the Inland Construction Company to the firm of Hamill, Ryan and Harris. By the fall of 1915 this work was finished, and in the following year considerable rock was excavated at the Sparrow Lake Chute by the same firm. But after the Swift Rapids power plant was put into operation, not much further work was done on section 2. The contractors had difficulty obtaining labourers because of the war, and so work was suspended for a year. Finally, because it was experiencing financial difficulties, Inland Construction asked to be relieved of its contract. On 28 October 1919 the government paid the contractors $101,322.88, on the basis of which the company discharged all claims against the government. In all, the government paid the company $682,005.31 for five years of work, which was only $40,000 less than the tendered price, but a good deal of the contract was still unfinished when the government took it back.

After the war Inland Construction tried to get a contract, on the basis of cost plus 8 per cent, to finish the work on section 2, but by then the government had decided not to finish the lock at Swift Rapids. Using W.H. Bennett (now a senator) as a mediator, the minister of railways and canals persuaded the Orillia Water, Light and Power Commission, which had been pressing the government for completion of the Swift lock, to accept a marine railway "as a temporary measure to tide over until the financial stringency occasioned by the war had passed."[2] Accordingly, in the summer of 1919 a marine railway, identical to the one built earlier at Big Chute, was constructed by York Construction at the Swift Rapids. Using day labourers, the Department of Railways and Canals built a new high-level railway bridge at Hydro Glen, which had been part of the original contract but was not started before Inland Construction went out of business. The government did intend to finish the lock at Swift Rapids some day, but nothing was done until the present lock was built in 1965.

Section 3

Section 3 extended from Sparrow Lake to deep water in Lake Couchiching. The contract included one lock with a 20-foot lift, two highway swing bridges, one railway swing bridge, several small dams at the mouth of the river near Washago, and a considerable amount of earth and rock excavation. The value of the contract awarded to the Randolph Macdonald Company was $901,140. This limited company was, like almost all the others, established for the specific purpose of acquiring contracts on the Trent canal. When the contracts were completed, the companies were generally dissolved, but Randolph Macdonald was one of the fortunate ones that continued to win contracts. Originally chartered by federal letters patent in August 1905, Randolph Macdonald received an Ontario charter in 1908. Unlike most of the other bidders, Macdonald seems not to have had any particular political affiliation to help him win contracts; he relied solely on the tendering process. Because his tenders were reasonable and usually quite close to the estimated costs, he succeeded in getting contracts from both Liberal and Conservative governments. He tendered for at least three of the Trent River contracts, winning the contract for the Hastings – Healey Falls section in 1909. He tendered for all three of the Severn River contracts but was successful on only one. In 1919 he was awarded a contract for rebuilding the Bobcaygeon lock. Randolph Macdonald was a good contractor.

Work on section 3 started in the fall of 1914, the main construction camp being at Washago. Because the construction sites were easily accessible from the CNR depot at Washago, work progressed smoothly for the first two years. Then both materials and labourers became hard to obtain because of the war, and so Macdonald asked to be relieved of his contract without penalty. By mutual agreement the contract was cancelled on 1 December 1917, about 56 per cent of the work having been completed. Some of the small control dams had been built, the lock pit had been excavated, some of the concrete had been poured, much of the canal prism between the lock and Lake Couchiching had been dug, and the superstructures for some of the bridges were in place.

As we shall see in the next chapter, Randolph Macdonald resumed work on the section in January 1919.

The Marine Railways

Because of war conditions the government decided not to call for tenders for section 1, which was to include construction of the locks at Go Home Bay and Big Chute. Because the Port Severn lock was opened in 1915 and because the Swift Rapids and Couchiching locks were expected to be finished in the summer of 1917, the only obstacle to through navigation from Lake Simcoe to Georgian Bay would have been the Big Chute. W.H. Bennett, who had been doing everything short of pouring concrete to expedite completion of the Severn River division, proposed a temporary measure to eliminate the Big Chute bottleneck. On 15 February 1916 he wrote to Frank Cochrane, asking him to consider construction of a "500 foot tramway connection from below Big Chute to the waters above the

Chute."[3] Bennett's request brought swift action from the canal authorities. Two days later A.J. Grant ordered divisional engineer F.S. Lazier to begin preparing plans for the tramway, and a month later the minister gave permission for construction to begin.

It is not clear where the idea of an electrically powered tramway, or "marine railway" as it was soon called, originated; certainly not with W.H. Bennett. The first marine railway on the Trent canal was to have been built at Swift Rapids as a supplement to the lock. The Orillia *Packet* reported in 1914 that the construction plans for the Swift Rapids works shown to the representatives from Orillia in the negotiations for relocation of the power plant included "a device for transferring canoes and skiffs between the upper and lower pools."[4] The device was reputed to be a "narrow gauge railway about 540 feet long with a car to carry boats,"[5] operated by electric-powered machinery. This marine railway was probably planned for economic reasons. The lock that was to be built at Swift Rapids would have been (as it now is) the highest standard lift lock on the waterway. The single lower gate was to be opened (as it now is) on the window principle, instead of in the ordinary way. That is, the large wooden gate was to be raised on steel towers by means of a lifting device powered by electricity. If it had been built in 1914 it would have been a unique design indeed. To have used this massive lock for the transfer of canoes and small boats, which comprised a good deal of the traffic on the Severn River in those days, would have wasted a good deal of both water and electricity. The proposed marine railway, although also electrically driven, would use much less power than the lock machinery and would waste no water at all.

Where Jost got the idea for this marine railway, if in fact it was his idea, is not known. Similar devices had been used on the Morris Canal in New Jersey as early as 1830. The 102-mile-long Morris Canal, which connected the Delaware River with the Hudson, had been built to move coal from Pennsylvania to Newark. Some of the elevations on the canal were too high to be surmounted with locks, and so an ingenious system of "incline planes,"as they were called, was built. Coal barges were floated onto wooden cradles attached to three-inch-thick endless cables, by which the cradles were hauled to the top of the incline on rails. The device was powered by a water turbine fastened to the cable, the canal being tapped at the upper level and the water channelled to the bottom of the hill to turn the turbine. Remains of some of the incline planes can still be seen in parts of Morris county on the abandoned canal.

Another possible origin of the marine railways built on the Severn was the "ship's railway," originally proposed by Capt. James B. Eads in 1878. Eads proposed building a colossal railway to carry ships across the Tehuantopec Isthmus in Mexico, as being more satisfactory than the canal being planned at Panama by Ferdinand de Lesseps. A company was actually formed to promote the idea, but de Lesseps's canal proposal won general approval, and Eads's "ship's railway" was never built.

It was R.B. Rogers's father-in-law, Henry Calcutt, who introduced the term "marine railway" into the engineering vocabulary of Canada's Department of Railways and Canals. In November 1880, when the Trent canal scheme was being revived by the Macdonald government, Calcutt wrote to Sir Charles Tupper, drawing his attention to an article in the August 1879 issue of the *Scientific American* describing Eads's proposal. Calcutt thought the ship's railway, which he called a marine railway, might be appropriate for some of the expensive sections of the Trent canal. "If you can see the feasibility of it," he wrote Tupper, "by being the first to introduce it into Canada, it would hand down your name to posterity and make our party very popular in this section of Ontario." Whether inspired by a vision of immortality, or merely by a desire to enhance the popularity of the Conservative party, Tupper instructed an engineer to examine Calcutt's suggestion. The engineer advised Tupper against constructing marine railways on the Eads principle on the Trent system because there would not be "a sufficient amount of traffic to keep the required machinery in almost constant use";[7] therefore the plan would not be economic.

A marine railway, similar in principle to the marine railways built on the Severn River, was developed by Messrs. Day, Summers, and Company of the Northam Iron Works in Southampton, England, in 1878. It may in fact have been the prototype of the one built at Big Chute. In the Northam model, vessels were floated into a cradle, blocked, and hauled out of the water on rollers, the device being pulled by a steel wire hawser coiled around a drum, which was rotated by a steam engine. Although the Northam marine railway was used only for hauling steam boats out of the water for inspection and repair, it could easily have been adapted for portaging boats over a land obstacle.

The marine railways designed for the Severn River combined both principles. Like the Northam marine railway, the cradle or car, on the Big Chute version, was hauled by a steel cable wrapped around a drum, and, like Eads's ship's railway, the car was placed on tracks instead of rollers. The drum on the Severn marine railways was turned by electric motors rather than steam engines.

Divisional engineer F.S. Lazier was instructed to conduct a survey of boat owners and boat manufacturers between Orillia and Penetang to determine how large the proposed marine railway need be. His survey revealed that a conveyance capable of carrying vessels 30 feet in length, 9 feet in the beam with 3-foot draft, and weighing five tons, would accommodate all the boats in the area with the exception of five large cruisers. Based on the information gathered by Lazier, A.J. Grant hastily prepared a design and submitted it to Bowden along with an estimate of cost. Typically, Grant, who seemed to have a penchant for designing structures larger than necessary (remember the locks on the Newmarket canal and the Trent River), designed a device capable of transporting 10-ton boats. Grant thought it should be a permanent structure; his estimate was $25,000. The minister rejected Grant's plan and asked for a smaller and cheaper railway to be designed, as "it was not proposed to permanently maintain it."[8] J.B. Jost, now Bowden's assistant in Ottawa, designed a new version that was estimated to cost only $4,000. Jost's plan, perhaps identical to the one originally planned for Swift Rapids, was approved by the minister and sent to Grant, with instructions to proceed with construction at once. Grant was given the liberty to change the plans as he saw fit, as long as the cost did not exceed $5,000 and no delay in construction was caused by the changes.

The original plan was to have the marine railway built by the Inland Construction Company as an "extra" under the section 2 contract, but Grant advised against this because of the labour problems being encountered by that company. He recommended instead that the department make arrangements with the York Construction Company to build the railway as additional work on the Port Severn contract. This is what was done, although, curiously, the Port Severn work had been finished for nearly a year. Under war conditions, the government could do almost anything it chose without parliamentary approval, because it had given itself extraordinary powers to pursue the war effort under the War Measures Act. So although the Big Chute marine railway could hardly be considered essential to the war effort, the government used its powers under the act to enter into an agreement with York construction, without tender, to build the marine railway and a new dam in Six Mile Channel. The generous standard wartime contract rate of cost plus 10 per cent was applied.

The little marine railway at Big Chute, designed by Jost and built by York Construction, was the first of its kind to be built anywhere in the world. With its construction the Trent canal then had two unique tourist attractions: the highest concrete hydraulic lift lock in the world, at Peterborough, and the world's first electrically operated marine railway, at Big Chute. For the Big Chute railway a standard-gauge track, 730 feet long, was laid north of the power plant, across the land barrier between the upper and lower levels of the river, with about 125 feet of track at each end submerged under the water. The land on which the railway was built belonged to the Hydro Electric Power Commission (HEPC), under its provincial lease, and so permission had to be obtained from the HEPC before construction could start. Naturally the uneven rock terrain had to be smoothed out for the roadbed, and at the summit a wooden trestle was built to carry the rails over the HEPC's water intake from the forebay, which fed water to the boarding-house and the superintendent's residence. Timber wharfs, running the full length of the submerged portion of track, were built for landing passengers and to facilitate the placing of boats on the car.

A steel frame for the car was custom built by the William Hamilton Company under subcontract. The car ran on four 18-inch wheels; it was 24 feet long, slightly more than 9 feet wide, and open at both ends, with sides just over 6 feet high. The floor and sides were made of two-inch Douglas fir planks. The car was pulled by a five-eighths-inch steel cable hooked onto one end of the car; the other end was fastened to an electric winch housed in a control shack, located at the summit on the north side of the track. A 20-horsepower reconverted electric motor powered the winch. The car was designed to carry a boat 35 feet long, with a 9-foot beam and weighing no more than 5 tons. Everyone knew that this was just a temporary device until the locks at Big Chute were built, and so not too much care was taken in building it and a good deal of second-hand material went into its construction.

The operation of transferring a boat across the land barrier involved floating the boat onto the partly submerged car – the water covering the downhill end of the car was seldom more than three feet deep – resting it on a pair of adjustable cushions fore and aft, and securing the boat with ropes. The car was then pulled out of the water and along the track to the summit, where it was brought to a halt and the cable transferred to the other end. The car was jimmied over the crest of the hill and lowered with the winch down the hill and into the water at the other end. A portage lasted about half an hour.

Two problems complicated the operation: the control house was placed in such a position that the operator could not see the downstream side of the railway and therefore could not tell when the car had entered the water or when it was ready to be pulled up, and the quantity of wood on the car in relation to the amount of metal was such that the car tended to float off the track. The first problem was solved by placing a mark on the cable so that the operator could judge when the car was entering the water. But when raising a boat from the lower level, the operator had to leave the control house, cross the crest of the hill, and watch for the signal of his assistant to start the winch when the boat was properly placed. The flotation problem was solved by placing heavy concrete wedges in each corner of the car.

Because of the acute shortage of labour and the difficulty in obtaining materials, the marine railway was not ready for operation until July 1918. As the work neared completion, a question arose regarding the appointment of an appropriate operator. The complexity of the electrical equipment and the potential risk involved in portaging boats with this novel device required higher-level skills than were required on standard locks. A.J. Grant recommended that the job be given to Peter Ritchie, superintendent of the power plant at Big Chute. Ritchie had helped the contractors install the electrical equipment and, being a man with mechanical interests, had offered many suggestions and assistance as the railway was being built. He was, in fact, the only one who really knew how to operate the unique contraption when it was finished. Grant had thought that the railway would have only limited use and that Ritchie could manage the job on a part-time basis along with his duties as superintendent of the power plant. But Ritchie did not get the job. It went to John Sinclair of Orillia, a brother-in-law of W.A. Finlayson, who had strong ties through W.H. Bennett with the Conservative government in Ottawa. Sinclair arrived at Big Chute on 8 July. The railway was officially placed in operation the next day. Ritchie helped Sinclair put the first three or four boats over and instructed him in the railway's operation. Sinclair was lodged in the HEPC's boarding-house.

It was well that a full-time operator had been appointed, as the railway soon proved to be very popular, and much busier than its planners had anticipated. In July, 149 portages were made; in August, 312; in September, 219; in October, 153, and in November, 71, for a first season's total of 904 trips. Most of the craft portaged were skiffs and canoes, seven or eight at a time, but larger boats were transferred too. The largest boat to pass over the marine railway during the first summer was 33 feet long, with a 9-foot beam. It belonged to John O'Hara of Waubaushene.

When the Severn division was opened for through traffic in 1920 it became apparent that Sinclair would need a full-time assistant. The man hired was the author's father, William N. Angus, who had been working on the division as an axeman since April 1919. The two Scots, Jack Sinclair and Scotty Angus, formed an excellent team. They were practical men in their mid-thirties, returned soldiers, conscientious and dedicated public servants. Both had boundless energy and engaging personalities. Under their management the Big Chute marine railway became more than a unique machine; it became a national institution. The railway with its two charming Scots attendants was well known from Cleveland to Collingwood, wherever tourists, many of whom passed through the canal annually, resided.

In those days the marine railway was operated 24 hours a day, seven days a week. There were no roads leading to the Severn River between Port Severn and Severn Bridge. The only way out to civilization was by water, and, although few normally travelled on the river after dark, there was always the possibility of an emergency or a delay in getting home because of a faulty engine. The marine railway had to be available at all hours of the day or night. So when boats arrived, whether at 2 p.m. or 2 a.m., one of the operators was always there to "put them over."

It was obvious by 1920 that the Trent canal would never be used for transporting grain. Principally the canal would be, as its most recent promoters had been predicting, a tourist convenience. Without any direction from Ottawa, Jack and Scotty saw themselves not so much in the transportation business as in the tourist trade. They considered themselves to be not just government functionaries, efficient though they were in executing their official duties, but goodwill representatives of Canada serving as unofficial hosts to tourists, especially American yachtsmen who passed through Big Chute in increasing numbers after 1923. They played this role superbly well. Always friendly, co-operative, and helpful, they explained the operation of the marine railway several times a day and answered dozens of foolish questions with patience and good humour. They repaired engines, caulked leaking boats, and assisted many who found themselves in distress for one reason or another. Although the rules forbade passengers from riding in their boats on the car, the men made exceptions for the elderly and handicapped, one of them frequently riding along to assure the nervous passenger that the ride was safe, even enjoyable. Tourists always left the Big Chute happy and informed. And year after year they came back. Scotty and Jack received a flood of cards, letters, and sometimes gifts every Christmas from grateful tourists all over North America.

These irrepressible Scots enriched the lives of permanent summer residents as well. Both men liked a good time and ensured that other people enjoyed themselves too, making the Severn River a happy place to spend the summer. Whether at a shore party sing-song, at a dance at the Mordolphton Club on Gloucester Pool (now Severn Lodge), or at the new community hall at Severn Falls, one or the other of the two men was usually there, leading the dance, propping up quavering melodies with his own powerful voice, and entertaining with his wit and inexhaustible supply of party games and tricks. Jack and Scotty contributed their considerable talents without remuneration to make the summer social season successful, not only because they enjoyed themselves doing it but because their unique sense of duty made them want to contribute.

Jack Sinclair was a bachelor. He had invested his life savings in the stock market and lost them all in the crash of 1929. Like thousands of others in similar circumstances, he suffered a nervous collapse and was forced to leave the river in 1930. Scotty was a married man with a large family. Having saved no money, he had nothing to invest and hence nothing to lose; consequently, he was unaffected by the crash. When Jack left, he took over the chief operator's position which he held until his retirement in 1948. By then a road had come to Big Chute, strangers began appearing in the community, and residents began locking their doors for the first time. Summer life on the Severn River had changed. Day tourists now raced up and down the river in fast boats. To them the marine railway was no novelty, only a nuisance, an obstacle on the frenzied drive to nowhere.

Scotty would miss the river, but he was happy to leave. His time there had passed. When he retired, King George vi awarded him the Imperial Service Medal for 41 years of meritorious service. Apparently, someone in high places had discovered the unselfish contribution this Scots working man had made to the development of his adopted country: 9 years on railway surveys in northern Canada, 3 years in the Canadian army, and 29 years on the Trent canal.

Scotty Angus (left) and
Jack Sinclair, marine
railway operators, Big Chute.

CHAPTER TWENTY-NINE

The Couchiching Lock

As the First World War neared an end, it became clear that the government would have to find employment for returning soldiers and for the thousands of immigrants expected to enter Canada after the war. Accordingly, a decision was taken in the spring of 1918 to resume work on sections 2 and 3, suspended in 1917, and to let a contract for section 1. The Department of Railways and Canals included $500,000 for this purpose in its estimates, which were approved reluctantly by Parliament in May. Section 1 included a good deal of rock excavation for the bypass canal at Big Chute, which could be done in the winter months. Consequently, after the armistice in November the government was anxious to proceed, but a question arose as to how to find a contractor willing to take on the work under the unsettled conditions of the immediate post-war period.

Railways and Canals Minister J.D. Reid wanted the York Construction Company to have the contract for section 1, ostensibly because of "the special knowledge, experience, organization and facilities possessed by the York Construction Company,"[1] but more probably because the company's secretary, Strachan Johnston, had just been hired to argue the government's side in *The King* v. *John M. Kilbourn*, a case dealing with the crucial question of ownership of the water in the Trent canal.[2] Johnston was also retained, in view of his "experience in connection with water power matters in Ontario"[3] (gained while acting as counsel and later president of the Electric Power Company), to defend the dominion government in the event that the long-standing threat by the Ontario government to challenge dominion ownership of the Trent waters before the Exchequer Court were ever carried out. Also, Johnston was a friend of Reid's.

York Construction was asked to submit a tender but refused to submit one based on schedule rates, because of "the uncertain conditions respecting labour and materials."[4] The company did, however, express willingness to sign a contract under the fail-safe wartime condition of "cost plus 8%, the term 'cost' to comprise a fair and reasonable rental for the plant employed on the work."[5] The government accepted the condition and in January 1919 let a contract, without tender, worth well over a million dollars, using the extraordinary power of the War Measures Act which was still in force.

The contract included construction of a dam at White's Falls, excavation of the mile-long canal around Big and Little chutes, and construction of two locks, each with a lift of 29 feet, and of regulating dams at each end of the canal. Actually, the canal did not require as much excavation as one might think, because situated on the line of the canal were two large marshy areas, separated by a ridge of rock which, when cut through, would connect the marshes and create a natural channel. Three retaining walls had to be built on the river side of the marshes where the ground was low. These retaining walls were to consist of concrete core walls several hundred feet long, against which rock – excavated from the "centre cut," the strip of excavation between the marshes, and from the lock pits – would be piled to provide greater strength. Significantly, the contract did not include a lock at Honey Harbour, that idea apparently having been abandoned after Frank Cochrane retired in 1917.

The company moved quickly after signing the contract. On 6 January, 1919, company engineer W.B. Russell and construction superintendent W.H. Monroe examined the canal site, as a consequence of which they decided to build a construction camp in a deep bay on the south side of the river just above Little Chute, roughly at the centre point of the canal right of way and only a few hundred yards' walk to the site of the proposed lock pits. Materials, delivery of which started on 15 January, were unloaded at Buckskin station and hauled by team to the camp site. By the end of January the contractor had 40 labourers, 5 carpenters, and 6 teams unloading box cars, hauling material, clearing brush, and erecting the camp.

The contractors built the largest and finest camp of any of those used anywhere on the Trent canal construction. It was also the last. Cost was no obstacle; indeed, cost worked to the contractors' advantage, every dollar spent generating a profit for them of 8 per cent. Eventually 25 buildings were erected, including a kitchen, dining-room, bath-house, blacksmith's shop, office, saw mill, machine shop, store-house, root cellar, stables, ice-house, and boat-house, five large dormitories, and a dynamite house situated in a valley about a half-mile from the main camp. The buildings were single-boarded, covered with rubberoid, lined with heavy building paper, and heated with wood stoves. Each of the sleeping camps accommodated about 50 men. A 1,500-gallon tank provided running water, and a telephone line connected the camp with the outside world through the North River Telephone Exchange at Lovering. By the end of the first summer some 230 men were employed on the construction, most of them housed at the camp.

The labourers were mainly European immigrants, employed through the Robert Verity Employment Agency of Toronto; the contractor paid the agency a fee of one dollar per head. Verity recruited the workers in Europe, brought them to Toronto, and shipped them out on the first train to Severn Falls. The bewildered recruits, many fresh from the battlefield, former friends and former foes, marched in bunches of 50 or 60 along the six-mile stretch of blackfly-infested bush trail between the station and the construction camp and within hours of having left Toronto found themselves clearing brush, hauling rock, or wheeling concrete, most of them not even knowing where they were.

Labourers were paid 35 cents per hour, later raised to 40 cents, carpenters received 55 to 60 cents, and teams with drivers earned 70 cents. Workers paid $1 per day for room and board, and $1.40 per day was deducted from each teamster for the maintenance of his team. The working day was 10 hours long. Despite the good wages, immigrants could not take the hard work or stand the isolation. At least one worker went insane. Others quit in bunches of 30 or 40 and found their way back to Severn Falls and eventually to Toronto. During the year and a half that the construction camp was used, Verity shipped 419 labourers to Big Chute, but so great was the turnover that the work was often badly handicapped and at times almost completely tied up. So much for the government's post-war employment plan.

Gravel for the concrete was hauled all the way from Beausoleil Island on Georgian Bay with a tug and three scows, each holding about 62 cubic yards. Boulders and rock ledges had to be blown out of the Little Chute to ensure a six-foot navigation channel for the tug and scows to reach the camp. The concrete was mixed on the shore and wheeled in barrows by a continuous line of labourers, moving past the mixing machines and up a plank runway several hundred yards to the site of the core walls, where the concrete was dumped from platforms into the constantly rising wooden forms. The main core wall, curving for 500 feet between two rock hills, was built about 30 feet high at midpoint, with an almost equal height below ground level, extending down to bedrock. The wall was 15 feet wide at its base, tapering to about 2 feet at the summit. A tunnel was built through the wall at ground level to permit the marsh to drain into the river until the canal was ready for flooding. A six-inch pipe was built into the wall from the tunnel to the surface, through which concrete was later to be poured to fill the drainage tunnel. The other two smaller core walls are similarly constructed, but being located on higher ground are much lower than the main wall. Thousands of cubic yards of concrete went into the core walls' construction.

In the fall of 1920 the funds appropriated earlier ran out and the government was forced to close down the work. By then the political situation in Ottawa had changed. Borden had resigned in July 1920 because of ill-health; he was replaced as prime minister by Arthur Meighen, the politically naïve former justice minister. Reid was kept on as minister of railways and canals. The Union government, formed by Borden in 1917 on a platform of conscription, was beginning to fall apart, causing division in the government ranks. Mackenzie King had replaced Wilfrid Laurier as leader of the Liberal party in 1919 and was anxious to confirm his leadership at the polls. He was calling for an election. Money was scarce because of the post-war depression, and once again the Trent canal had low priority on everyone's list.

J.D. Reid had promised Parliament that the work on section 1 would continue only after the calling of public tenders; consequently on 8 January 1921 the contract with York Construction was formally terminated. Altogether $441,760.24 had been spent, but the only thing of tangible value produced was the concrete dam built at White's Falls to control water levels in Six-Mile Lake. At the Big Chute the core walls had been finished, about half the rock had been removed from the centre cut, and part of the pit for the Little Chute lock had been excavated. This was a good start, but it represented less than half the contract.

All the equipment, including the valves and hardware for the locks, was put in storage, and tons of food were locked up in the warehouse, pending the early return of the workers. But the workers did not come back. Whether the Conservatives were serious about calling tenders and finishing the Big Chute contract is questionable, despite the promises made during the 1921 election campaign. Plenty of opposition to further expenditure on the Trent canal had been voiced on both sides of the House of Commons in 1920, the most vehement coming from western MPs, who resented federal tax money being spent on what was by then clearly an Ontario tourist facility. Contracts had been let for enlarging the Welland Canal, and the westerners wanted that work given top priority, so that the perennial problem of moving prairie grain could be solved once and for all. Moreover, urgency to complete the Severn River locks was removed because the two marine railways had proved adequate for transferring all but the largest pleasure craft. Whatever the Conservatives' true intentions, they did not have to reveal them because Meighen lost the election.

There are plenty of ruins in the vicinity of Big Chute for future archaeologists to ponder. A concrete spillway, for a control dam that was never built, stands like Hadrian's Arch in the forest near the Little Chute. A rabbit runway passes under it. An abandoned steam boiler, too heavy for scrap scavengers to move, rusts into oblivion beside the water-filled lock pit that is gradually filling up with rotting leaves and sediment. The core walls will probably endure for centuries. The two smaller ones had been banked with rock taken from the centre cut before the contractor left; the walls are now buried beneath trees and thick undergrowth. Without knowing where to look, one would never find them. The main wall still stretches stark and naked across the valley between the rocky hills – a puzzling structure to anyone who happens upon it. For many years the wall was hidden in a poplar bush that had grown up on both sides of it, but industrious beavers, impatient to finish man's work, plugged the drainage tunnel, converting the marsh above into a shallow lake, which killed the trees. Now, as a consequence of the beavers' hydraulic engineering, the south side of the wall is exposed and visible for miles. The wall stands there useless, like the gateless locks at Newmarket, an even more perplexing monument to government folly. This one commemorates the foolishness of a Conservative government.

With the two marine railways in place, all that was needed to open navigation from Georgian Bay through to Lake Simcoe, at least for 35-foot boats, was the Couchiching lock and canal, abandoned by Randolph Macdonald for want of workers in 1917. The government had no choice but to renew the contract with the company, also at cost plus 8 per cent. Work resumed in January 1919, at the same time that York Construction began building its camp at Big Chute.

With the opening of the canal assured, Senator Bennett became concerned about its use and its real value to the country. Between 1891, when he was first elected to Parliament, and the First World War, he, like all the other canal promoters, had viewed the canal as a possible avenue for the cheap movement of western grain to world markets and as a stimulant for the economies in the towns through which it would pass. But by 1913 he was no longer convinced that the canal would become a commercial transportation route. With Hughes of Lindsay, Hale of Orillia, and Mulock of York North, Bennett was one of those who could now see the potential of the waterway as a tourist attraction. On 29 May 1913, while defending in Parliament Cochrane's decision to open the Severn River outlet, he expressed his revised view of the canal: "I have no apology to offer for the Trent Canal System as a tourist route. If, when it is finished, it becomes the greatest tourist system on the continent, it will be well worth the money spent on it."[6] For the next 10 years he did everything in his power to see that this would be so.

By 1919 Bennett was appalled at the lack of interest in the canal by former promoters now that it was nearly finished. It seems that when the vision of barges full of wheat moving through central Ontario faded, all interest in the waterway faded too. Bennett started a one-man campaign to awaken the communities along the route of the waterway to its new potential as a tourist attraction. He also wrote letters to newspapers in Montreal, Toronto, and some American cities, advising the readers of the opportunities the waterway offered for motorboat travel. Through the Montreal *Gazette*, for example, he invited the people of Montreal to "come up from Quebec over this grand water system with your boats and stir up reciprocity from Ontario with your brother motorboat enthusiasts to go down to see the beauties of the magnificent St. Lawrence River and your cities."[7]

He offered more practical advice to the people of Orillia. In a letter to the *Packet* he exhorted the town to plan "a monstrous motorboat regatta on Lake Couchiching on some public holiday. Hang out big prizes," Bennett implored. "Secure the interests of the builders of motorboats and engines. Stir up Peterborough, Lindsay, Belleville and other towns along the route and secure the co-operaton of motorboat owners generally, and you will be able to draw in more people than one dreams of at first sight ... It is not only a crowd for the day but advertising for the future that will be done by them coming with motorboats ... Get your Board of Trade interested in this for a 1919 regatta ... The ball is at your feet; kick it."[8] And kick the ball, they did.

More than a regatta was planned. At the monthly meeting of the Orillia board of trade in April 1920, it was proposed that a "Trent Valley Waterways Association to promote the tourist and freight trade along the route"[9] be formed. The proposal was discussed with Sen. Bennett, and with his assistance the Trent Waterway Development Association was created. Delegates from all along the route of the waterway met in Peterborough on 15 June for the inaugural meeting. Bennett, the keynote speaker, was elected honorary president. G.K. Fraser of Burleigh Falls became the first president, F.D. Kerr and J.C. Miller vice-presidents, and Leon Fraser secretary-treasurer. The mayors and reeves of some 15 towns and municipalities formed the board of directors.

Whereas the first Trent Valley Canal Association had been formed in 1879 for the purpose of getting the canal built, the aim of the second association was to find some purpose for the finished canal: specifically, "the development of the commercial, industrial and agricultural interests of the Trent Waterway District and the promotion of tourist traffic."[10] Although only minimally successful in promoting industrial and agricultural matters, the Development Association was highly effective in increasing tourist traffic and hence commercial activity along the waterway. Working closely with canal superintendent A.L. Killaly, the association succeeded in accelerating the process of buoying and marking the navigation channel so that boaters could find their way through the waterway. Until charts were prepared and published, the Orillia board of trade volunteered the services of two pilots to guide boats from Beaverton to Washago and Orillia. The Ontario government was encouraged to stock the waters with game fish and to provide more stringent enforcement of game protection laws. But it was through its advertising campaign, which peaked in 1923, that the association was most effective, Bennett being the prime mover.

Not since the days of steamer tours on the Kawartha Lakes in the 1890s had the waterway been so vigorously advertised. Forty thousand copies of a pamphlet promoting it were prepared for the 1923 season and distributed to railway companies and other tourist agencies across North America. Considerable publicity was gained from a visit by the governor-general to the waterway, arranged co-operatively by the city of Peterborough and the Development Association. On 31 March, at Bennett's suggestion, the Windsor Border Cities Star printed a full-page, illustrated article extolling the beauties of the Trent canal. Bennett also encouraged the Kermath Engine Manufacturing Company of Detroit to take out a full-page advertisement in the April issue of a boating magazine, describing the canal's route and pointing out its many tourist attractions. But the most fruitful promotional scheme was an impressive display at the New York Motorboat Show in February. The highlight of the display, which was consequently taken to other American cities, was a two-reel travel movie of the waterway produced by the Ontario government. The display also contained posters, pamphlets, and live specimens of game fish exhibited in an aquarium, also provided by the Ontario government. As a result of the publicity given the canal by the show in Rochester, New York, a flotilla of 15 yachts travelled the canal in the summer of 1923, harbingers of the fleets of American vessels that would come in the 1920s and 1930s. Because of the increased traffic of large boats resulting from these promotional campaigns, and in response to direct lobbying by the Development Association in Ottawa, the government enlarged the marine railways in 1923 to accommodate boats 60 feet long.

After 1924, as local cottagers' associations began to take over much of the work of the association, and as the Ontario and dominion governments began to expand their publicity services, the Trent Waterway Development Association disbanded. But during its brief existence, it did much to ensure that the Trent canal would become "the greatest tourist system on the continent."The Friends of the Trent-Severn Waterway Association, formed at Peterborough in 1982 to further public awareness, understanding, and appreciation of the waterway, is now the third generation of such promotional associations to be formed on the Trent waterway. It is to be hoped that the Friends, emphasizing historical interpretation and conservation, will be just as effective in achieving its aims as its two predecessors were.

On 23 June 1920, just eight days after the inaugural meeting of the Trent Waterway Development Association, the last dynamite blast was exploded, removing the final barrier to through navigation on the Trent canal. During the previous year the Randolph Macdonald Company had been digging the mile-long canal between Lake Couchiching and the Severn River. Excavation and bank lining had advanced from both ends, daily drawing closer to the CNR line that crossed the canal and that would have to be rerouted. Meanwhile construction of the lock and the railway swing bridge to which the railway would be diverted was going on. By 23 June the lock was finished, the bridge was built, the new track was laid, and the old one was torn up. A dredge, brought up from the Lake Couchiching end, stood by while the last charge was buried, deep in the narrow strip of land along which the railway track had recently run. In the morning the dynamite was set off, blasting skyward the last bit of rock and earth as the workmen stood at a safe distance, witnessing this historic event that was comparable to driving the last spike on the continental railway. A Department of Railways and Canals photographer recorded the event for posterity.

Within two minutes of the blast, water released by the workmen's shovels began to trickle through the gap; in 20 minutes it was a flood. Within an hour the water had found its level on both sides of the gap, and the dredge was brought up to remove the remaining earth. Two weeks later the canal was ready for use.

The official opening of this last lock took place quietly on 6 July 1920 at 1:30 in the afternoon. It was to have been a big event. In April the Orillia board of trade instructed its secretary "to communicate with Senator Bennett and suggest that arrangements should be made for a gathering of representatives from along the route of the canal at the time of the opening of the Washago [Couchiching] lock."[11] At the inaugural meeting of the Trent Waterway Development Association in June the lock opening was discussed again. There was talk of Lt.-Gov. Clark officiating, and the executive of the association planned to attend and to hold its first meeting at the lock. In the end, hardly anyone came. So the Couchiching lock was opened almost as inauspiciously as the first lock at Bobcaygeon 82 years earlier.

Only two small motorboats participated. In the lead boat was W. Hill, superintendent for the contractor, Mrs William Macdonald, the contractor's wife, and Mrs J.S. McLeod, wife of the assistant engineer. The second boat belonged to George Carson of Washago, later divisional superintendent but then only a rodman with the Department of Railways and

Canals. With Carson were several friends from the village. The only official present was divisional engineer George Kydd. He and several workmen stood on the lock walls, smiling, as the two small boats were lowered 20 feet into the lower reach. There were no speeches because no politicians were present, not even Sen. Bennett. The political value of the Trent canal had come, at least temporarily, to an end.

It was not until the next day that word of the lock's opening reached Orillia. The enterprising Thomas Woods, captain of the *Modello*, arranged a hasty excursion to the lock on the Wednesday afternoon bank holiday, but, regrettably, the CNR swing bridge had no operator yet, and so the steamer could not pass the bridge. On Thursday afternoon the Orillia town council and officers of the board of trade travelled to the Orillia power plant at Swift Rapids as guests of the Orillia Water, Light and Power Commission, on the commission's new boat, the *Owl*. On 3 July a small motor launch, the *Irene*, left Trenton, found its way through the still uncharted canal, and reached Port Severn on 20 July – the first vessel to make a through trip.

The early settlers in the Newcastle District would have been disappointed had they seen the 30-foot-long *Irene* knifing its way westwards through the Kawartha Lakes, only a token image of their grand vision of steamboats bringing trade goods all the way from England to exchange for farm products grown on their large estates. Regattas, and even pleasure travel on the canal, they would have understood. But that not one steamer, or one kernel of wheat, would ever move through the canal, those practical visionaries would not have comprehended.

If surprised at its eventual use, the canal's first promoters would have been dumbfounded at the cost. Nichol Hugh Baird's price tag of $3 million nearly ended the dream before it began, in 1835. Tom Rubidge's enormous estimate of $9 million nearly stopped it in 1888. But eventually the total cost of construction, including the $8,000 spent by Bethune at Bobcaygeon in 1833, would mount to $19,027,762.21. A further $3,203,099.81 would be spent on maintenance and repairs through the years, and it would cost $1,136,968.20 to operate the canal, making a grand total of $23,367,834.22 by 1923. To the settlers, who rarely saw cash, the amount would have been staggering. Today it is nothing. Spread over 90 years, it was really not very much at all.

Was the Trent canal worth the cost? Given the millions of dollars it has poured into the economy, to say nothing of the thousands of man-hours of pleasure it has given to its users, the canal is worth every cent the politicians reluctantly spent on it. Even John Carroll, who never did get a contract from John A. Macdonald for any of the Kawartha Lakes locks, would agree that the Trent canal turned out to be much, much more than a "respectable ditch."

APPENDIX

Major Construction Projects on the Trent Canal

Works	Contractor	Duration of Contract	Contract Price ($)	Final Cost ($)
THE COLONIAL YEARS: 1833 – 41				
Bobcaygeon	Pierce, Dumble			
First lock	and Hoar	1833 – 4	8,000	11,830
Second lock	William Hartwell	1836 – 7	8,250	Abandoned
	Commissioners	1837 – 8	–	12,108
Whitla's Rapids	William Hartwell	1836 – 7	25,565	Abandoned
Lindsay lock	Homer Hecox	1836 – 7	12,500	Abandoned
Hastings lock	Sidey and Craigie	1836 – 8	25,000	Abandoned
Buckhorn dam	Hall, Madge and Dixon	1837 – 8	3,300	3,300
Healey Falls dam	Homer Hecox	1836 – 8	3,750	Abandoned
Myers Island lock	Francis and Hay	1837 – 8	29,165	Abandoned
Chisholm's Rapids lock	Robert Barclay	1837 – 9	76,346	Abandoned
THE UNION YEARS: 1841 – 67				
Locks				
Lindsay	Board of Works	1842 – 4		
Whitla's Rapids	Board of Works	1842 – 4		
Hastings	Board of Works	1842 – 4		
Chisholm's Rapids	Board of Works	1842 – 4		
Dams				
Frankford	Board of Works	1842 – 4		
Fiddler's Island	Board of Works	1842 – 4		
Crowe Bay	Board of Works	1842 – 4		
Healey Falls	Board of Works	1842 – 4		

Works	Contractor	Duration of Contract	Contract Price ($)	Final Cost ($)
Slides				
Buckhorn	Board of Works	1842 – 5		
Hastings	Board of Works	1842 – 5		
Healey Falls	Board of Works	1842 – 5		
Crowe Bay	Board of Works	1842 – 5		
Ranney Falls	Board of Works	1842 – 5		
Booms				
Crowe Bay	Board of Works	1845		
Percy Boom	Board of Works	1845		
Bridges				
Bobcaygeon	Board of Works	1842 – 4		
Lindsay	Board of Works	1842 – 4		
Buckhorn	Board of Works	1842 – 4		
Peterborough	Board of Works	1842 – 4	↓	↓
Hastings	Board of Works	1842 – 4		
Campbellford	Board of Works	1842 – 4	(200,000)	(410,395*)

THE MACDONALD YEARS: 1867 – 96

Works	Contractor	Duration of Contract	Contract Price ($)	Final Cost ($)
Ontario (Provincial) Works				
Lindsay	Thomas Walters	1870 – 1	16,000	21,000
Young's Point	McDonnell and McDonald	1870 – 1	26,950	27,000
Rosedale	William Whiteside	1869 – 73	19,800	22,000
Locks				
Fenelon Falls	A.F. Manning and Co.	1882 – 5	105,700	114,355
Buckhorn	George Goodwin	1883 – 7	67,280	108,138
Burleigh and Lovesick	George Goodwin	1884 – 7	155,926	268,676
Dams				
Young's Point	Charles Wynn	1884 – 6	Unknown	12,600
Lakefield	Charles Wynn	1884 – 6	Unknown	17,750
Bridges				
Fenelon Falls	Robert Waddell	1887 – 9	Unknown	14,830
Buckhorn				
Burleigh Falls				
Lock Gates				
Fenelon Falls	Charles Wynn	1887	Unknown	11,175
Buckhorn	George Goodwin	1887	Unknown	20,356
Burleigh				
Lovesick				

408   Appendix

Works	Contractor	Duration of Contract	Contract Price ($)	Final Cost ($)
THE LAURIER YEARS: 1896 – 1911				
Peterborough-Lakefield Division				
Section 1	Brown, Love and Aylmer	1895 – 9	363,000	423,208
Section 2	Corry and Laverdure	1896 – 9	Unknown	300,538
Peterborough	Corry and Laverdure	1899 – 1903	Open	354,899
lift lock	Dominion Bridge Co.	1902 – 4	244,000	244,000
Simcoe – Balsam Lake Division				
Section 1	Andrew Onderdonk	1895 – 1900	492,000	483,874
Section 2	Larkin and Sangster	1900 – 7	Unknown	419,823
	Dominion Bridge Co.	1905 – 7	297,300	297,300
Section 3	Brown, Love and Aylmer	1900 – 7	Unknown	505,550
Additional Costs of the Above Two Divisions				
Bridges and road diversions				150,000
Land purchase and flood damage				193,000
Survey and engineering				350,278
Legal, court, land evaluation				25,285
Cement				451,415
Holland River Division				
Section 1	Simcoe Dredging Co.	1906	46,497	Abandoned
Section 2	York Construction	1908 – 12	652,000	Cancelled
Total cost (construction, land purchase, surveying, engineering)				818,642
Ontario – Rice Lake Division				
Section 1	Larkin and Sangster	1907 – 14	969,237	1,106,883
Section 2	Rogers and Dennon	1908 – 18	618,804	774,038
Section 3	Canadian General Development Co. Fred A. Robinson	1908 – 18	289,520	302,803
Section 4	Haney, Quinlan and Robertson	1910 – 18	1,428,466	1,286,496
Section 5	Brown, Love and Aylmer	1907 – 9	551,688	631,232
Section 6	Haney, Quinlan and Robertson	1910 – 18	525,000	465,089
Section 7	Randolph Macdonald Co.	1909 – 16	429,097	460,029

Major Construction Projects on the Trent Canal   409

Works	Contractor	Duration of Contract	Contract Price ($)	Final Cost ($)
Additional Costs of the Above Two Divisions				
Lock gates				136,923
Lock valves				117,892
Bridges				202,641
Flood damage and land purchase				99,255
Survey and engineering				1,107,550
Cement				711,347

THE BORDEN YEARS: 1911 – 20

Works	Contractor	Duration of Contract	Contract Price ($)	Final Cost ($)
Severn River Division				
Port Severn lock	York Construction	1913 – 15	130,000	137,000
Section 1	York Construction	1919 – 20	Cost plus 8%	441,760
Section 2	Inland Construction Co.	1914 – 17	712,258	682,000
Section 3	Randolph Macdonald Co.	1914 – 17	910,140	573,574
	Randolph Macdonald Co.	1919 – 20	Cost plus 8%	429,104
Big Chute marine railway	York Construction	1916 – 18	Cost plus 10%	11,016
Swife Rapids marine railway	York Construction	1919	Cost plus 8%	10,000
Additional Costs				
Lock valves				34,951
Operating machines for locks				17,941
Bridges				102,253

TOTAL COSTS: 1833 – 1923

Works				Final Cost ($)
Construction				19,027,762
Maintenance				3,203,099
Operation				1,136,986

* Costs of individual works not available.

Notes

CHAPTER ONE

1 Upper Canada, *Statutes, 1833*, 3 Wm. IV, c. 33, An Act to Provide for the Improvement of Certain Inland Waters in the District of Newcastle.
2 Ibid.
3 Ibid.
4 W.A. Langton, *Early Days*, 78.
5 Robinson, "Report," in Guillet, *Valley of the Trent*, 122.
6 *Cobourg Star*, 8 October 1833.
7 Upper Canada, *Journals of the House of Assembly*, 1836, Appendix 124.
8 Langton, *Early Days*, 99.
9 John Bannister to the Lieutenant Governor, 15 December 1820, in Guillet, *Valley of the Trent*, 146.
10 Upper Canada, *Journals, 1832 – 33*, 220.
11 *Cobourg Star*, 31 July 1833.
12 Ibid.
13 Traill, *The Backwoods of Canada*, 95.
14 Need, "Six Years in the Bush," in Guillet, *Valley of the Trent*, 389.
15 Upper Canada, *Journals, 1832 – 33*, 220.
16 Archives of Ontario (AO), Thomas Need Papers, Need Diary, 1832, Appendix B.
17 Upper Canada, *Journals, 1836*, Appendix 124.
18 Need, *Six Years in the Bush*, 65.
19 Upper Canada, *Journals, 1833 – 34*, Appendix 222.

CHAPTER TWO

1 Upper Canada, *Journals, 1833 – 34*, Appendix 205.
2 Ibid., 22.
3 Ibid.
4 W.A. Langton, *Early Days*, 98.
5 AO, Robinson Papers, James G. Bethune to Peter Robinson, 19 May 1836.
6 Ibid., Bethune to Robinson, 2 August 1834.
7 Langton, *Early Days*, 141.

8 AO, Robinson Papers, Bethune to Robinson, 5 August 1834.

9 Guillet, *Valley of the Trent*, 296.

10 AO, Robinson Papers, Bethune to Robinson, 5 August 1834.

11 Langton, *Early Days*, 56.

12 AO, Thomas Need Papers, Need Diary, 11 June 1834.

13 Ibid., 4 November 1834.

14 Ibid., 5 November 1834.

15 Ibid., 8 November 1834.

16 Baird, "Report no. 12," in Guillet, *Valley of the Trent*, 166.

17 Ibid.

18 Langton, *Early Days*, 173.

19 AO, Need Diary, May 1833.

20 AO, Robinson Papers, Bethune to Robinson, 28 September 1833.

21 Upper Canada, *Journals, 1836*, Appendix 124.

22 Ibid.

23 The village was named Rockeby by Sir John Colborne during a visit in 1834; the name was later changed to Bobcaygeon.

24 AO, Robinson Papers, Bethune to Robinson, 19 May 1836.

CHAPTER THREE

1 Public Archives of Canada (PAC), Upper Canada Sundries, RG 5, AL, vol. 135, 74128.

2 Upper Canada, *Journals, 1832*, 7 November.

3 Upper Canada, *Journals, 1833*, 13 February, 121.

4 *Cobourg Star*, 14 September 1833.

5 Baird, "Report no. 12," in Guillet, *Valley of the Trent*, 152.

6 Ibid.

7 Ibid.

8 Ibid., 159.

9 Ibid., 160.

10 PAC, RG 5, AL, vol. 154, 73580 – 2, Richard Bullock to Rowan, 4 October 1833.

11 PAC, RG 5, AL, vol. 134, 73923, Baird to Rowan, 30 October 1833.

12 *Cobourg Star*, 30 October 1833.

13 PAC, RG 5, AL, vol. 135, 74291 – 6, Bullock to Rowan (undated).

14 Upper Canada, *Journals, 1834*, 7 January.

15 Ibid., 87.

16 Upper Canada, *Journals, 1833 – 34*, Appendix, 154.

17 W.A. Langton, *Early Days*, 129.

18 Ibid.

19 Upper Canada, *Journals, 1835*, 26 January.

20 Upper Canada, *Journals, 1835*, 404.

21 *Cobourg Star*, 8 July 1835.

22 Ibid.

23 Ibid., 26 August 1835.

24 Ibid., 8 July 1835.

25 Upper Canada, *Journals, 1836*, Appendix, Report no. 12.

26 AO, Simcoe Papers, Vol. 3, 227.

27 *Cobourg Star*, 23 December 1835.

28 Kingston, *Chronicle*, quoted in ibid., 20 January 1836.
29 *Cobourg Star*, 26 January 1836.
30 Upper Canada, *Journals, 1836*, 3 February.
31 Ibid.
32 Upper Canada, *Journals, 1836*, 3 March.
33 Ibid.
34 Ibid.
35 Ibid.
36 Upper Canada, *Journals, 1837*, Appendix no. 12.
37 Ibid.
38 PAC, RG 5, AL, vol. 135, 96,730 – 2, George S. Boulton to J. Joseph, 7 April 1837.
39 Upper Canada, *Statutes, 1837*, 7 Wm. IV, c. 66, An Act granting to His Majesty a sum of money, to be raised by Debenture, for improvement of the navigation of the River Trent.
40 PAC, RG 5, AL, vol. 135, 96,730 – 2 , Boulton to Joseph, 7 April 1837.

CHAPTER FOUR

1 Upper Canada, *Statutes, 1836*, 6 Wm IV, c. 39, An Act to Improve the Navigation of the Inland Waters of the District of Newcastle.
2 PAC, RG 5, AL, vol. 185, George S. Boulton to J. Joseph, 1 June 1837.
3 AO, Baird Papers, Thomas McNeil to N.H. Baird, 15 December 1837.
4 Ibid., Report of Sidey and Craigie to the Commissioners for Improvements on the Inland Waters of the Newcastle District, 14 February 1840.
5 Ibid.
6 Ibid., Report of N.H. Baird to the Commissioners for Improvements on the Inland Waters of the Newcastle District, 10 September 1839.
7 Ibid., Report of Sidey and Craigie to the Commissioners, 14 February 1840.
8 Ibid.
9 Ibid., Report of Baird to the Commissioners, 10 September 1839.
10 Ibid.
11 PAC, Records of the Department of Railways and Canals, RG 43, B2(a). vol. 222, file 18344, Report of Baird to the Commissioners, 7 July 1837.
12 Ibid., 18 August 1837.
13 Ibid., 22 August 1837.
14 PAC, Records of the Department of Public Works, RG 11, vol. 69, file 122, Report of Baird to the Commissioners, 11 November 1837.
15 Ibid.
16 AO, Baird Papers, McNeil to Baird, 2 February 1838.
17 Ibid.
18 Ibid.
19 Ibid., McNeil to Baird (undated).
20 PAC, RG 43, B2(a), vol. 222, file 18344, Report of Baird to the Commissioners, 27 June 1838.
21 Ibid., Baird to the Commissioners, 6 August, 1838.
22 AO, Baird Papers, Minutes: Board of Commissioners for Improvements on the Inland Waters of the Newcastle District, 11 August 1838.
23 Ibid., Baird to McNeil, 5 January 1839.

24 Ibid., McNeil to Baird, 4 December 1838.
25 Ibid., Specifications for the Buckhorn Dam (undated).
26 PAC, RG 43, B2(a), vol. 222, file 18344, Report Baird to Commissioners, 27 June 1838.
27 Upper Canada, *Journals, 1839 – 40*, Appendix, 266.
28 AO, Baird Papers, Thomas Carr and Samuel Walles to the Commissioners, 31 August 1838.
29 Ibid., David Brodie to Baird, 8 November 1838.
30 W.A. Langton, *Early Days*, 48.
31 Upper Canada, *Journals, 1836*, Appendix, Report no. 13.
32 Ibid.
33 Ibid.
34 Upper Canada, *Journals, 1839*, Appendix, Report of the Commissioners for Improvement to the Navigation of the Inland Waters of the Newcastle District.
35 PAC, RG 43, B2(a), vol. 222, file 18344, Report of Baird to the Commissioners for Improvement to the Navigation of the Newcastle District.
36 Upper Canada, *Journals, 1839*, ibid.
37 Upper Canada, *Journals, 1840*, Appendix, 266, Report of Commissioners on the Improvement of the Navigation of the Inland Waters.
38 AO, Baird Papers, Baird to Mr. Shea, 10 November 1837.
39 H.H. Langton (ed), *A Gentlewoman in Upper Canada*, 41.
40 AO, Baird Papers, McNeil to Baird, 1 March 1838.
41 *Cobourg Star*, 9 December 1835.

CHAPTER FIVE

1 Upper Canada, *Statutes, 1837*, 7 Wm. IV c. 66, An Act granting to His Majesty a sum of money to be raised by Debenture, for Improvement of the navigation of the Trent River.
2 PAC, RG 43, B2(a), vol. 222, file 18344, Minutes: Board of Commissioners for Improvements on the River Trent, 2 September 1837.
3 Ibid.
4 AO, Baird Papers, Boulton to Baird, 2 September 1837.
5 Ibid.
6 Ibid., John Cliff to Baird, 21 December 1837.
7 PAC, RG 43, B2(a), vol. 222, file 18344, Report of Baird to the Commissioners, 14 January 1837.
8 Upper Canada, *Journals, 1840*, Appendix, 256, Report of the Commissioners for Improvements on the River Trent.
9 Ibid., 262.
10 AO, Baird Papers, Boulton to the Secretary of the Lieutenant Governor, 8 November 1840.
11 Upper Canada, *Journals, 1840*, Appendix, 255, Report of Commissioners for Improvements on the River Trent.
12 Ibid.

13 Ibid., 256.
14 PAC, RG 43, B2(a), vol. 222, file 18344, Report of Baird to the Commissioners, 2 July 1838.

CHAPTER SIX

1 PAC, RG 5, AL, vol. 208, J.H. Dunn to the Honourable John Macaulay, 5 November 1838.
2 Canada (Province), *Journals, 1844 – 45*, vol. 4, 113, Return of an Address from the Legislative Assembly.
3 PAC, Records of the Department of Public Works, RG 11, vol. 69, file 122, Minutes: Board of Commissioners for Improvements on the River Trent, 16 April 1838.
4 Ibid.
5 Ibid.
6 AO, Baird Papers, Report of Baird to the Commissioners, 17 April 1838.
7 W.A. Langton, *Early Days*, 193.
8 PAC, RG 5, AL, vol. 208, 114997, Cartwright, McDonell, and Boulton to Macaulay, 30 October 1838.
9 PAC, RG 5, AL, vol. 209, 115267, Dunn to Macaulay, 9 November 1838.
10 AO, Baird Papers, Boulton to Baird, 27 April 1839.
11 PAC, RG 11, vol. 77, file 169, Report of Baird to the Commissioners, 22 July 1839.
12 Ibid.
13 PAC, RG 43, B2(a), vol. 222, file 18344, Baird to the Commissioners, 12 August 1839.
14 AO, Baird Papers, Minutes: Board of Commissioners Meeting, 31 October 1839.
15 Ibid.
16 Ibid.
17 Ibid.
18 PAC, RG 43, B2(a), vol. 222, file 18344, Baird to the Commissioners, 8 July 1840.
19 AO, Baird Papers, Charles Green to Baird, 3 July 1841.
20 PAC, RG 11, vol. 69, file 122, Boulton to Thomas Begley, 2 December 1841.
21 Ibid., Boulton to the Honourable G.B. Harrison, 1 December 1841.
22 Traill, *The Backwoods of Canada*, 94.
23 Langton, *Early Days*, 52.

CHAPTER SEVEN

1 H.H. Langton (ed), *A Gentlewoman in Upper Canada*, 154.
2 Ibid., 152.
3 Canada (Province), *Statutes, 1841 – 42*, 4 and 5 Vic., c. 38, An Act to repeal certain Ordinances therein mentioned and to establish a Board of Works in this Province.

4 *Cobourg Star*, 4 November 1840.
5 Davin, *The Irishman in Canada*, 434.
6 Ibid.
7 Ibid.
8 Ibid.
9 For complete details of the Public Works program, see Canada *Journals, 1841*, Appendix c.c.
10 Canada (Province), *Journals, 1844 – 45*, Appendix AA.
11 W.A. Langton, *Early Days*, 24.
12 Canada (Province), *Journals, 1843*, Appendix Q.
13 PAC, RG 11, vol. 70, Petition from the Residents of the District of Newcastle to the Governor-General, 20 July 1841.
14 Canada (Province), *Journals, 1844 – 45*, Appendix AA.
15 Ibid.
16 AO, Baird Papers, Begley to Baird, 24 January 1842.
17 Considerable sums were also paid for damages caused by flooding of land and damage to mill property. This would be a common practice until the canal was finished in 1920. Of the $23,650 paid on 21 claims in 1845, John Gilchrist received $11,315. George Boulton did well, too. A large landholder, Boulton received thousands of dollars through the years for flood damages.
18 Canada (Province), *Journals, 1846*, Appendix o.
19 When John Langton became auditor-general in 1855 he discovered that conditions had not changed much in the Board of Public Works. He found the administration of the board in a dreadful mess, with corruption of the grossest kind prevailing. See Langton, *Early Days*, 269 – 70.
20 AO, Baird Papers, Walter Croften to Hamilton Killaly, 22 October 1842.
21 Ibid., Wilson to Begley, 24 September 1843.
22 Ibid., Begley to Baird, 2 September 1842.
23 As an example of how costs increased under the Board of Works, the wooden lock contracted for by Homer Hecox in 1838 for $12,000 cost $34,510 to build just six years later.

CHAPTER EIGHT

1 Baird in Guillet, *Valley of the Trent*, 185.
2 Ibid.
3 PAC, RG 43, vol. 222, Thomas Wilson to Killaly, 14 April 1845.
4 Ibid., Wilson to Begley, 17 May 1845.
5 John White lost his leg but recovered from the accident. He was recommended for a pension by the Board of Works on account of being "disabled from earning a livelyhood [sic]"; but the recommendation was turned down by the executive council (PAC, RG 11, vol. 19).
6 Bonnycastle, *Canada and the Canadians*, 235.
7 AO, Baird Papers, Baird to Killaly, 13 November 1843.
8 Ibid.
9 Ibid., Minutes of the Board of Works, 19 April 1845.

10 Ibid., Hawley to Adam Baird, 12 March 1844.

11 Ibid., Sir Dominick Daly to N.H. Baird, 3 June 1844.

12 Ibid., N.H. Baird to Killaly, 13 November 1843.

13 On 17 February 1845, a select committee of the legislature did award Baird $350 for expenses incurred in attending a meeting of the house of assembly prior to Union.

CHAPTER NINE

1 The St Lawrence canals were completed in 1848.

2 PAC, Minutes of the Executive Council, Canada, RG 1, Order-in-Council, 20 February 1855.

3 Canada (Province), *Journals, 1844 – 45*, Appendix AA.

4 PAC, RG 43 B2(a), vol. 222, file 18344, Wilson to Begley, 17 May 1845.

5 Canada (Province), *Journals, 1847*, Appendix QQ.

6 Ibid.

7 Canada (Province), *Journals, 1851*, Appendix CC.

8 Canada (Province), *Journals, 1854*, Appendix O.

9 Ibid.

10 Ibid.

11 Ibid.

12 By 1859 British imports of squared timber from the Baltic exceeded imports from British North America for the first time since 1816.

13 PAC, RG 11, vol. 191, James Cumming to the Secretary of the Department of Public Works, 24 July 1866.

14 Ibid.

15 The six lumbermen named to the management committee were James Cumming of Trenton, Henry Fowlds of Hastings, E.W. Myers of Trenton, Charles Perry of Peterborough, Ronald Campbell of Colborne, and Charles Townsend of Percy.

16 PAC, RG 11, vol. 191, G.F. Baillarge to the Secretary of the Department of Public Works, 16 March 1866.

17 PAC, RG 1, Order-in-Council, 22 April 1857.

18 PAC, RG 11, vol. 191, Baillarge to the Secretary of the Department of Public Works, 16 March 1866.

19 When the Conservative government of John A. Macdonald was defeated in 1873, the committee members resigned and a new committee was appointed by Alexander Mackenzie.

20 PAC, RG 11, vol. 191, Minutes of the Lumbermen's Committee, 11 August 1870.

CHAPTER TEN

1 Canada (Province), *Journals, 1844 – 45*, Appendix AA.

2 For complete details of Lyon's survey and Keefer's revision see Canada (Province), *Journals, 1844 – 45*, Appendix AA.

3 PAC, RG 11, vol. 189, George Ranney to the Secretary, Department of Public Works, 18 December 1862.
4 Ibid., Samuel Keefer to John Rose, 18 July 1860.
5 Ibid.
6 Henry Foulds bought James Crooks's mills, water powers, and property in 1851 and changed the name of the village of Crooks' Rapids to Hastings.
7 PAC, RG 11, vol. 191, Ranney to F. Braun, 31 July 1866.
8 PAC, RG 11, vol. 192, Ranney to Braun, 17 September 1867.
9 Ibid., Petition from the Cobourg, Peterborough and Marmora Railway and Mining Company to the Department of Public Works, 17 September 1867.
10 Ibid., John Beatty to Fred Boseville, 14 September 1867.
11 Ibid., John Page to the Secretary, Department of Public Works, 1 October 1867.
12 PAC, RG 11, vol. 192, Captain A. Mills, Captain George Crandell, Captain George Rose, and Captain John Turner to Ranney (no date).
13 PAC, RG 11, vol. 191, Ranney to the Secretary, Department of Public Works, 9 August 1866.

CHAPTER ELEVEN

1 Canada, *Sessional Papers, 1877*, Paper no. 36, Order-in-Council, 15 March 1870.
2 PAC, RG 11, vol. 192, Joseph Bigelow to William McDougall, 15 April 1868.
3 Ibid.
4 Ibid., Petition from Bigelow and others to His Excellency the Right Honourable Charles Stanley Viscount Monck, 13 May 1868.
5 Ibid., Memo from McDougall to J.H. Langevin, 16 May 1868.
6 Ontario, *Sessional Papers, 1869*, Paper no. 6, Report of T.N. Molesworth.
7 PAC, RG 11, vol. 192, Bigelow to the Minister of Public Works, 4 November 1869.
8 Ibid.
9 PAC, RG 11, vol. 192, Bigelow to McDougall, 18 June 1869.
10 Ibid., Petition from the Port Whitby and Port Perry Railway Company to His Excellency Sir John Young, 11 May 1869.
11 Ontario, *Sessional Papers, 1870*, Paper no. 2, Report of T.N. Molesworth.
12 In 1844 Kivas Tully emigrated from Ireland to Toronto, where for many years he practised architecture and engineering. Many public buildings in Ontario were designed by him. In 1847 his first wife, Elizabeth Drew, died. In 1852, he married Maria Strickland, daughter of Lt.-Col. Samuel Strickland.
13 Strickland, *Twenty-Seven Years in Canada West*, 228.
14 AO, Records of the Ontario Department of Public Works, RG 15, S-1, Molesworth to the Honourable John Carling, 23 February 1871.
15 Ontario, *Statutes, 1872*, 35 Vic., c. 53, An Act to Incorporate the Gull Waters Improvement Company.
16 AO, RG 15, S-1, Petition from Mossom Boyd et al. to the Ontario Commissioner of Public Works (undated).
17 Ibid., Boyd to Thomas Fairbairn, 25 January 1873.

1 AO, Need Papers, Mossom Boyd to Thomas Need, 6 July 1881.
2 Mossom Boyd arrived in Canada in 1834 at the age of 19. He settled on Sturgeon Lake, becoming the only original settler to remain in the area. After engaging in the square timber trade, for a time in partnership with John Langton, Boyd bought Thomas Need's mills at Bobcaygeon in 1849. He died in 1883 . His business was taken over by his oldest son, Mossom M. Boyd, who is often confused in the literature with his father.
3 Joseph Keeler was elected in the general elections of 1867 and 1872 but was defeated by the Liberal, Charles Biggar, in 1874. In 1878 he was swept back into power in the Macdonald victory.
4 James Ferris was the postmaster in Cambellford. He was first elected to the Ontario legislature in January 1875 but was unseated on a petition in October. He was re-elected (in a by-election) in November and again in 1879.
5 Toronto *Globe*, 19 February 1879.
6 Canada, *Debates*, 24 February 1879, 104.
7 Canada, *Sessional Papers, 1879*, no. 35, Report of C.F. Fraser to the Lieutenant Governor in Council, 3 October 1878.
8 Canada, *Statutes, 1867*, 31 Vic., c. 12, Public Works Act of Canada.
9 Ibid.
10 Canada, *Debates*, 2 April 1879, 904.
11 PAC, RG 11, vol. 190, Petition from the Residents of Seymour to the Governor General in Council, 16 August 1865.
12 The ridings of Victoria East and West, Peterborough East and West, Northumberland East and West, Durham East, and Hastings East had replaced Liberals with Conservatives in the 1878 dominion election. Only in Hastings West and Durham West did Liberals manage to hold their seats.
13 Canada, House of Commons, *Debates*, 2 April 1879, 905.
14 Ontario, *Statutes, 1874*, 37 Vic., c. 80, An Act to Incorporate the Huron Trent Valley Canal Company.
15 Canada, *Debates*, 2 April 1879, 907.
16 Ibid.
17 Ibid., 908.
18 Ibid.
19 Ibid., 909.
20 Ibid., 912.
21 Ibid.
22 Ibid.
23 Ibid.
24 The figure quoted by Macdonald was for construction of all the works including those above Rice Lake, thus adding to the confusion in the mind of the public as to how many of the dominion works had actually been transferred to Ontario. The transfer order included only the works on the Trent River.
25 Canada, *Debates*, 2 April 1879, 912.
26 PAC, RG 11, vol. 522, David Gilmour to the Minister of Public Works, 17 March 1879.

27 Ibid., Petition from Mossom Boyd et al. to Sir John A. Macdonald (undated).
28 Canada, *Debates*, 2 April 1879, 913.
29 Ibid.
30 Canada, *Journals of the House of Commons, 1879*, Appendix no. 3, Report of the Select Committee Appointed to Examine the Transfer of the Trent River Works to Ontario, 10 May 1879.
31 Ibid.
32 Ibid.
33 Joseph Keeler, who served as chairman of the committee, became trapped in a political backlash. Although he fully concurred with the general recommendation of the committee, he was obliged to dissent from the recommendation regarding the retention of the dam at Chisholm's Rapids because the committee had received a petition from 238 of Keeler's constituents, asking that the dam be removed even if the dominion government repossessed it.

CHAPTER THIRTEEN

1 PAC, RG 11, vol. 522, Report of D. Stark upon the Navigation of the River Trent, 20 August 1879.
2 Ibid.
3 Ibid.
4 Toronto *Tribune*, quoted in the Peterborough *Examiner*, 6 November 1879.
5 PAC, Sir John A. Macdonald Papers, MG 26 A, 167576, Henry H. Smith to Sir John A. Macdonald, 12 November 1879.
6 Peterborough *Examiner*, 25 December 1879.
7 PAC, RG 43. B1(a), vol. 292, A. McQuade to Sir Charles Tupper, 27 November 1880.
8 Canada, *Journals, 1879*, Appendix no. 3, Report of Select Committee, 10 May 1879.
9 Peterborough *Examiner*, 10 June 1880.
10 Ibid., 3 June 1880.
11 Ibid., 10 June 1880.
12 PAC, RG 43, B1(a), vol. 292, Joseph Keeler to the Honourable Mackenzie Bowell, 15 October 1880.
13 Ibid.
14 Peterborough *Examiner*, 31 March 1881.
15 Ibid., quoted in the *Debates* of the House of Commons, 15 February 1882.
16 PAC, Macdonald Papers, vol. 323, 145982, Petition to Sir John A. Macdonald from the Counties of Peterborough, Hastings, Victoria and Northumberland 28 March 1881.
17 Canada, *Sessional Papers, 1885*, Paper no. 96, F. Braun to John Page, 31 March 1881.
18 Barrie *Gazette*, 1 November 1879.
19 Toronto *Tribune*, quoted in the Peterborough *Examiner*, 6 November 1879.
20 PAC, Macdonald Papers, vol. 381, 177446, John Carnegie to Macdonald, 26 December 1881.
21 Ibid.

22 Canada, *Sessional Papers, 1885*, Paper no. 96, Tom S. Rubidge to Braun, 20 February 1882.
23 Ibid., T. Matchett to Tupper, 6 February 1882.
24 Ibid., Rubidge to Braun, 20 March 1882.
25 Ibid., Report of a Committee of the Privy Council approved by the Governor General in Council, 17 April 1882.
26 Ibid.

CHAPTER FOURTEEN

1 Canada, *Sessional Papers, 1885*, Paper no. 8, Report of Tom S. Rubidge.
2 PAC, Macdonald Papers, vol. 228, 97207, Hector Langevin to Macdonald, 16 August 1882.
3 PAC, RG 43, B1(a), vol. 293, A.F. Manning to A.P. Bradley, 3 September 1885.
4 Canada, *Sessional Papers, 1885*, no. 8, Report of Tom S. Rubidge.
5 Trent-Severn Waterway Office (hereafter TSWO), Statement of Quantities prepared by J.A. Aylmer, 15 June 1887.
6 TSWO, Aylmer to David Stark, 20 December 1887.
7 Canada, *Sessional Papers, 1885*, no. 8, Report of Tom S. Rubidge.
8 The three small locks built by the Ontario government in the Muskoka Lakes in the 1870s were located in granite, but these were formed of rock-filled timber cribs and like the Rosedale locks required little or no excavation.
9 PAC, RG 43, B1(a), vol. 294, George Goodwin to Bradley, 7 December 1887.
10 Ibid.
11 Ibid.
12 Strickland, *Twenty-Seven Years in Canada West*, 237
13 Guillet, *Valley of the Trent*, 165.
14 Ibid.
15 Strickland, *Twenty-Seven Years in Canada West*, 238.
16 The Burleigh locks were replaced with a single-lift lock in 1968.
17 PAC, RG 43, B1(a), vol. 293, Goodwin to Bradley, 1 April 1885.
18 Ibid., 9 May 1885.
19 Ibid., Telegram Rubidge to Bradley, 20 April 1885.
20 Ibid., Goodwin to Bradley, 10 July 1885.
21 Ibid., Page to Bradley, 23 July 1885.
22 Canada, *Sessional Papers, 1886*, no. 13, Report of Tom S. Rubidge.
23 In addition to being paid the exorbitant price of $5,000 for the old dam at Lakefield, in a ruinous condition, Roland Strickland was paid $750 for flood damages.
24 Chalmers received $5,500 for the Young's Point dam, also in dilapidated condition.
25 Canada, *Sessional Papers, 1886*, no. 13, Report of Tom S. Rubidge.
26 Peterborough *Examiner*, 12 March 1885.
27 Ibid.
28 Ibid.
29 PAC, RG 43, B1(a), vol. 293, George Hilliard to Henry John Pope, 3 August 1885.

30 Ibid.
31 Ibid.
32 PAC, RG 43, B1(a), vol. 293, Goodwin to Bradley, 12 August 1885.
33 Ibid., 24 August 1885.
34 PAC, RG 43, B1(a), vol. 294, Goodwin to Bradley, 8 April 1886.
35 Ibid., 30 April 1886.
36 Ibid.
37 PAC, RG 43, B1(a), vol. 293, Goodwin to Bradley, 12 April 1885.
38 PAC, RG 43, B1(a), vol. 294, Goodwin to Bradley, 26 August 1885.

CHAPTER FIFTEEN

1 Peterborough *Daily Examiner*, 5 April 1883.
2 Ibid., 7 February 1884.
3 Ibid., 27 August 1885.
4 Ibid., 25 February 1886.
5 Toronto *World*, 16 February 1887.
6 Ibid.
7 Ibid.
8 A.L. Killaly, superintendent of the Trent Canal 1914 – 35, was Hamilton Killaly's grandson.
9 The seven-and-a-half-mile-long Murray Canal connects Presquille Bay and the Bay of Quinte. Designed to shorten the distance from Cobourg to Trenton, the canal turned historic Prince Edward county into an island. The canal was dug between 1882 and 1889.
10 Peterborough *Daily Examiner*, 27 August 1885.
11 Ibid., 25 February 1885.
12 PAC, Macdonald Papers, 206302, T.M. Cabe to Macdonald, 8 March 1886.
13 Ibid., 206410, R.C. Strickland to Macdonald, 12 March 1886.
14 Ibid., 205740, Strickland to Macdonald, 13 February 1886.
15 Ibid., 205744, John Henry Pope to Macdonald, 16 February 1886.
16 Ibid., 205740, Strickland to Macdonald, 19 February 1886.
17 Ibid., 96370, C.S. Malers to Mr. Kirkpatrick, 9 January 1887.
18 Ibid.
19 Ibid., 215741, Emma Rubidge to Macdonald, 21 February 1887.
20 Ibid.
21 Ibid., 215709, Strickland to Macdonald, 19 February 1887.
22 Ibid., 215709, Macdonald to Strickland, 19 February 1887.
23 TSWO, Aylmer to Stark, 15 April 1887.
24 PAC, RG 43, B1(a), vol. 295, Rubidge to the Secretary, Department of Railways and Canals, 20 March 1887.
25 PAC, Macdonald Papers, 62531, Petition presented to the Government by the Trent Valley Canal Association, 15 June 1887.
26 PAC, RG 43, B1(a), vol. 295, Page to Rubidge, 1 September 1887.
27 Ibid., Rubidge to Page, 3 September 1887.
28 Peterborough *Daily Examiner*, 19 January 1888.
29 Ibid., 26 December 1887.
30 TSWO, Survey Report of David Stark, January 1885.

CHAPTER SIXTEEN

1 PAC, RG 43, B1(a), vol. 295, James Stevenson to Pope, 20 September 1887.
2 Canada, *Debates*, 15 May 1888, 1458.
3 Ibid.
4 Canada, *Sessional Papers, 1892*, no. 47, Report of the Commissioners Appointed to Consider the Advisability of Extending the Trent Canal and to what Extent.
5 PAC, RG 43, B1(a), vol. 295, Order-in-Council, 16 January 1886.
6 Canada, *Debates*, 15 May 1888, 1458.
7 Toronto *World*, 16 December 1887.
8 Ibid.
9 TSWO, Report of R.B. Rogers, 15 July 1887.
10 Barrie, *Northern Advance*, 21 April 1888.
11 Canada, *Sessional Papers, 1891*, no. 10, Report of the Minister of Railways and Canals, 31 December 1890.
12 Canada, *Sessional Papers, 1892*, no. 47.
13 Ibid.
14 Ibid.
15 Ibid.
16 Pope, *Memories*, vol. 2, 336.
17 Toronto, *Empire*, 18 February 1891.
18 Erasmus Wiman was born in Peel county, Upper Canada, in 1834. Originally a journalist with the Toronto *Globe*, in 1860 he joined the staff of R.G. Dunn and Co., a mercantile agency with headquarters in New York. Wiman advanced to become general manager of the company. He was a strong advocate of commercial union between Canada and the United States and is generally credited with being the founder of the unrestricted reciprocity movement. He became a US citizen in 1897 and died in New York in 1904.
19 Pope, *Correspondence*, 485, Macdonald to George Stephen, 31 March 1891.
20 Ibid, 17.
21 Ibid.
22 Saunders, *Life and Letters*, vol. 2, 140, Macdonald to Tupper, 5 June 1890.
23 PAC, Macdonald Papers, 239721, D.R. Murphy to Macdonald, 2 March 1891.
24 Canada, *Debates*, 1 September 1891, 4774.
25 PAC, Macdonald Papers, 27927, Murphy to Macdonald, 18 March 1891.
26 Ibid.
27 Ibid., 251438, Stevenson to Macdonald, 8 April 1891.
28 Canada, *Debates*, 1 September 1891, 4798.
29 Peterborough, *Daily Examiner*, 15 May 1896.
30 Ibid.
31 PAC, Mossom Boyd Papers, MG 28, vol. 155, Rogers to Mossom Boyd, 11 January 1896.

CHAPTER SEVENTEEN

1 PAC, Boyd Papers, MG 28, vol. 155, Rogers to Boyd, 1 October 1896.
2 Ibid.

3 Canada, *Debates*, 5 June 1914, 4942.
4 Beaverton, *Express*, 8 October 1896.
5 Ibid.
6 Cannington *Echo*, 6 November 1896.
7 Ibid.
8 PAC, Boyd Papers, Vol. 155, Andrew G. Blair to Boyd, 31 October 1896.
9 Peterborough *Daily Examiner*, 27 March 1897.
10 Ibid., 7 April 1897.
11 Ibid., 9 April 1897.
12 Ibid.
13 Ibid., 16 April 1898.
14 Ibid.
15 PAC, Boyd Papers, vol. 155, John Carnegie to Boyd, 19 May 1898.
16 Canada, *Debates*, 31 May 1898, 6538.
17 Ibid.
18 PAC, Sir Wilfrid Laurier Papers, MG 26 G, vol. 104, 31308 – 9, Richard Hall, J.R. Stratton, and Peter Hamilton to Sir Wilfrid Laurier, 13 March 1899.
19 Canada, *Debates*, 17 July 1899, 7300.
20 Ibid.
21 Ibid., 7302.
22 PAC, Laurier Papers, vol. 159, 46719, D.G. Sagan to Laurier, 21 June 1900.
23 Canada, *Debates*, 7 February 1900, 156.
24 PAC, RG 43 B2(a), vol. 19, Collingwood Schreiber to R.B. Rogers, 11 January 1900.
25 Ibid., Rogers to Schreiber, 31 January 1900.
26 PAC, Laurier Papers, vol. 163, 47525, Joseph Bigalow to Laurier, 17 July 1900.
27 Ibid., 47526, Laurier to Bigalow, 24 July 1900.

CHAPTER EIGHTEEN

1 Guillet, *Valley of the Trent*, 171.
2 Ibid.
3 Ibid., 172.
4 Peterborough *Review*, 20 January 1888.
5 The original locks were still in operation at the time of writing (1984), but the timber dams were replaced by concrete structures in 1922.
6 Canada, *Sessional Papers, 1898*, no. 10, Report of R.B. Rogers to Collingwood Schreiber.
7 Rogers, "Trent Canal," 202.

CHAPTER NINETEEN

1 Originally water was used as the hydraulic in the Peterborough and Kirkfield lift locks, after the fashion of the prototype at Anderton.
2 Ontario, *Journals, 1879*, Appendix no. 2, Report of the Select Company Committee on the Huron and Ontario Ship Canal.

3 For a full description of the specifications and construction techniques of the Peterborough lift lock see Walter J. Francis, "Mechanical Locks."
4 PAC, Laurier Papers, vol. 309, 83379 – 98, Specifications of the Work to be done on Section no. 2 of the Peterborough-Lakefield Division (no date).
5 Ibid.
6 AO, (Uncatalogued), Testimony given by R.B. Rogers at the Lift Lock Investigation in Peterborough, 18 December 1905.
7 PAC, Laurier Papers, vol. 309, 83405, Collingwood Schreiber to Corry and Laverdure, 23 May 1899.
8 Ibid.
9 Ibid., 83373, Corry and Laverdure to Laurier, 19 December 1903.
10 PAC, Laurier Papers, vol. 305, 82482 – 3, Corry and Laverdure to Rogers, 28 July 1900.
11 Ibid., 82473 – 5, Corry and Laverdure to Schreiber, 16 October 1900.
12 PAC, RG 43, B3(c), vol. 8, Rogers to Schreiber, 30 July 1904.
13 Ibid., 21 May 1904.
14 Ibid., 21 June 1904.
15 Toronto, *Globe*, 11 July 1904.
16 Ibid.
17 Ibid.
18 Ibid.
19 Ibid.
20 Ibid.
21 Ibid.

CHAPTER TWENTY

1 John Collins, Survey notes 1790, in Guillet, *Valley of the Trent*, 142.
2 Ibid.
3 Lieutenant J.P. Catty's Survey of a Route Between Lake Simcoe and the Ottawa River, 1819, in ibid., 145.
4 Report of Nichol Hugh Baird to Sir John Colborne, December 1835, in ibid., 176.
5 Woodville *Advocate*, 10 June 1880.
6 Ibid., 4 August 1881.
7 Beaverton *Express*, 13 October 1882.
8 Ibid., 3 November 1882.
9 Ibid.
10 Ibid., 10 June 1887.
11 Ibid.
12 Ibid., 3 August 1884.
13 Ibid.
14 Ibid., 17 August 1884.
15 Ibid., 21 December 1894.
16 Ibid., 11 October 1895.
17 PAC, RG 43, B3(c), vol. 9, L.K. Jones to Rogers, 2 September 1905.

18 Ibid., Rogers to M.J. Butler, 30 August 1905.

CHAPTER TWENTY-ONE

1 PAC, Laurier Papers, vol. 205, 38318, E. Musgrove to Sir Wilfrid Laurier, 24 August 1901.
2 Ibid.
3 PAC, Boyd Papers, vol. 156, George McHugh to W.C.T. Boyd, 23 March 1901.
4 Ibid.
5 For a full account of the irregularities and fraudulent practices of the Trent canal office in Peterborough under superintendent McClellan's supervision, see Canada, *Sessional Papers, 1914*, No. 190, Report of the Commission to Investigate the Matter of the Trent Valley Canal.
6 PAC, RG 43, B2(a), vol. 401, Reply of Richard B. Rogers to the Report of Henry Holgate re alleged defects in the construction of the hydraulic locks at Kirkfield and Peterborough.
7 Ibid., vol. 19, Memorial from Hope Township to the Minister of Railways and Canals, 2 August 1904.
8 PAC, Laurier Papers, vol. 373, 99356, J.A. Culverwell to Laurier, 5 July 1905.
9 Port Hope, *Guide*, 5 July 1905.
10 Peterborough *Evening Examiner*, 3 November 1905.
11 PAC, Boyd Papers, vol. 74, Rogers to Willie Boyd, 6 December 1907.
12 PAC, Laurier Papers, vol. 385, 102594, R.R. Hall to Laurier, 30 October 1905.
13 Ibid.
14 Ibid., 102592, Laurier to Hall, 31 October 1905.
15 Ibid., vol. 163, M.J. Haney to Laurier, 22 January 1901.
16 PAC, RG 43, B2(a), vol. 401, Rogers's reply to Holgate Report.
17 Ibid.
18 Peterborough *Evening Examiner*, 6 November 1905.
19 PAC, RG 43, B2(a), vol. 401, Rogers' Reply to Holgate Report.
20 Ibid.
21 PAC, RG 12, vol. 477, Butler to H.R. Emmerson, 28 November 1905.
22 AO, (Uncatalogued), Testimony given by R.B. Rogers at the Lift Lock Investigation in Peterborough, 18 December 1905.
23 PAC, RG 43, B2(a), vol. 401, Henry Holgate to Emmerson, 3 January 1906.
24 PAC, RG 12, vol. 478, Internal Memo, Department of Railways and Canals, 3 January 1906.
25 Canada, *Debates*, 14 May 1906, 3255.
26 PAC, RG 43, B2(a), vol. 401, Holgate to Emmerson, 3 January 1906.
27 Ibid.
28 PAC, RG 43, B2(a), vol. 401, Rogers's reply to Holgate Report.
29 AO, (Uncatalogued), Testimony given by R.B. Rogers at the Lift Lock Investigation in Peterborough, 18 December 1905.
30 PAC, RG 43, B2(a), vol. 401, Holgate to Emmerson, 3 January 1906.
31 Toronto *Globe*, 27 January 1906.
32 Peterborough *Evening Examiner*, 2 February 1906.
33 PAC, RG 43, B2(a), vol. 112, L.K. Jones to Rogers, 14 February 1906.

34 Ibid., Rogers to Jones, 16 February 1906.
35 Ibid., Jones to Rogers, 19 February 1906.
36 Ibid., Rogers to Jones, 19 February 1906.
37 Ibid., Rogers to Emmerson, 29 March 1906.
38 In March, public charges of immorality were made against H.R. Emmerson by George Fowler, MP, from Fredericton, NB. Emmerson proclaimed his innocence, but Laurier dated the letter of resignation 2 April 1906 and Emmerson announced it in the House.
39 PAC, Boyd Papers, vol. 74, Rogers to Willie Boyd, 16 February 1908.
40 PAC, RG 43 B2(a) Vol. 401, Holgate to Frank Cochrane, 18 March 1912.
41 PAC, RG 12, vol. 478, Cochrane to Gus Porter, 13 February 1914.
42 Ibid., Cochrane to Porter, 18 December 1914.
43 Ibid., Rogers to Cochrane, 3 April 1915.
44 Ibid., Holgate to Cochrane, 3 February 1915.
45 Ibid., Charles Keefer, A review of the Construction of the Hydraulic Lift Locks at Kirkfield and Peterborough, 19 November 1914.

CHAPTER TWENTY-TWO

1 Toronto *Globe*, 5 January 1912.
2 PAC, Laurier Papers, vol. 622, 168870 – 4, Sir William Mulock to Sir Wilfrid Laurier, 3 April 1910.
3 Ibid.
4 Ibid.
5 Newmarket *Era*, 16 September 1904.
6 Ibid., 9 September 1904.
7 Ibid., 16 September 1904.
8 Ibid.
9 Ibid.
10 Ibid.
11 Ibid.
12 PAC, Laurier Papers, vol. 352, 94023 – 4, Mulock to Laurier, 23 January 1905.
13 Ibid.
14 PAC, Laurier Papers, vol. 352, 94026, Laurier to Mulock, 26 January 1905.
15 Ibid., vol. 622, 168906 – 8, E.J. Walsh to H.S. Cane, 5 April 1910.
16 Ibid.
17 Ibid.
18 PAC, RG 43, B3(c), vol. 10, M.J. Butler to Alex J. Grant, 20 November 1906.
19 Ibid.
20 *Saturday Night*, 12 September 1908.
21 Orillia *Packet*, 18 February 1909.
22 Newmarket *Express-Herald*, 24 November 1909.
23 Toronto *Mail and Empire*, quoted in Bradford *Witness*, 18 February 1909.
24 Newmarket *Express-Herald*, 28 October 1910.
25 Canada, *Debates*, 23 March 1909, 3114.
26 Ibid.
27 Ibid., 3132.

28 Ibid., 3135.
29 Toronto *Weekly Sun*, quoted in Bradford *Witness*, 15 April 1909.
30 Canada, *Debates*, 6 April 1909, 4049.
31 PAC, Laurier Papers, vol. 619, 168369, Laurier to Mulock, 17 March 1910.
32 Ibid., 168370 – 4, Mulock to Laurier, 3 April 1910.
33 Ibid.
34 Canada, *Debates*, 28 July 1911, 10508.
35 Ibid., 23 March 1909, 3119.
36 Ibid., 3131.
37 PAC, Laurier Papers, vol. 622, 168903 – 8, Walsh to Cane, 5 April 1910.
38 Canada, *Sessional Papers, 1914*, no. 190, Report of the Commission to Investigate the Matter of the Trent Canal.
39 PAC, Laurier Papers, vol. 622, 168903 – 8, Walsh to Cane, 5 April 1910.
40 Ibid.
41 Neither Walsh nor Grant got the chief engineer's position. It was given to W.A. Bowden, a 38-year-old design engineer who had joined the department only in 1908, coming from Haney's Locomotive and Machine Company in Montreal.
42 PAC, Laurier Papers, vol. 622, 168903 – 8, Walsh to Cane, 5 April 1910.
43 Ibid., vol. 659, 179169 – 72, Mulock to Laurier, 3 January 1911.
44 E.J. Walsh to the Honourable George P. Graham, 20 January 1911, recorded in Canada, *Debates*, 28 July 1911, 10475 – 89.
45 Ibid.
46 Although Butler had qualified as a land surveyor in his youth, he later studied law and was called to the bar in Illinois in 1897. Before joining the Department of Railways and Canals he had been manager of the Rathbun Lumber Company at Deseronto. Hence Walsh's disparaging remarks.
47 E.J. Walsh to the Honourable George P. Graham, 20 January 1911, recorded in Canada, *Debates*, 28 July 1911, 10475 – 89.
48 Ibid.
49 Canada, *Debates*, 28 July 1911, 10475 – 89.
50 Ibid.

CHAPTER TWENTY-THREE

1 PAC, RG 43, B2(a), vol. 19, Petition from the City of Toronto to His Excellency the Right Honourable Sir John Gilbert Elliot Murray, 28 April 1904.
2 Ibid., R.R. Hall to H.R. Emmerson, 12 October 1905.
3 Ibid.
4 Toronto *Globe*, 14 October 1904.
5 PAC, Laurier Papers, vol. 339, 90745 – 6, Laurier to A.B. Aylesworth, 13 October 1904.
6 PAC, Laurier Papers, vol. 340, 90996, Laurier to Aylesworth, 14 October 1904.
7 PAC, RG 43 B2(a), vol. 19, M.J. Butler to Emmerson, 26 January 1907.
8 Ibid.
9 Ibid.
10 Ibid., W.J. Doxsee to Laurier, 26 January 1907.
11 PAC, Boyd Papers, vol. 74, R.B. Rogers to Willie Boyd, 13 November 1907.

12 PAC, RG 43, B2(a), vol. 249, L.B. Powers et al. to George P. Graham, 7 May 1910.

CHAPTER TWENTY-FOUR

1 PAC, RG 43, B2(a), vol. 122, W.A. Bowden to A.W. Campbell, 13 May 1910.
2 Canada, *Debates*, 28 July 1911, 10486.
3 Canada, Sessional Papers, *1907 – 08*, Paper no. 154, Royal Commission Quebec Bridge Inquiry, 1907, Minutes of Proceedings, 43.
4 Ibid., 45.
5 Ibid., 9.
6 Ibid., 10.
7 PAC, RG 43, B2(a), vol. 123, J.A. Culverwell to George P. Graham, 26 September 1907.
8 Ibid.
9 Ibid.
10 PAC, RG 43, B2(a), vol. 122, L.K. Jones to A.J. Grant, 14 October 1907.
11 Ibid., vol 124, Grant to Butler, 4 November 1908.
12 Ibid., Grant to Butler, 2 July 1909.
13 Ibid., Grant to Butler, 4 October 1909.
14 Ibid., Grant to Butler, 5 November 1909.
15 Ibid., Grant to Bowden, 10 May 1910.
16 Ibid., vol. 129 Grant to Butler, 14 February 1908.
17 Ibid., vol. 131, Grant to Butler, 9 April 1909.
18 Ibid., A Reformer to Butler, 28 September 1908.
19 Federal Court of Canada, Trial Division, "The Corporation of the Town of Cambellford vs. Her Majesty the Queen," 28 September 1981.
20 Toronto *Telegram*, 4 January 1911.
21 Midland *Free Press*, 20 June 1918.
22 Ibid., 8 August 1918.

CHAPTER TWENTY-FIVE

1 PAC, RG 43, B2(a), vol. 249, J.G.G. Kerry to R.C. Smith, 5 May 1910.
2 Ibid.
3 The low rental charged for this lease and the equally small amount charged for a similar lease issued by the dominion government indicate how little value governments placed on this important natural resource in 1899.
4 PAC, Laurier Papers, vol. 378, 100542 – 3, Allen B. Aylesworth to Wilfrid Laurier, 11 August 1905.
5 PAC, RG 43, B2(a), vol, 298, The Montreal Engineering Company to M.J. Butler, 21 July 1909.
6 Ibid., Butler to the Montreal Engineering Company, 22 July 1909.
7 Beaverbrook, *My Early Life*, 118.
8 PAC, Sir Robert Borden Papers, MG 26 H, vol. 256, 145139, A Brief from the Electric Power Company to the Minister of Railways and Canals, November 1911.
9 PAC, RG 43, B2(a), vol. 249, Kerry to Smith, 5 May 1910.

10 Ibid., Tom S. Rubidge to the Secretary, Department of Railways and Canals, 2 July 1881.

11 Ibid., L.K. Jones to A.J. Grant, 22 February 1910.

12 Ibid., R.J. McLaughlin to W.A. Campbell, 8 March 1910.

13 Ibid., Campbell to McLaughlin, 12 March 1910.

14 Ibid., Kerry to Smith, 5 May 1910.

15 Ibid.

16 Ibid.

17 Ibid.

18 Ibid.

19 Ibid.

20 Ibid., Smith to Campbell, 7 June 1910.

21 Ibid.

22 Ibid.

CHAPTER TWENTY-SIX

1 Baron de Lahontan, *New Voyages to North America*, quoted in Murray, *Muskoka and Haliburton*, 9.

2 PAC, RG 11, vol. 38, Joseph Portlock, "Remarks on the Severn River, 1819," *Report on Water Communications*.

3 Murray, *Muskoka and Haliburton*, 9, Robert Mathews to Lieutenant Colonel Mason Bolton, 19 May 1780.

4 Guillet, *Valley of the Trent*, 134, Benjamin Frobisher to Henry Hamilton, 2 May 1785.

5 Murray, *Muskoka and Haliburton*, 14, Lord Dorchester to Gother Mann, 29 May 1788.

6 Ibid., 15, Mann to Dorchester, 6 December 1788.

7 PAC, RG 11, vol. 38, Portlock, "Remarks."

8 Murray, *Muskoka and Haliburton*, 33, Extracts from Smyth's Report on Water Communications, 9 September 1825.

9 Ibid.

10 Guillet, *Valley of the Trent*, 180, Nichol Hugh Baird to Sir John Colborne, December 1835.

11 Canada, *Sessional Papers, 1892*, Paper no. 47, Report of the Commissioners to Consider the Advisability of Extending the Trent Canal.

12 Ibid.

13 PAC, RG 43, B2, vol. 112, E.J. Walsh's Survey of the Severn River and the Coldwater Cut-Off Routes for a Canal, 28 February 1907.

14 Ibid., The Mayor of Barrie to H.R. Emmerson, 13 December 1905.

15 Ibid., The Secretary of the Department of Railways and Canals to the Mayor of Barrie, 28 December 1905.

16 Orillia *Packet*, 25 January 1906.

17 PAC, RG 11, vol. 38, Portlock, "Remarks."

18 PAC, RG 43, B2, vol. 112, E.J. Walsh's Survey, 28 February 1907.

19 Ibid.

20 Ibid.

21 Barrie *Northern Advance*, 18 July 1907.

22 Orillia *Packet*, 27 February 1908.

23 PAC, RG 43, B2, vol. 112, E.J. Walsh's Survey, 28 February 1907.
24 Leighton McCarthy was more than just a footnote in the Trent canal story. Although he never again ran for Parliament, he maintained close ties with the Liberal party, especially Mackenzie King. A trustee of the National Foundation for Infantile Paralysis of the United States of America and of the Georgia Warm Springs Foundation, McCarthy became a close friend of Franklin D. Roosevelt, a relationship that Mackenzie King exploited by appointing McCarthy Canada's first ambassador to Washington in 1943.

CHAPTER TWENTY-SEVEN

1 Orillia *Packet*, 5 December 1912.
2 Ibid.
3 Ibid.
4 Ibid.
5 PAC, RG 43, B2(a), vol. 179, York Construction Company to L.K. Jones, 6 September 1915.
6 Ibid.

CHAPTER TWENTY-EIGHT

1 Orillia *Packet*, 9 September 1915.
2 Department of Indian and Northern Affairs, Canal Division, Records Branch, vol. 4, C. Hale to George Drew, 26 August 1959.
3 TSWO, Washago Files, W.H. Bennett to Frank Cochrane, 15 February 1916.
4 Orillia *Packet*, 19 March 1914.
5 Ibid.
6 PAC, RG 43, B1(a), vol. 292, H. Calcutt to Sir Charles Tupper, 25 November 1880.
7 Ibid., J. Tomlinson to F. Braun, 24 December 1880.
8 Department of Indian and Northern Affairs, Canal Division, Records Branch, vol. 4, W.A. Bowden to A.J. Grant, 14 July 1916.

CHAPTER TWENTY-NINE

1 PAC, RG 43, B2(a), vol. 180, Order-in-Council, 19 December 1918.
2 The dominion government won this case. The judge ruled that surplus water in the Trent canal belonged to the dominion government, thus discouraging Adam Beck from proceeding with the province's claim to the water.
3 PAC, Borden Papers, vol. 180, 99018, J.D. Reid to C.J. Doherty, 20 March 1916.
4 PAC, RG 43, B2(a), vol. 180, Order-in-Council, 19 December 1918.
5 Ibid.
6 Canada, *Debates*, 29 May 1913, 112265.
7 Orillia *Packet*, 3 July 1919.
8 Ibid., 30 January 1919.
9 Ibid., 22 April 1920.
10 Ibid., 17 June 1920.
11 Ibid., 22 April 1920.

Bibliography

UNPUBLISHED SOURCES

ARCHIVES OF ONTARIO, MANUSCRIPT DIVISION
Baird Papers
Department of Crown Lands Records (RG 1)
Department of Public Works Records (RG 15)
Thomas Need Papers (RG 15)
Provincial Secretary Records (RG 8)
John Beverley Robinson Papers (RG 8)
John Graves Simcoe Papers (RG 8)

DEPARTMENT OF INDIAN AND NORTHERN AFFAIRS
Canals Branch Records

ONTARIO MINISTRY OF CONSUMER AND COMMERCIAL
RELATIONS
Companies Branch Records

PUBLIC ARCHIVES OF CANADA, MANUSCRIPT DIVISION
Robert Borden Papers (MG 26 H)
Mossom Boyd Papers (MG 28)
George Brown Papers (MG 24)
Department of Public Works (RG 11)
Department of Railways and Canals Records (RG 43)
Department of Transport Records (RG 12)
Executive Council Minutes (RG 1)
Wilfrid Laurier Papers (MG 26 G)
John A. Macdonald Papers (MG 26A)
Arthur Meighen Papers (MG 26)
Upper Canada Sundries (RG 5)

TRENT-SEVERN WATERWAY OFFICE (PETERBOROUGH)
Records

GOVERNMENT PUBLICATIONS

CANADA
Exchequer Court Reports, 1919, 1920
Gazette
House of Commons, *Debates*, 1874 – 1923
Journals of the House of Commons, 1879, Appendix no. 3, Report of the Select Committee Appointed to Take into Consideration the Return of an Address of the 24th February last Relating to the River Trent and Newcastle District and Canal Work, 10 May 1879.
Ministry of Transport, *Canal Regulations Governing the Use and Management of Navigational Canals; St. Peters, Canso, St. Ours, Chambly, Ste. Anne, Carillon, Rideau, Murray, Trent*, 1976.
Parks Canada, *1971 – 76 Canal Statistics*. Ottawa, December 1976.
  100 Ton Marine Railway Station 41 – Big Chute. Ottawa 1977.
  Peterborough Lift Lock. Ottawa 1975.
Sessional Papers, 1867 – 1925
  – Reports of the Auditor General, 1880 – 1925
  – Reports of the Department of Public Works, 1867 – 79
  – Reports of the Department of Railways and Canals, 1880 – 1925
  – Statements of Public Accounts, 1867 – 1925
  – 1879, Paper no. 35, Report of C.F. Fraser.
  – 1892, Paper no. 47, Report of the Commissioners Appointed to Consider the Advisability of Extending the Trent Valley Canal and to What Extent.
  – 1906, Paper no. 19a, Report of the Royal Commission on Transportation.
  – 1907, Minutes of Proceedings.
  – 1907-8, Paper no. 154, Royal Commission Quebec Bridge Inquiry, 1907, Minutes of Proceedings.
  – 1914, Paper no. 190, Report of the Commission to Investigate the Matter of the Trent Valley Canal.
Statutes, 1867, 31 Vic., c. 12, Public Works of Canada.

CANADA, PROVINCE OF
Legislative Assembly, *Appendix to the Journals, 1841 – 59*.
  – Public Accounts, 1841 – 59.
  – Reports of the Commissioner of Public Works, 1851 – 9.
Legislative Assembly, *Debates, 1841 – 66*.
Legislative Assembly, *Journals, 1841 – 59*.
Legislative Assembly, *Sessional Papers, 1860 – 6*.
  – Public Accounts, 1860 – 6.
  – Reports of the Commissioners of Public Works, 1860 – 6.
Statutes, 1841 – 1842, 4 and 5 Vic., c. 38, An Act to repeal certain ordinances therein mentioned and to establish a Board of Works in this Province.

ONTARIO

Journals, 1879, Appendix no. 2, Report of the Select Committee on the Huron and Ontario Ship Canal.
Sessional Papers, 1868 – 83.
 – Reports of the Department of Public Works, 1868 – 83.
Statutes, 1872, 35 Vic., c. 53, An Act to Incorporate the Gull Waters Improvement Company.
 – 1874, 37 Vic., c. 80, An Act to Incorporate the Huron Trent Valley Canal Company.
 – 1906, 6 Edw. VII, c. 15, Act to Provide for the Transmission of Electrical Power to Municipalities.

UNITED STATES

The Congressional Globe, 1835 – 6
International Deep Waterways Association, First Annual Convention, 1895.

UPPER CANADA

Appendix to the Journals of the House of Assembly, 1832 – 40.
 – 1832 – 3, Report of a Select Committee on the petitions of James G. Bethune and Thomas Ward.
 – 1833 – 4, Report of the Commissioners for Superintending the Improvements of the Navigable Waters of the Newcastle District.
 – 1836, Report of a Select Committee on a petition of Pearse Dumble and Hoar.
 – 1839, Report of the Commissioners for Improvements to the Navigation of the Inland Waters of the District of Newcastle.
 – 1840, Report of the Commissioners for Improvements on the River Trent.
Journals of the House of Assembly, 1827 – 40.
Statutes, 1833, 3 Wm. IV, c. 33, An Act to Provide for the Improvement of Certain Waters in the District of Newcastle.
 – 1834, 4 Wm. IV, c. 28, An Act to Incorporate certain persons under the style and title of the Cobourg Rail Road Company.
 – 1834, 4 Wm. IV, c. 30, An Act to Incorporate certain persons under the Style and title of the President, Directors and Company, of the Port Hope and Rice Lake Canal Company.
 – 1836, 6 Wm. IV, c. 34, An Act to Improve the Navigation of the Inland Waters of the District of Newcastle.
 – 1837, 6 Wm. IV, c. 46, An Act for the relief of John Pearse, William Dumble and William Hoar.
 – 1837, 7 Wm. IV, c. 53, An Act to Amend an Act passed during the last session, entitled "An Act to improve the Navigation of the Inland Waters of the District of Newcastle."
 – 1837, 7 Wm. IV, c. 66, An Act granting to his Majesty a sum of money, to be raised by Debenture, for the improvement of the navigation of the River Trent.

– 1839, 2 Vic., c. 55, An Act to make further provision for the completion of the improvement of the Navigation of the Inland Waters of the District of Newcastle.

NEWSPAPERS

Barrie, *Gazette*.
Barrie, *Northern Advances*.
Beaverton, *Express*.
Bradford, *Witness*.
Canningon, *Echo*.
Cobourg, *Star*.
Midland, *Free Press*.
Newmarket, *Era*.
Newmarket, *Express-Herald*.
Orillia, *Packet*.
Peterborough, *Daily Examiner*.
Peterborough, *Evening Examiner*.
Peterborough, *Examiner*.
Port Hope, *Guide*.
Toronto, *Globe*.
Toronto, *Mail and Empire*.
Toronto, *Telegram*.
Toronto, *Tribune*.
Windsor, *Border Cities Star*.
Woodville, *Advocate*.

BOOKS AND ARTICLES

Ainslie, Mary E. *Sunny Inland Waterways of Ontario: The Trent*. Toronto: Department of Travel and Publicity 1946.
Armstrong, Christopher. *Politics of Federalism: Ontario's Relations with the Federal Government 1867 – 1942*. Toronto: University of Toronto Press 1981.
Armstrong, Christopher, and H.V. Nelles. "Contrasting Development of the Hydro-Electricity Industry in the Montreal and Toronto Regions, 1900 – 1930." *Journal of Canadian Studies*. XVIII, no. 1 (1983): 5 – 27.
Bain, J.W. "Surveys of a Water Route between Lake Simcoe and the Ottawa River by the Royal Engineers 1819 – 1827." *Ontario History*. L, no. 1 (1958): 15 – 28.
Bannister, John William. *Sketches of Plans for Settling in Upper Canada a Portion of the Unemployed Labourers of Great Britain and Ireland*. London: F. Marshall 1826.
Baskerville, Peter A. "Donald Bethune's Steamboat Business: A Study of Upper Canadian Commercial and Financial Practice." *Ontario History*, LXVII, no. 3 (1975): 135 – 52.
– "Entrepreneurship and the Family Compact, York-Toronto, 1822 – 55." *Urban History Review*. IX, no. 3 (1981):15 – 34.

Beahen, William. *Development of the Severn River and Big Chute Lock Station*. Ottawa: Parks Canada 1977.

Beaverbrook, Lord. *My Early Life*. Fredericton: Brunswick Press 1965.

Bleasdale, Ruth Elizabeth. "Unskilled Labourers on the Public Works of Canada, 1840 - 1880." Unpublished PHD, thesis, University of Western Ontario 1984.

Bonnycastle, R.M. *Canada and the Canadians in 1846*. London: Henry Colburn 1846.

Boyce, Gerald E. *Historic Hastings*. Belleville, Ont.: Ontario Intelligencer 1967.

Camerson, Wendy. "Selecting Peter Robinson's Irish Emigrants." *Social History*. Ottawa: University of Ottawa Press. May 1976, Vol. IX: 29 - 46.

Canada-Ontario-Rideau-Trent-Severn Waterway (CORTS). *The Rideau, Trent, Severn: Yesterday, Today, Tomorrow*. Toronto: 1973.

– *The Simcoe Couchiching Area*. 1973.

Canadian Parliamentary Guide, 1862.

Canniff, William. *History of the Settlement of Upper Canada*. Toronto: Dudley & Burns 1869.

Chapman, L.J., and D.F. Putnam. *Physiography of Southern Ontario*. Toronto: University of Toronto Press 1951.

Clay, Charles. *Rice Lake District Guide*. Bewdley 1975.

Craig, John. *By the Sound of Her Whistle*. Toronto: Peter Martin Associates 1966.

Craven, Paul. *An Impartial Umpire: Industrial Relations and the Canadian State, 1900 - 1911*, Toronto: University of Toronto Press 1980.

Creighton, Donald. *John A. Macdonald: The Old Chieftain*. Toronto: Macmillan 1955.

– *John A. Macdonald: The Young Politician*. Toronto: Macmillan 1952.

Cross, Michael S., "The Lumber Community of Upper Canada." *Ontario History*. LII, no. 4 (1960): 213 - 34.

Davin, Nicholas Flood. *The Irishman in Canada*. London: Sampson Low, Marston and Co. 1877.

Daw, J.S. *A Resource Guide to the Trent-Severn Waterway*. Ottawa: Parks Canada 1978.

Daw, Jocelyne, and Evelyn Raab. *The Trent-Severn Waterway's Activity Book for Children*. Peterborough: Friends of the Trent-Severn Waterway 1983.

De Bondt, John. *Canada on Wheels: A Portfolio of Early Canadian Cars*. Ottawa: Oberon 1970.

Denison, Merrill. *The People's Power*. Toronto: McClelland and Stewart 1960.

Easterbrook, W.T. and Hugh G.J. Aitken. *Canadian Economic History*. Toronto: Macmillan 1975.

Ennals, Peter Morley. "Land and Society in Hamilton Township, Upper Canada, 1797 - 1861." Unpublished PHD thesis, Johns Hopkins University 1978.

Epp, Abraham Ernest. "Cooperation among Capitalists: The Canadian Merger Movement, 1909 - 13." Unpublished PHD thesis, Johns Hopkins University 1978.

Evans, Margaret L. *Debate and Interpretation: Newspaper Opinion about the Trent Canal in the Latter 19th Century.* Ottawa: Parks Canada 1980.
Preliminary History of Bobcaygeon Lock Station. Ottawa: Parks Canada, undated.
Francis, Daniel. *I Remember: An Oral History of the Trent-Severn Waterway.* Peterborough: Friends of the Trent-Severn Waterway 1984.
Francis, Walter J. "Mechanical Locks in Canada." *Transactions.* 19 and 20 (1906): 77 – 100.
Frost, Leslie M. *Forgotten Pathways of the Trent.* Don Mills, Ont.: Burns & MacEachern 1973
Guillet, E.C. *Cobourg 1798 – 1948.* Oshawa: Goodfellow Printing 1948.
– *The Valley of the Trent.* Toronto: The Champlain Society 1957.
Hale, Charles H. *Reminiscences of Orillia 1874 – 1963.* Orillia: 1963.
Hastings and Prince Edward Counties. *Illustrated Historical Atlas.* Toronto 1878, Reprint, Belleville 1972.
Heisler, John P. *The Canals of Canada.* Ottawa: Department of Indian Affairs and Northern Development, National and Historic Parks Branch 1973.
Helleiner, Frederick M. "A Geographical Interpretation of Recreational Waterways, with Special Reference to the Trent-Severn Waterway." Unpublished PHD thesis, University of Western Ontario 1972.
Humphries, Charles Walter. "The Political Career of Sir James P. Whitney." Unpublished PHD thesis, University of Toronto 1967.
Hunter, A.F. "The Founding of Kirkfield, Ontario." *Ontario Historical Society Papers and Records.* Toronto, 1918, Vol. XVI.
– *A History of Simcoe County.* Barrie: Historical Committee of Simcoe County 1948.
Jackman, Sydney W. *Galloping Head: The Life of the Right Honourable Sir Francis Bond Head ... 1793 – 1875.* London: Phoenix House 1958.
Johnson, J.K. (ed.). *Historical Essays on Upper Canada.* Ottawa: Carleton University Press 1975.
Keefer, Charles H. *A Review of the Construction of the Hydraulic Locks at Peterborough and Kirkfield.* Peterborough: Review Printing and Publishing 1913.
Keefer, Thomas. *Report of Thomas Keefer of Survey of Georgian Bay Canal Route to Lake Ontario by Way of Lake Scugog.* Whitby 1863.
Kingsford, William. *The Canadian Canals: Their History and Cost.* Toronto: Rollo & Adam 1865.
Kirkconnell, Watson. *County of Victoria Centennial History.* Lindsay, Ont. 1967.
Langton, H.H. (ed.). *A Gentlewoman in Upper Canada: The Journals of Anne Langton.* Toronto: Clarke Irwin & Co. 1950.
Langton, W.A. (ed.). *Early Days in Upper Canada: Letters of John Langton.* Toronto: Macmillan 1926.
Legget, Robert F. *Canals of Canada.* Vancouver: Douglas, David & Charles 1976.
Lower, A.R.M. *The North American Assault on the Canadian Forest.* Toronto: Ryerson 1938.

McCullough, A.B. *Money and Exchange in Canada to 1900*. Toronto: Dundurn Press 1984.

Maltby, Peter, and Monica Maltby. "A New Look at the Peter Robinson Emigration of 1823." *Ontario History*. LV no. 1 (March 1963): 15 – 22.

Mills, G.K. "The Nottawasaga River Route." *Ontario Historical Society Papers and Records*. VIII (1907): 40 – 8.

Moodie, Susanna. *Life in the Clearings versus the Bush*. London: Richard Bentley 1853.

– *Roughing It in the Bush*. London: Richard Bentley 1852.

Murray, Florence B. *Muskoka and Haliburton 1615 – 1875*. Toronto: The Champlain Society 1963.

Need, Thomas. *Six Years in the Bush: Or Extracts from the Journal of a Settler in Upper Canada*. London: Simpkin, Marshall 1838.

Nelles, H.V. *Politics of Development: Forests, Mines and Hydro-Electric Power in Ontario, 1849 – 1941*. Hamden, Conn.: Shoe String Press 1974.

– "Public Ownership of Electrical Utilities in Manitoba and Ontario, 1906 – 1930." *Canadian Historical Review*. LVII, no. 4 (December 1976): 461 – 84.

Nickels, Nick. *Indian River Mills*. Lakefield, Ont.: Paddle Press 1975.

Northumberland and Durham Counties. *Historical Atlas*. Toronto: H. Belden 1878.

Oberdorf, Charles and Mechtild Hoppenrath. "Trent-Severn Waterway: Houseboating through Ontario's Heartland." *The Financial Post*. 1 September 1985.

Pammett, Howart T. *Lilies and Shamrocks: History of Emily Township*. Municipality of Emily 1974.

– "Steamboat Era on the Trent-Otonabee Waterway: 1830 – 1950." *Ontario History*. LVI, no. 2 (June 1964): 67 – 103.

Peterborough: Land of Shining Waters, An Anthology [ed. Ronald Borg] Peterborough 1968.

Peterborough County. *Illustrated Historical Atlas 1825 – 1875*. Peterborough 1975.

Piva, Michael Y. "Continuity and Crisis: Francis Hincks and Canadian Economic Policy." *Canadian Historical Review*. 66 (June 1985): 185 – 210.

Pool, Thomas W. *A Sketch of the Early Settlement and Subsequent Progress of the Town of Peterborough*. Peterborough: Robert Romaine 1867.

Pope, Joseph. *The Correspondence of Sir John Macdonald: Selections from the Correspondence of the Right Honourable Sir J.A. Macdonald, G.C.B., First Prime Minister of the Dominion of Canada*. Toronto 1921.

– *Memories of the Right Honourable Sir John Alexander Macdonald, G.C.B., First Prime Minister of the Dominion of Canada*. Ottawa 1894.

Raudzens, George. *The British Ordnance Department and Canada's Canals, 1815 – 1855*. Waterloo: Wilfrid Laurier University Press 1979.

Redish, Angela. "The Optimal Supply of Bank Money: Upper Canada's Experience on and off the Specie Standard." Unpublished PHD thesis, University of Western Ontario 1982.

"Why Was Specie Scarce in Colonial Economics?: An Analysis of the Canadian Currency." *Journal of Economic History*. XLIV, no. 3 (1984): 713 – 28.

Rogers, Richard B. "Trent Canal." *Canadian Society of Civil Engineers Proceedings*. XII, no. 138 (1899): 192 – 204.

Saunders, F.M. (ed.). *The Life and Letters of the Rt. Hon. Sir Charles Tupper, Bart., K.C.M.G.* London 1916.

Simcoe County. *Illustrated Atlas*. Toronto 1970.

Stevens, G.R. *Canadian National Railways, Vol. I, Sixty Years of Trial and Error, 1836 – 1896*. Toronto: Clarke, Irwin 1960.

Stevens, Paul Douglas. "Laurier and the Liberal Party in Ontario, 1887 – 1911." Unpublished PHD thesis, University of Toronto 1966.

Stewart, Frances. *Our Forest Home*. Montreal: Gazette Printing and Publishing 1902.

Strickland, Maj. *Twenty-Seven Years in Canada West*. London: Richard Bentley 1853.

Tatley, Ricard. *Steamboating on the Trent-Severn*. Belleville: Mika Publishing 1978.

Theberge, Clifford B., and Elaine Theberge. *The Trent-Severn Waterway: A Traveller's Companion*. Toronto: Samuel Stevens 1978.

Traill, Catharine Parr. *The Backwoods of Canada: Being Letters from the Wife of an Emigrant Officer*. London: Charles Knight 1836.

Trout, J.M., and Edward Trout. *The Railways of Canada for 1870 – 1*. Toronto: Monetary Times 1871.

Wallis, Hugh M. "James Wallis, Founder of Fenelon Falls and Pioneer in the Early Development of Peterborough." *Ontario History*. LIII, no. 4 (1961): 257 – 71.

Wells, Kenneth M. *Cruising the Trent-Severn Waterway*. Toronto: McClelland and Stewart 1964.

Wood, David J. (ed.). *Perspectives on Landscape and Settlement in Nineteenth Century Ontario*. Toronto: McClelland and Stewart 1975.

Wurtele, D.J. "Mossom Boyd: Lumber King of the Trent Valley." *Ontario History*. L, no. 4 (1958): 177 – 89.

Index

Index   443

Honey Harbour, 375, 377, 379, 381, 399
Howland, O.A., 202
Hudson River, 391
Hudspeth, F., 195
Hughes, Col. Sam, 211, 215, 245–7
passim, 251, 268, 376, 402
Humber River, 281, 285–6
Huron and Ontario Ship Canal Co., 165,
193, 196, 197, 230, 277
Huron Indians, 360
Huron Trent Valley Canal Co., 147, 157,
210
Huronia, 360
Huston, John G., 19, 23
hydraulic lift locks: history and principle
of operation, 229–30; see also Kirkfield
lift lock; Peterborough: lift lock
Hydro Electric Power Commission (HEPC),
304–7, 312, 320, 325, 329, 332, 335–8,
342–6, 371, 378, 381, 393
Hydro Glen, 385, 388–9; see also Ragged
Rapids
Hyman, V., 327

Idyl Wild Hunting Lodge, 156
Imperial Alaska Boundary Tribunal, 299
Indian River, 41
Inland Construction Co., 385–6, 389, 393
inland waters, 8, 97, 152–3; im-
provements, 36–53 passim
Institute of Civil Engineers, 257
Intercolonial Railway, 262, 292
"Interlake Communication," 201
Irene (motor launch), 406
Irish Catholic voters, 187, 262–3
Iroquois Indians, 183, 361
Italian canal workers, 173, 178, 269, 313,
316, 382–3

Jameson, Robert, 27, 38, 52, 69, 169–70
Jesuit fathers, 360
Jewett, F.C., 314, 317
Johnson, Andrew, 268
Johnston, Strachan, 346–7, 379, 398
Jones, L.K., 252, 270, 311
Jost, E.B., 377, 387, 391, 393; see also
Trent canal surveys

Kawartha Lakes, 117–18, 142, 156–8,
168–9, 191, 242, 249, 404, 406; see also
Back Lakes; inland waters
Keefer, Charles, 234, 268, 273, 274
Keefer, Samuel, 106, 109, 113
Keefer, Thomas, 145, 149, 202

Keeler, Joseph, 143–4, 146, 153, 160–2,
187, 244, 419n3, 420n33
Keeler's Mill, 40
Keene, 41–2
Keewatin, ss, 375
Kempenfelt Bay, 362–3
Kennedy, John, 193, 195
Kermath Engine Manufacturing Co.,
404
Kerr, F.D. 403
Kerr, Sen. William, 238
Kerry, J.G.G., 259–60, 306, 308; Quebec
Bridge inquiry, 308–10, 335; Seymour
Power and Electric Co., 310–12; Sidney
Electric Power Co., 311–14, 316;
Campbellford canal, 320–1; North-
umberland Paper and Electric Co.,
320–3, 337, 443, 445, 449; Electric
Power Co., 325, 342–7; background,
328, 347; power agreement with
Dominion government, 333; Miller
Brothers, 339, 343; competition with
Culverwell, 335–43 passim
Kerry and Chace, 347
Kerry, Smith and Chace, 303, 311, 337–9
Kilbourn, J., 260–1
Killaly, A.L., 182, 273, 403, 422n8
Killaly, Hamilton Hartley, 8, 68, 96, 106,
144, 152, 210; chairman, Board of
Public Works, 76–7; background, 77;
cancels Trent waterway, 78–81; plans
for the Trent, 83–4; assistant commis-
sioner of public works, 84; timber
slides, 88; dismissal of Baird, 92–3
King, W.L. Mackenzie, 293, 313, 401
King township, 279
King's Arms Hotel (Peterborough), 23
King's Topographical Collection, 361
Kingston, 31, 196–8; Chronicle, 31
Kiondacharia, 360; see also Severn River
Kirkfield, 209, 240, 243, 246, 251
Kirkfield lift lock: construction, 249–50;
leaks, 251–3, 264–5; official opening,
253–4; Holgate investigation, 267–8
Kitchener (motor launch), 327
Kydd, George, 406

La Louvrière, Belgium, 229
La Salle, Cavalier de, 360
LaFontaine, Louis, 96
Lahontan, Baron de, 361
Lake Algonquin, 240, 253
Lake Couchiching, 191, 240, 327, 360,
364–5, 368, 370, 374, 389–90, 405

Ritchie, Peter, 395
Rivard, mayor of Montreal, 160
Robert Fair and Co., 236
Robert Verity Employment Agency, 400
Robertson, Fred A., and Co., 317, 409
Robertson, William, 26, 33
Robinette, R.C., 293
Robinson, Peter, 5-7, 19
Robinson Island, 109
Rochester, NY, 404
Rockeby, 20, 412n23
Rogers, James Z., 257
Rogers, Richard B.: superintendent, Trent
canal, 99, 182, 186, 194, 197, 201-9
passim; concrete construction, 222-8,
231-4, 250-3; lock gate openers, 225-6;
Corry and Laverdure, 227-36 passim;
Balsam Lake – Simcoe division,
247-53; background, 256-7, 272-3;
political enemies, 258-65, 331; and lift
lock investigation, 266-9; resignation
270, 275, 283; Trent canal contract,
271, 303, 315-17, 407, 409; Camp-
bellford Water Power Syndicate, 338;
see also Trent canal surveys
Rogers, Robert, 257, 360
Rogers, Robert David, 259
Rogers Rangers, 257
Roman Catholic voters, 86, 167, 187
Rose, John, 103, 113
Rosedale: Ontario lock, 132, 139-40, 209,
408, 421n8; dam, 248
Ross government (Ontario), 282
Rowan, Lt.-Col., 23, 28
Rowdon township, 145
Royal Academy, 182
Royal Life Assurance Co., 329
Royal Securities Corporation, 333-4, 339
Rubidge, Capt. Charles, 183
Rubidge, Emma, 184, 188
Rubidge, Frederick P., 13, 15, 30, 45, 183,
242
Rubidge, Joseph William, 183
Rubidge, Mary, 182, 184
Rubidge, Tom S.: opposition to the Trent,
165, 182, 190-2; superintendent,
Kawartha construction, 170, 226, 257;
and George Goodwin, 172-80 passim;
background, 182-4; political
difficulties, 184-8 passim; survey
report, 190-1; see also Trent canal
surveys
Romanian canal workers, 383

Russell, W.B., 284, 379, 399
Russell House Hotel (Ottawa), 212
Ruttan, Henry, 33-4, 63, 66

St Amand, Billy, 383
St Catharines, 167, 312
St Lawrence River, 75, 81, 332, 377, 388,
403; canals, 74-5, 84, 96, 172, 182-3,
196, 211, 243
Sarnia, 82
Sault Ste Marie, 198
Saw Mill Island, 380
sawdust pollution, 118-19
Schomberg, 279
Schreiber, Collingwood, 203, 218, 225,
231-5, 237, 252, 263, 283, 291, 310
Scientific American, 392
Scott's Mills lock, 42, 94, 308; see also
Whitla's Rapids
Scugog River, 10, 47-8, 113, 134, 136
Severn Bridge, 368, 395
Severn Falls, 374, 378, 386, 400
Severn Lodge, 396
Severn River, 156, 165, 191, 197, 240,
243, 277, 359-80 passim; see also Trent
canal surveys
Severn River division: section 2, 386-9,
398-402, 410; section 3, 389-90, 398,
402-6, 410; section 1, 398-401, 410
Seymour Power and Electric Co., 303,
311-12, 322, 342
Seymour township, 37, 145, 319
Sidey and Craigie, 39-42 passim, 59, 69,
407
Sidney Electric Power Co., 312, 344
Silver Creek, 365
Simcoe Dredging Co., 285, 409
Simcoe, John Graves, 241, 361-3, 373
Simcoe, Lady, 361, 374
Simcoe East (riding), 367, 370
Simcoe North (riding), 287, 364-6, 370
Simcoe Railway and Power Co., 371, 373,
378-9, 387
Simcoe South (riding), 366-7, 370, 379,
385
Sinclair, John "Jack," 395-6
Sir Francis Bond Head (steamboat), 51-2
Sir George Arthur (steamboat), 47
Six Mile Channel, 374, 387, 393
Six Mile Lake, 376, 387, 401
Smith, Cecil B., 335, 337, 347
Smith, Henry H., 159-66, 201
Smith, John, 19

Smith, Kerry and Chace, 259–60
Smith, R.C., 169
Smith, R.C. (Millers' lawyer), 330, 342–3
Smith township, 44, 137, 187
Smith's Creek, 9
Smyth, Sir James Carmichael; see Trent canal surveys
Snowden House Hotel (Peterborough), 239
Soulanges Canal, 284, 308
South Bay, 246
Southampton, England, 392
Sovereign (steamboat), 253
Sparrow Lake, 368, 389
Sparrow Lake Chute, 374, 389
Spohn, Dr., 283
squared timber, 89–91 passim
Stark, David, 179, 187–8, 191–2; see also Trent canal surveys
Stayner, 370
Steamboat Committee, 51–2
steamboat navigation: on Back Lakes, 50–3, 87, 116; absence of regulations, 107; conflict with milling, 107; obstructions, 109, 118–19; on Otonabee River, 109; on Rice Lake, 109–10, 115, 160; on Trent River, 114–17, 149, 152, 155; emerging regulations, 116–19; conflict with logging, 118; on Kawartha Lakes, 156, 171
Stephen, George, 198
Stevenson, James, 188, 193–5, 199–200, 202
Stewart, Thomas A., 8, 27, 31–2
Stirling, 344
Stoney Lake (steamboat), 237, 253–4, 274
Stony Lake, 137, 139, 156, 174–5
Stratton, J.R., 211, 215–16, 236, 238, 248, 258–9, 333
Stratton, William A., 261
Strickland, George, 137
Strickland, Maria, 418n12
Strickland, Roland C., 137, 159, 185, 187–8, 213, 421n23
Strickland, Walter, 138
Sturgeon (steamboat), 10, 15, 20, 24, 27, 51, 117
Sturgeon Lake, 3, 18, 37, 45, 47, 111, 118, 134, 137, 204
Sturgeon Point Hotel, 156
Sully, 21, 26
Sun Life Assurance Co., 344
Sutherland, James, 219

Sutherland, Mr., 42
Sutton, 279
Swift Rapids, 375, 385–9; power plant, 376, 388, 406; lock, 389–90; marine railway, 389, 391, 393, 410
Sydenham, Lord, x, 64, 67, 73–84 passim, 89, 96, 210
Szlapka, P.L., 310

Taggest's Mill, 12
Talbot Portage, 241, 243–4
Talbot River, 209, 241, 243, 249
Tarte, J. Israel, 211
Tehuantopec Isthmus, 391
Tesla, Nicola, 302
Thompson, Charles Poulett, 73; see also Sydenham, Lord
Thompson, Mr., 90
Thomson, Tilley and Johnston, 379
Thornton, C.J., 299
Tiger (steamboat), 139
timber making, 89
timber trade, 88–92, 97–102 passim
Toronto, 135, 140, 157, 196, 209, 214, 259, 294, 297–8, 305, 360–2, 379; Globe, 143, 163, 198, 269–70; Tribune, 159, 163, 167–8; Irish Canadian, 168; board of trade, 211, 214–15; Carrying-Place, 241, 277, 361, 363; Liberal Club, 262; Saturday Night, 285; Mail and Empire, 286; News, 286; Telegram, 286; Electric Light Co., 305; Street Railway Co., 305; Weekly Sun, 396
Toronto and Nipissing Railway, 108, 139, 209, 243
Toronto Georgian Bay Ship Canal, 243, 362, 364; see also Huron and Ontario Ship Canal Co.
tourism, 156–7, 278, 367, 376–7, 379, 382, 396–7, 402–4
Traill, Catharine Parr, 11, 69
Transportation Commission (1903), 364
Trent canal, 254–9 passim, 275–6, 298, 322–3, 327, 331, 341, 359, 362, 372, 377, 385, 390–3, 396; politics (1830s), 21–3; no policy, 36; reasons for building, 47, 79–80; first lockage, 47; cancellation of, 80, 83–4; revival of, 154, 166; promoters, 157, 181–2, 210–14, 238–9, 376; barge canal, 158–9, 298, 300, 308, 336, 369, 375–6, 381; seats, 166, 190, 200, 203, 216, 232; first through boat, 406

Wallis, James, 27, 51-2, 111, 169-70
Walsh, Edmund J., 203, 271, 279-84
  passim, 290-3, 305, 308, 332, 364,
  366-75 *passim*, 428n41; *see also* Trent
  canal surveys
Walters, J.W., 330
Walters, Thomas, 110, 136, 408
War Measures Act, 393, 399
War of 1812, 241, 362
Ward, Col. H.A., 219, 259, 297, 299-301
Ward, Messrs., and Co., 52
Ward, Thomas, 43
Warsaw, 43
Warsaw Road, 227, 269
Wasaga Beach, 369
Washago, 327, 374, 376, 389, 404
water control: storage basins, 115-18;
  reservoir dams, 140-2
water leases: *see* Trent canal water
  powers
Waubaushene, 191, 378, 381-2, 395
Welland Canal, 29, 79, 96, 157, 172, 185,
  191, 211, 271, 313
Weller, Judge, 194
Weller, William, 51, 87, 99, 109, 114
Wellington, Duke of, 241, 363
West Bay, 242
Western Canada Power, 333, 343
Weston Shoe Co., 319
Whitby, 52, 83, 93, 112, 134-5, 159, 344
Whitby and Port Perry Railway, 108,
  133-6 *passim*
White, Andrew, 94
White, Joe, 383
White, John, 91, 416n5
White Rose Stream, 281

White's Falls, 376, 384, 399, 401
Whiteside, William, 140, 408
Whitla, George, 6
Whitla, William, 6
Whitla's Rapids, 9; lock, 37, 42-4, 65-6,
  407; restoration, 109-10
Whitney, James P., 261, 282, 332
Widdifield, A.E., 282
Widdifield, Henry, 282
Widow Harris', 54-5
Wilcocks Lake, 285
Wildman, J.W., 289
William Hamilton Co., 394
Williamsburg Canal, 183
Willow Creek, 362
Wilson, Thomas, 85-6, 90-1, 99, 101
Wiman, Erasmus, 198, 423n18
Windsor *Border Cities Star*, 404
Windsor harbour: *see* Whitby
Windsor Hotel (Ottawa), 212
Wisconsin Glacier, ix, 240
Woodman (steamboat), 52, 87, 99, 110,
  113
Woods, Thomas, 406
Wood's Bay, 365
woods rangers, 131
Woodville *Advocate*, 343
Wynn, Charles, 168, 186, 224, 408

Yankee Bonnet, 42, 109, 160
York Construction Co., 284, 288, 294,
  379, 389, 393, 398, 401-2, 409-10
Young, P.P., 253
Young, S.J., 217
Young's Point, 132, 180; Ontario lock,
  137-9, 209, 408